D1530450

Business, Government, and Society

**A Managerial Perspective
Text and Cases**

Tenth Edition

George A. Steiner
*Harry and Elsa Kunin
Professor of Business and
Society and Professor of
Management, Emeritus, UCLA*

John F. Steiner
*Professor of Management
California State University,
Los Angeles*

Boston   Burr Ridge, IL   Dubuque, IA   Madison, WI   New York   San Francisco   St. Louis
Bangkok   Bogotá   Caracas   Kuala Lumpur   Lisbon   London   Madrid   Mexico City
Milan   Montreal   New Delhi   Santiago   Seoul   Singapore   Sydney   Taipei   Toronto

McGraw-Hill Higher Education

A Division of The **McGraw-Hill** Companies

BUSINESS, GOVERNMENT, AND SOCIETY:
A MANAGERIAL PERSPECTIVE, TEXT AND CASES

This book is printed on acid-free paper.

domestic   2 3 4 5 6 7 8 9 0 DOC/DOC 0 9 8 7 6 5 4 3
international 1 2 3 4 5 6 7 8 9 0 DOC/DOC 0 9 8 7 6 5 4 3 2

ISBN 0-07-248834-4

Publisher: *John E. Biernat*
Senior sponsoring editor: *Andy Winston*
Editorial coordinator: *Sara E. Ramos*
Marketing manager: *Lisa Nicks*
Producer, Media technology: *Jennifer Becka*
Project manager: *Jim Labeots*
Production supervisor: *Debra R. Sylvester*
Coordinator freelance design: *Mary L. Christianson*
Photo research coordinator: *Judy Kausal*
Supplement producer: *Susan Lombardi*
Freelance cover designer: *Trudi Gershenov Design*
Cover photos: *top left to right,* © *Getty News;* © *Corbis Images;* © *Corbis Images; bottom left to right,* © *Eyewire;* © *Getty News;* © *Getty News.*
Typeface: *10/12 Palatino*
Compositor: *Shepherd Incorporated*
Printer: *R. R. Donnelley*

Library of Congress Cataloging-in-Publication Data

Steiner, George Albert, 1912–
    Business, government, and society : a managerial perspective / George A. Steiner, John
F. Steiner.—10th ed.
        p. cm.
    Includes bibliographical references and index.
    ISBN 0–07–248834–4 (alk. paper)—ISBN 0–07–119899–7 (international : alk. paper)
    1. Industries—Social aspects—United States. 2. Industrial policy—United States. I.
Steiner, John F. II. Title.
HD60.5.U5 S8 2003
658.4—dc21

                                                                                    2002066013

www.mhhe.com

We dedicate this book to the memory of Jean Wood Steiner

Brief Contents

Contents

Preface

AN OVERVIEW OF THE NEW EDITION

Rapidly changing interrelationships among business, government, and society are the subject of this book. It is written primarily for students and faculty. However, we believe its contents are also of interest to managers who must function in complex and dynamic global environments. In these pages readers will find many challenging and informative ideas, perspectives, and facts. A glance at the table of contents will reveal the broad scope of the book.

Since the last edition, a stream of events has mandated widespread and, in some places, fundamental revision. Each chapter is updated and many are substantially rewritten to include new trends, ideas, laws, personalities, and publications. As in the previous edition, we continue our effort to give more prominence to global dimensions of the subject matter. More areas of the text that were once focused solely on the United States have been broadened to include comparative material about other nations. In revising, we emphasize current events, issues, and conditions. As in preceding editions, however, we sometimes provide a historical background. We abide in our belief that the evolution of values, laws, theories, policies, and events is an important dimension of this field.

THE CHAPTERS

There are many changes in the new edition. Key updates and additions in the chapters are listed here:

- Chapter 1 is revised and updated. It retains its pragmatic approach to the field based on four models of the business–government–society relationship.

- Chapter 2 is extensively rewritten to emphasize the importance of industrial growth and technological change. Discussion of population growth as a deep historical force is introduced, and the legal environment is added as a key dimension in the business environment.

- Chapter 4 contains a revised and extended analysis of the worldwide movement to limit corporate power.

- Chapter 5 includes a new discussion of global corporate responsibility and an examination of codes of conduct created by multilateral agencies, governments, and corporations.

- Chapter 6 on implementing social responsibilities has been redone to emphasize management processes. It includes new discussions of strategic philanthropy, cause-related marketing, and international developments in social auditing.

- Chapter 7 contains an updated description of corporate ethics programs.

- Chapter 10 incorporates new data and materials on antitrust law in the European Union countries and elsewhere.

- Chapter 11 is rewritten to describe and assess state-of-the-art methods of corporate lobbying and rapidly evolving campaign contribution practices.

- Chapter 12 has new material on international corruption.

- Chapter 13 adds new emphasis on expanding regional trade agreements and on critics of globalization.

- Chapter 14 extends its description of the impacts of industrial growth on the natural environment and human populations. The discussion about environmental laws is updated. A new section assessing the effectiveness of regulations concludes the chapter.

- Chapter 16 contains new sections on consumerism as an ideology and Internet privacy issues.

- Chapter 17 has an expanded discussion of global competitiveness among workers of many nations.

THE CASE STUDIES

Case studies appear at the end of each chapter, except Chapter 1. They concretely illustrate one or more central themes of the chapter. The main issues in these case studies have strong pro and con sides and will generate classroom debate and controversy.

Our philosophy of case writing is based on a few key ideas. We believe that cases should raise substantial and, if possible, multiple issues. We believe that these issues should be developed, but not in exhausting detail. So our cases are of moderate length. We believe that cases should be written to raise questions rather than answer them. Therefore, we try to open lines of inquiry and we list central questions at the end of each case. And we believe that, with the exception of historical incidents, cases should be current. Therefore, except for the historical cases in Chapters 2 and 3, we have revised the cases carried over from the last edition, often substantially.

Six new case studies have been written for this tenth edition.

- "Genetically Modified Foods" follows Chapter 4. Activists are angry with companies that engineer and sell genetically modified foods. How valid are their complaints?

- "General Electric Company Under Jack Welch" follows Chapter 5. The business press applauds Jack Welch, GE's recently retired CEO, for his financial successes, but critics argue that under his leadership the company was not always a responsible corporate citizen. Who is correct?

- "The FDA and Tobacco Regulation" follows Chapter 9. It tells the story of how an agency went through the rule-making process, trying to regulate a deadly product, but ultimately failed. Should it have succeeded?

- "The World Trade Organization and Its Critics," following Chapter 13, invites discussion of the WTO's impact on global stakeholders. What are the benefits and costs of growing international trade?

- "Commercialism in Schools" is added to Chapter 16. Corporations now fund elementary and secondary schools in return for promotion of their brands and viewpoints on campus. Should education be a sanctuary from commercial appeals?

- "Disney Shareholders Attack Executive Pay" follows Chapter 19. Critics of rising executive compensation brought a proposal to the annual shareholder meeting for a vote. Should Disney's use of stock options for top executives be changed?

CHAPTER-OPENING STORIES

As in past editions, we begin each chapter with a true story, a vignette that introduces the theme forthcoming in the chapter text. Most of them are about companies. Eight new ones have been added.

- "The Royal Dutch/Shell Group of Companies" explains how a large energy company uses scenarios in its global planning.

- "Exxon Mobil Corporation, Petronas, ChevronTexaco Corporation" is the story of a landmark agreement between transnational corporations, nations, activists, and the World Bank to develop oil fields in a responsible way.

- "Realtors in the Wilderness" tells the tale of a small limited partnership that uses hardball tactics in real estate deals.

- "California Deregulates Electricity" is a story of failed policy in the Golden State.

- "Carl Lindner and Chiquita Brands International" illuminates the recesses of Washington, D.C., policy-making to reveal the alchemy that turns money into power.

- "The Coca-Cola Company" illustrates the adjustments that a large multinational corporation needs to make as it operates in many nations.

- "DaimlerChrysler" is the story of a company altered by global winds of change.

- "Enron's Governance Debacle" tells how one firm's board of directors failed to discharge its oversight duties.

SUPPORT MATERIALS FOR INSTRUCTORS

An *Instructor's Resource Manual* includes the following sections: sample course outlines, chapter objectives, case study teaching notes with answers to the case questions, and a list of term paper topics for each text chapter. The manual also contains a test bank covering chapters and case studies, including multiple-choice, true/false, fill-in, and essay questions.

A set of *PowerPoint® slides* highlighting chapter topics is available for use in classroom lectures.

A *Computerized Test Bank* contains all of the questions in the print test bank. It is a powerful system that allows tests to be prepared quickly and easily. Instructors can view questions as they are selected for a test; scramble questions and answers; add, delete, and edit questions; create multiple test versions; and view and save tests.

A *Video Series in Business, Government, and Society* will help students connect topics covered in class with current events discussed in video clips.

A book-specific *Online Learning Center* features resources for both instructors and students. The site offers downloadable supplements for instructors, and interactive exercises and self-quizzes designed to enhance student understanding of text material: www.mhhe.com/steiner10e.

Acknowledgments

We are deeply indebted to many authors who have inspired and informed us. Where appropriate we have cited their works. Many others have been helpful with their contributions and suggestions during preparation of the book. We are especially grateful to the following: Bryan Adams, Mergerstat; Suzanne Beck, Levi Strauss & Co.; Barbara Breen, Pfizer Inc.; Mark V. Buckingham, Monsanto Company; Kathryn Gordon, Organisation for Economic Co-operation and Development; Charles A. Kothe, Oral Roberts University; William A. Krohley, Kelley Drye & Warren LLP; John Musser, Dow Chemical Company; Melinda Warren, Center for the Study of American Business; J. Fred Weston, University of California at Los Angeles; and Marsha Zelinski, Exxon Mobil Corporation.

The following reviewers provided many helpful comments and suggestions for this edition: Susan Key, Kamal Dean Parhizgar, Douglas McCabe, Caroline Rider, and Dennis Wittmer.

At California State University, Los Angeles, we want to thank G. Timothy Haight and Paul Washburn for their generous support throughout the writing of this volume. At the John F. Kennedy Memorial Library, Alan Stein gave valuable advice on the research process.

We are grateful to the editorial team at McGraw-Hill/Irwin, especially to Andy Winston, our sponsoring editor, for his conceptual advice and encouragement; to Sara Ramos, editorial coordinator, for her graceful guidance as the manuscript was written; and to Jim Labeots, project manager, for his skill in creating a finished product. In addition, we appreciate the contributions of our copyeditor whose insights about language and attention to detail enabled us to express our ideas more effectively. We also are grateful to Judy Kausal and Amy Bethia for permissions research.

Finally, special thanks is owed to Deborah Luedy for her generous support and artistic contributions.

George A. Steiner
John F. Steiner

About the Authors

George A. Steiner

is one of the leading pioneers in the development of university curriculums, research, and scholarly writings in the field of business, government, and society. In 1983 he was the recipient of the first Sumner Marcus Award for distinguished achievement in the field by the Social Issues in Management Division of the Academy of Management. In 1990 he received the Distinguished Educator Award, given for the second time by the Academy of Management. After receiving his B.S. in business administration at Temple University, he was awarded an M.A. in economics from the Wharton School of the University of Pennsylvania and a Ph.D. in economics from the University of Illinois. He is the author of many books and articles. Two of his books received "book-of-the-year" awards. In recognition of his writings, Temple University awarded him a Litt.D. honorary degree. Professor Steiner has held top-level positions in the federal government and in industry, including corporate board directorships. Past president of the Academy of Management and co-founder of *The California Management Review,* he is Harry and Elsa Kunin Professor of Business and Society and Professor of Management, Emeritus, Anderson School, UCLA.

John F. Steiner

is Professor of Management at California State University, Los Angeles. He received his B.S. from Southern Oregon University and received an M.A. and Ph.D. in political science from the University of Arizona. He has coauthored two other books with George A. Steiner, *Issues in Business and Society* and *Casebook for Business, Government, and Society.* He is also the author of *Industry, Society, and Change: A Casebook.* Professor Steiner is a former chair of the Social Issues in Management Division of the Academy of Management and former chair of the Department of Management at California State University, Los Angeles.

Part One

A Framework for Studying Business, Government, and Society

Chapter **One**

Introduction to the Field

Exxon Mobil Corporation

Every business exists in the embrace of one or more governments and societies. The story of one large corporation, ExxonMobil, reveals complex and profound relationships among these entities.

ExxonMobil* descends from the original Standard Oil trust. Incorporated by John D. Rockefeller as Standard Oil of New Jersey in 1882, it once controlled more than 90 percent of the American oil industry. Its power so offended public values that in 1890 Congress passed the Sherman Antitrust Act to strike at its near monopoly. In 1911, after years of legal battles, the trust was finally broken into 39 separate companies. However, after the breakup Standard Oil of New Jersey continued to exist, and although it shed 57 percent of its assets to create the new firms, it remained the world's largest oil company. Some companies formed in the breakup were Amoco, ARCO, Cheeseborough-Ponds (a company that made petroleum jelly), Chevron, Conoco, Mobil, and Sohio. In 1972 Standard Oil of New Jersey changed its name to Exxon, and in 1999 it merged with Mobil Corporation, formerly Standard Oil of New York, to form ExxonMobil, a recombination of two firms from the old-time trust.

ExxonMobil is headquartered in Irving, Texas, listed by *Fortune* magazine as America's largest corporation, and generally thought of as an American firm, but it does business in 118 countries and gets 80 percent of its revenues from outside America. Its main business is exploring for, producing, and selling oil and natural gas, and that is where 92 percent of these revenues come from; but it also runs chemical plants, coal and copper mines, and power plants. It employs 99,000 people.

*The company prefers that Exxon and Mobil be written as two words when followed by the word corporation, but combined as one word when not followed by the word corporation.

ExxonMobil faces a competitive *business environment*. Although it is the largest private energy firm, it has only 5.6 percent of the world's daily output of barrels of oil. It competes not only with other investor-owned energy companies but with larger government-owned firms and with the Organization of Petroleum Exporting Countries (OPEC), which has 40 percent of world output. In the energy industry rivals know ExxonMobil as a fierce competitor. The company itself recently noted that it "employs all methods of competition which are lawful and appropriate."[1] It has an authoritarian corporate culture focused on twin strategies of cost-cutting and growth. Its energy philosophy is that no practical alternative to hydrocarbon energy will soon exist, so it gets new oil and natural gas fields into production as fast as possible. In recent years, the company has been more profitable than its peers.

ExxonMobil faces a complex *government environment*. The laws and regulations of each country in which it does business restrict operations. In the United States, for example, there are about 300 federal regulatory agencies, most of which impose rules and standards. In foreign countries ExxonMobil faces import and export restrictions, price controls, and rules that restrict production, for example, to protect nature. Beyond such restrictions, it faces political risks. In Indonesia it recently defied the government and suspended natural gas production when a rebel army threatened the lives of workers. In 2000 it supported governments by paying $68 billion in taxes worldwide, a sum so huge that it exceeds the revenues of all but seven other corporations on the *Fortune* 500 list for that year. Governments also subsidize ExxonMobil in various ways. At a cost of billions annually, the U.S. military defends Middle Eastern oil fields that it pumps. The Army Corps of Engineers dredges harbor channels for its supertankers.

ExxonMobil faces a complex *social environment*. Energy is the fuel of society, and the energy industry is the world's largest and most important because it makes economies run. Energy-poor countries are backward, their people impoverished. So ExxonMobil provides a vital resource; however, because it is so large and because of the physical nature of its products, its operations are widely felt and closely scrutinized by environmental, civil rights, animal rights, labor, and consumer groups—many of which are hostile. Sometimes its impacts on society are negative. For example, there are cancer-causing chemicals such as benzine in ExxonMobil gasoline, as in the gasoline of all oil companies, and the costs of the disease they cause, while difficult to estimate and perhaps great, are not reflected in the price at the pump. These costs, not paid by ExxonMobil, are a hidden subsidy of the company by its customers.

In 1989 a company tanker, the *Exxon Valdez,* spilled 11 million gallons of oil into Alaskan waters. The disaster created enormous legal, political, and social problems for Exxon. Relations became tense and bitter with the State of Alaska and several federal agencies, including the Department of

[1] Exxon Mobil Corporation, *Form 10-K,* March 28, 2001, p. 1.

Justice and the Environmental Protection Agency. In 1990 a punitive federal law, the Oil Protection Act, was passed. One provision, inserted by Senator Ted Stevens (R-Alaska), barred the *Exxon Valdez* from ever again entering Prince William Sound, where the oil spill occurred.

ExxonMobil spent $2.5 billion to clean up the spill, $1.1 billion to settle lawsuits by the State of Alaska and the federal government for harm to the environment, and $300 million to pay damage claims by people and businesses. Still, in 1996 a jury in Alaska ordered the company to pay an additional $5 billion in punitive damages. The company called the award outrageous, and in 2001 an appeals court ordered a reduction, but no final amount is yet determined.[2]

The spill tarnished the company's long reputation for environmental responsibility. Critics accused it of lax operations, a grudging response to public concerns about the damage, and a slow cleanup. The previous year Exxon ranked sixth on *Fortune* magazine's list of most admired companies; the year of the spill, it dropped to 110.[3] Fifty thousand consumers tore up their Exxon credit cards.

ExxonMobil angered Alaska residents by challenging the law prohibiting return of the *Exxon Valdez* to their shores. The tanker, which was renamed *SeaRiver Mediterranean,* now sails around the Mediterranean Sea, but its large capacity could benefit the company more in Alaska because profit margins on Alaskan crude are higher. ExxonMobil believes that under maritime law no precedent exists for banning a ship from navigable waters. One of its lawyers compared the ban with a prohibition on driving a car past the point of a prior accident. Alaska residents see it differently. According to a fisheries professor at the University of Alaska, returning the ship "would be like telling the people of Hiroshima you want to bring the Enola Gay back to Japan for passenger service."[4] Nonetheless, the company is pressing in court for its return.

ExxonMobil funds worldwide programs to benefit nature and communities. These range from a $6.6 million campaign to save from extinction the world's five remaining tiger species, an appropriate project since the tiger is the company's symbol, to sponsorship of free poetry readings in Singapore, where the company has a $2 billion chemical plant. In 2000 the company funded $92 million of such charitable programs. This sounds like a large sum from the perspective of an individual. However, for ExxonMobil it is four ten-thousandths of 1 percent of its $210.4 billion revenues, the equivalent of a person making $100,000 a year giving 44 cents to charity. Although nearly 70 percent of ExxonMobil's revenues come from outside the United States and it drains oil and gas from some

[2] *In re: the Exxon Valdez v. Joseph Hazelwood and Exxon Corporation,* 270 F.3d 1215 (2001).
[3] Paul Wiseman, "Dark Days for Oil Giant," *USA Today,* April 26, 1990, p. 1B.
[4] Rick Steiner, quoted in Stanton H. Patty, "In the Wake of the Valdez," *San Francisco Examiner,* February 8, 1998, p. T1.

of the most abject areas on the globe, only 21 percent of the $92 million given for social causes goes outside the country. Does this pattern of giving live up to the elegant example of founder John D. Rockefeller, the great philanthropist of his era? In September 2001 ExxonMobil was a leading contributor to relief efforts after the World Trade Center terrorist attacks, giving $10 million within days.

Infinite relationships exist among businesses, governments, and societies. The story of ExxonMobil illustrates why the study of these relationships—the subject matter of this text—is so important to managers. In this first chapter we begin by defining the field and discussing its importance. Then we present four basic models that reveal alternative ways of seeing the business–government–society relationship. Finally, we explain our approach to the field.

WHAT IS THE BUSINESS–GOVERNMENT–SOCIETY (BGS) FIELD?

In the universe of human endeavor, we can distinguish subdivisions of economic, political, and social activity—that is, business, government, and society—in every nation throughout time. The interplay among these activities creates an environment in which business operates. The BGS field is the study of this environment and its effect on management.

First, we define the basic terms. *Business* is a broad term encompassing a range of actions and institutions from hamburger stands to giant corporations. The term covers manufacturing, finance, trade, service, and other economic activities. The fundamental purpose of business activity is to satisfy human needs by creating products and services.

Government refers to structures and processes in society that authoritatively make and carry out policies and rules. Like business, it encompasses a wide range of organizations at many levels, from international to local. One focus in this book is on the economic and regulatory powers of government and their impact on business.

A *society* is a network of human relations that includes three interacting elements: (1) ideas, (2) institutions, and (3) material things.

Ideas, or intangible objects of thought, include values and ideologies. Values are enduring beliefs concerning fundamental choices in personal and social life. Ideologies—for example, democracy and capitalism—are bundles of values that create a certain world view. They establish the broad goals of life expressed in terms of what is considered good, true, right, beautiful, and acceptable. Ideas shape the institutions of society, including business.

Institutions are formal patterns of relations that link people together to accomplish a goal. Examples are corporations, governments, labor unions, universities, and legal systems. Rules and procedures determine how they work. Institutions reflect prevailing ideas in a society.

They are essential to coordinate the work of individuals who have no personal relationship with each other.[5]

The third element in society is *material things,* including natural resources, land, and manufactured goods. These help shape, and are partly products of, ideas and institutions. Economic institutions, together with the extent of resources, mainly determine the type and quantity of society's material goods.

The BGS field studies the interaction of the three broad areas defined above, and it does so primarily by focusing on the interaction of business with the other two elements. The primary focus, therefore, is on how business shapes and changes government and society, and how it, in turn, is molded by political and social pressures. Of special interest is how forces in the BGS nexus affect the manager's task.

In every country, the BGS relationship is unique and changes over time. In the United States, for example, business was much more free of restraint by government 100 years ago than it is now. In Russia, due to the fall of communism, private companies are freer from government restraint now than just 15 years ago, but they face a population in which hostility toward profits is widespread due to the persistence of socialist values.

WHY IS THE BGS FIELD IMPORTANT TO MANAGERS?

To succeed in meeting its objectives, a business must be responsive to both its economic and its noneconomic environment. ExxonMobil, for example, must be efficient in producing and transporting energy to consumers. Yet swift response to market forces is not always enough. There are powerful nonmarket forces to which every business, especially a large one, is exposed. Their importance is clear in the two dramatic events that punctuate Exxon Mobil Corporation's history—the 1911 court-ordered breakup and the 1989 *Exxon Valdez* oil spill.

In 1911 the Supreme Court, in a decision that reflected public opinion and political will as well as interpretation of the law, forced Standard Oil to conform with social values that favored open, competitive markets. With unparalleled economic genius, courage, and perspicacity, John D. Rockefeller and his lieutenants built a wonder of efficiency that spread fuel and light throughout America at lower cost than otherwise would have prevailed. They never understood why this remarkable commercial performance was not the full measure of Standard Oil. But beyond efficiency, the public demanded fair play and justice. Thus, the great company was dismembered. In the Alaska disaster, it was not a slow accretion of growing discontent but a sudden accident that instantly changed

---

[5] Arnold J. Toynbee, *A Study of History,* vol. XII, *Reconsiderations* (London: Oxford University Press, 1961), p. 270.

Procter & Gamble Acknowledges a Social Contract

Procter & Gamble does business in 70 countries. Its understanding of the social contract shows in these excerpts from its policy statement "Our Role in Society."

> A corporation like Procter & Gamble traces its existence to laws established by society. In establishing the corporation, society gave it certain rights to encourage its success and longevity. In return, we believe a corporation has certain responsibilities to society—to the governmental entities which authorize its existence, to our employees, our shareholders, our consumers, and the communities and nations where we operate. . . .

Source: "Corporate Citizenship" at www.pg.com.

ExxonMobil's political and social environments, ending in billions of dollars of sanctions. Today ExxonMobil operates its tanker fleet with extreme care. It has new environmental safeguards, avoids high-risk areas, and randomly tests crew members for drugs and alcohol. Remarkably, over a recent four-year period it lost only 10 barrels of oil out of 2.8 billion barrels moved on its ships.[6]

Recognizing that a company operates not only within markets but within a society is critical. If the society, or one or more of the power interests within it, does not accept a company's actions, that firm will be punished and constrained. There exists in every era a basic agreement between business institutions and society known as the *social contract*. This contract defines broad relationships between business and society. It is partly expressed in statutes and laws, but it also resides in social values. To illustrate, after high unemployment throughout Europe in the 1930s depression years, public faith in free markets wavered, and to ensure full employment, countries took over and ran companies in major industries. Nationalizing these enterprises enforced the implicit obligation of business under the social contract to provide jobs. More recently, the state-run firms in Europe, grown inefficient and bloated, became uncompetitive in world markets and were forced to lay off workers. Many have been reprivatized. Laws or rules designed to create full employment in another era have been relaxed—all to ensure continued high employment.

Unfortunately for managers, the social contract is not as clear-cut as are the economic forces a business faces, as complex and ambiguous as the latter often are. For example, the public widely believes that business

[6] Exxon Mobil Corporation, "Pounds of Prevention, Tons of Cure," *National Journal,* March 31, 2001, p. 953 (advertisement).

has social responsibilities beyond making profits and obeying regulations. If a business does not meet them, it may suffer. But precisely what are they? How can we measure a corporation's performance with respect to them? To what extent must a business comply with ethical obligations not written into law? What is the priority when meeting social expectations conflicts with maximizing profits? Nevertheless, the social contract expresses the normative expectations of a society, and managers who ignore or violate it are courting disaster.

FOUR MODELS OF THE BGS RELATIONSHIP

People view the interplay of BGS forces with mental models that lead them to reach varying conclusions about central issues. There is no exact or consensual model of the BGS relationship. Depending on the prism used by a person to view these forces, they will think differently about the scope of business power in society, criteria for managerial decisions, the extent of corporate social responsibility, the ethical duties of managers, and the need for regulation.

The following four models are basic alternatives for seeing the BGS relationship. As abstractions they simplify reality, but each is a strong lens for focusing on central issues. With one exception, each model can be both descriptive and prescriptive; that is, it can be both an explanation of how the BGS relationship does work and, in addition, an ideal about how it should work.

The Market Capitalism Model

The market capitalism model, shown in Figure 1.1, describes business as substantially sheltered from direct impact by sociopolitical forces and focuses on the primacy of economic forces. It depicts business as existing within a market environment shaped both by business operations and by social and political pressures. The market in the model is a buffer between business units and nonmarket forces.

The system depicted here is called classical capitalism. In it, most economic activity is carried on by private firms in competitive markets. The pricing mechanism of the market allocates resources. The efficient operation of this system is based on some fundamental assumptions.[7]

One assumption is that government interference in economic life is slight. This is called *laissez-faire,* a term first used by the French to mean literally that government should "let us alone." This stood for the idea that government intervention in the market is both inappropriate and

[7] The model was built in consideration of the way in which the ideal operation of the free enterprise system was first enunciated by Adam Smith in his *Wealth of Nations* (New York: Modern Library, 1937), first published in 1776.

FIGURE 1.1
The Market Capitalism Model

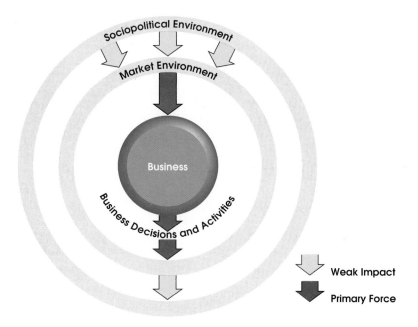

unnecessary. It is inappropriate because it lessens the efficiency with which free enterprise operates to benefit consumers. It is unnecessary because market forces are more efficient than government in channeling economic resources to meet society's needs. Noneconomic goals or performance measures are not legitimate yardsticks for judging business. Market performance should be the only accepted measure of social performance. It is for governments, not the free enterprise system, to minister to social problems. Managers, therefore, should define company interests narrowly, as profitability and efficient use of scarce resources. Business makes its primary contribution to society by creating wealth, jobs, taxes, goods, and services.

Another fundamental assumption is that individuals have freedom to pursue their own self-interest. Every person, it is reasoned, is motivated to make money. Acting through markets, the greed of each individual is harnessed to create economic progress. In market competition, individuals and companies enrich themselves and society only by creating value for customers.

The model assumes also that individuals can own private property and are free to risk investments. Under these circumstances, managers are powerfully motivated to make a profit. If free competition exists in the market, it will hold profits to a minimum and the quality of products and services will rise as firms try to attract more buyers. If one enterprise tries to increase profits by charging higher prices, consumers will go to a competitor. If one producer makes higher-quality products, others will be

Full Production and Full Employment under Our Democratic System of Private Enterprise, **ca. 1944, a crayon and ink drawing by Michael Lenson, an artist working for the Works Progress Administration Federal Art Project. Lenson focuses on the virtues of market capitalism.** Source: Courtesy of The Library of Congress.

forced to follow. In this way, markets convert selfish competition into broad social benefits.

Space does not permit elaboration of all the assumptions but we can mention others. Consumers are informed about products and prices and make rational decisions; moral restraint accompanies the self-interested behavior of business; basic institutions such as banking and laws exist to ease commerce; and there are many producers in competitive markets.

The perspective of the market capitalism model encourages the following conclusions about the BGS relationship. Government regulation should be limited. Markets discipline private economic activity to promote social welfare. The proper measure of corporate performance is profit. The ethical duty of management is to promote the interests of shareholders; by doing so, managers inevitably serve society and meet the requirements of the social contract.

In the United States, the idea of laissez-faire economics dominated the public imagination from the colonial era to the 1930s depression years. Over this time, the model accurately described the BGS relationship. Beginning in the 1930s, however, faith in the market was tarnished by visible failures of the business system, including high unemployment, monopoly, unethical behavior, income inequality, and pollution. Popular disenchantment with laissez-faire led to massive intrusions of government into markets to correct these flaws.

Today the concept of free market capitalism still inspires. In addition, corporation law formed in earlier eras enshrines its assumptions, making it the duty of management to run firms for shareholder benefit. However, as a description of today's BGS relationship it is distorted in light of current realities.[8] The social responsiveness of business is not as limited as this model implies, and other assumptions in the model are contrary to reality. Self-interested behavior of business is no longer seen as entirely benign and beneficent. It has become apparent with the growth of enterprises in

[8] For a perceptive commentary on the assumptions underlying market capitalism, see Charles E. Lindblom, *The Market System: What It Is, How It Works, and What to Make of It* (New Haven: Yale University Press, 2001).

FIGURE 1.2
**The Dominance
Model**

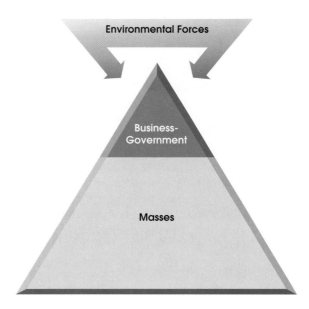

size and reach that sole reliance on the profit motive creates harmful spillover effects such as the destruction of nature. Therefore, government regulation is now extensive. Contemporary managers must respond to sociopolitical forces outside markets. And society demands additional measures of corporate responsibility beyond just efficiency and profitability.

Nevertheless, the model is still widely used as a lens through which many, particularly managers and economists, view the BGS relationship. The ideology of market capitalism remains the dominant source of economic values in the United States and is of growing importance in other nations.

The Dominance Model

The dominance model is a second basic way of seeing the BGS relationship. It represents primarily the perspective of business critics. In it, business and government dominate the great mass of people. This idea is represented in the pyramidal, hierarchical image of society shown in Figure 1.2. Those who subscribe to the model believe that a small elite sits astride a system that works to increase and perpetuate wealth and power for a privileged few at the expense of the many. Such a system is, of course, undemocratic. In democratic theory, government and leaders represent interests expressed by the people.

Proponents of the dominance model focus on the defects and inefficiencies of market capitalism. They believe that corporations are insulated from pressures that promote responsibility to society, that regulation by a government in thrall to big business is feeble, and that market forces are inadequate to ensure ethical management. Unlike other models, the dominance model does not represent an ideal in addition to a description of how things are. For its advocates, the ideal is to turn it upside down so that the BGS relationship conforms to democratic principles.

In the United States, the dominance model gained a following during the latter half of the nineteenth century when large trusts such as Standard Oil emerged, buying politicians, exploiting workers, monopolizing markets, and sharpening income inequality. Beginning in the 1870s, farmers and other critics of big business rejected the ideal of the market capitalism model and based a reform movement called populism on the critical view of the BGS relationship implied in the dominance model.

This was an era when, for the first time, on a national scale the actions of powerful business magnates shaped the destinies of common people. And they openly displayed their contempt for commoners. "The public be damned," snapped William H. Vanderbilt when a reporter told him that as a railroad owner he had a responsibility to the public, "I am working for my stockholders."[9] Later, Edward Harriman, the aloof and arrogant president of the Union Pacific Railroad, allegedly reassured industry leaders worried about reform legislation, saying "that he 'could buy Congress' and that if necessary he 'could buy the judiciary.' "[10] It was with respect to Harriman that President Theodore Roosevelt once noted that "men of very great wealth in too many instances totally failed to understand the temper of the country and its needs."[11]

The populist movement in America ultimately fell short of reforming the BGS relationship to a democratic ideal. Other industrializing nations, notably Japan, had similar populist movements. Marxism, an ideology opposed to industrial capitalism, emerged in Europe at about the same time as these movements, and it also contained ideas resonant with the dominance model. In capitalist societies, according to Karl Marx, an owner class dominates the economy and ruling institutions. Many business critics worldwide advocated socialist reforms that, based on Marx's theory, could achieve more equitable distribution of wealth and power.

Critical attitudes about business in a capitalist society live on. Ralph Nader, declaring his 2000 candidacy for president, spoke the language of the dominance model.

> Over the past twenty years, big business has increasingly dominated our political economy. This control by corporate government over our political government is creating a widening "democracy gap." . . . The unconstrained behavior of big business is subordinating our democracy to

[9] Cited in Clifton Fadiman, ed., *The Little Brown Book of Anecdotes* (Boston: Little Brown, 1985), p. 560.
[10] Quoted from correspondence of Theodore Roosevelt in Maury Klein, *The Life & Legend of E. H. Harriman* (Chapel Hill: University of North Carolina Press, 2000), p. 369.
[11] Ibid., p. 363.

This 1900 political cartoon illustrates a central theme of the dominance model, that powerful business interests act in concert with government to further selfish money interests. Although the cartoon is old, the idea remains compelling for many.

IN THE HANDS OF HIS PHILANTHROPIC FRIENDS.

the control of a corporate plutocracy that knows few self-imposed limits to the spread of its power to all sectors of our society.[12]

In the United States today, the dominance model, in its most unadulterated form, is a theory opposed by considerable research suggesting that multiple forces in society channel and control corporate and government power. It may have been more accurate in the late 1800s when it first arose to conceptualize a world shaken by industrialization. However, it remains popular, and in recent years the growing size and power of transnational corporations has given it new life in a global context.

The Countervailing Forces Model

The countervailing forces model, shown in Figure 1.3, depicts the BGS relationship as a flow of reciprocal interactions among the major elements of society. It suggests complex exchanges of influence among them, attributing dominance to none.

This is a model of multiple, or pluralistic, forces. Their strength waxes and wanes depending on factors such as the subject at issue, the power of competing interests, the intensity of public opinion, and the influence

[12] "Statement of Ralph Nader," in *The Ralph Nader Reader* (New York: Seven Stories Press, 2000), pp. 3 and 4.

FIGURE 1.3
The Countervailing
Forces Model

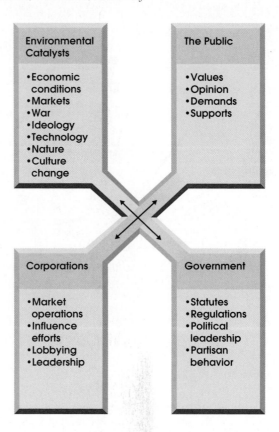

of leaders. The countervailing forces model reflects the BGS relationship in industrialized nations with democratic traditions. It differs from the market capitalism model, because it opens business directly to influence by nonmarket forces. Many important interactions implied in this model would be evaluated as negligible in the dominance model.

What overarching conclusions can be drawn from this model?

1. Business is deeply integrated into an open society and must respond to many forces, both economic and noneconomic. It is not isolated from its social environment, nor is it dominant.

2. Business is a major initiator of change in society through its interaction with government, its production and marketing activities, and its use of new technologies.

3. Broad public support of business depends on its adjustment to multiple social, political, and economic forces. Incorrect adjustment leads to failure. This is the social contract at work.

4. BGS relationships continuously evolve as changes take place in the main ideas, institutions, and processes of society.

FIGURE 1.4   **The Stakeholder Model**

The Stakeholder Model

In the stakeholder model, as shown in Figure 1.4, the business firm is at the center of a set of mutual relationships with persons and groups known as *stakeholders.* Stakeholders are those whom the firm's operation has benefited or burdened; that is, they have a stake in it. For a large corporation, this definition of a stakeholder includes a wide range of entities, which can be divided into two categories based on their relative importance. *Primary stakeholders* have an immediate, continuous, and powerful impact on a firm. They are stockholders (owners), customers, employees, communities, and governments and may, depending on the firm, include others such as suppliers or creditors. *Secondary stakeholders* include a wide range of entities that have less power to influence the firm's activities but that effect or are affected by its operations. Examples are environmentalists, the media, trade associations, universities, and religious orders.[13]

Exponents of the model debate how to identify who or what is a stakeholder.[14] Some use a very broad definition and include, for example, future generations and natural entities such as the earth's atmosphere, oceans, terrain, and living creatures because corporations have an impact on them.[15]

The stakeholder model reorders the priorities of management away from what they are in the market capitalism model. There, the corporation is the private property of those who invest capital in it. Its dominant goal is to benefit just one group—the investors. In the stakeholder model, however, the welfare of each stakeholder must be considered as an end; stakeholder interests have intrinsic worth, they are not valued only to the extent that they enrich investors. Put differently, "stakeholders are defined by *their* legitimate interest in the corporation, rather than simply by the corporation's interest in *them*."[16] Managers should be strongly responsive to multiple stakeholders, and because of this, the investor's interests receive less priority.

The view of the corporation prescribed by the stakeholder model, then, emphasizes duties toward groups in society, duties not recognized in classical economic theory, which encourages domination of the environment and maximization of stockholder wealth. Stakeholder theory asserts a moral duty for management to raise its gaze above profits to see and respond to a range of other values. One group of scholars, for example, urges that corporations "should adopt processes and modes of behavior that are sensitive to the concerns and capabilities of each stakeholder constituency."[17]

The stakeholder model is more than a descriptive model of corporations in their environment. Advocates intend it to redefine the corporation; they reject the shareholder-centered view of the firm in the market capitalism model. "The plain truth is," write two of its advocates, "that the most prominent alternative to stakeholder theory (i.e., the 'management serving the shareowners' theory) is morally untenable."[18]

---

[13] See, for example, Max Clarkson, "A Stakeholder Framework for Analyzing and Evaluating Corporate Social Performance," in Max E. Clarkson, ed., *The Corporation and Its Stakeholders: Classic and Contemporary Readings* (Toronto: University of Toronto Press, 1998).

[14] Ronald K. Mitchell, Bradley R. Agle, and Donna J. Wood, "Toward a Theory of Stakeholder Identification and Salience: Defining the Principle of Who and What Really Counts," *Academy of Management Review,* October 1997, pp. 853–64.

[15] See, for example, Edward Stead and Jean Garner Stead, "Earth: A Spiritual Stakeholder," *Business Ethics Quarterly,* Ruffin Series no. 2, 2000, pp. 231–44.

[16] Thomas Donaldson and Lee E. Preston, "The Stakeholder Theory of the Corporation: Concepts, Evidence, and Implications," *Academy of Management Review,* January 1995, p. 76.

[17] Clarkson Centre for Business Ethics, *Principles of Stakeholder Management* (Toronto: Clarkson Centre for Business Ethics, 1999), also at http://mgmt.utoronto.ca/stake/Principles.htm.

[18] Donaldson and Preston, "The Stakeholder Theory of the Corporation," p. 88.

The stakeholder model seeks to create a doctrine of ethical duties toward multiple constituents that would replace the market economic doctrines at the heart of corporate life. But not everyone agrees. Critics of the model argue that it is not a realistic assessment of power relationships between the corporation and other entities. It seeks to give power to the powerless by replacing force with moral duty, a timeless and often futile quest of moralists. In addition, it sets up too vague a guideline to substitute for the clear yardstick of maximizing profits for investors. There are some mysteries in stakeholder theory. It is not clear who or what is a legitimate stakeholder, to what each stakeholder is entitled, or how managers should balance competing demands among a range of stakeholders. And, unlike the old criterion of return of capital in traditional capitalism, there is no single, clear, and objective measure to evaluate the combined ethical/economic performance of a firm. According to one critic, this lack of a criterion "would render impossible rational management decision-making for there is simply no way to adjudicate between alternative projects when there is more than one bottom line."[19] Predicts another critic, "it promises to make the boardroom (populated . . . by representatives of all stakeholding groups) the site of wasteful, inefficient interest-group politicking."[20]

WHAT ARE THE MAIN CHARACTERISTICS OF THE ANALYSIS IN THIS BOOK?

Discussion of the BGS field could be organized in many ways. The following comments describe our approach.

Comprehensive Scope

This book is comprehensive. We try to cover many subjects. This method contrasts with intensive focus on a few areas. We believe that for those new to the field seeing a panorama is better than receiving in-depth treatment of a few issues.

Interdisciplinary Approach with a Management Focus

This is a field in which the limited perspectives of single academic disciplines impede understanding. Many disciplines illuminate its theory, practice, and issues. These include the business disciplines, particularly management; the social sciences, including economics, political science, philosophy, history, and sociology; the professional disciplines, including medicine, law, and theology; and from time to time,

[19] John Argenti, "Stakeholders: The Case Against," *Long Range Planning,* June 1997, p. 444.
[20] Alexei M. Marcoux, "Business Ethics Gone Wrong," *CATO Policy Report,* May–June 2000, p. 11.

the natural sciences such as biology and chemistry. Thus, our approach is eclectic; we cross boundaries to find insight.

Our dominant orientation, however, is the discipline of management and, within it, the study of *strategic management,* or actions that adapt a company to its changing environment. To compete and survive, firms must create missions, purposes, and objectives; the policies and programs to achieve them; and the methods to implement them. We discuss these elements as they relate to corporate social performance, illustrating successes and failures.

Use of Theory, Description, and Case Studies

Theories simplify and organize areas of knowledge by describing patterns or regularities in the subject matter. They are important in every field, but especially in this one, where innumerable details from broad ranges of human experience intersect to create a new intellectual universe. Where theory is missing or weak, scholarship must rely more on description and the use of case method.

Right now there is no underlying theory to integrate the entire field. Fortunately, the community of scholars studying BGS relationships is building two broad platforms of theory. The first is theory describing how corporations interact with stakeholders. This theory is rudimentary today, but a growing body of scholarship shows increasing sophistication and wider agreement on basic ideas. The second is theory explaining corporate social performance and how it can be measured. This area of theory building focuses on defining exactly what a firm does to be responsible in society and on creating scales and rulers with which to weigh and measure its actions.[21]

Despite the lack of a single unifying theory in the field, useful theories abound in relevant disciplines. For example, there are tested economic theories about the impact of government regulation, scientific theories regarding industrial pollution, political theories explaining corporate power, and legal theories concerned with subjects such as manufacturer liability for dangerous products. When fitting, we discuss such theories; elsewhere we rely on description of events. We also present case studies at the end of each chapter that raise unsettled, controversial issues for discussion and contemplation.

Global Perspective

A central focus in this book is the BGS relationship in the United States. Yet the spread of a global economy makes it impossible to isolate the BGS relationship in one country from international forces. Besides

---

[21] For an overview of theory-building efforts in the field, see Donna J. Wood, "Theory and Integrity in Business and Society," *Business and Society,* December 2000; and Jeffrey S. Harrison and R. Edward Freeman, "Stakeholders, Social Responsibility, and Performance: Empirical Evidence and Theoretical Perspectives," *Academy of Management Journal,* October 1999.

ExxonMobil, with 80 percent of its sales in foreign countries, a growing number of the largest American corporations have most of their sales in other countries—examples are Coca-Cola (63 percent), Dow Chemical (60 percent), IBM (57 percent), and Hewlett-Packard (55 percent). Many of the largest foreign transnationals also get the bulk of their revenue outside their home countries—examples are Nestlé of Switzerland (98.5 percent), Unilever of the Netherlands and the United Kingdom (88 percent), DaimlerChrysler of Germany (81 percent), and Sony of Japan (72 percent).[22] The growth of global markets has had a profound impact on governments, which find their economic and social welfare policies judged by world financial markets. And on a societal plane, issues such as the environment, human rights, and income inequality challenge the international community. Therefore, in this book the perspective is often global.

Historical Perspective

History is the study of phenomena moving through time. The BGS relationship is a stream of events, of which only one part exists today. Historical perspective is important for many reasons. It helps us see that today's BGS relationship is not like that of other eras; that current ideas and institutions are not the only alternative; that historical forces are irrepressible; that corporations both cause and adapt to change; that our era is not unique in undergoing rapid change; and that we are shaping the future now. When appropriate, we examine the antecedents of current arrangements.

[22] Figures are based on 1998 sales data in United Nations Conference on Trade and Development, *World Investment Report 2000* (New York: United Nations, 2000), pp. 72–74.

Chapter **Two**

The Dynamic Environment

The Royal Dutch/Shell Group of Companies

Royal Dutch/Shell is the second-largest private energy company in the world. Like ExxonMobil, it engages in worldwide exploration, production, and marketing of oil, natural gas, fuels, chemicals, and electricity. It employs 416,500 workers in 135 countries. In 2000 it had revenue of $149 billion, making it a little more than two-thirds the size of ExxonMobil. Its net profits were 8.5 percent of revenues, slightly exceeding ExxonMobil's 8.4 percent.[1]

Shell is a beehive of 1,700 separate companies. The stock of each of these is owned by one of three holding companies that are themselves owned by two partners, Royal Dutch Petroleum Company, a Dutch company that owns 60 percent, and Shell Transport and Trading Company, a United Kingdom company that owns 40 percent. This partnership began in 1907. The shell in the company's yellow and red logo symbolizes the distant origin of the English partner, which started back in 1833 as a small London shop selling sea shells.

Royal Dutch/Shell has a unique and pioneering method of analyzing its environment using scenarios, or stories, about the future.[2] A *scenario* is a plausible projection of the future based on assumptions about how current trends will develop. Carefully written scenarios challenge complacent thinking since they force consideration of alternative worlds that may come to exist. They are like mental wind tunnels in which environmental forces are shifted around the form of the company to see how it "flies."

In 1971 Shell staff members developed a scenario in which oil-rich countries cut their exports to raise prices. This was thought unlikely in the con-

---

[1] "The Global 500," *Fortune,* July 23, 2001, p. F1.
[2] See Peter Schwartz, *The Art of the Long View* (New York: Doubleday Currency, 1991). Schwartz helped Shell with its scenarios, and the book explains how they are created.

ventional wisdom of the day. Nevertheless, it influenced Shell's planning, and when the first OPEC oil embargo occurred in 1973, Shell was the only major oil company prepared for it. This readiness was reflected in its profits for years afterward.

Today global forces, historically unprecedented in their strength and scope, act on the business environment. Shell has a complex structure in which geographically separate companies in different product lines have great autonomy. Imposing a common strategic direction is a critical task. Shell believes that its scenarios foster a common intellectual outlook, helping to bind the organization.

In the early 1990s Shell planners formed a theory of change in the global business environment that has been the foundation of every subsequent scenario. They saw three strong forces shaping the future: liberalization (meaning growing freedom for business from trade restrictions and domestic regulations), globalization, and technology. These forces are inescapable, so businesses, governments, and other entities must adapt to them. Shell planners bottle this belief in a phrase, "THERE IS NO ALTERNATIVE," and use its acronym, TINA, as shorthand for the three forces and their unrelenting nature. According to Shell, "TINA is a rough, impersonal game, involving stresses and pressures akin to those of the Industrial Revolution."[3] The existence of these peremptory forces does not in itself explain how they shape history, so Shell uses scenarios to examine a range of possibilities.

In 1995 two scenarios projecting events out to 2020 were created. Their purpose was to learn what kind of corporations, governments, and economies were best adapted to thrive in the world of TINA. The scenarios were given colorful names serving as shorthand for their content.

- In the *Just Do It* scenario, the values glamorized in the Nike ad campaign based on this slogan prevail. Forces in TINA resonate with Western values promoting extreme individualism, hypercompetition, abundance-based materialism, and fast technological change. Free markets flourish and spread. Fierce global competition erupts. Companies survive and win in this environment by spotting "bubbles of value" in markets and quickly exploiting them before other firms copy their actions. They rapidly introduce new and customized products for customers. They give more freedom and creative opportunity to employees.

- *Da Wo (Big Me)* is a scenario named after a Chinese proverb that reads "Sacrifice 'small me' to benefit 'Big Me.' " It is based on an Asian ideal of community. As opposed to exhibiting excesses of individualism and competition, the world's social, political, and economic systems adapt to the forces in TINA by growing more cooperative. A vision of common welfare

[3] Shell International Limited, *Global Scenarios 1995–2020,* Public Scenarios PX96-2, 1996, p. 2. A longer description of scenarios discussed in this section is at www.shell.com/royal-en/content/0,5028,25432-50913,00.html.

unites humanity, weakening ideologies of individualism and diversity. Asian economies built on networks of trust and long-term relationships prosper and dominate world commerce. Successful companies build webs of alliances with other firms, governments, and civil society groups. They also exhibit high levels of social responsibility to meet rising public expectations.

Another set of scenarios for the years 1998 to 2020 explored the idea that TINA operates on two levels: a level of global markets, financial systems, governments, and other institutions; and an individual level affecting people by making them freer, better educated, and more affluent.[4] What changes could this bring?

- The *New Game* scenario explores the global level. Existing economic, social, and political institutions evolve and new ones emerge to solve problems created by TINA. Yet as the game unfolds with new players, rules, and tactics, it grows more complex. Communications technology spreads ideas and experience quickly. Businesses and other organizations thrive by emphasizing learning and continuously reinventing themselves. Entities that cling to the status quo wither.

- The *People Power* scenario explores how TINA works at the individual level. As wealth, democracy, and education spread there is an explosion of individual diversity, creativity, and free expression. This undermines traditional institutions such as marriage and weakens governments designed in past eras to impose formal and central authority on society. Governments and institutions are unable to cope with TINA at the global level. Because they are slow to fix problems the public loses confidence in them. Frustrated people take action themselves. Local forms of government grow stronger. Nongovernmental organizations gain power. Activist groups bypass governments to take direct, sometimes violent, action against polluters and irresponsible corporations.

All the scenarios are developed at length; each fills a separate volume. Much in them focuses on the future of the energy industry, but they nonetheless represent cutting-edge thoughts about global change. They influence Shell in many ways. The response to TINA guides its global business strategy.[5] The vision of a more open, interconnected world has led to more public disclosure about its operations. The company's website now contains environmental and social responsibility reports and hosts candid discussions.

Scenarios about sustainability written in 2000 led the company to invest more heavily in wind farms, biomass plants, and solar energy systems.[6] It

---

[4] Shell International Limited, *Global Scenarios 1998–2020,* summary brochure, 1998.
[5] See "Strategy" in Royal Dutch Petroleum Company, N. V. Koninklijke Nederlandsche Petroleum Maatschappij, *Annual Report and Accounts 2000* (Amsterdam and London, 2001), p. 20.
[6] World Business Council for Sustainable Development, *Exploring Sustainable Development: Global Scenarios 2000–2050,* summary brochure, p. 21.

revised its statement of core business principles to include sustainability and protection of human rights. In 2001 it endowed an international Shell Foundation with $250 million to fund projects that promote energy sustainability and poverty reduction in less developed nations.

The scenarios have not prevented missteps. Shell was savaged by environmentalists in 1997 over plans to dispose of its Brent Spar oil drilling platform by sinking it in the North Sea.[7] Its reputation was also damaged by human rights activists accusing it of complicity in human rights abuses by Nigerian troops protecting its oil fields. However, scenario learning may have prevented worse misadventures.

Shell uses scenarios to direct its course in a stormy world. In this chapter we explain how a few deep historical forces underlie what is perceived as rapid, turbulent change in the global business environment. Then we discuss specific dimensions of the current business environment, describing major trends and challenges in each. Much in this discussion focuses on subjects at the heart of Shell's scenarios.

VOLATILITY IN THE BUSINESS ENVIRONMENT

In 1844 Philip Hone, the mayor of New York City, was baffled by the volatility of his environment. "This world is going on too fast," he wrote.

> Improvements, Politics, Reform, Religion—all fly. Railroads, steamers, packets, race against time and beat it hollow. Flying is dangerous. By and by we shall have balloons and pass over to Europe between sun and sun. Oh, for the good old days of heavy post-coaches and speed at the rate of six miles an hour![8]

Hone's views reflect what people have experienced throughout history, including today. From ancient to modern times, environments have been volatile and generally unpredictable. For example, the Black Death in the middle of the fourteenth century killed one-third of the population of Europe and completely changed that world. The industrial revolution in the eighteenth century in England was unforeseen and changed the world significantly for all time. After 1870 world trade grew remarkably and early multinationals such as Bayer, Colt, Ford, Lever Bros., Singer, and Standard Oil invested heavily in foreign assets. However, following World War I many nations raised tariffs, and by 1930 foreign investment by companies fell to just half its prewar level. Then, in a climate of international depression, trade collapsed and the world's first experiment

---

[7] John F. Mahon and Richard A. McGowan, "Corporate Reputation, Crises, and Stakeholder Management," *Global Focus* 11, no. 3 (1999), pp. 45–47.
[8] Quoted in John Steel Gordon, "When Our Ancestors Became Us," *American Heritage,* December 1989, p. 108.

with global economic integration ended in failure, changing the destinies of people and businesses.

Throughout history, managers who have been ignorant or unaware of changing environments have, at best, lost opportunities for profit and, at worst, led their companies to failure. Look at the Baldwin Locomotive Works, for example. Matthias W. Baldwin, a watchmaker, started the firm to build steam locomotives. The first engine he produced—"Old Ironsides"—was built in 1832, one of the earliest steam engines made in America. By the time of Baldwin's death in 1866, the plant had made 1,500 locomotives for railroads around the world. As the years went by, Baldwin's company prospered and held a near monopoly on domestic production of steam locomotives. However, its management failed to see the significance of the diesel engine and the company went bankrupt. General Electric seized the opportunity offered by diesel technology and built a prosperous diesel locomotive division to exploit the world market.

Today's changing conditions in the United States and around the globe bewilder people in and out of business with their volatility and scope. For instance, worldwide markets exist for the first time in many industries. Product innovations are so quickly seen and copied that seizing an advantage over competitors is difficult. And societal expectations about the ethical duties of corporations dictate new, elevated performance standards. What insights exist to help us make sense of such pervasive change?

UNDERLYING HISTORICAL FORCES CHANGING THE BUSINESS ENVIRONMENT

We believe that, in a broad sense, order can be found in the swirling patterns of current events; that there is a deep logic in the passing of history; and that change in the business environment is the result of elemental historical forces moving in roughly predictable directions. Henry Adams defined a historical force as "anything that does, or helps to do, work."[9] The work to which Adams refers is the power to cause events. Change in the business environment is the work of nine deep historical forces or streams of related events discussed below.

The Industrial Revolution

The first historical force is the industrial revolution. It is a powerful force that grips the imagination of humanity. The term *industrial revolution* refers to transforming changes that turn simple economies of farmers

---

[9] In the essay "A Dynamic Theory of History (1904)," in Henry Adams, *The Education of Henry Adams* (New York: Modern Library, 1931), p. 474; originally published in 1908.

FIGURE 2.1
**World GDP Growth
in 50-Year Intervals**

Source: Bradford J. DeLong,
"Estimating World GDP, One
Million B.C.–Present,"
available at
http://econ161.berkeley.edu.

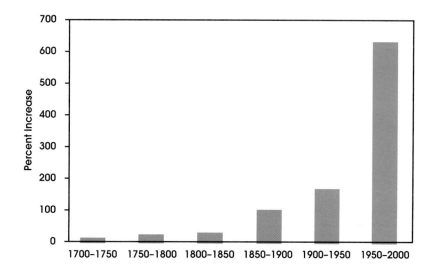

and artisans into complex industrial economies. Such change requires specific conditions, including a sufficiency of capital, labor, natural resources, and fuels; transportation; strong markets; and the ideas and institutions to combine effectively these ingredients. In world history, these conditions first arose in England during the late eighteenth century, then spread to Western Europe and the United States during the nineteenth century. Japan and Russia took off in the first half of the twentieth century, and other Asian nations, including Taiwan, South Korea, and China, followed in the second half. Industrialization continues to spread as less developed nations try to create the conditions for it.

Industrial growth remakes societies. It elevates living standards, alters life experiences, and shifts values. Since institutions built on older ideas change more slowly than people's lives, industrialization generates huge strains in the social fabric. It continues today to generate these strains in both developing and developed economies. The striking thing about economic growth is its astounding size and acceleration in the twentieth century. The total amount of goods and services produced in the twentieth century exceeds all that produced in recorded human history. Indeed, as Figure 2.1 shows, output for just the second half of the century, from 1950 to 2000, exceeds all that came before.

Inequality

From time immemorial, status distinctions, class structures, and gaps between rich and poor have defined societies. Inequality is ubiquitous, as are its consequences—jealously, demands for equality, and doctrines to justify why some people have more than others. The basic political conflict in every nation, and often between nations, is the antagonism between rich and poor.[10] This is the conflict, manifest in the competition between Athens' commercial democracy and Sparta's oligarchy, that debilitated and eventually tore apart ancient Hellenic civilization.

Today industrialism has accelerated the accumulation of wealth without solving the persistent problem of its uneven distribution. Explosive economic growth of the twentieth century has widened the gap between rich and poor around the globe. Most of the increases in output, and so rise in income and living standards, have come in the wealthiest industrialized nations, creating a growing wealth gap between rich and poor nations. After 1900 per capita gross domestic product (GDP) increased 600 percent for the richest quarter of the world's population compared with only 300 percent for the poorest quarter. Although citizens of the poorest nations were still better off by 2000, many had not reached income levels achieved in advanced nations by 1900. For example, in 2000 GDP per person in Africa averaged only $1,290, far below the average of $3,092 for the countries of Western Europe in 1900.[11] Over the twentieth century, the Gini coefficient—a measure of inequality in which 0 is perfect equality and 1 is absolute inequality (in theory a single person would have all wealth)—rose from 0.40 to 0.48.[12] This is the result of accelerating output in highly developed nations, which pulls them away from underdeveloped countries.

Contrary to popular opinion, industrial development does not itself increase income inequality within modernizing nations. A recent study of 137 countries shows that during industrialization the incomes of the poor, defined as the lowest fifth of the income distribution in a country, rose in proportion to the rise in average income for the country as a whole. The authors conclude that "income of the poor has a very tight link with overall incomes" and "as overall income increases, on average incomes of the poor increase equiproportionately."[13] Thus, where industrialization occurred, incomes of the poorest rose as fast as the average income rise for their nation.

Today about 1.2 billion people suffer from extreme poverty, defined as living on incomes of less than $1 per day. Another 2.8 billion live on less than $2 a day.[14] The vast majority live in underdeveloped economies not yet enriched by industrial growth. Their presence creates expectations that the ethical duties of global corporations include helping the poor and equitably distributing the fruits of commerce.

[10] Mortimer J. Adler, *The Great Ideas* (New York: Macmillan, 1992), pp. 578–79.
[11] International Monetary Fund, *World Economic Outlook 2000* (Washington, DC: IMF, May 2000), pp. 155–56.
[12] Ibid., p. 155.
[13] David Dollar and Aart Kraay, "Growth Is Good for the Poor," working paper, Washington, DC, World Bank, March 2001, p. 5.
[14] United Nations Development Programme, *Human Development Report 2001: Making New Technologies Work for Human Development* (New York: Oxford University Press, 2001), p. 9.

The Human Development Index

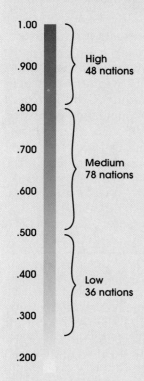

1.00
.900 — High 48 nations
.800
.700 — Medium 78 nations
.600
.500
.400 — Low 36 nations
.300
.200

The Human Development Index (HDI) is a statistical tool used by the United Nations for measuring the progress of humanity. It is based on the theory that income alone is not an adequate measure of the standard of living, let alone a rich and fulfilling life. If this theory is correct, discussions of inequality based on income differences within and between nations do not give a complete picture of differences in human welfare.

The HDI is a scale running from 0 to 1, with 1 representing the highest possible human development and 0 the lowest. It measures the development of nations as an average of scores in three equally-weighted categories.

Of the 162 nations in the *Human Development Report 2001,* 48 rank high with HDI scores of 0.800 or above, 78 rank medium with scores of 0.500 to 0.799, and 36 rank low with scores of 0.499 or below. Highest ranked is Norway, with an HDI value of 0.939. Lowest is Sierra Leone with only 0.258. The United States ranks sixth with 0.934. The world average HDI value is 0.716.[15]

Historical HDI values show enormous increases in human welfare since the late nineteenth century. This is mainly because of progress in medical technology leading to spectacular mortality declines. In 1870 the United States had an HDI value of 0.467, a score that would today tie it with Haiti in the low human development category.[16] In 1913 it had an HDI value that would today rank it just below Turkey, deep in the medium human development category. Since 1950 the absolute gap between the highest- and lowest-rated countries has narrowed substantially, indicating that inequality in living standards around the world, as measured by the HDI, is declining even while income inequality, as measured by per capita GDP, is rising. Thus, inequality is greater if measured by monetary income and less if longevity and education, two traditional measures of a good life, are taken into consideration using the HDI.

- *Longevity,* or life expectancy at birth.

- *Knowledge,* or the adult literacy rate plus the ratio of students enrolled in school as a percentage of the population of official school age.

- *Income,* or gross domestic product per capita (in equivalent U.S. dollars).

[15] UNDP, *Human Development Report 2001,* app. 1.
[16] Nicholas Crafts, "Globalization and Growth in the Twentieth Century," IMF working paper, WP/pp/44, Washington, DC: International Monetary Fund, March 2000, pp. 6–7.

Population Growth

The basic population trend throughout human history is growth. World population grew very slowly until the great transition to intensive agriculture about 10,000 years ago. As more food was raised using new methods,

FIGURE 2.2
World Population Growth and United Nations Projections to 2050

Source: U.S. Bureau of the Census, "Historical Estimates of World Population," available at www.census.gov/ipc/www/worldhis.html and U.S. Bureau of the Census, "Total Midyear Population for the World: 1950–2050," May 10, 2000, available at www.census.gov/ipc/www/worldpop.html.

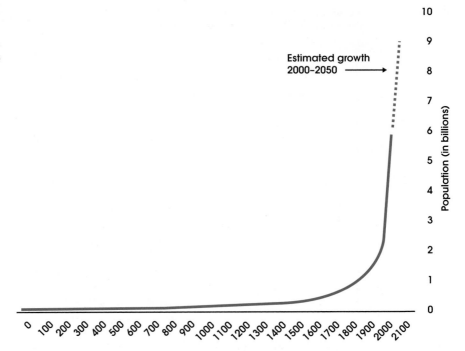

the population began to grow faster. Then the growth rate accelerated remarkably in the twentieth century. This new growth spurt had two causes. First, advances in water sanitation and medicine reduced deaths from infectious disease, and second, mechanized farming further expanded the food supply. It had taken until 1825 for the world population to reach one billion; then each billionth additional person was added faster and faster—first in 100 years, then in 35, then 15, then only 12.[17]

The world's population in 2001 was 6.1 billion, up from just 2.5 billion in 1950. However, an end to this exponential growth rate is in sight, and world population is predicted to grow more slowly to 9.3 billion by 2050. Fastest growth is expected in the least developed regions, where fertility rates are highest. By 2050 the population in Africa will have grown 152 percent, despite the HIV/AIDS epidemic, which is estimated to reduce growth there only about 8 percent. But in high-income areas, growth is slowing as a result of declining fertility rates. The North American population will increase by only 71 percent and the European population will actually fall about 17 percent.[18] The population graph in Figure 2.2 shows a dramatic

---

[17] Clive Ponting, *A Green History of the World* (New York: Penguin Books, 1991), p. 240.
[18] Figures in this paragraph are from data in Population Division, Department of Economic and Social Affairs, *World Population Prospects: The 2000 Revision, Highlights,* draft, New York, United Nations, February 28, 2001, p. 1. Projections are calculated from medium assumptions.

FIGURE 2.3   **World GDP and Population since 1750**

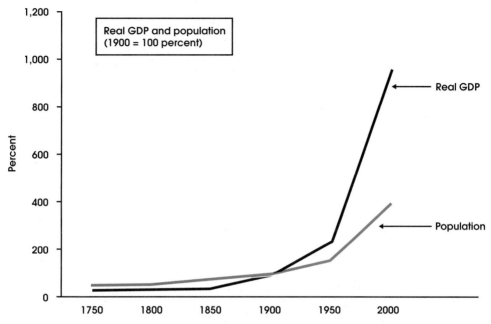

Source: Bradford J. DeLong, "Estimating World GDP, One Million B.C.–Present," available at http://econ161.berkeley.edu.

rise in population. Note, however, that when this population growth is shown relative to the increase in industrial output, as in Figure 2.3, it appears much less dramatic.

Population trends have many implications. First, although the overall population rise is slowing, growth will be highest in less industrialized regions, reducing per capita income and widening further the wealth gap between high- and low-income countries. Second, population growth will continue to strain the earth's ecosystems, especially as industrial activity rises and spreads. Third, the West is in demographic decline compared with other peoples. In 1900 Western nations held 30 percent of the world's population and had colonial rule over another 15 percent. But today they are stripped of their former colonies and hold only 13 percent of the world's population.[19] In the future, growing non-Western peoples will be stronger economically, militarily, and politically and will push to expand their influence. This can be seen today in Islamic societies, which have young, rapidly growing populations. Although Western market values and business ideology seem ascendant now, they may be less widespread in the future as Western power wanes. In addition, demographers

---

[19] Samuel P. Huntington, *The Clash of Civilizations and the Remaking of World Order* (New York: Simon & Schuster, 1996), p. 84.

FIGURE 2.4   **Waves of Innovation Since the Beginning of the Industrial Revolution**

Source: "A Survey of Innovation in Industry," *The Economist*, February 20, 1999, p. 8. Reprinted with permission.

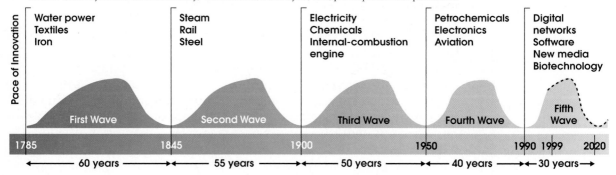

predict that over the next 50 years immigration from low- to high-growth areas will be extensive and that workforces in high-income countries will age. All these demographic changes will alter the business environment and create new societal expectations for corporate behavior.

Technology

Throughout recorded civilization inventions and new techniques have fueled the engine of commerce. The waterwheel and the printing press are early examples. However, in the nineteenth and twentieth centuries new inventions and innovations have been pivotal in accelerating economic and population growth. The invention of the steam engine in the late eighteenth century and its widespread use beginning in the early 1800s, together with increased use of water power and new iron production methods, triggered the modern industrial revolution.

As Figure 2.4 shows, this was the first of five distinct waves of technological revolution. In each wave, innovations spread stimulating economic booms of increased investment, rising productivity, and output growth. In the second half of the nineteenth century, steam power revolutionized economies when new steel-making techniques turned out iron rails for railroads and the railroads created national markets. In the early twentieth century, electricity, chemicals, and the internal-combustion engine emerged; and in mid-century, petrochemicals, electronics, and aviation came forth. Today the world is experiencing a fifth wave based on information technology and biotechnology. The shortening of successive waves reveals a speeding up of technological innovation.

Technological advances bring great gains. New technologies foster the productivity gains that sustain long-term economic progress, and they promote human welfare. In the process, they also disrupt societies. For example, before the 1860s a transatlantic voyage took a month, cost a year's wages for a European worker, and was risky. About 5 to 10 percent of passengers died from sinkings and shipboard transmission of diseases. Then advances in steamship technology cut the cost by 90 percent and reduced the travel time to a week, thereby lowering mortality to 1 percent or less. The consequence was that European immigrants poured into the American east, creating gluts of labor that caused wage depressions and fueled political movements against the gold standard, financiers, and big companies.[20] The technology of the steamship thereby shaped the American political agenda.

In the nineteenth and twentieth centuries, technology reshaped human civilization by stimulating economic growth and accelerating population growth to yearly percentage rises unknown in previous recorded history. This has created many benefits, including higher living standards and longer life spans, but because technology changes faster than human beliefs and institutions, it has also imposed strains.

Globalization

Globalization occurs when networks of economic, political, social, military, scientific, or environmental interdependence grow to span worldwide distances.[21] In the economic realm, globalization refers to the development of an increasingly integrated commercial system based on free markets in which nations are open to foreign trade and capital. The current rise of such a system began after World War II when developed nations dropped many trade barriers and loosened capital controls.

Multinational corporations are central forces of globalization. In the last half of the twentieth century, they grew more numerous, larger, and more transnational in their assets and operations. In 2000 there were 63,000 parent multinationals, with approximately 700,000 foreign affiliates. The value of goods and services produced by the foreign operations of these firms is growing faster than world gross domestic product, showing that accelerating economic growth is due more to growth of transnational investment than to rising domestic production.[22]

Economic globalization has been speeded by the rise of *multilateral organizations,* or organizations set up to administer policies and rules affecting more than one country. There are hundreds of such organizations regulating global dimensions of everything from civil aviation to telecommunications standards, but the organizations that are most significant in promoting economic globalization are the International Monetary Fund, the World Bank, the World Trade Organization, and the United Nations. We will write more about these elsewhere.

---

[20] Robert William Fogel, *The Fourth Great Awakening & the Future of Egalitarianism* (Chicago: University of Chicago Press, 2001), p. 54.
[21] Joseph Nye, Jr., "Globalization's Democratic Deficit," *Foreign Affairs,* July–August 2001, p. 2.
[22] United Nations Conference on Trade and Development, *World Investment Report 2000* (New York: United Nations, 2000), chap. 3.

Between the 1950s and the 1980s, a small number of developed countries opened their borders to international flows of trade and capital. Later, more developing nations opened themselves until today no national economy of any significance remains isolated from world markets. Yet globalization is incomplete.[23] Although openness to trade and capital flows has increased, labor mobility is still limited. Immigration controls throughout the world are tighter today than they were a century ago.

Globalization expands the social role of transnational corporations. Their investments quicken societal change in all nations, creating problems and anxieties that lead to heightened expectations of responsible behavior. Doing business around the world multiplies the number and kind of stakeholders. Double standards in operations are no longer acceptable. The high expectations and ethical standards of corporate performance found in affluent nations are learned and manifest everywhere.[24] Transnational corporations are pressured to help with global problems such as spread of the HIV virus and climate warming. In addition, there is a strong antiglobalization movement supported mainly by groups in rich nations that see the growing velocity of trade with alarm because it clashes with their values on the environment, human rights, and democracy. These groups seek to restrain and regulate the activities of corporations, with some success.

Nation-States

The modern nation-state system arose in an unplanned way out of the wreckage of the Roman Empire. The institution of the nation-state was well-suited for Western Europe, where boundaries were contiguous with the extent of languages. However, the idea was subsequently transplanted to territories in Eastern Europe, Southwest Asia, and the Middle East, partly by force of colonial empires and partly by mimicry among non-Western political elites for whom the idea had attained high prestige. Where it was transplanted, nations were often irrationally defined and boundary lines split historic areas of culture, ethnicity, religion, and language.

The nation-state is the unit of human organization in which individuals and cultural groups can influence their circumstances and future. This is its paramount function and the reason it has survived over centuries. Today the world is a mosaic of independent countries, and the dynamics of this system are a powerful force in the international business environment. Conflict between nations seeking to aggrandize wealth and

---

[23] Martin Wolf, "Will the Nation-State Survive Globalization?" *Foreign Affairs,* January–February 2001, p. 184.

[24] See Ian Wilson, *The New Rules of Corporate Conduct: Rewriting the Social Charter* (Westport, CT: Quorum Books, 2000), pp. 27 and 52.

power is frequent, though due to economic globalization its nature has changed. In the past, nations increased their power by seizing territory from other nations. With more territory they acquired new natural resources, agriculture, and labor. Hence, in the 1930s Japan colonized South Asian countries to gain access to oil and bauxite. Now, however, the wealth of high-income nations is based on the operation of global corporations that use flows of capital and knowledge to provide goods and services in many nations. Seizing the headquarters or a few manufacturing facilities or sources of raw materials of one of these corporations would not enable the aggressor nation to take advantage of the value chain in the firm's worldwide operations, particularly where wealth creation was based on brainpower. So nations today increasingly prefer to aggrandize themselves through trade, where they can transfer wealth more efficiently to themselves than through traditional warfare designed to seize land and stocks of material resources.[25]

Although economic trends discourage war to seize resources, conflict between ethnic and religious groupings across nation-state boundaries is prominent today.[26] For example, the nationalistic feelings of Palestinians have affected global companies in many industries, from oil firms caught in Middle East conflicts to airlines losing passengers afraid of terrorism.

Dominant Ideologies

Thought shapes history. An ideology is a set of reinforcing beliefs and values that constructs a worldview. The industrial revolution in the West was facilitated by a set of interlocking ideologies, including capitalism, but also constitutional democracy characterized by protections for rights that allowed individualism to flourish; progress, or the idea that humanity was in upward motion toward material betterment; Darwinism, or Charles Darwin's finding that constant improvement characterized the biological world, which reinforced the idea of progress; social Darwinism, or Herbert Spencer's idea that evolutionary competition in human society, as well as the natural world, weeded out the unfit and advanced humanity; and the Protestant ethic, or the belief that hard work, saving, thrift, and honesty led to salvation.

Ideology has enormous consequences. A principle reason some areas undergo successful economic development and others do not is the cultural worldviews that shape the behavior and expectations of populations. In the early 1960s South Korea and Ghana were poor countries with similar low levels of economic development and per capita income.

[25] This thesis is elaborated in Richard Rosecrance, *The Rise of the Virtual State* (New York: Basic Books, 1999).
[26] See Huntington, *The Clash of Civilizations, part IV.*

Both were mainly agricultural economies, both got similar amounts of international aid, and both were well endowed with natural resources—coal, tungsten, and molybdenum in South Korea, and gold, diamonds, bauxite, manganese, and rubber in Ghana. Over the next 30 years, however, South Korea experienced an amazing ascent, becoming one of the world's leading industrial nations, while Ghana suffered decades of per capita income decline. Today per capita GDP in South Korea is seven times that of Ghana.

Though many factors affected both nations' performance, South Koreans, in the words of one observer, "valued thrift, investment, hard work, education, organization, and discipline."[27] Ghanaians, on the other hand, hold values consistent with sub-Saharan African culture and inconsistent with economy building. They attach low priority to the future, live in the present, and spend rather than save. Although there are large Christian and Muslim elements in Ghana, most citizens follow indigenous religions that see the world as an uncertain place changing only at the whim of supreme beings. Such belief breeds passivity, lack of individual initiative, distaste for work, and reliance on irrational, superstitious behavior to cope with life.[28] This story of two nations teaches that some values assist industrial development while others impede it.

Great Leadership

Leaders have brought both beneficial and disastrous changes to societies and businesses. Alexander the Great imposed his rule over the ancient Mediterranean world and created new trade routes on which Greek merchants flourished. Adolf Hitler of Germany and Joseph Stalin in the Soviet Union were strong leaders, but they unleashed evil that retarded industrial growth in their societies.

There have been many business leaders whose actions had great impact. In America, probably none has had a more lasting influence than John D. Rockefeller. His Standard Oil Company, between its inception in 1870 and its breakup in 1911, dominated the industrial landscape, arousing the public, testing restraints, shaping the nation. Today William Gates of Microsoft inspires comparisons to Rockefeller as the strategies of his company define how telecommunications technologies will be used in society. However, Gates is constrained by Rockefeller's legacy. The Sherman Act of 1890, the hammer originally forged by Congress to break up Rockefeller's empire, is the same tool the government used to try and split Gates's corporation.

---

[27] Samuel P. Huntington, "Cultures Count," in Lawrence E. Harrison and Samuel P. Huntington, eds., *Culture Matters: How Values Shape Human Progress* (New York: Basic Books, 2000), p. xiii.
[28] Daniel Etounga-Manguelle, "Does Africa Need a Cultural Adjustment Program?" in Harrison and Huntington, *Culture Matters,* pp. 65–77.

There are two views about the power of leaders as a historical force. One is that leaders simply ride the wave of history. "Great men," writes Arnold Toynbee, "are precisely the points of intersection of great social forces."[29] The other is that leaders themselves change history rather than being pushed by its tide. "The history of the world," wrote Thomas Carlyle, "is at bottom the History of the Great Men who have worked here."[30] Cases and stories of business leaders in this text provide instances for debate of this provocative clash of views.

Chance

Scholars are reluctant to use the notion of chance, accident, or random occurrence as a category of analysis. Yet some changes in the business environment may be best explained as the product of unknown and unpredictable causes. No less perceptive a student of history than Niccolò Machiavelli observed that fortune determines about half the course of human events and human beings the other half. We cannot improve on this estimate, but we note it. Its significance is that managers must be prepared for the most unprecedented events and have faith in Machiavelli's counsel that when such episodes arrive those who are ready will prevail, as fortune "directs her bolts where there have been no defenses or bulwarks prepared against her."[31] No doubt Machiavelli would think Shell's scenarios are praiseworthy.

SEVEN KEY ENVIRONMENTS OF BUSINESS

Figure 2.5 shows the seven most important environments affecting business today. In these environments are forces of revolutionary proportion bringing epic and rapid change. Understanding and adapting to changes is no longer the sole responsibility of a company's top managers. Managers throughout an organization must continuously pay attention to them.

We turn now to thumbnail sketches of each of the dominant environments and selected forces operating in them. We will dig deeper into these environments throughout the book.

The Economic Environment

The economic environment consists of forces that influence market operations, including overall economic activity, commodity prices, interest rates, currency fluctuations, wages, competitors' actions, technology

[29] *A Study of History,* vol. XII, *Reconsiderations* (London: Oxford University Press, 1961), p. 125.
[30] In "The Hero as Divinity," reprinted in Carl Niemeyer, ed., *Thomas Carlyle on Heroes, Hero-Worship and the Heroic in History* (Lincoln, NE: University of Nebraska Press, 1966), p. 1. This essay was originally written in 1840.
[31] Niccolò Machiavelli, *The Prince,* trans. George Bull (New York: Penguin Books, 1961), chap. XXV, p. 73.

FIGURE 2.5
The Seven Key Environments of Business

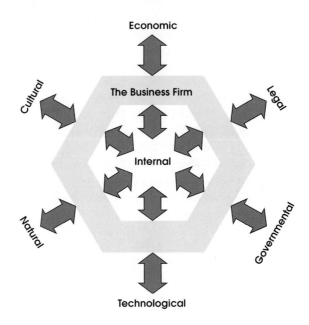

change, and government policies. Today three trends dominate the global economic environment.

First, economic output is growing over the long term. In the United States, the economic environment of the recent past has been favorable to business. The "New Economy" of the 1990s was characterized by long-term expansion, GDP growth, low unemployment, low inflation, and high productivity that created widely shared gains for both low- and high-income households.[32] Global production accelerated, but the elements of long-term prosperity and wealth-creation characteristic of the United States eluded many developing and underdeveloped nations.

Second, both investment and production are becoming more international. Large transnational firms, and increasingly small- and medium-sized ones, create some complex networks of facilities and affiliations that span national borders. According to the United Nations, foreign direct investment in 1999 was 14 percent of all domestic capital investment, compared with only 2 percent 20 years before. And sales of goods produced by international production networks accounted for 10 percent of global GDP as opposed to only 5 percent 20 years ago.[33] This internationaliza-

---

[32] Council of Economic Advisers, *Economic Report of the President 2001* (Washington, DC: U.S. Government Printing Office, January 2001), chap. 1.
[33] United Nations Conference on Trade and Development, *World Investment Report 2000: Cross-Border Mergers and Acquisitions and Development* (New York: United Nations, 2000), pp. xv–vi.

tion of economic activity is due to technology advances and the lowering of trade barriers by governments. Because of its interconnectedness, the world economy is also fragile. Following the terrorist attacks of September 11, 2001, the World Bank forecast declines in exports, tourism, commodity prices, and foreign investment, slowing global GDP growth over the following year enough to condemn 10 million more people to poverty.[34]

Third, markets are expanding. Speeded communications and reduced transportation costs expose businesses to new competitors and more intense competition. Bigger and more competitive markets force managers to consider changes in corporate structure. Many corporations have decided to expand operations across borders and grow in size to gain competitive advantage. One result has been a sharp increase in the number of transnational firms from about 7,000 in the most developed countries in the late 1960s to more than 63,000 today.[35] Also, firms have grown and internationalized through an explosive increase in mergers and acquisitions (M&A). In 1980 the value of global mergers and acquisitions was less than three-tenths of 1 percent of world GDP, but in 1999 it was 8 percent.[36] Firms have engaged in M&A activity for many reasons, including to gain strategic assets such as patents or brand names, to enter new markets, to gain size efficiencies, to stimulate stock gains, to reduce risks, and to gain market power. Since mergers have increased concentration and created oligopoly in some industries, they have led to rising fears of corporate control over markets.

In some industries, companies have responded to economic forces by choosing to shrink rather than grow. They sell plants and equipment and build virtual firms in which contract manufacturers in distant, low-wage settings supply products. Other elements of the business, such as advertising, distribution, and pension management, may also be provided by contract suppliers. Some firms adopting this restructuring model, including Levi-Strauss and Nike, were criticized when foreign plants making their brands had low human rights standards.

The Technological Environment

Today new scientific discoveries and incremental development of old innovations create a business environment filled with mind-boggling technology. For example, semiconductor manufacturing can create microchips with components the size of one ten-millionth of a meter. Nanotechnology, the ability of scientists and engineers to work with materials the size of a nanometer (one billionth of a meter), now can manipulate single atoms

[34] "Poverty to Rise in Wake of Terrorist Attacks in U.S.," Washington, DC, World Bank, news release no. 2002/093/S, October 1, 2001, p. 1.
[35] UNCTAD, *World Investment Report* 2000, pp. 8–9.
[36] Ibid., pp. 106–7.

and molecules. When this ability is harnessed to manufacturing it will create chips of astonishing computing power with transistors about one ten-thousandth the thickness of a human hair and microcircuits that operate on an atomic scale comparable to the process of photosynthesis in plants. Human genome mapping promises new biogenetic products that will cure intractable human diseases. In process today is a cornucopia of new genetically engineered plants that will revolutionize agriculture. Fuel cells and methods of harnessing renewable energy may dramatically reduce use of fossil fuels. Advancing digital telecommunications technology has created a global network of computers, software, and electronic devices that promises to reshape every facet of life. Forces generated by these new technologies will shake the foundations of the most secure businesses and powerfully affect consumer choices, the rate and growth of different business sectors, standards of living, and the duties of corporations to society.

A turbulent technological environment has surrounded business for more than two centuries. It creates difficult choices and problems. Companies tend to focus on the immediate commercial and strategic possibilities of technology, but making correct decisions can be difficult because the ultimate use of a new technology is not always clear. Western Union was the dominant communications company of the nineteenth century, but it took a catastrophic misstep rejecting the telephone. When Alexander Graham Bell invented the telephone in 1876 it had a range of only three miles. Western Union considered hooking the new device to its lines, but it thought the range was inadequate and rejected the telephone as simply a toy. In response, the inventor formed his own company. When engineers began to lengthen the range of the phone, by using copper instead of iron wire, for example, Western Union saw its mistake and got into the business with a phone device of its own. The mighty company used "every devious and underhanded method," including political pressure and bribes, to prevent towns and cities from adopting the Bell phone.[37] However, in 1878 it lost a patent infringement suit to the Bell Telephone Company and was forced out of the business. Tiny Bell Telephone went on to become AT&T, one of the great firms of the twentieth century. Today the Internet has created a similar strategic junction in telecommunications. Companies are rising and falling based on new ideas about its application, and it will be many years before its implications are fully understood.

New technologies have unforeseen consequences for society when they are put into widespread use for commercial gain. Sometimes these implications are unanticipated. The cigarette rolling machine was invented before dangers of smoking were discovered. The manufacturing technologies that mixed asbestos into hundreds of common materials were put

---

[37] Page Smith, *The Rise of Industrial America,* vol. 6 (New York: Penguin Books, 1984), p. 115.

into use before the unhealthy aspects of its fibers were well understood. In other cases, the implications of new technologies are more predictable. When Napster, Inc., went online offering free file-sharing of music among Internet users, it challenged existing copyright laws and created an ethical debate. One critic wrote that it "made innocent, college-style theft possible on a global scale."[38] Users argued that MP3 file-sharing was inevitable in a networked age and that laws, standards, and opinion should adapt to new technology, just as they had when VCR machines were first introduced. The music industry saw Napster's business model as piracy, and it was shut down by courts upholding copyright laws. The ethical debate caused by Napster was predictable, although long-run changes it introduced in the music industry were unpredictable.

As these stories illustrate, technology can have both good and bad effects. Corporations have a duty to avoid harming society; so besides the challenges of incorporating new technologies into strategy, businesses must carefully weigh the consequences of the stresses they may impose on society.

The Governmental Environment

Business is simultaneously encouraged and constrained by governments. There are two long-term, global trends in the government environment today.

First, governments have greatly expanded their activities. One way of measuring government activity is by the size of public expenditures relative to gross domestic product, and around the world this has been rising. In the United States, for example, government spending in 1913 was 8 percent of GDP, but by 1998 it had risen to 33 percent.[39] The increases have been higher in European countries and lower in less developed nations, but broadly the trend is up because governments have taken on new functions. For one, governments have taken on social welfare roles and make huge and growing transfer payments to their citizens. This role grew importantly in the years between the two world wars when there was a wave of democratization and many nations expanded their electorates. The new voters included women and the less privileged, groups that voted to expand government by supporting assistance programs. The other main source of growth in government is expanded regulation of domestic industries to protect citizens against abuses. In the United States, for example, there is today practically no aspect of business that governments cannot and will not regulate if the occasion arises and popular support exists. New laws, added to past laws, result in more government restriction of business than ever before.

---

[38] Paul Kedrosky, "Napster Should Be Playing Jailhouse Rock," *The Wall Street Journal,* July 31, 2000, p. A22.
[39] IMF, *World Economic Outlook 2000,* table 5.4.

Of course, governments also support business. The current increase in international trade results in part from lowering of barriers by many nations to stimulate growth. In 1950 tariffs on manufactured goods averaged 25 percent in industrialized Europe and 14 percent in the United States. However, they have now fallen to an average of 5 percent for European Union countries and 3 percent in the United States.[40] In addition, governments grant enormous subsidies to business. One study of 20 industries estimated that over a two-year period 250 major corporations received $98 billion in tax breaks from the U.S. government.[41]

The second long-term environmental trend is that governments are becoming more open and democratic. In 1900 no nation was a full democracy with multiparty elections and universal suffrage. The United States and Great Britain were close, but both lacked female suffrage, and the United States additionally lacked black suffrage. Yet by 1950 there were 22 democracies, and in 2000 there were 119 (out of 192 existing countries) in which lived 62 percent of world population.[42] A consequence of increased openness to popular majorities is that governments increasingly enforce public demands regarding corporate social performance.

The Legal Environment

The legal environment consists of legislation, regulation, and litigation. All three are on the increase, and the general trend is toward constraint of business behavior. Early in American history, and especially before the rise of big corporations, the legal environment was permissive. Congress passed laws encouraging business activity. There was no restrictive federal regulation, and states regulated little business activity. Most business law revolved around enforcing the common law of small business.

With the growth of large corporations in the nineteenth century this legal climate permanently changed, creating trends that continue to this day. First, laws and regulations have steadily grown in number and complexity. Second, corporations have continuously expanding duties to protect "rights" of stakeholders, including employees, consumers, the public, and even competitors. Thus, businesses must comply with a range of laws, including those on discrimination, sexual harassment, advertising, antitrust, the environment, products liability, and intellectual property. Third, globalization has increased the complexity of the legal environment by exposing corporations to international law and laws of foreign countries. In addition, advocacy groups promoting human rights and environmental causes push corporations to adopt so-called *soft laws,*

[40] Crafts, "Globalization and Growth in the Twentieth Century," table 2–4.
[41] David Cay Johnston, "Study Finds that Many Large Companies Pay No Taxes," *New York Times,* October 20, 2000, p. C2. The study covered the years 1996–98.
[42] Figures are from *Democracy's Century: A Survey of Global Political Change in the 20th Century* (Washington, DC: Freedom House, 2001), p. 2.

or voluntarily-adopted codes of conduct that set forth rules exceeding the laws of nations in which business is done. Fourth, although the requirements of ethical behavior and corporate social responsibility go beyond legal duty, they are continuously plucked from the voluntary realm and encoded into law. For instance, it was always unethical to save money by firing an employee of many years the week before he or she was vested with pension rights. Since 1974 the Employee Retirement Income Security Act has made such firings not only unethical but illegal.

Fifth, the law is constantly changing and emerging. Because of technological change, for example, corporations have always needed to anticipate expanding liability. In this respect, the old *T. J. Hooper* case is useful reading for corporate counsel today. The tug *T. J. Hooper* headed out to sea on a sunny day in March 1928 hauling a coal barge. Two days later it encountered stormy weather off New Jersey, and the barge with its load of coal was lost. The owners of the cargo of coal sued, claiming that the tug was unseaworthy because it lacked a receiving radio. Lacking this radio, the *T. J. Hooper* did not hear a radio weather report that caused other shipping to put into a harbor before the gale hit. Although there was no law requiring a radio and no general industry custom of installing them, the great judge Learned Hand held that "there are precautions so imperative that even their universal disregard will not excuse their omission."[43] Thus, even in the absence of law and custom, the tug owners were held negligent and had to pay for the loss of coal because they had not adopted a cutting-edge technology. Moving ahead to the present, a parallel example is the existence of defibrillators capable of restarting a heart. No Federal Aviation Administration rule yet requires airlines to carry them on passenger jets, but their availability opens any airline that does not to charges of negligence by the survivors of a heart-attack victim.[44]

The Cultural Environment

A *culture* is a system of shared knowledge, values, norms, customs, and rituals acquired by social learning. No universal culture exists, so the environment of a multinational corporation can include a variety of cultures, each with differing peoples, languages, religions, and attitudes.

On one level, this variation causes conflicts of business custom, and managers operating in foreign countries must absorb both subtle and striking differences in areas such as employee loyalty, group versus individual initiative, the place of women in organizations, ethical values, norms of giving and gratuities, attitudes toward authority, the meaning of time, and clothing worn in business settings. The consequences of cultural

---

[43] *In re The* T. J. Hooper, et al., 60 F.2d 737 (1932), at 740.
[44] Milton Bordwin, "Your Company and 'THE LAW'," *Management Review,* January 2000, p. 58.

difference are often trivial, even humorous. Thus, a consulting firm that specializes in helping managers avoid social blunders in foreign business settings counsels Americans not to force the custom of name tags at business meetings on Europeans, who feel they are being treated as children when wearing them.[45] However, consequences can be serious too. In France, the notion is widespread that American fast food causes obesity and, worst of all, is bad tasting and insults the refined French palate. Recently, President Jacques Chirac said that national ways of eating should be preserved in the face of an assault by cross-Atlantic invaders; and the minister of agriculture said the United States was "home to the world's worst food."[46] For McDonald's, the consequences of these cultural feelings were deadly. A mob wrecked one of its restaurants and another was bombed, killing an employee.

On a deeper level, although no uniform world culture exists there is a fundamental divide between the culture of Western economic development and the rest of the world's cultural groupings. The culture of the advanced West promotes a core ideology of markets, individualism, and democratic government. It is sustained by Western nations that dominate international organizations, contain the most powerful corporations, and have the strongest militaries. However, although developing nations tend to adopt elements of Western culture, some nations and cultures have resisted its spread. Islamic nations and China see spreading Western values as a form of cultural aggression. They have resisted adopting them, particularly participatory forms of government.

Over the last half of the twentieth century, some cultural values in developed nations began to shift, creating changes in the global business environment. In these societies, beginning in the 1960s, traditional values based on historical realities of economic scarcity were transformed. In their place came what are called *postmodern values,* or values based on assumptions of affluence. For example, in older industrializing societies materialism was a dominant value. People sacrificed other values such as leisure time and environmental purity to make money and buy necessities, then luxuries. While consumption is still a powerful value in developed nations, their affluent citizens grow more concerned with quality of life and self-expression.

The World Values Surveys, a series of surveys in 65 countries now spanning more than 20 years, shows that the rise of postmodern values has uniformly shifted the social, political, economic, and sexual norms of rich countries.[47] Despite some resistance in non-Western cultures, surveys show the rise of these norms in all modernizing nations, including, for ex-

[45] Lalita Khosla, "You Say Tomato," *Forbes,* May 21, 2001, p. 36.
[46] John-Thor Dahlburg, "To Many French, Ugly American Is McDonald's," *Los Angeles Times,* April 22, 2000, p. A10.
[47] Richard Inglehart, "Globalization and Postmodern Values," *Washington Quarterly,* Winter 2000.

ample, China, where surveys find a rising and "surprisingly high" high score for the Chinese public on values linked to democracy.

Postmodern norms are a strong influence in the operating environments of multinational corporations. To illustrate, there is a powerful global movement to promote fundamental human rights by stamping out racism, sexism, authoritarianism, intolerance, and xenophobia. This movement is energized by West-dominated coalitions of individuals, advocacy groups, governments, and international organizations such as the United Nations.[48] Similar and interrelated movements have risen to promote sustainable development and humanitarian assistance to poor areas. This global tide of morality, based on the postmodern values of the West, elevates expectations about the behavior of multinational corporations. Increasingly, they must follow proliferating codes and rules developed by moral reformers and must define their basic purposes as promoting human welfare above narrow profit-making. For example, Coca-Cola, including its bottlers, is the largest employer on the African continent. Activists pressured the company to take major steps in the fight against Africa's AIDS epidemic. The company began to pay for AIDS drugs for its employees. However, the groups and organizations in the activist coalition believed Coca-Cola could do much more. Eventually, the firm formed a partnership with a United Nation's agency, using its trucks to distribute condoms and educational materials and applying its marketing sophistication to make AIDS education entertaining and compelling.[49]

The Natural Environment

Economic activity is a geophysical force with power to change the natural environment. Output growth in the twentieth century depleted mineral resources, reduced forest cover, killed species, released molecules not found in nature, unbalanced the nitrogen cycle, and probably triggered climate change by altering the chemistry of earth's atmosphere. The Living Planet Index of the World Wide Fund, which measures the health of the earth's biosphere, has declined by 33 percent since 1970, meaning that in contrast to the phenomenal economic growth of these years the earth has lost about a third of its natural capital.[50] Figure 2.6 shows how this decline compares to the growth in world real GDP and population.

Attitudes about the relationship of economic activity to nature are now rapidly changing. When the twentieth century began, dominating and consuming nature was justified by a variety of doctrines, not the

[48] See, for example, United Nations Development Programme, *Human Development Report 2000* (New York: Oxford University Press, 2000), "Overview," pp. 1–18.
[49] Betsy McKay, "Coke to Help Fight Aids in Africa," *The Wall Street Journal,* June 20, 2001, p. B1.
[50] World Wide Fund International, *Living Planet Report: 2000* (Gland, Switzerland: WWF International, 2000), p. 1.

FIGURE 2.6

Rates of Change of GDP, Population, and Living Planet Index

Sources: Bradford J. DeLong, "Estimating World GDP, One Million B.C.–Present," available at http://econ16l. berkeley.edu; World Wide Fund International, *Living Planet Report: 2000* (Gland, Switzerland: WWF International: 2000).

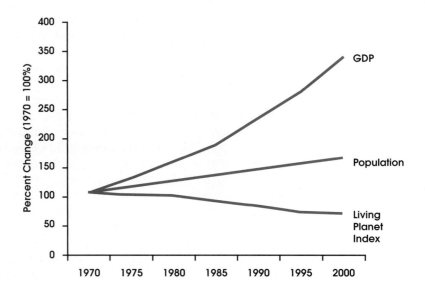

least being capitalism, which valued nature as a production input. By the time the century ended, global opinion demanded preservation and co-existence with nature. Managers must adapt to this changed thinking.

An example is the story of a Louisiana jury that punished ExxonMobil for behavior that placed profits above protecting nature. In the 1960s a Louisiana family leased property to a company that cleaned and refur-bished pipes used by Exxon for oil drilling. During oil drilling, pipes build up scale that cuts oil flow, and the deposits contain naturally occur-ring radium that make them radioactive. For over 30 years, Exxon sent millions of feet of pipe to the company for processing. There workers used equipment that pulverized the scale into fine dust that blew around and settled on the leased property. Exxon admitted it knew that the residue in the pipes was radioactive, though there was some question as to how long. Yet it did not warn the company until 1987, at least a year after an internal document indicated that the company knew. The owners of the property sued Exxon for $56 million, the cost of removing radioac-tive soil. Exxon dug more than 1,000 bore holes on the property, and re-sults showed it was necessary to clean up only eight-tenths of 1 percent of the land to restore it to full use and value. This would cost only $46,000. Notwithstanding, a jury gave the property owners the $56 million they asked for and $1 billion in punitive damages to punish the company.[51] ExxonMobil believes the verdict is unwarranted and is appealing. Even if it is overturned, however, it suggests the cost of business operations that pass below a rising bar of perfectionism in stewardship of nature.

---

[51] *Grefer v. Alpha Technical Services Inc.*, No. 97-15003 (Dist. Ct., Orleans Parish, LA), 2001.

FIGURE 2.7
A Depiction of the
Internal Business
Environment

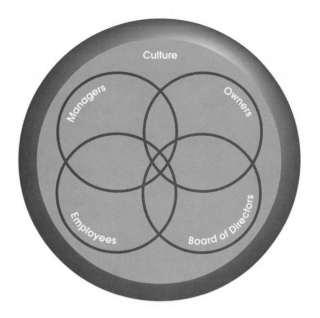

The Internal Environment

The internal environment consists of four groups of people in a corporation, as shown in Figure 2.7. Each group in the chart has different goals, beliefs, needs, and functions that managers must coordinate to achieve overall company goals. In this process, a corporate culture that transcends the values of any single internal group is created.

Like external environments, the internal environment changes over time. Forces in external environments are causing declines in the power of major internal groups in corporations. Employees are losing power due to globalization of labor markets that puts them in competition with lower-wage workers elsewhere. Managers are limited in their decisions by government and forced to accommodate a range of outside constituents expecting some right to influence an entity with power over them. Shareholders, and boards of directors as their representatives, are losing power to external groups demanding socially responsible actions that conflict with profit maximization.

CONCLUDING OBSERVATIONS

The environments of business have profound implications for managers. Figure 2.8 summarizes the chapter discussion by illustrating the dynamic interconnection of business with historical forces and current environments. The deep historical forces act to shape the seven key environments,

FIGURE 2.8 The Dynamic Interaction of Historical Forces, Business Environments, and Corporate Actions

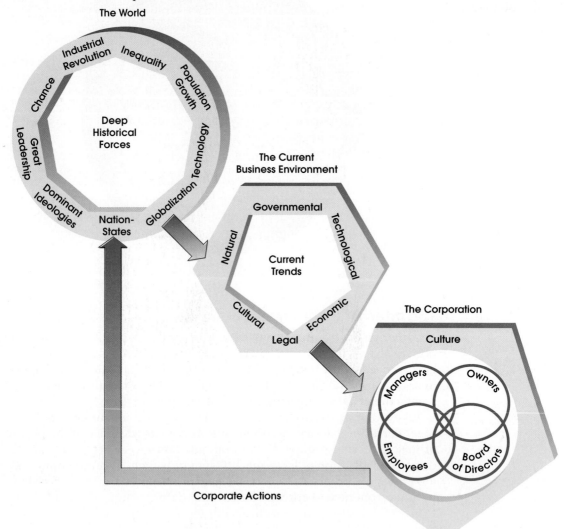

while the actions of business constantly influence not only current environments but, in addition, the deeper course of history. As the arrow running from the corporation to the world in Figure 2.8 indicates, business is not simply a passive entity that moves with historical and environmental forces like a billiard ball reacting to impacts. On the contrary, although strongly constrained by its environment, business has a powerful capacity to shape society and change history in ways small and large.

For example, when Eastman Kodak wanted to demonstrate the speed of its fast film and Flashmatic shutter in 1940, it ran ads showing pictures of the "Kodak Moments" when people blew out the candles on their birthday cakes. The ads so popularized this custom that it became universal among Americans.[52] In contrast to this small change, the story of the automobile illustrates how industries can much more deeply affect lives. Perhaps no twentieth century industry created more intentional and unintentional change. It was a prime mover of the American economy and once accounted directly or indirectly for one of every eight jobs. It encouraged an expansive highway system, brought decline to the railroads, depleted oil reserves, created pollution, altered cities, encouraged a connection between status and ownership of material objects, and changed patterns of crime. In the next chapter we will discuss the nature of this power that business has to shape the world.

[52] James B. Twitchell, *Lead Us Not into Temptation* (New York: Columbia University Press, 1999), p. 26.

The American Fur Company

The American Fur Company was a relentless monopoly operating in the climactic era of the fur trade. It was created in 1808 by John Jacob Astor, a poor German immigrant, in an environment so favorable that it grew to have a more powerful presence than the federal government over vast areas. But by the 1830s its situation so deteriorated that it and a thriving 300-year-old trade in furs fell apart. Nevertheless, in its time, this company shaped the destiny of a young nation and its peoples. It made Astor the richest American of his day.

ASTOR ARRIVES IN A YOUNG NATION

Astor was born in 1763 in the small German village of Waldorf, the son of a butcher. Young John Jacob found the village dull, so at the age of 15 he left for London, working there four years to save money for a trip to America and finally embarking on a ship in 1783. During the long voyage, he met an expert fur trader who taught him how to appraise and handle skins. This instruction gave Astor the knowledge he needed for an occupation, and he soon put it to use.

At this time, the fur trade on the North American continent was almost 300 years old. It had begun early in the sixteenth century among Spanish and French explorers who made contact with native forest dwellers, and it soon included the British. The Europeans wanted beaver, martin, ermine, mink, otter, bear, deer, muskrat, wolf, raccoon, and other animal skins for fashionable hats and clothing. The Native Americans, who had not yet entered the age of metal, were anxious to have even the simplest manufactured goods such as knives, mirrors, blankets, ornaments, buttons, and firearms. This simple mutual advantage proved durable over time.

For the most part, the British, French, and American fur traders of Astor's time depended on the American Indians to trap animals and then negotiated with them to buy the pelts in exchange for trinkets and manufactured goods. Indian women performed the work of skinning and preparing them. In this way, Indians became the production workers of the fur industry and overhead costs were reduced since no wages had to be paid. Instead of wages, trade goods worth a fraction of a fur's ultimate value were used. Since furs were light and compact, they could be transported economically over long distances by mules, barges, and ships to eastern ports and thence to Europe. Profits on furs were enormous.

Fur trading had transforming effects on society because it promoted settlement. Typically, fur traders were explorers who established their industry on the frontiers of Euro-American settlement. Over time, however, production always dropped as fur-bearing animals such as beaver with slow biological regeneration rates were depleted and Indian trappers became debilitated, their tribal cultures buckling under the pressure of new economic motives, tools, and values. When productivity in an area fell, the traders moved just over the horizon, and rolling in their wake came settlers using maps and trails created by the fur trade. Farms and towns cropped up, then Indians were killed or moved by the government. This unsentimental cycle of the fur trade, repeated over and over, created the settlement pattern in much of the United States as it exists today.

ASTOR ENTERS THE FUR BUSINESS

Astor made his way to New York where he got a job selling bakery goods. He invested most of his $2-a-week pay in small trinkets and in his spare time prowled the watefront for Indians who might have a fur to trade. Within a year he had picked up enough skins to take a ship back to London, where he established connections with fur-trading houses. This was a phenomenal achievement for an immigrant lad of 21 who had been nearly penniless on his arrival in America, but it revealed Astor's deadly serious and hard-driving personality.

Astor worked briefly with a fur dealer in New York City during which time he trekked into the forests of upstate New York to bargain for furs. He soon left his employer and by 1787 was working solely for himself. He demonstrated sharp negotiat-

ing skills in trading trinkets for furs and soon built up an impressive business. One neighbor said:

> Many times I have seen John Jacob Astor with his coat off, unpacking in a vacant yard near my residence a lot of furs he had bought dog-cheap off the Indians and beating them out, cleaning them and repacking them in more elegant and salable form to be transported to England and Germany, where they would yield him 1,000 percent on the original costs.[1]

Astor made great profits and expanded his business but, like other Americans, he was blocked from harvesting furs in the forests of the Northwest Territory. The Northwest Territory was the huge unsettled area between the Ohio River and the Mississippi River bounded on the north by the Great Lakes. After the Revolutionary War, Great Britain had ceded this area to the United States but continued to maintain forts and troops there because the American government was too weak to enforce its rights. British fur-trading companies exploited the area and incited Indians to attack traders and settlers who dared enter.

This imperiousness of the British pushed Congress near to declaring war. To avoid hostilities, England agreed to a treaty in 1794 that required removal of British troops and gave both British and Americans the right to trade in the Northwest Territory.[2] When Astor heard the news he said, "Now I will make my fortune in the fur trade."[3] But he was stunned when President George Washington proposed that the government promote friendly relations with Indians by setting up its own fur-trading posts to be run with benevolent trading policies. These would compete with private traders such as Astor. Congress approved the plan, which allowed trade goods to be sold at cost, prohibited the use of liquor, and required payment of fair prices for furs.

The government-run trading posts infuriated Astor, who moved quickly to undermine them. He saturated the territory with his agents, in-

---

[1] A "Gentleman of Schenectady," quoted in John Upton Terrell, *Furs by Astor* (New York: Morrow, 1963), p. 55.
[2] The treaty was negotiated for the United States by John Jay and is known as Jay's Treaty.
[3] Terrell, *Furs by Astor*, p. 93.

structing them to buy every fur they could get their hands on before competitors did. He bought trade goods in huge quantities to lower the cost, and his agents paid for furs with these trinkets. And he allowed liquor to flow freely during trade negotiations, creating an advantage the government could not match.

Astor had great success with these tactics. The government lacked his nimbleness and commitment, and he outwitted other rivals. In less than 10 years he was the second-richest man in America (after only Stephen Girard, the shipping magnate and banker). Having accumulated deep resources, the Astor juggernaut turned toward the West.

THE LOUISIANA PURCHASE

In 1803 the territory of the United States more than doubled with the Louisiana Purchase. President Thomas Jefferson agreed to purchase from France for $15 million approximately 800,000 square miles of land between the Mississippi River and the Rocky Mountains and running north from New Orleans to the forty-ninth parallel, which is now the Canada–U.S. boundary. At the time, little was known about the area called the Louisiana Territory. No accurate or complete maps existed; even its exact boundaries were vague. But Louisiana was beautiful in its mystery. Some geographers thought it was largely an arid desert. Others predicted a lush, fertile land over which Jefferson's ideal of an agrarian republic could spread. Rumors of geological wonders, horrific animals, and strange natives circulated, including the story of a tribe of bow-hunting, man-hating female savages in which the archers had their right breasts removed to keep them from interfering the bowstrings.[4]

Jefferson himself had a clear vision of how to use the new territory. He did not believe it could be settled right away, and until it could, he wanted to populate it with Indians and fur traders. In his 1803 message to Congress, he proposed to relocate into Louisiana eastern tribes getting in the way of American settlers, and over the next 50 years this

occurred many times.[5] He also ordered an Expedition of Discovery headed by Meriwether Lewis and William Clark to explore on foot the unknown territory. A primary purpose of the Lewis and Clark expedition was to determine the suitability of Louisiana for the fur trade. The adventurers set out on a round-trip march between St. Louis and the Pacific Ocean, going where no white American had gone before, and on their return reported a wondrous land "richer in beaver and otter than any country on earth."[6] They also reported that most Indian tribes in the territory were friendly to Americans and the fur trade. These discoveries were not lost on fur traders, among them John Jacob Astor.

THE AMERICAN FUR COMPANY IS BORN

The Lewis and Clark expedition was a catalyst for fur-trading in the new territory. Beaver production in the Northwest Territory was already beginning to fall off. Beavers reproduce slowly, and their populations quickly decline when trapping begins, especially when no restraint is practiced, as was the case in those days. Immediately, the North West Company, Astor's main competitor in the old Northwest Territory, began to move down from Canada to trade for beaver skins with Great Plains Indian tribes. Its intention was to harvest the newly discovered fur resources in the Louisiana Territory as rapidly as possible.

However, they had to reckon with Astor, who wanted the prize himself. In his distant New York City study, Astor poured over maps of the fur-rich areas discovered by Lewis and Clark, hatching a vast and daring plan for a new company that would string trading posts over a 2,000-mile route. In those days, state legislatures had exclusive power to create a company by issuing a charter that

[4] Ben Gilbert, *The Trailblazers* (New York: Time-Life Books, 1973), p. 18.

[5] For a list of 24 relocations, see Cardinal Goodwin, *The Trans-Mississippi West (1803–1853)* (New York: Appleton, 1922), plate following p. 88.
[6] Quoted in David J. Wishart, *The Fur Trade of the American West (1807–1840): A Geographical Synthesis* (Lincoln: University of Nebraska Press, 1979), p. 19, citing the original journals of the trip.

listed the conditions of its existence. So he approached the governor and legislature of New York seeking to charter a company to be known as the American Fur Company. To sell the idea, he cloaked his mercenary scheme with a veil of patriotism. He argued that most of the furs taken from the new Louisiana territory went to Canadians and British, thereby depriving America of trade revenue. His new company would drive the foreigners out. He announced plans to join with 10 or 12 other wealthy entrepreneurs to capitalize the new company, which would then issue stock to others. The new company would enhance U.S. security by establishing a strong presence of American citizens over unpopulated areas. And finally, Astor promised that his company would deal honestly with the Indians and drive out smaller, irresponsible traders. The legislators of New York, responding more to Astor's open pocketbook than to the credibility of his arguments, passed a charter setting up the American Fur Company. Soon President Jefferson wrote a letter to Astor giving his blessing to the new company also.

Astor proceeded to take on four partners and establish a board of directors for the American Fur Company as the charter required. However, he retained 99.9 percent of the stock, elected himself president, and subsequently declared dividends whenever he wanted to compensate himself. The partnership was a fiction; Astor never intended to share either the proceeds of the company or any portion of the fur trade that he could control.

In 1810 he made his first move. His ship, the *Tonquin,* sailed to the mouth of the Columbia River on the Pacific Coast and set up a trading post named Astoria. At this time, Britain and the United States contested the wild area known as Oregon territory, consisting of present-day Oregon and Washington. Astor got diplomatic support for his trading post by arguing that its presence established an American claim to the territory. Secretly, however, he hoped to form a new nation called Astoria and make himself king.

Meanwhile, he would make Astoria one end of a vise that would squeeze competitors out of the new fur areas. Furs taken in the west would come to Astoria and then be shipped to China, which was a major fur market, or to New York. By this time, Astor owned a fleet of ships with which to do this.

The other end of the vise would be St. Louis. Furs from Astor's planned string of trading posts on the eastern slopes of the Rocky Mountains would come down the Missouri River system to St. Louis and from there go overland to New York or on to the port of New Orleans to be shipped to Europe. It was a megalomaniac scheme, and no one but Astor had both the audacity and the resources even to attempt it. But it was too grandiose. Only part of it was to work, and the rest worked only until the fur trade fell apart.

THE ROAD TO MONOPOLY

In 1813 Astor's plan suffered a great reversal when he was forced to sell Astoria to the British during the War of 1812. He sold out at a fraction of its value because British soldiers were in a position to seize it as a war prize. Without Astoria as a foothold in the Oregon territory, he was unable to compete with British and Canadian fur companies. And 61 of Astor's employees died pursuing the settlement, along with hundreds of natives they came in conflict with.[7] Unbowed, Astor later commissioned Washington Irving, the best-selling author of the day, to write a book about the intrepid adventurers and himself as the great mind behind them.[8]

Despite the loss of Astoria, Astor nonetheless predominated. In 1816 his lobbying efforts succeeded in getting Congress to pass a law forbidding foreigners from trading furs in U.S. territories. This prevented Canadian and British companies from operating in the Northwest Territory, and Astor immediately bought out their interests, giving him a monopoly in furs east of the Missouri River. Blocked from the Pacific Coast trade by the British presence, he turned his attention to the upper-Missouri fur trade.

Astor bided his time as other fur companies pioneered trading in the northern Great Plains and then, after discovery of rich valleys of beaver, in the Rocky Mountains. By 1822 Astor had established a presence selling trade goods and buying

[7] Axel Madsen, *John Jacob Astor: America's First Multimillionaire* (New York: Wiley, 2001), p. 163.
[8] *Astoria; or, Enterprise beyond the Rocky Mountains* (New York: The Century Co., 1909); originally published in 1839.

furs in St. Louis, but he waited as other companies sent expensive expeditions of traders and mountain men up the Missouri, absorbing heavy losses of men and money. Despite losses, these pioneering companies found tremendous reserves of beaver in Rocky Mountain valleys, mapped new routes, and discovered advantageous locations for trading posts.

Then he began to crush the competition. In 1826 he merged with Bernard Pratte & Company, an established firm, using it as an agent. He bought out and liquidated another competitor, Stone, Bostwick & Company. In 1827 he broke the Columbia Fur Company by building his own trading posts next to every one of theirs, engaging in cutthroat price competition for furs, and plying Indians liberally with whiskey. His trappers shadowed Columbia Fur Company trapping parties to discover where the rich sources of beaver were, then worked the areas. Using similar tactics, he bankrupted Menard & Valle. Now, according to Astor's biographer Terrell:

Portrait of John Jacob Astor. © Bettman/Corbis.

> Competition on the Missouri River was all but nonexistent. What remained was inconsequential, and might have been likened to a terrier yapping at a bear. The bear lumbered on, ignoring the noise until it became aggravating. Then with the sudden swipe of a paw, the yapping was forever stilled.[9]

Astor made astonishing profits. He would buy, for example, a 10-pound keg of gunpowder for $2, or 20 cents a pound, in London and transport it to his trading posts using his ships. He paid himself a 2 percent commission for buying the trade goods, or $.04 cents on the keg of gunpowder. He paid himself a freight charge for carrying the gunpowder on his ship to New Orleans. From there the keg was transported up the Missouri using the inexpensive labor of his hired trappers and traders. The gunpowder was valued at $4 a pound to the Indians, who were not allowed to pay money for it but got it only by exchanging furs or on credit. In the 1820s Astor charged one 2-pound beaver skin for each pound of gunpowder, getting 10 skins weighing 20 pounds for the key of gunpowder.

These skins were transported back to London, where they were worth $7 a pound or $140. From the $140 Astor deducted a 5 percent commission, or $7, for brokering the sale of the furs. Astor also subtracted 25 percent, or $35 from the $140, for the estimated costs of transportation and wages.

All told, this left a net profit for the American Fur Company of $97.96, or 4,900 percent on the original $2 investment.[10] And Astor owned over 99 percent of the company's shares. This profitable arithmetic was repeated on a wide range of trade goods.

The importance of trade goods lies in the nature of Indian cultures. Indians coveted them so much that they considered the whites foolish to exchange even the smallest trinkets for beaver skins in free supply. In general, the concept of material acquisition beyond basic needs was foreign to Indian cultures based on ideas of sufficiency. The Arikaras, for example, believed that a person who had more than

---

[9] Terrell, *Furs by Astor*, p. 391.

[10] These calculations are based on figures in Terrell, *Furs by Astor*, pp. 397–98.

needed to survive ought to divided it with others. It was difficult to motivate Indians to trap and process furs for Astor and other traders by using money; they were indifferent to accumulating currency. Trade goods such as rifles, knives, clothing, blankets, beads, and trinkets did have some utility for Indians, which made them attractive, but frequently native-made equivalents were just as good or better.

For the Indians, trade goods had mystic significance beyond their monetary value or utility. The appeal of trade goods in their eyes lay in certain magical, spiritual values not apparent to Europeans and Americans. They believed that the future could be divined by looking in a reflection of the self. Manufactured mirrors gave a clearer reflection than water and were, therefore, a wondrous advance in prophecy. Guns were seen as supernatural beings because they could create thunder, an event associated with the spiritual world. Kettles were regarded as having life because they rang or sang out when hit. In this way, Indians found supernatural qualities in trade goods that were lost on Europeans.[11]

Astor encouraged Indians to take trade goods on credit. As a result, some tribes—the Winnebagos, Sacs, Foxes, Cherokees, Chickasaws, and Sioux—were hopelessly mired in debt, owing the American Fur Company as much as $50,000 each. Since trade goods had sky-high markups, Astor could not lose much even if tribal debts grew, but indebtedness forced tribes to trade furs with him rather than with competitors.

His traders and trappers fared no better. He marked up trade goods heavily before selling them to traders. Often, traders were in debt to Astor or had mortgaged their trading posts to him and were forced to mark up trade goods heavily themselves before selling them to Indians and trappers. Trappers employed by the American Fur Company were ruthlessly exploited. They worked unlimited hours in hazardous conditions and extreme weather, but when Astor achieved dominance in an area, he cut their salaries from $100 a year to $250 every three years. They had to buy trade goods and staples at markups that were higher than those charged Indians to get furs. Whiskey costing $.30 a gallon in St. Louis was diluted with water and sold to them at $3 a pint. Coffee and sugar costing $.10 a pound was marked up to $2 at the trading posts up the Missouri. Clothes and trade goods to be used with the Indians were marked up 300 to 400 percent.

Overall, Astor contrived a lucrative, pitiless system that amplified his fortune by diminishing those caught in its workings. Though never venturing out west, he was not out of touch, working long hours, his shrewd mind obsessed with the most minor details and with squeezing out the smallest unnecessary expenses. In 1831 his son William estimated revenues for the American Fur Company of "not less than $500,000" yearly.[12] Astor was by now the richest man in America and had begun to buy real estate in and around New York City.

ASTOR RACES ON

In the early 1830s it seemed nothing could slow Astor. Competing firms were started by men who hated the American Fur Company, but few lasted. Astor destroyed them by outbidding for furs and debauching the Indians with alcohol.

In 1832 Congress prohibited import of alcohol into territories occupied by Indians, but the law was widely ignored. Astor never favored using alcohol, but many competitors who could not match his resources saw it as their only hope of seducing Indians with furs away from him, and so they continued to use it. So Astor, never squeamish about meeting the competition, let the spirits freely flow despite ruinous consequences.

Alcohol was unknown in native cultures; Indians developed a craving for it only after European traders introduced intoxication into the process of negotiating fur prices. Some believed that spirits occupied their bodies when they drank. Among Indians who took to whiskey, a new desire was created where none existed before, a desire that motivated them to produce furs. A few tribes, notably the Pawnee,

---

[11] Richard White, "Expansion and Exodus," in Betty Ballantine and Ian Ballantine, eds., *The Native Americans: An Illustrated History* (Atlanta: Turner Publishing, 1993), chap. 14.

[12] Gustavus Myers, *History of the Great American Fortunes* (New York: Modern Library, 1936), p. 102; originally published in 1909.

Crow, and Arikara, never would drink. But most did, and some tribes were so debilitated by its effects that their fur production fell and traders moved on.

Astor had no intention of obeying the new prohibition statute and smuggled as much liquor as needed past Indian Agents. One of Astor's agents built a still at the confluence of the Yellowstone and Missouri rivers that produced enough spirits to keep tribes in several states in a constant state of inebriation. The fact was that Congress could not enforce its will because the federal government had almost no presence in the vast areas of the West. Written laws were meaningless where no civil authorities existed to back them up. In Indian country, the only law was the will of leaders of trading companies and brigades of trappers who wore self-designed, military-style uniforms and could rob, cheat, and murder both Indians and whites with impunity. An 1831 report to Lewis Cass, Secretary of War, stated:

> The traders that occupy the largest and most important space in the Indian country are the agents and engagees of the American Fur Trade Company. They entertain, as I know to be the fact, no sort of respect for our citizens, agents, officers of the Government, or its laws or general policy.[13]

Government officials such as Cass were disinclined to thwart Astor in any case since they were frequently in his pay. Cass, who was the federal official in charge of enforcing the prohibition law, was paid $35,000 by the American Fur Company between 1817 and 1834.[14] At one time, Astor even advanced a personal loan of $5,000 to President James Monroe. Over the years, the Astor lobby achieved most of its objectives in Washington, D.C., and state capitals, including exclusion of foreign companies from the United States, heavy tariffs on imported furs, and abolition of the government fur-trading posts so beloved to Washington and Jefferson. Under these circumstances, it is not surprising that the government failed to regulate the fur trade.

In 1831 Astor introduced a new technological innovation, the steamboat *Yellowstone,* which could travel 50 to 100 miles a day up the Missouri, transporting trade goods and supplies to his posts. Keelboats used by competitors made only 20 miles upriver on a good day and exposed men pulling them with ropes from the bank to hostile Indian fire. Upriver Indians were awestruck by the *Yellowstone* and traveled hundreds of miles to see the spirit that walked on water. Some tribes refused to trade with the Hudson Bay Company any longer, believing that because of the *Yellowstone* it could no longer compete with the American Fur Company.

THE ENVIRONMENT OF THE FUR TRADE CHANGES

Although the American Fur Company was ascendant, unfavorable trends were building that would bring it down. Demand for beaver was falling as the fashion trends that made every European and American gentleman want a beaver hat waned. Silk hats became the new rage. Also, new ways of felting hats without using fibrous underhair from beaver pelts had developed, and nutria pelts from South America were entering the market.

These were not the only problems. In 1832 trade came to a near standstill during a worldwide cholera epidemic because many people thought the disease was spread on transported furs. Beaver populations were depleted by overtrapping. The fur companies made no conservation efforts; the incentive was rather to trap all beaver in an area, leaving none for competitors. In the 1820s the Hudson Bay Company tried to prevent Astor from moving into Oregon territory by exterminating beaver along a band of terrain to create a "fur desert" that would be unprofitable for Astor's trappers to cross.

Losses of human life rose as mountain men entered the shrinking areas where beaver was still abundant, leaving behind somewhat friendly Indians such as the Snake and Crow to encounter more hostile tribes such as the Blackfeet, who poisoned their arrows with rattlesnake venom and conducted open war against trappers.[15] One study of

---

[13] Report of Andrew S. Hughes, quoted in Myers, *History of the Great American Fortunes,* p. 99.
[14] Myers, *History of the Great American Fortunes,* p. 103.

[15] Trappers also attacked Blackfeet without provocation. See Osborne Russell, *Journal of a Trapper* (Lincoln: University of Nebraska Press, 1955), pp. 52, 86.

446 mountain men actively trapping between 1805 and 1845 found that 182, or 41 percent, were killed in the occupation.[16]

Astor saw that the fur industry was doomed. Beaver pelts that had fetched $6 a pound in 1830 brought only $3.50 a pound by 1833, and in that year he liquidated all his fur-trading interests. He spent the rest of his years accumulating more money in New York real estate. For a time, the American Fur Company continued its ruthless dominion under new owners, but the industry environment continued to worsen. In 1837 the firm's steamboat *St. Peters* carried smallpox up the Missouri, killing more than 17,000 natives, and an agent observed that "our most profitable Indians have died."[17] By 1840 the firm had withdrawn from the Rocky Mountains and focused on buffalo robes, which remained profitable for some time.

ASTOR'S LAST YEARS

Astor lived on in New York, wringing immense profits from rents and leases as the city grew around his real estate holdings. By 1847 he had accumulated a fortune of $20 million that towered above any other of that day. This sum has been estimated to be the equivalent of $78 billion today, more than the wealth of Microsoft's Bill Gates.[18] In his last years, he was weak and frail and exercised by having attendants toss him up and down in a blanket. Yet despite his physical deterioration, he remained focused on getting every last penny from his tenants, poring over the rents for long hours behind the barred windows of his office.

Astor gave little to charity, and social critics attacked him for his stinginess. When he died in 1848, his major gift to society was $460,000 in his will for building an Astor Library. In addition, he left $50,000 to the town of Waldorf, Germany, his birthplace; $30,000 for the German Society of New York; and $30,000 to the Home for Aged Ladies in New York City. This totaled, in the words of one commentator, less than "the proceeds of one year's pillage of the Indians."[19] The rest of his wealth went to his heirs.

THE LEGACY OF THE FUR TRADE

For 300 years the fur trade shaped the economic, political, and cultural life of both native and European inhabitants of the raw North American continent. Its climactic era has often been depicted as a progressive and romantic period when trading posts represented "civilization which was slowly mastering the opposition of nature and barbarism."[20] According to historian Dan Elbert Clark:

> The fur traders, with all their faults and shortcomings, were the pathfinders of civilization. They marked the trails that were followed by settlers. They built trading posts where later appeared thriving towns and cities. They knew the Indians better than any other class of white men who came among them.[21]

The American Fur Company and its competitors greatly advanced geographical knowledge and blazed trails. The fur industry reinforced central American values such as rugged individualism, the frontier spirit, and optimism about the inevitability of progress. Yet there is also a dark side to the story. Traders undermined Indian cultures by introducing new economic motivations. Tribal societies were destroyed by alcohol, smallpox, and venereal disease. "The fur trade," according to Professor David J. Wishart of the University of Nebraska, "was the vanguard of a massive wave of Euro-American colonisation which brought into contact two sets of cultures with disparate and irreconcilable ways of life."[22]

[16] William H. Goetzmann, "The Mountain Man as Jacksonian Man," *American Quarterly*, Fall 1963, p. 409.
[17] Jacob Halsey, a clerk at Fort Pierre, quoted by Wishart, *The Fur Trade of the American West*, p. 68.
[18] This is the estimate of Michael Klepper and Robert Gunther in "The American Heritage 40," *American Heritage*, October 1998, p. 56.

[19] Myers, *History of the Great American Fortunes*, p. 149.
[20] Arthur D. Howden Smith, *John Jacob Astor: Landlord of New York* (Philadelphia: Lippincott, 1929), p. 131.
[21] Dan Elbert Clark, *The West in American History* (New York: Thomas Y. Crowell, 1937), p. 441.
[22] Wishart, *The Fur Trade of the American West*, p. 215.

The industry also left extensive ecological damage in its wake. Animal populations were decimated and whole riverside forest areas were denuded to get wood that fueled steamboats. The mentality of pillage exhibited by Astor's agents set a destructive standard. Argues Wishart: "The attitude of rapacious, short-term exploitation which was imprinted during the fur trade persisted after 1840 as the focus shifted from furs to minerals, timber, land, and water."[23]

The American Fur Company, a company no longer remembered by most Americans, was the largest actor in a powerful industry that shaped the country. Its operation was like a test-tube experiment revealing the social consequences of raw, laissez-faire capitalism unrestrained by government. It would be many years before the nation learned all the lessons.

QUESTIONS

1. How would you evaluate Astor in terms of his motive, his managerial ability, and his ethics? What lesson does his career teach about the relationship between virtue and success?

2. How did the environment of the American Fur Company change in the 1830s? What deep historical forces are implicated in these changes?

3. Evaluate the impact of the fur trade on society in major dimensions of the business environment, that is, economic, cultural, technological, natural, governmental, legal, and internal.

4. Who were the most important stakeholders of the nineteenth-century fur industry? Were they treated responsibly by the standards of the day? By the standards of today?

5. On balance, is the legacy of the American Fur Company and of the fur trade itself a positive legacy? Or is the impact of these companies predominantly negative?

6. Does the story of the American Fur Company hint at how and why capitalism has changed and has been changed over the years?

7. Do one or more models of the business–government–society relationship discussed in Chapter 1 apply to the historical era set forth in this case? Which model or models have explanatory power and why?

[23] Ibid., p. 212.

Chapter **Three**

Business Power

The American Tobacco Company

James B. Duke was born in 1856 on a North Carolina farm. At the end of the Civil War, his father returned home and found a shed of tobacco miraculously intact after the Union Army occupation and began selling the contents. Soon the elder Duke built a small factory to manufacture a brand of chewing tobacco named Pro Bono Publico (a Latin phrase meaning "for the public good"). Young James Duke entered the business with his father. He was a precocious, energetic boy who became the driving force behind the company.

During the 1870s James Duke's visions of grandeur for the little factory were thwarted by the dominance of a huge rival firm, the Bull Durham Co. Its brand of chewing tobacco, Bull Durham, was so dominant and well entrenched that head-on competition seemed hopeless. So he decided on a new strategy. He would manufacture an unproven tobacco product—cigarettes. This was a venturesome move, because at the time cigarettes were a tiny segment of the tobacco market and their use was associated with degenerate dudes and dandies in big cities.

Duke brought 10 professional tobacco rollers from Europe to his factory in North Carolina and set them to work. Each could roll a little over 2,000 cigarettes per day. At first he had trouble selling his Duke of Durham brand. Tobacco shops refused to buy them because customers didn't request them. So Duke innovated with his marketing strategy. In Atlanta, he put up a billboard of a famous actress holding Duke cigarettes in her outstretched hand. This was the first time a woman had been used to advertise cigarettes, and the novelty created demand. In St. Louis, Duke's salesmen found extreme prejudice against cigarettes. Tobacco shop proprietors simply would not buy. So Duke hired a young, redheaded widow to call on the tobacconists, and she got 19 orders on her first day.

When a young Virginia engineer, James Bonsack, invented a mechanical cigarette-rolling machine capable of rolling 200 per minute, Duke negotiated an exclusive agreement to operate the machine. With the new Bon-

This ad for one of Duke's brands appeared in *Puck* magazine in 1886. Courtesy of the Valentine Museum.

sack machines, Duke simultaneously cut manufacturing costs from $.80 per thousand to $.30 and multiplied factory output many times.[1]

To find new markets for this swollen output, he first tried to open New York City as a foothold in the East. There he ran into competition from local firms, and he also encountered resistance to machine-rolled cigarettes among smokers. But both these barriers yielded to an array of ingenious promotional practices. He advertised widely. He put pictures of actresses and athletes in cigarette packs and numbered them so that compulsive collectors would want complete sets. He hired people to go into tobacco

[1] John K. Winkler, *Tobacco Tycoon: The Story of James Buchanan Duke* (New York: Random House, 1942), p. 56.

shops and demand his new machine-rolled Cameo and Cross Cuts brands. Immigrants entering New York were handed free samples.

Overseas, Duke's minions were at work also. One great conquest was China. At the time a few Chinese, mostly older men, smoked a bitter native tobacco in pipes. Cigarettes were unknown. Duke sent experts to Shantung Province with bright leaf from North Carolina to cultivate a milder tobacco. His sales force hired "teachers" to walk village streets showing curious Chinese how to light and hold cigarettes. He installed Bonsack machines in four huge manufacturing plants in China that soon ran 24 hours a day. And he unleashed on the Chinese a full range of promotional activities. At one time his cigarette packs contained pictures of nude American actresses, which proved to be a big hit with Chinese men. Duke turned China into a nation of cigarette smokers.

Back home his tactics wore down competitors, and in 1889 he engineered a combination of his firm and other large firms into the giant American Tobacco Company. As president, Duke built the company into a monopoly that controlled 93 percent of the cigarette market by 1900 and dominated the snuff, cheroot, and smoking tobacco markets as well. Duke ruthlessly swallowed or bankrupted 250 competing firms during the next 22 years while continuing to spread the gospel of smoking around the globe.

Duke's monopoly lasted until 1911, when the Supreme Court ordered it broken up.[2] Duke himself sat down and figured out how to divide the giant trust into four independent companies: Ligget & Myers Tobacco Company, P. Lorillard Company, R. J. Reynolds Company, and a new American Tobacco Company. After the breakup, Duke retired from the the tobacco industry to start an electric utility, Duke Power & Light. He also gave money to a small North Carolina college, which became Duke University.

Duke's career illustrates the power of commerce to shape society. He made the cigarette an acceptable consumer product and spread it around the world. To find a market for the copious production of the new Bonsack machines, he turned China into a nation of smokers. His monopoly defined the structure of the tobacco industry and destroyed rivals; its power flattened the comparatively feeble efforts of antitobacco leagues to publicize health hazards. Duke's ads made smoking glamorous. His bribes to legislators killed antismoking laws. And, due largely to Duke's forcefulness, the tobacco industry resuscitated the crippled post–Civil War southern economy and created a powerful, enduring political coalition in Congress. Although he encountered a limit on business power when the Supreme Court dismantled his mammoth trust, its legacy endures in the roll call of smokers across 130 years.

---

[2] *United States v. American Tobacco Company,* 221 U.S. 106 (1911).

THE NATURE OF BUSINESS POWER

Business has tremendous power to change society, and the extent of this power is underappreciated. In past eras, rising companies and new industries furrowed the social landscape, altering ideas, values, and institutions. This effect is visible in the stories of dominant companies such as the American Fur Company, the Standard Oil Company, and the American Tobacco Company. Such examples show the power of just one company to alter the world. The cumulative power of all business is an even more massive force for change. In this chapter we discuss how this power to change society works and explain its limits.

WHAT IS POWER?

Power is the force or strength to act. It exists on a broad spectrum ranging from coercion at one extreme to weak influence at the other. Its use in human society creates change. Although power is sometimes exerted to prevent change, such resistence is, of course, itself a force that alters history. There are many sources of power, including wealth, position, knowledge, law, arms, social status, charisma, and public opinion. Power is unevenly distributed, and all societies have mechanisms to control and channel it for wide or narrow benefit. These mechanisms, which are imperfect, include governments, laws, police, cultural values, and public opinion. Also, multiple, competing power formations limit discretion.

Business power is the force or strength behind business actions that change the world. Its source is a grant of authority from society to convert resources efficiently into needed goods and services. In return for doing this, society gives corporations the authority to take proper actions and permits a return on investment. This agreement between business and society is called a *social contract.*

The social contract legitimizes business power by giving it a moral basis. *Legitimacy* is the rightful use of power. The power of giant corporations is legitimate when it is exercised in keeping with the agreed-upon contract.[3] The philosopher John Locke wrote that for governments the opposite of legitimacy is tyranny, defined as "the exercise of power beyond right."[4] Corporations can also breach the social contract, exercising "power beyond right" when they corrode social values, harm the public, or act illegally.

---

[3] For an effort to stipulate social contract norms that should guide business behavior, see Thomas Donaldson and Thomas W. Dunfee, *Ties That Bind: A Social Contracts Approach to Business Ethics* (Boston: Harvard Business School Press, 1999).

[4] John Locke, *The Second Treatise of Government* (New York: Bobbs-Merrill, 1952), p. 112; originally published in 1690.

Business power is legitimate when it is used for the common good. The grounds of legitimacy vary between societies and over time. Child labor, once widespread in the United States, is no longer permitted, but it exists in other nations. As we will see in subsequent chapters, the definition of the common good that business must serve has expanded throughout American history and is now expanding globally.

LEVELS AND SPHERES OF CORPORATE POWER

Corporate actions have an impact on society at two levels, and on each level they create change. On the *surface level*, business power is the direct cause of visible, immediate changes, both great and small. Corporations expand and contract, hire and fire; they make and sell products.

On a *deep level*, corporate power shapes society over time through the aggregate changes of industrial growth. At this level, corporate power creates many indirect, unforeseen, and invisible effects. Multiple lines of events converge and interact in complex networks of cause and effect. At this deep level, the workings of corporate power are unplanned, unpredictable, and slow to appear, but they are far more significant. Corporate power "is something more than men," wrote John Steinbeck. "It's the monster. Men made it, but they can't control it."[5] This is a poetic description of business power at a deep level.

On both the surface and deep levels, business power is exercised in spheres corresponding to the seven business environments set forth in Chapter 2.

- *Economic power* is the ability of the corporation to influence events, activities, and people by virtue of control over resources, particularly property. At the surface level, the operation of a corporation may immediately and visibly affect the well-being of its stakeholders, for example, by making stockholders rich. At a deeper level, the accumulating impact of corporate economic activity has sweeping effects. For example, over many years corporations have created enough wealth to raise dramatically living standards in industrialized nations.

- *Technological power* is the ability to influence the direction, rate, characteristics, and consequences of physical innovations as they develop. On a surface level, in 1914, assembly lines run by new electric motors allowed Henry Ford to introduce transportation based on the new internal combustion engine. Using this new method, he turned an expensive luxury of the rich into a mass consumer product. But at a deeper level, as the auto took hold in American society it created

[5] In *The Grapes of Wrath,* quoted by Rich Jaroslovsky, "It Lives among Us . . . and Employs Us Too," *The Wall Street Journal,* April 11, 2001, p. A20.

unanticipated consequences. One juvenile court judge in the 1920s called the automobile a "house of prostitution on wheels," something that the puritanical Henry Ford doubtless never intended to create.[6]

- *Political power* is the ability to influence government decisions. On the surface, corporations give money to candidates and lobby legislatures. On a deeper level, as noted in Chapter 2, all around the world industrialism engenders values that radiate freedom and erode authoritarian regimes.

- *Legal power* is the force to shape the laws of society. On the surface, big corporations have formidable legal resources that intimidate opponents. On a deeper level, the law of the United States—including constitutional, civil, and criminal law—has been shaped in many ways by the consequences of industrial activity.

- *Cultural power* is the ability to influence cultural values, institutions such as the family, customs, lifestyles, and habits. John Wanamaker, founder of a department store chain and an early advertising genius, started Mother's Day in the early 1900s. He ran full-page newspaper ads in the *Philadelphia Inquirer* featuring a woman mourning her mother, creating the sentiment that gratitude for mothers should be expressed by a gift on a special day.[7] At a deeper level, the cumulative impact of ads has altered American society by reinforcing values selectively, for example, materialism over asceticism, individualism over community, or personal appearance over character development.

- *Environmental power* is the impact of a company on nature. On the surface, a steel mill may pollute the air; on a deeper level, since the seventeenth century, the burning of wood, coal, and oil to power industry has turned the earth's atmosphere into a gigantic chemistry experiment.

- *Power over individuals* is exercised over employees, managers, stockholders, consumers, and citizens. On the surface, a corporation may determine the work life and buying habits of individuals. At a deeper level, industrialism sets the pattern of daily life. People are regimented, living by clocks, moving in routes fixed by the model of an industrial city with its streets and sidewalks. Their occupation determines their status and wealth.

Activity in the economic sphere is the primary force for change. From this, change radiates into other spheres. The story of the railroad

---

[6] Frederick Lewis Allen, *Only Yesterday: An Informal History of the 1920s* (New York: Harper & Brothers, 1931), p. 100.
[7] Richard Wolkomir and Joyce Wolkomir, "You Are What You Buy," *Smithsonian,* May 2000, p. 107.

industry in the United States illustrates how an expanding industry with a radical new technology can change its environments.

THE STORY OF THE RAILROADS

When small railroads sprang up in the 1820s, most passengers and freight moved by horse and over canals. The railroad was a vastly superior conveyance and was bound to revolutionize transportation. Tracks cost less to build than canals and did not freeze in winter. Routes could be more direct. For the first time in history, people and cargo traveled overland at faster than the speed of a horse. The trip from New York to Chicago was reduced from three weeks to just three days. And the cost of moving goods and passengers was less; in a day a train could go back and forth many times over the distance that a canal boat or wagon could traverse once.

The initial boom in railroading came at mid-century. In 1850 trains ran on only about 9,000 miles of track, but by 1860 more than 30,000 miles had been laid down. During that decade, 30 railroad companies completed route systems, which had significant consequences for the financial system. Tracks were expensive, and each of these enterprises was a giant for its day. Many needed $10 to $35 million in capital, and the smallest at least $2 million. Companies in other industries did not approach this size; only a handful of textile mills and steel plants had required capitalization of more than $1 million.[8]

The call for this much money transformed capital markets. The only place such huge sums could be raised was in large northeastern cities. Since interest rates were a little higher in Boston at the time, New York became the center of financial activity and has remained so to this day. Railroads sold bonds and offered stocks to raise capital, and a new investment banking industry was created. The New York Stock Exchange went from a sleepy place, where only a few hundred shares of stock might change hands each week, to a roaring market. Speculative techniques such as margin trading, short-selling, and options trading appeared for the first time. Later, the finance and speculative mechanisms inspired by railroad construction were in place when other industries needed more capital to grow. This changed American history by accelerating the industrial transformation of the late 1800s. It also put New York bankers such as J. P. Morgan in a position to control access to capital.

At first the railroads ran between existing trade centers, but as time passed and track mileage increased, they linked ever more points. The 30,626 miles of track in 1860 increased to 93,267 miles by 1880 and

---

[8] Alfred D. Chandler, Jr., *The Visible Hand: The Managerial Revolution in American Business* (Cambridge, MA: Belknap Press, 1977), pp. 83, 86, and 90.

163,597 miles by 1890.[9] This required enormous amounts of wood, and led to extensive clear-cuts where forests were harvested to make ties and stoke fires in early steam locomotives. A deeper consequence of extending the tracks was a society transformed.

Before the tracks radiated everywhere, the United States was a nation of farmers and small towns held together by the traditional institutions of family, church, and local government. Since long-distance travel was time-consuming and arduous, these towns often were isolated. Populations were stable. People identified more with local areas than with the nation as a whole. Into this world came the train, a destabilizing technology powered by aggressive market capitalism.

Trains took away young people who might have stayed in rural society but for the lure of wealth in distant cities. In their place came a stream of outsiders who were less under the control of community values. Small-town intimacy declined, and a new phenomenon appeared in American life—the impersonal crowd of strangers. Trains violated established customs. Sunday was a day of rest and worship, so many church-goers were angered when huffing and whistling trains intruded on services. But new capital accounting methods used by railroad companies dictated using equipment an extra day each week to increase return on investment. This imperative trumped devoutness. In early America, localities set their own time according to the sun's overhead transit, but this resulted in a patchwork of time zones that made scheduling difficult. An editorial in *Railroad Age* argued, "Local time must go."[10] For the convenience of the railroads, a General Time Convention met in 1882 and standardized the time of day, though not without resistence from holdouts who felt that "[s]urely the world ran by higher priorities than railroad scheduling."[11]

As the railroads grew, they spread impersonality and an ethic of commerce. Towns reoriented themselves around their train stations. Shops and restaurants sprang up nearby so that strangers would spend money before moving on. The railroads gave more frequent service to cities with commercial possibilities and bypassed small towns or let them wither from less frequent service. This speeded urbanization and the centralization of corporate power in cities. Rural areas were redefined. Once the cultural heartland, they now were seen as backward and rustic—places best used for vacations from urban stress.

The railroads also changed American politics. On the surface, their lobbyists could dominate legislatures. On a deeper level, the changes

---

[9] Bureau of the Census, *Statistical Abstract of the United States,* 77th ed. (Washington, DC: U.S. Government Printing Office, 1956), table 683.
[10] Bill Kauffman, "Why Spring Ahead," *The American Enterprise,* April–May 2001, p. 50.
[11] Ibid., p. 50, quoting Michael O'Malley, *Keeping Watch: A History of American Time* (Washington, DC: Smithsonian Institution Press, 1996).

were more profound. Congress had always selected nominees before presidential elections, but now trains brought delegates to national party nominating conventions, changing the way candidates were picked. Trains enabled all sorts of associations to have national meetings, and the rails spread issues that might in an earlier era have remained local. The movement to give women the vote, for example, succeeded after Susan B. Anthony took trains to all parts of the country, spreading her rhetoric and unifying the cause.[12]

At first government encouraged and subsidized railroads. All told, federal and state governments gave them land grants of 164 million acres, an area equal to the size of California and Nevada combined.[13] But later the challenge was to control them. When Congress passed the Interstate Commerce Act in 1887 to regulate railroads, the approach of the statute, with all its strengths and weaknesses, set the example for regulating other industries later.

Many other changes in American society are traceable to the railroads. They were the first businesses to require modern management structures. Due to the need for precise coordination of speeding trains over vast reaches, railroads pioneered professional management teams, division structures, and modern cost accounting—all innovations later adopted by other industries.[14] Railroads lay behind Indian wars. For the plains Indians, the tracks that divided old hunting grounds were the main barrier to peace.[15] Thousands of laborers came from China to lay rail, and their descendants live on in communities along the lines. Railroads changed the language. The word *diner,* meaning a place to eat, appeared after the introduction of George M. Pullman's first dining car in 1868.[16] And social values changed. The tracks were channels for infusing eastern commercial values into the byways of America.

TWO PERSPECTIVES ON BUSINESS POWER

There is agreement that business has great power. There is considerable disagreement about whether its power is adequately checked and balanced for the public good. Views about business power cover a wide spectrum, but there are two fundamental and opposing positions.

First is the *dominance theory,* which holds that business is preeminent in American society, primarily because of its control of wealth, and that

---

[12] These and other social and political changes are treated at length in Sarah H. Gordon, *Passage to Union* (Chicago: Ivan R. Dees, 1996).

[13] Page Smith, *The Rise of Industrial America,* vol. 6 (New York: Viking Penguin, 1984), p. 99.

[14] Chandler, *The Visible Hand,* chap. 3.

[15] Smith, *The Rise of Industrial America,* p. 89.

[16] Daniel J. Boorstin, *The Americans: The Democratic Experience* (New York: Random House, 1973), p. 335.

American Landscape, **a 1930 oil painting, depicts Ford Motor Company's River Rouge plant. Here artist Charles Sheeler makes a comment on the power of business to change and shape society. Outwardly, this vista seems to beautify and ennoble the architecture of industry, making it appear almost pastoral. Yet on another level the painting provokes anxiety. Factory buildings run nature off the scene, dominating a landscape that is now, but for the sky, entirely artificial. A tiny human figure in the middle ground is overwhelmed and marginalized by the massive complex; its movement is limited and regimented by the surrounding industrial structure. Here, then, art reveals emotions about industrial growth in a way that words cannot. This theme is found in many other Sheeler paintings and photographs.** Source: Charles Sheeler, *American Landscape*. 1930. Oil on Canvas, 24″ × 31″ (61 × 78.8 cm). The Museum of Modern Art, New York. Gift of Abby Aldrich Rockefeller. © Charles Sheeler. The Museum of Modern Art, New York.

its power is both excessive and inadequately checked. Corporations can alter their environments in self-interested ways that harm the general welfare. This was the thesis of Karl Marx, who wrote that a ruling capitalist class exploited workers and dominated other classes. The dominance theory is the basis of the dominance model of the BGS relationship set forth in Chapter 1.

Second is the *pluralist theory,* which holds that business power is exercised in a society where other institutions such as markets, government, labor unions, advocacy groups, and public opinion also have great power. Business power is counterbalanced, restricted, controlled, and subject to defeat. Adam Smith was convinced that by market forces alone, business power could be channeled to benefit society. The pluralist theory is the basis of the countervailing forces model in Chapter 1.

The Dominance Theory

In industrializing societies, business organizations grow in size and concentrate wealth. According to the dominance theory, business abuses the power its size and wealth confer in a number of ways. The rise of huge corporations creates a business elite that exercises inordinate power over public policy. Asset concentration creates monopoly or oligopoly in markets that reduces competition and harms consumers. Corporations wield financial and organizational resources unmatched by opposing interests. For example, they use campaign contributions to corrupt politicians, hire lobbyists to undermine the independence of elected officials, employ accountants and lawyers to avoid taxes, and run public relations campaigns that shape opinion in their favor. Moreover, large corporations achieve such importance in a nation's economy that elected officials are forced to adopt probusiness measures or face public wrath. "If enterprises falter for lack of inducement to invest, hire, and produce," writes one advocate of the dominance theory, "members of the political elite are more likely than those of the entrepreneurial elite to lose their positions."[17] We will discuss further the growth in size and wealth of corporations and the presence of elites in the American context.

Corporate Asset Concentration

The idea that concentration of economic power results in abuse arose, in part, as an intellectual reaction to the awesome economic growth of the late nineteenth century. Until then, the United States had been primarily an agricultural economy. But between 1860 and 1890, industrial progress transformed the country. Statistics illustrating this are striking. During these 30 years, the number of manufacturing plants more than doubled, growing from 140,433 to 355,415; the value of what they made rose more than 400 percent, from $1.8 billion to $9.3 billion; and the capital invested in them grew 650 percent, from $1 billion to $6.5 billion.[18]

This growth did more than create wealth; it also concentrated it. At the end of the century, between 1895 and 1904, an unprecedented merger wave assembled dominant firms in industry after industry. Since then, there have been other great merger waves, but this was the first. It made

---

[17] Charles E. Lindblom, *The Market System: What It Is, How It Works, and What To Make of It* (New Haven: Yale University Press, 2001), p. 247.
[18] Figures in this paragraph are from Arthur M. Schlesinger, *Political and Social Growth of the United States: 1852–1933* (New York: Macmillan, 1935), pp. 132–44.

a definitive impression on the American mind, and its legacy is an enduring fear of big companies.

Merger waves are caused by changes in the economic environment that create incentives to combine. The main stimulus for the 1895–1904 wave was the growth of the transcontinental railroads, which reduced transportation costs, thereby creating new national markets. Companies rushed to transform themselves from regional operations to national ones. Combinations such as James Duke's American Tobacco Company gorged themselves, swallowing competitors. They crowded into formerly isolated markets, wiping out small family businesses. The story was repeated in roughly 300 commodities, including oil, copper, cattle, smelting, and such items as playing cards and tombstones. A 1904 study of the 92 largest firms found that 78 controlled 50 percent of their market, 57 controlled 60 percent or more, and 26 controlled 80 percent or more.[19]

At the time, the public failed to see the growth of huge firms as a natural, inevitable, or desirable response to new economic incentives. Instead, it saw them as colossal monuments to greed. Companies of this size, or *trusts* as they were called then, were something new. They inspired a mixture of awe and fear. In 1904, when the United States Steel Corporation became the first company with more than $1 billion in assets, people were astounded. Previously, such numbers applied in the realm of astronomy, not business.

In the twentieth century, corporations continued to grow in size, but the marked rise in asset concentration slowed and leveled off. By 1929 the 200 largest nonfinancial corporations in the United States (less than 0.7 percent of all nonfinancials) controlled nearly 50 percent of all corporate wealth.[20] But by 1947 the nation's top 200 corporations had 46 percent of corporate wealth, and this fell to 34 percent in 1984. After that, asset concentration rose only slightly to a high of 36 percent in 1996.[21]

However, today concentration of assets is growing in global firms, giving rise worldwide to the same fears that gripped Americans a century ago. In the universe of approximately 63,000 transnational corporations the foreign assets of the largest 100 are 13 percent of total foreign

---

[19] John Moody, *The Truth about Trusts: A Description and Analysis of the American Trust Movement* (New York: Greenwood Press, 1968), p. 487; originally published in 1904.

[20] Adolph Berle and Gardner Means, *The Modern Corporation and Private Property* (New York: Macmillan, 1932).

[21] J. Fred Weston, Kwang S. Chung, and Juan A. Siu, *Takeovers, Restructuring, and Corporate Governance,* 2d ed. (Upper Saddle River, NJ: Prentice Hall, 1998), p. 116. See also J. Fred Weston, "Mergers and Economic Efficiency," in *Industrial Concentration, Mergers, and Growth,* vol. 2 (Washington, DC: U.S. Government Printing Office, June 1981). These figures allow rotation of new firms into the top 200 firms. If the same 200 firms had been followed over the years, asset concentration would have fallen even faster.

assets and growing.[22] Market share for a range of industries is consolidating because of a global wave of mergers and acquisitions that began about 1995. This merger wave parallels that in the United States at the turn of the twentieth century in interesting ways. It is comparable in scope. At the height of activity in the turn-of-the-century United States, merging companies accounted annually for about 10 percent of GDP; in the global merger wave, merging companies accounted for 8 percent of world GDP in 1999, and the ratio is rising.[23] Forces behind the mergers are also similar. As in the United States a century ago, transnational companies are restructuring because of new technologies that have lowered transportation costs, increased the size of markets, and raised competitive exposure. Yesterday it was the growth of railroads and introduction of electricity; today it is the Internet.

Adherents of the dominance theory believe that the increasing size and financial power of global corporations will be converted into the same old abuses. Their power will bring "exploding inequalities of income and wealth" to the world and "the conversion of the major political parties into mailboxes for corporate money" in the United States.[24] However, the link between market power and this abuse this remains to be seen. Larger firms in many industries do not necessarily even have increased market power because they face formidable competitors, emerging competition from new industries, enlarged market boundaries, and antitrust enforcement. In the social and political dimension, these firms face growing global pressure to act responsibly.

Also, no corporation, no matter how large, is assured of survival. Over time, poor management, competition, and technological change have continuously revised the roster of America's biggest companies. Of the 100 largest corporations in 1909, only 36 remained on the list until 1948. Between 1948 and 1958, only 65 of the new top 100 held their place. The winnowing continues. Only 116 company names remained on the *Fortune* 500 list of industrials from its inception in 1955 to 1994, when industrial and service corporations were combined. Now attrition is beginning on the new list. Between 1995 and 2000, 251 companies, almost exactly half the original list, were dropped.[25] Many firms dropping from the list were, of course, acquired by other firms.

---

[22] United Nations Conference on Trade and Development, *World Investment Report 2000: Cross-Border Mergers and Acquisitions and Development* (New York: United Nations, 2000), p. 71.
[23] Ibid., p. 10.
[24] Richard B. DuBoff and Edward S. Herman, "Mergers, Concentration, and the Erosion of Democracy," *Monthly Review,* May 2001, p. 14.
[25] Figures in this paragraph are derived from Neil H. Jacoby, *Corporate Power and Social Responsibility* (New York: Macmillan, 1973), p. 32; John Paul Newport Jr., "A New Era of Rapid Rise and Ruin," *Fortune,* April 24, 1989, p. 77; Carol J. Loomis, "Forty Years of the 500," *Fortune,* May 15, 1995, p. 182; and successive listings of the *Fortune* 500.

Chapter 3 *Business Power* **69**

The Rise and Decline of Powerful Corporations

In 1896 journalist Charles H. Dow created a list of 12 companies as an index of stock market performance. Each firm was a leader in an important industry and represented its fortunes. As America's industrial structure changed over the years, companies came and went; and the list, today called the Dow Jones Industrial Average Index, grew from 12 to 30. The most recent additions and deletions were made in 1999.

The leading firms in 1896 reflect a different world. Farming was much more important in the American economy, and four firms dealt in agricul-

tural products. They included James B. Duke's American Tobacco Company, cotton and sugar producers, and a company that made livestock feed. Other firms represented the prominence of industrial technologies based on iron, lead, and coal. U.S. Leather made a product in the shadow of imminent obsolescence, leather belts used for power transmission in factories. General Electric, which made electric motors, was the technology company of that era. Chicago Gas and Laclede Gas Light Co. of St. Louis were utilities supplying natural gas for new gas streetlamps in cities. North American Co. ran streetcars.

1896	2001	
American Cotton Oil	AlliedSignal	Intel
American Sugar Refining	Aluminum Co. of America	International Paper
American Tobacco	American Express	J. P. Morgan
Chicago Gas	AT&T	Johnson & Johnson
Distilling & Cattle Feeding	Boeing	McDonald's
General Electric	Caterpillar	Merck
Laclede Gas Light	Coca-Cola	Microsoft
National Lead	DuPont	3M
North American	Eastman Kodak	Philip Morris
Tennessee Coal & Iron	ExxonMobil	Procter & Gamble
U.S. Leather	General Electric	SBC Communications
U.S. Rubber	General Motors	Travelers Group
	Hewlett-Packard	United Technologies
	Home Depot	Wal-Mart Stores
	IBM	Walt Disney

The 2001 list registers the rise of new technologies and shifting patterns of demand. The only company remaining on the list from 1896 is General Electric, and it was taken off for nine years between 1898 and 1907. Of the other 11 original firms, 2 (American Tobacco and North American) were broken up by antitrust action, 1 (U.S. Leather) was dissolved, and

8 continue to operate as less important companies or as parts of other firms that acquired their assets.

As a biography of American industry, the index dramatizes the rise and fall of powerful companies and industries. Over more than a century, 97 different firms have been listed. The index teaches that dominance of even the largest firms is transient.

Elite Dominance

Another argument that supports the dominance theory is that there exist a small number of individuals who, by virtue of wealth and position, control the nation. The members of this elite are alleged to act in concert and in undemocratic ways. There is a long history of belief in an economic elite dominating American society. In the debates preceding adoption of the Constitution in 1789, some opponents charged that the delegates were wealthy aristocrats designing a government favorable to their businesses. Later, farmers suspected the hand of an economic elite in the probusiness policies of Alexander Hamilton, George Washington's secretary of the treasury, who had many ties to wealth and commercial power. Since the colonial era, charges of elitism have surfaced repeatedly in popular movements opposed to big business.

The modern impetus for the theory of elite dominance comes from the sociologist C. Wright Mills, who wrote a scholarly book in 1956 describing a "power elite" in American society. "Insofar as national events are decided," wrote Mills, "the power elite are those who decide them."[26] Mills described American society as a pyramid of power and status. At the top was a tiny elite in command of the economic, political, and military domains where they made decisions that shaped society. Mills never gave a specific estimate of its numbers, but he said it was small. Just below was a group of middle-class lieutenants who carried out the elite's policies. They included professional managers of corporations, politicians beholden to the elite for their election, and bureaucrats appointed by the politicians. The large base of the pyramid was composed of a mass of powerless citizens, including feeble groups and associations with little policy impact. This image of a pyramid corresponds to the dominance model in Chapter 1.

Mills did not believe that America was a democracy and thought that the elite simply used government "as an umbrella under whose authority they do their work."[27] Although he never suggested that the economic segment of the elite was dominant over the political and military, he noted that "the key organizations, perhaps, are the major corporations."[28]

The Power Elite is a book in which there is more speculation than substantiation. It is based on cursory evidence. There is none of the statistical research that would be required to support such sweeping generalizations in a similar work of sociology today. Yet the book came out right at the time when the ideology of the Marxists and the belief in a capitalist ruling class was losing its grip on the American left. Mills's sociological perspective of a power elite, with its scholarly patina, provided a new vi-

---

[26] C. Wright Mills, *The Power Elite* (New York: Oxford University Press, 1956), p. 18.
[27] Ibid., p. 287.
[28] Ibid., p. 283.

sion for left-wing critics. Ever since, the anticorporate left has been inspired by Mills's idea that a small group with inordinate economic power unfairly dominates society. Mills would have been pleased. In correspondence, he once expressed indignation about the power of "the sons of bitches who run American Big Business."[29]

Scholars inspired by Mills have pressed the study of elites and are less reluctant to suggest business dominance. One is G. William Domhoff, who has for more than 30 years researched a "governing class" in American society.

> There is a social upper class in the United States that is a ruling class by virtue of its dominant role in the economy and government. . . . This ruling class is socially cohesive, has its basis in the large corporations and banks, plays a major role in shaping the social and political climate, and dominates the federal government through a variety of organizations and methods.[30]

In the mid-1990s political scientist Thomas R. Dye tried to find out precisely which individuals occupied positions of great power. In America today, power comes with leadership roles in corporations, government, and other large organizations. So Dye defined a "national institutional elite" that consists of

> individuals who occupy *the top positions in the institutional structure of American society.* These are the individuals who possess the formal authority to formulate, direct, and manage programs, policies, and activities of the major corporate, governmental, legal, educational, civic, and cultural institutions in the nation. . . . For purposes of analysis we have divided American society into 12 sectors: (1) industrial corporations, (2) utilities and communications, (3) banking, (4) insurance, (5) investments, (6) mass media, (7) law, (8) education, (9) foundations, (10) civic and cultural organizations, (11) government, and (12) the military.[31]

Applying this method, Dye identified 7,314 elite positions and found that they were held by 5,778 individuals (because some persons, for example, business leaders who served on several boards of directors, held more than one position). This is a much larger elite than that suggested by Mills, but it is still only two ten-thousandths of 1 percent of the American population.

Economic elites are inevitable, but their legitimacy is not. In a democracy, this rests on openness and public-mindedness. The American business elite

---

[29] In a letter to his parents quoted in John B. Judis, "The Spiritual Wobbly," *New York Times Book Review,* July 9, 2000, p. 9.

[30] G. William Domhoff, *Who Rules America Now? A View for the 80s* (Englewood Cliffs, NJ: Prentice Hall, 1983), p. 1.

[31] Thomas R. Dye, *Who's Running America? The Clinton Years,* 6th ed. (Englewood Cliffs, NJ: Prentice Hall, 1995), pp. 8–9; emphasis is in the original.

J. P. Morgan and the Panic of 1907

In the first decade of the twentieth century, J. P. Morgan (1837–1913), head of J. P. Morgan & Co. in New York, was often called the most powerful man in the country. He specialized in buying competing companies in the same industry and merging them into a single, monopolistic firm. He joined separate railroads into large systems. He combined smaller electrical concerns into General Electric in 1892 and then pulled a collection of manufacturers into the International Harvester Company, which started with 85 percent of the farm machinery market. In 1901 he created the first billion-dollar company when he merged 785 separate firms to form the United States Steel Company with capitalization of $1.4 billion.

Morgan and two of his close associates together held 341 corporate directorships. His power was very independent of government controls since at the time antitrust laws were unenforced, there was no national bank to regulate the money supply, and existing securities and banking laws were rudimentary. One awestruck biographer said that Morgan "was a God" who "ruled for a generation the pitiless, predatory world of cash."[32] His critics were less kind. Senator Robert W. La Follette once called him "a beefy, red-faced, thick-necked financial bully, drunk with wealth and power."[33]

In October 1907 panic swept Wall Street and stocks plummeted as frantic investors sold shares. Soon a number of banks suffered runs of withdrawals and were on the verge of failure. Liquidity, or the free flow of money, was fast vanishing from financial markets, and the nation's banking system teetered on the verge of collapse. So influential was Morgan that he commanded the New York Stock Exchange to stay open all day on October 24 to maintain investor confidence. To support it, he raised $25 million of credit.

The federal government could do little to ease the crisis. President Theodore Roosevelt was off hunting bears in Louisiana, an ironic pursuit in light of the crashing stock market. Without a national bank, the government had no capacity to increase the money supply and restore liquidity. Powerless, Secretary of the Treasury George B. Cortelyou traveled to New York to get Morgan's advice.

On the evening of October 24, Morgan gathered members of the New York banking elite at his private library. He played solitaire while in another room the assembled bankers discussed methods for resolving the crisis. Periodically, someone came to him with a proposal, several of which he rejected. Finally, a plan was hatched in which $33 million would be raised to support the stock exchange and failing banks. Where would this money come from? The secretary of the treasury was to supply $10 million in government funds, John D. Rockefeller contributed $10 million, and Morgan the remaining $13 million.

This action stabilized the economy. Perhaps it demonstrates that elite power may be exercised in the common good. It should be noted, however, that the panic of 1907—and other panics of that era—came after Morgan and other titans of finance repeatedly choked the stock exchange with the colossal stock offerings needed to finance their new combinations.

Morgan was widely criticized for his role in ending the panic of 1907. Conspiracy theorists, suspicious of so much power resident in one man, attacked him. Upton Sinclair, for example, accused him of inciting the panic for self-gain, a wildly erroneous accusation. In 1912 Morgan was the focus of congressional hearings by the Pujo Commission, which concluded that he led a "money trust" that controlled the nation's finances and that this was unfortunate. Death claimed him in 1913 just before Congress passed the Federal Reserve Act to set up a central bank and ensure that no private banker would ever again be sole caretaker of the money supply.

[32] John K. Winkler, *Morgan the Magnificent* (New York: Doubleday, 1950), p. 3; originally published in 1930.
[33] Quoted in Jean Strouse, *Morgan: American Financier* (New York: Random House, 2000), p. x.

comes from the ranks of top corporate executives and directors, and those who hold these positions do so based overwhelmingly on ability. Turnover is frequent. However, those selected at these rarified levels come from a narrow range of backgrounds. Every study of them finds that disproportionately they are male, white, and Christian; that they come from upper-class families; and that they graduate from a few prestigious universities.[34] Diversity among the elite grows only slowly. Evidence suggests that inclusion of blacks, Latinos, and women is based on their similarity in background and thinking to the existing elite.[35]

However, since the rise of industrial America, elite organizations have sometimes transcended self-interest. To give examples, the National Civic Federation, founded by business leaders in 1900, set up committees of business, labor, and civic leaders that worked to end child labor, regulate companies, and settle strikes. The Federation stimulated much reform in its time. More recently, the Ford Foundation nurtured environmental and consumer groups that sought liberal reforms. In the early 1970s it was the source of nearly 90 percent of the grants given these groups. Among its gifts was the start-up money for the Environmental Defense Fund, an organization that aggressively sued polluting companies.[36]

Pluralist Theory

The counterpoint to the dominance theory is the pluralist theory, or the argument that in democratic settings business must compete in an open society and in open markets with other strong interests and institutions. Pluralists argue that the United States is such a setting as are many other nations and, to a growing extent, so is the global business environment. Even if corporations or elites have unmatched wealth and power, they cannot engage in tyranny because offsetting forces hem them in.

A *pluralistic society* is one that has many groups and institutions through which power is diffused. No one group has overwhelming power, and each may have direct or indirect effects on others. The countervailing forces model in Chapter 1 illustrates how, in such a society, business must interact with many constraining forces in its environments. It may have considerable influence over some of them; but over most it has limited influence, and over a few none at all. American society has several features that contribute to its pluralistic nature.

First, it is infused with democratic values. Unlike many nations, America has no history of feudal or authoritarian rule, so there is no entrenched

---

[34] Richard L. Zweigenhaft and G. William Domhoff, *Diversity in the Power Elite* (New Haven: Yale University Press, 1998).

[35] Richard L. Zweigenhaft and G. William Domhoff, *Diversity in the Power Elite: Have Women and Minorities Reached the Top?* (New Haven: Yale University Press, 1998), chap. 7.

[36] John B. Judis, *The Paradox of Democracy: Elites, Special Interests, and the Betrayal of Public Trust* (New York: Pantheon, 2000), pp. 19 and 100.

deference to an aristocracy of wealth. In colonial days, Americans adopted the then-revolutionary doctrine of natural rights, which held that all persons were created equal and entitled to the same opportunities and protections. The French aristocrat Alexis de Tocqueville, who toured America and wrote an insightful book about American customs in the 1830s, was forcibly struck by the "prodigious influence" of the notion of equality. Belief in equality, he wrote, ran through American society, directing public opinion, informing the law, and defining politics. It was, he wrote, "the fundamental fact from which all others seem to be derived."[37] Thus, in America laws apply equally to all. All interests have the right to be heard. To be legitimate, power must be exercised for the common good.

Second, American society encompasses a large population spread over a wide geography and engaged in diverse occupations. It has a great mixture of interests, more than some other countries. Economic interests, including labor, banking, manufacturing, agriculture, and consumers, are a permanent fixture. A rainbow of voluntary associations (whose size, longevity, and influence vary) compete in governments at all levels.

Third, the Constitution encourages pluralism. Its guarantees of rights protect the freedom of individuals to form associations and freely to express and pursue interests. Thus, business is challenged by civil rights, environmental, and other groups. In addition, the Constitution diffuses political power through several branches of the federal government and between the federal and state governments and to the people of the United States. This is a remarkably open system with many points of access.

In addition, business is exposed to constraining market forces, forces that can fell even the mighty. Henry J. Kaiser seemed unerring in business. The son of German immigrants, he worked his way up from store clerk to owner of 32 companies, including seven shipyards that launched one finished ship a day during most of World War II. When he started an auto company in 1945, nobody thought he would fail. Eager customers put down 670,000 deposits before a single car was built.[38] But his cars, the Kaiser and the Frazier, were underpowered and overpriced, and the market eventually rejected them. The venture failed.

Market forces are the most significant restraints on management. They force a stream of resource allocation decisions to center on cost reduction and consumer satisfaction. Kaiser never got costs under control; he had to negotiate the prices of many parts with competing auto companies that made them. Toward the end, he built a model that was sold at Sears as the Allstate. This was a terrible mistake because it gave the car a low-quality image with consumers. In addition to old-fashioned competitive drubbings, markets also register the force of disruptive new technologies.

---

[37] Alexis de Tocqueville, *Democracy in America* (New York: New American Library, 1956), p. 26; originally published as two volumes in 1835 and 1850.
[38] Robert Sobel, "The $150 Million Lemon," *Audacity,* Winter 1997, p. 11.

the measure of a person with a withering stare, and few were his match. He was formidable in negotiations because he was invariably informed in detail about the other's business. And he was still a pious churchgoer who read the Bible every night before retiring.

Late in 1871 Rockefeller hatched a brazen plan for stabilizing the oil industry at the refining level. In clandestine meetings, he worked out a rebate scheme between a few major refiners and the three railroads that connected to the Pennsylvania oil regions. This scheme was called the South Improvement Plan. In it, the railroads agreed to a big increase in published rates for hauling oil. But Rockefeller's Cleveland refineries and a small number of major refineries in other states would be given large rebates on every barrel shipped. For example, the regular rate between the oil regions and Cleveland would be $.80 a barrel and between Cleveland and New York $2.00 a barrel. It would cost a total of $2.80 per barrel for any other refinery in Cleveland to bring in a barrel of crude oil and ship a barrel of refined oil to New York for sale or export. Rockefeller, on the other hand, would be charged $2.80 but would receive a rebate of $.90. The other conspiring refineries got similar rebates.

In addition, the refineries participating in the South Improvement Plan received *drawbacks,* or payments made on the shipment of oil by competitors! Thus, Rockefeller would receive a drawback of $.40 on every barrel of crude oil his competitors shipped into Cleveland and one of $.50 on every barrel of refined oil shipped to New York. Under this venal scheme, the more a competitor shipped, the more Rockefeller's transportation costs were lowered. While competitors paid $2.80 for this critical transportation route (Pennsylvania oil regions–Cleveland–New York), Rockefeller paid only $1.00. Also nefarious was the requirement that railroads give the conspirators waybills detailing competitors' shipments—a more perfect espionage system could not be imagined.

Why did the railroads agree to this scheme? There were several reasons. First, it removed the uncertainty of cutthroat competition. Oil traffic was guaranteed in large volume and apportioned so that the Pennsylvania got 45 percent of eastbound shipments from the oil regions, the Erie 27.5 percent, and the New York Central 27.5 percent. Sec-

ond, the refiners agreed to provide services to the railroads, such as tank cars, loading facilities, and insurance. And third, railroad executives were offered stock in the participating refineries. This gave them a large stake in their success.

The consequences of the South Improvement Plan were predictable. Nonparticipating refineries would face unreasonably high transportation costs and be noncompetitive with the conspirators. They would have two choices. Either they could sell to Rockefeller and his cohorts, or they could stand on principle and go bankrupt. The appeal of the former would encourage horizontal integration, the acquisition of other firms at the refining level. Refinery capacity would be limited and price stabilization would occur because a combination of refiners could keep down the price of crude. Rockefeller believed that the industry could thus be rationalized.

THE CONSPIRACY PLAYS OUT

In February 1872 the new freight rates went into operation. Their advent was greeted by widespread and explosive rage in the industry, and the full outlines of the agreement were quickly revealed. Producers and refiners in the oil regions rebelled and boycotted the conspirators and the railroads. Rockefeller was correctly regarded as the prime mover behind the South Improvement Plan, and his reputation was scorched by public attacks. His wife feared that Rockefeller's life was in danger, but he was steadfast in his belief that the plan was right. He said of the plan: "It was right. I knew it as matter of conscience. It was right between me and my God."[4] Indeed, as historian Ida Tarbell noted, Rockefeller was not squeamish about such business affairs.

> Mr. Rockefeller was "good." There was no more faithful Baptist in Cleveland than he. Every enterprise of that church he had supported liberally from his youth. He gave to its poor. He visited its sick. He wept with its suffering. Moreover, he gave unostentatiously to many outside charities of whose worthiness he was satisfied. . . . Yet he

---

[4] Peter Collier and David Horowitz, *The Rockefellers: An American Dynasty* (New York: New American Library, 1976), p. 11.

was willing to strain every nerve to obtain himself special and unjust privileges from the railroads which were bound to ruin every man in the oil business not sharing them with him.[5]

Within a month, the weight of negative public opinion and loss of revenue caused the railroads to cave in. They rescinded the discriminatory rate structure. All appearances were of a Rockefeller defeat. But in this case, appearances deceived. After the South Improvement Plan had been drawn up, but before it was exposed, Rockefeller quickly met one by one with rival refiners in Cleveland. Because of overcapacity and vicious price-cutting, most were doing poorly. He explained the rebate scheme and its salutary effect on the industry and then asked to buy out his competitor. He offered the exact value of the business in cash or, preferably, in stock of the Standard Oil Company.

By the time the railroads reset their rates, Rockefeller had purchased 21 of his 26 Cleveland competitors. Some acquisitions were simply dismantled to reduce surplus capacity. He now dominated Cleveland, the country's largest refining center, and controlled over a quarter of U.S. capacity. Furthermore, he soon negotiated a secret new rebate agreement with Commodore Vanderbilt's Erie Railroad, giving him renewed advantage in transportation costs. Of these actions, Ida Tarbell noted sardonically: "He had a mind which, stopped by a wall, burrows under or creeps around."[6] If any circumstance cast a shadow over this striking victory, it was that public opinion had turned against him. Henceforth, he was reviled as an unfair competitor, hatred of him growing apace with his burgeoning wealth. He never understood why.

ONWARD THE COURSE OF EMPIRE

By this time Rockefeller, now 33, was wealthy. But he drove on, compelled to finish a grand design, to spread his pattern over the entire industry landscape, to conform it to his vision.

He continued the strategy of horizontal integration at the refinery level by absorbing more and more of his competitors. He branched out from Cleveland and began a relentless campaign of refinery acquisitions in other cities.

As the size of Standard Oil increased, Rockefeller gained added leverage over the railroads. Like an orchestra conductor he played them against each other, granting shares of the oil traffic in return for rebates and drawbacks that gave him a decisive advantage over competitors.

Some competitors stubbornly clung to their businesses, but Rockefeller made them "sweat" and "feel sick" until they sold.[7] He owned large numbers of tank cars, and these were often "unavailable" to ship crude oil to competing refiners. Rockefeller kept many of his acquisitions a secret to conceal the full sweep of his drive to monopoly. These companies were the Trojan horses of Rockefeller's war against independent refiners. They appeared to be independent but secretly conspired to undermine Standard's competitors by participating in elaborate conspiracies involving code words used in letters and telegrams, such as "morose" for Standard, "doubters" for refiners, and "mixer" for railroad drawbacks. The phantom competitors bought some refiners who refused in principle to sell out to Standard Oil. Their existence confronted independents with a dark, mysterious force that could not be brought into the light in order to be fought.

THE STANDARD OIL TRUST

By 1882 Rockefeller's company was capitalized at $70 million and produced 90 percent of the nation's refining output. Its main product, illuminating oil, was changing the way people lived. Prior to the availability of affordable illuminating oil of good quality, most Americans had gone to bed at dark because they could not afford expensive candles or whale oil and feared using the explosive kerosene made by Standard's early, small competitors. They now had inexpensive light and stayed up, and their lives were changed.

---

[5] Ida M. Tarbell, *The History of the Standard Oil Company*, vol. 1 (Gloucester, MA: Peter Smith, 1963), p. 43.
[6] Ibid., p. 99.

[7] Abels, *The Rockefeller Billions*, p. 35.

Rockefeller reorganized Standard Oil as a trust.[8] His purpose in doing so was to make state regulation more difficult. The trust form that he adopted became the model for many other dominant firms of that era. Rockefeller directed his far-flung empire from headquarters at 26 Broadway in New York City. He worked with a loyal inner circle of managers. As he had absorbed his competitors, so had he co-opted the best business minds in industry, and business historians attribute much of Standard's success to this stellar supporting cast. Though dominant, Rockefeller delegated great responsibility to his managers by running the giant company with a system of committees.

His management style was one of formal politeness. He never spoke harshly to any employee. The perfectionist instinct remained strong. He insisted on having a statement of the exact net worth of Standard Oil on his desk every morning. Oil prices were always calculated to three decimal places. On the way to work, he penciled notes on the cuff of his sleeve. At night he prowled the headquarters turning down oil lamps. Compared to other moguls of that era, he lived simply. He had two large estates, in Cleveland and New York, but neither was overly ostentatious. He read the Bible daily, continued regular attendance at a Baptist church, and gave generously to charities.

EXTENDING DOMINATION

By the 1880s Standard Oil had overwhelming market power. Its embrace of refining activity was virtually complete, and it had moved into drilling, pipelines, storage facilities, transportation, and marketing of finished products. By now the entire world was becoming addicted to kerosene and other petroleum products, and Standard branched out into international sales.

In all these efforts, Rockefeller's dominating competitive philosophy prevailed. Regional marketing agents, for example, were ordered to destroy most independent suppliers. To suppress competition, Rockefeller's employees pioneered fanatical customer service. More questionable tactics were used as well. A competitor intelligence-gathering network was established. A bookkeeper at one independent refinery was offered $25 to pass information to Standard Oil. Railroad employees were turned into company detectives and bribed to misroute shipments. Standard employees climbed on competitor's tank cars and looked into the contents. Price warfare was used. A competitor often found Standard selling kerosene to its customers at a price substantially below production cost.

Rockefeller himself was never proved to be personally involved in any flagrant misconduct. He blamed criminal and unethical actions on overzealous employee behavior. His critics said the strategy of suffocating small rivals and policies such as that requiring regular written intelligence reports encouraged degenerative ethics among his minions.

Rockefeller, however, saw Standard Oil as a stabilizing force in the industry and as a righteous crusade to illuminate the world. How, as a good Christian devoted to the moral injunctions of the Bible, was Rockefeller able to suborn such vicious behavior in business? His biographer Allan Nevins gives one explanation:

> From a chaotic industry he was building an efficient industrial empire for what seemed to him the good not only of its heads but of the general public. If he relaxed his general methods of warfare . . . a multitude of small competitors would smash his empire and plunge the oil business back to chaos. He always believed in what William McKinley called "benevolent assimilation"; he preferred to buy out rivals on decent terms, and to employ the ablest competitors as helpers. It was when his terms were refused that he ruthlessly crushed the "outsiders." . . . It seemed to him better that a limited number of small businesses should die than that the whole industry should go through a constant process of half-dying, reviving, and again half-dying.[9]

---

[8] A trust is a method of controlling a number of companies in which the voting stock of each company is transferred to a board of trustees. The trustees then have the power to coordinate the operations of all companies in the group. This organizing form is no longer legal in the United States.

[9] Allan Nevins, *Study in Power: John D. Rockefeller*, vol. 2 (New York: Scribner, 1953), p. 433.

THE STANDARD OIL TRUST UNDER ATTACK

Standard Oil continued to grow, doubling in size before the turn of the century and doubling again by 1905.[10] But eventually its very size brought a flood of criticism that complicated operations. Predatory monopoly was at odds with prevailing social attitudes about individual rights and free competition. The states wanted to regulate Standard Oil and filed antitrust cases against it. Muckraking journalists scorched Standard Oil as a company by whose acts, in the words of one, "hundreds and thousands of men have been ruined."[11] Rockefeller was the personification of greed in political cartoons. Some politicians not suborned by his bribery lambasted him.

Rockefeller, by now the richest man in the nation, was shaken by public hatred. Feeling that his life was endangered, he hired bodyguards and slept with a revolver. At church on Sundays gawkers and shouters appeared, forcing the hiring of Pinkerton detectives to guard services. He developed a digestive disorder so severe that he could eat only a few bland foods, and upon his doctor's advice he stopped daily office work. By 1896 he appeared only rarely at 26 Broadway. Soon he was afflicted with a nervous disorder and lost all his hair.

As attacks on Rockefeller grew, the vise of government regulation slowly tightened on Standard Oil. A swarm of lawsuits and legislative hearings hung about the company. Finally, in 1911, the Supreme Court in an 8–1 opinion ordered its breakup under the Sherman Antitrust Act, holding that its monopoly position was an "undue" restraint on trade that violated the "standard of reason."[12] The company was given six months to separate into 39 independent firms. The breakup consisted mainly of moving the desks of managers at 26 Broadway and was a financial windfall for Rockefeller, who received stock shares in all the companies, the prices of which were driven up by frenzied public buying. All the companies prospered primarily because of skyrocketing demand for gasoline to run a growing number of automobiles. Prior to 1910 kerosene sales had buoyed the company. But just as electric light bulbs were replacing oil lamps, the automobile jolted demand for another petroleum distillate—gasoline. In 1900 only 8,000 autos were registered, but by 1910 the number had grown to 458,000, by 1915 to 2,491,000, and by 1925 to 19,941,000.[13] Rockefeller, who was 71 at the time of the breakup and would live another 26 years, would earn new fortunes simply by maintaining his equity in the separate companies.

THE GREAT ALMONER

Since childhood Rockefeller had made charitable donations and, as his fortune accumulated, he increased them. After 1884 the total was never less than $100,000 a year, and after 1892 it was usually over $1 million and sometimes far more. In his mind, these benefactions were linked to his duty as a good Christian to uplift humanity. To a reporter he once said:

> I believe the power to make money is a gift from God—just as are the instincts for art, music, literature, the doctor's talent, yours—to be developed and used to the best of our ability for the good of mankind. Having been endowed with the gift I possess, I believe it is my duty to make money and still more money and to use the money I make for the good of my fellow-man according to the dictates of my conscience.[14]

Over his lifetime, Rockefeller gave gifts of approximately $550 million. He gave, for example, $8.2 million for the construction of Peking Union Medical College in response to the need to educate doctors in China. He gave $50 million to the University of Chicago. He created charitable trusts and endowed them with millions. One such trust was

---

[10] Ibid., app. 3, p. 478.

[11] Henry Demarest Lloyd, "Story of a Great Monopoly," *The Atlantic,* March 1881, p. 320.

[12] *Standard Oil Company of New Jersey v. United States,* 31 U.S. 221.

[13] Hastings Wyman Jr., "The Standard Oil Breakup of 1911 and Its Relevance Today," in Michael E. Canes, ed., *Witnesses for Oil: The Case against Dismemberment* (Washington, DC: American Petroleum Institute, 1976), pp. 72–73.

[14] Quoted in Abels, *The Rockefeller Billions,* p. 280.

John D. Rockefeller at age 65. This photograph was taken shortly after a disease, generalized alopecia, caused him to lose his hair.
Courtesy of the Library of Congress.

the General Education Board, set up in 1902, which started 1,600 new high schools. Another, the Rockefeller Sanitary Commission, succeeded in eradicating hookworm in the South. The largest was the Rockefeller Foundation, established in 1913 and endowed with $200 million. Its purpose was "to promote the well-being of mankind throughout the world." Rockefeller always said, however, that the greatest philanthropy of all was developing the earth's natural resources and employing people. Critics greeted his gifts with skepticism, thinking them atonement for years of plundering American society.

In his later years, Rockefeller lived a secluded, placid existence on his great Pocantico estate in New York, which had 75 buildings and 70 miles of roads. As years passed, the public grew increasingly fond of him. Memories of his early business career dimmed, and a new generation viewed him in the glow of his huge charitable contributions. For many years, he carried shiny nickels and dimes in his pockets to give to children and well-wishers. On his 86th birthday he wrote the following verse.

> I was early taught to work as well as play,
> My life has been one long, happy holiday;
> Full of work and full of play—
> I dropped the worry on the way—
> And God was good to me every day.

He died in 1937 at the age of 97. His estate was valued at $26,410,837. He had given the rest away.

QUESTIONS

1. With reference to the levels and spheres of corporate power discussed in the chapter, how did the power of Standard Oil change society? Was this power exercised in keeping with the social contract of Rockefeller's era?

2. How does the story of Standard Oil illustrate the limits of business power? Does it better illustrate the dominance theory or the pluralist theory discussed in the chapter?

3. Did Rockefeller himself ever act unethically? By the standards of his day? By those of today? How could he simultaneously be a devout Christian and a ruthless monopolist? Is there any contradiction between his personal and business ethics?

4. In the utilitarian sense of accomplishing the greatest good for the greatest number in society, was the Standard Oil Company a net plus or a minus? On balance, did the company meet its responsibilities to society?

5. Did strategies of Standard Oil encourage unethical behavior? Could Rockefeller's vision have been fulfilled using "nicer" tactics?

Chapter **Four**

Critics of Business

McDonald's Corporation

Imagine a machine so colossal that it casts a shadow over much of the earth. At the back moves a stream of farmers pouring potatoes and lettuce through an opening, while beside them a line of cows, pigs, and chickens glides in and disappears. Inside, a crew of 364,000 people works levers and buttons. And out the front, to a waiting crowd, flow 2,035 meals a second, 24 hours a day. A side door regularly opens and big bags of money drop out. A vent releases bursts of paper, polystyrene, and other waste material. As you watch, the machine slowly expands and quickens.

McDonald's Corporation is such a machine. It all started in 1948 when two brothers, Richard and Maurice "Mac" McDonald, built several hamburger stands with golden arches in southern California. One day a traveling salesman named Ray Kroc came by selling milkshake mixers. The popularity of their $0.15 hamburgers impressed him, so he bought the world franchise rights from them and spread the golden arches around the globe.

McDonald's grows rapidly. In 2000 it had 28,707 restaurants, a 243 percent increase over 1990. About half of them are outside the United States, and these bring in 60 percent of company revenues. The percentage of foreign earnings is rising because most of the 1,500 to 1,600 new restaurants opened every year are in one of 119 foreign countries where McDonald's does business.[1] The key to the company's success is its ability to standardize a formula of quality, service, cleanliness, and value and apply it everywhere.

McDonald's is not the world's largest company. Its systemwide sales are only about one-fifth those of ExxonMobil or Wal-Mart Stores. However, it owns one of the world's best known brands, and the golden arches are familiar to more people than the Christian cross.[2] This prominence, and its conquest of global markets, makes the company a focal point for inquiry and criticism.

[1] *McDonald's Corporation Annual Report 2000* (Oak Brook, IL: McDonald's Corp., 2001), pp. 1 and 2.
[2] Eric Schlosser, *Fast Food Nation* (Boston: Houghton Mifflin, 2001), p. 4.

Scholars have studied it. For example, a group of anthropologists documented its influence on east Asian cultures. They found that in Hong Kong and Taiwan the company's clean rest rooms and kitchens set a new standard that elevated expectations throughout the country. in Hong Kong, children's birthdays had traditionally gone unrecognized, but McDonald's introduced the practice of birthday parties in its restaurants, and now birthday celebrations are widespread in the population.[3] A journalist recently set forth a "Golden Arches Theory of Conflict Prevention" based on the notion that countries with McDonald's restaurants do not go to war with each other.[4] A British magazine, *The Economist,* prints a yearly "Big Mac Index" that uses the price of a Big Mac in foreign currencies to assess exchange-rate distortions.[5]

McDonald's also attracts barrages of criticism. It conveniently symbolizes evils of globalization that agitate a range of ideologues, including leftists, anarchists, nationalists, farmers, labor unions, environmentalists, consumer advocates, protectors of animal rights, religious orders, and intellectuals. For others, it symbolizes an evil America. Within hours after U.S. bombers began to pound Afghanistan in 2001, angry Pakistanis damaged McDonald's restaurants in Islamabad and an Indonesian mob burned an American flag outside another.[6]

A defining moment for McDonald's and its critics was a confrontation over a six-page leaflet that a group called London Greenpeace wrote for protests at McDonald's restaurants in England. The leaflet, entitled "What's Wrong with McDonald's?", was illustrated with a grotesque caricature of a businessman hiding his leering face behind a Ronald McDonald clown mask. A parody of the golden arches logo replaced the company's name with the words "McDollars," "McGreedy," "McCancer," and "McMurder." Its text accused the company of destroying rain forests to raise beef; littering cities; exploiting children with its ads; encouraging the "torture and murder" of food animals; serving fatty, cancer-causing food; and abusing employees with low wages. In short, said the leaflet, the company hid its "ruthless exploitation of resources, animals and people behind a facade of colorful gimmicks and 'family fun.' "[7]

McDonald's executives suffered indigestion over the brochure and brought suit for libel against two young anarchists who were handing it out, David Morris and Helen Steel. McDonald's said that the leaflet contained lies and sought damages of £120,000 while offering to drop the suit

---

[3] James L. Watson, ed., *Golden Arches East: McDonald's in East Asia* (Stanford, CA: Stanford University Press, 1997), pp. 103 and 134.

[4] Thomas L. Friedman, *The Lexis and the Olive Tree* (New York: Farrar Straus Giroux, 1999), chap. 10.

[5] "Big Mac Currencies," *The Economist,* April 21, 2001, p. 74.

[6] David Barboza, "When Golden Arches Are Too Red, White and Blue," *The New York Times,* October 14, 2001, p. C1.

[7] The leaflet is at www.mcspotlight.org/case/pretrial/factsheet.html.

"Modern Man Followed by the Ghosts of His Meat," by Sue Coe. Coe is an artist who attempts to provoke anger and unease. Her paintings are often bleak because she believes that the presence of injustice in her subjects leaves no beauty. This painting is one of a series Coe did after visiting slaughterhouses and meatpacking plants. The series and this image challenge values that support meat eating. The haunted subject clutches a McDonald's bag.
Source: Sue Coe. "Modern Man Followed by the Ghosts of His Meat." 1988. Copyright © 1988 Sue Coe. Courtesy Galerie St. Etienne, New York.

if the two signed an apology. But they would not; on principle, Steel and Morris elected to fight. The trial began in 1994. A prominent British libel lawyer represented McDonald's; Morris and Steel could not afford counsel and defended themselves.

Court proceedings revealed that the corporation and its critics lived in different worlds. Morris and Steel called witnesses who said that a diet of the high-fat, low-fiber foods such as those on McDonald's menu caused cancer and heart disease. In response, a McDonald's executive testified that all foods are nutritious, even Coca-Cola because it contains water. Morris and Steel got expert testimony that children were enticed to eat junk food at McDonald's by ads encouraging them to pester their parents into going. In reply, a McDonald's senior vice president proudly testified that its ads all over the world were calculated to create brand loyalty in children between the ages of two and eight. The company believed this promoted profamily values. So it went as the opposing parties dueled over each sentence in the leaflet.[8]

In 1997, after three years of trial, the British court handed down a judgment of £60,000 against Morris and Steel, just half the damages sought by McDonald's, because the judge found compelling evidence that

[8] See John Vidal, *McLibel* (New York: New Press, 1977).

some statements were accurate, for example, that the company was cruel to cows and chickens and that it manipulated children. Morris and Steel appealed the judgment, and in 1999 a higher court reduced it to £40,000. Further appeals have so far failed, but the company has never tried to collect.

The McLibel trial, as it was called, quickened the battle between McDonald's and its critics. The curiosity of a giant corporation suing two people of limited means galvanized activists. They created a website to post news of the trial and coordinate efforts such as a Global Week of Action against McDonald's held each year in October.[9] In addition, an array of international groups posted information about their campaigns against the company. For example, McDonald's Workers Resistance, a group of company employees in England seeking a union, felt that McDonald's "pioneered methods of exploitation" for other global companies "geared to profiteering" and stated their specific complaints thusly.

> Most of us agree that working for McDonald's is #@*%—late nights, skin irritations, no overtime, harassment from management, low wages, stupid uniforms, unlawful business practices, imbecilic propaganda, cuts and burns, oppressive controls on how we should look, never being able to finish on time—there's a lot we object to.[10]

Another group, People for the Ethical Treatment of Animals (PETA), announced a campaign entitled "McCruelty to Go," dedicated to improving the conditions in which animals are raised for McDonald's restaurants. PETA organized more than 400 demonstrations at restaurants around the world using clever "Unhappy Meal" boxes holding bloodied toy animals. McDonald's Corporation raises no animals itself, but in 2000 it adopted a set of "guiding principles" for suppliers to improve conditions of animals they raise. These principles did not go far enough to satisfy PETA, but the group wrote a letter to the company's CEO, informing him that it had granted a breathing spell.

> [W]e are declaring a one-year moratorium on our campaign against McDonald's, effective immediately. We are doing this to afford McDonald's a decent amount of time to make other important changes in line with its public pledge to keep moving forward with animal welfare improvements. . . . [M]illions of animals continue to live miserable lives and die badly on factory farms and in slaughterhouses directly supported by McDonald's.[11]

Worldwide, the company remains a lightning rod for the discharges of critics angry about Americanization, capitalism, fast food, meat eating, commercialism, and environmental degradation. According to its CEO, Jack

---

[9] See www.mcspotlight.org.
[10] "McDonalds' UK Workers Fight Back," www.mcspotlight.org/campaigns/current/mwr.html.
[11] Letter to Jack Greenberg, at www.meatstinks.com/mcd/moratorlet.html.

Greenberg, these people "are more interested in using McDonald's as a convenient symbol than in understanding the facts of our business."[12] In many foreign countries, the presence of a McDonald's is regarded as a sign of modernization. The company is often one of the first foreign corporations to enter a developing country, and one commentator regards it as "the canary in the coal mine of economic success" because it arrives when disposable income rises and there is promise of more growth and progress.[13]

Contrary to the view that McDonald's is a wedge for entry of American low culture, foreign customs seem resistant to broad change based on what people eat for lunch. In any case, most McDonald's restaurants are franchises, run as local businesses. Although in 2000 sales of all its restaurants exceeded $40 billion, most of this revenue went to franchise owners, not to McDonald's Corporation, which had total revenue of only $14.2 billion. Thus, just as many McDonald's serve local dishes, they also use local suppliers, pay local taxes and payrolls, and respond to local cultural sensitivities.

Some think the company to be highly responsible. In *Fortune* magazine's 2000 listing of America's Most Admired Companies, McDonald's was ranked first in the category of social responsibility. The ranking, based on a survey of managers in other companies, recognized broad efforts to protect the environment and support communities. The company pays tuition for employees in schools, promotes massive recycling efforts, and, through its Ronald McDonald House Charities, supports children's health.

Perhaps the most important truth about McDonald's Corporation is that on a typical day 175 million people eat in its restaurants, attracted by brand attributes such as cleanliness, service, and value. This reveals the wide gulf between millions of average people and a small number of activists. This gulf is characteristic of attitudes toward other corporations and of business criticism in general.

Like McDonald's, other big corporations today are attacked by a wide range of critics. As with McDonald's, conflict resolution is difficult or impossible where there are deep and irreconcilable differences in values. There are, however, many types of critics and levels of criticism. In this chapter we elaborate on the origins, nature, and extent of anticorporate feeling.

ORIGINS OF CRITICAL ATTITUDES TOWARD BUSINESS

There are two fundamental sources of criticism of business. The first is the belief that people in business prioritize profit over other values that are more worthy, such as honesty, truth, justice, love, devoutness, aesthetic merit, tranquillity, and respect for nature. This view arose in ancient Greece. The second fundamental source is the strain that economic

---

[12] In Moises Naim, "McAtlas Shrugged," *Foreign Policy,* May 2001, p. 26.
[13] Jonah Goldberg, "The Specter of McDonald's," *National Review,* June 5, 2000, p. 30.

development imposes on societies. During industrialization and later, after an economy has grown large and complex, corporations both create and symbolize a range of ills. We will discuss both these sources of criticism. We begin our discussion in the ancient Mediterranean world.

The Greeks and Romans

The earliest societies were agrarian in nature. An *agrarian society* is a preindustrial society in which economic, political, and cultural values are based on agricultural experience. In them, the great mass of people tilled land for subsistence. No industry or mass-consumer markets existed, so business activity beyond barter and exchange was only a tiny part of the overall economy. In this setting, the activities of merchants were often viewed as indecent because their sharp trading practices and temporizing ethics clashed with the traditional, more altruistic values of family and clan relations among farmers. Merchants were typically given lower class status than government officials, farmers, soldiers, artisans, and teachers.

Both Greece and Rome were based on subsistence agriculture, and economic activity by merchants, bankers, and manufacturers was limited. The largest factory in Athens, for example, employed 120 workers making shields.[14] Commercial activity was greater in Rome, but it was still mainly an agrarian society. Perhaps because industrial activity was so limited in Hellenic civilization, inaccurate economic doctrines arose to explain or justify commercial activity.[15] For example, greed was suspect because of the popular belief that the amount of wealth was fixed. If so, an individual seeking to increase wealth did it only by subtracting from the share of others. This was a believable chain of logic in an agricultural society because the land on which the economy is based is fixed in amount.

Into this realm of intellectual error moved some of the early philosophers who encoded the idea that profit-making was an inferior motive and that commercial activity led to excess, corruption, and misery. Their views are of great significance because, as with many other topics of discourse in Western civilization, they first defined the terms of debate over the relative ranking of profit with other values. Both Plato and Aristotle created the lasting, fundamental indictment that has cast a shadow over business ever since.

Plato believed that in each person existed insatiable appetites that could be controlled only by inner virtues painstakingly acquired with character development. The pursuit of money was one of these appetites, and Plato thought that when people engaged in trade they inevitably suc-

---

[14] Will Durant, *The Life of Greece* (New York: Simon & Schuster, 1939), p. 272.
[15] John Kenneth Galbraith, *Economics in Perspective* (Boston: Houghton Mifflin, 1987), pp. 9–10.

cumbed to the temptation of excess and became grasping. Once wealth was acquired in a society, it spawned terrible evils, including inequality, envy, class conflict, and war. "Virtue and wealth," argued Plato, "are balanced against one another in the scales."[16] Rulers of the utopian society he created in *The Republic* were prohibited from owning possessions for fear they would be corrupted and turn into tyrants. So troubled was he about this that they were forbidden even to touch gold or silver.

Aristotle believed that there was a natural form of acquisition, common to families in agrarian societies, that consisted of getting things needed for subsistence. This kind of acquisition was limited and moderate. However, with the rise of trading and monetary systems, the art of acquisition was no longer practiced this simple way. Instead, merchants studied techniques of commerce to figure out how to make the greatest profit and soon pursued not the necessities, but unlimited pools of money. This is a lower form of acquisition, thought Aristotle, because it leads to unhappiness.

According to Aristotle, happiness is the ultimate goal of life. It comes to those who develop character virtues such as courage, temperance, justice, and wisdom. He calls these virtues "goods of the soul" and holds them superior to "external goods," defined as possessions and money. Aristotle believed that the amount of happiness a person gained in life was equal to the amount of virtue accumulated in the soul. Since material possessions beyond what was needed for subsistence added nothing to the amount of virtue in the soul, it followed that they contributed nothing to happiness; thus, it was a waste or "perversion" of any virtue to apply it toward acquisition of excess. "The proper function of courage, for example, is not to produce money but to give confidence," wrote Aristotle.[17]

Thus, both of these preeminent thinkers relegated the profit motive to the sphere of lower or base behaviors, a place from which it would not escape for centuries and then only partially. Soon, Roman law would forbid the senatorial class from making business investments (and the law would be widely circumvented). Likewise, the Stoic philosophers of Rome, such as Epictetus and Marcus Aurelius, taught that the truly rich person possessed inner peace rather than capital or property. "Asked, 'Who is the rich man?' Epictetus replied, 'He who is content.' "[18] These thinkers looked down on merchants of their day as materialists who, in pursuit of wealth, sacrificed the opportunity to develop character. Of course, this did not deter the merchants from accumulating fortunes and neglecting the study of ideals.

---

[16] *The Republic*, trans. F. M. Cornford (New York: Oxford University Press, 1945), p. 274.
[17] In *Politics*, trans. Ernest Barker (New York: Oxford University Press, 1962), book I, chap. X, §17. See also book VII, chap. 1, §§ 1–10.
[18] *The Golden Sayings of Epictetus*, trans. Hastings Crossley, in Charles W. Eliot, ed., *Plato, Epictetus, Marcus Aurelius* (Danbury, CT: Grolier, 1980), p. 179.

The Medieval World

During the Middle Ages, the prevailing theological doctrines of the Roman Catholic Church were intolerant of profit-making. One reason for this was that the Church's most influential theologian, St. Thomas Aquinas, was deeply influenced by Aristotle when he set forth authoritative Church doctrine about the ethics of profit-making and lending money. But there were other reasons as well. At its start, Church doctrine opposed the values of the wealthy ruling class of Rome, which had persecuted early Christians and debilitated civilization in its waning years. The Church, then, naturally rejected a focus on wealth accumulation and sought special status for the poor. It was also deeply suspicious of commerce because business activity diverted merchants from devoutness.

Under Church doctrine, merchants were exhorted to charge a *just price* for their wares, a price that incorporated a modest profit just adequate to maintain them in the social station to which they were born. The just price stands in contrast to the modern idea of a *market price* determined by supply and demand without moral dimensions. Today we hear echoes of medieval theology when consumers complain that high prices for a scarce product are unjust. Catholicism also condemned *usury*, or the lending of money for interest. By the twelfth and thirteenth centuries, however, the money supply and economic activity had greatly expanded and interest-bearing loans were commonplace. "Commercial activity," notes historian Will Durant, "proved stronger than fear of prison or hell."[19] In time, Church scholars began to back away from the dogma of just price and usury, though they never fully embraced market pricing or lending for interest. In fact, Church doctrine making lending money for interest a sin was not officially repealed until 1917.

The Modern World

As business activity accelerated during the Renaissance, new economic theories arose to justify previously condemned practices. Two are of particular interest. First, the rise of the Protestant ethic in the sixteenth century confronted the Church's antagonism toward commerce with a new doctrine that removed moral suspicion of wealth. The Protestant reformers Martin Luther and John Calvin believed that work was a means of serving God and that if a person got great wealth through hard work it was a sign of God's approval. This contradicted Aristotle's belief that the pursuit of money corrupted the soul. Second, in 1776 Adam Smith published his theory that free markets harnessed greed for the public good and protected consumers from price gouging. This defied the Church's insistence on the idea of a just price. Moreover, visible wealth creation in expanding economies forcefully countered the notion that only a fixed

[19] In *The Age of Faith* (New York: Simon & Schuster, 1950), p. 631.

amount of wealth existed in a society. These developments ended the domination of doctrines that made business activity morally suspect and released new energies into commerce. However, the broom of doctrinal reform failed to make a clean sweep, and many business critics clung to the old approbations of Aristotle and the Church.

In addition, just when old beliefs loosened their hold, the industrial revolution created new tensions that led to critical attitudes about business. These new tensions arose as industries and inventions transformed agrarian societies and challenged traditional values with modern alternatives. During industrialization, rural, slow-paced, stable societies are swiftly and dramatically altered. They become urban and fast-paced. More emphasis is placed on commerce, and people's values change. Wealth creation overwhelms self-restraint. Consumption supplants thrift and saving. Conquest of nature replaces awe of nature.

As societies modernize, the antiquarian values of Greece nevertheless live on in the charges of critics. Always, the fundamental critique is altered to fit changed circumstances. We will see how this happened in the United States.

The American Critique of Business

High levels of public confidence in business existed during the early years. Historians record generally positive feelings toward entrepreneurs, companies, and the business system until the growth of giant trusts in the latter half of the nineteenth century.

Privately owned English companies established the earliest colonies. Sometimes the motive for colonization was to avoid religious persecution, but the backers of the Pilgrims, for instance, hoped to make a profit. The commercial spirit manifested itself in different ways in colonial America, but it was dominant in most walks of life. The farmer was not a peasant bound to the soil with a pattern of life dictated by custom. Although his way of life was different from that of the retail merchant in the town, both engaged in buying and selling. As the farmers accumulated wealth, they built and ran grain mills and in other ways employed their capital exactly like the merchants.

By 1850 America was a predominantly rural, agrarian society of small, local businesses. But explosive industrial growth rapidly reshaped it, creating severe social problems in the process. Cities grew as farmers left the land and immigrants swelled slum populations. Corrupt political machines that failed to improve parlous conditions ran large cities. Simultaneously, in many industries companies merged into huge national monopolies. These changes were the raw material of two movements critical of big business.

The first was the *populist movement,* a farmers' protest movement that began in the 1870s and led to formation of a national political party, the Populist Party, which assailed business interests until its decisive defeat in 1896. The movement arose soon after the Civil War, when farmers experienced declining crop prices. Falling prices were caused mainly by overproduction due to the efficiencies of new farming machinery, and by competition from foreign farms because of new transportation methods. At the time, farmers did not understand these factors and blamed their distress on railroad companies, the largest and most visibly corrupt businesses of the day, which frequently overcharged farmers when hauling crops, and on "plutocrats" such as J. P. Morgan and others in the eastern banking community, who controlled finance, industry, and the loan companies that sometimes foreclosed on their farms.

In a typical tirade, Mary Lease, a powerful speaker who whipped up large crowds of farmers at picnics and fairs, explained:

> Wall Street owns the country. It is no longer a government of the people, by the people and for the people, but a government of Wall Street and for Wall Street. The great common people of this country are slaves, and monopoly is the master. The West and South are bound and prostrate before the manufacturing East.[20]

To solve agrarian ills, the populists advocated government ownership of railroads, abandonment of the gold standard, and measures to control the influence of companies in politics, including direct election of U.S. senators, who at the time were picked by state legislatures corrupted with money from big business.

Historian Louis Galambos believes that despite the populist critique, there existed a great reservoir of respect for and confidence in business until the late 1880s.[21] After that, analysis of newspaper and magazine editorials shows mounting hostility toward large trusts. Soon the populists succeeded in electing many state and local officials, who enacted laws to regulate the railroads and provided the political groundswell behind the creation of the Interstate Commerce Commission in 1887 to regulate railroads. The populist movement attracted a diverse, unstable coalition of interests, including farmers, labor, prohibitionists, antimonopolists, silverites, and suffragists. These groups were held together for a time by their common, deep-seated hostility toward big companies. This tentative affinity is markedly similar to the coalition of disparate interests that has coalesced today to oppose the expansion of global trade. Despite efforts, populists were unable to forge an effective national coalition with labor and other groups, and the movement was moribund even before

[20] In John D. Hicks, *The Populist Revolt* (Minneapolis: University of Minnesota Press, 1931), p. 160.
[21] Louis Galambos, *The Public Image of Big Business in America, 1880–1940* (Baltimore: Johns Hopkins University Press, 1975), chap. 3. Galambos examined 8,976 items related to big business that were printed in newspapers and journals between 1879 and 1940, using content analysis to reconstruct rough measures of opinion among certain influential groups.

Was President McKinley the Wizard of Oz?

The Wonderful Wizard of Oz is one of the all-time best-selling children's books.[22] It was written by Lyman Frank Baum (1856–1919), an actor, sales clerk, and small-town newspaper editor who loved creating stories for children. On the surface, the book is a magical adventure in a fairyland where children are as wise as adults. However, the book has a deeper dimension. It is a parable of populism.[23]

The Wonderful Wizard of Oz satirizes the evils of an industrial society run by a moneyed elite of bankers and industrialists. "Oz" is the abbreviation for ounce, a measure of gold. It and the Yellow Brick Road allude to the hated gold standard. The main characters represent groups in society. Dorothy is the common person. The Scarecrow is the farmer. The Tin Woodsman is industrial labor. His rusted condition symbolizes factory closings in the depression years of the 1890s, and his lack of a heart hints that factories dehumanize workers. The Cowardly Lion is William Jennings Bryan, the defeated Populist Party candidate,

whom Baum regarded as lacking sufficient courage. The Wicked Witch of the East is a parody of the capitalist elite. She kept the munchkins, or "little people," in servitude. At the end of the Yellow Brick Road lay the Emerald City, or Washington, D.C., where on arrival the group was met by the Wizard, representing the president of the United States. At the time Baum wrote the book, William McKinley was president, having defeated Bryan in 1896. Populists reviled McKinley because he had the backing of big trusts and he supported the hated gold standard.

At the conclusion, Dorothy melted the Wicked Witch of the East, the Wizard flew off in a balloon, the Scarecrow became the ruler of Oz, and the Tin Woodsman took charge of the East. This ending is the unrealized populist dream.

Baum's first motive was to be a child's storyteller, not to write political satire for adults. He never stated that the book contained populist themes, leading to debate over whether finding such symbolism is fair. Yet Baum lived in South Dakota while populism was emerging and he marched in Populist Party rallies. *The Wonderful Wizard of Oz* was written in 1898, at the height of ardor for reform. Therefore, it seems reasonable to think that Baum's tale was inspired by the politics of the day.

[22] L. Frank Baum (Chicago: Reilly & Britten, 1915), first published in 1900.
[23] The classic interpretation of symbolism is by Henry W. Littlefield, "The Wizard of Oz: Parable on Populism," *American Quarterly*, Spring 1964.

1900 when William Jennings Bryan, the Populist Party's presidential candidate, was decisively defeated for a second time.

However, the populists refined a logic and lexicon for spotlighting the business system as the source of social ills. They blamed adverse consequences of industrialization on monopoly, trusts, Wall Street, "silk-hatted Easterners," the soulless "loan sharks" and shameless "bloodhounds of money" who foreclosed on farms, and corrupt politicians who worked as errand boys for the "moneybags" in a system of "plutocracy" (or rule by the wealthy). Their criticisms were harsh and colorful. In an essay on the virtues of farming as an occupation, Bryan wrote that for farmers "even the dumb animals are more wholesome companions than the bulls and bears of Wall Street."[24]

[24] "Farming as an Occupation," *Cosmopolitan*, January 1904, p. 371.

Art Young, a radical
cartoonist of the
Progressive era, had
an impish ability to
highlight the excesses
of the industrial age.
This cartoon, typical
of many then drawn
by Young and others,
first appeared in 1912.

CAPITALISM

It was, of course, too late for America to be a farming economy. This
did not diminish the appeal of the populist message to large segments of
the population. On the contrary, continued industrial growth has caused
it to resurface time and again up to the present day, each time its vocabulary recycled and its critical message refined to fit current circumstances.

The second critical movement was the *progressive movement*, a broader
reform effort lasting from about 1900 until the end of World War I in
1918. Fueled by wide moral indignation about problems of industrialization, it incorporated the urban middle class and also farmers. Although a short-lived Progressive Party was formed and unsuccessfully

nominated Theodore Roosevelt for president in 1912, both the Democratic and Republican parties had powerful progressive wings. Unlike populism, progressivism was a mainstream political doctrine. Like populism, it was at root an effort to cure social ills by controlling perceived abuses of big business.

Because of broad popular support, progressives were far more effective than populists in their reform efforts, and during their era a reform tide washed over business. Progressives broke up trusts and monopolies, made campaign contributions by corporations illegal, imposed federal regulation on consumer products, restricted child labor, passed a corporate income tax and an inheritance tax, and regulated safety conditions in factories. "Turn the waters of pure public spirit into the corrupt pools of private interests," wrote Ernest Crosby, editor of *Cosmopolitan* magazine, "and wash the offensive accumulations away."[25] Progressivism further refined the antibusiness lexicon of the populists and carried their legacy into the twentieth century.

After the triumph of progressive reforms, there was a period of high public confidence in big business during the prosperous, expansive 1920s. This rosy era ended abruptly with the stock market crash of 1929, and business again came under sustained attack. During the 1920s, the idea that business knew how to achieve continuing prosperity was widely accepted. The depression of the 1930s disproved this and, in addition, brought to light much ineptness, criminal negligence, and outright fraud by prominent executives. There was a popular feeling that the economic collapse would not have occurred if business leaders had been more capable.

As the depression deepened, anger at business grew and the old rhetoric of populism reemerged. In the Senate, for example, Huey Long, a colorful populist Democrat from Louisiana who claimed to be the advocate of the poor against the rich, rose to condemn a "ruling plutocratic class."[26] One of Long's favorite rhetorical tactics was to use the analogy of a great barbecue to show how the economic elite was cheating depression-era Americans.

> The 125 million people of America have seated themselves at the barbecue table to consume the products which have been guaranteed to them by their Lord and Creator. There is provided by the Almighty what it takes for them all to eat: yea, more. . . . But the financial masters of America have taken off the barbecue table 90 percent of the food placed thereon by God, through the labors of mankind, even before the feast begins, and there is left on that table to be eaten by 125 million people less than should be there for 10 million of them.

---

[25] "The Man with the Hose," August 1906, p. 341.
[26] *Congressional Record,* 73d Cong., 2d sess., 1934, p. 6081, speech of April 5.

What has become of the remainder of those things placed on the table by the Lord for the use of us all? They are in the hands of the Morgans, the Rockefellers, the Mellons, the Baruchs, the Bakers, the Astors, and the Vanderbilts—600 families at the most either possessing or controlling the entire 90 percent of all that is in America. . . . Like the dog in the manger, they command a wagon load of hay, which the dog would not allow the cow to eat, though he could not eat it himself. . . . I hope none will be horror-stricken when they hear me say that we must limit the size of the big man's fortune in order to guarantee a minimum of fortune, life and comfort to the little man.[27]

These remarks are consistent with the ancient Greek view that wealth in a society is limited and the accumulation of one person is a subtraction from all others—that great material wealth reflects greed. Long used these views to gain moral authority for his proposals. In 1934 he introduced a plan to redistribute wealth by collecting annual taxes on corporate assets and large fortunes and then giving every family a $5,000 initial gift followed with a guaranteed annual income of $2,500. In a collapsed economy, this populist-like plan had tremendous appeal, and Long attracted millions of followers. However, he was assassinated before it could be enacted, leaving the milder reforms of President Franklin D. Roosevelt's New Deal to carry the day.

During World War II, support for business rebounded. Industry wrapped itself in patriotism, and its high output of war material proved essential to Allied victory. As a result, business was seen as the "arsenal of democracy," not as a bloated plutocracy. In a postwar poll, only 10 percent of the population believed that where "big business activity" was concerned "the bad effects outweighed the good."[28] This renascence of respect lasted into the 1960s before the populist seed sprouted again.

The 1960s to the Present

Strong public support for business collapsed in the mid-1960s. It was a time of redefinition of values due to rising affluence and of unrest. Social movements attacked business not, as in the past, for failure to provide wages, incomes, and general prosperity, but for its failure to solve or prevent societal problems such as pollution, racism, sexism, consumer fraud, denigrating work, and other conditions that lowered quality of life. The attacks of critics coincided with a negative trend in public opinion toward business. In 1968, for example, 70 percent of Americans agreed that business tried to strike a fair balance between profits and the public interest. However, by 1970 the figure declined to 33 percent,

---

[27] Radio speech broadcast March 7, 1935, inserted in the *Congressional Record,* March 12, 1935.
[28] Burton R. Fisher and Stephen B. Withey, *Big Business as the People See It* (Ann Arbor, MI: University of Michigan Microfilms, December 1951), p. xiii.

FIGURE 4.1   **Percentage of American Public Expressing Confidence in Leaders of Major Companies**

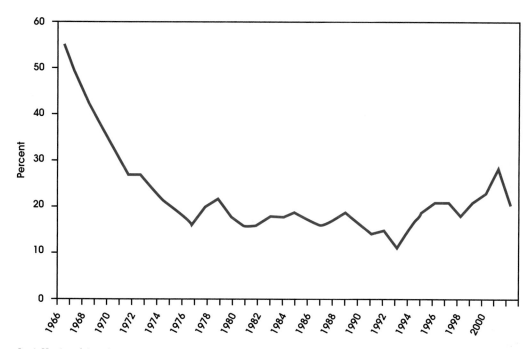

Source: Louis Harris and Associates.

and in 1976 it plummeted to 15 percent. This was a drop of 55 points in eight years.[29]

Scholars who studied the polls theorized that the period of turmoil in American society in the 1960s created a "confidence gap," or a gap between public expectations about how corporations *should* act and public perceptions of how they actually *did* act. This gap has now persisted for almost 40 years and continues to define the climate of public opinion. An illustration, shown in Figure 4.1, is the long-term trend of the percentage of Americans expressing "a great deal of confidence" in "people in charge of running major companies." In 1966, about 55 percent of the public expressed such confidence, but by the early 1970s the number fell into the low 20s. It dropped further to 11 percent in 1992 and has since recovered back to the low 20s. The large number of Americans lacking confidence in business suggests a broad reservoir of cynicism that, as we will see, radical critics can sometimes tap into to support their attacks on corporations. In addition, beginning in the late

[29] Seymour M. Lipset and William Schneider, "How's Business: What the Public Thinks," *Public Opinion,* July–August 1978.

1960s, this broad reservoir of cynicism provided political support for enactment of a huge network of regulations, covering many areas of business activity.

CURRENT CRITICISM OF BUSINESS

The list of specific criticisms of business is virtually endless. Recent criticism has focused mainly on global corporations and international bodies that are leading expansion of the world economy. Criticism comes from an *antiglobalism coalition* that includes labor unions, human and civil rights organizations, environmentalists, religious orders, farmers, consumer defenders, animal rights crusaders, neo-Luddites opposed to expansion of new technologies, and anarchists opposed to any emerging world order. This coalition encompasses diverse, sometimes inconsistent ideologies and agendas, so ascribing to it a specific goal or platform is difficult.

The critique of the antiglobalists exhibits the two fundamental sources of criticism of business earlier discussed. First, it is filled with the perception that transnational corporations place profit before other lofty and enduring values. In the words of one business critic, the coalition is united in opposing "corporate-led globalization at the expense of social goals like justice, community, national sovereignty, cultural diversity and ecological sustainability."[30] Second, its complaints center on problems generated by economic growth. Following is a list of generic categories of antiglobalist criticism. Each broad category, in turn, includes many specific criticisms.

- Transnational corporations have too much power. This power is concentrated in too few hands and is inadequately checked in transnational corporations because no adequate countervailing force exists. "The reality of our world, seems more like a global powerocracy," writes one critic.[31]

- Multilateral agencies such as the World Trade Organization, International Monetary Fund, and World Bank are undemocratic. They are dominated by the governments of a few developed nations that, in turn, corporate elites have dominated and corrupted. Third World countries must conform to their dictates. Ralph Nader asks, "How can we sign on to something that subordinates democracy to corporate power?"[32]

---

[30] Walden Bello, "Lilliputians Rising 2000: The Year of Global Protest against Corporate Globalization," *Multinational Monitor*, January–February 2001, p. 33.
[31] Eduardo Galeano, "Rule of the Few," *The Progressive*, August 2001, p. 16.
[32] In "Retro Cool," *Time*, April 24, 2000, p. 46.

- Globalization creates inequality. Rich corporations and nations benefit more than the poor and seek to hold power and wealth rather than share it. According to one critic, this is a form of "recolonization."[33]

- Corporations spread a gospel of Western-style development around the world, erasing distinct local cultures. Capitalism creates undesirable structural trends such as industrialization, growth of mass consumer markets, and reliance on intrusive, large-scale technologies, including autos, bioengineered crops, dams, and nuclear power plants. This technology is objectionable because it both harms the environment and centralizes power in corporations that control it. Thus, industrialization cannot define progress because it reduces the life-satisfactions of those it affects.

- Corporations exploit stakeholders. "To ask corporations to behave better by making growth and profit a lower priority or to act foremost in the interests of local communities, the environment, or the workers is like asking armies to give up guns," notes one critic.[34]

Classifying business critics is difficult. They exhibit a wide range of values, opinions, methods, and goals. It is important to distinguish between average people who have some cynicism about business but largely accept the current situation and a small number of others who have deep-seated, emotional, and principled objections to the system and want to reform or change it. To oversimplify, there are four basic groups of these more vociferous critics.

Progressive Activists

Progressive activists come largely from a community of antiglobalist interests that has coalesced into a worldwide movement to limit corporate power and reform corporate behavior. This movement shares a common ideology and common goal with historical movements of prior centuries that fought for reforms in business and government. The ideology is one of deep suspicion of markets and corporations, and the goal is that of regulating corporate power so that the economic system works to advance human welfare.

The global network of progressive activists has no single leader, but in the United States a prominent figure and senior statesman is Ralph Nader. Nader began his activist career more than 30 years ago by writing *Unsafe at Any Speed,* a book that attacked the auto industry for putting styling ahead of safety.[35] The popularity of the book helped Congress

---

[33] Martin Khor, "The United Nations and Globalization," speech to the Millennium Forum, May 22, 2000, at www.corpwatch.org/un/background/2000/mkhor.html.
[34] Jerry Mander, "The Rules of Corporate Behavior," in Jerry Mander and Edward Goldsmith, *The Case against the Global Economy* (San Francisco: Sierra Club Books, 1996), p. 309.
[35] New York: Grossman, 1965.

pass auto safety legislation. Based on this success and his belief that it was important to be involved in seeking change through government, Nader created more than 50 organizations to research consumer issues and lobby government for protective regulations. With the passage of time, Nader's general hostility toward corporations has deepened. In speeches, he rails against "a government of the Exxons, by the General Motors and for the DuPonts."[36]

Announcing his candidacy for President of the United States in 2000, Nader said he was running to challenge "rampaging corporate titans," "runaway commercial imperatives," and "global corporations . . . astride our planet."[37] He declined to seek the nomination as either a Republican or a Democrat because, he explained, both parties "feed at the same corporate trough."[38] Instead, he ran as a candidate for the Green Party, a global political movement that began as an antinuclear movement in Great Britain and New Zealand and has broadened its platform to include "nonviolence, social justice, environmentalism, respect for diversity, global responsibility and community-based economics and democracy."[39] Although Nader got only 2.7 percent of the popular vote in 2000, he prevented Democrat Al Gore from winning the electoral votes of key states, allowing Republican George W. Bush, the more probusiness candidate, to win. Liberal Democrats who seek moderate regulation of corporations are angry with Nader for this, but they fail to understand that Nader is, in his own words, challenging "the accepted concentration of power and wealth in the hands of global corporations who dominate our government."[40]

Activists, by definition, take action. In recent years, elements in the antiglobalism coalition have created networks of advocacy to correct perceived problems or abuses. An example is the International Campaign to Ban Landmines, composed at its height of 800 groups in 50 countries. As part of its work, activist groups such as Human Rights Watch attacked corporations making antipersonnel mines. As a result, Raytheon stopped making mine components, and others, including Motorola, Hughes Aircraft, and General Electric, quit selling parts used to make antipersonnel mines.[41] Similar advocacy networks have formed to

---

[36] In Hector Tobar and Bill Stall, "Green Party Nominates Nader for President," *Los Angeles Times,* August 20, 1996, p. A3.

[37] "Closing the Democracy Gap," *The Progressive Populist,* October 15, 2000, pp. 13 and 14.

[38] Ibid., p. 14.

[39] Kevin Graham, *Ralph Nader: Battling for Democracy* (Denver: Windom Publishing Company, 2000), p. 106.

[40] "Restraining Corporate Power," *Nader 2000,* at www.votenader.com/issues/corp-quotes.html, undated.

[41] Christina Del Valle and Monica Larner, "A New Front in the War on Land Mines," *Business Week,* April 28, 1997, p. 43.

Ralph Nader (1934–).
Portrait by Deborah Luedy.

fight sweatshop contracting by clothing makers and environmental abuses by energy and mining companies.

Antiglobalism activists have also staged massive protests intended to disrupt meetings of international economic bodies. The first big assault came in Seattle, Washington, when a mass of 40,000 protestors disrupted meetings of the World Trade Organization in 1999. Other large-scale demonstrations followed. Anticorporate assaults attracted widespread attention in the last decade due to increased use of the Internet and more media coverage. But such campaigns are not new. In the 1800s a remarkably similar advocacy network led the global antislavery campaign.[42] In the 1970s powerful international campaigns against Nestlé and other infant-formula makers led to reforms of infant-formula sales in less developed countries. And in the 1980s a powerful human rights coalition forced large corporations to leave racially divided South Africa.[43]

Activists use a wide range of tactics to accost companies. Common pressure tactics include letter writing, speeches, lobbying, research, and editorial writing. Groups such as the Natural Resources Defense Council and the Environmental Defense Fund specialize in using lawsuits to challenge business. Following is a list, hardly exhaustive, of other widely used tactics.

- *Consumer boycotts.* A boycott is a call to pressure a company by not buying its products and services. In recent years, there have been hundreds of boycott calls by advocacy groups. Here are some current examples: INFACT, a group that fights "life-threatening abuses by

[42] Margaret E. Keck and Kathryn Sikkink, *Activists Beyond Borders* (Ithaca, NY: Cornell University Press, 1998), pp. 8–12.
[43] S. Prakash Sethi and Oliver F. Williams, *Economic Imperatives and Ethical Values in Global Business: The South African Experience and International Codes Today* (South Bend, IN: University of Notre Dame Press, 2001).

transnational corporations," is boycotting Kraft Foods until its corporate parent, Philip Morris, withdraws the Marlboro Man ad campaign.[44] PETA is boycotting PETsMART for mistreatment of animals sold in its stores. Purchasing bans by governments are a variant on boycotting (see box on page 106).

- *Shareholder proposals.* Rules permit shareowners of public companies to sponsor resolutions on which all stockholders may vote at annual meetings. If passed, they are binding on management. Religious groups have led in sponsoring them. The Interfaith Center on Corporate Responsibility coordinates a coalition of more than 200 religious orders and denominations that, in 2001, generated 226 proposals to 160 companies. Examples are a proposal asking Boeing to link executive pay to promotion of basic human rights and one asking H. B. Fuller, a glue manufacturer, to stop selling adhesives to tobacco companies for use in making cigarettes.[45]

- *Harassment.* When Citigroup employees set up booths on college campuses to market credit cards, activists upset with the big bank over its investment practices set up a booth right next to them, warning students away. Forms of harassment are limited only by the imagination. Activists have brought lawsuits based on trumped-up charges such as racketeering. They have disrupted the lives of executives and their families by picketing their homes, protesting at their children's schools, and interrupting services at their churches. They attract attention by climbing corporate buildings to unfurl large signs.

- *Principles and codes of conduct.* Some advocacy groups and coalitions have developed codes of conduct that essentially enact their agendas. Corporations are pressured to sign on to these codes, after which they generally must submit to compliance monitoring. An example is Social Accountability 8000, a detailed code created by organizations in the worldwide campaign against sweatshop labor. The code sets forth principles for ethical treatment of workers consistent with the progressive ideology and requires that corporate signers meet many conditions to achieve certification and then submit to periodic monitoring by teams of examiners trained to enforce the code. A few progressive-leaning companies helped in developing the code, including Avon Products and The Body Shop.

---

[44] "Taking Our Message to the Top: Give the Marlboro Man the Boot!" *INFACT at Work*, Summer 2001, p. 2.
[45] "Corporate Responsibility Challenges 2001," *The Corporate Examiner*, February 28, 2001, pp. 13 and 15.

- *Corporate campaigns.* A corporate campaign is a broad, sustained attack on a corporation, usually by a coalition of groups, that employs a wide range of tactics trying to force more socially responsible behavior.[46] They are a primary means of mobilizing activists for coordinated warfare against the targeted firm. The organizers of a corporate campaign pressure a corporation by depicting it to its stakeholders as engaging in antisocial behavior to make a profit while presenting themselves as crusaders for the public interest. When activists attack corporations, there is a huge imbalance of power. A large transnational corporation has enormous financial resources, strong influence in government bodies, and frequently a trusted brand name. Activists have little financing, slight political influence, and low public recognition. However, they invariably have one key source of strength: the tendency of the public to perceive an environmental, religious, or human rights group as selfless and out to do something in the public interest. Using this perception, activists seize the ethical high ground and engage the corporation with an assault that might be likened to warfare because the action sometimes stretches or breaks the bonds of civil society.

For example, a few years ago a coalition of environmental groups began a corporate campaign targeting Home Depot for irresponsibly selling wood from endangered old-growth forests. Home Depot was picked because it is the world's largest home improvement chain selling enormous amounts of lumber around the world. The coalition, which included Rainforest Action Network, Earth First!, Greenpeace, Sierra Club, and many others, then organized an extraordinary assault. More than 250,000 people signed petitions, sent postcards, or called the company asking it to desist. Elementary school children were recorded singing a song about forest preservation that was sent to the CEO of Home Depot. When the company tried to build new stores, activists fought zoning permits. At its annual meeting, sympathetic shareholders presented resolutions that management was forced to oppose. A team of climbers hung a five-story banner on the company's corporate headquarters building in Atlanta reading, "HOME DEPOT: STOP SELLING OLD GROWTH."

Over a two-year period, there were more than 600 demonstrations outside Home Depot outlets. Inside, activists prowled the aisles and put stickers on products made from old-growth wood. A Forest Action Network activist dressed in a bear costume tied himself to the

---

[46] For an extended discussion, see Jarol B. Manheim, *The Death of a Thousand Cuts: Corporate Campaigns and the Attack on Corporations* (Mahwah, NJ: Lawrence Erlbaum Associates, 2001).

The Massachusetts Burma Law

Under pressure from activist groups and labor unions, some states, counties, and cities have passed laws, known as *selective purchasing laws*, prohibiting agencies under their jurisdictions from buying goods and services from targeted corporations. These laws first achieved prominence during the 1970s and 1980s, when almost 200 states and localities made it illegal for their agencies to buy from corporations doing business in South Africa, a country that ran on a system of racial separation called *apartheid*.

The laws were powerful tools. They forced companies to leave South Africa or risk losing considerable business in the United States. When the white-run South African regime ended, it was due in part to this pressure on the country's economy. Similar laws then appeared banning contracts with companies for a range of reasons. For example, New York targeted Swiss banks that withheld assets of Holocaust victims. Berkeley, California, barred companies doing business in Nigeria.

In the 1990s some states and cities adopted laws to penalize corporations doing business in Burma. Burma is run by military leaders who refer to the country as Myanmar and silence opponents with repression. In 1990 the nation had a democratic election in which an opposition party advocating democracy won an overwhelming 82 percent of the vote. However, the military refused to give up its power and placed the opposition's leader, Aung San Suu Kyi, under house arrest, on the trumped-up excuse that she needed protection from "terrorists." Such events outrage human rights activists, who conclude that corporations doing business in Burma are complicit in the repression since their commercial activities and taxes support the military.

In 1996 a Massachusetts state legislator took an anti-apartheid law he had written years before, revised it by inserting "Burma" for "South Africa," and got it passed. The law effectively barred corporations doing business in Burma from selling goods or services to any Massachusetts agency. It did so by automatically adding 10 percent to their bids, invariably making them noncompetitive. Immediately, Japan and the European Union strenuously objected, arguing that the law was an illegal trade barrier violating World Trade Organization rules. Then, Apple Computer, Eastman

rafters over the cash register in a Canadian Home Depot, remaining there for several hours to talk with customers. An Indian named Qwatsinas, the hereditary chief of a tribe in a Canadian rainforest, entered Home Depot's flagship store in Atlanta to engage in "ethical shoplifting." He took Red Cedar lumber believed to have been illegally logged from his native land and turned it in to the FBI as stolen property.[47]

This pressure, which escalated over time, led Home Depot to announce that it would phase out purchase of wood from endangered forests by the end of 2002. It agreed to begin using wood certified by the Forest Stewardship Council, a group that verifies sustainability in wood harvesting using criteria acceptable to environmentalists. Logging and lumber companies have resisted the Council's program, but when Home

---

[47] Jill Krill, "Felling the Lumbering Giants," *Multinational Monitor,* January–February 2001, p. 17.

Kodak, and Hewlett-Packard left Burma, saying that the Massachusetts law was responsible.

Later in the same year, Congress passed a Burma Act banning any aid and giving the president broad power to impose trade sanctions and to work with other nations to bring democracy to the country. After Congress acted, a group representing American companies engaged in overseas commerce brought suit claiming that the Massachusetts law was unconstitutional for two reasons. First, as a state law it improperly interfered with the foreign affairs power reserved for the national government. Second, it conflicted with the Burma Act passed by Congress, and when a state law clashes with a national law it is *preempted,* or superseded, by the national law. Two federal courts agreed with the business group, but Massachusetts appealed to the Supreme Court.

In 2000 the Supreme Court handed down a 9–0 opinion holding that Congress's sanctions against Burma preempted the Massachusetts law. In *Crosby v. National Foreign Trade Council,* the Court said that the state law undermined the ability of the president to carry out the objectives set by Congress. "[T]he President's maximum power to persuade," it noted, "rests on his capacity to bargain for the benefits of access to the entire national economy with-

out exception for enclaves fenced off willy-nilly by inconsistent political tactics."[48]

Business groups applauded the ruling. By invalidating the Massachusetts law, the Court made it harder for activists to use selective purchasing laws to leverage the power of commerce in achieving their goals. Big transnational corporations are now freer to trade in undemocratic settings. Human rights advocates were disturbed. It showed, said one, "the supremacy of trade over all other human concerns."[49] Some commentators noted an irony in the situation. Colonists at the Boston Tea Party threw British tea overboard rather than pay unjust taxes. Now, when the people of Massachusetts again applied an ethical criterion to their purchasing, they were stopped because this violated the Constitution, the nation's most fundamental guarantee of rights. "It would be ironic," noted the *Harvard Law Review,* "if, in protecting Congress's ability to promote democracy abroad, the Court were to weaken democracy at home."[50]

[48] 120 S. Ct. 2288 (2000) at 2299.
[49] Mark Weisbrot, "Trade Trumps Human Rights in Court Decision," *The Progressive Populist,* July 15, 2000, p. 17.
[50] "The Supreme Court, 1999 Term: Leading Cases," November 2000, p. 359.

Depot, the giant of its industry, agreed to buy certified wood, its competitors felt pressured to do likewise or risk appearing heartless about the environment.

Intellectuals

This group is composed of thinkers who illuminate the social costs of industrialization, expressing their concern with the pen rather than the sword of activism. Often they are in the vanguard; they see emerging social problems caused by corporate activity, frame issues for public discussion, and suggest reforms. Usually, they believe in protection of human rights, restraint of corporate power, and solution of social problems through government action.

The intellectual critique surfaced as America industrialized. When economic activity accelerated, intellectuals began to be bothered. "Commerce," complained Ralph Waldo Emerson in 1839, "threatens to upset the balance of man and establish a new, universal Monarchy more tyrannical than Babylon or Rome."[51]

By the end of the nineteenth century, factories had proliferated and a mass consumer society formed to buy their output. In 1899 Thorstein Veblen gave an unflattering description of "conspicuous consumption" in *The Theory of the Leisure Class.* He said that in an industrial society, material possessions replaced knowledge and character as sources of status. Therefore, people bought expensive things to compete with their neighbors. The more extravagant and wasteful a possession, the more it gave "pecuniary strength" to its owner. A circuitous driveway over flat land, for example, was much preferred to a straight one. The indirect route was less efficient, but the wasteful extra expense of constructing it showed that the owner was opulent and inspired "invidious comparison."[52] As a critic of consumer society, Veblen was decrying the deterioration of thrift as a central value.

By the 1950s a new class of white-collar workers had emerged. In his 1956 book *The Organization Man,* sociologist William H. Whyte Jr. argued that big corporations forced conformity on their employees.[53] Industry was whittling away at the American tradition of rugged individualism. Around this time, economist John Kenneth Galbraith wrote the first of many books over 40 years advocating government control of business to reverse the loss of consumer sovereignty that he attributes to the growth of corporations.[54]

Some writers never challenge business directly, but their work changes public values. In the 1962 book *Silent Spring,* naturalist Rachael Carson warned of the danger of pesticides and wrote at just the right time to galvanize a dawning environmental movement and quicken the attack on industrial pollution.[55] Peter Singer's 1975 philosophical tract *Animal Liberation* created a moral justification for animal rights that changed the environment for the animal agriculture, cosmetics, fur, and restaurant industries.[56]

Socialists

Socialist critics reject current institutions and demand replacement with a collectivist state. Unlike reform-oriented critics, this group believes that the faults of capitalism cannot be ameliorated through gradual reform. Basic institutions such as the free market and private capital must be swept away.

Socialists base their critique on the philosophical and economic theories of Karl Marx (1818–1883). They attack classical economists for blind-

---

[51] Quoted from Emerson's *Journals,* vol. V, pp. 284–86, in Vernon Louis Parrington, *Main Currents in American Thought* (New York: Harcourt, Brace, 1927), p. 386.
[52] New York: Penguin Books, 1979, pp. 27 and 137; originally published in 1899.
[53] New York: Simon & Schuster, 1956.
[54] See, for example, *The Affluent Society* (Boston: Houghton Mifflin, 1958); and *The New Industrial State* (Boston: Houghton Mifflin, 1967).
[55] Boston: Houghton Mifflin, 1962.
[56] New York: New York Review of Books, 1975; revised edition by Avon Books, 1990.

ness to the abusive aspects of markets. Orthodox views of the market, they say, fail to acknowledge worker exploitation, imperialist foreign expansion, resource waste, race and sex discrimination, income inequality, militarism, and other evils.

Historically, socialist critics have been persistent antagonists of business. An early landmark of American socialism was Edward Bellamy's popular 1888 novel *Looking Backward*. Bellamy began the book with a metaphor comparing industrial society "to a prodigious coach which the masses of humanity were harnessed to and dragged toilsomely" while the privileged few sat in "breezy and comfortable seats on the top."[57] But the plot made its way to a new cooperative society in the year 2000, in which businesses nationalized by the government worked for the benefit of everyone, not to satisfy the greed of a few. The book ignited the public's imagination and sold more copies—over 500,000—than any book ever had before. It spawned "Nationalist" clubs across the country and inspired several hundred people to form a colony in Tennessee to bring Bellamy's vision to life. This colony was a living critique of capitalism. It required members to pass a socialist entrance exam, used a loud steam whistle to regiment activity from wake-up to evening meal, and tried to instill egalitarian values with communal readings of the Declaration of Independence.[58] It lasted only seven years.

Although the tide of history has gone against socialism, its advocates reached high-water marks in two historical eras. The first was the progressive era, when in 1912 the Socialist Party presidential candidate, Eugene V. Debs, attracted 6 percent of the popular vote. The second was the depression era of the 1930s, when its radical prescriptions made sense to desperate people and Marxists achieved prominence in labor unions. In both eras, however, moderate reform defeated the socialist agenda.

In the United States, socialists were thrown on the defensive in the 1950s by Senator Joseph McCarthy's (R–Wis.) histrionics about revealing communists hiding in government. Subsequently, the union movement purged radical socialists, removing Marxists from their only base of power. And in the 1960s a New Left movement emerged on college campuses that rejected Marxism in favor of a modern sociological view of corporate elites dominating society. Today the influence of Marxist thinkers has waned elsewhere as formerly socialist countries convert to market economies. This historical development blunts the appeal of their critique. Though the movement is moribund, to dismiss it now might be premature.

[57] *Looking Backward: 2000–1887* (Boston: Ticknor and Company, 1888), p. 6. Bellamy advocated "nationalism" and avoided the word socialism because he believed it had frightening connotations for Americans.
[58] W. Fitzhugh Brundage, *A Socialist Utopia in the New South* (Urbana: University of Illinois Press, 1996); pp. 50, 109, 125.

Radical Nonsocialists

Radical nonsocialist critics see industrial society as beyond redemption and want to overthrow its basic principles and restructure its institutions. Unlike socialists, who get their prescription for change from Karl Marx, they do not coalesce around a specific theory of what is wrong, what should be done, and how to do it.

Radical criticism of industry has a long, colorful history in American society. In the nineteenth century, the first radical critics tried to cling to the values and life of an agrarian society being swept away before their eyes. In the 1840s Brook Farm in Massachusetts and similar agrarian communes were founded to display an alternative way of life. In them, values prized in industrial society—materialism, competition, individualism, and tireless labor—were rejected. Instead, an effort was made to substitute moderation, group harmony, and leisure. These utopias soon failed, their example overwhelmed by the allure of industry.

In 1863 Henry David Thoreau wrote to reject a world in which commercial values smothered the poetry and grace of everyday life.

> This world is a place of business. What an infinite bustle! I am awakened almost every night by the panting of the locomotive. It interrupts my dreams. There is no sabbath. It would be glorious to see mankind at leisure for once. It is nothing but work, work, work. I cannot easily buy a blank-book to write thoughts in; they are commonly ruled for dollars and cents. . . . I think that there is nothing, not even crime, more opposed to poetry, to philosophy, ay, to life itself, than this incessant business.[59]

The ideas of Brook Farm and Thoreau failed to spread. Nevertheless, the tradition of radical rejection of industrial society has been continuously renewed. In 1896 Henry Demarest Lloyd wrote *Wealth Against Commonwealth*, a popular book that moved public sentiment against big business. The argument in Lloyd's book makes the same points as today's critics. He attacked the drive of "corporate caesars" to "control production, not by the needs of humanity, but by the desires of a few for dividends"; he wrote that across the globe, "corporations are grown greater than the State," and that common people are "slaves to market tyrants."[60] Lloyd rejected government as a solution, advocating instead a curative based on brotherly love. Like many radical critics of industrialism, the arc of reasoning never returns to earth; the faults of capitalism are laid bare, but the remedy is nebulous. He was unable to offer a concrete substitute for the way of life he rejected.

More recently, E. F. Schumacher wrote *Small Is Beautiful*, in which he urged a new society of small-scale organization in which people harmo-

---

[59] Henry David Thoreau, "Life without Principle," *The Atlantic Monthly*, October 1863, pp. 484–85.
[60] New York: Harper & Brothers Publishers, 1989, pp. 2, 1, 494, and 521.

nize with nature instead of dominating it.[61] Dave Foreman, a founder of Earth First!, believes in dismantling much of industrial civilization, tearing up roads, and returning to an earlier kind of life.[62] Another recent radical critic, Kirkpatrick Sale, writes that corporations must be reoriented to have "spiritual identification" with all species, large global organizations must be replaced by small communities, and industrial capitalism must be converted from a competitive to a cooperative system."[63] These ideas were applauded at the Brook Farm commune more than 150 years ago.

CONCLUDING OBSERVATIONS: WHAT TO THINK OF CRITICS?

In this chapter we have narrated a history of negative attitudes toward business. In doing so, we have not analyzed the merits of particular criticisms, many of which deserve serious thought. Nor have we set forth a response to them.

There is no question that industrial capitalism as it exists in the United States and elsewhere is a historical force that creates continuous, turbulent social change; it is, as the economist Joseph Shumpeter wrote in 1942, "a perennial gale of creative destruction" that destroys institutions and challenges existing authority.[64] The great issue is how to regard this change.

The defense of industrial capitalism is that, for the most part, the changes it brings represent progress, a condition of improvement for humanity. All the while that critics have been objecting, it has steadily improved living standards for millions. In the United States, it operates in a democratic political system that has reformed its greatest abuses over the years. As against promoting greed and avarice, it has instead promoted positive cultural values such as imagination, innovation, organized cooperation, hard work, and the interpersonal trust necessary to conduct millions of daily business transactions. In the words of one defender, market capitalism is a soaring triumph.

> If the principles of commerce and technology, on which America is founded, are in some ways less noble than those of the ancient world, they are also more realistic and more practical. Moreover, they have produced not just material but also moral progress: the abolition of slavery, the elevation of countless people from poverty to comfort, the relief of suffering produced by disease, humanitarian campaigns against torture

[61] New York: Harper & Row, 1973.
[62] Dave Foreman, *Confessions of an Eco-Warrior* (New York: Harmony Books, 1991).
[63] Kirkpatrick Sale, *Rebels against the Future* (Reading, MA.: Addison-Wesley, 1995), pp. 276–77.
[64] *Capitalism, Socialism and Democracy* (New York: Harper & Row, 1976), p. 143; originally published in 1942.

and famine all over the world, and a widely shared conception of human rights, human freedom, and human dignity.[65]

Whether or not we agree with shrill ideologues, a broad spectrum of criticism is an important check on business power. Many legitimate criticisms demand attention by corporations, governments, and multilateral organizations. If criticism is properly channeled, it can preserve the best of the business institution and bring wide benefit. In Ralph Nader's words: "Whenever, in our nation's history, people successfully challenge the excessive power of commercial interests, whether over workers, child labor, minorities, consumers and the environment, the country became better and the economy stronger."[66]

[65] Dinesh D'Souza, *The Virtue of Prosperity* (New York: The Free Press, 2000), pp. 186–87.
[66] "Human Need Trumps Corporate Greed," *The Wall Street Journal,* October 25, 2000, p. A22.

Genetically Modified Foods

Soon after the introduction of gene-altered soybeans in the United Kingdom in 1996, a truck driven by Greenpeace activists dumped five tons of the beans on the sidewalk in front of Prime Minister Tony Blair's residence. Other activists busied themselves destroying fields of genetically modified (GM) crops and demonstrating at headquarters of companies making or using the soybeans. Greenpeace wants a complete ban on the use of gene-altered foods. With activist allies, it has been very successful in turning public opinion against them in Europe and is now focused on waging war against them in the United States.

In early 2001 Greenpeace organized a campaign against Trader Joe's, a specialty grocery store chain operating in nine states. The campaign began with a press conference in Los Angeles near Trader Joe's headquarters. Other groups and activists interested in the issue were recruited for a series of actions. They set up tables outside stores. They handed out leaflets. They asked customers to sign petitions, call the company and send e-mails and faxes. They organized store tours during which activists led groups of customers from aisle to aisle pointing to products with genetically engineered corn, soy, cotton seed oil, and other ingredients. At some stores, Greenpeace "shoppers" put loads of these items in shopping carts and left them in the front of the stores with signs on top.

TRADER JOE'S:
We, your customers, have removed these products from your shelves because they contain unsafe genetically engineered ingredients. Now it's your turn.

Late in 2001 Trader Joe's gave in, agreeing to ban genetically modified ingredients from the private-label products that make up about 70 percent of its stock.[1] It is the first U.S. grocer to take this action. Greenpeace announced that it will begin to target other supermarket chains.

[1] Melinda Fulmer, "For Trader Joe's, No GMOs," *Los Angeles Times,* November 15, 2001, p. C2.

WHAT IS BIOTECHNOLOGY?

The science of genetic modification is a subset of the larger field of biotechnology. According to the U.S. Office of Technology Assessment, biotechnology includes any technique "that uses living organisms (or parts of organisms) to make or modify products, to improve plants and animals, or to develop microorganisms for specific uses." Biotechnology is an old science. For example, the fermentation process in making wine uses microorganisms to convert sugar into alcohol. Most of the foods consumed today are the products of farmers and scientists who experimented for decades with cross-fertilization of plants. In the 1920s, for example, a farmer in Anaheim, California, named Rudolph Boysen crossed a loganberry, a blackberry, and a red raspberry. He abandoned his experiments, but a nearby farmer named Walter Knott rescued his dying plants and produced what he called a "boysenberry." Knott built his boysenberry business into one of the largest amusement parks in California.[2] While today's genetic modification can be considered an extension of this history, it is such a significant technical leap forward that it has been rightfully called an agricultural revolution.

WHAT IS GENETIC MODIFICATION?

GM refers to "sophisticated artificial techniques capable of transferring genes from other organisms directly to recipient organisms."[3] Genes determine traits such as color, insect resistance, size, or taste. Such traits can be moved from one plant to another to introduce a new plant not found in nature.

Scientists use many techniques to do GM, and all of them are extremely expensive, arduous, and time-consuming. One observer reported that the process can take a dozen or more years and involve thousands of transfers before one successful new product is produced.[4] An oversimplified sequence of steps is as follows. First, a plant exhibiting the desired gene, such as color or resistence to a particular pesticide, is identified. A bit of deoxyribonucleic acid (DNA) or gene is removed and inserted in the DNA of the recipient plant. This is then placed in a petri dish with plant cells and a new plant grows. It is then planted in soil for field testing. If the results are satisfactory, a new plant line is born and may be commercialized.[5] The fundamental process is shown in more detail in the accompanying box.

INTRODUCTION OF GM FOODS IN THE MARKETPLACE

In May 1994 a GM tomato was the first to enter the U.S. market. It was called SavrFlavr and developed by Calgene Inc. (a California firm), later acquired by Monsanto Company. This tomato could be picked vine ripened and was claimed by the company to retain its flavor from farmer to consumer. It did not sell well largely because consumers thought the taste was unsatisfactory and it cost too much.[6] The first GM food product introduced in the European market was a tomato paste bred by Zeneca (a Swiss firm) in the spring of 1996. This product was designed to deteriorate more slowly than similar non-GM foods and was well received by consumers. A few months later, Monsanto introduced in the U.K. market a new GM soybean called Roundup Ready, which can resist a powerful pesticide called Roundup, also produced by Monsanto. Roundup can kill virtually any green plant. With this product, a farmer plants Roundup Ready soybeans knowing that spraying fields will

---

[2] Nancy Wride, "The Knott Family Legacy, *Los Angeles Times Magazine,* July 15, 2001.
[3] Jane Rissler and Margaret Mellon, *The Ecological Risks of Engineered Crops* (Cambridge, MA: MIT Press, 1996), p. 9.

[4] Laura Tangle, "How to Create a Life without Sex," *U.S. News & World Report,* July 2, 1999.
[5] For a scientific explanation of the process, see Committee on Genetically Modified Pest-Protected Plants, Board on Agriculture and Natural Resources, National Research Council, *Genetically Modified Pest-Protected Plants: Science and Regulation* (Washington, DC: National Academy Press, 2000).
[6] For a complete story of this product from one who was involved through its life, see Belinda Martineau, *First Fruit* (New York: McGraw-Hill, 2001).

Genetic Engineering

Advances in a number of fields have allowed agricultural scientists to take genetic material responsible for a desired trait — from any plant, animal, insect, bacterium or virus — and introduce it to a given crop.

HOW IT IS DONE   There are two common methods for introducing the genetic material:

1. The first uses Agrobcaterium, a bacterium that naturally alters a plant's DNA. Researchers place the desired genes into the bacterium, then infect the plant. The bacterium inserts the new genetic codes into the plant's DNA. The cells are then grown to maturity, producing future generations with the desired characteristic.

PRIMARY CROPS   Wide-leafed plants like tobacco, tomato, apple and pear.

Altered genes

Cell's DNA

Modified cells grow into plants

2. The second method uses a "gene gun" to propel genetic material coating thousands of microscopic shards of tungsten into a group of plant cells. The tungsten penetrates the cells and carries the DNA to the area of the nucleus. The DNA makes its way to the nucleus and joins with the genes inside.

PRIMARY CROPS   Narrow-leafed plants like grasses and grains.

LIMITATIONS   Traits can be bred more accurately, but some complex traits remain difficult if not impossible. Also, there is some risk of achieving unexpected results.

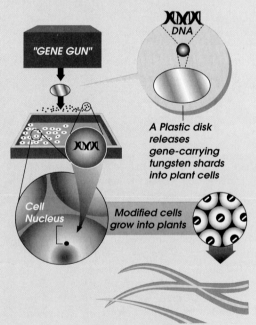

DNA

"GENE GUN"

A Plastic disk releases gene-carrying tungsten shards into plant cells

Cell Nucleus

Modified cells grow into plants

Source: Carol K. Yoon, "Reassessing Ecological Risks of Genetically Altered Genes," *The New York Times,* November 3, 1999, p. A22.

kill weeds but not harm the soybeans. Flour made from the bean found a use in many foods. This soybean and foods containing it triggered an angry storm of criticism that has continued to this day.

Despite the criticism, dozens of new GM products are being developed. For example, biotechnology companies have been working on pest-resistant crops such as apples, tomatoes, corn, cotton, canola, potatoes, sugar beets, squash, and papaya. Scientists have developed new versions of all the major food crops in the world.

GM crops were first planted commercially in the 1995 growing season, and according to the U.S. Department of Agriculture (USDA), acreage devoted to them rapidly expanded. By the spring of 2001, farmers had planted 82.3 million acres of GM crops, an 18 percent increase over the year 2000. Sixty-eight percent of all soybeans were planted with Roundup Ready seeds. This was 27.5 percent more than the previous year. Farmers planted 1.8 million acres of GM corn seed, amounting to 26 percent of total corn acreage. U.S. farmers planted 11.2 million acres of GM cotton seed, or 69 percent of total cotton acreage planted in 1999. These are remarkable numbers in light of domestic criticism and outright rejection in some foreign markets.[7]

PUBLIC DISTRUST OF GM FOODS

Consumer activists in the U.K. derided foods with GM soybean ingredients with the epithet "Frankenfoods." The Monsanto Company was the primary target of their wrath, and they called the company "Frankenstein food giant." Demonstrations took place at Monsanto's London headquarters as well as those of other companies such as Unilever and Nestlé, demanding they stop using soybeans in their products. Monsanto's test plots in the U.K. were destroyed. Objections to GM products moved to France, where similar demonstrations took place. Several McDonald's restaurants were vandalized.

At Montpelier University, a program of experiments with rice was destroyed. There was little public indignation about these events.[8]

Activist groups pressured governments in the U.K. and other European countries to place a moratorium on imports of GM soybeans. Many companies went along with the moratorium idea. Nestlé U.K. and Unilever U.K. promised to end the use of GM ingredients in their foods. Gerber and H. J. Heinz said they would not include GM corn or soybeans in baby foods. McDonald's in the U.K. told its suppliers to look for beef and chicken not raised on GM feeds and to purchase non-GM potatoes.

Part of the explanation for the aggressive anti-GM criticism in the U.K. was the unfortunate timing of the introduction of GM soybeans into the country. U.K. consumers were fearful of health threats of GM foods and concerned about adverse environmental impacts of GM plants. There were, however, other forces inflaming the public.[9] Outbreaks of different strains of salmonella and botulism made people apprehensive about food safety. Of major significance was the appearance of bovine spongiform encephalopathy (BSE), a bacterial disease causing brain tissue of cows to deteriorate. The disease was thought by many to be transmittable to humans, and consumers avoided eating beef. Tens of thousands of cattle were eventually killed to stop the spread of BSE, and some foreign countries banned the importation of British beef. Salmonella infected egg production in the U.K. The Ministers of Health banned baby milk containing high levels of aluminum. The Department of Health warned pregnant women not to eat brie and Camembert cheese because of risk of listeriosis. Slow and often inept government action on these problems sustained public distrust.

Monsanto and other major biotechnology companies failed to understand that European consumers were more skeptical of GM foods than the Americans. They sought support of government officials and farmers and assumed this would satisfy consumers. Eventually, Monsanto realized its

[7] Scott Kilman, "Use of Genetically Modified Seed by U.S. Farmers Increased 18%," *The Wall Street Journal,* July 2, 2001, p. B2, reporting USDA surveys.
[8] Robert Graham, "Concern is Mounting: Food Safety," *Financial Times* (London), June 14, 2000, p. 8.

[9] Kim Brooks, "History, Change and Policy: Factors Leading to Current Opposition to Food Biotechnology," *Georgetown Public Policy Review,* Spring 2000.

error and launched a $1.5 million advertising campaign to acquaint Europeans with the safety and benefits of GM foods. It was too late and did not lessen widespread distrust.

FUTURE DEVELOPMENTS OF GM FOOD PLANTS

Biochemical companies are currently spending billions of dollars on research, despite organized and vocal criticism of GM technology. For example, they are working on cereals tolerant of drought, plants that boost yields per acre in amounts considered impossible, rice and other plants that produce vitamins when eaten, plants that tolerate poor climate and soil conditions, plants that can grow in salty soil, fruits that spoil quickly made to delay ripening, corn that will find and poison cancer cells, fruits and vegetables that will produce vaccines against various diseases, cotton plants that grow selected colored fibers, and plants that better resist insects and viruses.

CORE ISSUES IN THE GM FOOD FIGHT

RISKS

An overarching criticism of GM plants and foods is that unknown risks are too great to take. Critics assert we do not know enough about the risks to environment and public health to accept GM plants and foods. Among the more moderate critics, for example, is Ralph Nader, who wrote: "Genetic *engineering*—of food and other products—has far outrun the *science* that must be its first governing discipline."[10]

At the other end of the spectrum of critics are those who recognize that there may be some risks but that they are no greater than in traditional food

plants. For example, the National Academy of Sciences concluded in a study of the effects of GM products that

> There is no evidence that unique hazards exist either in the use of DNA techniques or in the movement of genes between unrelated organisms. . . . The risks associated with the introduction of DNA-engineered organisms are the same in kind as those associated with the introduction of unmodified organisms and organisms modified by other methods.[11]

Gordon Conway, president of the Rockefeller Foundation, which has funded $100 million of research on bioengineered crops, added another dimension to GM risks: "the risks of GM foods seem pretty low compared with those posed by aflatoxin (a potent carcinogen) and E. coli (toxic bacteria) sometimes found in normal foods. Are organic peanuts guaranteed to be free of aflatoxin?"[12]

In dealing with environmental and other issues concerned with GM, it is important to note that generalizations are frequently less convincing than specific cases. On the latter point, the United Nations in a seminal report on world human development said

> Environmental risks in particular are often specific to individual ecosystems and need to be assessed case by case. In considering the possible environmental consequences of genetically modified crops, the example of European rabbits in Australia offers a warning. Six rabbits were introduced there in the 1850s. Now there are 100 million, destroying native flora and fauna and costing local industries $370 million a year.[13]

THE ENVIRONMENT

Critics complain that not nearly enough is known about the impact on the environment and human

[10] Ralph Nader, "Forward," in Martin Teitel and Kimberly A. Wilson, *Genetically Engineered Food, Changing the Nature of Nature* (Rochester, VT: Park Street Press, 1999), p. ix.

[11] Committee on Genetically Modified Pest-Protected Plants, *Genetically Modified Pest-Protected Plants,* p. 5.
[12] Gordon Conway, "The Voice of Reason in the Global Food Fight," *Fortune,* February 21, 2000.
[13] *Human Development Report 2001, Making New Technologies Work for Human Development* (New York: Oxford University Press, 2001), p. 4.

health of GM food plants. Prince Charles is often quoted on this point:

> I am not convinced we know enough about the long-term consequences for human health and the environment of releasing plants . . . bred in this way. . . . Major problems may, as we are assured, be very unlikely, but if something does go badly wrong the GM crops will be faced with a form of pollution that is self-perpetuating. . . . I don't think anyone knows how to clean up after that sort of incident, or who would pay for it.[14]

Critics of GM assert that these crops will devastate the environment in ways that cannot be reversed. Some specific areas of concern are gene flows that pollute other plants, toxins that kill non-target insects and birds, growth of pest-resistance plants, increased use of pesticides, and adverse impacts on agricultural ecosystems. Some defenders, such as the National Academy of Sciences, say there may be some truth to these concerns but risks are low. Monsanto Company and others claim that GM food crops can benefit the environment. For example, they claim GM crops can reduce significantly the need to use pesticides on croplands.

GENE FLOWS

Gene flow refers to the spread of pollen from GM plants, carried by wind or insects, that pollinates plants in adjacent fields. Once these plants are grown, there is no way to prevent the spread of their pollen. Furthermore, there is no way to predict precisely what will be the consequence of this pollenation. One great fear of critics is that genes from herbicide-resistant plants will spread to other related plants to produce "superweeds" resistant to pesticides. The herbicide-resistant canola plant is one major source of this fear. This form of pollination, they say, will create weeds that are expensive to control and impossible to eradicate.

To support their fears they point to instances around the world where the introduction of new species of plants introduced into an environment

stimulated the growth of unwanted weeds that created serious problems. One example is the kudzu introduced into the United States in the late 1880s as an ornamental vine to shade porches and courtyards in southern homes. In the early 1990s it was used as a forage crop. In the 1930s it was used to reduce soil erosion. It soon defied control efforts and now infests about seven million acres in the south.[15]

Advocates of GM crops maintain that risks of superweeds are small or nonexistent. A National Research Council Committee on Genetically Modified Pest-Protected Plants examined these concerns and concluded that

> Pollen dispersal can lead to gene flows, but only trace amounts of pollen are typically dispersed further than a few hundred feet. The transfer of resistance traits to weed relatives could potentially exacerbate weed problems, but such problems have not been observed or adequately studied.[16]

GM PLANTS KILL GOOD INSECTS

Some GM pest-resistant plants contain the toxin *bacillus thuringiensis (Bt)*. Critics point to a study of the monarch butterfly as indicative of the damage GM crops can cause to nontarget insects and birds. This study, made by scientists at Cornell University, reported that when monarch butterfly larvae were fed milkweed dusted with Bt pollen the result was far higher mortality than when the larvae were fed ordinary corn pollen. When the larvae were fed milkweed (which the larvae feed on) dusted with Bt maize pollen, mortality was 44 percent compared to zero when they were fed non-GM plant pollen.[17]

This result, some researchers say, must not be viewed as conclusive. For one thing, this was a laboratory study. The degree to which the results

---

[14] Prince Charles, www.princeofwales.gov.uk.

[15] Jane Rissler and Margaret Mellon, *The Ecological Risks of Engineered Crops* (Cambridge, MA: MIT Press, 1996), p. 23.
[16] Committee on Genetically Modified Pest-Protected Plants, *Genetically Modified Pest-Protected Plants,* p. 92.
[17] Indur M. Goklany, *Applying the Precautionary Principle to Genetically Modified Crops* (St. Louis: Washington University, Center for the Study of American Business, Policy Study no. 157, August 2000), p. 17.

apply to field conditions is far from clear. Furthermore, the dosage of Bt pollen fed the larvae was far higher than would exist in field conditions. Most other studies conclude that more research clearly is needed before decisive results are reached.[18]

GROWTH OF PEST-RESISTANT INSECTS

It is well known that insects exposed for a long time to insecticides such as Bt will eventually develop an immunity to the toxin. This poses many problems. One is that biotechnology companies are faced with a need to develop at considerable cost a plant with a new toxin to resist the insects. Another problem is created for farmers who must find new pesticides to control the insects.

This situation poses a regulatory problem for the Environmental Protection Agency (EPA), which has authority to control pesticides. The EPA has acted to combat the problem. For example, farmers who are growing GM corn having Bt toxins are required to plant 20 percent to 50 percent of their corn acreage with conventionally bred corn.[19]

INCREASED USE OF PESTICIDES

One important claim made by the GM industry is that its pesticide-resistant crops permit farmers to use less pesticide than on conventional varieties. Two critics who challenge this claim say, "It is estimated that this (GM pest-resistant plant) will triple the amount of herbicides used on crops, resulting in even more chemicals in our food and water."[20] Greenpeace says data from the USDA show that use of Monsanto's Roundup Ready soybeans led to a substantial increase in the use of herbicides, ranging from 11.4 to 30 percent.[21]

Bob Shapiro, CEO of Monsanto, contradicted such assertions. In a speech he gave at the Fourth Annual Greenpeace Business Conference in 1999, he said that a major benefit of biotechnology was that it reduced a current agricultural practice of excessive pesticide usage. He added,

> In recent tests . . . in India, cotton that was genetically modified to control an important pest on the crop reduced the number of insecticide sprays used by seven. In other words, there were seven insecticide sprays that are normally used in the growing seasons that were not needed at all while producing a 40 percent increase in the yield.

He went on to refer to an article by Dr. Paul Christou, a scientist at the John Innes Center in Norwich, U.K., reporting that USDA statistics clearly showed a 30 to 40 percent reduction in herbicide use with herbicide-resistant plants.[22] Ronald Bailey, science correspondent for *Reason* magazine, supports this view. He says,

> With biotech corn, U.S. farmers have saved an estimated $200 million by avoiding extra cultivation and reducing insecticide spraying. U.S. cotton farmers have saved a similar amount and avoided spraying two million pounds of insecticides by switching to biotech varieties.[23]

FOOD SAFETY

Potential hazards of GE foods are high-priority targets of critics. They also, of course, are of concern to scientists, biotech companies, and consumers, not to mention protestors in the United States, the U.K., and other countries. In a June 2001 Roper poll, more than 1,000 persons were asked, "Do you think genetically modified food, also known as bio-engineered food, is or is not safe to eat?" Fifty-two percent said "not safe." Only 35 percent said "safe." When asked whether they would buy a food in the market labeled as genetically modified 57 percent said they would be less likely to purchase it. However, 34 per-

[18] Committee on Genetically Modified Pest-Protected Plants, *Genetically Modified Pest-Protected Plants*, p. 37; and Goklany, ibid., p. 17.
[19] Committee on Genetically Modified Pest-Protected Plants, ibid., p. 35.
[20] Laura Ticciati and Robin Ticciati, *Genetically Engineered Foods* (Los Angeles: Keats Publishing, 1998), p. 4.
[21] Greenpeace, "New Study Finds Monsanto Soya Means More Pesticides in the Environment," www.greenpeace.org/press releases/geneng/2001m4.html.

[22] Speech of Bob Shapiro at Fourth Annual Greenpeace Business Conference, 1999, http:newsvote.bbc.co.uk/hi/english/sci/tech/newsid_468000/468147.stm.
[23] Ronald Bailey, "Dr. Strangelunch," *Reason,* January 2001, p. 24.

cent said it would make no difference. When people were asked whether they thought the new GM foods "will be poisonous or cause diseases in people who eat them," 14 percent said "very likely," and 31 percent said "likely."[24] These numbers show the American public has misgivings.

Juan Enriquez, researcher at the David Rockefeller Center for Latin American Studies at Harvard University, and Ray A. Goldberg, an emeritus professor of the Harvard Business School, observe that when people are asked about GM foods they focus "not on the potential benefits—cures for diseases, healthier and longer lives, more nutritious foods, less pollution—but on the potential for accidents and abuse."[25] Alan McHughen, senior research scientist at the University of Saskatchewan, Canada, has written: "There have been no environmental disasters or health issues attributable to GM or GMOs (Genetically modified organisms), despite their being grown on millions of acres and consumed by millions of humans over several years."[26]

POTENTIAL ALLERGIES

Between 1 and 3 percent of adults and 5 to 8 percent of children are subject to food allergies, which can cause serious and sometimes fatal reactions. Each year, 135 people die of food allergies and thousands are treated in hospitals.[27] Most people are aware of such dangers and are, therefore, concerned about food safety when a particular food allergy is given wide publicity. This is the case with soybeans modified with a protein from StarLink corn and the Brazil nut.

In September 2000 it was discovered that StarLink corn flour was in taco shells at Taco Bell. Adventis Crop/Science, the creator of StarLink, immediately announced an agreement with three federal regulatory agencies to recall all foods containing the flour. Why?

StarLink was developed to produce a protein (Cry 9C) toxic to the corn borer. It was known that this protein could cause an allergic reaction in some people but not in animals. In 1998, when it was approved only for animal feed or nonfood use, the EPA wrote strict rules to prevent the corn protein from reaching the food chain for people. For example, all farmers who bought the corn seed were ordered to leave 600-foot buffer zones around their StarLink fields to prevent windblown pollen from reaching traditional corn fields destined for human consumption. The EPA required all farmers who bought the seed to sign a form stating they understood the restrictions and would comply.

There were consumer complaints of allergic reaction from foods produced with the corn. The Food and Drug Administration in October 2000 asked the Center for Disease Control (CDC) to investigate the human health effects of StarLink exposure. The CDC found no evidence of allergic reactions to StarLink in any of the cases of people who complained about allergic effects from it.[28] Nevertheless, StarLink was taken off the market.

In 1996 scientists were working on injecting a protein (methionine) from a Brazil nut into soybeans. The object was to enhance the nutritive value of the soybean. It was generally known that Brazil nuts caused allergic reactions in some people, so the scientists tested the nut for its allergic effect. They concluded that the protein in the soybeans would cause allergic reactions in some people, and as a result, the bean with the protein was never produced.[29]

[24] "Public Opinion Online," Roper Center at the University of Connecticut, June 26, 2001.

[25] Juan Enriquez and Ray A. Goldberg, "Transforming Life, Transforming Business: The Life-Science Revolution," *Harvard Business Review,* March–April 2000, p. 102.

[26] Alan McHughen, *Pandora's Picnic Basket* (New York: Oxford University Press, 2000), p. 260.

[27] Reported by Goklany, *Applying the Precautionary Principle,* p. 19. From U.S. Senate Committee on Agriculture, Nutrition, and Forestry, *The Science of Biotechnology and Its Potential Applications to Agriculture,* Hearings before the Committee on Foreign Relations, 106th Cong. 1st sess., October 6, 1999; www.senate.gov/-agriculture/Hearings/Hearings_1999/buc99106.htm-(11 January 2000).

[28] Center for Disease Control, *Investigation of Human Health Effects Associated with Potential Exposure to Genetically Modified Corn, a Report to the U.S. Food and Drug Administration from the Center for Disease Control and Prevention,* June 11, 2001.

[29] For further details, see Julie Nordlee et al., "Identification of a Brazil Nut Allergen in Transgenic Soybeans," *New England Journal of Medicine* 334, no. 11 (1996), pp. 688–92.

Activists have used these two cases to contend that scientists mix a variety of genes from different species, and as a result, no one knows which foods now being produced contain allergens harmful to people. Defenders of GM respond by reiterating that there have been no food disasters from GM products.

LABELING

Many consumers are becoming more aware of GM foods and risks such as those posed by Star-Link. It is not difficult to predict, therefore, that when they are asked whether they would like labeling of GM ingredients in their foods they respond affirmatively.

The European Union, Japan, and South Korea have required food labels for GM ingredients in foods. Other countries, such as Mexico, Australia, and New Zealand, are developing labeling requirements. But the United States has not required labeling. The FDA, however, has permitted companies voluntarily to label.

In 2000 the EU began requiring strict labeling of foods whose ingredients exceeded a 1 percent limit on genetically engineered content. This requirement and prior restrictions of other countries, especially the U.K., have effectively blocked the import of many GM products to Europe. Japan decided to label all GM foods but specified a limit of 2 to 5 percent of GM ingredients before mandatory labeling. A U.N. commission called the Codex Alimentarious Commission is working on labeling requirements for GM foods.

A wide range of organizations opposes mandatory labeling of GM ingredients in food from corporations to the U.S. Congress. Many reasons are given for opposition. For example, such labeling would raise costs, resulting in higher prices to consumers or a reduction of profits, or both. There are questions about how informative such information on labels would be for consumers. For example, companies fear that labeling could convey irrelevant information, such as warning of a potential danger, and turn consumers away from the product. Anyway, opponents of labeling assert the current system of regulation is operating effectively.[30]

Nevertheless, as noted above, consumers favor labeling. Some shareholders have taken the issue directly to corporations at annual shareholder meetings. The Interfaith Center on Corporate Responsibility reports that by mid-2001, 18 companies received resolutions for labeling. A surprising number of shareholders voted for such resolutions. At Kroger, for example, 15 percent favored a labeling resolution. This is the highest favorable vote so far for a GM resolution.[31]

REGULATING GM FOODS

Critics of GM plants and foods, from radical environmentalists to reputable scientists and even some companies, have called for more government regulation. Their demands range from banning sale of GM foods to selected reforms. Critics were partially successful in the late 1990s in Europe in persuading governments to ban certain GM foods, such as Monsanto's soybeans. The U.K. was the first country to enact a moratorium on some GM foods. Other countries, such as France, Japan, Brazil, and Australia, followed.[32] In April 2001 the EU Parliament passed a measure that would put new strict rules on planting and sale of GM crops and foods.

Critics failed to get the U.S. government to place a moratorium on GM plants and foods, but pressures continue for stricter regulations. There are three federal agencies in the United States overseeing the safety of GM plants and foods: the USDA, the FDA, and the EPA. Each operates

---

[30] For an extended discussion of problems with labeling, see Alan McHughen, *Pandora's Picnic Basket,* chap. 12.

[31] Interfaith Center on Corporate Responsibility, "2001 Proxy Season Report," *The Corporate Examiner,* August 20, 2001, p. 1.

[32] For a brief resume of laws in various countries, see Ronnie Cummins and Ben Lilliston, *Genetically Engineered Food* (New York: Marlow & Co., 2000), chap. 5.

under many statutes, and many of these laws give these agencies considerable authority to control GM plants and foods. The USDA oversees the planting of GM crops, the FDA deals with the impact of GM ingredients in foods, and the EPA with outdoor plant technology. Companies and individuals must get government approval for field testing and report in detail their activities. The government evaluates the reports and approves or disapproves commercialization of the product.

The environment for biotechnology innovations has been more congenial in the United States than anywhere else. Indeed, the federal government has had a powerful role in funding biomedical and other fundamental research in biology, biochemistry, and genetics. These disciplines form the basis for the new biotechnology.

CRITICS VERSUS DEFENDERS: A FINAL OVERVIEW

Critics have many additional complaints. For example, they fear a loss of biodiversity in crops, the spread of disease, and the power of big corporations to risk public health to make a profit. Peter Melchett, the executive director of Greenpeace U.K., voices the position of many activists groups as follows: "Everything we've actually seen of GM food and farming so far is bad and is taking us in the wrong direction."[33]

Opposed to these critics, the defenders claim GM crops and foods have and will likely continue to have minimal and correctable negative impacts on human health and the environment but will have great benefits. Backing up the defenders is a report from the U.N. describing how GM plants can significantly increase plant yields, improve human nutrition, provide cheap medicines and vaccines and, because of all this, save millions—perhaps hundreds of millions—of lives of people throughout the world.[34] The President's Council of Economic Advisors writes that this new GM technology "has the potential to usher in a new agricultural revolution." They note that it can be particularly significant in underdeveloped countries, where an estimated 840 million people live, a large part of them suffering from malnutrition.[35]

QUESTIONS

1. How are plants and foods genetically modified? Explain the process.

2. Do genetically modified crops and foods pose a significant risk to humans? To the environment? With respect to each of these questions, what arguments are made by critics and defenders? Which side do you agree with?

3. Should the FDA mandate labeling for foods containing genetically-modified ingredients? Why or why not?

[33] "Peter Melchett: In His Own Words," Speech at the Fourth Annual Greenpeace Business Conference, London, October 8, 1999.

[34] United Nations, *Human Development Report 2001: Making New Technologies Work for Human Development* (New York: Oxford University Press, 2001).
[35] *Economic Report of the President,* Washington, DC: January 2001, p. 183.

Part Two

The Nature and Management of Social Responsibility

Chapter **Five**

Corporate Social Responsibility

Merck & Co., Inc.

Corporate social responsibility takes many forms. The story that follows stands out as extraordinary.

For centuries river blindness, or *onchocerciasis* (on-ko-sir-KYE-a-sis), has tortured humanity in equatorial regions. A parasitic worm that lives only in humans causes the disease. When bitten by the female black fly, which swarms near fast-moving rivers and streams, people are infected by the worm's tiny, immature larvae. The larvae settle in human tissue and form colonies, often visible outside the body as lumps the size of tennis balls, where adults grow up to 2 feet long. Mature adults live for 7 to 18 years coiled in these internal nodes, where they mate and release tens of thousands of microscopic new worms, called *microfilariae.* The offspring migrate from the internal nodes back to the skin, where they produce disfiguring welts, lumps, and discoloration. The resulting itch is so terrible that suicide is frequent. Eventually they migrate to the eyes, causing blindness. They renew the cycle of infection when the black fly bites a person with onchocerciasis, ingesting tiny microfilariae with the blood, and then bites uninfected individuals, passing on the parasitic larvae.

More than 17 million people have the disease, most of them in river regions of African nations. About a third of these people suffer pronounced itching, and another 770,000 are visually impaired or blind.[1] The disease saps economies by blinding and enervating workers and by driving people away from fertile, riverside land.

Until recently, no practical treatment for river blindness existed. In 1974 the World Health Organization began pesticide spraying in Africa to kill the

---

[1] Frank Richards and Donald Hopkins, "Programmatic Goals and Approaches to Onchocerciasis," *The Lancet,* May 13, 2000, p. 1663.

black fly, but it was tough going. The breeding cycle has to be suppressed for 14 years to stop reinfections. Winds carry flies up to 100 miles from the breeding grounds.

Then in 1975 scientists at Merck & Co., a pharmaceutical firm headquartered in New Jersey, discovered a compound that killed animal parasites. By 1981 they synthesized it and introduced it as a veterinary drug. Yet they had a strong hunch it also would be effective in humans against *Onchocerca volvulus,* the river blindness parasite.

Merck faced a hard decision. It cost an average of $230 million to bring a new drug to market and more to manufacture it later.[2] Yet the people who had the disease were among the world's poorest. Their villages had no doctors. Should Merck develop a drug that might never be profitable? The company chose to go ahead, largely because humanitarian and scientific goals motivated its researchers, and restraining them in a corporate culture that strongly valued innovation was difficult. Donations from governments and foundations could pay for much of the cost later, management reasoned.

Clinical trials of the drug, called *ivermectin,* confirmed its effectiveness. A single low dose dramatically reduced the population of the tiny worms migrating through the body and impaired reproduction by adult worms, alleviating symptoms and preventing blindness.[3]

Eventually, it became clear that neither those in need nor their governments could afford to buy ivermectin. So in 1987 Merck decided that it would manufacture and ship it at no cost to areas where it was needed for as long as it was needed to control river blindness. The company asked governments and private organizations to set up distribution programs.

Since then, Merck has given away more than 100 million doses in a treatment program put together by humanitarian groups with the help of the United Nations and the World Bank. With this program and continued black fly spraying, the disease is close to eradication in 11 African nations, and 25 million hectares of farmland, enough to grow food for 17 million people a year, has returned to production.[4] A new program covering 50 million people in 19 more countries is under way and aims to wipe out onchocerciasis by 2008.

For a drug company to go through the new drug development process and then give the drug away was unprecedented. However, Merck's management believes that although developing and donating ivermectin has cost hundreds of millions of dollars, humanitarianism and enlightened self-interest vindicate the decision.

[2] David Bollier, *Merck & Company* (Stanford, CA: Business Enterprise Trust, 1991), p. 5.
[3] Mohammed A. Aziz et al., "Efficacy and Tolerance of Ivermectin in Human Onchocerciasis," *The Lancet,* July 24, 1982.
[4] World Health Organization, "The Control of River Blindness: The Leopard Must Change Its Spots," press release, April 17, 1998.

In countries ravaged by river blindness, young children sometimes lead the blind by having them hold on to a stick. Merck commissioned this bronze sculpture, which stands at its headquarters in New Jersey, to symbolize the concern for humanity in its program to develop and give away a river blindness drug. Photo courtesy of Merck & Co., Inc.

Few corporations have such a singular opportunity to drive evil from human life and the mind-set to take advantage of it, but most firms today go beyond normal business to improve society in some way. Merck's donations of medicine are a stellar example of old-fashioned philanthropy the way it has been done in America since the rise of big companies. The program also pioneered a form of global social action in partnership with other nations, international organizations, and civil society groups. In this chapter we define the idea of corporate social responsibility and explain how it has expanded in meaning and practice over time.

THE EVOLVING IDEA OF SOCIAL RESPONSIBILITY

Corporate social responsibility is the duty a corporation has to create wealth by using means that avoid harm to, protect, or enhance societal assets.[5] As we explain in the following section, both the practice and the idea have broadened over time, though not without considerable resistence by business. Over time the doctrine expanded because, first, stakeholder groups gained increasing power to defeat antisocial business behavior, and second, the ethical and legal philosophies underlying it evolved to support broader action by managers. Today we see a new wave of expansion, a wave fashioning new norms and practices of corporate responsibility on a global level.

Social Responsibility in Classical Economic Theory

Throughout American history, classical capitalism, which is the basis for the market capitalism model in Chapter 1, has been the basic inspiration for business. In the classical view, a business is socially re-

[5] The phrase "corporate social responsibility" is a modern one. It did not enter common use until the 1960s, when it appeared in academic literature.

sponsible if it maximizes profits while operating within the law, because an "invisible hand" will direct economic activity to serve the good of the whole.

This ideology, derived from Adam Smith's *Wealth of Nations,* is compelling in its simplicity and its resonance with self-interest.[6] In nineteenth century America, it was elevated to the status of a commandment. However, the idea that markets harness low forms of selfishness and work them into social progress has always attracted skeptics. Smith himself had a surprising number of reservations about the market's ability to protect human welfare.[7] Thus, businesses have, in practice and more so over time, modified the strict profit-maximizing rule. Today the classical ideology still commands the economic landscape, but, as we will see, ethical theories of broader responsibility have worn down its prominences.

The Charitable Impulse of the Eighteenth and Nineteenth Centuries

The idea that corporations had social responsibilities awaited the rise of corporations themselves. Meanwhile, the most prominent expression of duty to society was the good deed of charity by owners.

Colonial era businesses were very small. Merchants practiced thrift and frugality, which were dominant virtues then, to an extreme. Benjamin Franklin's advice to a business acquaintance reflects the penny-pinching nature of the time: "He that kills a breeding sow, destroys all her offspring to the thousandth generation. He that murders a crown, destroys all that it might have produced, even scores of pounds."[8] Yet charity was a coexisting virtue, and respectability came to business owners who gave to churches, orphanages, and poorhouses. In doing this, they exemplified the historical lesson that although American commerce is often depicted as a jungle of profit maximization, people in it have always been concerned citizens.[9]

In the early nineteenth century, however, companies were not effusive in their social actions. Charity by owners continued and grew as great fortunes were made. Mostly, entrepreneurs endowed social causes as individuals, not through the companies that were the fountainheads of their wealth. One of the earliest was Steven Girard, a shipping and

---

[6] Adam Smith, *An Inquiry into the Nature and Causes of the Wealth of Nations* (New York: Modern Library, 1967), originally published in 1776.

[7] Jacob Viner, "Adam Smith and Laissez-Faire," *Journal of Political Economy,* April 1927.

[8] Benjamin Franklin, "Advice to a Young Tradesman [1748]," in *The Autobiography of Benjamin Franklin and Selections from His Other Writings,* ed. Nathan G. Goodman (New York: Carlton House, 1932), p. 210. A crown was a British coin on which appeared the figure of a royal crown.

[9] Mark Sharfman, "The Evolution of Corporate Philanthropy, 1883–1952," *Business & Society,* December 1994.

Andrew Carnegie's Philanthropy

After selling United States Steel for $250 million, Carnegie retired to devote his life to what he called "scientific philanthropy." He found this to be hard work. Every day he received hundreds of requests for money. So he developed a set of priorities for giving, listing the areas of worthy projects in order of their importance to him.[10]

1. Universities

2. Free libraries

3. Hospitals

4. Parks

5. Concert and meeting halls

6. Swimming baths

7. Churches

Eventually, Carnegie wore out and set up a philanthropic foundation in New York, endowing it with $125 million presided over by a staff paid to cull through the supplicants.

[10] Alex Groner et al., *The History of American Business and Industry* (New York: American Heritage Publishing Co., 1972), p. 206.

banking tycoon. When he died in 1831, the richest person in the nation, he made generous charitable bequests in his will, the largest of which was $6 million for a school to educate orphaned boys from the first grade through high school.[11] This single act changed the climate of education in the United States because it came before free public schooling, when a high-school education was still only for children of the wealthy.

Following Girard, others donated generously and did so while still living. John D. Rockefeller systematically gave away $550 million over his lifetime. Andrew Carnegie gave $350 million during his life to social causes, built 2,811 public libraries, and donated 7,689 organs to churches. He wrote a famous article entitled "The Disgrace of Dying Rich" and argued that it was the duty of a man of wealth "to consider all surplus revenues . . . as trust funds which he is called upon to administer."[12]

However, Carnegie's philosophy of giving was highly paternalistic. He believed that big fortunes should be used for grand purposes such as endowing universities and building concert halls like Carnegie Hall. They should not be wasted by paying higher wages to workers or giving gifts to poor people; that would dissipate riches on small indulgences

[11] The school became known as Girard College, which the senior author of this book attended; it still exists in Philadelphia.

[12] Andrew Carnegie, *The Gospel of Wealth* (Cambridge, MA: Harvard University Press, 1962), p. 25; originally published in 1901.

Andrew Carnegie (1835–1919).
Portrait by Deborah Luedy.

and would not, in the end, elevate the culture of a society. Thus, one day when a friend of Carnegie's encountered a beggar and gave him a quarter, Carnegie admonished the friend that it was one of "the very worst actions of his life."[13]

In this remark, Carnegie echoed the doctrine of *social Darwinism,* which held that charity interfered with the natural evolutionary process in which society shed its less fit to make way for the better adapted. Well-meaning people who gave to charity interfered with the natural law of progress by propping up failed examples of the human race. The leading advocate of this astringent doctrine, the English philosopher Herbert Spencer, wrote the following heartless passage in a best-selling 1850 book.

> It seems hard that a laborer incapacitated by sickness from competing with his stronger fellows should have to bear the resulting privations. It seems hard that widows and orphans should be left to struggle for life or death. Nevertheless, when regarded not separately, but in connection with the interests of universal humanity, these harsh fatalities are seen to be full of the highest beneficence—the same beneficence which brings to early graves the children of diseased parents and singles out the low-spirited, the intemperate, and the debilitated as the victims of an epidemic.[14]

Spencer approved of some charity, though only when it raised the character and superiority of the giver. Still, the overall effect of Spencer's arguments was to moderate charity by business leaders and retard the growth of a modern social conscience.

More than just faith in markets and social Darwinism constrained business from undertaking voluntary social action. Charters granted by states when corporations were formed required that profits be

---

[13] Quoted in Page Smith, *The Rise of Industrial America,* vol. 6 (New York: Penguin Books, 1984), p. 136.
[14] Herbert Spencer, *Social Statics* (New York: Robert Schalkenbach Foundation, 1970), p. 289; first published in 1850, p. 289.

disbursed to shareholders. Courts consistently held charitable gifts to be *ultra vires,* that is, "beyond the law," because charters did not expressly permit them. To use company funds for charity or social works took money from the pockets of shareholders and invited lawsuits. Thus, when Rockefeller had the humanitarian impulse to build the first medical school in China, he paid for it out of his own pocket; not a penny came from Standard Oil. Although most companies took a negative view of philanthropy, by the 1880s the railroads were an exception. They sponsored the Young Men's Christian Association (YMCA) movement, which provided decent housing and religious indoctrination for rail construction crews. A few companies also built schools and churches in company towns. Yet such actions were narrow exceptions to the reality of the 1800s that support of even the most worthy causes invited hard-to-win lawsuits.

As the twentieth century approached, classical ideology was still a mountain of resistance to expanding the idea of business social responsibility. A poet of that era, James Russell Lowell, captured the spirit of the times.

> *Not a deed would he do*
>
> *Not a word would he utter*
>
> *Till he's weighed its relation*
>
> *To plain bread and butter.*

Social Responsibility in the Late Nineteenth and Early Twentieth Centuries

Philanthropic giving was often unrelated to a company's impacts on society. As such, it was a very narrow kind of social responsibility. When industrialization created massive social problems, business was pushed to do more. Many questioned the ultimate benevolence of a doctrine as cruel as social Darwinism. Business feared calls for more regulation and sought to blunt their urgency.

By the 1920s three interrelated themes emerged to justify broader responsibility. First, managers were *trustees,* that is, agents whose corporate roles put them in positions of power over the fate of not just stockholders, but of others such as customers, employees, and communities. This power implied a duty to promote the welfare of each group. Second, managers had an obligation to *balance* these multiple interests. They were, in effect, coordinators who reconciled competing claims. And third, many managers subscribed to the *service principle,* a near-spiritual belief that individual managers served society by making each business successful; if they all prospered, the aggregate effect would eradicate social injustice, poverty, and other ills. This belief was only a fancy reincarnation of classical ideology and in itself did not broaden the idea of social responsibility. However, many of its adherents conceded that although capitalism elevated humanity, companies were still obligated to undertake social projects that helped, or "served," the public.[15]

Despite their limitations compared with modern thinking, these three interrelated ideas—trusteeship, balance, and service—expanded the idea of business social responsibility beyond simple charity. Now daily impacts on society had to be considered. Giving magnanimously long after the damage was done no longer sufficed.[16] Nevertheless, most managers of the day were not diverted from an underlying Scrooge-like mentality.

Railroad car manufacturer George M. Pullman conspicuously displayed the service principle, hiring an architect to incorporate the latest principles of science and public health in a model community for his employees called Pullman, Illinois. Pullman was lauded for bringing blissful living to workers, but his actions soon revealed that he saw the town as a way to make more money. In the depression of 1893 he laid off half the workers and cut the wages of the rest by 25 percent. Despite this, he refused to reduce house rent payments pegged to give the company a 6 percent return on its investment. When union leaders demanded rent cuts, he fired them, starting the notorious Pullman strike of 1894, a long, bloody deadlock that paralyzed the nation's economy. Although the workers no longer lived in unsanitary, crime-plagued tenements, they were now shot at by thugs hired to discourage strikers, and, as the strike dragged on, they grew malnourished from hunger. Pullman, previously known as a great humanitarian, became, in the eyes of the *Chicago Tribune,* "a cold-hearted, cold-blooded autocrat" whose "small piggish eyes" contained "the glitter of avarice."[17]

Like Pullman, there were many others for whom profits came first, service to society a distant second. One was Henry Ford, who had an aptitude for covering cruelty toward workers with a shining veneer of citizenship. In the winter of 1914 Ford thrilled the public by announcing the "Five-Dollar Day" for Ford Motor Co. workers. Five dollars was about double the daily pay for manufacturing workers at the time and seemed very generous. In fact, although Ford took credit for being bighearted, the $5 wage was intended to cool unionizing and was not what it appeared

---

[15] Rolf Lunden, *Business and Religion in the American 1920s* (New York: Greenwood Press, 1988), pp. 147–50.

[16] Wallace B. Donham, "The Social Significance of Business," *Harvard Business Review,* July 1927, pp. 406–7.

[17] Smith, *The Rise of Industrial America,* vol. 6, p. 524.

on the surface. The offer attracted hordes of job seekers from around the country to Highland Park, Michigan. One subzero morning in January, there were 2,000 lined up outside the Ford plant by 5:00 A.M.; by dawn there were 10,000. Disorder broke out, and the fire department turned hoses on the freezing men.

The few who were hired had to serve a six-month apprenticeship and comply with the puritanical Ford Motor Co. code of conduct (no drinking, marital discord, or otherwise immoral living) to qualify for the $5 day. Many were fired on pretexts before the six months passed. Thousands of replacements waited outside each day hoping to fill a new vacancy. Inside, Ford speeded up the assembly line. Insecure employees worked faster under the threat of being purged for a younger, stronger, lower-paid new hire. Those who hung on to qualify for the $5 wage had to face greedy merchants, landlords, and realtors in the surrounding area who raised prices and rents.

Ford was a master of image. In 1926 he announced the first five-day, 40-hour week for workers, but with public accolades still echoing for this "humanitarian" gesture, he speeded up the line still more, cut wages, and announced a program to weed out less-efficient employees. These actions were necessary, he said, to compensate for Saturdays off. Later that year, Ford told the adulatory public that he had started a social program to fight juvenile delinquency. He proposed to employ 5,000 boys 16 to 20 years old and pay them "independence wages."[18] This was trumpeted as citizenship, but as the "boys" were hired, older workers were pitted against younger, lower-paid replacements.

The stories of Pullman and Ford illustrate how weak was the sense of moral duty that the new service notion aroused in the leaders of some large companies. A few business leaders, however, carried out practices consistent with the new themes of business responsibility. One was General Robert E. Wood, who led Sears, Roebuck and Company from 1924 to 1954. He believed that a large corporation was more than an economic institution; it was a social and political one as well. In the Sears *Annual Report* for 1936, he outlined the ways in which Sears was discharging its responsibilities to what he said were the chief constituencies of the company—customers, the public, employees, sources of merchandise supply, and stockholders.[19] Stockholders came last because, according to General Wood, they could not attain their "full measure of reward" unless the other groups were satisfied first. In thought and action, General Wood was far ahead of his time.

Nevertheless, in the 1920s and after that, corporations found various ways to support communities. Organized charities were formed, such

---

[18] Keith Sward, *The Legend of Henry Ford* (New York: Rinehart & Company, 1948), p. 176.
[19] James C. Worthy, *Shaping an American Institution: Robert E. Wood and Sears, Roebuck* (Urbana: University of Illinois Press, 1984), p. 173.

as the Community Chest, the Red Cross, and the Boy Scouts, to which they contributed. In many cities, companies gave money and expertise to improve schools and public health. In the 1940s corporations began to give cash and stock to tax-exempt foundations set up for philanthropic giving.

The Late Twentieth Century

During this period, corporations continued to grow in size and power. Fear of this power combined with the rise of postmodern quality-of-life values to expand further the idea of corporate social responsibility. By the end of the century, the idea was broader and more widely practiced in the United States than in other nations.

An early and influential statement of the modern idea of social responsibility was made in 1954 by Howard R. Bowen in his book *Social Responsibilities of the Businessman.*[20] Bowen said that managers knew of strong public expectations to act in ways that went beyond profit-seeking and were, in fact, meeting those expectations. Then he laid out the basic arguments for social responsibility: (1) managers have an ethical duty to consider the broad social impacts of their decisions; (2) businesses are reservoirs of skill and energy for improving civic life; (3) corporations must use power in keeping with a broad social contract, or lose their legitimacy; (4) it is in the enlightened self-interest of business to improve society; and (5) voluntary action may head off negative public attitudes and undesirable regulations. This book, despite being 50 years old, remains an excellent encapsulation of the modern case for corporate social responsibility. If unburdened of its sexist title, given fresh examples, and rereleased, it would shine forth as better argued than some recent books.

Resistance to the Theory of Social Responsibility

Not everyone accepted Bowen's arguments, particularly managers who wanted to avoid the inconvenience of lower profits. Their cause was elevated to an ideological plane by conservative economists who claimed that business is *most* responsible when it efficiently makes money, not when it misapplies its energy on social projects. The best-known advocate of this view, then and now, is Nobel laureate Milton Friedman.

> There is one and only one social responsibility of business—to use its resources and engage in activities designed to increase its profits so long as it stays within the rules of the game, which is to say, engages in open and free competition, without deception or fraud. . . . Few trends could so thoroughly undermine the very foundations of our free society as the

---

[20] New York: Harper, 1953.

acceptance by corporate officials of social responsibility other than to make as much money for their stockholders as possible. This is a fundamentally subversive doctrine.[21]

Friedman argues that in a free enterprise, private-property system, a manager is an employee of the owners of the business and is directly responsible to them. Stockholders want to make as much profit as possible, so the manager's sole objective is to accommodate them. If a manager spends stockholder money on social projects, he or she is diverting dollars to projects they might not even favor. Similarly, if the cost of social actions is passed on to consumers in higher prices, the manager is spending their money. This "taxation without representation," says Friedman, is wrong.[22] Furthermore, if the price on the market for a product does not truly reflect the relative costs of producing it, but includes costs for social programs, then the market's allocation mechanism is distorted. The market will also punish corporations that add to their costs by assuming social responsibilities.

A corollary argument of Friedman is that social responsibility threatens political freedom. A company running social programs is performing both a political and an economic function. This fusion of power in the hands of corporate executives is dangerous. Moreover, if business takes on political functions it will be evaluated by political criteria and that is undesirable. Others agree with Friedman, including Peter Drucker:

> Milton Friedman's position that business should stick to its business . . . is indeed the only consistent position in a free society. Any other position can only mean that business will take over power, authority, and decision making in areas outside of the economic sphere, in areas which are or should be reserved to government or to the individual or to other institutions.[23]

The Doctrine Is Reinforced

The opposition of Friedman and adherents of classical economic doctrine to corporate social responsibility has been a principled, rearguard action. The futility of it was immediately evident when business itself articulated a vision of expanded duty. In 1971 the Committee for Economic Development, a group of corporate leaders, published a report boldly stating the case for expansive social responsibility. Society, said the re-

---

[21] *Capitalism and Freedom* (Chicago: University of Chicago Press, 1962), p. 133.
[22] "The Social Responsibility of Business Is to Increase Its Profits," *New York Times Magazine,* September 13, 1970.
[23] Peter Drucker, *Management: Tasks, Responsibilities, Practices* (New York: Harper & Row, 1973), p. 348.

port, has broadened its expectations outward over "three concentric circles of responsibilities."[24] Paraphrased, these were

- An *inner circle* of clear-cut responsibility for efficient execution of the economic function resulting in products, jobs, and economic growth.

- An *intermediate circle* encompassing responsibility to exercise this economic function with a sensitive awareness of changing social values and priorities.

- An *outer circle* that outlines newly emerging and still amorphous responsibilities that business should assume to improve the social environment broadly, even if they are not directly related to specific economic activities of the firm.

Classical ideology focused solely on the first circle. Now business leaders argued that managerial responsibilities went further. The report was followed in 1981 by a *Statement on Corporate Responsibility* from the Business Roundtable, a group of 200 CEOs of the largest corporations. It said,

> Economic responsibility is by no means incompatible with other corporate responsibilities in society. . . . A corporation's responsibilities include how the whole business is conducted every day. It must be a thoughtful institution which rises above the bottom line to consider the impact of its actions on all, from shareholders to the society at large. Its business activities must make social sense just as its social activities must make business sense.[25]

These statements from top executives undermined conservatives of the Friedman school. After they appeared, the range of social programs assumed by business expanded rapidly in education, the arts, public health, housing, the environment, literacy, employee relations, and other areas.

Corporate Social Responsibility in Other Nations

By the turn of the century, both the doctrine and practice of corporate social responsibility were most expansive in the United States. The idea developed differently elsewhere, because unique histories, cultures, and institutions combined to form distinctive social contracts.

Europe

In European nations with mixed economies, or economies where some industries are nationalized and others remain privately run, governments have taken responsibility for alleviating social problems. Traditionally, governments have used high taxes to fund broad social programs and

---

[24] Committee for Economic Development, *Social Responsibilities of Business Corporations* (New York: CED, 1971), p. 11.
[25] New York: Business Roundtable, October 1981, pp. 12 and 14.

have tried to achieve social objectives through state-owned firms. As a result, less pressure has existed in Europe than in America for private firms to address social problems voluntarily. The rise of an expansive social responsibility ideology similar to that in the United States has, therefore, been slow. European companies are more likely to believe that they have met their obligations by paying taxes and obeying laws.

Japan

In Japan, because of historical tradition and the influence of Confucianism, the idea of corporate social responsibility developed slowly. In 1868 the Emperor Meiji called on the country to modernize as a way of avoiding humiliation by stronger Western nations. Support for industry became a patriotic duty. The Japanese people, who had a long cultural tradition of loyalty to feudal lords, transferred their loyalty to companies. Since then, big companies have built housing, roads, and public facilities for workers. Japanese companies accept all-encompassing responsibility for their community of employees. However, while they cosset their workers, they lack a broad conception of societal involvement. This narrow perspective on duty is partly a consequence of Confucian values. Confucianism spells out strict ethical duties and responsibilities, but traditionally they apply only to persons in direct relationships. Thus, companies embrace responsibility for workers but do not feel as obligated to external stakeholders such as consumers. Government must legislate solutions for other groups, and corporate responsibility is then to follow the law.

Japanese culture supports an emphasis on corporate economic performance. The tax code does not make charitable contributions tax-deductible. Compared with those in the United States, stakeholder groups in Japan apply less pressure for social performance. Consumer and environmental interests have far less support. Labor unions are company-based and weak. There are few minorities in Japan, where racial purity is openly discussed as a virtue. Wide acceptance of the Confucian teaching that women are subordinate has slowed a nascent feminism. Thus, no strident civil rights movement confronts business. With the maturing of Japan's industrial society, its corporations are adopting more expansive social programs, but the Japanese idea of social responsibility is still narrower than the American.[26]

Less Industrialized and Industrializing Nations

In less developed countries, there is often no indigenous sense of corporate responsibility. Many small African and Latin American nations have massive social problems, and their economies limp along because of low

---

[26] For more about this expansion, see Richard E. Wokutch and Jon M. Shepard, "The Maturing of the Japanese Economy: Corporate Social Responsibility Implications," *Business Ethics Quarterly,* July 1999.

incomes, high inflation, weak currencies, and capital flight. Economic success is the primary duty of business in such situations.

A few less industrialized nations emphasize strong corporate social responsibility if their history, culture, and stage of development support this. One example is the Philippines, where in 1970 a group of corporations joined to fight poverty and social problems. Today there are 180 firms in Philippine Business for Social Progress, each of which agrees to give 1 percent of its net income before taxes to social programs.

India is another example. There thinking is influenced by the *doctrine of trusteeship* set forth by Mahatma Gandhi in the 1940s. Gandhi felt that all money and property belong to society. Rich people and companies hold their wealth in trust and are obligated to use it for social welfare.

> Suppose I have earned a fair amount of wealth. . . . I must know that all that belongs to me is the right to an honourable livelihood no better than that enjoyed by millions of others. The rest of my wealth belongs to the community and must be used for the welfare of the community.[27]

Since the mid-1960s, Indian business groups have produced a series of statements that connect Gandhi's doctrine to the ideology of business responsibility. As a result, Indian companies undertake widespread and significant social actions to an extent unusual for a developing nation.

ENTERING THE TWENTY-FIRST CENTURY: GLOBAL CITIZENSHIP

Today the environment of transnational corporations supports further expansion of corporate social responsibility to a global plane. Trade is expanding. Economic interdependence is increasing. Corporations are becoming larger, more transnational, and less subject to the controls of individual nations, even as their impact on peoples and cultures grows. International law is imbalanced; commercial rights are extensively protected, but social duties of corporations are little codified. Negative aspects of globalization persist. Markets have not overcome severe poverty, wide inequality, deprivations of human rights, rampant corruption, environmental damage, and lack of access by most of the world's population to leading technology.

In this situation, a moral argument exists that the widened trade freedoms of transnational firms imply a stronger obligation to protect and enhance global society. Pressures are rising on corporations to expand social programs internationally, including heightened stakeholder expectations,

[27] In *Young India,* November 6, 1932, quoted in K. M. Mital, *Social Responsibilities of Business* (Delhi: Chanakya Publications, 1988), p. 134.

threats of new regulation, the spotlight thrown on operations by the Internet, campaigns by activist groups, and moral exhortations by international agencies such as the United Nations.

The United Nations and the Global Compact

The United Nations promotes the idea of *global corporate citizenship,* meaning that transnational corporations have both rights and duties in an emerging global society in which they operate.[28] In this new global society, corporations must recognize a set of social values transcending those of single countries and, indeed, even conflicting with the norms of some countries. The term global corporate citizenship, with its emphasis on transnational rights and duties, is intended to be broader than the term corporate social responsibility, which some argue refers mainly to corporate obligations in home countries. This is a hairsplitting semantic distinction, but it does serve to emphasize the expansion of the idea.[29]

In a 1999 speech, U.N. Secretary-General Kofi Annan challenged the leaders of global corporations to "embrace and enact" a set of "universal values" by signing the Global Compact. The Global Compact is a set of nine principles distilled from several statements of rights proclaimed under U.N. auspices over many years (see the accompanying box). Corporations that join agree to write these principles into their mission statements, apply them in their operations, and publicize their concrete progress on a U.N. website.[30] Annan emphasized that the Global Compact is not a rigid set of rules nor a legally binding code with bureaucratic compliance requirements. Corporations do not even sign anything when they join. It is, rather, a way of getting companies to apply widely agreed-upon principles to individual situations. "We have to choose," said Annan, "between a global market driven only by calculations of short-term profit, and one which has a human face."[31]

More than 300 corporations have signed on, including BP Amoco, DuPont, DaimlerChrysler, Royal Dutch/Shell, and Unilever. However, some activists oppose the Global Compact because they think it is toothless. Since fidelity to the nine principles is not enforced, they believe that corporations engage in what they call "bluewashing," a word that references the color of the U.N. flag, a powerful, worldwide symbol of peace and justice.

---

[28] United Nations Commission on Trade and Development, *World Investment Report 1999* (New York: U.N., 1999), pp. 352–53.

[29] For analysis of semantic distinctions, see Jeanne M. Logsdon and Donna J. Wood, "Business Citizenship: From Domestic to Global Level of Analysis," *Business Ethics Quarterly,* April 2002, pp. 157–60.

[30] The website is www.unglobalcompact.org.

[31] Quotes in this paragraph are from Annan's "A Compact for the New Century," speech at the World Economic Forum, Davos, Switzerland, January 31, 1999, at www.un.org/partners/business/davos.htm.

The Global Compact Principles

In the area of human rights, businesses should:

1. Support and respect the protection of internationally proclaimed human rights.

2. Make sure they are not complicit in human rights abuses.

In the area of labour, businesses should:

3. Uphold the freedom of association and the effective recognition of the right to collective bargaining.

4. Eliminate all forms of forced and compulsory labour.

5. Work for the effective abolition of child labour.

6. Eliminate discrimination in respect of employment and occupation.

And in the area of the environment, businesses should:

7. Support a precautionary approach to environmental challenges.

8. Undertake initiatives to promote greater environmental responsibility.

9. Encourage the development and diffusion of environmentally friendly technologies.

Sources of these principles are the Universal Declaration of Human Rights (1948), the Rio Principles on Environment and Development (1986), and the International Labor Organisation's Fundamental Principles on Rights at Work (1998).

In bluewashing, corporations use the appearance of U.N. approval to launder their commercial predations. A coalition of 70 groups monitors the actions of some Global Compact signatories, reporting violations over the Internet. Recently, for example, it berated Aventis for violating Principle 7, the precautionary principle, by selling genetically engineered StarLink corn.[32]

Proliferating Codes of Corporate Conduct

The Global Compact is not the only global conduct code for corporations. In the past decade, code-making has exploded. One estimate is that 246 codes now exist.[33] Most of these are voluntary codes written by corporations, but there are many others. To oversimplify, there are four categories of such codes based on their origin.

Single Corporation Codes

Many U.S. corporations have codes of conduct that specifically address global operations, including, for example, Caterpillar, Procter & Gamble, Levi Strauss, and Unocal. Fewer European and Asian transnationals

[32] See www.corpwatch.org/un/updates/2001/gcseries.html.
[33] This is an estimate by the Organisation for Economic Co-operation and Development reported by Gary Gereffi, Ronie Garcia-Johnson, and Erika Sasser, "The NGO-Industrial Complex," *Foreign Policy,* July 2001, p. 56.

have them. Typically, these codes express a mission, duties to stakeholders, and a set of principles to guide behavior. In addition, large transnationals frequently have separate, additional codes on the environment and labor. The advantage of corporate codes is that they are voluntary and flexible approaches to corporate social responsibility. Their disadvantages are that they are often vague and lack strong implementation.

In practice, corporate codes can reflect very different philosophies. One of the oldest and best known is Johnson & Johnson's "Our Credo," written more than 50 years ago and now translated into 36 languages. A central feature is that it lists the order of the firm's responsibilities to stakeholder groups, putting customers first, employees second, communities third, and stockholders last because prioritizing duties to the first three groups should ultimately assure profits for the last. This logic is the reverse of Unilever's "Our Principles," which sets forth a duty of caring for customers, employees, and communities, but states: "Our first priority is to be a profitable business."

Corporate codes, with some exceptions, emphasize high-minded generalizations, typically lack concreteness, and rarely base their provisions on statements of global norms such as the Universal Declaration of Human Rights. They usually do not specify methods for tying stated principles into daily operations. Fewer than 1 percent of corporations with codes allow external parties to check their compliance. And public reports about code compliance (or noncompliance) are rare. Because of these shortcomings, most corporate codes engender skepticism among critics.[34] However, there is a trend toward more serious implementation and monitoring.

Industry Codes

The most developed voluntary global initiative by a major industry is Responsible Care, a set of 10 guiding principles and six codes of management practices adopted by the chemical industry. Responsible Care arose out of the need to restore the reputation of the industry. The 1984 gas leak that killed more than 4,000 people at a Union Carbide pesticide plant in India created alarm about chemical plants. In the United States, public opinion about chemical companies in general fell to abysmal lows. One survey showed only 14 percent of Americans had a favorable view of the industry.[35]

---

[34] S. Prakash Sethi, "Codes of Conduct for Global Business: Prospects and Challenges of Implementation," in *Principles of Stakeholder Management* (Toronto: University of Toronto, Clarkson Centre for Business Ethics, 1999), pp. 9–11.
[35] Andrew A. King and Michael J. Lenox, "Industry Self-Regulation without Sanctions: The Chemical Industry's Responsible Care Program," *Academy of Management Journal,* August 2000, p. 700.

To defuse pressure for more regulation, and because no single company acting alone could calm the public, the industry's trade association, the American Chemical Council (ACC), set up Responsible Care in 1988. It is a voluntary program, but chemical companies must adopt it as a condition of joining the trade association, and 180 have, including all the largest firms. They are then expected to follow more than 100 guidelines and practices, reporting on these annually to the association. Many of these go beyond legal requirements.[36] The ACC reports aggregate data for the industry as a whole. Compliance is not monitored, and there are no sanctions short of expulsion from the ACC. No firm has ever been thrown out.

The trade associations of 45 other nations have adopted Responsible Care programs, so nearly all of the world's largest chemical firms are participants. However, practices differ among countries. For example, American companies have community advisory panels for dialogue with the public, but Japanese companies do not see the need for them. American firms operating plants outside the country are not required to use U.S. Responsible Care standards; instead, they comply with host-country standards.

Environmental groups such as Friends of the Earth are critical of Responsible Care for two reasons. First, it fails to require consistent practices in all countries. Second, its main focus is accident prevention and it lacks sufficient emphasis on sustainable resource use.[37] For example, the standards do not minimize greenhouse gas emissions. The International Council of Chemical Associations, a group that represents the trade associations of many countries, is working to harmonize requirements among nations and to introduce new sustainability measures.

Codes Created by External Groups

Activist groups also write codes of conduct. Their codes would overcome the perceived laxity of corporate and industry codes by tying performance standards to norms expressed in international protocols and proclamations, by making the standards concrete and measurable, and by requiring external checks on compliance. Generally, business is not supportive of these codes, although a handful of progressive corporations work with code-writing activists. Codes written by coalitions made up of labor, human rights, religious, or environmental groups are often intended to embarrass corporations by pronouncing high ethical standards the companies cannot or will not meet. By spotlighting behavior that falls short of the code, activists weaken the corporation's reputation.[38] Two sets of standards set up by activists have gotten limited support.

---

[36] Aseem Prakash, "Responsible Care: An Assessment," *Business & Society,* June 2000, p. 184.
[37] "Michael Warhust, "Chemicals Need Global Controls," *Chemistry and Industry,* June 18, 2001, p. 368.
[38] Jarol B. Manheim, *Corporate Conduct Unbecoming: Codes of Conduct and Anti-Corporate Strategy* (St. Michaels, MD: Tred Avon Institute Press, 2000), chap. 6.

The first is Social Accountability (SA) 8000, a set of nine core standards for workplaces. A coalition of labor, human rights, and progressive business interests created it at the instigation of the Council for Economic Priorities, a group that does research to evaluate the social performance of corporations for interested investors and consumers. Standards in SA8000 require companies to accept principles in nine International Labor Organisation conventions, the U.N. Convention on the Rights of the Child, and the Universal Declaration of Human Rights. They invent a uniform global workplace standard in place of numerous self-adopted and conflicting corporate standards. The SA8000 organization trains auditors to visit workplaces and certify them as meeting standards. Fewer than 100 factories have been certified under the code, mainly contract manufacturers in Asia. No large transnational corporation has so far opened factories it owns to SA8000 certification.

The second set of standards is the CERES Principles (CERES stands for Coalition for Environmentally Responsible Economies). Galvanized by the *Exxon Valdez* oil spill, a coalition of environmental groups, socially responsible investors, and religious orders in 1989 drafted a set of 10 principles for corporate environmental responsibility. Signing corporations pledge to go beyond the law in reducing pollution, conserving resources, correcting damage, and reducing risks. They also install management practices to carry out these objectives, audit their compliance, and publish a yearly report card. About 60 companies have signed on, including Bank of America, Bethlehem Steel, Ford, General Motors, Nike, Polaroid, and Sunoco. However, most CERES companies are smaller, progressive firms such as The Body Shop and Earth Friendly Products.

The coalition introduces shareholder resolutions at company annual meetings, hoping that stockholders will vote to have their firm join. Dozens of resolutions have been introduced, but none have passed. For example, the Episcopal Church submitted a proposal to join CERES at the 2001 annual meeting of Raytheon. Raytheon management recommended a vote against it, stating that many groups, with varying priorities, advanced codes for corporations and Raytheon was better off following its own environmental policies "rather than trying to keep up with and accommodate the ever-changing agendas of these various groups."[39] In the end, only 8.7 percent of Raytheon shares were voted for the Church's resolution.

Government or Multilateral Agency Codes

There are many statements of rules and principles in the protocols and treaties signed by governments. The U.N. Global Compact, previously discussed, is a prominent voluntary code of conduct from a multilateral

---

[39] Raytheon Co., *Proxy Statement 2001*, March 26, 2001, p. 57.

The OECD Guidelines for Multinational Enterprises

GENERAL POLICIES

Enterprises should take fully into account established policies in the countries in which they operate, and consider the views of other stakeholders. In this regard, enterprises should:

1. Contribute to economic, social and environmental progress with a view to achieving sustainable development.

2. Respect the human rights of those affected by their activities consistent with the host government's international obligations and commitments.

3. Encourage local capacity building through close co-operation with the local community, including business interests, as well as developing the enterprise's activities in domestic and foreign markets, consistent with the need for sound commercial practice.

4. Encourage human capital formation, in particular by creating employment opportunities and facilitating training opportunities for employees.

5. Refrain from seeking or accepting exemptions not contemplated in the statutory or regulatory framework related to environmental, health, safety, labour, taxation, financial incentives, or other issues.

6. Support and uphold good corporate governance principles and develop and apply good corporate governance practices.

7. Develop and apply effective self-regulatory practices and management systems that foster a relationship of confidence and mutual trust between enterprises and the societies in which they operate.

8. Promote employee awareness of, and compliance with, company policies through appropriate dissemination of these policies, including through training programmes.

9. Refrain from discriminatory or disciplinary action against employees who make *bona fide* reports to management or, as appropriate, to the competent public authorities, on practices that contravene the law, the *Guidelines* or the enterprise's policies.

10. Encourage, where practicable, business partners, including suppliers and sub-contractors, to apply principles of corporate conduct compatible with the *Guidelines*.

11. Abstain from any improper involvement in local political activities.

Source: Organisation for Economic Co-operation and Development, *The OECD Guidelines for Multinational Enterprises: Revision 2000* (Paris: OECD, 2000). Reprinted with permission.

agency. Another example is the "Guidelines for Multinational Enterprises," of the Organisation for Economic Co-operation and Development (OECD). The Guidelines were written in 1976 but revised in 2000 after negotiations between corporations and activist groups. The OECD is a group of 29 nations in Europe and North America formed in 1961. Its main purpose is to boost economic growth of its members by expanding trade. However, the Guidelines emphasize that corporations must act responsibly if global economic progress is to continue.

The OECD Guidelines are the only comprehensive global code of corporate conduct endorsed by governments. Besides the 29 OECD nations,

Argentina, Brazil, Chile, and the Slovak Republic have adopted them, bringing the number of countries to 33, including the those that are home to nearly all large transnationals. The Guidelines begin with general policies (see the accompanying box). Following these are guidelines for information disclosure, employment, the environment, combating bribery, consumer protection, technology use, fair competition, and paying taxes. Recommended practices derive legitimacy from their basis in international policy statements such as the Universal Declaration of Human Rights. However, the Guidelines can hardly claim to define universal duties since most of the world's nations are not in the OECD and did not join in defining the rules.

The OECD Guidelines are often broad. For example, General Policy 11 asks that a corporation refrain from "improper involvement in local political activities." But what is "improper"? Reasonable responses will differ. Is it a large, legal campaign contribution that gives one party a financial advantage? Is it paying for the vacation of an official where laws do not prohibit such favors? Of course, ambiguity is natural in conduct codes. Provisions must be general, so their meaning invites interpretation. No compliance monitoring and no sanctions for violation exist in the Guidelines. However, governments receive complaints of violations and mediate settlements.

Support for the OECD Guidelines is mixed. In business, there are reservations about General Policy 10, to encourage suppliers and subcontractors to comply with the Guidelines. This kind of recommendation is known as a *snowball clause*, or a requirement that the corporation use its power over smaller companies to extend the reach of a code. Snowball clauses are found in other codes, for example SA8000. Managers dislike them because they imply a duty to monitor independent businesses. Unions and activists approve of the high ideals in the Guidelines, but they are skeptical about their impact given lack of enforcement by governments and believe that voluntary codes cannot substitute for regulation.[40]

Assessing the Codes

Corporate conduct codes have distinct advantages and disadvantages. On the positive side, codes that distill principles from international policy statements on human rights, the environment, and labor build recognition of global norms for commerce. As these norms jell, dodging them in weaker countries that cannot protect their citizen's rights or the environment is harder for corporations. In addition, codes address corporate behavior that has raised the hackles of activists. Their groups have succeeded in connecting trade liberalization with human rights, labor, and

---

[40] See, for example, John Sweeny of the AFL-CIO in "Putting the Guidelines to Work," *Bank Accounting & Finance*, March 2001, p. 33.

environmental abuses. Many leaders of business groups and international organizations realized that the issues raised by critics needed addressing. The U.N.'s Global Compact and the OECD Guidelines are efforts to protect the global expansion of free trade by raising corporate behavior standards. If such codes attract the support of business, governments, and activist groups, they may protect corporations from more costly and inflexible regulations down the road.

Yet codes promote mainly standards of the developed world and sometimes override political and social custom of other regions. For example, codes based on norms from International Labor Organization protocols require corporations to support collective bargaining as a basic right of workers. However, in some countries, for example, China, the government does not recognize this right. Child labor and bribery are other examples of practices where cultures differ. In addition, overgrowth of codes causes "code fatigue" among corporations.[41]

Codes are based on the agendas of entities that create them, and they mandate differing, sometimes contradictory, actions. Critics point out that they often require meeting standards of environmentalism and human rights that have evolved in the richest nations. The trade-offs encountered when imposing these high standards on the developing world are often ignored. For example, activists besieged companies, including Nike and Reebok, for contracting with small factories in Pakistan in which children made soccer balls. A storm of adverse publicity pushed the companies to do something, so they built a new, well-monitored facility that employs no children. However, the places where soccer balls used to be made suffered. Previously employed workers, mostly women and children, lost income and also lost what they, in contrast to rich-country activists, may have perceived as a lifesaving opportunity.[42] Finally, the great advantage of many codes to business, their flexibility and voluntariness, is also their great weakness. Because most codes that are acceptable to the largest corporations, including self-adopted codes, lack monitoring and external auditing requirements, cynicism about them and demands for formal regulation go on.

THE BASIC ELEMENTS OF SOCIAL RESPONSIBILITY

Three principal elements of social responsibility are market actions, externally mandated actions, and voluntary actions. Figure 5.1 illustrates the relative magnitudes of the three basic elements of social responsibility, how they have changed over three historical eras, and how they can

---

[41] United Nations Conference on Trade and Development, *World Investment Report 1999*, p. 367.
[42] Ethan B. Kapstein, "The Corporate Ethics Crusade," *Foreign Affairs*, September–October 2001, p. 110.

FIGURE 5.1
Principal Elements of Social Responsibility and Their Evolving Magnitudes

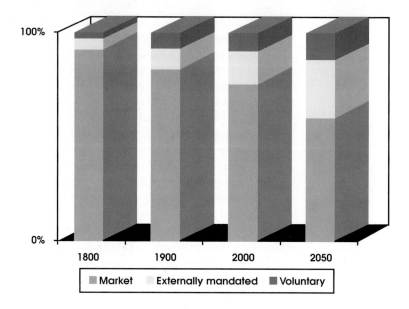

be predicted to change if the idea of corporate social responsibility continues to expand.

The first element is *market actions,* or competitive responses to forces in markets. Such actions have always dominated and will continue to do so. When a corporation responds to markets, it fulfills its first and most important social responsibility. Some critics believe that certain businesses, for instance, gambling, defense, tobacco, animal agriculture, and alcohol, are irresponsible no matter how profitable. Such value judgments do not invalidate the general rule that the overriding impact of a corporation on society—therefore, the greatest test of responsibility—is from normal market operations.

General Motors illustrates this. In 2000 it had a profit (net income) of $4.5 billion from $185 billion in sales. It employed 386,000 people in 51 countries and had a worldwide payroll of $21.6 billion. It made 8.5 billion vehicles using 30,000 suppliers and sold them through more than 14,000 dealers that employed as many as 500,000 people. GM paid $2.4 billion in taxes of all kinds. General Motors customers paid another $6.6 billion in taxes worldwide when purchasing GM products. In the United States, GM withheld an additional $3.7 billion from employees' paychecks, which it remitted to the federal government for income and social security taxes. It also paid $4.6 billion in employee benefits and $2.38 billion in benefits to its retirees.[43] These statistics illuminate the huge aggregate im-

---

[43] Figures in this paragraph are from General Motors Corporation, Form 10-K 2000, filed March 7, 2001. Figures for dealerships, dealer employees, U.S. withholding, and customer taxes paid are prorated from figures in General Motors Corporation, *1994 Public Interest Report* (Detroit: General Motors Corporation, 1994), p. 3.

pact of GM's routine, everyday business operations. Around the globe, the company directly and indirectly sustains more than a million workers and their dependents, paying billions of dollars in wages and medical benefits. It pays billions of tax dollars to governments and generates a larger sum in taxes on the sales of its products, taxes used to build and maintain societies. And it creates the cars and trucks that speed people through their lives. This broad support for economic welfare is GM's biggest social responsibility program.

The second element includes *mandated actions,* or programs required either by government regulation or by agreements negotiated with stakeholders, such as union contracts. For corporations in developed nations, the size of this element grew in the second half of the twentieth century.

GM is exposed to multiple regulations in many nations, dictating a range of decisions. For example, many regulations force GM to reduce harmful environmental impacts. Its fleet must achieve an average fuel economy of 27.5 miles per gallon (it averaged 27.9 miles per gallon in 2000). Its passenger cars must meet a noise standard of 80 decibels as measured from 50 feet away. Their tailpipe emissions must meet not only federal standards but stricter standards adopted by five states. In European Union countries, GM and other automakers must comply with a new regulation that they dismantle their "end-of-life" cars and recycle the materials in them.

The third element is *voluntary actions,* within which are three zones of action. First, there are voluntary programs that can be described as "legal plus." They go beyond regulatory mandates in areas such as minority advancement, worker safety, or pollution control. Second are voluntary programs that respond to a national consensus, such as contributing to charity or improving adult literacy. In the third zone are actions taken in areas lacking a public consensus. Few programs exist in this zone. Benetton Group discovered the reason in its recent anti-death-penalty ad campaign in the United States. Ads showing the faces of murderers on death row were intended to provoke debate on the death penalty. They did, but they also led Sears, Roebuck to drop Benetton clothing from its stores and ignited a boycott of Benetton outlets by the murdered children's relatives.[44]

General Motors undertakes many voluntary social programs. Some of these fall into the legal plus category. In 1994 GM became a signatory of the CERES Principles, which require actions and reporting standards exceeding government mandates. Other voluntary efforts commit GM to helping society in nonregulated areas. There are hundreds of such projects worldwide, many responding to duties that arise from GM's unique characteristics. As an automaker, GM is a major supporter of Mothers Against Drunk Driving, the national SAFE KIDS Campaign to educate

[44] Jerry Della Famina, "Benetton Ad Models Are Dressed to Kill Sales," *The Wall Street Journal,* March 20, 2000, p. A34.

parents about child restraints and seat belt use, and the Glow Power initiative that gives reflective armbands to British children. As a company headquartered in Detroit, GM supports a wide range of urban programs from minority scholarships to charity animal hospitals. Similar projects are supported in other countries. As the largest auto company in the United States, it has a wide range of community support programs nationwide. GM also places special emphasis on helping victims of disasters worldwide. In 1999 it raised more than $700,000 for tornado victims in Oklahoma by donating $250 to the Red Cross for every new vehicle financed through General Motors Acceptance Corporation, and it gave special deals on vehicles to residents of the disaster areas. When terrorists collapsed the World Trade Center towers, GM immediately donated $1,000,000 and more than 150 vehicles to assist rescue efforts. After an earthquake in Columbia, it donated cars and trucks worth $800,000 to deliver food and medicine. It has a special website, GM Global Aid, set up to collect donations to the American Red Cross, United Way, and other relief agencies from any person.

GENERAL PRINCIPLES OF CORPORATE SOCIAL RESPONSIBILITY

No universal rule of social responsibility applies to every company. Managers must decide carefully what their firms will do. The following are general principles to guide them.

- Corporations are economic institutions run for profit. Their greatest responsibility is to provide economic benefits. They should be judged primarily on economic criteria and cannot be expected to meet purely social objectives without financial incentives. However, corporations must incur short-run costs to correct social problems that threaten long-term sustainability. Solving social problems can sometimes be profitable.

- All firms must follow multiple bodies of law, including (1) corporation law that creates fiduciary duty toward stockholders, (2) civil and criminal law, and (3) the body of regulation that protects stakeholders. However, obeying the law is a minimum. Law is reactive and lags behind emerging norms and duties.

- Corporations have a duty to correct the adverse social impacts they cause. They should try to internalize *external costs,* or costs of production borne by society. A factory dumping toxic effluent into a stream creates costs such as human and animal disease imposed on innocents, not on the company or its customers.

- Social responsibility varies with company characteristics such as size, industry, strategies, marketing techniques, locations, internal cultures, stakeholder demands, and manager's values. Thus, a global pharmaceutical company such as Merck has a different impact on society than a local insurance company; its responsibilities are both different and greater.

- Managers should try to meet legitimate needs of stakeholders. Studies report general agreement by managers that their primary responsibilities are to three groups: customers, stockholders, and employees, with governments and communities also recognized but given lesser emphasis.[45] However, the multiple demands of stakeholders sometimes conflict, and each company must set priorities. Research suggests that the effort made by companies to respond to the primary stakeholders varies significantly between firms and between industries.[46]

- Corporate behavior must comply with norms in an underlying social contract. To understand this contract and how it changes, managers can study the direction of national and global public policy as evidenced in laws, treaties, protocols, and policy statements. They can also study the "broad pattern of social direction reflected in public opinion, emerging issues, formal legal requirements, and enforcement or implementation practices."[47]

ARE SOCIAL AND FINANCIAL PERFORMANCE RELATED?

Is there a reward for virtue? Scholars have done many studies to see if companies that are more socially responsible are also more profitable. A recent review of 95 such studies over 30 years found that a majority (53 percent) showed a positive relationship between profits and social responsibility. However, 24 percent of them found no relationship, 19 percent a mixed relationship, and 5 percent a negative relationship.[48] Overall, these studies generally support the thesis that social responsibility and profits go together. Yet since many studies have mixed, inconclusive, or negative findings, this conclusion cannot be stated with highest confidence.

[45] This is the order of priority revealed in surveys of 220 CEOs of large U.S. companies. See Linda D. Lerner and Gerald E. Fryxell, "CEO Stakeholder Attitudes and Corporate Social Activity in the Fortune 500," *Business & Society,* April 1994, table 2. See also Steven F. Walker and Jeffrey W. Marr, *Stakeholder Power* (Cambridge, MA: Perseus, 2001), pp. 24–25 and 156, for reinforcing survey results.
[46] Catherine Lerme Bendheim, Sandra A. Waddock, and Samuel Graves, "Determining Best Practice in Corporate Stakeholder Relations Using Data Envelopment Analysis: An Industry-Level Study," *Business & Society,* September 1998. This study includes the environment as a stakeholder and not government.
[47] Lee E. Preston and James E. Post, *Private Management and Public Policy: The Principle of Public Responsibility* (Englewood Cliffs, NJ: Prentice Hall, 1975), p. 57.
[48] Joshua Daniel Margolis and James Patrick Walsh, *People and Profits: The Search for a Link between a Company's Social and Financial Performance* (Mahwah, NJ: Lawrence Erlbaum, 2001), p. 10. See also Jennifer J. Griffin and John F. Mahon, "The Corporate Social Performance and Corporate Financial Performance Debate," *Business & Society,* March 1997.

The inconsistency of results from study to study is not surprising given the difficult problems of method that researchers face. To begin, because no universal definition of social responsibility fits every firm, an objective ranking of corporations as more or less responsible is impossible. Many studies use rankings of companies done by the Council on Economic Priorities or the Domini Social Equity Fund, which have liberal perspectives. Others rely on social responsibility rankings made by executives of *Fortune* 500 companies, who have a more conservative perspective.[49] It might seem that financial performance can be gauged more objectively; but among measures of profitability such as return on assets, earnings per share, or net income, which is best? In the above-mentioned review of 95 studies, the authors report that researchers drew on 27 different information sources to rate social performance and used 70 different methods of calculating financial performance. This ensures that the findings of one study will not be exactly comparable to the findings of others.

Thus, while most academic studies suggest that more responsible companies are more profitable, there are still enough methodological questions to reserve final judgment. Yet it seems fair to say that corporations rated high in social responsibility are no less profitable than lower-rated firms and are probably doing a little better.

CONCLUDING OBSERVATIONS

Historically, corporations have been motivated primarily by the classical economic ideology of profit-making. However, as they have grown in size and power, so has the sphere of their behavior called corporate social responsibility. This is because (1) the idea of corporate social responsibility as an ethical duty has expanded and (2) the power of stakeholders in the corporation's environment has grown.

Recently, both the idea and practice of social responsibility have evolved. Whereas only a short time ago the norms and power equations of individual countries defined the responsibilities of corporations, the explosive growth of global trade and global corporations now creates standards and practices of social responsibility tied to global norms and pressures. The rise of these new standards and practices is reflected in proliferating corporate codes of conduct.

The future appears to hold further expansion of corporate responsibilities. If the past is any guide, wide variation in the responses and behaviors of corporations will continue. The largest firms with internationally known brands are most vulnerable to boycotts and other stakeholder

---

[49] For an analysis of ranking systems, see Eugene Szwajkowski and Raymond E. Figlewicz, "The Social Performance Component of Corporate Reputation Ratings," paper delivered at the Annual Meeting of the Academy of Management, San Diego, CA, August 12, 1998.

pressures, and, often under pressure, they will be the first to manifest behavior in keeping with expanding public expectations.

In this chapter we focused on defining and explaining the idea of corporate social responsibility. In the next chapter we look at the methods corporations adopt to ensure that they carry out their responsibilities to society.

General Electric Company under Jack Welch

In April 1981 John Francis "Jack" Welch, Jr. became chief executive officer of General Electric. He held the position for 20 years until retiring in September 2001. During that time, he transformed GE, taking a solidly profitable manufacturing company and turning it into an exceptionally profitable conglomerate dominated by service businesses. If you had invested $100 in GE stock when Welch took the reins and held it for 20 years, it would have been worth $6,749.

Welch is lauded for his creative management style and became a national business hero. A fawning *Business Week* article called him "America's #1 Manager."[1] *Fortune* magazine gushed that GE under Welch was "the best-managed, best-regarded company in America."[2] Yet the intense, aggressive Welch made fortunes for GE shareholders using methods that had mixed impacts on employees, unions, communities, other companies, and governments. As a result, not everyone sees the GE performance as a model for corporate social responsibility. Upon Welch's retirement, the *Multinational Monitor*, a progressive magazine founded by Ralph Nader, devoted an entire issue to making "The Case Against GE." The lead editorial branded Welch as a corporate titan opposed to rules of society and said that his actions were "disastrous" for workers and communities.[3]

Did General Electric under Jack Welch carry out the full range of its duties to society? Did it fall short? Readers of this case are invited to assess how closely the company's actions conformed to ideals of corporate social responsibility found in the abstract definitions, explanations, and guidelines from this chapter.

GE'S ORIGINS

The genesis of General Electric lies in a clash between two legendary figures from separate walks of life—Thomas Edison and J. P. Morgan. In the 1870s inventor Thomas Alva Edison (1847–1931) was experimenting to find a filament that would hold up in an electric light bulb. The pre-electric era was a different world. Kerosene lamps lit cities and dwellings. Cleaning soot-covered glass chimneys and trimming wicks was a daily household chore. Every night on city streets, lamplighters moved from post to post lighting lamps. On windy nights the lamps blew out, and on moonlit nights towns with budget problems left them unlit.[4] Horse-drawn trolleys transported the crowds in hundreds of cities.

In 1879 Edison made the first commercially successful electric lamp. With the backing of J. P. Morgan he formed the Edison Electric Light Company, not only to make the lamps but to build direct current electrical distribution systems consisting of dynamos, transformers, wiring, and household sockets. Cities rushed to build central power plants where steam engines rotated shafts attached to flapping leather pulleys that turned the dynamos

[1] John A. Byrne, "Jack: A Close-Up Look at How America's #1 Manager Runs GE," June 8, 1998, p. 91.
[2] Jerry Useem, "It's All Yours, Jeff. Now What?" September 17, 2001, p. 64.
[3] "You Don't Know Jack," July–August 2001, p. 5.
[4] John Winthrop Hammond, *Men and Volts: The Story of General Electric* (Philadelphia: J. B. Lippincott, 1948), pp. 3–4.

to make current. Electric street lights appeared. Overhead wires soon hung above routes for electric trolley cars powered by Edison motors, and streets were freed of the dung from tens of thousands of horses. Buildings rose taller as Edison motors powered new elevators.

Then Edison made a great mistake. A rival company formed by George Westinghouse emerged making systems based on alternating current, and these began to drive out Edison's system. Edison stubbornly clung to his direct current model as it lost ground. As a result, in 1892 he was forced to merge with another company, and this is how General Electric was born. J. P. Morgan, who engineered the merger, plotted a reduction of Edison's influence in the new company, disposing of his top managers and dropping the word Edison so that the firm's name became simply General Electric Company. Morgan sat as a commanding figure on the new company's board. Although Edison was also a director, he attended only the first meeting and never appeared again.[5]

After the merger, General Electric and its competitor Westinghouse became a duopoly in lighting and electrical equipment, absorbing or driving out smaller companies. By 1905 GE controlled 97 percent of the incandescent bulb market. Twice the government challenged it with violating the Sherman Antitrust Act. In 1911 the company agreed to minor changes in its practices, and in 1926 it escaped completely when the Supreme Court held that both it and Westinghouse were innocent of conspiring to fix light bulb prices.[6]

Of the two big companies, GE was the more creative, and what emerged from it over the years changed American life. In the early years of the twentieth century, its motors worked the Panama Canal locks, powered battleships, and ran locomotives. GE's research lab bred a profusion of new electrical appliances, including fans, toasters, refrigerators, vacuum cleaners, ranges, garbage disposals, air conditioners, and irons. At first they were expensive, but as more people used them production costs fell and they became commodities within the reach of every family. By 1960 GE was credited with a remarkable list of other inventions, including the x-ray machine, the motion picture with sound, flourescent lighting, the diesel-electric locomotive, the jet engine, synthetic diamonds, the hard plastic Lexan, and Silly Putty.[7]

GE grew, and by 1981, just before Jack Welch took over, it had become a company of $27 billion in revenues and 404,000 employees. It was organized into approximately 50 separate businesses that reported to a layer of six sector executives at company headquarters in Fairfield, Connecticut, who in turn reported to the CEO. The company also had a large staff of researchers and planners who created detailed annual plans setting forth revenue goals and other objectives for each of GE's businesses.

JACK WELCH RISES

Most top executives come from upper-class backgrounds of wealth and privilege. Jack Welch is an exception. He was born in 1935 to working-class Irish parents in a small Massachusetts town. His father was a quiet, passive man who endured as a railroad conductor punching tickets on a commuter train. Welch's mother was a strong, dominant woman who caused her husband to wilt but instilled a strong will and drive in her son. Welch was an excellent student who attended the University of Massachusetts at Amherst and went on to get a doctorate in chemical engineering at the University of Illinois.

After graduating, he started working at a GE plastics factory in 1960, and his tremendous energy and ambition quickly became apparent. He was so competitive in weekend softball games that his aggressive play alienated co-workers and he stopped going. After one year, he threatened to quit when he got the same $1,000 raise as everyone else. He wound up staying and was promoted to higher and higher levels.

---

[5] Thomas F. O'Boyle, *At Any Cost: Jack Welch, General Electric, and the Pursuit of Profit* (New York: Knopf, 1998), p. 55.

[6] *United States v. General Electric, et al.*, 272 U.S. 476 (1926). This was a unanimous opinion written by Chief Justice William Howard Taft.

[7] Thomas F. O'Boyle, " 'At Any Cost' Is Too High," *Multinational Monitor*, July–August 2001, p. 41.

As he rose, Welch exhibited a fiery temperament and expected those around him to share his intensity. He was blunt, impatient with subordinates, and emotionally volatile. He loved no-holds-barred discussions in meetings but frequently put people on the spot saying "My six-year-old kid could do better than that."[8] With every promotion, he sized up his new staff with a cold eye and purged those who failed to impress him. "I'm the first to admit," he says, "I could be impulsive in removing people during those early days."[9] This was just preparation for the big leagues to come. GE had a polished corporate culture reflecting the eastern establishment values of its leadership over many decades. Welch did not fit. He was impatient, frustrated by the company's bureaucracy, and lacking in deference. With this mismatch GE might have repulsed Welch at some point, but his performance was outstanding. Several times he got mixed reviews for a promotion, but because of exemplary financial results he was never blocked. In 1981 he took over as CEO.

THE WELCH ERA BEGINS

Welch believes that managers must confront reality and adapt to the world as it is, not as they wish it to be. As he studied GE's situation in the early 1980s, he saw a corporation that needed to change. GE's manufacturing businesses were still profitable, but margins were shrinking. Wages of American workers were rising even as their productivity was declining. International competition was growing, particularly from the Japanese, who had cost advantages due to a weak yen. In addition, GE was bloated with layers of bureaucracy that slowed decisions and frustrated change. Although GE seemed healthy on the surface, powerful forces were gathering in the environment. The company, as currently operated, could not weather them well. It would have to change.

Welch articulated a simple guiding vision. Every GE business would be the number one or number two player in its industry. If it failed this

Jack Welch (1935–).
Portrait by Deborah Luedy.

test it would be fixed, closed, or sold. In addition, Welch said that all GE businesses would have to fit into one of three areas—core manufacturing, technology, or services. Any business that fell outside these three strategic hubs was a candidate for sale or closure. This included manufacturing businesses that could not sustain high profit margins.

In the next five years, Welch executed his strategy by closing 73 plants, selling 232 businesses, and eliminating 132,000 workers from GE payrolls.[10] As he conformed GE to his vision, he also bought hundreds of other businesses large and small. Within GE businesses he eliminated jobs through attrition, layoffs, and outsourcing. In the largest acquisition of that period, Welch acquired RCA in 1985. RCA was a giant electronics and broadcasting conglomerate with a storied history as the company that developed radio technology. After paying $6.7 billion for RCA, Welch chopped it up, keeping NBC and selling other businesses one by one, in effect, destroying the

---

[8] Jack Welch, *Jack: Straight from the Gut* (New York: Warner Books, 2001), p. 43.
[9] Ibid., p. 43.

[10] Frank Swoboda, "GE Picks Welch's Successor," *Washington Post*, November 28, 2000, p. E1.

giant company as an organizational entity. As jobs vanished, Welch got the nickname "Neutron Jack," comparing him with a neutron bomb that left buildings standing but killed everyone inside.

Welch also attacked the GE bureaucracy. One problem was its size. There were too many vice presidents, too many layers, and too many staffs who had authority to review and approve decisions. A second problem was the bureaucratic mentality in which headquarters staff practiced a "superficial congeniality" that Welch interpreted as smiling to your face and getting you behind your back.[11] He demolished the hierarchy by laying off thousands of central staff in strategic planning, personnel, and other areas. Then he set out to change GE's culture by promoting the notion of a "boundaryless" organization, or one in which ideas were freely exchanged so that organizational learning could occur rapidly. Welch compared GE to an old house:

> Floors represent layers and the walls functional barriers. To get the best out of an organization, these floors and walls must be blown away, creating an open space where ideas flow freely, independent of rank or function.[12]

Later, Welch introduced the practice of "workout" sessions in which employees in every GE business had an opportunity to confront their bosses to express frustration with bureaucratic practices and suggest more efficient alternatives. Managers in these sessions sat in front of a room filled with subordinates and had to agree or disagree on the spot to carry out suggestions. Thousands of such sessions were held to drive out the bureaucratic mentality. Welch also used Crotonville, the company's campus-like training center on the Hudson River, to meet with managers and instill his vision. He invited candid discussions, and gradually the company culture became more informal and open.

Welch introduced other initiatives that transformed GE. In 1986 he emphasized globalization. The manager of each GE business was held responsible for globalizing that business. This worked so well that by 1998 GE ranked number one in foreign assets among transnational corporations.[13] In 1990 the idea of "best practices" was introduced. GE businesses were encouraged to share ideas so that something that worked well in one part of the company could be spread to all parts. In 1996 Welch adopted companywide a statistical program called Six Sigma to eliminate defects. Finally, in 1999 he digitized GE, requiring every manager to incorporate the Internet into their operations.

DIFFERENTIATION

Welch is convinced that having the right people in management positions is the single most important cause of success in a business. Early in his career, he developed a colorful vocabulary to differentiate between players. Inept managers were "turkeys" and "dinks," standouts were called "all-stars." As CEO he reinforced strategic initiatives with a system of "differentiation" that generously rewarded managers who achieved performance goals and got rid of those who missed them. In this system, every year each GE business was forced to evaluate its managers and rank them on a "vitality curve" that differentiated among As, Bs, and Cs. The As were committed people, filled with passion for their jobs, who took initiative and exceeded performance goals. They had what Welch called "the four Es of GE leadership":

> very high *energy* levels, the ability to *energize* others around common goals, the *edge* to make tough yes-and-no decisions, and finally, the ability to consistently *execute* and deliver on their promises.[14]

The vitality curve was Darwinian. The As were the top 20 percent, Bs were the middle 70 percent, and Cs were the bottom 10 percent (see Exhibit 1). The As received salary increases, promotions, and stock options. Welch followed their careers closely. He kept large loose-leaf notebooks containing evalu-

---

[11] Welch, *Jack*, p. 96.
[12] Ibid.

[13] United Nations Conference on Trade and Development, *World Investment Report 2000* (New York: U.N., 2000), table III.1.
[14] Welch, *Jack*, p. 158.

EXHIBIT 1
The Vitality Curve

Source: Jack Welch, "Jack: Straight From the Gut," (New York: Warner Books, 2001), p. 95. © 2001 by John F. Welch, Jr. Foundation. Reprinted by permission of Warner Books, Inc.

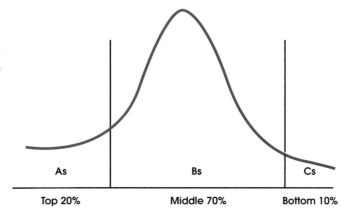

As

Bs

Cs

Top 20%   Middle 70%   Bottom 10%

ations of the top 750 of GE's 4,000 managers. Bs were considered vital to the success of the company and were coached so that some would become As. Cs were not worth wasting time on and were dismissed. The process was repeated annually, and each time the bottom 10 percent had to go. The curve applied to every GE business. No business leader could claim that his or her group was an exception, though some tried. Filling the A, B, and C categories forced difficult decisions. If 20 managers were evaluated, 2 had to be placed at the bottom and their careers at GE ended. After several years of getting rid of low performers, the leaders of GE businesses resisted classifying anyone as a C, but Welch was relentless. If they didn't identify the bottom 10 percent, he refused to carry out stock option and salary recommendations for the entire group until they did. In this way, the bar of performance was continually raised.

Welch compared people to plants. "If they grow, you have a beautiful garden," he said. "If they don't, you cut them out."[15] He disagreed with those who found the system heartless:

> Some think it's cruel or brutal to remove the bottom 10 percent of our people. It isn't. It's just the opposite. What I think is brutal and "false

kindness" is keeping people around who aren't going to grow and prosper. . . . The characterization of a vitality curve as cruel stems from false logic and is an outgrowth of a culture that practices false kindness.[16]

AN ASSESSMENT OF THE WELCH YEARS

With Jack Welch at the helm GE sustained exceptionally high rates of profitability, and shareholders were enriched. Even with five stock splits, earnings per share rose from $.46 in 1981 to $1.07 in 2000, his last full year as CEO, and total return on GE shares averaged 21.5 percent.[17] In 2000 GE reported a net operating margin of 19 percent and earned 27 percent on invested capital. These are high figures for a large transnational corporation.[18]

Welch also reshaped GE. He continuously bought and sold businesses both large and small. During his last four years alone he made more than 400 acquisitions. One underlying reason for the increasing profitability of GE is that through

[15] Quoted in Carol Hymowitz and Matt Murray, "Raises and Praise or Out the Door—How GE's Chief Rates and Spurs His Employees," *The Wall Street Journal,* June 21, 1999, p. B1.

[16] Welch, *Jack,* p. 162.
[17] Swoboda, "GE Picks Welch's Successor," p. E1; Julie Schlosser, "Jack? Jack Who?" *Fortune,* September 17, 2001, p. 52.
[18] General Electric Company, *GE Annual Report 2000* (Fairfield, CT: General Electric Company, 2001), p. 42.

EXHIBIT 2 GE Businesses Segments, Sales, and Profits in 2000

Business Segment	2000 sales (in billions)	2000 profits (in billions)
Aircraft Engines (commercial and military jet engines)	$10.8	$2.5
Appliances (refrigerators, washers, ranges, ovens, air conditioners)	5.9	0.7
Industrial Products and Systems (locomotives, lighting, electric motors, transformers)	11.9	2.2
NBC (television network with 220 affiliated stations)	6.8	1.8
Plastics (polymers, silicones, industrial diamonds)	7.8	1.9
Power Systems (power plants, gas and steam turbines)	14.9	2.8
Technical Products and Services (x-ray machines, MR and CT scanners)	7.9	1.7
GE Capital Services (credit cards, loans, insurance, aircraft leasing)	66.2	5.2
Corporate adjustments, elimination of businesses	(2.3)	
Totals	**$129.9**	**$5.2**

Source: *GE Annual Report: 2000.*

this churning of businesses GE's center of gravity shifted from manufacturing to services. The GE he inherited earned 85 percent of its revenues from manufacturing; the GE he created got 70 percent of its revenues from services.[19] Exhibit 2 shows the main business segments of GE and their contribution to revenues. The bulk of service revenue comes from GE Capital Services, but manufacturing businesses also engage in services; for example, the company not only makes aircraft engines, it services them over their lifetimes. Welch wrung profits from GE by creating a performance culture. Managers were energized. Plants grew more efficient. For instance, when Welch became CEO, GE's locomotive plant in Erie, Pennsylvania, needed 7,500 hourly employees to make 350 locomotives a year. By 2000 productivity improvements enabled 4,000 workers to make more than 900 locomotives a year.[20]

The story of the Welch years has the elements of legend. An ambitious son of working-class parents rises through hard work to command one of America's great companies, inspires managers everywhere, and becomes rich along with the company's shareholders. To reward his long-term leadership, in 2000 the GE board awarded him a salary and bonus of $16,754,019 plus a special stock award valued at $48,715,625 and options estimated to be worth a minimum of $108,130,570 over the next 10 years and perhaps much more if GE shares do well.[21] Together this package was

[19] James Flanigan, "New Boss' Challenge: To Keep GE Together," *Los Angeles Times,* August 26, 2001, p. C1.

[20] "Dignity and Defiance: An Interview with John Hovis," *Multinational Monitor,* July–August 2001, p. 35.

[21] General Electric Company, *Notice of 2001 Annual Meeting* and *Proxy Statement,* March 9, 2001, pp. 22 and 27.

worth $174 million. Beyond this wealth, Welch has accumulated 22 million shares of stock and options worth an estimated $917 million on the day he retired. This is astronomical compensation for one person, but $917 million is only two one-thousandths of 1 percent of the $460 billion in equity value created during his tenure.

Not everyone, however, sees the actions of GE during the Welch years as something to admire or emulate. Early in his career, Welch was compared with a speedboat going down a narrow canal, leaving considerable turbulence in its wake.[22] His detractors say that once Welch was at the master controls of GE he piloted the mammoth organization through global straits the same way. There is no denying positive impacts, particularly wealth creation, but also no denying negative ones.

LOSS OF JOBS

Early on, Welch was caricatured as a ruthless job cutter. When he became CEO in 1981, the corporate culture reinforced loyalty. People went to work at GE directly out of college, stayed for 40 years, retired in communities of GE people, and attended GE alumni clubs until rigor mortis set in.

As Welch remodeled GE there were mass layoffs. Within a few years, one of every four employees was gone. Welch believed that the idea of loyalty in GE's culture retarded change, so he rooted it out. At meetings he told employees it was out of fashion. He instructed staff never to use the word *loyalty* in any company document, press release, or publication. He wanted each GE manager to prove their value every day and said people who knew they could be fired worked harder.

In the Welch years there was great churning in the workforce, and no total number exists for workers who lost jobs. When he took over there were 404,000 GE employees, when he left there were 313,000. In between, tens of thousands came and went. Union leaders estimate that in his last 15 years GE eliminated 150,000 jobs in the United States through layoffs, subcontracting, and outsourcing to foreign countries.[23] Welch expressed his feelings about these layoffs in his memoirs:

> Removing people will always be the hardest decision a leader faces. Anyone who "enjoys doing it" shouldn't be on the payroll and neither should anyone who "can't do it." I never underestimated the human cost of those layoffs or the hardship they might cause people and communities.[24]

Welch stressed globalization of production to lower costs. Many jobs still exist, but they have left the United States. In 1985 the electrical worker's union had 46,000 members working at GE, but by 2001 the number had declined to 16,000. Ed Fire, the union's president, estimates that two-thirds of the 30,000 lost jobs were simply transferred to low-wage countries.[25] GE has eliminated additional jobs in the United States by pressuring its suppliers to migrate along with it. After moving production to Mexico, for example, GE Aircraft Engines held a 1999 conference in Monterrey for supplier companies and told them to cut costs by moving their facilities (and jobs) to Mexico's low-wage labor market or face inevitable loss of their GE business.[26] Says Fire:

> GE is the quintessential American corporation that has engaged in what has been referred to as the "race to the bottom"—finding the lowest wages, the lowest benefit levels and most intolerant working conditions. . . . I don't think they have given enough consideration to the consequences, particularly the human consequences, of the decisions they make. In my opinion, the decisions are designed too much to increase the company's profitability at the expense of the employees.[27]

---

22 O'Boyle, *At Any Cost,* p. 59.

23 "GE Fast Facts," GE Workers United, May 7, 2001, at www.geworkersunited.org/news/fast_facts.asp.
24 Welch, *Jack,* p. 128.
25 Ed Fire, president of the International Union of Electronic, Electrical, Salaried, Machine and Furniture Workers—Communications Workers of America, the Industrial Division of CWA, "Resisting the Goliath," *Multinational Monitor,* July–August, 2001, p. 31.
26 Robert Weissman, "Global Management By Stress," *Multinational Monitor,* July–August 2001, p. 20.
27 Fire, "Resisting the Goliath," pp. 31 and 33.

A DEFECTIVE EVALUATION SYSTEM

The vitality curve rating method is flawed. Forced ranking hurts the morale of employees who are not placed on top. At first, GE ranked employees in five categories instead of three, but it was soon discovered that everyone who failed to land in the top category was demoralized. Hence, three categories were combined into one to create the "vital" 70 percent of Bs in the middle. Disheartening classifications as 2s, 3s, and 4s were abolished. The system also hurts teamwork by pitting people against each other. It may encourage back-stabbing behavior. Its inflexibility produces unfair results when high-performing and low-performing units must classify managers the same way. The bottom 10 percent in an outstanding business may be better than middle- or top-ranked managers on a weaker team. If the sublimated murder of the bottom 10 percent goes on for many years, people who were once in the middle range may find themselves lopped off. Of course, the curve calls the recruiting system into question if recent hires are lost. Finally, finding objective performance criteria may be impossible if managers in the evaluation pool do not have identical jobs.

Forced ranking was just one source of pressure on GE managers, who were expected to meet high profit goals and knew that if there were too many mistakes or misjudgments Welch would get rid of them. His confrontational style reduced some to tears. He reportedly believed that overweight people were undisciplined. At GE businesses these people were hidden when he visited for fear they would catch Welch's eye and lose their jobs. One large manager trying to save his career had surgery to staple his colon.[28] Working at GE was also hard on marriages because of the long hours required to be a player. Welch himself divorced and remarried.

Welch's status as a management icon led other corporations to adopt similar forced rankings. Sun Microsystems, for example, uses an identical 20–70–10 percent curve. Ford Motor Company used a 10–80–10 percent curve until dropping the system in 2001 due to morale problems and lawsuits by low-ranked employees. Yet many other companies retain the system, hoping to emulate GE by raising the bar of performance. The practice has spread far. Welch tells the story of being taken aside by the manager of a Fifth Avenue store where he went to buy a sweater. The manager explained he had 20 sales workers. "Mr. Welch," he asked, "do I really have to let two go?" "You probably do," replied Welch, "if you want the best sales staff on Fifth Avenue."[29]

POLLUTION IN THE HUDSON RIVER

For 35 years several GE manufacturing plants in New York released polychlorinated biphenyls (PCBs) into the Hudson River. They followed permits that set release levels and stopped in 1977 when PCBs were outlawed because of evidence that they were toxic to humans and animals. There is widespread scientific agreement that PCBs cause cancer in test animals and probably cause cancer and a range of other illnesses in humans.

In 1983 the Environmental Protection Agency (EPA) made the Hudson River a Superfund site because more than 100,000 pounds of PCBs released by GE still lay on the river bed. Although the biggest deposits were covered by new sediments, slowing their release into the river, fish were unsafe to eat and the chemicals gradually spread downstream from hot spots of contamination. PCBs are stable molecules that persist in the environment, and because they are fat soluble, they accumulate in human tissue. The GE plants released more than a million pounds of PCBs, and most of this had already floated down 200 miles of river to the ocean, from there migrating around the planet.

The EPA and independent experts studied the river, concluding that dredging the bottom was necessary to remove the dangerous deposits. This would be extremely expensive, and GE was liable for the cost. GE objected. It sponsored studies showing that PCBs were not harmful to health, but these were rejected by the EPA and outside experts. It argued that removing the contaminated sediment would stir up embedded PCBs, doing more harm than good, but the EPA planned to

[28] O'Boyle, *At Any Cost,* p. 76.

[29] Welch, *Jack,* p. 434.

monitor the dredging to prevent this. GE undertook an extensive public relations campaign in the Hudson River region to convince the public that dredging would be an ineffective nuisance. It ran television and print ads and succeeded in dividing the public to such an extent that people began to shop only at stores where the owners supported their position and classmates teased children over their parent's views.[30] GE hired 17 lobbyists, including a former senator and six former House members, to fight a lengthy political battle against the cleanup.[31] After many years of delay, the EPA finally ordered dredging in 2001.[32] The cost to GE is now estimated at $460 million.

Environmentalists believe that Welch acted aggressively to obscure the clear scientific basis for the dredging and avoid the expense. Welch argues that "[e]xtremists have latched onto issues like PCBs to challenge the basic role of the corporation."[33]

THE GE PENSION FUND

GE has a pension fund covering 485,000 people, including 195,000 who are now retired. As the stock market rose in the 1990s, the fund rose also, and by 2001 it totaled $50 billion. Its liabilities, the future payments it must make to retirees, were only $29 million, leaving a surplus of more than $20 billion. GE's retirees and their unions requested increased benefits and automatic cost-of-living increases for pensioners, but the company has rejected these demands. By law, it does not have to raise pensions over the original obligations. Under current accounting rules, GE can put interest earned by the pension fund on the corporate balance sheet as revenue, and in recent years these earnings increased GE's net by as much as 13.7 percent.[34]

After being pressured by unions and pensioners, GE announced increases of 15 to 35 percent in 2000; but since 1965 prices had risen by 60 percent, retirees were still losing ground.[35] Helen Quirini, 81, is part of a group protesting GE's failure be more generous. After working 39 years at a GE factory, one year less than Welch's 40-year tenure, she retired in 1980 and receives $737 a month, or $8,844 a year. Jack Welch will get an annual retirement benefit of $7.9 million. As part of his retirement package, he must be available to consult up to 30 days a year at GE. On these days, he is entitled to be paid a "daily consulting fee" based on the equivalent of a day's salary during 2000. This is $45,984 per day, or $5,748 per hour based on an eight-hour day.

Welch understood that there are several benefits to GE management in letting the plan remain overfunded. First, it generates bottom-line profits. Second, these "vapor profits" increase the salaries of top GE executives, whose bonuses are tied to corporate profits. And third, the excess funding makes it easier for GE to acquire companies with underfunded pension plans. This eases deal making, but involves sharing funds set aside for GE workers and retirees with people who get a windfall coming in after careers in other companies.[36] Quirini sees GE management as "out all the time trying to figure out how to screw us" using "accounting gimmicks."[37]

CRIMINALITY AT GE

Pressure for performance tempts employees to cut corners. Welch knew this.

> If there was one thing I preached every day at GE, it was integrity. It was our No. 1 value. Nothing came before it. We never had a corporate meeting where I didn't emphasize integrity in my closing remarks.[38]

[30] John M. Glionna, "Dredging Up Ill Will on the Hudson," *Los Angeles Times,* October 1, 2001, p. A17.
[31] Charlie Cray, "Toxins on the Hudson," *Multinational Monitor,* July–August 2001, pp. 9–18.
[32] "Mrs. Whitman Stays the Course," *The New York Times,* August 2, 2001, p. A20.
[33] Welch, *Jack,* p. 283.
[34] Rob Walker, "Overvalued: Why Jack Welch Isn't God," *The New Republic,* June 18, 2001, p. 22. See *GE Annual Report 1999* and *GE Annual Report 2000,* Notes to Consolidated Financial Statements, 6, "Pension Benefits."

[35] "GE Pension Fund Story: Workers Pay, GE Benefits," GE Workers United, April 1, 2001, at www.geworkersunited.org/pensions/index.asp?ID+61.
[36] Vincent Lloyd, "Penny Pinching the Retirees at GE," *Multinational Monitor,* July–August 2001, p. 23.
[37] Quoted in Lloyd, "Penny Pinching," p. 23.
[38] Welch, *Jack,* pp. 279–80.

Yet during his tenure, GE committed a long string of civil and criminal transgressions. The *Multinational Monitor* compiled a "GE Rap Sheet," listing 39 law violations, court-ordered remedies, and fines in the 1990s alone.[39] Many are for pollution hazards from GE facilities. Others are for consumer fraud, including a $165,000 fine for deceptive advertising of light bulbs and a $100 million fine on GE Capital for unfair debt-collection practices. Still others are for defense contracting fraud, including a $69 million fine for diverting fighter contract funds to other purposes and other fines for overcharging on defense contracts.

Since GE is such a large company, technical violations of complex regulations and incidents of wrongdoing by individual managers are inevitable. The *Multinational Monitor* sees "a consistent pattern of violating criminal and civil laws over many years."[40] The key question is whether GE's malfeasance increased due to relentless performance pressure on its managers.

ASSESSING THE SOCIAL RESPONSIBILITY OF GE

Corporate social responsibility is multidimensional. No company achieves the ideal. Profit pressures and other environmental forces dictate the need for compromise. Therefore, we must weigh overall achievement against what is possible, not against perfection.

General Electric in the Welch years fulfilled its primary economic responsibilities to society. It was remarkably profitable. It paid taxes—$5.7 billion in 2000. Shareholders, including pension and mutual funds, were enriched. Many of its managers became multimillionaires in GE stock. In the Welch system, however, there was a transfer of wealth from workers to shareholders. He insulated himself from the pain this caused by rationalizing that what he did was for the greater good.

> I believe social responsibility begins with a strong, competitive company. Only a healthy enterprise can improve and enrich the lives of people and their communities. . . . That's why a CEO's primary social responsibility is to assure the financial success of the company. Only a healthy, winning company has the resources and the capability to do the right thing.[41]

General Electric engages in a broad range of community activities. In 2000 its philanthropic foundation, the GE Fund, made $40 million in grants to colleges, universities, and nonprofit groups in the United States and in other countries. The Elfun Society, a global group of GE employees and retirees, undertakes community projects, including tutoring, playground construction, repairing school equipment and recording machines for the blind, blood drives, and Special Olympics. In 2000 current and former GE employees volunteered one million hours of community service. Doing these things, GE clearly fulfills a range of voluntary responsibilities. On the other hand, the company has pressured cities, counties, and states to lower taxes by threatening to move operations elsewhere, and this lowers budgets for schools and infrastructure.

General Electric obeys the law and complies with government regulations. However, critics believe that the company is too politically powerful and that it succeeds in having many laws and regulations written in favorable ways. Jack Welch emphasized integrity to managers. There were some lapses, and some of his actions related to employees will rise to the heavens for ultimate evaluation.

QUESTIONS

1. Corporate social responsibility is defined in Chapter 5 as the corporate duty to create wealth by using means that avoid harm to, protect, or enhance societal assets. Did GE in the Welch era fulfill this duty? Could it have done better? What should it have done?

2. Does GE under Welch illustrate a narrower view of corporate social responsibility closer to Fried-

[39] "GE: Decades of Misdeeds and Wrongdoing," *Multinational Monitor*, July–August, 2001, p. 26.
[40] Ibid., p. 30.
[41] Welch, *Jack*, pp. 381–82.

man's view that the only social responsibility is to increase profits while obeying the law?

3. How well did GE comply with the "General Principles of Corporate Social Responsibility" set forth in the section of that title in the chapter?

4. What are the pros and cons of ranking shareholders over employees and other stakeholders? Is it wrong to see employees as costs of production? Should GE have rebalanced its priorities?

Chapter **Six**

Implementing Social Responsibility

Exxon Mobil Corporation, Petronas, ChevronTexaco Corporation

In 1974 an exploratory well in the southern desert of Chad struck oil. Further exploration led to the discovery of huge oil pools. Now ExxonMobil is leading a joint venture with Petronas of Malaysia and ChevronTexaco to extract the oil. The project began in late 2000 and will be completed in 2003. More than 300 wells are being drilled. Since Chad is a landlocked country, the companies have set in motion an ambitious, expensive plan to build a pipeline running 650 miles from the oil fields through the highland tropical forests of neighboring Cameroon to an offshore loading facility for tankers in the Atlantic Ocean. Among many remarkable aspects of this project is the unprecedented, detailed plan of corporate social responsibility being followed by the three companies.

The origins of this plan lie in Chad's plight. Located in central Africa, it is one of the world's poorest nations. Per capita GDP is $850 a year. Its 8 million people have an average life expectancy of 46 years, and only 3 percent of the population reaches 65 years of age.[1] It has a preindustrial economy. Although only 3 percent of the land is arable, 85 percent of people work in agriculture. In a country three times the size of California, there are only several hundred miles of paved road. Electric service is spotty. Few people have televisions, radios, telephones, or refrigerators.

Chad gained independence from France in 1960 and went through several decades of civil war characterized by bitter tribal rivalries. Today the country is in the grip of a repressive government. President Idress Déby seized power in a 1990 coup and has since then maintained relative politi-

---

[1] United Nations Development Programme, *Human Development Report 2001,* indicator tables 1 and 5.

cal stability. Limited progress toward democracy has been made. The Déby regime inaugurated a new constitution, and in 1996 the first elections were held. An overwhelming majority elected Déby, though widespread fraud was reported. In 2001, when he was reelected, human rights groups and unions in Chad called a week of national mourning for the death of democracy. On the evening of election day, Déby briefly jailed the leading opposition candidates. During his rule, state security forces have conducted a reign of terror and are accused of ethnic massacres, rapes, and beatings. Along with this political turmoil there is economic weakness. The nation's GDP is in decline.

In 1996 environmental and human rights groups learned of the big oil company project in its planning stage and drummed up a worldwide campaign to stop it. Environmentalists feared that a pipeline would degrade the pristine rain forests of Cameroon inhabited by tribes of Pygmies. They pointed to a record of environmental damage by the giant energy companies in Africa including, for example, flaring of large quantities of natural gas for which there is no commercial market. Satellite pictures of Africa taken at night show a dark continent, unlit except by the electrified cities of industrial South Africa. However, on the west coast there is a large band of light from natural gas burning into the atmosphere. The governments of Chad and Cameroon have weak environmental laws. Oversight of the companies would be weak.

Human rights groups were aghast at the prospect of billions of dollars flowing into the hands of the corrupt oligarchs and militarists in the Déby regime. In other African nations where oil and diamonds produce windfall revenues, undemocratic regimes have misused the money, diverting it from projects to help the poor and into offshore bank accounts of officials, to military spending, and to gold-plated projects such as new airport terminals that benefit only elites. As one African activist noted, "There is not one example in Africa where oil has led to development."[2] There was no reason to believe that Chad would be different.

Critics also saw potential for the abuse of corporate power. In 2000 Exxon-Mobil, Petronas, and ChevronTexaco had combined revenues of $329 billion, more than 40 times Chad's gross domestic product. Could the corrupt and unstable political system of a repressive African nation, lacking both laws and willpower, take on these giants and force them to operate responsibly?

Advocacy groups in the developed world concluded that the project should be stopped. However, they soon faced opposition from groups within Chad that abhorred the project but also knew it was the country's only hope for betterment. Economic benefits will be potentially enormous. ExxonMobil estimates that besides $3.7 billion in foreign direct investment,

---

[2] Quoted in Norimitsu Onishi, "Pygmies Wonder if Oil Pipeline Will Ease Their Poverty," The *New York Times,* July 10, 2000, p. A3.

construction of the pipeline will generate oil revenues of $5 to $8 billion over the oil field's 25- to 30-year lifetime. Chad's government budget, now about $230 million yearly, will be increased at least 90 percent by oil revenue of as much as $200 million a year. During the construction phase, nearly 7,000 jobs will be created.

Advocacy groups refocused their energies and began to think about molding the project for the better. They pressured the World Bank, which has leverage over the Chad government because of debt relief and loan arrangements, and the bank obtained an unprecedented agreement with the Déby regime that the oil revenue will be spent to benefit Chad's poor. A revenue management plan was put into law under which payments from the oil companies will initially go into a special account controlled by an independent monitoring group. The group will then disburse it to banks in Chad for expenditure on development projects. Under the plan, 72 percent of the revenues will go to health, education, agriculture, and environmental projects; 4.5 percent to development of towns near the oil fields; 10 percent to a fund for the benefit of future generations; and the remaining 13.5 percent to government expenses related to oil development, primarily loan repayments.

For its part, the consortium of companies agreed to seek approval for the project from the World Bank, based on strict policies and rules built up by the World Bank for development projects it sponsors. Although World Bank loans are only a token 3 percent of project money, the oil companies understood that without the bank's participation they faced a prolonged battle against belligerent advocacy groups. The bank's standards are designed to promote its primary goal of alleviating poverty. They also protect both the natural and sociocultural environments in less developed countries with weak and inept governments. And in the Chad project, they would shield the oil companies from raging critics.

To comply with their commitment to gain World Bank validation, Exxon-Mobil and the other companies went to extraordinary lengths. Among many actions taken, the consortium

- Prepared a 19-volume environmental impact study. The study proposed safeguards to protect fragile rain forests from ecological damage and harm due to increased logging and hunting once construction roads to the pipeline opened wild areas.

- Committed funding for an Environmental Foundation that will create two new national parks in Cameroon to compensate for wilderness land lost along the pipeline route.

- Sent trained facilitators to gatherings at more than 900 villages along the pipeline route to inform people and get comments and suggestions. The meetings led to hundreds of route and design adjustments.

- Undertook 165 consultations with Pygmy settlements in meetings attended by sociologists and representatives of advocacy groups.

- Held 145 meetings to consult with 250 international and Chadian environmental and social advocacy groups about the environmental assessment.

- Set up a website on the project containing voluminous documentation. This was done to ensure overall "transparency."[3]

- Agreed to submit quarterly and annual reports to the World Bank on progress and actions taken.

- Committed a staff of 33 people to monitor environmental impacts as the project unfolds.

The approach of the companies in Chad and Cameroon is unique in the annals of corporate responsibility. They must follow exacting standards to mitigate the project's impact on nature and society. Both companies and governments are operating under scrutiny, because two outside groups will monitor progress. A nine-member national supervisory board in Chad oversees spending of oil revenues. The board consists of five government officials and four advocacy group representatives. A six-member international advisory group audits progress of the oil field and pipeline projects and reports its findings to the World Bank.

The project sets a precedent, affirming expansive duties of transnational energy corporations in the Third World. However, it got off to a rocky start. President Déby received a $25 million bonus from the oil companies and used $4.5 million of it to buy weapons. The World Bank responded by suspending, then resuming, its debt-relief program for Chad.

In the last chapter we explained the social responsibilities that corporations have; in this one we discuss management methods used to carry them out. Few companies have guidelines for social programs that are as specific and extensive as those used by the pipeline consortium. However, many firms attempt to define a social mission and then use a range of organizational tools to implement it.

PRESSURES FOR UNDERTAKING SOCIAL PROGRAMS

There is no end to the actions that individuals, government, and organized groups want corporations to take. The point is underscored in Figure 6.1, which shows major sources of pressure for social actions. For each source there are many specific needs and demands, and they are not mutually exclusive. For example, pressures for reduction of harmful impacts on the environment come from every area. With this chart, visualizing the huge number of potential demands placed on a large multinational corporation is easy.

---

[3] The website is www.esssochad.com.

FIGURE 6.1
Pressures on
Business to
Undertake Social
Programs

KEY ELEMENTS OF MANAGING SOCIAL RESPONSE

There is no simple way to evaluate the many demands on a typical large company. Sometimes, the top executive acting alone decides how to respond. In large corporations, both functional areas and corporate staff evaluate pressures and proposals. The manufacturing function, for example, may be faced with issues related to building plants in disadvantaged areas. A corporate community affairs or public affairs staff will handle demands from communities in which the firm operates, often in the form of reports and recommendations sent in by local managers. Outside consultants can be engaged in the evaluation. The formality of the process by which social pressures are weighed and social actions carried out varies widely among companies. In some firms the process is informal, temporary, and reactive. In other firms it is highly formal, institutionalized, and anticipatory. Much depends on leadership, experience, and the nature of pressures. However, in a large corporation the following key elements are involved in implementing social programs.

Executive Leadership

Top management sets the tone for a company's social response. Commitment at the top, or lack of it, determines the extent of a wide range of organizational responses. When founders or CEOs have a strong social responsibility philosophy, it is reflected throughout the organization.

Anita Roddick, for example, developed The Body Shop as a beacon of ethical and social activism in a world darkened by capitalist greed. She believed that cosmetics was "an industry dominated by men trying to create needs that don't exist," and she devoted herself to "harnessing commercial success to altruistic ideals."[4] Many of the company's ads encourage women to accept their natural appearance. A company booklet points out that "[t]here are 3 billion women who don't look like supermodels and only 8 who do." In its products and marketing, the company fights animal testing and promotes sustainability and human rights.

There are only a handful of companies founded by social visionaries. Other examples include ice-cream-maker Ben & Jerry's and the environmentally conscious clothing firm Patagonia Inc. None of the largest transnational corporations fall into this category. In some of them, however, top management is more devoted to social issues, which is reflected in the extent of organizational response. In the 1990s Royal Dutch/Shell was assaulted by activists. It was accused of aiding a brutal Nigerian government crackdown on native peoples opposed to oil drilling, and it suffered a worldwide protest over its plan to sink a drilling platform in the North Sea. All this resulted in a boycott of the company's products at one point. At the time, Royal Dutch/Shell was perceived as an arrogant firm, fixated on commerce and disdainful of its social impacts. However, one top executive, Mark Moody-Stuart, emerged as a champion of change and led the company to set up management systems that built in greater social responsiveness. Moody-Stuart was heavily influenced by an encounter with an activist who convinced him that it was wrong to see the corporation at the center and all else revolving around it. Rather, he came to believe that the corporation was only one stakeholder dependent on a broader society. His views on human rights have also been influenced by his wife, who is a Quaker, and Royal Dutch/Shell is now one of the few large corporations to endorse the United Nation's Universal Declaration of Human Rights.[5]

Mission, Values, and Vision Statements

Many corporations write statements to express guiding philosophies. Most such statements emphasize high-quality products and profitability. R. J. Reynolds, for example, says it aspires to "meet the preferences of adult smokers better than our competitors" and to "deliver an attractive return to shareholders." However, some companies state additional purposes, for instance, protecting the environment and improving society. Kellogg Co. says that

> Social responsibility is an integral part of our heritage. We are committed to be, and be recognized as, an economic, intellectual, and social asset in each community, region, and country in which we operate.

The Kellogg statement goes on to list actions that promote its values, such as encouraging employee volunteers.

---

[4] Anita Roddick, *Business as Unusual* (London: Thorsons, 2000), pp. 97 and 172.
[5] Martha M. Hamilton, "Shell's New Worldview," *Washington Post,* August 2, 1998, p. H1.

The best mission statements are specific and explain a direction for action. The "Mission Statement" of Ben and Jerry's Ice Cream Co. includes a statement of a "Social Mission:"

> To operate the company in a way that actively recognizes the central role that business plays in the structure of society by initiating innovative ways to improve the quality of life of a broad community.

This idea of "initiating innovate ways" led over the years to creative actions. The company planted trees to replace the wood used in its popsicle sticks and donated a percentage of the sales of its Peace Pops to fund research on world peace. Unfortunately, many mission or values statements are filled with generalizations, platitudes, and motherhood statements. In a paragraph entitled "Our Vision," Bayer Corporation sets a lofty goal of "being good corporate citizens in the communities in which we work and live." However, in 14 subsequent sections the only direct elaboration on the meaning of community citizenship is a nonspecific admonition about "[t]aking an active role in the communities in which we work and live." In its "Vision" statement Ciba Specialty Chemicals Corporation asserts: "We act responsibly in environmental and social matters." Statements such as these lack specific meaning and unless top management spells out action they are like the notes of national anthems that fade away when the ball game starts.

Mission statements are increasingly popular. Ideally, they should be based on an effort to discover or shape core values that can then be articulated in a written statement. At Johnson & Johnson managers meet periodically to discuss the currency of its "Credo." Employees are also surveyed for their opinions about it. The purpose of a mission statement is to express the company's values to employees and other stakeholders. Some companies are very serious about using these statements to spread values. At children's clothing maker Hanna Andersson, managers accost workers anytime to quiz them on their knowledge of company values. If they can answer the questions they get an "I know it" button entitling them to $5 of food in the cafeteria.[6]

Issues Management

Because of the social movements of the 1960s, demands on corporations for action increased. The social environment of companies became more hostile when critics of that era generated boycotts, lawsuits, adverse publicity, and pressure for more government regulation. Managers reacted to this worsening environment by developing strategies to find and analyze issues before they could be surprised by them and the reputation of

[6] Steven Voien, ed., *Corporate Social Responsibility: A Guide to Better Business Practices* (San Francisco: Business for Social Responsibility Education Fund, 2000), p. 210.

FIGURE 6.2
The Issue Life Cycle

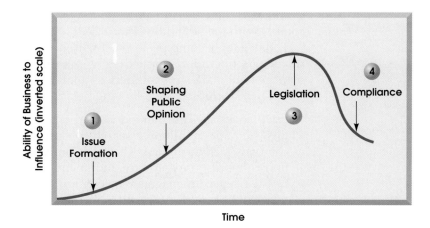

the company harmed. This is *issues management,* or the process of identifying, assessing, and tracking environmental issues. The importance of issues management is clear. There is no end to the list of actions that large companies are pressured to undertake. Some issues, if not addressed, may result in severe damage to the business. It therefore is important for a company to identify critical issues and decide what action, if any, should be taken.

The Issues Management Process

One assumption of the issues management process is that issues have a life cycle, as shown in Figure 6.2. As they form (1) they have only a narrow following. At this point, some issues, such as demands of an activist group focused on the company, are obvious. Others, however, may be vague, unfocused, and lack urgency. It is extremely difficult to predict if or when an issue will grow in importance. Events or promotion by interested groups may, sometimes after many years, cause issues to emerge in the media and get wider attention (2). When they do, debate grows; and it is on this part of the issue life-cycle curve that corporations can most effectively use public relations and communications tactics to shape public opinion. This is the point at which corporations and industries propose voluntary codes of conduct and other forms of self-regulation. Over time, strong opinions on the issue form, fewer alternatives attract support, and corporations have less ability to influence outcomes. Meanwhile, pressure on government to resolve the issue has grown strong and laws or regulations are likely to appear (3). During the legislative process or the rule-making process in agencies, corporations exert influence through lobbying, campaign contributions, coalition formation, and other methods. However, when laws and rules appear, opportunities for influence narrow to interpretation of wording and methods of enforcement. Now proposals for voluntary action are too late, options have evaporated, and the issue can no longer be "managed." The task is to comply with the new rules (4).

Today a large company is faced with hundreds of issues that could influence its operations immediately or in the future. Some have issues management staffs and committees analyzing the field using a range of techniques, including the following.

- *Intuitive search.* This method is used when a manager does a random, unsystematic, qualitative search for information about issues in the company's environment. The selection of information and its evaluation is based on experience, judgment, insight, and feel. When done by experienced managers who continuously survey the evolving environment, it is more powerful than any other technique.

- *Scenarios.* Scenarios are descriptive narratives of the future. They are written, disciplined, and structured depictions of what the world will be like based on alternative assumptions about the direction and interaction of social, political, and economic trends. Writing a single scenario is possible, but more frequently planners create several or more. As discussed at the beginning of Chapter 2, Royal Dutch/Shell is a leader in the use of scenarios, having used them for more than 25 years to predict change in the global business environment. United Distillers used the technique more narrowly, when it constructed scenarios about the future of India, where statutes and cultural values hamper sales of its Scotch whisky.[7] Well-structured scenarios force managers to contemplate the impact of current trends and the possibility of unlikely events. History teaches that there is enormous potential for surprise. Scenario learning invites preparation for discontinuities before they occur.

- *The probability/impact matrix.* In this technique, demands for social action arising from a range of issues are analyzed as to their probability and potential impact on the company. This is a powerful tool. If evaluation places a demand in the upper-left corner of the matrix in Figure 6.3, attention to it should become a high priority for the firm. If, on the other hand, a demand is judged to fall into the lower-right corner, it has low priority. Demands placed in medium-priority areas on the chart require assessment. General Electric used a matrix like this for many years in its strategic planning.

Alignment of Structure and Processes

If the structure and processes of a company are not aligned with social goals in its mission statement and strategic vision, those goals will be slighted. Organizational elements must be in place to channel aspiration and inspiration.

---

[7] Peter Bartram, "Prophet Making," *Director,* July 2001, p. 76.

FIGURE 6.3
Probability/Impact
Matrix

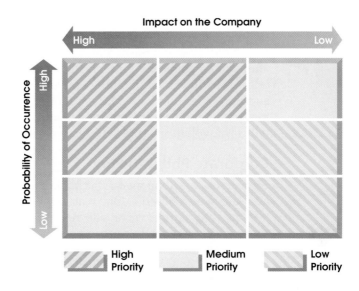

Creating committees and positions ensures that there is a location for decisions related to corporate responsibilities. Many corporations have committees at high levels charged with oversight of social actions. Examples of companies with such committees on their boards of directors are General Electric, Royal Dutch/Shell, Kellogg, Target Corporation, and 3M. When carrying out an activity is important, corporations assign a manager to do it. Starbucks and Eddie Bauer have created vice presidents of corporate social responsibility, but these are unique positions. More typically, separate departments are created for various elements of the social response, for example, environmental health and safety, equal employment, ethics and compliance, community relations, and philanthropic giving. Reebok International set up a department of human rights charged with monitoring treatment of workers in the factories that make its shoes. Training departments in many corporations educate employees about a range of social programs.

Corporations also build in social action through changes in the reward structure. In some companies, job descriptions include elements of social concern and part of a manager's compensation is based on meeting social goals. Executive pay is linked to environmental performance at Alcoa, Dow Chemical, and Phillips Petroleum. At Coca-Cola and Texaco, which have suffered highly publicized discrimination suits, pay is linked to achieving diversity goals. At Eastman Kodak, up to one-third of a manager's compensation depends on employee satisfaction and responsibility to the public.[8]

---

[8] "Linking Manager Pay to Social Performance," *Business Ethics,* March–April 2001, p. 8.

Some companies formally recognize employees who undertake social projects. General Electric sponsors the Phillippe Awards, named after a former executive distinguished in public service. Each GE business nominates annually an employee with creative or heroic community service. Recent winners include a GE Lighting employee in Rio de Janeiro who organized support for 40 elderly people abandoned by their families and a GE Power Systems employee in California who directs "GE Thursday Nights" on which GE volunteers cook and serve meals at a homeless shelter.

Corporate Philanthropy

Businesses have long made charitable contributions. Until 50 years ago the amounts were not large. One reason was that courts held that such contributions were *ultra vires,* or acts beyond the powers given the corporation by law. This restrictive doctrine was strong in the days when businesses were small and most charity came from individuals. As corporations grew big and rich, however, the public expected alms-giving from them too.

The first major break from narrow legal restrictions on giving was the Revenue Act of 1935. This law allowed corporations to deduct from taxable earnings their charitable contributions, up to 5 percent of net profits before taxes. (The Economic Recovery Tax Act of 1981 raised this to 10 percent.) Despite the Revenue Act, the legality of corporate giving remained doubtful, and charity dollars trickled slowly out of corporations because managers feared stockholder suits. Eventually, in the *A. P. Smith* case (see the accompanying box) the courts cleared away outdated rigidities in the law, freeing companies to be generous. Since then, corporations in the United States have given a larger portion of overall charitable contributions than in other nations, though their contributions still lag far behind those of individuals.

Patterns of Corporate Giving

Corporations give both from contributions budgets and through foundations. Foundations provide tax benefits, but they also attract more requests for funds. Either way, most firms do not give a significant amount compared to their potential. Only about one-third of American businesses set aside philanthropic funds; two-thirds do not even engage in active giving.[9] In 2000 the philanthropic third of the business sector gave $10.9 billion in cash and gifts of products or services. This is only a little more than 5 percent of all charitable contributions in the United States, which totaled $203 billion. Individuals gave 75 percent, or $152 billion, and the rest came from noncorporate foundations and through bequests.[10] According to a 1999 Conference Board survey, the largest

---

[9] Shirley Sagawa and Eli Segal, *Common Interest, Common Good: Creating Value through Business and Social Sector Partnerships* (Boston: Harvard Business School Press, 2000), p. 15.
[10] *Giving USA 2001* (New York: AAFRC Trust for Philanthropy, 2001).

A. P. Smith Manufacturing Company v. Barlow, et al., 13 N.J. 145 (1953)

A. P. Smith was a New Jersey corporation set up in 1896. It made valves and hydrants. In 1951 the firm gave $1,500 to Princeton University's annual fund-raising drive. This was not its first charitable contribution. It gave to a local community chest fund and had donated to other nearby colleges.

These contributions were made in a legal environment clouded by inconsistency. On the one hand was the law of corporate charters. These charters were issued by states, and corporations were not allowed to act beyond the powers expressly granted in them. The assumption in the charters was that the corporation's duty was to maximize profits for shareholders. A. P. Smith's incorporation papers, like those of most firms at the time, did not grant specific authority to make charity gifts. On the other hand was a statute. New Jersey passed a law in 1930 giving its corporations the right to make such donations if they did not exceed 1 percent of capital.

Ruth Barlow and four other angry owners of common and preferred stock thought the company had no right to give away any amount of money, because it was rightfully theirs as share-holders. They sued and in due course a trial was held. Luminaries from the business community appeared as witnesses for A. P. Smith to assert the merits of corporate charity. A Standard Oil of New Jersey executive argued that it was "good business" to show the kind of citizenship the public demanded. A U.S. Steel executive said that maintaining universities was essential to preserving capitalism. Nevertheless, the judge ruled against A. P. Smith, saying that the company had acted beyond its legitimate power.

A. P. Smith appealed. In 1953 the Supreme Court of New Jersey overturned the lower court, arguing that rigid interpretation of charters to restrict charitable giving was no longer fitting since, unlike the old days when corporations were small and had limited assets relative to individuals, they now had enormous assets and it was reasonable for the public to expect generosity from them.

The *Smith* case settled the legal question of whether corporations could give to charity. After it, the legal cloud of acting *ultra vires* dissipated, clearing the way for greater corporate giving.

portion of corporate contributions, 35 percent, went to education. Of the rest, 30 percent went to health and human services, 14 percent to civic and community causes, 9 percent to culture and the arts, and 13 percent to a variety of other areas.[11]

Few corporations have ever given enough to approach 10 percent of their pretax revenues, the level at which tax deductibility ceases. For the past 50 years, contributions have been remarkably consistent, hovering around 1 percent of earnings before taxes, rarely deviating more than two-tenths of a percent, and rising above 2 percent only in one year, 1986, when a record of 2.38 percent was set.[12] The amount given by corporations

---

[11] Audris D. Tillman, *Corporate Contributions in 1999* (New York: The Conference Board, 2000), p. 19. Percentages exceed 100 percent due to rounding.
[12] Paul Ostergard, "Should Corporations Be Praised for Their Philanthropic Efforts, Yes: A Golden Age," *Across the Board,* May–June, 2001, p. 46.

Corporations Respond to Tragedy

Within 10 days of the September 11 terrorist attacks on the World Trade Center and the Pentagon, corporations contributed $289 million to funds for victims and relief efforts. Here are the biggest givers during this time (in millions of dollars).

Lily Endowment	$30
Citigroup	$15
AXA Group	$10
Bear Stearns	$10
Carnegie Corp.	$10
DaimlerChrysler	$10

ExxonMobil	$10
Ford Foundation	$10
Johnson & Johnson	$10
Microsoft	$10
Morgan Stanley	$10
Pfizer	$10
Philip Morris	$10

Source: Anne-Marie O'Connor, "Donations Pour In for Victims of the Attacks," *Los Angeles Times,* September 21, 2001, p. A10.

is closely correlated with their profits, rising and falling from year to year with their fortunes.[13] However, cash donation statistics understate overall corporate philanthropy. They fail to include contributions that are not dollar expenditures, for example, employee volunteers, managerial talent lent to nonprofit organizations, use of facilities, reduced income from below-market loans, gifts of the company's products, and donations of used equipment. All told, noncash giving is about one-quarter of total giving.[14]

Historically, wealthy entrepreneurs contributed large sums separately from their companies. Among the pioneers were John D. Rockefeller and Andrew Carnegie. More recently, others have followed in their footsteps. Bill Gates of Microsoft is the leading philanthropist of any era. He has endowed the Bill and Melinda Gates Foundation with more than $23 billion by giving Microsoft stock that is sold and invested in a diversified portfolio. The foundation focuses primarily on supporting worldwide distribution and development of vaccines. Besides Gates, there are today other philanthropists from business making a conspicuous impact. Financier George Soros, who is best known for making $1 billion in a week by currency speculation that undermined the British pound in 1992, funds a global network of foundations to promote democracy. Since 1990 these foundations have expended almost $3 billion to fund prodemocracy groups in formerly com-

[13] Sophia A. Muirhead, *Corporate Contributions: The View From 50 Years* (New York: The Conference Board, 1999), p. 6.
[14] Ibid., p. 26.

The George Feeney Story

George Feeney, 68, is one of the greatest living philanthropists. In a technique reminiscent of the old television program "The Millionaire," he has given hundreds of millions of dollars using cashier's checks that do not reveal his name.

Feeney is an Irish-American who grew up in a working-class New Jersey neighborhood. With a partner he founded the Duty Free Shoppers stores in airports around the world. In 1984 he experienced a revelation. "I simply decided I had enough money," he told a reporter. Without even informing his business partner, he set up a foundation in Bermuda that is not subject to U.S. laws requiring disclosure of contributions. Then he irrevocably transferred his ownership interest in Duty Free Shoppers to the foundation. At the time, this was worth about $500 million; today the foundation has assets of at least $4.8 billion, making it one of the world's 10 largest.

Feeney could now be worth over $5 billion, but his personal assets are only about $5 million. According to a friend, he does not own a house or a car and wears a $15 watch. He prefers casual clothes and calls himself a "shabby dresser."

Most of Feeney's gifts go to hospitals, universities, and mainstream charities around the world.

His passion for secrecy stems from a desire to live life without constant importuning from seekers of funds and from his belief in the teachings of Maimonides, a twelfth-century philosopher who taught that the highest form of giving was anonymous and selfless. Feeney's staff painstakingly seeks out and probes charity recipients. Unsolicited requests for money are always disqualified. Feeney sometimes attends staff meetings with potential recipients, who are not told the identity of the quiet observer.

Feeney's unassuming nature stands in contrast to the publicity that goes with large gifts made by some others. However, there is a tradition of anonymous contribution in American history. Chester F. Carlson, the inventor of xerography, gave away $300 million that way in the late 1960s (in today's dollars, about $1 billion). Feeney also holds in contempt billionaires who fail to give large gifts for fear of jeopardizing their position on lists of the most wealthy.

munist countries. They played a central role in bringing down Yugoslavian president Slobodan Milosevic by supporting student organizations that fomented his overthrow.[15] In 1997 AOL/Time Warner executive Ted Turner gave $1 billion of stock in the company to the United Nations.

Most corporate donations still go to communities and causes in the United States. For instance, although GE has more foreign assets than any other firm, only 5 percent of the $40 million donated by the GE Fund in 2000 went outside the United States.[16] As the largest firms become more transnational, overseas giving has risen. However, there are formidable obstacles. Many nations lack a tradition of charitable giving. In them, nonprofits are not well developed and cannot handle large donations. Foreign tax laws often discourage gifts. And administering grants at a great distance is harder for a corporate foundation in the United States.

[15] David Holley, "The Seed Money for Democracy," *Los Angeles Times,* January 26, 2001, p. A1.
[16] The GE Fund lists international contributions of $1,787,483 in 2000. See "GE Fund Grant Initiatives," www.ge.com/community/fund/grant_initiatives/grant_lists.html.

Strategic Philanthropy

With historical roots in religious teachings, the act of philanthropy presumes a selfless motive of giving out of moral duty to benefit the needy or to improve society. Traditionally, corporate philanthropy conformed to such ideals of altruism and magnanimity. Companies, and their foundations, gave to help the destitute, underprivileged, and deserving and funded social goods such as education, culture, and the arts. Of course, there was always a measure of self-interest in these donations. It was recognized that generous giving enhanced the corporate image, elevated reputation, created goodwill, and improved the economy by enhancing society.

Strategic philanthropy is the alignment of a corporation's business mission with its charitable mission. It exists when giving is used to support both business goals and worthy causes. As corporations gained experience with philanthropic activity, many concluded that the traditional approach of scattershot giving to myriad worthy causes was noble but flawed. Over time, the number of causes grew; and as gift giving became more splintered, the shrinking sums given to each charity had little impact on problems. Results were never measured. Top executives and their spouses diverted corporate support into pet artistic and cultural projects unimportant to the firm's main stakeholders. This passive approach to philanthropy lacked any underlying logic. In addition, in the 1980s and 1990s it became awkward for companies to give money away just when they were laying off groups of employees. For these reasons, many firms decided to change their philosophy of giving from one of pure generosity to one that aligns charity with commercial objectives.

There are many examples of strategic philanthropy. Here are several:

- The General Mills Foundation was set up in 1954 after the green light of the *A. P. Smith* decision. For many years, it emphasized giving to prestigious cultural and arts programs in the Minneapolis headquarters area. In 1997, however, it decided to target its support for projects helping families, children, and youth in 22 U.S. and Canadian communities where it had facilities. This connected charity giving with the concerns of average grocery shoppers who buy Cheerios and Betty Crocker cake mixes.

- Mattel donated $25 million to put its name on the children's hospital at UCLA, now called Mattel Children's Hospital. The company has no role in running the hospital, although it gives toys to patients. Its large gift contributes to a compassionate corporate image among toy buyers. Adding the company name to the hospital increases brand recognition. These benefits reinforce the commercial goals of a toy company. A Mattel competitor, Hasbro, made a similar donation to establish Hasbro Children's Hospital in Providence, Rhode Island.[17] In both examples, the companies reinforced their commercial interests while helping sick children.

- Dell Computer Corporation has a large economic impact on central Texas, where it is headquartered and does manufacturing. It has 22,000 employees in the region and estimates it is responsible directly or indirectly for the creation of 28,000 other jobs and $5 billion in annual economic activity. Recently, Dell expanded its manufacturing to Tennessee, becoming one of that state's largest employers. The Dell Foundation only funds charities and projects in two Texas counties and two Tennessee counties where it is a major presence. In these counties it focuses on funding oriented toward youth and gives to a range of health and welfare charities. It emphasizes funding for projects that improve access to computers in schools.[18] In this way, Dell has aligned its charitable activity with the goals of strengthening the local economy and promoting use of its products among future consumers.

Not everyone approves of strategic philanthropy. The mixed motive of the corporation departs from the pure altruism found in religious parables. One critic calls it "self-serving and self-interested," just "business by other means."[19] Defenders retort that looking behind good deeds to disparage the benefactor's motive is arrogant. This raises a question. Does it matter why a corporation does a good deed?

Venture Philanthropy

Ben Cohen, the co-founder of Ben & Jerry's, is dedicated to social action. He left the company after Unilever bought it in 2000 and, with money from the sale, set up a philanthropic fund for helping poor neighborhoods. This fund—called the Barred Rock Fund since Unilever prohibited use of the Ben & Jerry's name—started by investing $5 million in a small Philadelphia cleaning products company in return for 80 percent ownership. With the injection of this money, the company's 14 workers got health insurance for the first time and wage increases of up to 23 percent. However, Cohen is not giving a passive gift like a corporate foundation engaging in either traditional or strategic philanthropy. He considers the $5 million an investment, is advising company managers, and plans to use profits from the company to buy other companies that can be helped in the same way.[20]

---

[17] Julie Edelson Halpert, "Dr. Pepper Hospital? Perhaps, for a Price," The *New York Times,* February 18, 2001, sec. 3, p. 1.

[18] An extensive list of these projects is on the Dell website at www.dell.com.

[19] Benjamin R. Barber, "Should Corporations Be Praised for Their Philanthropic Efforts, No: Always an Angle," *Across the Board,* May–June 2001, p. 49.

[20] Jim Hopkins, "Ben & Jerry's Co-Founder to Try 'Venture Philanthropy,' " *USA Today,* August 7, 2001, p. 1B.

Cohen's method is an example of *venture philanthropy*, or charitable giving as an investment that is actively managed to meet the goals of the investors. It is an attempt to bring the philosophy of venture capital, which funds entrepreneurs and new business ideas, to the world of charitable giving and nonprofits. Unlike the world of venture capital, however, the criteria for investment are not purely financial gain. The performance of the nonprofit or social entrepreneur is usually measured using nondollar indicators. Like venture capitalists, venture philanthropists such as Ben Cohen actively participate in their investments.

The software company webMethods set up a venture philanthropy foundation to invest in nonprofits that work for low-income housing in its Washington, D.C., headquarters area. The webMethods Foundation entered into a partnership with Jubilee Enterprise, a nonprofit that refurbishes lower-rent apartments. A large foundation grant supports the nonprofit, but webMethods also provides employees who volunteer their labor and give management assistance. This active support reflects the underlying feeling in the venture philanthropy movement that traditional corporate contributions are limp gestures—splintered, made largely to improve corporate reputations, and untracked for results.[21] Venture giving, on the other hand, is focused, designed for concrete change, and measured for result.

Venture philanthropy is only a tiny fraction of all philanthropy. It has received much attention recently because newly wealthy entrepreneurs in technology companies have favored it. Yet the notion is old. A prominent example of venture philanthropy is Newman's Own, a food company set up in 1982 by actor Paul Newman that donates all of its profits to a spectrum of charities, for example, summer camps for seriously ill children.

Cause-Related Marketing

Cause-related marketing is a marketing method linking a corporation or brand to a relevant social cause so that both benefit.[22] Brands are used in marketing to differentiate products, especially mass-produced products that consumers might see as interchangeable commodities if they lacked brand qualities. Companies spend heavily to endow brands with values that will attract consumers and allow them to charge a price premium. In the past, branding created attributes in the consumer's mind in two dimensions. One was a description of products and the benefits of using them that appealed to the logical mind. The other was image creation designed to engage consumers on an emotional level.

Due to the rise of postmodern values in developed markets, consumers are now more focused on social issues than in the past, and their buying decisions reflect this. A recent survey of U.S. consumers found

---

[21] Curt Weeden, *Corporate Social Investing* (San Francisco: Berrett-Koehler, 1998), chap. 3.
[22] Hamish Pringle and Marjorie Thompson, *Brand Spirit* (New York: Wiley, 2001), p. 3.

that 79 percent have taken into account the social responsibility of a company before buying that firm's product.[23] Corporations realize that if their brand is associated with a social cause it creates a third attribute dimension by appealing to the conscience of consumers. In cause-related marketing the corporation calculates it will add this ethical dimension to its brand while also doing a philanthropic good deed. Examples follow.

- In the early 1990s American Express encountered restaurant owners who felt its card fees were too high. Enough restaurants refused the cards when they were tendered that, rather than face rejection, many cardholders chose to use a competing card instead. To counteract this, the company started a cause-related marketing campaign called "Charge Against Hunger" in which it donated $.03 per transaction to nonprofit antihunger groups during the holiday months of November and December each year. The campaign created a clear link between using the card to pay for restaurant meals and fighting hunger. It raised $21 million in four years for donations to 600 antihunger groups. It also increased charge volume by 12 percent and raised the opinion of restaurant owners about the card.[24]

- In Australia, Kellogg's faces intense competition from two stronger cereal brands, Sanitarium and Uncle Toby's. To strengthen the value of its brand, it started a cause-related campaign to link Kellogg's cereals with social concern for young consumers. It began a partnership with Kid's Help Line, a 24-hour telephone number that 5- to 18-year-olds can call 24 hours a day to get free, confidential counseling. Kellogg's donates $.05 per package sold to Kid's Help Line and advertises the service on television and on cereal boxes. The help line has now received more than $1 million, enabling it to hire more counselors and field a rising number of calls. Kellogg's cereal sales have had a strong increase.

- Avon Products is the world's largest seller of beauty products. Almost all of its revenues come from direct sales through 3.4 million part-time, predominately female, sales representatives in 139 countries. The Avon brand is internationally known, but the company's reliance on direct selling carries an old-fashioned, downmarket connotation.[25] Avon decided to use cause-related marketing to burnish its brand image. The vast majority of Avon's sales are to women. Its CEO is a woman as are 71 percent of its managers.[26] Research showed that the cause of fighting breast cancer struck a responsive chord among its

[23] Hill & Knowlton, *2001 Corporate Citizen Watch Survey* (New York: Hill & Knowlton Corporate Citizen Watch, 2001), p. 3.
[24] Sagawa and Segal, *Common Interest,* p. 119.
[25] Pringle and Thompson, *Brand Spirit,* p. 33.
[26] "Avon Calls on the World of Retail," *Retail Week,* September 7, 2001, p. 14.

customers and sales representatives, so Avon began donating to breast cancer detection, treatment, and research when customers bought products (such as the $4 "Courageous Spirit" lipstick, of which $1 becomes a donation). Since 1993 Avon has collected $150 million for breast cancer causes, and its brand increasingly carries this connotation of caring.

Cause-related marketing raises big sums of money for worthy causes but, like other forms of strategic philanthropy, its mixture of altruism and self-interest invites criticism. Critics note that companies pick causes based on research about what consumers care about, instead of research to find the most desperate needs. The campaigns offer a quick and easy way for consumers to relieve their sense of guilt at living comfortable, material lives while others suffer. Moreover, what happens to the needy beneficiaries of brand-enhancement drives when the marketing benefits of the cause wear off and the campaign ends?[27] Corporations, however, do not see commercial interests as ethically inferior to other motives the way critics do and believe that the concrete benefits of cause-related projects far outweigh any truth behind clever arguments about base motives. Many nonprofit organizations actually favor marketing links with corporations. Some have sought out marketing directors to pitch the mutual benefits of a tie-in with their cause.

Social Auditing and Reporting

A *social audit* is an assessment of the impacts of a corporation on society. Unlike a traditional audit based on financial measures, it is an accounting of social performance based on a range of qualitative and quantitative measures. With a social audit, managers may compare the impacts of a firm to its aspirations and the expectations of its stakeholders.

The idea of a social audit is simple, and companies have long practiced it in rudimentary and informal ways. However, doing a rigorous, objective, and credible social audit is an arduous task, and the results can be inconvenient for the corporation. This has retarded the practice of social auditing. The idea of systematic, publicly reported audits by companies emerged as a serious topic in the 1960s and 1970s. At the time, a few large firms, including Bank of America, Chase Manhattan Bank, Exxon, and Philip Morris, did widely publicized social audits. Atlantic Richfield Company published a social balance sheet in which it weighed the pluses and minuses of its social performance. A 1974 survey found that 76 percent of 284 companies did some form of social auditing by assessing social activities.[28]

---

[27] Warren Smith and Matthew Higgins, "Cause-Related Marketing: Ethics and the Ecstatic," *Business & Society*, September 2000.
[28] John J. Corson and George A. Steiner, *Measuring Business's Social Performance: The Corporate Social Audit* (New York: Committee for Economic Development, 1974), pp. 24–25.

Early interest in social auditing waned. One reason was the massive increase in environmental and social regulation that hit business in the 1970s. These regulations contained heavy reporting requirements that were, in effect, government-mandated social audits. However, recent emphasis on social performance by corporations has renewed development of formal social auditing. No single form of social audit exists. Many approaches are adopted, and what is done depends on who is doing it and for what purpose.

External groups do some social auditing of corporations. The primary source of systematic external assessment is socially responsible investors and funds. Corporate social audits have a variety of forms and purposes. Some smaller firms driven by social responsibility strategies, such as The Body Shop and Ben & Jerry's, have made public detailed and candid social audits to underline their progressive philosophies. Larger corporations tend to do forms of social auditing and reporting in limited areas. Many big multinationals have annual publications assessing their environmental, health, and safety performance or their philanthropic activities. These reports tend to publicize positive actions and rarely contain discussion of shortcomings or poor performance. A few reports come in response to criticism. Under attack by activists for its operations in impoverished, war-torn Sudan, Talisman Energy, a Canadian oil company, produced an extensive report of its impacts and activities in that nation.[29] PricewaterhouseCoopers, U.K., verified information in the report. A recent surge of interest in social auditing has created a new market, and global accounting firms such as PricewaterhouseCoopers, KPMG, and Arthur Andersen have entered the field. Their verification efforts increase believability of the reports, but some critics charge that companies have an incentive to hire "soft" and "friendly" auditors from firms that have a financial conflict of interest.[30]

One notable effort to create a social audit format is the Global Reporting Initiative (GRI), a partnership of the United Nations Environment Programme and the Coalition for Environmentally Responsible Economies (CERES). In the late 1990s, the GRI developed guidelines for reporting what it calls a *triple bottom line,* that is, a calculation of corporate economic, environmental, and social performance. These guidelines were crafted by consulting with corporations, advocacy groups, universities, and accounting firms. They introduce a standard format and simplify comparisons between companies. The GRI is voluntary, but large companies around the world have begun to adopt its template, including American Home Products, AT&T, British Airways, Ford, General Motors, Royal Dutch/Shell, Nokia, and Ricoh.

---

[29] *Corporate Social Responsibility Report 2000—Sudan,* Talisman Energy, 2001.
[30] Brendan O'Dwyer, "Social and Ethical Accounting, Auditing and Reporting," *Accountancy Ireland,* December 2000, p. 14.

GRI Indicators

Listed below are a few examples of indicators for the triple bottom line. These are among the indicators recommended as generally applicable to all companies. Note that some are numerical and others are discursive.

Environmental Performance
- Total energy use.
- Total water use.
- Greenhouse gas emissions in tons of CO_2 equivalent.
- Major environmental issues and impacts associated with the use of principal products and services, including disposal, where applicable. Include qualitative and quantitative estimates of such impacts, where applicable.

Economic Performance
- Net profit/earnings/income.
- Debt/equity ratio.
- Total wage expense, by country.
- Total benefits, by country.
- Taxes paid to all taxing authorities.

- Jobs, by type and country, absolute and net change.
- Philanthropy/charitable donations.

Social Performance
- Job satisfaction levels.
- Customer satisfaction levels.
- Investment per worker in illness and injury prevention.
- Ratio of lowest wage to local cost of living.
- Percentage of women in senior executive and senior and middle management ranks.
- Discrimination-related litigation—frequency and type.
- Verified incidences of noncompliance with child labor laws.
- Evidence of indigenous representation in decision making in geographic areas containing indigenous peoples.
- Number and cause of protests.

Source: Global Reporting Initiative, Sustainability Reporting Guidelines (Boston: GRI, June 2000), pp. 29–35.

The key to the GRI is the set of indicators (see the accompanying box) that have been generated and refined by working groups. Some are generally applicable to all companies. Others are appropriate only for certain firms or industries. For example, statistics on fuel consumption by fleet vehicles are appropriate for an express carrier but not for a software manufacturer that downloads products online. Some indicators are designed to frame corporate activity in the context of broader society. Companies are encouraged to state emissions, for example, discharges of sulfur compounds by an electrical utility, as a percentage of total sulfur emissions in a region. Companies are also encouraged to use indicators that connect the triple bottom lines. For example, an estimate of human health effects from the sulfur emissions of a utility links the environmental and social bottom lines.

Social auditing and reporting by companies is increasing. Although the GRI and other initiatives to develop and standardize it are promising, there are major obstacles to its becoming widespread. First, measuring social performance is far more complex than measuring financial performance. There is no agreement about what social performance should be. Even if there were, core elements of it such as ethical behavior are not easily captured by numbers. Second, candid and verifiable audits increase corporate credibility but leave firms open to criticism. Does any chemical plant really want to estimate a number of deaths in its vicinity based on statistical risks of exposure to substances in its emissions? Should General Motors report not only the number of vehicles it makes but also the number of people who die in them? However, none of these difficulties stand in the way of voluntary, limited, and partial auditing of social performance or the slow evolution of standards.

SOCIALLY RESPONSIBLE INVESTING

Mutual funds that assemble socially responsible portfolios for principled investors also do systematic evaluations of companies. There are almost 200 such funds. They include index, growth, balanced, international, small company, bond, and money market funds. The funds purchase shares of companies that pass through *screens,* or tests based on specific criteria used by the fund to define what is and is not responsible. The subjective nature of corporate responsibility is revealed in the wide variety of criteria used by different funds.

The Domini Social Equity Fund, perhaps the best known, is an index fund of approximately 400 companies. To pick these 400 companies, analysts examined about 650 firms, sifting through them to weed out the less responsible ones. Exclusionary "sin" screens block companies in alcohol, tobacco, and gambling. Two other exclusionary screens cut companies that produce nuclear weapons or nuclear power. Remaining companies are subjected to positive screens that assess philanthropy, employee relations, diversity, environmental performance, product quality, and support for human rights in non-U.S. operations. This philosophical approach to screening in and screening out is widely copied by other social responsibility funds. Several studies show that over multiyear periods the Domini Social Equity Fund has outperformed its benchmark, the Standard & Poor's 500, but by only a tiny margin.[31]

Other funds for principled investors use screens that reflect divergent social values. The Timothy Plan Mutual Fund for conservative Christian

[31] Beatrix Payne, " 'Engagement' Picked over Screens," *Pensions & Investments,* April 30, 2001, p. 14; and "Very Well Then, I Contradict Myself," *Business Ethics,* September–October 2001, p. 21.

investors screens out companies that engage in activities it considers un-biblical. It cuts out companies in the alcohol, tobacco, and gambling busi-nesses; in addition, it eliminates firms that produce sexually explicit and violent entertainment, firms that make medical products used in abor-tions, and firms that recognize gay employee groups or give benefits to domestic partners. The Myers Pride Value Fund, on the other hand, was established to invest in firms with gay- and lesbian-friendly policies. The American Trust Allegiance Fund, a fund for Christian Scientists, screens out the health care industry.

The use of screens is an art. Exclusionary screens invite in-or-out choices, but their boundaries are not always sharp. For example, if on principle a screen excludes tobacco companies, should it also block forest products firms that make cigarette paper or the cellulose in filters? Chemical companies that make cellophane for cigarette packs? Super-market chains that sell cigarettes? Companies owned by tobacco compa-nies in unrelated industries? To what extent should principled objection travel a chain of complicity in the disfavored product? As one fund man-ager notes, "It's difficult to be a purist in this. You can draw the line so sharply that all your investments are in environmentally friendly facto-ries where nuns make choir robes."[32] Some funds try. The Amana Growth Fund invests according to Islamic law and screens out not only companies that produce alcohol but also restaurant chains, hotels, and supermarkets that get sales revenue from it. The fund also screens out banks, because in Islam it is considered wrong to profit from interest. However, tobacco and nuclear power companies are acceptable. Positive screens may also present difficult choices. How should various actions be weighed? What criteria should be evaluated in each area? How much can information from a company be trusted?

This brief survey of socially responsible funds confirms that when the definition of corporate social responsibility moves from abstract princi-ple to specific criteria, disagreement arises. Contrasting values cause this disagreement. At the level of specific criteria, the definition of responsi-bility is subjective. There is no evidence that, as a group, socially screened funds perform better over the long run than unscreened funds.

CONCLUDING OBSERVATIONS

In the global business community, only a few companies seek to align their competitive and financial strategies with strong aspirations of social responsibility. In this chapter we discussed the methods of these leading companies in the belief that they are more representative of the future

[32] Quoted in Laurent Belsie, "Fending Off Stealthy Growth of Porn," *Christian Science Monitor*, February 5, 2001, p. 20.

than of the past. The history of the idea of social responsibility is one of expansion, and today's pressures and rewards in the corporate environment encourage more expansion. Although some programs and practices described in the chapter are not widespread now, the business world will more and more embrace them.

Levi Strauss & Company in China

Levi Strauss has long been admired for its high social and ethical standards. Perhaps no other large company has surpassed it as a leader in businesses' assumption of social responsibilities. Its leadership position in American industry has been recognized with many prestigious awards. In 1994 the company was inducted into America's National Business Hall of Fame. In 1998 President Clinton awarded Levi Strauss CEO Robert Haas the first Ron Brown Award for Corporate Leadership—in recognition of the company's "sustained and passionate commitment to employee and community relations." There were many other awards. Business leaders voted Levi Strauss America's most ethical company. It received awards from both Harvard University and Columbia University for its leadership in ethical values and social responsibility.

Its remarkable history in balancing social values with business success has at times raised difficult problems for its management. This case focuses on that balance.

THE COMPANY

Levi Strauss for many years was the largest apparel producer in the world. While a number of firms have in recent years challenged Levi Strauss, the company said, in a special report to the Securities and Exchange Commission (SEC) in 2000, "We believe there is no other apparel company with a comparable global presence in either the jeans or casual pants segment of the apparel market. . . . Levi's® jeans have become one of the most successful and widely recognized brands in

the history of the apparel industry."[1] At the time of the SEC statement, Levi Strauss had operations in 40 countries. It maintained a network of about 750 franchised or independently owned stores dedicated to Levi's products outside the United States and had a few company-owned stores.

The operating performance of the company has recently declined. Sales reached a high of $7.1 billion in 1996 and fell steadily to $5.1 billion in 1999. Net income hit a peak of $735 million in 1995 and fell to $5 million in 1999. For the first three months of the 2000 fiscal year, the company reported an income deficit. In 2001 the staff of the company totaled about 17,000, most of whom were in foreign countries. This was about half the 1997 total. Its foreign operations include wholly owned-and-operated businesses, joint ventures, licensees, and distributors. The company generally manufactures goods in countries in which they are sold.

ORIGINS OF THE COMPANY

This global giant had humble beginnings. In the 1850s a Bavarian-born immigrant and dry goods merchant named Levi Strauss moved from New York to San Francisco. In San Francisco, he made sturdy work pants from the canvas-like material he used in making tents for miners. In 1973 he and a tailor named Jacob Davis joined forces and patented the process of putting rivets in pants for strength because miners complained their pockets ripped under the weight of ore samples. This was

---

[1] Levi Strauss & Co., Form S-4, Registration Statement under the Securities Act of 1933, May 4, 2000, p. 5.

the origin of the pants known throughout the world as blue jeans.

Levi Strauss prospered as a privately held firm, and by 1970 sales reached approximately $350 million. At that time, opportunities for significant growth were apparent, but it needed cash to exploit them. To finance expansion, the company in 1971 offered 13 percent of its stock to the public. In 1985, however, following a year in which sales and profits dropped precipitously, it bought back the publicly held stock for $1.6 billion. The company said this was the best way to continue its long tradition of following its basic values. A new family-controlled entity called Levi Strauss Associates, Inc., was created to hold the acquired stock. This action took the stock off the New York Stock Exchange.

WHAT CAUSED THE DECLINE AFTER 1996?

In an SEC report, the company identified a number of the causes of the deterioration. For example, a major cause was the decline in both industrywide and company-specific factors. Industrywide factors included consumer market trends toward more fashion denim and nondenim products and severe competition from designer and private-label brands. Company-specific factors included erosion of consumer preference for jeans and problems in the company's distribution system. Karl Schoenberger, a journalist, commented that complacency and loss of touch with young consumers were also difficulties.[2]

Important strategies were formulated to deal with the problems. For example, restructuring cut overhead cost. Production capacity in U.S. plants was reduced. More production was moved from the United States to lower-wage countries. From 1997 to 2001 the number of employees was reduced by 18,500, and 29 owned-and-operated production facilities were closed in North America and Europe. A new senior management team was put in place, including a new CEO in 1999. This new CEO was Philip A. Marineau, a skilled marketing expert who had been successful in reviving falling brands. This was the first time a member of the family did not hold that title.

A SOCIALLY CONCERNED COMPANY

Social concern began with founder Levi Strauss and has continued to the present. For example, when the great earthquake of 1906 devastated San Francisco, Levi Strauss bought space in newspapers to notify his 350 employees that their paychecks would continue. He was one of the first to integrate his plants, and he paid his employees salaries above the average for the industry. Levi Strauss was known in San Francisco as a generous supporter of charities and education.[3] His company continued that tradition.

When Robert D. Haas, the great-great-grandnephew of Levi Strauss, was CEO of Levi Strauss, he followed the company's founder in repeatedly asserting the tradition of social responsibility. In one of his speeches he said,

> Our firm's values include a commitment to ethical business conduct; quality in everything we do; respect for people; an openness to new ideas; valuing and embracing diversity; and dedication to socially responsible conduct. I contend that by following these values and taking into account the interests of multiple stakeholders in our decision making, we are able to make sounder decisions. We're able to promote innovation, and ultimately, enhance sales and earnings.[4]

Philip Marineau articulated the value system enunciated by his predecessor CEO in these words:

> For Levi Strauss & Co., the concept of achieving commercial success responsibly has been a fundamental aspect of our business since its

---

[2] Karl Schoenberger, *Levi's Children: Coming to Terms with Human Rights in the Global Marketplace* (New York: Atlantic Monthly Press, 2000), p. 159.

[3] "Levi Strauss, A Biography," San Francisco, Levi Strauss & Co., undated.

[4] Robert D. Haas, "Risks, Innovation and Responsibility: A Business Model for the New Millennium," speech to Business for Social Responsibility conference, Los Angeles, November 6, 1997.

founding. Integrity, ethical behavior, a respect for diversity and a strong commitment to the health and welfare of our communities where we live and work are characteristic of the values of Levi Strauss & Co., which help guide our decisions and our behavior as a company.[5]

ETHICAL AND SOCIAL RESPONSIBILITY POLICIES

The values expressed above by Robert Haas were not simply rhetoric. He was among the first business leaders to specify in writing for his employees and the general public exactly what they meant in practical terms. The values were set forth in 1987 in two documents: a "Mission Statement" and an "Aspiration Statement." These two statements became the foundation of Levi's ethical and social values. They read as follows:

Mission Statement

The mission of Levi Strauss & Co. is to sustain responsible commercial success as a global marketing company of branded apparel. We must balance goals of superior profitability and return on investment, leadership market positions, and superior products and service. We will conduct our business ethically and demonstrate leadership in satisfying our responsibilities to our communities and to society. Our work environment will be safe and productive and characterized by fair treatment, teamwork, open communications, personal accountability and opportunities for growth and development.

Aspiration Statement

We all want a Company that our people are proud of and committed to, where all employees have an opportunity to contribute, learn, grow and advance based on merit, not politics or background. We want our people to feel respected, treated fairly, listened to and involved. Above all, we want satisfaction from accomplishments and friendships, balanced personal and professional lives, and to

have fun in our endeavors. When we describe the kind of LS&CO, we want in the future, what we are talking about is building on the foundation we have inherited: affirming the best of our Company's traditions, closing gaps that may exist between principles and practices and updating some of our values to reflect contemporary circumstances. What type of leadership is necessary to make our Aspirations a reality?

These statements were followed with details about what leadership was required to meet Levi's mission and aspirations, including policies with respect to employees, product, service, and foreign operations. Since its first issuance, this Aspiration Statement, governing at the time of most of the events discussed in this case, has undergone what Levi Strauss calls "fine tuning." A current statement was formulated in May 1999, which is fundamentally the same as the original one but clarifies many of the principles.[6]

APPLICATION OF THE VALUES IN PRACTICE

Over the years, Levi Strauss management faced significant issues that tested the application of the value system. The following are selected events that illustrate difficulties management faced and how company values were applied in dealing with them.

Civil Rights

Philip Marineau tells the story of Levi's actions in the 1950s concerning the integration of a plant in a southern city. Levi's managers told the town leaders the company wanted to integrate its sewing facilities. The city leaders flatly refused. Walter and Peter Haas, running the company at the time, then threatened to move the plant, an important employer in the city. The city leaders suggested a compromise: build a brick wall down the center of the plant to separate black and white workers. The brothers refused. The leaders then suggested painting a line down the center of the plant to separate the two races. Again the brothers refused. Faced with the

[5] Philip A. Marineau, "Corporate Social Responsibility through Innovation and Risk-Taking," speech before Georgetown Business Ethics Institute, Georgetown University, McDonough School of Business, February 17, 2000.

[6] It can be found at www.levistrauss.com/about/vision.

serious impact on the town's economy of a plant move, the leaders accepted the position of the Haas brothers and the plant was integrated. The decision led to other plant integrations in the South.[7]

Child Labor

Another incident concerns a Levi Strauss contractor in Bangladesh who was found to employ underage girls. Rather than force the contractor to fire the girls, Levi Strauss sought another alternative. To discharge the girls would either force them to seek employment in another similar situation or be deprived of their income. In the conditions in Bangladesh at the time, young children were a main source of income for a family. An agreement was reached with the contractors to stop employing the girls but to pay them a salary provided they went to school. Levi Strauss agreed to pay for tuition, books, and uniforms for the young girls, and the contractor agreed to employ them when they finished school.[8] This story not only illustrates Levi Strauss's sense of social responsibility but also the company's skills of innovation.

COMPETITION FORCES LEVI STRAUSS TO CLOSE U.S. PLANTS

In the late 1980s and 1990s Levi Strauss faced unrelenting pressures from competitors who were employing foreign low-wage workers to make their garments at much lower prices than could Levi's U.S. production facilities. One result, as noted above, was that Levi lost market share.[9] These conditions led the company to rely more on foreign sources for its garments. This led to a new form of ethical considerations in its foreign operations. Here are a few illustrations.

SAIPAN

In 1991 one of Levi Strauss's contractors in Saipan was accused of employing Chinese women and paying them below the island's legal minimum wage, among other violations of human rights. The contractor was fired, and the company formed a committee of top managers to establish standards for contractors in foreign countries.

After nine months the committee produced a two-part policy statement that was published in 1992 and revised in 1994, as shown in Exhibit 1. (Over the years, this statement has been fine tuned. The revisions, however, contain basically the same principles. Some are identical with the older statement, such as "ethical standards," and others are modified. For example, the meaning of the principle "Freedom of Association" is spelled out in considerable detail, enumerating workers' rights to form and join organizations of their own choice.) "Guidelines" condemns doing business in countries where there are pervasive violations of basic human rights. That was used as a basis to sever all relations with Burmese contractors. Levi Strauss was the first major company to leave Burma for such a reason. Other companies soon followed Levi's lead.

The early 1990s was a period when deplorable human rights violations were brought to public attention by groups such as Amnesty International, Human Rights Watch, Global Watch, and the Lawyers Committee for Human Rights. Many plants in some foreign countries were what are called "sweatshops."[10] Intense pressure on corporations by activists forced them to help improve conditions for workers in their overseas operations.

Such conditions led 13,000 garment workers in Saipan to file a class action suit in January 1999 alleging sweatshop conditions. The complaint was upheld by a U.S. district judge in the Mariana Islands. The defendants complained they often worked 12-hour days, seven days a week, in unsafe, unclean conditions that violated U.S. labor law and international treaties. One complaint was that garment workers, often from China, were forced to pay "recruitment fees" as high as $7,000 to get jobs in the Saipan plants. One reporter, however, found some garment workers who were satisfied with pay that was five times what they

---

[7] Marineau, "Corporate Social Responsibility."

[8] Ibid.

[9] On the last point, see Nina Munk, "How Levi's Trashed a Great American Brand," *Fortune*, April 12, 1999.

[10] Barry Bearak, "Lives Held Cheap in Bangladesh Sweatshops," *The New York Times International*, April 15, 2001.

EXHIBIT 1 **Terms of Engagement and Guidelines for Country Selection**

BUSINESS PARTNER TERMS OF ENGAGEMENT

Terms of Engagement address issues that are substantially controllable by our individual business partners.

We have defined business partners as contractors and subcontractors who manufacture or finish our products and suppliers who provide material (including fabric, sundries, chemicals and/or stones) utilized in the manufacture and finishing of our products.

1. **Enviromental Requirements**
   We will only do business with partners who share our commitment to the environment and who conduct their business in a way that is consistent with Levi Strauss & Co.'s Environmental Philosophy and Guiding Principles.

2. **Ethical Standards**
   We will seek to identify and utilize business partners who aspire as individuals and in the conduct of all businesses to a set of ethical standards not incompatible with our own.

3. **Health & Safety**
   We will only utilize business partners who provide workers with a safe and healthy work environment. Business partners who provide residential facilities for their workers must provide safe and healthy facilities.

4. **Legal Requirements**
   We expect our business partners to be law abiding as individuals and to comply with legal requirements relevant to the conduct of all their businesses.

5. **Employment Practices:**
   We will only do business with partners whose workers are in all cases present voluntarily, not put at risk of physical harm, fairly compensated, allowed the right of free association and not exploited in any way. In addition, the following specific guidelines will be followed.

   - **Wages and Benefits**
     We will only do business with partners who provide wages and benefits that comply with any applicable law and match the prevailing local manufacturing or finishing industry practices.

   - **Working Hours**
     While permitting flexibility in scheduling, we will identify prevailing local work hours and seek business partners who do not exceed them except for appropriately compensated overtime. While we favor partners who utilize less than sixty-hour work weeks, we will not use contractors who, on a regularly scheduled basis, require in excess of a sixty-hour week. Employees should be allowed at least one day off in seven.

   - **Child Labor**
     Use of child labor is not permissible. Workers can be no less than 14 years of age and not younger than the compulsory age to be in school. We will not utilize partners who use child labor in any of their facilities. We support the development of legitimate workplace apprenticeship programs for the educational benefit of younger people.

   - **Prison Labor/Forced Labor**
     We will not utilize prison or forced labor in contracting relationships in the manufacture and finishing of our products. We will not utilize or purchase materials from a business partner utilizing prison or forced labor.

   - **Discrimination**
     While we recognize and respect cultural differences, we believe that workers should be employed on the basis of their ability to do the job, rather than on the basis of personal characteristics or beliefs. We will favor business partners who share this value.

   - **Disciplinary Practices**
     We will not utilize business partners who use corporal punishment or other forms of mental or physical coercion.

6. **Community Betterment**
   We will favor business partners who share our commitment to contribute to the betterment of community conditions.

GUIDELINES FOR COUNTRY SELECTION

The following country selection criteria address issues which we believe are beyond the ability of the individual business partner to control.

1. **Brand Image**
   We will not initiate or renew contractual relationships in countries where sourcing would have an adverse effect on our global brand image.

2. **Health & Safety**
   We will not initiate or renew contractual relationships in locations where there is evidence that Company employees or representatives would be exposed to unreasonable risk.

3. **Human Rights**
   We should not initiate or renew contractual relationships in countries where there are pervasive violations of basic human rights.

4. **Legal Requirements**
   We will not initiate or renew contractual relationships in countries where the legal environmental creates unreasonable risk to our trademarks or to other important commercial interests or seriously impedes our ability to implement these guidelines.

5. **Political or Social Stability**
   We will not initiate or renew contractual relationships in countries where political or social turmoil unreasonably threatens our commercial interests.

would earn in China and were heading home after two years work with $6,000 to $10,000.[11]

Three suits were filed. The first was against 18 companies, including well-known firms such as The Gap Inc., Target Corp., J.C. Penney, Lane Bryant, and The Limited. The second was filed against the same retailers plus 11 Saipan-based garment contractors. And the third was filed against 22 Saipan-based garment contractors. Later, in March 2000, six additional retailers were added, one of which was Levi Strauss & Co. Various settlements have been made, except for Levi Strauss & Co., Brooks Brothers Inc., Gap Inc., Associated Merchandising Corp Inc., J.C. Penney Co., and a number of others. The settlements have included a Saipan Code of Conduct, which every retailer, as a condition of settlement, has to include in future contracts with Saipan-based contractors. The Code mandates strict adherence to detailed standards governing working and living conditions in Saipan factories. It also requires on-site monitoring by Verite, a nonprofit international human rights monitoring organization based in Amherst, Massachusetts. The settlements provided fees for Verite. A part of the settlements involved payment to defendants for their rights violations.

PLANT CLOSINGS

Beginning in the 1980s and extending into the late 1990s, Levi Strauss began closing its U.S.-owned manufacturing plants. Closures up to 1990 were due primarily to unrelenting competition. After 1990 the company said that the main reason for closing plants was to reduce excess capacity brought about principally because of loss of market. In both cases, the impacts on management, on workers who lost jobs, and on local communities were traumatic.

Most managers of corporations say the hardest decisions they make concern laying off people. Levi Strauss held off making such decisions longer than other apparel companies in the United States. But the company had no alternative.

San Antonio and Costa Rica

In 1990 Levi Strauss shut down a plant in San Antonio, Texas, that made jeans and shifted production to independent contractors in Costa Rica. Wages in the San Antonio plant were from $6 to $9 dollars an hour, compared with 30 cents to $1 in Costa Rico. Most of the 1,100 employees of the San Antonio plant were Latino women. The economic impact of the plant closing on the city as well as the workers was severe. Levi Strauss notified the workers 90 days before closing the plant (30 days are required by law) and offered workers English classes, vocational training programs, and three months of extended medical benefits.[12]

The workers formed a militant union, Fuerza Unida, and vigorously protested the layoffs. They claimed racial discrimination, asked for compensation for on-the-job injuries, and picketed the plant and Levi Strauss headquarters in San Francisco. A federal court in 1993 rejected a class action suit filed by the union.[13]

El Paso

In 1993 an El Paso plant was closed, and workers filed a number of suits claiming discrimination against some who had filed disability claims for maladies such as carpal tunnel syndrome. Workers claimed they were harassed in ways that forced them to quit their jobs. After several court proceedings, Levi Strauss agreed to pay about $5 million to settle the claims.[14]

Treatment of Workers at Plant Closings

Levi Strauss was generous in the packages it gave to discharged employees. For example, when it decided in 1997 to close a number of U.S. facilities, it said it would allocate $200 million for employee benefits and have the Levi Strauss foundation make $8 million in grants to communities affected by plant closings. Employees were given eight

---

[11] Seth Faison, "Stretching Federal Labor Law Far into South Pacific," *The New York Times International,* February 20, 1999.

[12] See Gavin Power, "Texas Plant Closure Still Haunting Levi's," *The San Francisco Chronicle,*" November 10, 1992; and Reese Erlich, *Christian Science Monitor,* November 9, 1992.

[13] Schoenberger, *Levi's Children,* p. 50.

[14] Ibid., p. 51.

months notice; up to three weeks' severance pay per year of service; continuation of health benefits for 18 months; a $6,000 allowance for education, retraining, and other severance costs; and early retirement. Bruce Raynot, executive vice president of the Union of Needletrades, Industrial and Textile Employees, said this was "by far the best severance settlement apparel workers have ever gotten, which will enable the affected workers to move forward with their lives."[15]

THE DECISIONS TO LEAVE AND THEN RETURN TO CHINA

Levi Strauss had three types of arrangements in China in 1991: (1) contracts with local companies to produce a certain number of garments, (2) contracts for a company in China to import fabric for further production of garments in China, and (3) contracts for the purchase of fabrics. Although the company had been buying from China since 1986, the 1992 volume of garment purchases was only about 2 percent of Levi Strauss's total output.[16] The company bought about 5 million items of clothing from Chinese sewing and laundry contractors with a value of around $50 million.[17]

Human rights violations were endemic in China. For example, freedom of association and expression were severely restricted. Dissidents were jailed without due process or fair trial procedures. Arrests were often arbitrary and capricious. Prisoners were subject to maltreatment, sometimes tortured, and impressed into forced labor. Communist Party representatives on boards of directors were pressed upon companies. Such appalling conditions received widespread publicity and produced outrage in the United States.

Conditions within individual companies varied. In general, however, they were contrary to Levi

Strauss's values. The specific conditions prevailing in the facilities of Levi's contractors are not known, but studies for other companies revealed the employment of children, long hours, absence of trade unions, authoritarian management, inadequate communications between managers and workers, excessive unpaid overtime, fines for minor infractions (such as being late to work by a few minutes), and unsafe and unhealthful working conditions.

The question before Levi Strauss's top management in 1991 was, Can we operate in China without violating our policies? This question should be viewed in light of continuing tensions between the United States and China over many years about human rights behavior. Tensions were heightened with the massacre in Tiananmen Square in 1989 by Chinese troops who slaughtered students campaigning for democratic values. Democratic governments around the world condemned the massacre, and human rights issues were brought into sharp focus in the United States.

LEVI STRAUSS DECIDES TO LEAVE CHINA

The company established a China Policy Committee to examine the situation, and it gave its recommendations to the Executive Management Committee in March 1993. A majority of the committee recommended staying in China. The final decision was left to Robert Haas, who presented a recommendation to leave China to the board of directors in April 1993. It approved the recommendation.

Reasons for Staying in China

There were many reasons given for staying in China, including

- China is a rapidly growing economy, and the company can take advantage of opportunities there by staying.

- If Levi Strauss leaves, it will be difficult to get back in.

- Finding alternative sources in Asia will be costly.

- If the firm stays, it may have potential leverage in improving human rights in conformance with the company's basic values. If

[15] Quoted in David Cay Johnston, "At Levi Strauss, a Big Cutback, with Largess," *The New York Times,* November 4, 1997.
[16] Abraham Wu, "Levi Strauss & Co. in China," S–P–13 (Palo Alto, CA: Stanford University, Graduate School of Business, July 1994); p. 2.
[17] Jane Palley Katz, "Levi Strauss & Co.: Global Sourcing (A)" (Boston, MA: Harvard Business School, 1995).

the firm stays, it should insist that provisions of the terms of engagement be met and monitored.

Reasons for Leaving China

The more important reasons for leaving were

- Staying in China means tolerating a climate of repression inconsistent with the company's fundamental values.

- More and more customers of Levi Strauss's products are concerned with human rights, and if the company stays in China, the brand loyalty to Levi Strauss could be seriously damaged.

- Economic problems in China are increasing costs of operations.

- China offers little protection from piracy of intellectual property, patents, or products.

- Political instability is always possible in China.

The Final Decision

The board decided to phase out contracting in China and make no direct investments but to continue to buy fabric until the company's sourcing guidelines were reviewed for these products.

LEVI STRAUSS DECIDES TO RETURN TO CHINA

The company announced on April 8, 1998, that it would end its self-imposed restrictions on manufacturing in mainland China. Actually, Levi Strauss never completely withdrew. Through contractors in Hong Kong, it produced in China 800,000 units a year, compared with over 2,600,000 a year at the time of the pullout. More important reasons for restoring full operations in China were

- Since Hong Kong was now a part of China, where the company had continued operations, the decision to expand operations was compelling.

- The company believed it could find business allies who would honor the Levi Strauss code.

- To not return to China would threaten the commercial interests of the company because competitors would solidify a foothold in this fast-growing economy.

- The 1993 decision was not intended to change human rights policies in China nor to impose Levi Strauss's values on others. It was essentially a business decision. So is the decision to return.[18]

REACTION OF ACTIVISTS

Fifty-one human rights organizations and activists sent Haas a letter expressing deep disappointment in the decision. They said the human rights situation in China was worse than when the company left in 1993. Among other recommendations, the group wrote that if Levi Strauss did business in China it should disclose the subcontractors it uses together with such data as wages and work hours. It should also allow independent human rights groups to verify compliance with the company's Code of Conduct. David Samson, vice president of communication for Levi Strauss, replied to the letter and explained some of the reasons for the return. In addition, he said, "If we return, we will move back in a measured and cautious way. If we can't operate in ways consistent with our values, we won't be there any long period of time."[19] Charles Kernaghan, executive director of the National Labor Committee, said, "It sounds like Looney Tunes to me that they think they can go in there and guarantee the rights of these workers."[20]

Not all activists, however, were critical. For example, Han Dangfang, a prominent Chinese labor activist who formed the first independent labor union during the Tiananmen Square uprising, said that "he believed that the company could do more good by providing jobs in China, rather than by shunning the country."[21]

---

[18] "Talking Points on Conducting Business in China," press release, April 8, 1998, www.levistrauss.com/press/pr_pressrelease.asp?releaseid=15.
[19] Published in "Letters," *Business Ethics,* July–August 1998, p. 5.
[20] Carol Emert, "Levi's Expanding in China; Five Years Ago, Company Restricted Operations," *San Francisco Chronicle,* April 9, 1998.
[21] Mark Landler, "Reversing Course, Levi Strauss Will Expand Its Output in China," *The New York Times,* April 9, 1998.

WHAT IS THE RESPONSIBILITY OF A COMPANY FOR IMPROVING HUMAN RIGHTS?

A corporation does have social responsibilities, but precisely what they are is not always clear. This is particularly so with respect to China. A multinational company's social responsibilities for human rights in that country depend upon many variables.

For example, there are numerous non-Chinese entities with influence in China aside from MNCs, including other nations, the United Nations, and nongovernment organizations such as human rights groups. Each has some responsibility, but how much?

An important factor in determining the responsibility of an MNC is the type of human rights in question. For example, a company has responsibility for worker rights associated with employment, such as safety conditions, but not for the Chinese government using prison labor.

The government is far more sensitive to criticisms of the latter type of human rights than the former. As Michael A. Santoro of Rutgers Graduate School of Management writes:

> The rights of workers to minimum wages, safe working conditions, and limited working hours are not as problematical for the Chinese government as the rights to association and expression. Hence, when foreign companies uphold minimal labor standards through business partner terms of engagement, the risk of alienating the Chinese government is not nearly as great as when companies attempt to uphold the political rights of Chinese workers.[22]

However, the human rights issue may be extremely difficult for a company when the government seeks its help in enforcing a penalty for a worker's exercise of freedom of speech or association contrary to government rules. Santoro says executives of MNCs "need not concern themselves with human rights violations that have nothing to do with the firm's operations."[23] But what if the government insists?

Multinational firms employ only a small percentage of all workers in China and encounter only a small fraction of human rights abuses. Furthermore, few if any MNCs are invulnerable to retaliation from the Chinese government. The typical MNC is weak, therefore, in its ability to influence the government to change its actions respecting human rights outside the workplace. China is interested in attracting foreign capital and seems little concerned with the working conditions set up by MNCs so long as the companies do not get involved in political promotion of human rights.

Santoro suggests what he called a "fair share" theory of corporate responsibility for human rights issues in China. This theory requires an allocation of responsibilities among major entities operating there. As noted above, MNCs do have responsibilities, particularly those concerning working conditions in their organizations. The greatest influence on human rights conditions in China, however, rests with international institutions.

QUESTIONS

1. Can a company with exceptionally high values like Levi Strauss survive in an industry where cutthroat competition prevails?

2. Do you believe that Levi Strauss has lived up to the letter and spirit of its Aspiration Statement and Guidelines in the global involvements and decisions described in this case?

3. Do you believe the guidelines shown in Exhibit 1 are appropriate for most or all U.S. companies doing business abroad? Explain your position. Are companies that lack such guidelines irresponsible?

[22] Michael A. Santoro, "Engagement with Integrity: What We Should Expect Multinational Firms to Do About Human Rights in China," *Business & the Contemporary World*, 10, no. 1 (1998), p. 40.

[23] Ibid., p. 45.

4. Evaluate the pros and cons of Levi Strauss's decision to stay in or leave China in 1993. Did Levi Strauss make the right decision?

5. Evaluate the decision to reenter China in 1998. Did Levi Strauss make the right decision?

6. What is the responsibility of a company like Levi Strauss for improving human rights in China or in other nations?

Managing Ethics

Chapter Seven

Business Ethics

Correct Craft

Walter C. Meloon dropped out of high school to work in a print shop. The boss's daughter was a devout Christian, so he became a convert to win her hand in marriage. In 1925, when Meloon started a small boat-making business in Florida, he resolved to glorify God and follow the Golden Rule in his business dealings.

Meloon's company, Correct Craft, barely survived the depression years of the 1930s, but during World War II it prospered making boats for the armed services. In January 1945 General Dwight D. Eisenhower was driving toward Berlin ahead of schedule and set March 10, 1945, as the date for crossing the Rhine. However, there was a critical shortage of the 17-foot, spoon-shaped assault boats that carried soldiers on such river crossings.

Correct Craft was given an urgent order for 300 of these boats by the Army. The company had only 18 days to build them; its normal output was 48 boats per *month!* Immediately, a government expediter demanded that Meloon go to a seven-day workweek, but he refused, saying that it was not God's plan to work on the Sabbath. The expediter gave in. Correct Craft went on to produce 306 boats four days ahead of schedule, without working on Sundays, and another 100 boats when other companies were unable to meet their schedules.

At a second Correct Craft plant, where Meloon built boats for the U.S. Navy, a government inspector tried to speed production by stopping weekly chapel services for the employees. Meloon told him: "If we can't serve the Lord and the U.S. Navy at the same time, we just won't serve the Navy."[1] The inspector relented.

After World War II, Correct Craft prospered as the second-largest builder of sport boats and yachts in the nation. Then, in 1957 the company got a big U.S. Army contract for 3,000 fiberglass boats. One day a government inspector demanded that the Meloons set up a special account for "inspector's expenses." This was a request for a bribe.

[1] Quoted in Robert G. Flood, *On the Waters of the World: The Story of the Meloon Family* (Chicago: Moody Press, 1989), p. 18.

This picture from the December 1945 *National Geographic* magazine shows the road in front of Correct Craft littered with finished plywood assault boats. It was taken on Wednesday, February 21, 1945. Photo courtesy of Correct Craft.

By this time W. C.'s equally principled sons, Walter O. and Ralph, managed daily operations. The family prayed for guidance. The payments were small compared to the income at stake. But bribery was wrong. The payments were not made. "If you have made a decision based only on money," said W. C., "you have made a bad decision."[2] Soon the inspectors began to use trivial blemishes as pretexts for rejecting finished boats. In the end they rejected 640 boats. Correct Craft lost $1 million on the contract and in 1958 went into Chapter 11 bankruptcy proceedings. It owed $500,000 to 228 creditors.

Knowing the situation, every Correct Craft employee resigned. Walter O. and Ralph rehired only those with essential jobs. The two brothers' wives worked at the switchboard. Walter O. returned his new Lincoln to the dealer. Other family members mortgaged their homes and sold their cars. All adopted a frugal lifestyle.

The company barely avoided liquidation. First came a loan from a friend. Then the government of Pakistan bought 239 of the fiberglass boats that the inspectors had rejected. In early 1965, after years of hardship, the bankruptcy

[2] Quoted in John S. Tompkins, "These Good Guys Finish First," *Reader's Digest,* June 1992, p. 140.

judge released the company from Chapter 11 when 127 remaining creditors agreed to repayment at 10 cents on the dollar.

But despite the agreement, the Meloons struggled for the next 19 years to repay 100 percent of their debt. As the years passed, it became hard to locate some creditors. The family worked to find them. In some cases, they were deceased and payments were made to surprised widows or relatives. In one case, Ralph flew to Michigan to search for a creditor when telephone calls proved fruitless. In May 1984 the last payment was made. The family had paid 100 percent of its debt!

Today Correct Craft is a profitable company known for its line of inboard-engined recreational boats, including the Ski Nautique, a towboat preferred by water skiers because of its flat wake. Correct Craft boats are sold worldwide. The third generation of Meloons is in charge; Walter N., son of Walter O., is president. Walter O. and Ralph remain on the board of directors and a third brother, Harold, has been company chaplain since 1974.

Correct Craft is a company driven by ethical values. These values, derived from the philosophy and example of its founder, permeate the company culture to direct employees and influence strategic decisions. Its story illustrates how ethical values can have a continuous impact on the fortunes of a business.

In this chapter, the first of two on business ethics, we discuss the sources of ethical standards that constrain business, examine ethical behavior in companies, and explain methods of managing that promote higher ethics. In the next chapter we focus on making ethical decisions.

WHAT ARE BUSINESS ETHICS?

Ethics is the study of what is good and evil, right and wrong, and just and unjust. *Business ethics*, therefore, is the study of good and evil, right and wrong, and just and unjust actions in business. Ethical managers try to do good and avoid doing evil. A mass of principles, values, norms, and thoughts concerned with what conduct *ought* to be exists to guide them. Yet in this vaporous mass, the outlines of good and evil are at times shadowy. Usually they are distinct enough, but often not. So, using ethical ideas in business is an art, an art requiring judgment about both the motivations behind an act and the act's consequences.

Discussions of business ethics frequently emphasize refractory and unclear situations, perhaps to show drama and novelty. Although all managers face difficult ethical conflicts, applying clear guidelines resolves the vast majority of them. The Eighth Commandment, for example, prohibits stealing and is plainly violated by taking tools home from work or theft of trade secrets. Lies in advertising violate a general rule of the Western business world that the seller of a product must not purposely deceive a buyer. This general understanding stems from the Mosaic law, the Code of Hammurabi, Roman law, and other sources and is part of a general ethic favoring truth going back at least 3,000 years.

Overall, ethical traditions that apply to business support truth telling, honesty, protection of life, respect for rights, fairness, and obedience to law. Some beliefs in this bundle of traditions go back thousands of years. Others, such as the idea that a corporation is responsible for the long-term health of its workers, have emerged more recently. In keeping with this long and growing ethical heritage, most business actions can be clearly judged ethical or unethical; eliminating unethical behavior such as bribery or embezzlement may be difficult, but knowing the rightness or wrongness of actions is usually easy.

This does not mean that ethical decisions are always clear. Some are troublesome because although basic ethical standards apply, conflicts between them defy resolution.

> Lockheed Aircraft Corp. made large campaign contributions to Japanese officials intended to influence the Japanese government to buy airplanes. This saved jobs for American workers. However, though such contributions were common in Japan and for the international aerospace industry overall, they violated U.S. business norms. Lockheed's actions are still debated.

Some ethical issues are hidden, at least initially, and hard to recognize.

> The A. H. Robins Co. began to market its Dalkon Shield intrauterine device through general practitioners while competitors continued to sell them only through obstetricians and gynecologists. This strategy was wildly successful in gaining market share for Robins and did not, initially, seem to raise ethical issues; but when dangerous health problems with the Shield started to appear, the general practitioners were slower to recognize them than the specialists. Robins's failure to make extra efforts in tracking the safety of the device then emerged as an ethical shortcoming.

And some ethical issues are very subtle, submerged in everyday workplace behavior. Managers must often work in a world of uncertainty and act or pass judgment without complete knowledge of facts. The following case involves a commitment, a promise.

> A regional manager tells a factory manager that replacement equipment for a factory with production problems due to breakdowns will be ordered from this year's budget. At year's end, however, the equipment has not been ordered because, as the regional manager explains, "there just wasn't enough money left to do it." Is the factory manager entitled to expect the budget to be managed so that the commitment could be kept? Why was the commitment not kept? Poor planning? Disguised withdrawal of cooperation? Another reason?

TWO THEORIES OF BUSINESS ETHICS

There is a debate about whether ethics in business may be more permissive than general societal or personal ethics. There are two basic views.

The first, the *theory of amorality,* is that business should be amoral, that is, conducted without reference to the full range of society's ethical ideals. Managers may act selfishly because the market mechanism distills their actions into benefits for stakeholders and society at large. Adam Smith noted that the "invisible hand" of the market assures that "by pursuing his own interest [a merchant] frequently promotes that of the society more effectively than when he really intends to promote it."[3] In this way, capitalism provides moral justification for the pursuit of profit through behavior that is not purposefully ethical.

The apex of this view came during the latter half of the nineteenth century when doctrines of laissez-faire economics and social Darwinism were popular. It was widely believed that business and personal ethics existed in separate compartments, that business was an ethical sanctuary in which less idealistic ethics were permissible.[4] Dan Drew, a builder of churches and the founder of Drew Theological Seminary, summed up the nineteenth-century compartmentalization of business decision making in these words:

> Sentiment is all right up in the part of the city where your home is. But downtown, no. Down there the dog that snaps the quickest gets the bone. Friendship is very nice for a Sunday afternoon when you're sitting around the dinner table with your relations, talking about the sermon that morning. But nine o'clock Monday morning, notions should be brushed aside like cobwebs from a machine. I never took any stock in a man who mixed up business with anything else. He can go into other things outside of business hours, but when he's in the office, he ought not to have a relation in the world—and least of all a poor relation.[5]

[3] Adam Smith, *The Wealth of Nations,* ed. Edwin Cannan (New York: Modern Library, 1937), p. 423; originally published in 1776. Smith also believed that merchants must abide by prevailing societal ethics.

[4] This view was encouraged in the writings of the social Darwinist Herbert Spencer, who believed in two sets of ethics. *Family ethics* were based on the principle of charity and benefits were apportioned without relation to merit. *State ethics* were based on a competitive justice and benefits were apportioned on the basis of strict merit. Family ethics interjected into business or government by well-meaning people were an inappropriate interference with the laws of nature and would slowly corrupt the workings of Darwinian natural selection. See "The Sins of Legislators," in *The Man versus the State* (London: Watts, 1940), originally published in 1884. Dual ethical perspectives have developed in other cultures, such as Slavic cultures, that assert one set of ethical standards for personal relationships and a second set that justifies less perfection for business matters. See Sheila M. Puffer, "Understanding the Bear: A Portrait of Russian Business Leaders," *Academy of Management Executive,* February 1994, p. 47.

[5] Quoted in Robert Bartels, ed., *Ethics in Business* (Columbus: Bureau of Business Research, Ohio State University, 1963), p. 35.

The theory of amorality now has far less luster and public acceptance, but it lives on quietly. For many managers, competitive pressures still justify behavior that would be wrong in private life; the theory of amorality continues to release these managers from a burden of guilt that they otherwise might feel.

The second basic ethical view is the *theory of moral unity,* in which business actions are judged by the general ethical standards of society, not by a special set of more permissive standards. Only one basic ethical standard exists, so principled behavior and business decisions can be harmonized.

Many managers take this position today, and some did even in the nineteenth century. An example is James Cash Penney. We remember Penney for building a chain of department stores, but his first enterprise was a butcher shop. As a young man, Penney went to Denver where, finding the shop for sale, he wired his mother for $300 (his life savings) to buy it. The departing owner warned Penney that his success depended on orders from a nearby hotel. "To keep the hotel for a customer," the butcher explained, "all you have to do is buy the chef a bottle of whiskey a week." Penney regularly made the gift and business was good, but he soon had second thoughts. Resolving no longer to do business that way, he stopped the bribe, lost the hotel's business, and went broke when the shop failed. He was 23 years old. Penney later started the Golden Rule Department Store in Denver and always believed that principles of honesty contributed to its ultimate success.

To J. C. Penney, and other exemplars of the theory of moral unity, desire to succeed is never an excuse to neglect principled behavior. Actions are not moral just because they make money. Ethical conflicts cannot be avoided simply because they arise in the course of business. Although many managers still practice the theory of amorality, the theory of moral unity better shows the expectations of society today.[6]

We turn now to a related question. Are there any factors that excuse or diminish ethical responsibility in business? The answer is yes. More than 2,000 years ago, Aristotle recognized that being ethical requires voluntary choice. A person must be able to choose between alternatives to act unethically. If there is no choice, their behavior is involuntary and is excused. According to Aristotle, two factors restrict choice, leading to involuntary behavior. They are *ignorance* and *incapacity.*

A person or corporation may be ignorant of facts or the consequences of an act.

---

[6] This conclusion is reinforced in a discussion of the history of these two ideas. See Jon M. Shepard, Jon Shepard, James C. Wimbush, and Carroll U. Stephens, "The Place of Ethics in Business: Shifting Paradigms?" *Business Ethics Quarterly,* July 1995.

The South African government once used Polaroid film and cameras for the pictures on racial identity papers. Black employees of Polaroid Corporation in the United States raised the issue of its complicity with racists, so it prohibited sales to the government while continuing sales to the South African public. For six years this policy went on, but Polaroid's distributor secretly kept selling to the government. On the day that it learned about this deceit, Polaroid completely withdrew from South Africa.[7]

Here Polaroid cannot be condemned; ignorance absolved management from any blame for violation of its policy. Of course, in such cases, negligence in getting facts creates blame. A "willful blindness" doctrine exists in criminal law in recognition that intentional ignorance increases culpability. It applies in cases where a manager is suspicious of wrongdoing but elects not to investigate.

Incapacity arises from four circumstances that render actions involuntary. First, an action may impose *unrealistically high costs*—for example, an auto manufacturer cannot be expected to prevent all traffic deaths since the costs of a completely safe vehicle in materials, design, and production would be staggering. Second, there may be *no power to influence* an outcome.

Recently, Amnesty International investigated a south Lebanon prison in which captors hung people from an electricity pylon, wet them, and administered electric shocks. The handcuffs used in this torture were marked, "The Peerless Handcuff Co. Springfield, Mass. Made in USA."[8] Peerless is a family business started in 1914 that makes handcuffs, leg irons, and waist chains. The company restricts its sales to legitimate law enforcement agencies and refuses orders from some countries, including Israel, because it does not condone torture.[9] Although Peerless knows that its restraints could wind up in torture chambers, it lacks power to oversee the lifetime ownership and use of every device it manufactures.

Third, at times *no alternative exists*. In Nazi Germany, party officials allocated raw materials and controlled import-export licenses and other permissions necessary to do business. They demanded bribes, and businesses could not function without paying them. Fourth, *external forces may compel action*. For example, a manager may pay excessive and unjust taxes in a foreign country because a corrupt ruler demands them.

Aristotle cautioned, however, that "[t]here are some things such that a man cannot be compelled to do them—that he must sooner die than do,

[7] Tom L. Beauchamp, *Case Studies in Business, Society, and Ethics* (Upper Saddle River, NJ: Prentice Hall, 1998), pp. 275–81. Polaroid stayed out of South Africa for 17 years until the official system of race segregation ended.
[8] Amnesty International, *Stopping the Torture Trade* (London: Amnesty International Publications, 2001), p. 3.
[9] Robert Weissman, "The Torture Trade," *Multinational Monitor*, April 2001, p. 7.

though he suffer the most dreadful fate."[10] Unethical behavior involving coercion is voluntary if a manager can simply refuse to comply with the external force. Those who argue that the market is an irresistible force overriding individual choice give too little credit to the strength of human will.

MAJOR SOURCES OF ETHICAL VALUES IN BUSINESS

Four great repositories of ethical values influence managers. They are religion, philosophy, cultural experience, and law. A common theme, the idea of *reciprocity*, or mutual help, is found in each of these value systems. This idea reflects the central purpose of ethics, which is to bind individuals into a cooperative social whole. Ethical values are a mechanism that controls behavior in business and in other areas of life. Ethical restraint is more efficient with society's resources than are cruder controls such as police, lawsuits, or economic incentives. Ethical values channel individual energy into pursuits that are benign to others and beneficial to society.

Religion

The great religions, including the Judeo-Christian tradition prominent in American history, converge in the belief that a divine will reveals the nature of right and wrong behavior in all areas of life, including business. Despite doctrinal differences, major religions agree on ideas that form the basic building blocks of ethics in every society. For example, the principle of reciprocity is found, encapsulated in variations of the Golden Rule, in Buddhism, Confucianism, Hinduism, Islam, Judaism, and Christianity. These religions also converge in emphasizing traits such as promise-keeping, honesty, fairness, charity, and responsibility to others.[11]

Christian managers often seek guidance in the Bible. Donald V. Seibert, former chairman of J. C. Penney Company, advocated daily Bible reading for executives. He found two books relevant:

> Proverbs, is replete with references to the proper approach to business transactions, such as "A wicked man earns deceptive wages, but one who sows righteousness gets a sure reward." [11:18]. And Jesus's teachings and parables in Matthew have enough practical wisdom in them to provide a blueprint for almost an entire working experience.[12]

---

[10] *Nichomachean Ethics,* trans. J. A. K. Thomson (New York: Penguin, 1953), p. 112; originally written c. 334–323 B.C.

[11] See, for example, Rafik Issa Beekun, *Islamic Business Ethics* (Herndon, VA: International Institute of Islamic Thought, 1997), p. 58.

[12] Donald V. Seibert and William Proctor, *The Ethical Executive* (New York: Simon & Schuster, 1984), pp. 119–20.

The Bible, like the source books and writings of other main religions, was written in a premodern, agricultural society, and many of its ethical teachings require interpretation before they can be applied to problems in the modern workplace. Much of the ethical teaching in the Bible comes in parables. The parable of the prodigal son (Luke 15:11–32) tells the story of an unconditionally merciful father—an image applicable to ethical conflicts in corporate superior–subordinate relationships. The story of the rich man and Lazarus (Luke 16:19–31) teaches concern for the poor and challenges Christian managers to consider the less privileged, an apt pursuit in a world where billions of people live with incomes less than $1 a day.[13] In Islam the Koran is a source of ethical inspiration. The Prophet Muhammad says that "Every one of you is a shepherd and everyone is responsible for what he is shepherd of."[14] In a modern context, the Muslim manager is analogous to a shepherd and has a duty to rise above narrow self-interest to protect the good of the organization.

In the Jewish tradition, managers can turn to rabbinic moral commentary in the Talmud and the books of Moses in the Torah. Here again, ancient teachings are regarded as analogies. For example, a Talmudic ruling holds that a person who sets a force in motion bears responsibility for any resulting harm, even if natural forces intervene. This is discussed in the context of an agrarian society in which a person who starts a fire is responsible for damage from flying sparks, even if nature intervenes with high winds. In an industrial context, the ethics lesson is that polluting companies are responsible for problems caused by their waste.[15]

Parables and stories in bodies of literature from ancient worlds may seem so innocent as to have little value for managers in a complex, global economy. However, as one rabbinic scholar notes, "Our world has undergone tremendous technological changes, but the issues stay the same—egotism, jealousy, greed, among others."[16] Thus, the central wisdom remains. When Confucius told Chinese merchants of his age that "He who acts with a constant view to his own advantage *(li)* will be much murmured against," he planted a speck of truth visible in the atmosphere of any era.[17]

---

[13] See Oliver F. Williams and John W. Houck, *Full Value: Cases in Christian Business Ethics* (New York: Harper & Row, 1978), for discussion of these and other biblical sources of inspiration for managers.

[14] Quoted in Tanri Abeng, "Business Ethics in Islamic Context: Perspectives of a Muslim Business Leader," *Business Ethics Quarterly,* July 1997, p. 52.

[15] Moses L. Pava, *Business Ethics: A Jewish Perspective* (New York: Yeshiva University Press, 1997), pp. 72–73. For more examples of how Jewish teachings apply, see www.jewishethicist.com, an advice column on Jewish business ethics.

[16] Meir Tamari, quoted in Gail Lichtman, "Ethics Is Their Business," *The Jerusalem Post,* May 25, 2001, p. 13.

[17] *Analects,* book IV, chap. XII. Cited in Stephen B. Young, "The CRT *Principles for Business* as an Expression of Original Confucian Morality," *Caux Roundtable Newsletter,* Fall 2000, p. 9.

Philosophy

A Western manager can look back on more than 2,000 years of philosophical inquiry into ethics. This rich, complex tradition is the source of many notions about what is right or wrong in business. Every age has added new ideas, but it is a mistake to regard the history of ethical philosophy as a single debate that, over centuries, has matured to bear the fruit of growing wisdom and clear, precise standards of conduct. Even after two millennia, there remains considerable dispute among ethical thinkers about the nature of right action. If anything, standards of ethical behavior were arguably clearer in ancient Greek civilization than they are now.

In a brief circuit of milestones in ethical thinking, we turn first to the Greek philosophers. Greek ethics, from Homeric times onward, were embodied in the discharge of duties related to social roles such as shepherd, warrior, merchant, citizen, or king. Expectations of the occupants of these roles were clearer than in contemporary America, where social roles such as those of business manager or employee are more vague, overlapping, and marked by conflict.[18] Socrates (469–399 B.C.) asserted that virtue and ethical behavior were associated with wisdom and taught that insight into life would naturally lead to right conduct. He also introduced the idea of a moral law higher than human law, an idea that activists use to demand supralegal behavior from transnational corporations. Plato (428–348 B.C.), the gifted student of Socrates, carried this doctrine of virtue as knowledge further by elaborating the theory that absolute justice exists independently of individuals and that its nature can be discovered by intellectual effort. In the *Republic,* Plato set up a 50-year program for training rulers to rule in harmony with the ideal of justice.[19] Plato's most apt pupil, Aristotle, spelled out virtues of character in the *Nicomachean Ethics* and advocated a regimen of continuous learning to improve ethical behavior.[20]

The Stoic school of ethics, spanning four centuries from the death of Alexander to the rise of Christianity in Rome, furthered the trend toward character development in Greek ethics. Epictetus (A.D. 50–100), for instance, taught that virtue was found solely within and should be valued for its own sake, arguing that virtue was a higher reward than external riches or outward success.

In business, the ethical legacy of the Greeks and Romans remains a conviction that virtues such as truth telling, charity, obeying the law, justice, courage, friendship, and the just use of power are important ethical qualities. Today when a manager trades integrity for profit, we condemn it based on the teachings of the Greeks.

---

[18] Alasdair MacIntyre, *After Virtue: A Study in Moral Theory* (South Bend, IN: University of Notre Dame Press, 1981), p. 115.
[19] Trans. F. M. Cornford (New York: Oxford University Press, 1945).
[20] *Nicomachean Ethics,* trans. Thomson, p. 51.

Ethical thinking after the rise of Christianity was dominated by the great Catholic theologians St. Augustine (354–430) and St. Thomas Aquinas (1225–1274). Both believed that humanity should follow God's will; correct behavior in business and all worldly activity was necessary to achieve salvation and life after death. Christianity was the source of many ethical teachings, including specific rules such as the 10 Commandments. Christian theology created a lasting reservoir of ethical doctrine, but its domination of ethical thinking declined during the historical period of intellectual and industrial expansion in Europe called the Enlightenment. Secular philosophers such as Baruch Spinoza (1632–1677) tried to demonstrate ethical principles with logical analysis rather than ordain them by reference to God's will. So also, Immanuel Kant (1724–1804) tried to find universal and objective ethical rules in logic. Kant and Spinoza, and others who followed, created a great estrangement with moral theology by believing that humanity could discover the nature of good behavior without reference to God. To this day, there is a deep divide between Christian managers who look to the Bible for divine guidance and other mangers who look to worldly writing for ethical wisdom.

Other milestones of secular thinking followed. Jeremy Bentham (1748–1832) developed the idea of utilitarianism as a guide to ethics. Bentham observed that an ethical action was the one among all alternatives that brought pleasure to the largest number of persons and pain to the fewest. The worldly impact of this ethical philosophy is almost impossible to overestimate, because it validated two dominant ideologies, democracy and industrialism, allowing them first to arise and then to flourish. The legitimacy of majority rule in democratic governments rests in large part on Bentham's theory of utility as later refined by John Stuart Mill (1806–1873). Utilitarianism also sanctified industrial development by legitimizing the notion that economic growth benefits the majority; thus the pain and dislocation it brings to a few may be ethically permitted.

John Locke (1632–1704) developed and refined doctrines of human rights and left an ethical legacy supporting belief in the inalienable rights of human beings, including the right to pursue life, liberty, and happiness, and the right to freedom from tyranny. Our leaders, including business leaders, continue to be restrained by these beliefs.

A *realist school* of ethics also developed alongside the idealistic thinking of philosophers such as Spinoza, Kant, the utilitarians, and Locke. The realists believed that both good and evil were naturally present in human nature; human behavior inevitably would reflect this mixture. Since good and evil occurred naturally, it was futile to try to teach ideals. Ideals could never be realized because evil was permanent in human nature. The realist school, then, developed ethical theories that shrugged off the idea of perfect goodness. Niccolò Machiavelli (1469–1527) argued that important ends justified expedient means. Herbert Spencer (1820–1903) wrote prolifically of a harsh ethic that justified vicious competition among companies because it furthered evolution—a process in which humanity improved as the unfit fell down. Friedrich Nietzsche (1844–1900) rejected the ideals of earlier "nice" ethics, saying they were prescriptions of the timid, designed to fetter the actions of great men whose irresistible power and will were regarded as dangerous by the common herd of ordinary mortals.

Nietzsche believed in the existence of a "master morality" in which great men made their own ethical rules according to their convenience and without respect for the general good of average people. In reaction to this master morality, the mass of ordinary people developed a "slave morality" intended to shackle the great men. For example, according to Nietzsche, the mass of ordinary people celebrate the Christian virtue of turning the other cheek because they lack the power to revenge themselves on great men. He felt that prominent ethical ideals of his day were recipes for timidity and once said of utilitarianism that it made him want to vomit.[21] The influence of realists on managers has been strong. Spencer was wildly popular among the business class in the nineteenth century. Machiavelli is still read for inspiration. The lasting appeal of realism is that many managers, deep down, do not believe that ideals can be achieved in business life.

Cultural Experience

Every culture transmits between generations a set of traditional values, rules, and standards that define acceptable behavior. In this way, individuals channel their conduct in socially approved directions. Civilization itself is a cumulative cultural experience consisting of three stages; in each, economic and social arrangements have dictated a distinct moral code.[22]

For millions of generations in the *hunting and gathering stage* of human development, ethics were adapted to conditions in which our ancestors had to be ready to fight, face brutal foes, and suffer hostile forces of nature. Under such circumstances, a premium was placed on pugnacity, appetite, greed, and sexual readiness, since it was often the strongest who survived. Trade ethics in early civilizations were probably deceitful and dishonest by our standards, and economic transactions were frequently conducted by brute force and violence.

Civilization passed into an *agricultural stage* approximately 10,000 years ago, beginning a time when industriousness was more important than ferocity, thrift paid greater dividends than violence, monogamy became the prevailing sexual custom because of the relatively equal numbers of the

---

[21] His exact words were " 'the general welfare' is no ideal, no goal, no remotely intelligible concept, but only an emetic." In *Beyond Good and Evil* (New York: Vintage Books, 1966), p. 157; originally published in 1886.
[22] Will Durant and Ariel Durant, *The Lessons of History* (New York: Simon & Schuster, 1968), pp. 37–42.

sexes, and peace came to be valued over wars, which destroyed crops and animals. These new values were codified into ethical systems by philosophers and founders of religions. So the great ethical philosophies and theologies that guide managers today are largely products of the agricultural revolution.

Two centuries ago, society entered an *industrial stage* of cultural experience, and ethical systems began to reflect an evolving institutional, intellectual, and ecological environment. Powerful forces such as global corporations, population growth, the capitalist ideology, constitutional democracy, new technology, and ecological damage have appeared. Industrialism has not yet created a distinct ethic, but rising postmodern values put stress on ethical values that evolved in ancient, agriculture-based worlds. Postmodern values alter people's judgments about good and evil. For example, the copious outpouring of material goods from factories encourages materialism and consumption at the expense of older, scarcity-based virtues such as moderation and thrift. The old truism that nature exists for human exploitation is less compelling when reexamined in a cloud of industrial pollution.

Law

Laws codify, or formalize, ethical expectations. They proliferate over time as emerging regulations, statutes, court rulings, and litigation theories impose new conduct standards. However, it is impossible for law to anticipate and prohibit every possible wrong action. The law always lags behind opportunities for corporate expediency. Three main types of sanctions for illegal acts are fines, damage awards by courts, and prosecution of individual managers.

Fines

Fines are intended to punish, deter future lawbreaking, and cause companies to disgorge wrongful gains. In 1991 the United States Sentencing Commission, a judicial agency that standardizes penalties for federal crimes, released guidelines for sentencing corporations.[23] It set fines based on type of crime, amount of top-level management involvement, monetary gain to the company or loss to its victims, company size, past criminal convictions, cooperation with law enforcement, and the presence or absence of programs to prevent or detect illegal acts.

The largest recent fines stem from federal antitrust prosecutions in two price-fixing conspiracies. The largest fine ever paid by any company was $500 million paid by F. Hoffmann-LaRoche Ltd. for its leadership of a decade-long conspiracy to cheat buyers of common vitamin supplements. Its executives met with managers from six other European and

[23] United States Sentencing Commission, *Guidelines Manual* (Washington, DC: Government Printing Office, November 1, 1991), chap. 8.

Japanese companies to allocate market shares and fix prices for vitamin A, B2 (riboflavin), C, E, and beta carotene. The other companies shared smaller fines totaling $680 million. A second antitrust prosecution focused on a global scheme to fix prices of the graphite electrodes used in steelmaking furnaces to conduct heat-producing electrical arcs. An American company, UCAR International Inc., the world's largest producer of graphite electrodes, led this remarkable four-year conspiracy. As a result, it agreed to the second-highest criminal fine ever paid by an American company—$110 million—surpassed only by the $125 million paid by ExxonMobil in 1991 for charges related to the Alaska oil spill.

A cynical public doubts that fines are large enough to deter mighty corporations from wrongdoing. Sometimes they are, indeed, too small to mar balance sheets. The Environmental Protection Agency once threatened to impose a $27,500 fine on General Electric each day it failed to clean up toxic waste at a factory. It was the equivalent of threatening a person making $1 million a year with a fine of three cents a day. When GE recently paid the government $1.84 million in fines to settle a billing fraud case, it was the equivalent of a $25 parking ticket for a person making $50,000 a year.

However, large fines can also be very painful. The $110 million fine of UCAR International shows how. That amount was only 12 percent of the company's $947 million sales in 1998, but UCAR could not afford to pay the full amount. Its financial troubles started the previous year when it took a charge against earnings of $340 million to cover future liabilities related to the antitrust litigation that had begun. Beyond the potential $110 million fine by the U.S. government, UCAR faced fines by other governments, suits by steel companies overcharged for electrodes, and suits by shareholders claiming that when UCAR hid the conspiracy it withheld material information affecting the stock price. The charge resulted in a net loss of $160 million for 1997, and the consequences rocked the company. Over the next year, it was forced to restructure its debt, close factories in three countries, initiate 150 cost-reduction projects, shrink its headquarters, and take an additional $86 million restructuring charge.[24] Its board chairman and CEO resigned, and its share price fell from a high of $45 in 1997, to a low of $12.50 in 1998. UCAR's $110 million fine is below what the Department of Justice considered appropriate to punish the company and disgorge it of unlawful gains estimated at $170 million. However, the government balanced the need to punish the company against the risk of jeopardizing its survival to arrive at the $110 million figure. It also allowed UCAR to pay the fine in six yearly installments ending in 2004.[25] In sum, there is no doubt that the fine hurt badly.

[24] UCAR International Inc., *Form 10-K405*, March 26, 1999, pp. 3–4.
[25] "Government's Sentencing Memorandum," *U.S. v. UCAR International Inc.* (USDC, E.Dist. Penn., No. 98–177), April 21, 1998.

Damages

Courts may assess damages, or payments for harm that comes to others because of a corporation's actions. *Compensatory damages* are payments awarded to redress concrete losses suffered by injured parties. *Punitive damages,* or payments greater than a wronged party's actual losses, are awarded to deter similar actions and punish a corporation. Punitive damages may be awarded only if malicious and willful misconduct exists. For example, a regional manager for Browning-Ferris Industries ordered a district manager to drive a small competitor in Vermont out of business using predatory pricing. His instructions were: "Do whatever it takes. Squish him like a bug."[26] Subsequently, a jury awarded the competitor $51,146 in actual damages, then added $6 million in punitive damages.

Since the purpose of punitive damages is to punish and deter crime, they must be large enough to cause pain. Yet they raise many questions about fairness. There is no fixed standard for calculating their size and arbitrary sums may violate constitutional due process requirements. Given similar offenses, juries often assess higher damages against a big corporation than against a smaller one simply to make certain the penalty hurts. And sometimes the sums awarded are so large that they must be weighed against Eighth Amendment prohibitions on "excessive fines" and "cruel and unusual punishments."

The Supreme Court decided to rein in punitive damages in the case of an Alabama physician, Dr. Ira Gore Jr., who bought a BMW automobile for $40,751 and drove it for nine months without noticing any problem. After an auto detailer told him that part of the car had been repainted, the owner found out that BMW North America had been secretly repainting cars with shipping damage and selling them as new. Gore estimated his damages at $4,000, or 10 percent of the value of the new car, and sued, charging BMW with gross, oppressive, and malicious fraud. An Alabama jury awarded him $4 million in punitive damages—1,000 times his actual loss. On appeal, the Supreme Court held that the award was unconstitutionally excessive.[27] However, the Court did not set up any formula for calculating punitive damages, so the definition of excessive is still imprecise.[28] Subse-

---

[26] *Browning-Ferris Industries v. Kelko Disposal,* 57 LW 4986 (1989).

[27] *BMW of North America, Inc. v. Gore,* 116 S.Ct. 1589 (1996).

[28] Cooper Industries, a knife maker, planned to introduce a new folding tool knife that closely copied a competitor's product. It removed identifying features from the competitor's model, photographed it, and used it in ads for its copycat product. A jury found Cooper guilty of false advertising and assessed damages of $50,000 for the injured competitor. It also found that Cooper acted in a "reckless and outrageous" manner and awarded $4.5 million in punitive damages. Cooper appealed the award as "grossly excessive," but the Ninth Circuit affirmed it. A skeptical Supreme Court sent the case back to the Ninth Circuit for reconsideration based on standards in *Browning-Ferris* and *BMW*. See *Cooper Industries* v. *Leatherman Tool Group* 532 U.S. 424 (2001).

quently, the Alabama Supreme Court reconsidered the case and awarded Gore only $50,000.[29]

Prosecution of Managers

A third type of sanction for corporate crime is prosecution of individuals in companies. Two UCAR International executives were jailed for their leadership in the graphite electrode conspiracy. CEO Robert P. Krass was fined $1.25 million and sentenced to 17 months in prison and Senior Vice President Robert J. Hart was fined $1 million and sentenced to 9 months. However, for many reasons, managers are rarely jailed.

Investigating corporate crime is difficult for prosecuting attorneys. They must wade through thickets of documents finding evidence. Sorting out subtle organizational relationships and fixing responsibility for decisions is tricky. Corporations hire stellar defense lawyers; less experienced attorneys with thin staff support often champion the state's case. And even when prosecutors succeed, judges are reluctant to jail managers convicted of white-collar crimes, who ordinarily do not violently endanger society and would further crowd prisons. Adding to these frustrations, violent crimes and drug trafficking compete for resources, and collaring street criminals is easier than wallowing in complex corporate cases.

Other methods for punishing corporate crime exist. One guideline for applying them is that they should not cripple or render inefficient legitimate corporate activity. If UCAR International had been destroyed by a larger fine, innocent employees, stockholders, suppliers, and communities would all have suffered. Courts have required advertisements and speeches to show contrition for wrongdoing. Some corporations have paid their fines to charities, and executives have done community service. Some statutes allow government agencies to bar offending corporations from government contracts.

BUSINESS ETHICS IN OTHER COUNTRIES

Business practices differ between countries and regions because environmental factors shape ethical values. Here are some illustrations of how these factors work.

History

Historical experience shapes business environments that are radically different from that in the United States. For example, Italian history is punctuated by a series of devastating natural disasters—volcano eruptions, floods, earthquakes, and famines. The caprice of these events led Italians

---

[29] "Alabama Court Slashes Punitive Award in Case Involving Repainted BMW Car," *The Wall Street Journal*, May 12, 1997, p. B10.

to temporize with chance and live for the moment. An Italian manager may be more carefree than an American one about keeping a promise or fulfilling a contract because of this attitude about the future.[30] As a result, levels of trust between parties in business deals are low in some parts of Italy, opening the door for corruption and organized crime. According to one observer, a function of the Mafia is its ability to "enforce" business dealings where law and custom cannot.[31]

The Russian people suffered centuries of autocratic rule, first under the Orthodox Church and czarism, and later with communist rule. Past oppression shaped ethical values in many ways. High ethical standards were always right with friends and family, but deception and intrigue were justified when dealing with tyrannical officials. This ethical split carried over into business life, where it remains today.

Authoritarian rule in Russia also created a system of *blat*, or the custom of informal, sometimes corrupt, use of favors to get official action. Under communism, party officials planned business activity in intricate detail, promulgating blizzards of laws, rules, and orders affecting every industry. It was impossible to comply with all these dictates and still run an efficient business, so Soviet managers routinely broke rules, manipulated production data, and fabricated accounts to accomplish business goals. The use of *blat* to get government actions was widespread and fostered a climate of corruption.

With the downfall of the Soviet regime, an entrepreneurial, free enterprise system sprouted in Russia. However, the ethics of this new business system are low by American standards. Under communist ideology, entrepreneurship was considered unethical because people were supposed to work for the collective good of the state. The communist regime taught Russians to regard the American economy as a kind of "wild capitalism" that played out Karl Marx's worst nightmare. Now, not only are most Russians hostile toward people who start private companies, but the image of capitalism gone wild is the template that shapes the behavior of the new capitalists. As a result, free enterprise in Russia is chaotic, corrupt, devoid of trust, and unpredictable.[32] If we can view history as an experiment, Russia is an example of how not to create a climate of decorous ethics.

---

[30] Stephen J. Carroll and Martin J. Gannon, *Ethical Dimensions of International Management* (Thousand Oaks, CA: Sage Publications, 1997), p. 9.

[31] Amartya Sen, "Economics, Business Principles and Moral Sentiments," *Business Ethics Quarterly*, July 1997, p. 9.

[32] Sheila M. Puffer and Daniel J. McCarthy, "Finding the Common Ground in Russian and American Business Ethics," *California Management Review*, Winter 1995. See also Detelin S. Elenkov, "Can American Management Concepts Work in Russia?" *California Management Review*, Summer 1998, p. 134.

Culture

Culture is a wellspring of many ethical differences. One remarkable variation in business ethics arises from the emphasis on individualism in American culture as opposed to the emphasis on community in Asian cultures. Individualism in American social philosophy makes individual conscience a strong source of ethical control; the notion of individual sin in Christianity makes personal guilt a powerful penalty for wrong conduct. In Asian societies, duty toward the group is a much more powerful control on behavior; and because the idea of sin is foreign to Eastern religion and philosophy, the idea of shame by group disapproval is more developed than in the West.

Japanese, for instance, have a strong ethic of fidelity to work groups and corporations. Beginning in about the sixth century, Japan, like other Asian societies, began to borrow and adapt Chinese culture. Traditional values in China stressed that an individual's primary obligation was not to self but to others, including family, clan, and government. The Japanese also built a strong ethic of loyalty to superiors from the emphasis on fidelity in Chinese Confucianism. In medieval times, the extreme of loyalty was seen in the samurai, who gave their lives for feudal lords. Today it is seen in corporate employees who show extreme deference to their superiors and often do ordinary jobs with life-or-death urgency.

The collectivist ethic in Japan has many consequences. Japanese employees do not blow the whistle on their companies in the face of wrongdoing; they are restrained by loyalty to employers. A Japanese corporation will fire an employee for the breach of simply interviewing with another firm. Loyalty is so strong that if a company does wrong, all employees feel shame. Years ago, reporters from Japan visited Lockheed headquarters in Burbank, California, when the Lockheed payoff scandals were disgracing a prime minister and his government. They were amazed to see Lockheed employees walking around, looking happy, and behaving normally. They wrote that the Lockheed workers "had no sense of shame."[33]

Philosophy

Philosophy can have a deep impact on ethical values. Asian countries are influenced by lines of thought that originated in ancient China. Asian managers, who are inclined to philosophy, read Bing Fa, a form of strategic thinking developed in Chinese military doctrine beginning around 700 B.C.[34] Bing Fa is based on the study of historic warfare. Asians believe that all parts of human existence are interconnected and that universal

---

[33] Jack Seward and Howard Van Zandt, *Japan: The Hungry Guest,* rev. ed. (Tokyo: Yohan Publications, 1987), pp. 277–78.

[34] *Bing* literally means "soldier" and *Fa* means "doctrine." Together they may be translated as "the art of war." Min Chen, *Asian Management Systems* (New York: Routledge, 1995), p. 39. See also Chin-Ning Chu, *The Asian Mind Game* (New York: Rawson Associates, 1991), pp. 10–82.

principles discovered in one area are at work in all areas of life. So ancient battles and strategies are tirelessly studied to find universal truths that can be applied in business. For Asian managers, then, the conduct of business shades into warfare. A greater range of action is seen as legitimate than is the case in the West.

In Bing Fa texts, the most popular of which is Sun Tzu's *Art of War,* deception is a highly valued tactic.[35] Western managers are sometimes angered in business negotiations with Chinese, Japanese, or Korean managers when the Asians hide their purpose through indirection or distraction that to the Westerner is deceitful. Chinese, Japanese, and Koreans directly pry into trade secrets and delight in snooping on competitors. They may infringe on patents in part because they see the marketplace as a battlefield where manipulations considered unethical in America are seen as elegant by the standards of Bing Fa.

Stage of Economic Development

In countries where economic activity is not supported by institutions and values the way it is in developed economies, basic trust may be missing. The extent of cheating and fraud in China is extraordinary. Government figures estimate that corruption reduces GDP by 13 to 17 percent, private companies pay only half the taxes they owe, 40 percent of all goods produced are counterfeit or substandard, and half of all contracts signed contain fraudulent elements.[36] Much of this arises because standards for financial statements, bank loans, tax collection, and law enforcement are weakly developed. In China, as in many less developed nations, civil institutions fail to support high ethical standards.

In some countries, various pathologies of government create climates of corruption. In Uganda and Vietnam, for example, officials in government agencies, judges, and customs officials make such low salaries that they rely on bribes, or "silent fees," to survive.[37] If the government is highly bureaucratic, as in Venezuela or Italy, there are so many rules and restrictions that bribery, corruption, and personal favoritism are rampant. Red tape is avoided by bribes, and friends are given favors in preference to strangers. In both nations, officials can paralyze businesses by strictly applying laws until they get payoffs. Ethics in such countries sink to fit the business environment.

---

[35] Sun Tzu, *The Art of War,* trans. Samuel B. Griffith (London: Oxford University Press, 1963); originally written c. 500 B.C. Another popular text studied by Asian managers is Miyamoto Musashi, *A Book of Five Rings (Go Rin No Sho),* trans. Victor Harris (Woodstock, NY: Overlook Press, 1994); originally written in 1645.
[36] Bruce Gilley, "People's Republic of Cheats," *Far Eastern Economic Review,* June 21, 2001, p. 59.
[37] See John Hallows, "Uganda: Corruption's Costly Hold on Company Profit Margins," *Africa News,* December 21, 2000; and Lady Borton, "Working in a Vietnamese Voice," *Academy of Management Executive,* November 2000, p. 26.

Viewpoints about Ethical Variation

As this discussion shows, ethical behavior in business varies considerably around the world. Are some cultures correct about what is proper business ethics and others wrong? There are two ways to answer this question.

The school of *ethical universalism* holds that in terms of biological and psychological needs, human nature is everywhere the same. Ethical rules are transcultural because behavior that fulfills basic needs should be the same everywhere—for example, basic rules of justice must be followed. Basic justice might be achieved, however, through emphasis on group or individual ethics, leaving room for varying cultural tastes.

The school of *ethical relativism* holds that although human biology is everywhere similar, cultural experience creates widely diverging values, including ethical values. Ethical values are subjective. There is no objective way to prove them right or wrong as with scientific facts. A society cannot know that its ethics are superior, so it is wrong for one nation to impose standards on another.

We cannot settle this age-old philosophical debate. However, ethical variation is a practical and urgent issue. With the rise of a global economy, corporations struggle with the question of how to apply codes of conduct across cultures. If large multinationals based in developed countries decide to vary behavior based on local customs, they open themselves to disturbing practices, for example, in countries where women are held inferior. If, on the other hand, firms maintain absolute consistency in conduct standards, they operate with lack of respect for local norms. One U.S. company used the same sexual harassment training materials around the world, exposing managers in a Muslim country to culturally alien depictions of men and women interacting in suggestive ways.[38] Some flexibility seems appropriate, and a recent survey found that about one-third of companies with ethics codes modified their content in host countries.[39]

What guidelines exist for companies that want to introduce flexibility into their conduct codes? Some scholars argue that at a high level of abstraction, the ethical ideals of all cultures converge to basic sameness. Thomas Donaldson and Thomas W. Dunfee see a deep social contract underlying all human societies. This contract is based on what they call *hypernorms,* or principles at the root of all human ethics. Examples are basic rights, such as rights to life and to political participation. These hypernorms validate other ethical norms, which can differ from nation to nation but still be consistent with the hypernorms. For example, many

---

[38] Thomas Donaldson and Thomas W. Dunfee, "When Ethics Travel: The Promise and Peril of Global Business Ethics," *California Management Review,* Summer 1999, p. 61.
[39] "2000 EOA Member Survey: Public Version," www.eoa.org/Research/survey_2k.html, p. 15.

U.S. corporations prohibit people from hiring their relatives. In India, however, tradition places a high value on supporting family and clan members, and some companies promise to hire workers' children when they grow up. Although these practices are inconsistent, they exist in what Donaldson and Dunfee call *moral free space*, where inconsistent norms are permitted if they do not violate any hypernorms.[40]

FACTORS THAT INFLUENCE MANAGERIAL ETHICS

Most managers have high ethical standards and in surveys say that honesty is critical in business. Yet despite widespread efforts of companies to raise standards, high background levels of dishonest behavior defy reduction. In 2000 a national survey of American workers found that 38 percent believed their managers "would authorize illegal or unethical conduct to meet business goals." Worse, 76 percent had observed co-workers breaking the law or company rules in the last year and a half. These violations were so serious that if publicly revealed they would cause companies to "significantly lose public trust."[41]

Why do such large numbers of managers and employees act unethically? The answer is that there are strong forces at work in the corporate organization that can, depending on how they are managed, push people toward higher or lower ethics. We discuss here four prominent and interrelated forces that shape conduct.

Leadership

The example of leaders is perhaps the most significant influence on ethical standards in a company. Not only do leaders set formal rules, but by their example they show the importance of right behavior or they undermine it. Subordinates are keen observers and quickly notice if standards are, in practice, upheld or evaded. Exemplary behavior is a powerful tool available to all managers. It was used wisely by this executive, who tells about taking over a financially troubled manufacturing operation:

> Most of our management was flying first class. . . . I did not want . . . my first act to be to tell everybody that they are not gonna fly first class anymore, so I just quit flying first class. And it wasn't long before people noticed it and pretty soon everybody was flying coach. . . . I never put out a directive, never said a word to anybody. . . . People look to the leader. If the leader cuts corners, they say its okay to cut corners around

---

[40] Donaldson and Dunfee, "When Ethics Travel," p. 61.
[41] KPMG, *2000 Organizational Integrity Survey: A Summary*, KPMG Integrity Management Services, 2000, pp. 2–3.

here. If the leader doesn't cut corners, we must be expected not to do any of that around here.[42]

A common failing is for managers to show by their actions that there is a difference between formal policies and how things actually work. One large insurance company had formal rules against the illegal practice of "churning," or selling new policies to customers by making misleading statements. Yet churning was rampant in the organization. One sales agent explained why in an interview.

> The agent is out there churning, and he doesn't come into the business knowing how to do that. It has to be learned, it had to be taught . . . they're learning it from the people who are training them. Most of the time, as the manager would go out with a new agent, the manager would sell that way, and the agent would pick it up.[43]

To set an ethical tone, a manager must be a strong model of virtue. Many employees are prone to cynicism. Diverting blame for mistakes, breaking small promises, showing favoritism, and diversion of even trivial company resources for personal use is ill-advised—because if the leader does it, a cynical employee can rationalize his or her entitlement to do it also.

Strategy and Performance

A critical function of managers is to create strong competitive strategies that enable the company to meet financial goals without encouraging ethical compromise. In companies with deteriorating businesses, managers have great difficulty meeting performance targets and may feel pressure to compromise ethical standards. Even excellent overall strategies need to be carried out with policies that support honest achievement. Unrealistic performance goals can pressure those who must make them work.

> Chief Executive Richard McGinn of Lucent Technologies made the company's shares skyrocket by promising 20 percent yearly sales growth. When he twice missed quarterly targets, the stock plummeted. He could not miss again. Warned by subordinates that fourth quarter 2000 sales might fall short, he "went ballistic."[44] Under intense pressure to meet the

---

[42] Interview quoted in Linda Klebe Treviño, Laura Pincus Hartman, and Michael Brown, "Moral Person and Moral Manager: How Executives Develop a Reputation for Ethical Leadership," *California Management Review,* Summer 2000, p. 134.

[43] Interviewed by Tammy L. MacLean, "Thick as Thieves: A Social Embeddedness Model of Rule Breaking in Organizations," *Business & Society,* June 2001, p. 184.

[44] Quotes in this paragraph are from Dennis K. Berman and Rebecca Blumenstein, "Behind Lucent's Woes: All-Out Revenue Goal and Pressure to Meet It," *The Wall Street Journal,* March 29, 2001, pp. A1 and A8.

revenue goal, the sales staff reacted. They offered legitimate discounts to customers, but these did not bring in enough to meet goals. Soon other methods popped up. Customers were given credits booked in the fourth quarter toward future purchases. Products were sold to distributors, not final customers, in a procedure called "channel stuffing." BellSouth signed a $95 million "software pooling" deal booked in the fourth quarter, though it had a year to decide how much software it would actually buy. Told again by the head of sales that the revenue target was hopeless, McGinn simply "didn't take no for an answer." Ultimately, the target was missed. McGinn was fired. Lucent notified government regulators that $679 million in fourth quarter revenue was unallowable. One sales agent lost his job for falsifying documents about when revenue was received. McGinn assured reporters that he "never asked anyone to do anything untoward."

Reward and compensation systems can also expose employees to ethical compromises.

The Laser Vision Institute is a chain of 19 centers that does popular Lasik eye surgery to correct vision. The market for this surgery is extremely competitive. LVI's ads state a fee of $499 per eye, although an asterisk leads to small type stating "price may vary according to RX and astigmatism." When customers arrive they do not see physicians at first; instead, they meet with counselors who explain what type of surgery the person needs and collect a deposit. The deposit is not refundable unless the patient is later medically disqualified. There is no record of dissatisfaction with the outcome of LVI's laser treatments. What patients do not realize is that the counselors they see work on an incentive system. They make yearly base salaries of $40,000 but add to their income with bonuses paid when patients are upgraded to more expensive surgeries. For the $499 procedure they get a per-eye bonus of only $1. But the amount rises with the surgery's price—$2 for a $599 surgery, $6 for the $799 procedure, $16 for $999, and so forth, up to $40 for patients paying $1,599. To be eligible for these bonuses, however, the counselors must close on at least 75 percent of the people with whom they meet. It is no surprise, then, that prospects are subjected to aggressive tactics similar to those faced by car buyers and that, in the end, 88 percent of them pay more than $499.[45]

When companies adopt policies that put employees under pressure, they should build in strong ethical rules too. Otherwise, the repetitive message to achieve profit goals drowns out the principles in the ethics code framed on the wall. When the tide of money runs high, shore up the ethical dikes.

---

[45] Marc Borbely, "Lasik Surgery Sales Tactics Raise Eyebrows," *Washington Post,* September 4, 2001, p. A1.

Corporate Culture

Corporate culture refers to a set of values, norms, rituals, and behaviors that characterize a company. Every corporate culture has an ethical dimension reinforced not primarily by formal policies but by daily habit and shared beliefs about which behaviors are rewarded and which are penalized.

Recent graduates of the Harvard MBA program who were interviewed about the ethical atmosphere in their organizations revealed the strong presence of four informal but powerful "commandments" conveyed to them early in their careers.

> First, performance is what really counts, so make your numbers. Second, be loyal and show us that you're a team player. Third, don't break the law. Fourth, don't overinvest in ethical behavior.[46]

The young managers believed, in the face of these informal norms, that if questionable behavior was accompanied by achievement, it advanced careers. They were in fear of taking ethical stands or blowing the whistle, and not without reason. When one manager persisted in challenging false figures that her superior used, she discovered that she was in trouble.

> He started treating other people better. He wasn't on my side anymore, and you needed him on your side to do things. He wasn't my buddy anymore . . . there were other cases of this. He did it by acting like you weren't that smart anymore. It made it really difficult to get the kind of support you needed to be a really top performer.[47]

A factor that contributes to lowered ethical climates in corporations is the inability to raise and discuss ethical issues between managers. At one oil company, an employee requested time to raise an ethical problem during a meeting of division presidents. They refused saying, "If he wants to talk ethics, let him talk to a priest or a psychiatrist."[48] This phenomenon, which was studied by Bird and Waters and labeled "moral muteness," is widespread. In their study, Bird and Waters found that "managers seldom discuss with their colleagues the ethical problems they routinely encounter."[49] Indeed, of 300 cases of ethical issues their interviews uncovered,

---

[46] Joseph L. Badaracco Jr. and Allen P. Webb, "Business Ethics: A View from the Trenches," *California Management Review,* Winter 1995, p. 11.

[47] Ibid.

[48] Linda Klebe Treviño, Gary R. Weaver, David G. Gibson, and Barbara Ley Toffler, "Managing Ethics and Legal Compliance: What Works and What Hurts," *California Management Review,* Winter 1999, p. 143.

[49] Frederick B. Bird and James A. Waters, "The Moral Muteness of Managers," *California Management Review,* Fall 1989, p. 74.

only 12 percent were ever openly discussed. There are reasons for this inability to talk about ethics. Some managers think that verbalizing an ethical judgment is confrontational; it involves placing blame and creates anger or grudges. In organizations where formal standards are not followed and deceit is rewarded, ethical arguments lack legitimacy or force. In addition, many managers have a rich vocabulary and logic for parsing business issues but lack these assets in the moral realm. Thus, they tend to redefine ethical issues as business matters. For example, if someone lays out a fraudulent ad in a committee meeting, others will not accuse the person of dishonesty. Instead, they will discuss possible losses of sales and revenue if the misrepresentation is discovered—even if their primary motive for opposing the ad is a desire to be honest. The tendency toward moral muteness is probably present to some degree in every company.

Individual Characteristics

Behavior is motivated by a mixture of internal disposition and situational incentives. In a corporation with a poor ethical climate, corrupt leaders, and high pressure to achieve numbers, otherwise honest individuals may be pushed into compromise. However, all things being equal, having employees who are internally disposed to right action is better. People differ greatly in their drives, ambitions, neuroses, and penchants for ethical behavior.

Researchers have attempted to discover what characteristics of people are associated with ethical behavior. However, it proves very difficult to find a relationship between something concrete about an individual and that person's ethical disposition. There are indications that higher ethics come with advancing age and longer work experience.[50] Some studies show that women are more ethical than men, but results are mixed.[51] No studies find men to be more ethically sensitive than women, but some show no difference. A few studies suggest that people with more education are more ethical, but others do not. There is considerable evidence that the company environment influences conduct. Individuals seem to act less ethically as corporations increase in size, but they tend to be more ethical where companies have codes of conduct.[52]

[50] Terry W. Low, Linda Ferrell, and Phylis Mansfield, "A Review of Empirical Studies Assessing Ethical Decision Making in Business," *Journal of Business Ethics,* June 2000.
[51] Donald Robin and Laurie Babin, "Making Sense of the Research on Gender and Ethics in Business: A Critical Analysis and Extension," *Journal of Business Ethics,* October 1997, pp. 79–81.
[52] See, for example, Marshall Schminke, "Considering the Business in Business Ethics: An Exploratory Study of the Influence of Organizational Size and Structure on Individual Ethical Predispositions," *Journal of Business Ethics,* April 2001.

HOW CORPORATIONS MANAGE ETHICS

In the past, it was assumed that ethics are a matter of individual conscience. A few pioneers tried to elevate company ethics. In 1913 James Cash Penney introduced a conduct code for employees in his department stores (one that is still used today, despite somewhat archaic language). However, his effort was a lonely one, and until recently, most companies had more formal policies and procedures for managing petty cash than for elevating ethics. This has changed.

Today many companies set up what are called *ethics programs,* or coordinated applications of management techniques designed to instill values and promote more ethical behavior. There are two types. Ethics programs have a *compliance* orientation if their primary purpose is to keep employees from breaking the law. They have a *values* orientation when they are designed to instill ethical values in employees over and above the more pedestrian aim of simply getting them to obey laws. Whatever they are called, they operate similarly, relying on many of the same management tools and differing only in emphasis.

Ethics programs grew from the soil of scandal. In response to a run of contract billing frauds and cost overruns that plagued military contractors in the 1980s, the industry set up the Defense Industry Initiative, a project requiring firms to adopt ethics codes, train employees to obey laws, and create an open atmosphere for reporting violations. Today 50 of the largest defense contractors have extensive ethics programs and even get together once a year at a conference to share best practices. The rise of these programs dramatically reduced malfeasance in this industry. A second wave of scandal-spawned ethics programs came in the mid-1990s, when the federal government cracked down on hospitals and nursing homes for Medicare billing fraud. Corporations in the health care industry rushed to follow the defense industry model.

Meanwhile, the United States Sentencing Commission in 1991 set up sentencing guidelines that provided uniform punishment for corporations. It also established a system of penalty calculation that permitted massive fines exceeding any previously levied for egregious behavior. In 1990, the year before introduction of the guidelines, fines of lawbreaking companies averaged $177,990. As a result of the guidelines, by 1999 the average fine was $6.1 million.[53] The guidelines allowed major reductions in fines and penalties for companies having internal programs for preventing and reporting criminal behavior. These reductions were an impetus for all corporations, not just those in scandal-prone industries, to start ethics programs. If the company or its managers ever committed a

---

[53] Diana E. Murphy, "The Federal Sentencing Guidelines for Organizations: A Decade of Promoting Compliance and Ethics," *Iowa Law Review,* January 2002.

criminal act, the punishment would be lessened by a reasonably sincere ethics program—even one inadequate to prevent the crime.

The need for such a program was further underlined in the 1996 *Caremark* case. Caremark International, a health care company, was caught giving kickbacks to physicians who referred Medicare and Medicaid patients to its clinics. After being indicted, the company set up a compliance program, but it was too late to prevent $250 million in fines. Angry shareholders sued members of the board of directors for breach of duty because they had not set up an ethics program, thereby exposing the firm to a big fine. Caremark's directors narrowly escaped paying damages from their own pockets after a settlement. However, the judge who approved the settlement made it plain that if directors fail to setup management systems promoting lawful behavior they can be held liable for fines.[54]

What should these systems be like? Chapter 8 of the *Guidelines Manual* helps companies design compliance programs that may reduce culpability.[55] Following are listed the seven "minimum steps." The chapter does not spell out how each step must be carried out; however, we elaborate on common methods used by companies in each.

1. *Establish compliance standards and procedures for employees that are reasonably capable of reducing criminal acts.* Most companies meet this requirement with a variety of written documents. The centerpiece is usually a written code of conduct that sets forth basic values such as honesty, integrity, and fairness, often at a high level of abstraction. Here are some typical statements.

> We will always take the high road by practicing the highest ethical standards and by honoring our commitments. We will take personal responsibility for our actions and treat everyone fairly and with trust and respect.
>
> *Boeing Company*

> Business integrity is hard to define, but everybody knows it when they see it. Among other things, it means honesty, and obeying the law. It means treating those with whom we work with fairness and respect. And it means being accountable and taking responsibilities for actions and consequences.
>
> *Sara Lee Corporation*

---

[54] *In re Caremark International Inc. Derivative Litigation,* 698 A.2d 970 (1996).
[55] United States Sentencing Commission, *Guidelines Manual,* §8A1.2, application notes 3(k)(1)–(7), November 1, 2001.

GE Code of Conduct

- Obey the applicable laws and regulations governing our business conduct worldwide.

- Be honest, fair and trustworthy in all your GE activities and relationships.

- Avoid all conflicts of interest between work and personal affairs.

- Foster an atmosphere in which fair employment practices extend to every member of the diverse GE community.

- Strive to create a safe workplace and to protect the environment.

- Through leadership at all levels, sustain a culture where ethical conduct is recognized, valued and exemplified by all employees.

Source: General Electric Company, *Integrity: The Spirit & the Letter of Our Commitment,* October 2000.

> Each of our employees is expected to comply with the law, but our standard of business ethics goes beyond compliance with law. No list of rules can substitute for the exercise by anyone who represents our company of basic morality, common decency, high ethical standards and respect for the law.
>
> *Sealed Air Corporation*

Some codes of conduct, such as GE's (see the accompanying box), are brief statements of principle at a high level of abstraction. These short codes are usually reinforced by more detailed policy documents on subjects such as conflict of interest, bribery, gifts and entertainment, insider trading, antitrust violations, trade secrets, and political contributions. The Boeing code of "Ethical Business Conduct," for example, is only two and one-half pages, but it is supplemented by 10 more specific policies. Some company's codes are booklets running to dozens of pages. The Weyerhaeuser "Guidelines for Business Conduct" fill a 36-page booklet, and the Baxter International "Global Business Practice Standards" cover 46 pages.

Besides broad expressions of ethical values and longer statements of rules or procedures, conduct codes contain a variety of other elements. Some, for example, present brief cases in question and answer format. Raytheon's colorful *Standards of Business Ethics and Conduct* booklet contains this example on a page about gifts, entertainment, and bribes.

Q: One of my suppliers regularly gives away box seats to our local professional baseball team. I know that the tickets cost more than the $20 maximum for gifts, but this supplier gives tickets away to all his customers, not just us, and he has never, ever, asked to swap a baseball ticket for a business favor. Why shouldn't I accept the tickets?

A: In our relationships with suppliers, even the appearance of favoritism can damage our reputation. Although the baseball tickets probably aren't intended to influence a specific business decision, this gift could be perceived as favoritism by customers or suppliers. It could also be used in the future to influence a business decision.[56]

A recent survey reported that 97 of responding companies had a code of conduct.[57] They are usually distributed to all employees and frequently recipients must sign a form acknowledging that they have read the code and agree to comply with it. Many companies translate them into multiple languages.

2. *Assign responsibility for overseeing the program to high-level personnel.* The structures of ethics programs vary, but direct oversight usually comes from the company's board of directors. At Boeing, for example, the board appoints members of an Ethics and Business Conduct Committee that is responsible for the administration of the ethics program. This committee consists of Boeing's chairman and CEO, the president and COO, the presidents of operating groups, and senior vice presidents. Reporting to the committee is a vice president of ethics and business conduct, who administers the program's daily affairs and supervises ethics officers who work in Boeing business segments around the world. This internal structure is typical of a well-integrated program in a multinational corporation. Occasionally, ethics staffs are quite large. United Technologies, for example, has a network of 160 business ethics officers at its businesses around the world.[58] However, some companies have very lean structures in which overall responsibility is placed with a single corporate executive or in a legal department.

3. *Exercise due care not to delegate substantial discretionary authority to persons who are prone to engage in criminal behavior.* This requirement in the sentencing guidelines is important, but it has not led to major changes in the way companies operate. In one survey of the 1,000 largest American firms, only 56 percent did background checks before hiring managers and only 17 percent did them when employees were first put into sensitive positions.[59] About half the companies required major vendors to comply with provisions in their codes of conduct.

---

[56] August 2001, p. 13.
[57] Sherrie McAvoy and Carole Basri, "Measuring Your Compliance Program," *New York Law Journal,* May 14, 2001, p. S6.
[58] "Doing Well by Doing Good," *The Economist,* April 22, 2000, p. 67.
[59] McAvoy and Basri, "Measuring Your Compliance Program," p. S6.

4. *Take steps to communicate standards and procedures to all employees.* A key element of an ethics program is training. There are many approaches to training. Generally, ethics training is most effective when company managers do it, not outsiders, and when it steers away from abstract philosophy to focus on the work lives of attendees. A few companies offer in-depth seminars lasting one to three days that transmit policies and allow discussion of rules and case studies. More typical are one-hour sessions in which employees see a video or work through a series of exercises. At many companies, ethics training is given on a website or intranet.

Typically, training sessions and exercises are simple, practical, and short. They are not philosophical debates of amusing dilemmas. Usually they raise questions in areas of potential difficulty, and the company gives firm answers. At Lockheed Martin, employees play ethics games for one hour each year in which they score points based on responses to workplace situations. At Boeing, employees doing web-based training go through a gamelike sequence of short incidents that raise ethical issues.[60] After reading about a situation, they pick an action from among alternatives, each of which is scored based on its appropriateness at Boeing.

> A colleague is attending business school and wants everyone to know it. During team meetings, he peppers his speech with jargon like "synergy," "out of the box," "proactive," "win-win," and "empowerment," inserting at least one of these words into every sentence. Several team members have mentioned to you that they find this annoying. To poke fun at him, you have created a series of cards containing these words that look like bingo cards. During team meetings, players will check off these words when they hear your colleague use them. The first player to complete a row will shout "bingo!" and win the game. . . . Is this OK?
>
> A. You bet. It will bring him down a peg and let him know he is annoying others. It is also a fun way to build team spirit (scored as −10 because it violates "Boeing's commitment to treating each other with trust, fairness, and respect").
> B. Absolutely not. It would be OK if he was your manager, but it's not OK to do this to a peer (scored as 0 because although it is the right answer, the reasoning is faulty: "It makes no difference whether the colleague is a manager or not").
> C. No, it's not OK to play the game (scored as +10 because it is "just not right to humiliate a co-worker in this way").

5. *Take reasonable steps to achieve compliance with standards by using monitoring and auditing systems designed to detect lawbreaking and by having in place a reporting system that employees can use to report criminal conduct.* There are many options for monitoring, auditing, and reporting. Strong ethics/compliance programs have telephone *hotlines* on which employees can report unethical behavior. Effective hotlines are toll-free, operate

---

[60] At http://active.boeing.com/companyoffices/ethicschallenge/cfm/initial.cfm.

around the clock, and grant anonymity to callers. Since many employees are suspicious and fear retaliation, hotlines must be supported with strong policies against retaliation. One estimate is that each year 20 to 23 employees out of every 1,000 employees in a company will place a hotline call.[61] The calls create an enormous amount of work for ethics offices. Many employees seek advice: "Would it be a conflict of interest for me to work in the evening?" Others have trivial complaints, such as "My supervisor came back an hour late from lunch." Allegations must be investigated; for instance, "I think one of my team members is harassing a co-worker." Although very few calls reveal criminal wrongdoing, hotlines are an important channel of communication from workers who might be intimidated from speaking to their immediate superiors.

Companies also engage in other forms of monitoring, auditing, and reporting. GE's Aircraft Engines division monitors statistical indicators related to compliance. For example, it watches the number of sales representatives in foreign countries, and when that number rises, it takes action to reduce the risk of violating antibribery laws.[62] Some companies require reports of unusual financial transactions. BellSouth prepares a quarterly ethics report containing statistics and commentary about the number and disposition of hotline calls and other issues.

6. *Consistently enforce standards using appropriate disciplinary mechanisms and, as appropriate, disciplining individuals responsible for failure to detect an offense.* Most firms with ethics and compliance programs have written disciplinary policies. Although discipline is usually handled on a case-by-case basis there can be standards to insure consistency across organization levels and between business units. Discipline is usually based on factors such as seriousness of the violation, level in the organization of the violator, extent of cooperation in the investigation, prior misconduct, and willfulness of the action. A progressive range of disciplinary options—counseling, oral reprimand, written reprimand, probation, suspension, salary reduction, termination—can be used as fits the case.[63] Many companies publicize at least raw numbers of disciplinary actions, such as the number of firings for ethical transgression.

A related approach to standards enforcement is to make ethics a part of performance appraisals. This is done in many companies where an-

[61] Andrew Singer, "At Howmet Corporation, the Internal Auditor Wears the Ethics Hat," *Ethikos,* September–October 1999.
[62] Andrew Singer, "GE Extends Its 'Quality' Effort to Compliance," *Ethikos,* January–February 2001, p. 6.
[63] John D. Copeland, "The Tyson Story: Building an Effective Ethics and Compliance Program," *Drake Journal of Agricultural Law,* Winter 2000.

nual ratings require comment on such things as whether a manager encourages discussion of ethical concerns, maintains a reprisal-free environment, acts fairly, and instills trust and respect.[64]

Tenet Healthcare Corp., an $11 billion company with 115 hospitals in 17 states, is one of only a few companies that ties compensation to ethics. For the top 800 managers and executives, bonus amounts are increased or decreased by up to 25 percent based on an ethics score given in performance reviews. Tenet's senior vice president of ethics, business conduct, and administration visits all 115 facilities and conducts the assessment by gathering the manager's colleagues around a table and asking for comments reflecting the person's effort in ethics and compliance. Based on these comments, managers get a score between –5 and +5 points and each point increases or decreases their bonus by 5 percent. Negative scores are called "dings" in company slang, and the humiliation of being singled out far outweighs the lost dollars.[65]

7. *Immediately after an offense has been detected, respond appropriately and take reasonable steps to prevent further similar offenses.* The first response of a corporation learning of a crime should be to notify law enforcement voluntarily. This may greatly reduce subsequent penalties. After serious problems, companies can modify their ethics and compliance systems, making them better able to detect and prevent wrongdoing. This includes actions such as revising the code of conduct or adding more training.

ETHICS PROGRAMS: AN ASSESSMENT

Ethics programs are a set of interrelated policies and methods. A firm estimate of the number of companies having them is elusive. Many firms have one or more of the central elements of an ethics program, for example, a code of conduct; but only a small number, perhaps 100 to 200, have strong programs in which a full range of methods is integrated into organizational structures and processes. Among firms with full ethics programs, the compliance orientation predominates over the values orientation. This is not surprising because research has shown that the federal sentencing guidelines and fear of a corporate scandal hitting the media

---

[64] The Defense Industry Initiative on Business Ethics and Conduct, *2000 Annual Report to the Public and the Defense Industry,* February 15, 2001, pp. 44–45.
[65] Andrew W. Singer, "At Tenet Healthcare: Linking Ethics To Compensation," *Ethikos,* January–February 2001, pp. 4–5.

are the primary motives for setting them up.[66] Researchers have also shown that both orientations are effective in increasing employees' awareness of ethical issues at work and reducing unethical behavior, though the values orientation is most effective.[67]

CONCLUDING OBSERVATIONS

The business environment is rich in sources of ethical values. Yet strong forces in both markets and corporations act to depress behavior. Managers may use a range of methods to discourage transgression and encourage high ethics. While these methods achieve some success, there is no evidence that, overall, behavior is different or better today than in the past. Ethical problems in economic life stem from a timeless conflict between self-interest and fairness toward others. In the next chapter we take a close look at ethical decisions to explain why they are difficult.

[66] Gary Weaver, Linda Klebe Treviño, and Philip L. Cochran, "Corporate Ethics Programs as Control Systems: Influences of Executive Commitment and Environmental Factors," *Academy of Management Journal*, February 1999, pp. 50–53.

[67] Gary Weaver and Linda Klebe Treviño, "Compliance and Values Oriented Ethics Programs: Influences on Employees' Attitudes and Behavior," *Business Ethics Quarterly*, April 1999.

Dow Corning and Breast Implants

Dow Corning Corporation is a 50–50 joint venture of Dow Chemical Company and Corning Incorporated. It was set up in 1943 to develop commercial uses for a marvelous new material called silicone. Over the years, it has done this so successfully that it now makes more than 7,000 silicone-based products. In 2000 it had sales of $2.7 billion and employed 9,300 workers around the world.

Dow Corning has a history of pioneering. It pioneered in the development of the silicones that now are ubiquitous in daily life. It pioneered by setting up an ethics program in the 1970s, when such efforts were rare. And it pioneered breast implants made of silicone, which belong in a showcase of great twentieth century product disasters. What follows is the story of how honest, well-intentioned managers muddled their way into a quicksand of lawsuits and bankruptcy from which extrication is a work in progress.

DEVELOPMENT OF BREAST IMPLANTS

Before silicone, other substances were used to enlarge women's breasts, including stainless steel, rubber, and plastic sponges. The body rejects these materials, and the results often looked bad. When silicone came along, doctors tried injecting it directly into the breast, but loose silicone sometimes migrated into the chest, with disfiguring results.

In 1959 two Texas physicians had an idea for making better implants by filling silicone bags with saline solution. They contacted Dow Corning for help and the company put itself to the task. No reliable valve to contain such a fluid existed, so the company recommended filling a silicone bag with a semiliquid silicone gel that would feel much like natural breast tissue.

While Dow Corning chemists made a proto-type, the two doctors put silicone implants in a few dogs for 18 months. This would be the only testing done to check for biological reactions before the first implants were marketed. Dow Corning did no animal studies of its own but believed, based on experience with other silicone products such as shunts and catheters, that the substance was biologically inert and harmless in the human body. Neither did it do any clinical trials with human subjects. Because of a gaping loophole in the Food, Drug, and Cosmetic Act of 1938, these weren't required. This law required drug companies to do rigorous animal and human studies before selling a prescription drug. Yet it allowed "medical devices," even those put into the human body, to be sold without any testing. If Dow Corning had invented a pill to enlarge women's breasts, years of expensive animal tests and clinical trials would have been required to prove its safety. Yet a device to be placed in a woman's breast for a lifetime got a free pass. Therefore, when Dow Corning put the first silicone-gel breast implant on the market in 1963, no testing had proved it safe.

A CLOSER LOOK AT SILICONE

Silicones are long, heavy molecules based on a repeating chain of silicon and oxygen atoms. Silicon is the second most abundant elemental substance, comprising 28 percent of the earth's crust. It is the building block for the silica compounds in sand. To make its silicone products, Dow Corning buys large quantities of silicon from suppliers that refine it from sand.

Unlike silicon, silicones do not exist in nature. They are created in a high-temperature process during which chemists can manipulate them by adding organic molecules such as methyl or phenyl and raising or lowering the heat. This is how silicone powders, liquids, semiliquid gels (as in breast implants), and solids are made. A child's Silly Putty is a silicone molecule containing a methyl group cooked in a 5 percent boric acid solution for many hours at a temperature above 300° F.

Until the 1940s, silicones were experimental curiosities, but their practical properties were finally recognized. It was the military value of silicones that led to the formation of Dow Chemical at the height of World War II. For example, silicone gaskets for searchlights on antiaircraft guns retained their shape and shock absorbency within a temperature range of −55 to +570° F, so they could absorb recoil and withstand heat from the electric arc in the lights. Silicone fluids were made for the hydraulic systems of airplanes, where they retained viscosity over a broader temperature range than motor oils and were less flammable. In those days, silicones were regarded as wondrous substances.

After the war, the unique properties of silicones brought them into consumer products. At normal temperatures they are chemically inert, so in paints and coatings they resist oxidation. They are heat and flame resistant and do not conduct electricity, making them fine insulators. Their low surface tension makes them slippery, so they ease the application of waxes, polishes, hand lotions, and roll-on antiperspirants. Due to antifoaming qualities, they are added to fruit juices, molasses, soft drinks, shampoos, varnishes, and detergents. So on a daily basis the average American ingests or absorbs silicone molecules.

A NEW GENERATION OF IMPLANTS

Dow Corning's silicone-gel implants were thought to be completely safe, and demand surged as women took advantage of them. In the early 1970s, however, competitors hired away some of Dow Corning's scientists and attacked its market monopoly with a new generation of superior silicone-gel implants. The new implants had thinner envelopes and more flexible gel, giving them a more natural feel. By 1975 competitors selling them had seized two-thirds of the market from Dow Corning.

To counter the competition, Dow Corning created a new, thinner, silicone gel of its own called flo-gel. It projected sales of more than 50,000 a year and wanted to rush flo-gel to market. Great urgency was attached to meeting a deadline of June 1975. In January 1975 a mammary task force was set up to guide the project. Its leader, Arthur H. Rathjen, was a hard-driving manager whose memos featured a countdown to the June deadline. A January 31 memo began: "17 weeks, 121 days, 2,904 hours, 174,240 minutes."[1]

Although members of the task force shared a strong belief that silicone was safe in the human body, they decided to see if "gel-bleed" would be a medical problem with the new implants. Gel-bleed occurred when silicone molecules migrated through the thin plastic envelope surrounding the new liquid gel. The thinner formulation in flo-gel contained smaller molecules, which is why it was more flexible and felt more natural to the touch. However, these smaller molecules slipped through the larger molecular structure of the outer silicone envelope. Gel-bleed was so pronounced that the implants had a greasy, slippery feel in the hand. Sales managers found this molecular leakage to be a nuisance. A memo written on May 12, 1975, said that the implants on display at a trade show "became oily" and "were bleeding on the velvet in the showcase."[2] Some task force members were concerned that gel-bleed might cause adverse reactions in human tissue.

Dow Corning decided to do some testing on animals and humans. Early in February 1975, implants were sown into rabbits. Before the rabbit test ended, eight Canadian women received the new implants in experimental surgery. When the rabbit test report came in four days later, it showed significant inflammatory reactions in the animals but stated that these might be related to the surgery itself rather than bleeding gel. In another test, implants put in dogs migrated in their bodies. Weeks later the rabbits showed persistent inflammation.

Nonetheless, Dow Corning marketed its new implants on schedule without more testing. A consensus existed in the company that the gel was not a new material, only another formulation of biologically inert silicone. This sanguine view was not unanimous. Thomas Talcott, a product engineer on the implant team, believed that if the implant sac ruptured, the fluid gel would spread to surrounding tissue, posing unknown risks. He urged more study. When it was not forthcoming he resigned.

The company attributed his resignation to poor performance reviews.

The new flo-gel implants went on the market in the fall of 1975. Soon Dow Corning's sales force ran into inquiries and complaints from plastic surgeons about noticeable gel-bleed, migration of leaking gel, and ruptured implants. Sales representatives were angry. "To put a questionable lot of mammaries on the market is inexcusable," wrote one in a memo to his boss. "I don't know who is responsible for this decision, but it has to rank right up there with the Pinto gas tank."[3]

When physicians noticed severe inflammatory reactions in some women, Rathjen wrote an internal memorandum raising questions. "We are engulfed in unqualified speculation. . . . Is there something in the implant that migrates out of or off the prosthesis? Yes or no!"[4] The scientists in the company concluded that the case reports were medical anomalies and their faith in the safety of silicone was unshaken. So no clinical studies were initiated.

Despite this rocky start, the new flo-gel implants restored Dow Corning's market dominance. Over the next 15 years, the popularity of breast augmentation soared and plastic surgeons bought hundreds of thousands of them. Most women were pleased with their implants. Reports of problems continued, but they were not frequent or compelling enough to shake the company's belief that silicone was safe.

BREAST IMPLANT SURGERY

Although breast implants are used for reconstruction after accidents or cancer surgery, the vast majority—about 80 percent—are put in for cosmetic reasons.[5]

There are three basic types. *Gel-filled* implants contain viscous silicones held in place by a flexible silicone envelope. *Saline* implants contain sterile

---

[1] Marlene Cimons, "Implant Firm's Memos Linked to Full FDA Ban," *Los Angeles Times*, January 17, 1992, p. A32.
[2] Ibid.
[3] Quoted in John A. Byrne, *Informed Consent* (New York: McGraw-Hill, 1996), p. 78.
[4] "Maker of Implants Balked at Testing, Its Records Show," *The New York Times*, January 13, 1992, p. B1.
[5] Nancy J. Nelson, "Silicone Breast Implants Not Linked to Breast Cancer Risk," *Journal of the National Cancer Institute*, November 2000, p. 1715.

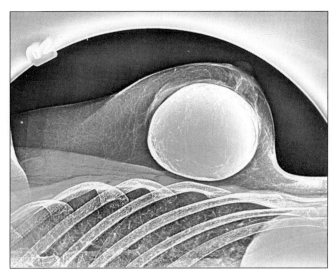

Mammograph showing a silcone-gel breast implant. © Custom Medical Stock Photo

saline solution inside a silicone envelope. They are like balloons filled with salt water. Saline implants can be inserted in collapsed form through a small incision and then filled in place. If the capsule ruptures, the salt water is harmlessly absorbed by the body within hours. The woman will, of course, wake up in the morning with a deflated breast. (Dow Corning never made saline implants.) *Double-lumen* implants contain a gel capsule surrounded by an envelope of saline (or sometimes the reverse). This design is thought to create a more natural-looking breast.

Most implant surgeries are performed as outpatient procedures. Either local or general anesthesia may be used. Incisions are usually made under the breast where the implant is inserted in a pocket cut out by the surgeon. It takes about two hours, and there can be pain afterward. For plastic surgeons, the procedure is simple: "like changing a tire," in the words of one.[6] The current cost of breast implantation is $4,000 to $8,000.

Women who get implants risk complications. After insertion the body forms scar tissue around them. As this tissue hardens it contracts, squeezing the implant into a round shape. The breast may feel hard and be painful. Capsular contracture, as this is called, occurs in about half of the recipients. Another common problem is loss of nipple sensation immediately following surgery. This also affects about half of all patients. Sometimes full or partial sensation returns in six to nine months. Less frequently, women may suffer a range of postsurgical complications such as skin necrosis from inadequate blood circulation when skin stretches to accommodate the implant, asymmetrical breasts, and palpable wrinkling of the implant's surface.[7]

CONTROVERSY RISES

Some women had trouble with their implants. In 1985 a San Francisco jury awarded a woman $1.7 million based on her claim that silicone had migrated from a ruptured flo-gel implant causing a painful immune system response. During the trial, her lawyers discovered Dow Corning memos questioning the safety of the flo-gel and reporting on

---

[6] Quoted in Susan M. Zimmermann, *Silicone Survivors* (Philadelphia: Temple University Press, 1998), p. 57.

[7] Package insert for "Silastic MSI Brand Mammary Implant H. P. Gel-Filled Design by Dow Corning Wright," rev. 3, June 1991, pp. 4–8.

the old animal studies in which rabbits and dogs suffered inflammation. The jury found the company guilty of fraud for its failure to disclose to women the risks alluded to in these documents. It was also found guilty of selling a defective product and breaching its written warranty that the implants would last a lifetime. The company's response was to change the wording on package inserts to reveal more risks.

There were no more lawsuits in the 1980s, but controversy over implants slowly grew. Discussions about them appeared in the media. Activists emerged to campaign for investigation and regulation. Their efforts soon bore fruit.

In 1976 Congress had amended the 1938 law that exempted medical devices from clinical trials, giving the Food and Drug Administration (FDA) authority to require safety tests before they were marketed. It took a while, but in 1988, over the persistent opposition of Dow Corning, breast implant manufacturers were given 30 months to submit evidence that silicone breast implants were safe.[8]

In 1991 Dow Corning handed over more than 10,000 pages of information intended to prove safety, but after some study, the FDA found the evidence insufficient, though not alarming enough to warrant banning them. It gave Dow Corning more time to collect and submit additional evidence of safety.

THE HOPKINS CASE LEADS TO AN FDA MORATORIUM

By this time, the media was filled with emotional and sensational stories about women made ill by breast implants. Then a San Francisco jury awarded $7.3 million to Marianne Hopkins, a woman who claimed that silicone molecules spreading from a ruptured Dow Corning implant into her lymph nodes had harmed her immune system. She suffered extreme fatigue and swollen, painful joints and was diagnosed with irreversible mixed connective tissue disorder. Dow Corning's lawyers argued that there was no scientific evidence showing silicone exposure caused immune reactions. Hopkins's attorneys introduced into evidence the internal memos used in the 1985 case. The jury held that the company had marketed a defective design and negligently failed to warn women of the risks.

The verdict stunned Dow Corning, which immediately issued a press release calling it "outrageous" and "an affront to the more than 8,000 Dow Corning employees worldwide."[9] After the trial, a court order sealed the Dow Corning documents, but one of Hopkins's attorneys leaked them to FDA Commissioner David Kessler. They so alarmed Kessler that on January 6, 1992, three days after getting them, he announced a 45-day moratorium on the sale of silicone-gel breast implants.

The FDA moratorium, following closely on the heels of the Hopkins decision, was a calamity for Dow Corning and other implant makers, setting them on a collision course with a mass of lawsuits. Attorneys who specialize in products liability cases noted Hopkins's huge $7.3 million award, of which $6.5 million was punitive damages, and the FDA's action, which suggested serious defects. Within a week there were more than 75 implant suits; by the end of the month about 1,000, and this was just the beginning.[10]

In February the FDA advisory panel met again. It concluded that there was insufficient evidence to make a causal connection between implants and the symptoms and diseases they were alleged to cause. It also said that manufacturers still had not proved the devices safe and recommended restrictions on their use. So Commissioner Kessler extended his moratorium indefinitely until medical research confirmed the safety of silicone-gel implants, knowing that this would take many years.[11] Saline implants remained available. At this point, Dow Corning stopped making silicone breast implants and never resumed.

[8] 53 FR 23856, June 24, 1988.

[9] Dow Corning, *Corporate News,* "Dow Corning and Its Employees Call San Francisco Jury Award Regarding Breast Implants 'Outrageous,' " December 13, 1991, pp. 1 and 2.
[10] Joseph Nocera, "Fatal Litigation," *Fortune,* October 16, 1995, p. 74.
[11] See David A. Kessler, "The Basis of the FDA's Decision on Breast Implants," *New England Journal of Medicine,* June 18, 1992, p. 1713.

LAWSUITS DRIVE DOW CORNING INTO BANKRUPTCY

Lawsuits against Dow Corning and its competitors accumulated. Attorneys for the women asked a federal court to certify the implant suits as a class so that a great many cases could be combined into one action. This would create a *class action suit,* which is used when multiple parties seek to redress similar injuries. All the cases are assigned to one court where the judge appoints a committee of lawyers to negotiate a settlement with manufacturers or take the case to trial on behalf of injured plaintiffs. The attorneys receive a percentage of any monetary settlement or trial award. By collecting many cases, plaintiffs' lawyers put extreme pressure on a corporation to settle, and the larger the settlement, the greater their own compensation.

A class certification was given in 1992, and a mass of breast implant cases was consolidated and assigned to federal judge Sam C. Pointer Jr. in Birmingham, Alabama. Lawyers around the country brought their cases into the class action, which quickly grew to about 10,000 women plaintiffs. Judge Pointer set up a committee of the women's attorneys to negotiate with Dow Corning and other manufacturers.

Some attorneys purposely kept their clients out of the class action, preferring to take them to trial one by one. In the first case that came to trial, the jury awarded $25 million against another implant maker, Bristol-Myers Squibb. After this, Dow Corning and the other companies preferred to settle most cases before they came to trial, and the settlements averaged $1 million per case. When they did go to trial, the companies sometimes won by focusing on the dearth of scientific evidence that implants were harmful. However, they lost other cases when women's attorneys convinced juries that women were inadequately warned of risks and that danger signals had been covered up. And the sheer mass of cases threatened astronomical legal costs if they went to trial one by one, even if the manufacturers prevailed in the majority. Moreover, the high settlement costs and jury awards in these lawsuits threatened to tear apart the class action. Why should women stay in the class and accept perhaps tens of thousands of dollars after years of drawn-out negotiations when they could go to trial right away and might get a much larger sum?

A FAILED SETTLEMENT LEADS TO BANKRUPTCY

In April 1994 Judge Pointer announced that a $4.25 billion settlement agreement had been reached in the class action. Under the agreement, women were to get 75 percent of the money; the rest, or a little more than $1 billion, would be divided by a few attorneys. However, the settlement fell apart because it was too generous—women with autoimmune disease could get up to $1.4 million—and any woman with implants could register to participate in it. Whereas 10,000 women had been enrolled in the class action, 40 times this number materialized to sign up for money, 400,000 in all, including 137,000 claiming current symptoms. There were so many women that the payment to each would have been less than 5 percent of original estimates. The plan collapsed.

With the class action settlement falling apart and independent attorneys prepared to take more cases to trial, Dow Corning faced a debilitating financial gauntlet. If nothing was done, it would eventually run out of cash for normal business operations. On May 15, 1995, the company filed a Chapter 11 bankruptcy petition. This froze all claims against it, including lawsuits, until a committee of creditors could be set up to resolve its financial problems. All implant claims against Dow Corning were moved to a federal bankruptcy court in Michigan.

Later in the year, the other implant makers that were being sued went ahead without Dow Corning and settled about 80 percent of the cases against them in an agreement of between $2 and $3 billion (depending on how many women filed claims).[12] Women who settled were entitled to payments

[12] These companies were Baxter International, Bristol-Myers Squibb Company, McGhan Medical Corporation, Minnesota Mining & Manufacturing Company, and Union Carbide Corporation. The latter two companies were sued for supplying the silicone used in breast implants sold by other companies.

from \$10,000 to \$250,000, with the average estimated at \$26,000. Although women who settle agree not to reveal amounts, only a few women have received more than \$50,000, and some have gotten as little as \$700.[13] Despite the settlement, the morass of litigation continued for these companies because 11,041 women opted not to settle and continued to pursue their own individual cases.

MEDICAL EVIDENCE ABOUT IMPLANTS

While Dow Corning and the other manufacturers struggled with lawsuits, medical researchers began publishing studies that shed more light on health risks. The most awaited ones examined the possibility that the silicone in implants causes serious diseases. There was no question that some women suffered inflammation, infection, capsular contracture, and implant rupture. But claims that implants were responsible for cancer and immune diseases were the ones that led to multimillion-dollar jury awards and placed a high cost on settling the class actions.[14]

Before the first large-scale studies came in, evidence of implant risks had been largely anecdotal, that is, based on single cases or small numbers of cases. About 1 percent of American women have implants and 1 percent have autoimmune disease. By coincidence then, a few women have both. So the individual cases written up in medical journals did not prove that implants caused immune disorders. What was needed were studies that compared a large group of women with implants to a similar group of women without them to see if disease was more prevalent in the implant group. Work on such studies had begun when the FDA called for evidence on the safety of the devices.

Research, as it came in, failed to show that silicone-gel implants increased the risk of serious disease in women. The first major study was published early in 1995. It compared connective tissue disease in 1,183 women with silicone-gel implants and 86,381 women with no implants. The authors found no association between implants and disease.[15] The next study, published in 1996, looked at connective tissue disease in 10,830 women with implants and 384,713 women without them. It found a statistically significant, but minor, increased risk of connective tissue disease among women with implants. The authors believed that this could have been because women in the study were allowed to self-report a diagnosis of disease. They concluded that "women with breast implants should be reassured that there is no large risk of connective tissue disease."[16] Soon additional large-scale studies were published, and not one showed any statistical connection between implants and a wide range of autoimmune disorders.

Cancer studies also failed to show evidence that women with implants are more likely to have cancer. A 1992 study, for example, found that 11,676 women with silicone implants experienced only about half the number of breast cancers that would be expected in the general population.[17]

The women's attorneys attacked the studies. They argued that the numbers of women in the group studies were too small to detect rare connective tissue disorders. For instance, in the 1995 study discussed above, out of 87,501 women, only 516 had a connective tissue disorder and of these

[13] Tinker Ready, "All but Forgotten," *Los Angeles Times,* October 1, 2001, p. S1.
[14] Connective tissue disorders of an autoimmune origin include scleroderma, a disfiguring hardening of the skin; lupus erythematosus, an inflammatory disease of the skin and internal organs; and rheumatoid arthritis, a painful inflammation of the joints. The yet-to-be-proven theory of women plaintiffs is that silicone molecules leak from implants and trigger the formation of antibodies, which, in turn, cause an autoimmune reaction.

[15] J. Sanchez-Guerrero et al., "Silicone Breast Implants and the Risk of Connective-Tissue Diseases and Symptoms," *New England Journal of Medicine,* June 22, 1995, pp. 1666–70.
[16] C. H. Hennekens et al., "Self-Reported Breast Implants and Connective-Tissue Diseases in Female Health Professionals: A Retrospective Cohort Study," *Journal of the American Medical Association,* February 28, 1996, p. 616.
[17] Hans Berkel, Dale C. Birdsell, and Heather Jenkins, "Breast Augmentation: A Risk Factor for Breast Cancer?" *New England Journal of Medicine,* June 18, 1992, pp. 1649–53.

only three had implants.[18] One group of researchers estimated that for a study to have sufficient statistical power to rule out any increased risk of connective tissue disorder, it would be necessary to have 64,000 women with implants in the study group, but organizing this number of women and verifying their medical conditions is an impossible research task.[19] Therefore, the studies do not provide definitive, scientific proof of total safety. They only rule out large risks, so the individual women in court could still be legitimate victims.

Women's lawyers also argued that the studies focused on classic symptoms of connective tissue disease; therefore, the researchers might have missed a new silicone-gel-related disorder. Such a disorder has never been identified and remains an unproven, theoretical possibility. Finally, some of the studies had been funded by Dow Corning, and physicians wrote to medical journals questioning the objectivity of these efforts. Yet the researchers made available their methods and data for others to analyze. Sometimes they established advisory committees of respected experts to monitor their efforts.[20] Never did evidence emerge of any Dow Corning influence.

By 2001 more than 1,100 studies of silicone-gel breast implants had been published. A few have found elevated risk of serious illness, but it would be unusual if this were not so among such a large number. Yet even studies finding risk do not find great risk or clear danger from silicone in implants. For example, a study of 13,488 women with implants over 13 years found an increased risk of brain and respiratory cancers and suicide. However, since the researchers could not record lifestyle data, including smoking behavior, for deceased women, they con-

cluded that "the significance of these findings is not clear."[21] Lifestyle data is important because studies of women who get cosmetic implants, as compared with all women, show that they drink more, have more sexual partners, have children at a younger age, are more likely to have had an abortion, and are more likely to use oral contraceptives and hair dyes.[22] Such differences are independent risk factors. Another study found that women with gel migration from ruptured implants were more likely to report having connective tissue disease.[23] However, the association between gel migration and any disorder was borderline and became statistically insignificant when multiple factors such as implant age or manufacturer were considered.

Overall, the scientific evidence shows that the significant risks with breast implants are "local complications" such as scar tissue formation, rupture, numbness, and postsurgical infection. For women having implants, the risk of experiencing one or more of these complications is high, particularly for rupture. Examination of one sample of 344 asymptomatic women found that 69 percent had ruptured implants.[24] The risks of major disease, including cancer, are statistically insignificant.

DOW CORNING IN BANKRUPTCY

In a Chapter 11 bankruptcy such as Dow Corning's, all lawsuits and financial claims against the company are frozen. Unlike a Chapter 7 bankruptcy filing, the company is not liquidated. Instead, it continues to operate and, under the

[18] Sanchez-Guerrero et al., "Silicone Breast Implants," p. 1666.
[19] S. E. Gabriel et al., "Risk of Connective Tissue Diseases and Other Disorders after Breast Implantation," *New England Journal of Medicine*, June 16, 1994, pp. 1697–1702.
[20] See the letter from Hennekens et al. in reply to criticism in the *Journal of the American Medical Association*, July 10, 1996, pp. 101–3.
[21] L. A. Brinton et al., "Cancer Risk at Sites Other than the Breast following Augmentation Mammoplasty," *Annals of Epidemiology*, May 2001, p. 248.
[22] Linda S. Cook et al., "Characteristics of Women with and without Breast Augmentation," *Journal of the American Medical Association*, May 28, 1997, p. 1612.
[23] S. L. Brown et al., "Silicone Gel Breast Implant Rupture, Extracapsular Silicone, and Health Status in a Population of Women," *Journal of Rheumatology*, May 2001, pp. 996–1003.
[24] Ibid., p. 996.

watchful eye of a bankruptcy court, it must produce a debt-restructuring plan. Once the company gets approval of the plan from its creditors, it can emerge from Chapter 11 protection and begin paying its debts.

In 1996 Dow Corning set forth the first of what would be three reorganization plans. It proposed a $2 billion fund to settle the implant lawsuits, but the women's attorneys refused to accept it. In 1997 it set forth a second proposal, this time offering $2.4 billion. Again they rejected it. As time passed, however, it was becoming harder for women to win at trial. Emerging medical evidence tended to exonerate silicone gel as the cause of serious disorders. The U.S. Supreme Court also hurt their cause in a 1993 decision when it gave judges the power to exclude so-called "junk science" testimony in trials.[25] Since research coming from establishment science consistently failed to find any connection between women's symptoms and implants, some attorneys relied on testimony by eccentrics with scientifically unsupported theories. After the court's decision, judges refused to permit testimony by experts who failed to meet standards of scientific validity.[26]

In 1998 Dow Corning made a third settlement offer of $3.2 billion. Women in the class would get $5,000 for implant removal, $25,000 for repair of rupture damage, and up to $300,000 for more serious illness. In making the offer, Dow Corning did not admit any guilt or accept the validity of theories that implants caused debilitating illness, but it agreed to compensate women anyway. Women who did not accept could opt out of the plan and individually sue the company, but only $400 million of the $3.2 billion was set aside for these independent litigants to fight over. No punitive damages were allowed, and when the $400 million fund was exhausted, they could not sue the company further. This plan was approved by 94 percent in a vote of women claimants and approved

by the bankruptcy court in 1999. Appeals continue to delay final confirmation.[27]

Why did Dow Corning still offer to settle when the tide of scientific evidence ran so strong in its favor? There are several reasons. First, the cost of defending lawsuits was high—about $1 million per case even when the company won. Second, women's lawyers kept trying to find legal theories that would crack open the bank accounts of Dow Corning's two large parents—Dow Chemical and Corning. There was fear that some novel legal theory might succeed in bankrupting these companies too. The planned settlement precludes any suits against Dow Corning's parents, which is one source of the appeals that are delaying final approval of the settlement. Finally, the implant controversy was draining in many ways. There was a strong desire to resolve the issues and refocus the company on business opportunities. Among its concerns was that GE Plastics, its biggest competitor, smelled blood and attacked its dominant position. Over the bankruptcy years, Dow Corning retained its lead, but GE had cut into it, increasing its global silicone sales by 40 percent.[28]

DOW CORNING'S ETHICS

How did a company with a history of concern for ethics fall into a morass of lawsuits alleging fraud and failure to reveal known health risks? Why did it go on selling a product it had not thoroughly tested, even as stories that women were ill multiplied?

In the early 1970s scandals emerged about overseas bribes by American companies. Since a third of its employees worked in other countries, Dow Corning set up a conduct code to guard against

[25] *Daubert v. Merrell Dow Pharmaceuticals, Inc.*, 509 U.S. 579 (1993).
[26] For example, *Hall v. Baxter Healthcare Corp.*, 947 F. Supp. 1387 (Dist. Ore. 1996), and *Kelly v. American Heyer-Schulte*, 957 F. Supp. 873 (W. Dist. Tex. 1997).
[27] There have been 28 appeals. They fall into four categories: (1) foreign women who object to lower payouts pegged to per capita GDP in their countries, (2) women who want to continue products liability suits against Dow Chemical and Corning that would be cut off by the settlement, (3) shareholders suing Dow Chemical and Corning for failure to adequately disclose Dow Corning's potential liabilities, and (4) the federal government, which wants $43 million from the fund as reimbursement for implant-related medical expenses it incurred under government health programs.
[28] David Hunter, "Dow Corning: An Update," *Chemical Week*, June 27, 2001, p. 41.

payoffs and promote integrity. In 1977 an ethics code was written and sent by the CEO to the home of every employee. It was translated into foreign languages, posted in lobbies and hallways, and emphasized in training. A business conduct committee that reported to the board of directors enforced it.

In 1977 this committee began ethics audits of Dow Corning facilities worldwide. In the audits, small groups of employees met face to face with at least two ethics committee members to discuss code-related issues. These audits were not superficial; sessions lasted up to a full day. Overall, Dow Corning's ethics program was an early, precedent-setting effort. It set up procedures to smoke out and manage ethical issues.

In fact, the propriety of selling implants was raised and discussed. John Swanson, the leader of the ethics program, became concerned over questions about the flo-gel implant's safety. In 1991 he succeeded in taking the issue to the board of directors, even drafting a hypothetical press release for their discussion, which stated that the manufacture and sale of implants would be suspended until there was more certainty about their safety. The board decided to continue making implants. It feared such a suspension would be seen as admitting that medical problems existed, which would invite catastrophic lawsuits.[29]

Besides fear of lawsuits, several other factors explain Dow Corning's sluggish response. The corporate culture held a conviction about the safety of silicone so strong that it was akin to religious belief. It was unthinkable that this miraculous, inert substance could be dangerous in the human body. Implants, which a small subsidiary in Tennessee made, were never more than one-tenth of 1 percent of Dow Corning's sales. They did not attract as much scrutiny as bigger product lines. And absence of strong ethical leadership at the top of the company may have contributed to problems.

Despite a response that is deficient in retrospect because it led to disaster, Dow Corning is not a company with an unethical culture. According to one of its former CEOs, ethical issues were discussed in some depth, and in his view, the company may even have made the right decisions. After noting the lack of scientific evidence for serious dangers from implants he says this:

> Certainly, withdrawing would have been the best short-term way to placate our critics, and maybe—in hindsight—the best business decision. But I don't think the moral dimension is quite that simple. For what about the woman who has just learned that she has breast cancer and who desparately wants the option of reconstructive surgery as part of her lifeline to hope? What was our moral responsibility to her . . . ?
>
> And what about the hundreds of thousands of women with implants who had no problems? . . . What impact would a decision to pull implants off the market have on the fears of these women, and thus, what was our moral responsibility to them?[30]

POSTSCRIPT

Today about two million women have breast implants. At a high point in the late 1980s, 150,000 women per year had augmentation surgery. The number plummeted to 31,000 in 1992 following the FDA moratorium but has steadily risen since then, and in 2000 almost 188,000 women underwent the procedure, an increase of 467 percent from 1992.[31] Since the FDA moratorium on gel implants is still in effect, the vast majority are saline implants.

Dow Corning has gotten out of its line of medical products. Beyond breast implants, it dropped knee, hip, and finger implants. It no longer conducts development research on products such as synthetic skin, eye fluids, and artificial eyes. As Dow Corning CEO Gary Anderson recently noted, "We could have continued the evolution toward a bionic person, so society has lost out. But until trial lawyers are reined in, and we get better laws, it's just not worth the aggravation of making anything that goes into the body."[32]

[29] Andrew Singer, "In Breast Implants Scandal, Where Was Dow Corning's Concern for Women?" *Ethikos,* May–June 1994.

[30] Richard A. Hazelton, "The Breast Implant Controversy: Threats and Lessons for All of Us," *Vital Speeches of the Day,* December 1, 1998, p. 117.
[31] American Society of Plastic Surgeons, "2000 Cosmetic Surgery Trends," at www.plasticsurgery.org.
[32] Quoted in Claudia H. Deutsch, "Away From the Glare, Dow Corning Recovers Its Footing," *The New York Times,* May 7, 2000, sec. 3, p. 7.

QUESTIONS

1. Did Dow Corning act in unethical ways? What did it do that was wrong or illegal?

2. What mistakes did Dow Corning make that led it into bankruptcy?

3. Could a strong manager, highly conscious of ethical issues in organizations, have taken actions that would have avoided the bankruptcy?

4. What changes could Dow Corning make to strengthen its ethics program?

5. Is the compensation in the final settlement plan fair to women? If women cannot prove by scientific method that silicone implants caused their serious illnesses, should they receive compensation at all?

6. Did the legal system work well to resolve the issues brought before it?

Chapter **Eight**

Making Ethical Decisions in Business

Realtors in the Wilderness

In ancient times the Gunnison River flowed through what is now western Colorado, carrying abrasive rock particles and debris, scouring away hard rock as it went to form a deep canyon 50 miles long. This spectacular cut in the earth reaches depths of 2,900 feet and at one point is just 40 feet wide. It is so narrow that sunlight shines on the floor only an hour a day, hence its name—Black Canyon.

In 1999 this geologic marvel was upgraded from a national monument to a national park, entitling it to uncompromising protection from human intrusion. Just before the park was created, a land speculation firm named TDX L.P. bought a 120-acre parcel of private land on the south side of the canyon. Small, privately owned tracts such as this in national monuments and parks are called *inholdings.* Property rights to inholdings were acquired years ago, usually back in the 1800s or early 1900s, as homesteads or mining claims. Under the Homestead Act of 1862 and various mining statutes, the government cannot take or buy them without the owner's consent.[1] Nor can it restrict the owner's right to mine and develop their property.

Using a realtor in the area named Tom Chapman, TDX had bought the Black Canyon acres for $240,000.[2] Soon Chapman created a sales brochure

---

[1] Although condemnation proceedings are difficult and rare, the federal government has acquired a few inholdings this way. See, for example, *United States v. 0.37 Acres of Land, More or Less,* 414 F. Supp. 470 (E. Dist. Mont., 1976).

[2] Aaron Porter, "Feds Sue to Stop Development of Land around Black Canyon," Cox News Service, December 4, 2000.

advertising lots for the construction of luxury homes. Then a billboard rose on the site of the lots along the main road into the monument: "For Sale. Forty-acre building sites. Beautiful canyon views. World-class sunsets."[3] TDX is asking $4,500 an acre for the lots, an amount that would return a gross profit of 110 percent. Environmentalists are enraged. Houses would be visible from canyon outlooks, blighting the atmosphere of wildness and natural splendor. The park superintendent is appalled but cannot afford to buy the property at such a high price.

Inholdings are a small but significant presence in the West, totaling 0.5 percent of park and wilderness acres. To protect the integrity of wilderness lands Congress years ago set up a fund to buy inholdings, but every president since Ronald Reagan raided it for money to lower the federal deficit. Now too little is left to buy much, and federal agencies generally offer owners below-market amounts for their trapped lands. This is where Thomas Chapman and TDX come in; they force the government to pay more.

In a prior foray into Black Canyon in 1984, Chapman represented a client who had been offered $200 an acre by the National Park Service for property in what was then the Gunnison National Monument. He picked part of his client's acreage, a highly visible area on the rim of the striking canyon, and threatened to build a subdivision. After he brought in a bulldozer, the agency was forced to pay $510 an acre to buy the land and halt construction.

By 1992 Chapman had become part of TDX, a limited partnership in Alabama with investors from around the country, formed for land speculation. He and the partners bought 240 acres of inholdings in the West Elk Wilderness of Colorado for $4,000 per acre. They offered to sell the land to the U.S. Forest Service, but the agency could not afford it. So Chapman started to build a lodge. Since there was no road access, construction proceeded with the roar of helicopters flying building materials over the surrounding forests. Soon the Forest Service caved in and offered to swap the TDX inholding for 107 acres it owned near Telluride, Colorado. That parcel was near a ski resort, and after the swap was made it quickly sold for $4.2 million, making a sizable profit for the investors. Chapman's share was about $1 million.[4]

This formula has been repeated at least two other times. It works because once virgin areas are developed, the wilderness is gone. Property rights are fundamental in America. Yet Chapman and TDX are criticized for extorting money that could be used for the welfare of pristine lands and their visitors. While the speculators profit, federal agencies that run parks and monuments are severely underfunded, rangers get low pay, and parks

---

[3] Richard Miniter, "Real-Estate Broker From Hell," *Reader's Digest,* February 2001, p. 114.
[4] Jason Blevins, "Real Estate Broker Defends Wilderness Tactics," *Denver Post,* August 13, 2000, p. M1.

deteriorate. Their tactics have been called immoral, unethical, and outrageous. Chapman, however, defends them.

> I will never apologize for being a capitalist because capitalism is what created the cornucopia of goods and services that we enjoy in this country. Everybody, everybody wants to sell something for more than they paid. It's all American. Unless of course you own property in a wilderness area or in a national park or a national forest. Then all of a sudden you are a greedy capitalist, a profiteer. . . . Why should capitalism be removed from wilderness areas?[5]

The story of TDX reveals an ethically complex situation. Its investors exercise basic property rights, but rights are not absolute. Their methods resonate with free market values dominant in American society, but markets exhibit flaws. In a just world, laws and rules are fair. When inholders pay taxes on their property but cannot use it as they wish or sell it for current market value, that seems unfair. Arm-twisting land deals create lavish profits for a few, but they foreclose alternative uses of money that may benefit many others.

In this chapter we set forth a wide range of principles and methods for making ethical decisions. These include principles great and small, character development, simple procedures that corporations give to their employees, and practical tips. Use of these devices makes ethical thinking more sophisticated. In themselves they do not resolve ethical issues. Judgment is still required. If you owned a pocket of land in a national park, would you threaten to build a subdivision of homes? If you decided to do that, would you feel comfortable explaining why on television? The material in this chapter can help to answer such questions. We begin by discussing some timeless ethical principles.

PRINCIPLES OF ETHICAL CONDUCT

We begin with a compendium of ethical principles—some ancient, some modern. There are dozens, if not hundreds, of such principles in the philosophical and religious traditions of East and West.

From a larger universe, we set forth 14 principles that every manager should know and think about. The 14 principles here are fundamental guides or rules for behavior. Each of them has strengths and weaknesses. Some were created to be universal tests of conduct. Others have a more limited reach and apply only in certain spheres of human relations. Some are ideals. Others accommodate balancing of interests where perfection is impossible. A few invite compromise and can be used to rationalize flawed behavior. One principle, might equals right, is a time-honored

---

[5] Ibid.

justification for ignoble acts, but we include it here because it has been the subject of discussion since time immemorial.

These principles distill basic wisdom that spans 2,000 years of ethical thought. To the extent that they offer ideas for thinking about and resolving ethical dilemmas, they are not vague abstractions but useful, living guides to analysis and conduct.[6] We present them alphabetically.

The Categorical Imperative

The categorical imperative (meaning, literally, a command that admits no exception) is a guide for ethical behavior set forth by the German philosopher Immanuel Kant in his *Foundations of the Metaphysics of Morals,* a tract published in 1785. In Kant's words: "Act only according to that maxim by which you can at the same time will that it should become a universal law."[7]

In other words, one should not adopt principles of action unless they can, without inconsistency, be adopted by everyone. Lying, stealing, and breaking promises, for example, are ruled out because society would disintegrate if they replaced truth telling, property rights, and vow keeping. Using this guideline, a manager faced with a moral choice must act in a way that he or she believes is right and just for any person in a similar situation. Each action should be judged by asking: "Could this act be turned into a universal code of behavior?" This quick *test of universalizability* has achieved great popularity.

Kant was an extreme perfectionists. He walked the same route each day at the same time, appearing at places along the route so punctually that neighbors set their clocks by him. Before leaving his house he attached strings to the top of his socks and connected them to a spring apparatus held by his belt. As he walked, the contraption would pull the slack out of his socks. To no one's surprise, his ethical philosophies are perfectionist also, and that is their weakness. Kant's categorical imperative is dogmatic and inflexible. It is a general rule that must be applied in every specific situation; there are no exceptions. But real life challenges the simple, single ethical law. If a competitor asks whether your company is planning to sell shirts in Texas next year, must you answer the question with the truth?

---

[6] Studies show that managers find principles helpful. See Phillip V. Lewis, "Ethical Principles for Decision Makers: A Longitudinal Survey," *Journal of Business Ethics,* April 1989; T. K. Das, "Ethical Principles in Business: An Empirical Study of Preferential Rankings," *International Journal of Management,* December 1992; and Scott K. Jones and Kenneth M. Hiltebeitel, "Organizational Influence in a Model of the Moral Decision Process of Accountants," *Journal of Business Ethics,* July 1995.

[7] Immanuel Kant, *Foundations of the Metaphysics of Morals,* trans. Lewis White Beck (Indianapolis: Bobbs-Merrill, 1969), p. 44; written in 1785.

The Conventionalist Ethic

This is the view that business is analogous to a game and special, lower ethics are permissible. In business, people may act to further their self-interest so long as they do not violate the law. This ethic, which has a long history, was popularized some years ago by Albert Z. Carr in *Business as a Game*.[8] "If an executive allows himself to be torn between a decision based on business considerations and one based on his private ethical code," explained Carr, "he exposes himself to a grave psychological strain."[9]

Business may be regarded as a game, such as poker, in which the rules are different from those we adopt in personal life. Assuming game ethics, managers are allowed to bluff (a euphemism for lie) and to take advantage of all legal opportunities and widespread practices or customs. Carr used two examples of situations where game ethics were permissible. In the first, an out-of-work sales agent with a good employment record feared discrimination because of his age—58. He dyed his hair and stated on his résumé that he was 45. In the second, a job applicant was asked to check off magazines he read, but decided not to check off *Playboy, The Nation,* or *The New Republic.* Even though he read them, he did not want to be labeled controversial. He checked tame magazines such as *Reader's Digest* instead.[10]

The conventionalist ethic is criticized by those who make no distinction between society's ethics and business ethics. They argue that commerce defines the life chances of millions and is not a game to be taken lightly. As a principle, the conventionalist ethic is a thin justification for deceptive behavior at the office.

The Disclosure Rule

Using the disclosure rule, a manager faced with an ethical dilemma asks how it would feel to explain the decision to a wider audience. This simple idea appears in many company ethics codes. It is stated in Baxter International's *Global Business Practice Standards* in tests of ethics that are set forth in two questions.

- What will my manager, supervisor, co-workers, or family think about what I plan to do? (The "Others" Test)

- If what I do is reported in a newspaper, or on television, will I be proud of my actions? (The "Press" Test)[11]

This rule screens out base motives such as greed and jealousy, which are unacceptable if disclosed, but it does not always give clear guidance for ethical dilemmas in which strong arguments exist for several alternatives.

---

[8] Albert Z. Carr, *Business as a Game* (New York: New American Library, 1968).

[9] "Is Business Bluffing Ethical," *Harvard Business Review,* January–February 1968, p. 149.

[10] Carr, *Business as a Game,* p. 142.

[11] Deerfield, IL: Baxter International Inc., 2000, p. 43.

A Promise, Sort Of

Are ethics and the law congruent? You be the judge.

Back in the 1960s and 1970s General Motors, like all companies, tried to recruit and retain outstanding managers. Attractive benefits such as a generous retirement plan helped. In 1968 GM began paying the full cost of basic medical insurance for salaried employees who retired and for their surviving spouses as well.

In a series of eight booklets written over two decades to explain benefits, GM made a clear commitment. "Your basic health care coverages will be provided at GM's expense for your lifetime," said one entitled *Your Benefits in Retirement,* printed in 1977. Although all eight booklets avowed lifetime coverage, four also gave notice that GM could change or end the health care coverage. "General Motors Corporation reserves the right to amend, change or terminate the Plans and Programs described in this booklet," stated *Your GM Benefits* in 1985.

Over the years, tens of thousands of GM salaried employees retired at the normal age of 65, and, as agreed, GM provided health insurance for them and their spouses at no cost. As GM's market share slipped and competition from foreign car makers increased, it also had to make reductions in the size of its salaried workforce. So it offered managers special early retirement packages. One inducement was lifetime health insurance for them and their spouses.

As health care costs rose, however, GM reconsidered its pledge. In 1987 it made major changes, eliminating vision and hearing aid coverage, adding annual deductibles of up to $250, and requiring co-payments for medical bills up to $500 a year. Suddenly, pensioners whose medical bills GM had paid in full found themselves billed up to $750 a year for medical care.

Outraged retirees sued, alleging that GM had bound itself to provide lifetime coverage. To back their claim, they argued that GM had violated parts of the Employee Retirement Income Security Act of 1974, a law that protects workers from arbitrary and unfair changes in pension and benefit plans. However, in *Sprague v. General Motors,* an appeals court disagreed and upheld GM's actions. It ruled that the disclaimer in some of GM's booklets was sufficient to put the retirees on notice that their benefits could be changed. The court was willing to overlook GM's failure to print the disclaimer in half the booklets because that did not show any deliberate intent to deceive. "There is, in our view, a world of difference between the employer's deliberate misleading of employees . . . and GM's failure to begin every communication to plan participants with a caveat," wrote Judge David A. Nelson.[12]

However, a powerful dissent came from Chief Judge Boyce F. Martin Jr., who believed the central question was, "Do the retirees have a right to the lifetime free health care General Motors promised them or can General Motors renege on its promise?" He noted that "General Motors profits from having a salaried workforce that operated under the assumption it would receive lifetime health care. When the bill came due, though, General Motors was allowed to walk away."[13]

Back when GM dominated the world auto industry and medical care cost less, a promise to provide lifetime medical care to retirees was untroubling. When keeping the agreement became a burden and those who had made it were no longer at GM, perhaps even themselves on the retirement rolls, the company released itself. GM kept its fingers crossed behind its back by issuing disclaimers in some of its brochures, so the American legal system supported its escape. The Supreme Court refused to review the case.[14] But could GM prevail in a court of business ethics?

[12] *Robert D. Sprague, et al. v. General Motors Corporation,* 133 F.3d 388 (6th Cir.1998), at 405.
[13] Ibid., at 410.
[14] *Sprague v. General Motors,* 118 S.Ct. 2312, cert. denied (1998).

Also, an action that sounds acceptable if disclosed may not, upon reflection, always be the most ethical.

The Doctrine of the Mean

This ethic, set forth by Aristotle in the *Nicomachean Ethics* and sometimes called the *golden mean,* calls for virtue through moderation.[15] Right actions are found in the area between extreme behaviors, which are labeled excess on the one hand and deficiency on the other. Facing an ethical decision, a person first identifies the ethical virtue at its core (such as truthfulness) and then seeks the mean or moderate course of action between an excess of that virtue (boastfulness) and a deficiency of it (understatement).

At ITT, Harold Geneen pushed managers to extraordinary personal sacrifices. Their time, energy, loyalty, and will were bent to corporate purposes. Obsessive work led to remarkable business successes but also to personal difficulties such as marital problems. While specific operations of ITT, taken one by one, were constructive and ethical, immoderation led some to sacrifice a balanced life.[16] To Aristotle, this would have been wrong.

The doctrine of the mean is today little recognized, but the underlying notion of moderation as a virtue lingers in Western societies. The doctrine itself is inexact. To observe it is simply to act conservatively, never in the extreme. The moderate course and specific virtues such as honesty, however, are defined as aspects existing between and defined in relation to polar extremes. What they are is open to wide interpretation.

The Ends-Means Ethic

This principle is age-old, appearing as an ancient Roman proverb, *existus acta probat,* or "the result validates the deeds." It is often associated with the Italian philosopher Niccolò Machiavelli. In *The Prince* (1513), Machiavelli argued that worthwhile ends justify efficient means, that when ends are of overriding importance or virtue, unscrupulous means may be employed to reach them.[17] When confronted with a decision involving an ethically questionable act, a person should ask whether some overall good—such as the survival of a country or business—justifies cutting corners.

In the 1980s Oracle Corporation grew rapidly. To get this growth, founder and CEO Lawrence J. Ellison pressed his sales managers to double revenues every year. Methods used by the frenzied sales force were watched less closely than its ability to hit targets. In 1993 the Securities and

---

[15] *Nicomachean Ethics,* trans. J. A. K. Thomson (New York: Penguin Books, 1982), book II, chap. 6.
[16] Manuel Velasquez and Neil Brady, "Catholic Natural Law and Business Ethics," *Business Ethics Quarterly,* March 1997, p. 95.
[17] Niccolò Machiavelli, *The Prince,* trans. T. G. Bergin, ed. (New York: Appleton-Century-Crofts, 1947); written in 1513 and first published in 1532.

Exchange Commission fined Oracle for overstating earnings by double-billing customers, invoicing companies for products never sold, and violating accounting standards by recording sales revenue before it was received.[18] However, by then Oracle had crushed its early competition in the relational database market. Today Oracle is an $11 billion corporation and Ellison is a billionaire. It employs 31,000 people and has made many of them millionaires. Its software makes governments, businesses, and universities more productive. It pays taxes in 60 countries. It has a wide range of social responsibility programs. Does this end result justify the competitive tactics used to build the company?

Any manager using unscrupulous means concedes the highest virtue and accepts the necessity of ethical compromise. In solving ethical problems, means may be as important, or more so, than ends. In addition, the process of ethical character development can never be furthered by the use of expedient means.

The Golden Rule

An ideal found in the great religions and in works of philosophy, the golden rule has been a popular guide for centuries. Simply put, it is: "Do unto others as you would have them do unto you." It includes not knowingly doing harm to others. A manager trying to solve an ethical problem places him- or herself in the position of another party affected by the decision and tries to figure out what action is most fair from that perspective.

A related principle called the *practical imperative* was set forward by Immanuel Kant. It is: "Act so that you treat humanity, whether in your own person or in that of another, always as an end and never as a means only."[19] This principle admonishes a manager to treat employees as ends in themselves, not to manipulate them simply as factors of production for the self-interested ends of the company.

Around 1900, when E. H. Harriman owned the Southern Pacific railroad, train accidents killed between 5,000 and 6,000 people a year. One day on an inspection tour, his train hit a rough section of track and nearly derailed because a work crew had neglected to post a flagman. Instead of firing the crew chief, Harriman insisted on firing the whole crew. A top executive spoke up, arguing it was cruel to punish them all. "Perhaps," responded Harriman, "but it will probably save a lot of lives. I want every man connected with the operation to feel a sense of responsibility. Now, everybody knew that the man hadn't gone back with the flag."[20] Harriman used this crew of workers to send a message to all

---

[18] Mike Wilson, *The Difference between God and Larry Ellison* (New York: William Morrow and Company, 1997), p. 239.

[19] *Foundations of the Metaphysics of Morals,* p. 54.

[20] Quoted in Maury Klein, *The Life & Legend of E. H. Harriman* (Chapel Hill: University of North Carolina Press, 2000), p. 266.

other crews. The workers were not treated as individuals; they were punished en masse to signal others in the company.

A manager may comply with both the practical imperative and the golden rule by using the *test of reversibility,* that is, by asking if he or she would change places with the person affected by the contemplated action. A problem with the golden rule is that people's ethical values differ, and they may mistakenly assume that their preferences are universal. In addition, it is primarily a perfectionist rule for interpersonal relations. So applying it in business life where the interests of individuals are subordinated to the needs of the firm is sometimes hard.

The Intuition Ethic

This ethic, as defined by philosophers such as G. E. Moore in his *Principia Ethica* (1903), holds that what is good is simply understood.[21] That is, people are endowed with a moral sense by which they intuitively know the difference between right and wrong. The solution to an ethical problem lies simply in what you feel or understand to be right.

Most people facing an ethical conflict have an emotional, gut reaction that occurs before reason illuminates the specific problem in logical terms. The situation just bothers them, even if they are not sure why. Something is wrong. This ethical intuition is not simply ungrounded self-judgment. A person's ethical instincts are the product of socialization, role expectations, and character development. Everyone carries a lifetime of moral lessons that can well up as strong emotions. Though fallible, intuition is usually accurate.

Some corporations recognize the intuition ethic in their conduct codes and offer it as a general guideline for employees. At Cummins Engine Company, Inc., for example, employees are told: "If . . . you are uncomfortable with a particular action . . . then DON'T DO IT."[22]

Drawbacks exist. The approach is subjective. Self-interest may be confused with ethical insight. No standard of validation outside the individual is used. It is unpersuasive to others for a manager to say, "It's wrong because I just think so." Also, intuition may fail to give clear answers.[23]

The Might-Equals-Right Ethic

This ethic defines justice as the interest of the stronger. It is represented by Friedrich Nietzsche's "master morality" and in the practiced ethics of organized crime. Some competitive strategies and marketing tactics reflect this thinking. What is ethical is what an individual or company has the

[21] New York: Cambridge University Press, 1948; reprint.
[22] Patrick E. Murphy, *Eighty Exemplary Ethics Statements* (South Bend, IN: University of Notre Dame Press, 1997), p. 117; emphasis in original.
[23] For an excellent discussion of intuition in manager's decisions, see Joseph L. Badaracco Jr., *Defining Moments* (Boston: Harvard Business School Press, 1997), chap. 4.

strength and power to accomplish. When faced with an ethical decision, people should seize what advantage they are strong enough to take, without regard for lofty sentiments.

In the 1860s Ben Holladay, owner of the Overland Stage Line, perfected a competitive strategy based on overbearing power. He entered new routes with lowball coach fares, subsidizing this service with profits from monopoly routes, waiting until local competitors failed. In 1863 a small stage line between Denver and Central City in Colorado charged $6 per run. Holladay put an elegant new Concord Coach with a leather interior on the line and charged only $2. The competitor soon folded, then Holladay replaced the new stagecoach with a primitive vehicle resembling a freight wagon and raised the fare to $12.

The weakness of the might-equals-right ethic lies in its confusion of ethics with force. Exercising power is different than acting from ethical duty. An ethical principle that can be invalidated by its foundation (e.g., physical force) is not consistent, logical, or valid. Might-equals-right is not a legitimate approach in civilized settings. It invites retaliation and censure, and it is not conducive to long-term advantage. Seizure by power violates the bedrock ethical duty of reciprocity on which all societies are based.

> You are sailing to Rome (you tell me) to obtain the post of Governor of Cnossus. You are not content to stay at home with the honours you had before; you want something on a larger scale, and more conspicuous. But when did you ever undertake a voyage for the purpose of reviewing your own principles and getting rid of any of them that proved unsound?
>
> **Source:** Epictetus, *The Discourses* (circa. A.D. 120).

The Organization Ethic

Simply put, this principle is: "Be loyal to the organization." It implies that the wills and needs of individuals are subordinate to the overall welfare of the organization (be it a corporation, government, university, or army). A member should act consistent with the organization's goals. This ethic leads to cooperation and mutual trust.

Many employees have such deep loyalty to an organization that it transcends self-interest. Some Americans jeopardize their health and work excessively long hours without pay out of devotion to the employer. In Asian societies, which have strong collectivist values, identification with and commitment to companies is exceptionally strong. In Japan, workers are so afraid of letting down their work group or employer that they come to work despite broken limbs and serious ailments. This behavior is so common that a word for death from overwork, *karoshi,* has entered the Japanese language.

The ethical limits of obedience are reached when duty to the organization is used to rationalize wrongdoing. The Nuremberg trials, which convicted Nazis of war crimes, taught that Western society expects members of organizations to follow their conscience. Just as no war criminal argued successfully that taking orders in a military chain of command excused their behavior, so no business manager may claim to be the helpless prisoner of corporate loyalties that crush free will and justify wrongdoing.

The Principle of Equal Freedom

This principle was set forth by the philosopher Herbert Spencer in his 1850 book *Social Statics*. "Every man may claim the fullest liberty to exercise his faculties," said Spencer, "compatible with the possession of like liberty by every other man."[24] Thus, a person has the right to freedom of action unless such action deprives another person of a proper freedom. Spencer believed this was the first principle of ethical behavior in society because only when individual liberty was protected against infringement by others could human progress occur.

To use the principle, a person asks if an action will restrict others from actions that they have a legitimate right to undertake. Most people know the colloquial version: "Your right to swing your fist ends where my nose begins."

The principle of equal freedom lacks a tie breaker for situations in which two rights conflict. Such situations require invocation of some additional rule to decide which right or freedom has priority. Ethically permissible management decisions may abridge the rights of some parties for the benefit of others. For example, all employees have broad privacy rights, but management invades them when it hires undercover detectives to investigate theft.

The Proportionality Ethic

Proportionality, an idea incubated in medieval Catholic theology, applies to decisions having both good and evil consequences. For instance, a maker of small-caliber, short-barreled, handguns that are irreverently called Saturday Night Specials has a dual impact on society. It makes available cheap, easily concealable weapons for criminals. Yet it also creates a supply of affordable self-defense weapons for poor people in crime-ridden areas who cannot buy high-quality handguns costing as much as $500. In this and similar cases, where a manager's action has a good effect but also entails a harm, the idea of proportionality fits.

A classic formulation of proportionality into a specific principle is Thomas M. Garrett's *principle of proportionality*. It states that managers are responsible for the consequences when they create situations leading to both good and evil effects. The principle allows them to risk predictable, but unwilled, harms to people (for example, innocent victims being shot by handguns) if they correctly weigh five factors.

[24] New York: Robert Schalkenbach Foundation, 1970, p. 69; first published in 1850.

First, managers must assess the *type of good and evil* involved, distinguishing between major and minor forms. Second, they should calculate the *urgency* of the situation. For example, would the firm go out of business unless employees were laid off? Third, they must estimate the *probability* of both good and evil effects. If good effects are certain and risks of serious harm are remote, an action is more favorable. Fourth, the *intensity of influence* over effects must be considered. In considering handgun injuries, for instance, manufacturers might assume that criminal action was an intervening force over which they had no control. Fifth, the existence of *alternatives* must be considered. If, for instance, an advertisement subtly encourages product misuse, the most ethical action might be to change it. Garrett believed that taking these five factors into consideration would reveal fully the ethical dimension of a decision.[25]

An alternative formulation of the idea of proportionality is the *principle of double effect,* which is that in a situation from which both good and evil consequences are bound to result, a manager will act ethically if (1) the good effects outweigh the evil, (2) the manager's intention is to achieve the good effects, and (3) there is no better alternative.[26]

These are intricate principles, requiring consideration of many factors. They force a manager to think about and weigh multiple factors in an organized way.

The Rights Ethic

Rights protect people against abuses and entitle them to important liberties. A strong philosophical movement defining *natural rights,* or rights that can be inferred by reason from the study of human nature, grew in Western Europe during the Enlightenment as a reaction against medieval religious persecutions. Over time, many such rights were given legal status and became *legal rights.*

Basic rights that are now widely accepted and protected in Western nations include the right to life; personal liberties such as expression, conscience, religious worship, and privacy; freedom from arbitrary, unjust police actions or unequal application of laws; and political liberties such as voting and lobbying. In Eastern societies, especially those transfused by the collectivist values of ancient Chinese culture, there is far less recognition of individual rights.

Rights imply duties. Because individuals have rights, many protected by law, other people have clear duties to respect them. For example, management should not permit operation of an unsafe machine because this would deprive workers of the right to a safe workplace. This right is based on the natural right to protection from harm by negligent actions of others and is legally established in common law and the Occupational

---

[25] Thomas M. Garrett, *Business Ethics* (New York: Appleton-Century-Crofts, 1966), p. 8.

[26] This is a simple version of the principle of double effect. For fuller treatment, see Lawrence Masek, "The Doctrine of Double Effect, Deadly Drugs, and Business Ethics," *Business Ethics Quarterly,* April 2000, pp. 484–87.

Safety and Health Act. If some risk in operating a machine is unavoidable, workers have the right to be given an accurate risk assessment.

Theories of rights have great importance in American ethical debates. A problem caused by our reverence for rights is that they are sometimes wrongly expanded into selfish demands or entitlements. Rights are not absolute and their limits may be hard to define. For example, every person has a right to life, but industry daily exposes people to risk of death by releasing carcinogens into the environment. An absolute right to life would require cessation of much manufacturing activity (for example, petroleum refining). Rights, such as the right to life, are commonly abridged for compelling reasons of benefit to the overall public welfare.

The Theory of Justice

A theory of justice defines what individuals must do for the common good of society. Maintaining the community is important because natural rights, such as the right to life, are reasonably protected only in a well-kept civil society. A basic principle of justice, then, is to act in such a way that the bonds of community are maintained. In broad terms, this means acting fairly toward others and establishing institutions in which people are subject to rules of fair treatment. In business life, justice requires fair relationships within the corporate community and establishment of policies that treat its members fairly.

In society, a person's chances for justice are determined by basic economic and political arrangements. The design of institutions such as business corporations and political constitutions has a profound effect on the welfare and life chances of individuals. A contemporary philosopher, John Rawls, has developed an influential set of principles for the design of a just society. Rawls speculates that rational persons situated behind a hypothetical "veil of ignorance" and not knowing their place in a society (i.e., their social status, class position, economic fortune, intelligence, appearance, or the like) but knowing general facts about human society (such as political, economic, sociological, and psychological theory) would deliberate and choose two rules to ensure fairness in any society they created. First, "each person is to have an equal right to the most extensive basic liberty compatible with a similar liberty for others," and second, "social and economic inequalities are to be arranged so that they are both (a) reasonably expected to be to everyone's advantage, and (b) attached to positions and offices open to all."[27] In general, inequality would only be allowed if it would make better the lot of the most disadvantaged members of the society.

The impartiality and equal treatment called for in Rawls's principles are resplendent in theory and may even inspire some business decisions, but they are best applied to an analysis of broad societal issues. Acting justly in daily business life, on the other hand, requires the application of

27 John Rawls, *A Theory of Justice* (Cambridge, MA: Harvard University Press, 1971), pp. 60–71.

maxims that more concretely define fairness. Managers can find such guidelines in three basic spheres of justice.

Distributive justice requires that the benefits and burdens of company life be distributed using impartial criteria. Awarding pay raises based on friendship rather than performance criteria is unfair. All laws, rules, and procedures should apply equally to each employee. *Retributive justice* requires punishment to be evenhanded and proportionate to transgressions. A cashier should not be fired for stealing $5 if an executive who embezzled $10,000 is allowed to stay on the job and pay it back. And *compensatory justice* requires fair compensation to victims. A corporation that damages nearby property must restore it to its original state; one that hurts a customer must pay damages. The general idea of fairness in such maxims of justice supports orderly communities and organizations in which people secure human rights and meet human needs.

The Utilitarian Ethic

The utilitarian ethic was developed between the late eighteenth century and the mid nineteenth century by a line of English philosophers, including Jeremy Bentham and John Stuart Mill. The principle of utility, on which this ethic is based, is that actions that promote happiness are right and actions that cause unhappiness are wrong. The utilitarians advocated choosing alternatives that led to the greatest sum of happiness or, as we express the thought today, the greatest good for the greatest number.

In making a decision using this principle, one must determine whether the harm in an action is outweighed by the good. If the action maximizes benefit, then it is the optimum choice over other alternatives that provide less benefit. Decision makers should try to maximize pleasure and reduce pain, not simply for themselves but for everyone affected by their decision. Utilitarianism facilitates the comparison of the ethical consequences of various alternatives in a decision. It is a popular principle. Cost-benefit studies embody its logic and its spirit.

The major problem with utilitarianism is that in practice it has led to self-interested reasoning. Its importance in rationalizing the social ills of capitalism can hardly be overestimated. Since the 1850s it has been used to argue that the overall benefits of manufacturing and commerce are greater than the social costs. Since the exact definition of the "greatest good" is subjective, its calculation has often been a matter of expediency. A related problem is that because decisions are to be made for the greatest good of all, utilitarian thinking has led to decisions that permit the abridgment of individual or minority group rights. Utilitarianism does not properly relate individual and community ends in a way that protects both.[28]

---

[28] See, for example, Mortimer Adler, *Desires: Right and Wrong* (New York: Macmillan, 1991), p. 61. John Stuart Mill's famous essay "Utilitarianism" deals directly and brilliantly with these and other criticisms. It is reprinted in Mary Warnock, ed., *Utilitarianism and Other Writings* (New York: New American Library, 1962), pp. 251–321.

Do Men and Women Reason Differently about Ethics?

Professor Lawrence J. Kohlberg of Harvard University became famous for research showing that from childhood on people pass through six stages of moral development.[29] These stages begin with utter selfishness and rise to the use of ethical principles. According to Kohlberg, not everyone gets to the highest, or principled-reasoning, stage—the moral development of most people is arrested at a middle stage.

To create and test his theory, Kohlberg measured changes over more than 20 years in the ethical thinking of 84 boys. Others who built on his work soon discovered that women, in particular, were unlikely to get to the higher stages. What was the reason? Were women less ethical than men? Professor Carol Gilligan, a colleague of Kohlberg's at Harvard, tried to answer these questions by studying the moral thinking of 144 men and women ranging in age from six to sixty.[30]

Gilligan learned that men and women approached ethical reasoning from different perspectives. The men in her studies grew to see themselves as autonomous, separate individuals in a competitive, hierarchical world of superior–subordinate relationships. As a result, male ethical thinking stressed protection of individual rights and enforcement of principled rules to channel and control aggression. The women, on the other hand, tended to see a world of relationships rather than individuals, a world in which people were interconnected in webs rather than arrayed in dominance hierarchies. Women did not think using abstract rules and principles that set sharp boundaries on individual behavior; they focused on the importance of compassion, care, and responsibility in relations with others. They were not ethically stunted; they just thought differently than men.

Kohlberg built his stages on the way ethical reasoning developed in men. Gilligan's work, however, indicated the existence of an equally valid but different developmental process in women. Based on her research, a *care ethic* exists; that is, a person should have compassion for others, avoid hurt in relationships, alleviate suffering, and respect the dignity of others. The care ethic is violated in business by, for example, cruelty toward subordinates, exploitation of consumers, deceit in relationships, or focus on individual performance that is indifferent toward the welfare of co-workers.

If Gilligan is correct, men emphasize rules, individual rights, and duties that can be fixed impartially; women emphasize caring and accept an intuitive emotional instinct as a valid criterion for behavior. However, even if this marked contrast exists, it seems to disappear in business. Studies of managers, as opposed to studies of young adults and students, fail to show gender differences in ethical decision making.[31]

[29] See, for example, Lawrence Kohlberg, "The Cognitive-Developmental Approach to Moral Education," in Peter Scharf, ed., *Readings in Moral Education* (Minneapolis: Winston Press, 1978).

[30] Carol Gilligan, *In a Different Voice* (Cambridge: Harvard University Press, 1982).

[31] See James Weber and David Wasieleski, "Investigating Influences on Managers' Moral Reasoning," *Business & Society,* March 2001; and Donald Robin and Laurie Babin, "Making Sense of the Research on Gender and Ethics in Business: A Critical Analysis and Extension," *Business Ethics Quarterly,* October 1997.

The use of ethical principles, as opposed to the intuitive use of ethical common sense, may improve reasoning, especially in complex situations. Say a bank teller pockets $20 at the end of the day. The person's supervisor strongly feels that stealing is wrong and fires the teller. Ethical common sense is all that is needed in this situation, but the following situation defies a simple solution.

> I was working as a manager in a division that was going to be closed. The secret clock was ticking away to the surprise mass layoff. Then a co-worker approached. He was thinking of buying a house. Did I think it was a good time to get into real estate?
>
> The man's job was doomed and I knew it. But spilling the secret, I believed, would violate my integrity as a corporate officer and doom the company to a firestorm of fear and rumor. There was no way to win and no way out.
>
> I considered it my fiduciary responsibility to the business to keep my mouth shut, and yet here was this person coming for advice as a friend and a business acquaintance and I had material information that would affect him. For someone with a sense of empathy and sympathy, which I like to think I have some of, it was very, very hard.
>
> In the end I swallowed my anguish and kept silent. The man bought the house and lost his job. The secret held. But now 10 years later I have many times relived the story and second-guessed what I did that day.[32]

This is a vexing situation, and one created by the complexities of modern organizational life. The last paragraph finds the narrator alerted by the intuition ethic to the presence of an ethical conflict. Something in the situation causes anguish. In this predicament, however, simple moral homilies such as "tell the truth" or "be fair" are insufficient to resolve conflicts. Let us apply to this case three ethical principles, each of which offers a distinct perspective—utilitarianism, the rights ethic, and the theory of justice.

The utilitarian ethic requires the manager to calculate which course of action, among alternatives, will result in the greatest benefit for the company and all workers. A frank response here will disrupt operations. People would resign, take days off, work less efficiently, and engage in sabotage. Keeping the secret will cause hardship for a single employee about to buy a house and perhaps others in a similar situation. On balance, the manager must protect the broader welfare of customers, stockholders, and remaining employees.

From the standpoint of rights, the employee is entitled to the truth and the manager has a duty to speak honestly. On the other hand, rights are not absolute. The corporation has the competing right to protect its property, and this right must be balanced against the right of an em-

---

[32] Paraphrased and quoted from Kirk Johnson, "In the Class of '70, Wounded Winners," *The New York Times*, March 7, 1996, p. A12.

ployee to straight talk. In addition, the manager, in effect, promised to keep the layoff confidential and has a duty of promise keeping.

In justice, corporations are required to promote fair, evenhanded treatment of employees. Distributive justice demands the impartial distribution of benefits and burdens. It would be partial to signal the layoff to one worker and not others.

Based on the application of utility, rights, and justice, the manager's decision to remain silent is acceptable. Some judgment is required in balancing rights, but the combined weight of reasoning with all three principles supports the manager's decision. Yet the manager's intuition was not wrongly aroused. The situation required, by commission or omission, a lie, and it violated the practical imperative by treating the employee as expendable while achieving a corporate goal. So both good and evil result from the resolution of this situation. In such cases, application of the principle of double effect is apppropriate. Here the welfare of the company outweighs the welfare of one employee, the manager's intention is not to hurt the employee but to help the company, and no better alternative presents itself (it is possible that the manager could be wishy-washy and evasive; however, this raises suspicion in the employee and, in any case, avoids resolution of the ethical dilemma). So the principle of double effect reconfirms the manager's action.

CHARACTER DEVELOPMENT

Character development is a source of ethical behavior separate from the use of principled reasoning. The theory that character development is the wellspring of ethical behavior can be called the *virtue ethic.* It originated with the Greek philosophers. Aristotle wrote that moral virtue is the result of habit.[33] He believed that by their nature ethical decisions require choice, and we build virtue, or ethical character, by habitually making the right choices. Just as we learn to play the piano through daily practice, so we acquire virtues by constant practice, and the more conscientious we are, the more accomplished we become. In a virtuous person ethical behavior comes from inner disposition, not from obeying external rules or applying abstract principles. Plato identified four fundamental traits—justice, temperance, courage, and wisdom—and these have come to be called the *cardinal virtues.* Numerous other virtues have been mentioned over the years, including prudence, reverence, charitableness, hopefulness, and integrity.[34]

---

[33] *Nichomachean Ethics,* trans. Thomson, p. 91.
[34] Dennis J. Moberg, "The Big Five and Organizational Virtue," *Business Ethics Quarterly,* April 1999, p. 246.

Application of the virtue ethic requires conscious effort to develop a good disposition by making right decisions over time. Then acts are generated by inner traits ingrained from repetition and reflect the disposition of a virtuous character. When Sholom Menora, CEO of Tri-United Technologies moved out of Chicago, he sent a check for $25 to the city, believing that over the years he had neglected to feed parking meters from time to time.[35] This is an act that reveals a trait of obsessive integrity, not the application of an abstract, high-level ethical principle.

The idea of acting from virtue does not require rejection of the ethical principles explained earlier in the chapter. Virtuous individuals might be more sophisticated in their principled reasoning than less virtuous individuals.

PRACTICAL SUGGESTIONS FOR MAKING ETHICAL DECISIONS

There are practical steps to better define and resolve ethical problems in business. Here are some suggestions.

First, learn to think about ethics in rational terms using ideas such as universalizability, reversibility, utility, proportionality, or others. Such ideas enhance the ability to see ethical problems clearly and to create solutions.

Second, consider some simple decision-making tactics to illuminate alternatives. The philosopher Bertrand Russell advocated imaginary conversations with a hypothetical devil's advocate as an antidote for certitude. Write an essay in favor of a position and then a second opposed to it. Seek out a more experienced, ethically sensitive person in the company as an adviser. This person can be of great value in revealing the ethical climate of the firm or industry.

Use a two-column balance sheet to enter pros and cons for various alternatives, crossing out roughly equal considerations until a preponderance is left on one side or the other. Balance sheets organize information and discipline scattered, emotional thinking. Also, the process of entering all relevant factors sometimes brings new or unconscious considerations to light.

Another tactic is the *critical questions approach*. Ask yourself a series of questions about the ethical implications of an action. More than 50 years ago, one scholar surveyed the great philosophers and wrote 36 critical questions for thoughtful executives.[36] Examples are "What is not within our power?" and "What are the undesirable extremes in human dispositions?" Today this approach is popularized in corporate ethics programs in the form of short quizzes. Here is the one used at Lockheed Martin.

---

[35] "Chicago Businessman Does Right by Jewish Law," *Ha'aretz,* October 6, 2000.
[36] John Leys, *Ethics for Policy Decisions* (Englewood Cliffs, NJ: Prentice Hall, 1952). For another list of questions, see Laura L. Nash, "Ethics without the Sermon," *Harvard Business Review,* November–December 1981.

Quick Quiz—When In Doubt, Ask Yourself

- Are my actions legal?

- Am I being fair and honest?

- Will my actions stand the test of time?

- How will I feel about myself afterward?

- How will it look in the newspaper?

- Will I sleep soundly tonight?

- What would I tell my child to do?

- How would I feel if my family, friends, and neighbors knew what I was doing?

If you are still not sure what to do, ask . . . and keep asking until you are certain you are doing the right thing.[37]

These eight questions are shorthand for a variety of approaches to ethical reasoning. Some invoke basic maxims such as "obey the law" and "tell the truth." Others summon up the disclosure ethic and the intuition ethic.

Third, sort out ethical priorities early. Serious ethical dilemmas can generate paralyzing stress. However, clear values reduce stress by reducing temptation and easing conscience as a source of anxiety. For example, when being honest means sacrificing a sale, it helps to clarify in advance that integrity is more important than money.

Fourth, be publicly committed on ethical issues. Examine the workplace and find sources of ethical conflict. Then tell co-workers about your opposition to padding expense accounts, stealing company supplies, price fixing, or other actions that might become issues. Colleagues will be disinclined to approach you with corrupt intentions, and public commitment forces you to maintain your standards or suffer shame.

Fifth, set an example. This is a basic managerial function. An ethical manager creates a morally uplifting workplace. An unethical manager can make money, but he or she (and the company) pay the price—and the price is the person's integrity. Employees who see unethical behavior by their supervisor always wonder when that behavior will be directed at them.

Sixth, thoughts must be translated into action, and ethical deeds often require courage. Reaching a judgment is easier than acting. Ethical stands sometimes provoke anger in others or cost a company business, and there are personal risks such as job loss.

Seventh, cultivate sympathy and charity toward others. The question "What is ethical?" is one on which well-intentioned people may differ. Marcus Aurelius wrote: "When thou art offended by any man's fault,

---

[37] At www.lockheedmartin.com/about/ethics/standards/print.html.

Warning Signs

Lockheed Martin gives this list of phrases to all employees, telling them that when they hear one they are coming up on an ethical problem.

- "Well, maybe just this once."

- "No one will ever know."

- "It doesn't matter how it gets done as long as it gets done."

- "It sounds too good to be true."

- "Everyone does it."

- "Shred that document."

- "We can hide it."

- "No one will get hurt."

- "What's in it for me?"

- "This will destroy the competition."

- "We didn't have this conversation."

Source: *Lockheed Martin Code of Ethics and Business Conduct, 2001.*

forthwith turn to thyself and reflect in what like manner thou dost err thyself; for example, in thinking that money is a good thing, or pleasure, or a bit of reputation, and the like."[38] Reasonable managers differ with respect to such matters as the rightness of factory closings or genetic testing of workers.

Ethical perfection is illusory. We live in a morally complex civilization with endless rules, norms, obligations, and duties that are like road signs, usually pointing in the same direction but sometimes not. No decision ends conflicts, no principle penetrates unerringly to the Good, no manager achieves sainthood. There is an old story about the inauguration of James Canfield as president of Ohio State University. With him on the inaugural platform was Charles W. Eliot, president of Harvard University for 20 years. After receiving the mace of office, Canfield sat next to Eliot, who leaned over and whispered, "Now son, you are president, and your faculty will call you a liar." "Surely," said Canfield, "your faculty have not accused you of lying, Dr. Eliot." Replied Eliot, "Not only that, son, they've proved it!"

WHY ETHICAL DECISIONS ARE DIFFICULT

Why are ethical problems refractory even in the face of principles and methods to guide resolution? In this section we list nine reasons.

First, managers confront a distinction between facts and values when making ethical decisions. Facts are statements about what *is,* and we can

---

[38] *The Meditations of Marcus Aurelius Antoninus,* trans. George Long (Danbury, CT: Grolier, 1980), p. 281; originally written circa A.D. 180.

observe and confirm them. Ethical values, on the other hand, are expressed as statements about what *ought* to be and are held by individuals independently of facts. For example, some years ago, Burroughs Wellcome Co., a British firm, was accused of overcharging for azidothymidine (AZT), the drug that slows replication of the AIDS virus. A capsule that cost $.30 to manufacture had a retail price of $1.60 to $1.80. For AIDS victims the annual cost was $10,000. AZT was expensive to research and develop and the company felt a high price was justified. Was Burroughs Wellcome exploiting desperate AIDS patients, or was it entitled to retrieve AZT's high cost of research and development and earn a profit above that? Facts, such as prices, do not logically dictate values about what is ethical in such a situation. What *is* never defines what *ought* to be. Pressure from gay activists led to price cuts. But yielding to political force does not answer the question "What ought to be?" either.

Second, it is often the case that good and evil exist simultaneously, in tandem and interlocked. Nestlé's sales of infant formula in countries such as Kenya and Zambia have led to infant deaths as mothers mixed the powdered food with contaminated local water and their babies died of dysentery. But evidence also shows that infant formula saves some infants' lives when the mother is not available, the infant will not breastfeed, or dietary supplements are needed. Evil should be minimized, but in some cases, it cannot be eliminated.

Third, knowledge of consequences is limited. Many ethical theories, for instance the utilitarian theory of the greatest good for the greatest number, assume that the consequences of a decision are knowable. But the impact of business policy is uncertain in a complex world. In 1977, for example, General Motors substituted Chevrolet engines in Pontiacs, Oldsmobiles, and Buicks, with a policy that extended an old industry practice of parts switching to entire engines. The intention of the policy was to achieve the salutary effects of making more large-block engines available over a wider range of automobiles to satisfy consumer demand. Unpredictably (for General Motors), consumers looked on the engine switching as an attempt to manipulate buyers and rob owners of status—an ethical implication perhaps entirely at odds with corporate motivations.

Fourth, the existence of multiple stakeholders exposes managers to conflicting ethical claims. To illustrate, tobacco firms are in a crossfire of competing ethical claims. Customers assert their right to smoke and demand cigarettes. Tobacco farmers, representing more than 200,000 farming families in the United States alone, give ethical priority to maintaining the tobacco economy. Stockholders urge the priority of profits. Governments in less developed nations such as Zimbabwe and Brazil encourage tobacco to generate sorely needed tax revenues. On the other hand, the World Health Organization and physicians worldwide condemn smoking. Feminist, minority, and consumer groups criticize tobacco ads that target women, minorities, and youth. Companies in many industries face such clashing stakeholder values.

Fifth, antagonistic interests frequently use incompatible ethical arguments to justify their intentions. Thus, the ethical stand of a corporation is often based on entirely different premises from the ethical stand of critics. Ralph Nader refers to ads on children's television programs as "electronic child molesting" because they undermine parental authority.[39] Animal rights groups draw an analogy between Nazi death camps and factory farms that raise chicken and cattle. Environmentalists in England and the United States engage in "ethical shoplifting," taking items made of rain-forest mahogany off retail shelves and turning them in to local police. The ethical values underlying what these activists say and do are so at odds with the ethical values of the companies they attack that reconciliation is hopeless.

Sixth, some ethical standards are variable; they may change with time and place. In the 1950s American corporations overseas routinely made payoffs to foreign officials, but managers had to curtail this practice when public expectations changed and a new law, the Foreign Corrupt Practices Act of 1977, prohibited most such expenditures. Certain bribes and payments are accepted in Asian, African, and Latin American countries that would not be condoned in the United States.

Seventh, ethical behavior is molded from the clay of human imperfection. Even well-intentioned managers can be mistaken in their judgment or motivation. Dennis Levine was an ambitious Wall Street executive who worked hard. He rose from humble origins to make more than $1 million a year honestly at Drexel Burnham Lambert. Yet for seven years he also traded on insider information through a Swiss bank account. He was prosecuted and jailed. He never intended to be a criminal, but temptation had gradually eroded his honesty. "My ambition was so strong," he later wrote, "that it went beyond rationality, and I gradually lost sight of what constitutes ethical behavior."[40]

Eighth, the effects of science and technology present managers with new ethical problems that lack settled solutions. For example, current ethical theory has not yet developed an adequate principle for weighing human life against economic factors in a decision. Cancer studies can predict that workers exposed to chemicals will become ill in small numbers far in the future. How should this information be balanced against costs of regulation or job loss? Other examples of tough, new ethical problems exist. In years past, big pension funds and mutual funds bought large positions in a stock in secrecy to prevent buying by short-term speculators who, if alerted in advance, would buy shares and drive prices higher than they would have risen due to fund buying. Giving advance information to speculators was considered unethical, since by their

[39] Quoted in George Skelton, "California and the West: An Old Reliable in Era of Spin and Empty Promises," *Los Angeles Times,* March 23, 2000, p. A3.
[40] Dennis Levine, "The Inside Story of an Inside Trader," *Fortune,* May 21, 1990, p. 82.

actions they took money from the pockets of fund investors, transferring it to themselves. However, day traders now use software that scans trading activity in thousands of companies, alerting them to large fund trades in progress and allowing them to dive in, make a quick speculative gain, and get out. Unlike past insider trading, this method is legal. Yet like insider trading, it enriches speculators at the expense of fund investors. Thus, software technology has outraced legal remedy and ethical consensus.

Finally, growth of huge corporate organizations gives added significance to ethical problems such as committee decision making that masks individual responsibility and organizational loyalty versus loyalty to the public. These are ethical complexities peculiar to large organizations.

CONCLUDING OBSERVATIONS

There are many paths to ethical behavior. Not all managers appreciate the repertoire of principles and ideas available to help resolve ethical problems arising in business. By studying ideas in this chapter, a person can become more sensitive to the presence of ethical issues and more resolute in correcting shortcomings. In addition, these principles and guidelines are applicable to ethical issues raised by the case studies throughout the book. We encourage students to refer to this chapter for conceptual tools.

Short Incidents for Ethical Reasoning

The following situations contain ethical conflicts. Try to define the ethical problems that exist. Then apply ideas, principles, and methods from the preceding two chapters to resolve them.

A CLOUDED PROMOTION

As chairman of an accounting firm in a large city, you were prepared to promote one of your vice chairmen to the position of managing partner. Your decision was based on a record of outstanding performance by this person over the eight years she has been with the firm. A new personnel director recently insisted on implementing a policy of résumé checks for hires and current employees receiving promotions who had not been through such checks. Unfortunately, it was discovered that although the vice chairman claimed to have an MBA from the University of Michigan, she dropped out before completing her last 20 units of course work. Would you proceed with the promotion, retain the vice chairman but not promote her, or fire her?

THE ADMIRAL AND THE THIEVES

When Admiral Thomas Westfall took command of the Portsmouth Naval Shipyard, theft of supplies was endemic. It was a standing joke that homes in the area were painted gray with paint stolen from the Navy. Admiral Westfall issued an order that rules related to supply practices and forbidding theft would be strictly enforced. Within a few days, two career petty officers were apprehended carrying a piece of Plexiglas worth $25 out of the base. Westfall immediately fired both of them and also a civilian storeroom clerk with 30 years' service, who lost both his job and his pension. According to Westfall, "the fact that I did it made a lot of honest citizens real quick." Did the admiral act ethically?

SAM, SALLY, AND HECTOR

Sam, Sally, and Hector have been laid off from middle-management positions. Sam and Hector are deeply upset by their misfortune. They are nervous, inarticulate, and docile at an exit meeting in the personnel department and accept the severance package offered by the company (two weeks' pay plus continuation of health benefits for two weeks) without questioning its provisions. Sally, on the other hand, manifests her anxiety about job loss by becoming angry. In the exit meeting, she complains about the inadequacy of the severance package, threatens a lawsuit, and tries to negotiate more compensation. She receives an extra week of pay that the others did not get. Has the company been fair in its treatment of these employees?

A PERSONALITY TEST

You are asked by a potential employer to take a psychological profile test. A sample segment includes these items.

Because you have read that it is best to fit into a "normal" range and pattern of behavior, and because it is your hunch that the personnel office will weed out unusual personalities, you try to guess which answers are most appropriate for a conservative or average response and write them in. Is this ethical?

AL

The CEO of a midwestern manufacturing company tells the following story.

I was looking over recent performance reviews in the household products division and one thing that struck me was the review of a star sales rep named Al. I know Al because he handles our Wal-Mart account. Al had the highest annual sales for the past five years and last year nearly doubled the next highest reps' total. The sales manager's written evaluation was highly laudatory as expected, but cautioned Al to adhere strictly to discount policy, shipping protocol, and billing protocol. I got curious.

A conversation with the division manager revealed that Al ingratiated himself with workers on the loading dock, socializing with them, sending them birthday cards, and giving them small gifts such as tickets to minor-league ball games. The loading dock supervisor complained that Al was requesting and sometimes getting priority loading of trucks for his customers despite the formal first-in, first-out rules for shipping orders. Second, Al had given several customers slightly deeper discounts than authorized, although the resulting orders were highly

	Yes	No	Can't Say
It is difficult to sleep at night.			
I worry about sexual matters.			
Sometimes my hands feel disjointed from my body.			
I sometimes smell strange odors.			
I enjoyed dancing classes in junior high school.			
Not all of my friends really like me.			
Work is often a source of stress.			

profitable for the company. And finally, late in December, Al had informally requested that one big account delay payment on an order by a week so that the commission would be counted in the next year. This would have gotten him off to a running start had not an accountant for the purchaser paid promptly and written to Al's manager in refusing the request.

The division head stuck up for Al. I didn't press or request that any action be taken. Did I do the right thing?

How would you answer the CEO's question?

A TRIP TO SEA WORLD

A sales representative for a large manufacturer of consumer electronics equipment headquartered in Los Angeles, California, has courted a buyer from a nationwide chain of 319 retail stores for over a year. At company expense the buyer was flown to Los Angeles from Trenton, New Jersey, with his spouse, for a three-day sales presentation. The company is paying all expenses for this trip and for the couple to attend a Los Angeles Dodgers baseball game and dine at fine restaurants.

During the second day of meetings, the buyer discusses a one-year, $40 million order. The chain that the buyer represents has not sold the company's products before, but once it starts, reorders are likely. At dinner that evening, the buyer mentions that he and his wife have always wanted to visit Sea World in San Diego. While they are in southern California and so close, they would like to fly down. It is clear that he expects the company to pay for this trip and that he will delay making a commitment for the $40 million order until he gets a response.

The company has already spent $2,200 for the buyer's trip to Los Angeles. The San Diego excursion would cost about $500. The marketing manager estimates that the company can make a 9 percent gross profit on the sale. The sales representative stands to receive a .125 percent commission over base salary.

What should the sales representative do?

MARY AND TOM

Mary P., an aerospace engineer, tells about a difficult career experience in which her friend Tom plays a central role.

"My friend Tom and I are employed by Republic Systems Corporation. We started about the same time after graduating from engineering school five years ago. The company does a lot of defense work, mostly for the Air Force, and it's big. Tom and I worked on project teams doing tests to make sure that electonics shipped to customers met specifications. We have very similar backgrounds and job records, and there has always been a little competition between us. But neither one of us pulled ahead of the other on the corporate ladder. That is until last winter.

"At that time, we were assigned a special project to modify the testing protocol on certain radar components. The success of the projects was critical; it had to be done before Republic bid for two more years on its big radar systems contract. About 40 percent of our people work radar.

"We rolled up our sleeves and put in long hours. After a month, though, Tom volunteered to be on a companywide task force developing a new employee privacy policy. Privacy is a big deal to Al Manchester, our CEO.

"Tom continued to work with me, but he gradually put more and more of his energy into the privacy project. I had to start taking up some of the slack. He enjoyed the task force meetings. They met in the dining room at the Kenthill Country Club and he could hobnob with Al and some of the other big shots. He worked overtime to impress them.

"We finally finished the testing project and it was a success. But toward the end I did the lion's share of it. One day, Tom made me angry by ending a capacitor test at 94 hours instead of the 100 hours you really have to have for validity. He did it because he was late for a privacy task force meeting. Overall, I guess Tom helped a lot, but he didn't do his share all the way through.

"Last month the assistant manager of the radar project left the company and Tom and I both applied for the position. It was a pay raise of several grades and meant getting a lot of recognition. They chose Tom. The announcement in the company newsletter said that he was a "strong team player" and mentioned both the testing project and the privacy task force as major accomplishments.

"I don't think it was fair."

Was Tom fair to Mary? Was Tom's promotion fair to Mary? Was the company wrong to promote Tom?

THE HONDA AUCTION

Dave Conant co-owned and managed Norm Reeves Honda in Cerritos, California. Naturally, he worked closely with Honda marketing executives to get cars for his dealership. One day, one of these executives, Dennis Josleyn, the new zone sales manager, approached him, asking him to submit a bid on 64 company cars. These were near-new cars previously driven by corporate executives or used to train mechanics. Company policy called for periodic auctions in which Honda dealers submitted competitive bids, and the high bidder got the cars to sell on its lot. It was Josleyn's job to conduct the auction.

"I want you to submit bids on each car $2,000 below wholesale market value," Joselyn told Dave Conant.

Conant dutifully inspected the 64 cars and submitted the asked-for bids. Meanwhile, Josleyn busied himself creating fake auction papers showing that other Honda dealers bid less than Conant. Of course, others bid near the wholesale price, so their bids were higher. Completing the phony auction, Josleyn announced the winner—Conant's dealership. The next day he showed up there and handed Conant an envelope.

"I have a little invoice for you," he said.

Conant went to his office, opened it, and found a bill for $64,000 payable to an ad agency co-owned by Josleyn and his brother. The message was clear. Josleyn wanted a 50–50 split with the dealer on the $2,000 windfall each car would bring, so he was billing Conant for half the extra $128,000 the entire batch of cars would bring in.

Conant faced a decision. If the invoice was paid, the dealership would make a $64,000 windfall. If he refused to pay, the cars would be rerouted to a dealer who was a "player" and future shipments of new Hondas might be slower. He decided to pay the invoice. In his own words: "I believed I had no choice. If I hadn't paid the amount, I would have incurred the wrath of Dennis Josleyn and possibly some of the other Honda gods, and I believe they would have taken our store down."[1]

Conant was not alone. Honda dealers around the country faced a dilemma. After investing large sums to build new showrooms and facilities and hire employees, they soon found themselves having to choose between two paths. If they gave bribes and kickbacks to Honda executives, they secured a copious flow of cars and made a fortune. On average, a favored dealer made almost $1,000,000 a year in personal income. However, if they stayed clean, no matter how modern their dealership and well trained its sales force, they received fewer cars and less profitable models. If they went bankrupt, and many did, the Honda executives arranged for less scrupulous owners to take over their dealerships. Many an honest dealer short on cars drove across town to see a rival's lot packed with fast-selling models in popular colors. Over time, it also became clear that the highest Japanese executives at Honda knew what was going on but chose to do nothing.

Did Conant make the right decision? What would you do in his position?

THE TOKYO BAY STEAMSHIP COMPANY

The Tokyo Bay Steamship Company operated a tourist ship between Tokyo and the volcanic island of Oshima 50 miles offshore. It also had a restaurant on the island. It was a modest business until February 1933, when Kiyoko Matsumoto, a 19-year-old college student, committed suicide by jumping into the crater of the volcano, which bubbled with molten lava. Ms. Matsumoto left a poetic suicide note and, through newspaper stories, the Japanese public became obsessed with her story.

---

[1] Quoted in Steve Lynch, *Arrogance and Accords: The Inside Story of the Honda Scandal* (Dallas: Pecos Press, 1997), p. 106.

Soon other Japanese emulated Ms. Matsumoto. In the next 10 months, 143 people threw themselves into the crater. Many more came to watch. One Sunday in April, for example, 31 people tried to jump; 25 were restrained, but 6 succeeded. People crowded around the edge of the crater waiting for jumpers. Shouts of "Who's next?" and "Step right up, there's plenty of room in front" could be heard.

The Tokyo Bay Steamship Company capitalized on the volcano's popularity. It increased its fleet to 30 ships and added 19 more restaurants. Meanwhile, the Oshima police chief met the boat and tried to weed out potential suicides using a crude behavioral profile (was someone too happy or too sad?). A police officer stood at the rim of the volcano. The Japanese government made purchase of a one-way ticket to Oshima a crime. Many suicides were prevented; others succeeded. Twenty-nine people who were stopped at the volcano killed themselves by jumping into the ocean on the return boat to Tokyo.

In the meantime, Tokyo Bay Steamship company prospered. Its shares rose on the Tokoyo exchange. But did it meet basic standards of ethics?

HCA—The Healthcare Company

This is the story of an aggressive corporation that brought business methods into a health care system unaccustomed to the rigors of market discipline. It ran hospitals for a profit—a big profit. Yet its success was also its undoing. As its star rose, jealous competitors, nervous regulators, and guardians of traditional values in medicine gave it a beating so severe that its top management has grown timid and its methods lie dormant, awaiting resurrection.

HCA—The Healthcare Company is still the nation's largest hospital chain. It has 196 hospitals across America with about 42,000 beds and, in addition, runs 78 surgery centers. This is far fewer hospitals than the 318 it ran at its peak, but it is still a sizable firm. In 2000 it had revenues of $16.6 billion, making it larger than such companies as Eastman Kodak and Anheuser-Busch.

RISING COSTS CHANGE THE HEALTH CARE SYSTEM

HCA's story is best begun by explaining long-term changes in the complex, chaotic network of entities and processes that is the U.S. health care system. The driving force behind these changes is rising costs. Health care in America is expensive. Its cost rose from 4.4 percent of GDP in 1950 to 13.6 percent in 2000, the highest of any nation.[1] Unfortunately, expenditure does not equal effectiveness. The World Health Organization recently ranked the United States only fifteenth among all nations in the attainment of better health for citizens, mainly because 44 million people lack health insurance, thus have only tenuous access to medical care.[2] Yet spending continues to rise.

The origins of rising expenditures lie in the years following World War II. Soon after the war, the federal government began to fund medical studies. This, along with research in companies, led to a steady stream of new machines, drugs, and treatments that increased the expense of medical intervention. As medical care began to cost more, demand for health insurance rose, and in the 1960s the majority of Americans enrolled in health plans, most of which were paid for by employers. These plans usually allowed people unlimited access to doctors and hospitals if they met small annual deductibles and co-payments. Insurers paid claims

[1] William B. Schwartz, *Life without Disease* (Berkeley: University of California Press, 1998), p. 8; and Alex Frangos, "Model vs. Model: A Comparison of Countries' Health-Care Systems," *The Wall Street Journal,* February 21, 2001, p. R4.
[2] "The Health of Nations," *The Economist,* June 24, 2000, p. 93.

one by one on a fee-for-service basis. Financial incentives to limit treatment costs that had existed when patients themselves paid vanished when insurance became widespread.

In 1965 the federal government set up Medicare to pay hospitalization and other expenses for people over 65 and, sharing expenses with the states, set up the Medicaid program to finance medical care for the poor. The two programs covered most people who were not in employer-sponsored plans. In effect, government gave every citizen access to medical treatment, and health care soon came to be seen as an entitlement. These government programs increased demand for medical services and, of course, expenditures climbed.

As costs rose, so did pressures to reduce them. By the early 1980s Medicare and Medicaid payments strained government budgets. Private employers and insurance companies complained loudly that paying for employee health care sapped productivity and held down wages. Hospital expenses were the primary reason; it was in hospitals that dazzling new machines and procedures escalated costs out of control.

MEDICARE CHANGES ITS BILLING PROCEDURE

To combat rising hospital costs, Medicare in 1983 changed its reimbursement method. Instead of paying one by one for each inpatient treatment and procedure, it now gave the hospital a lump sum based on one of 470 categories, or "codes," into which patient's illnesses were classified. The single payment that Medicare would make was based on the underlying costs of each hospital and the average severity of specific maladies. This coding system was intended to lower Medicare payouts by giving hospitals an incentive to cut the costs of treatment, and they did so.

When the 470 illness categories—or *diagnosis-related groups* (DRGs)—were introduced, the average length of hospitalizations shortened. There were cost savings in shortening patients' stays, but within two years Medicare payments began to creep up again. The incentive for hospitals was to spend less on patients and cut short their stays.

However, shorter hospital stays led to a big rise in outpatient procedures and follow-up care, as many Medicare patients walked from hospital rooms to outpatient clinics for treatments.

The DRG system, which still functions, is terribly complex. The coding procedure is a labyrinth of rules covering more pages than the notoriously intricate Internal Revenue Code.[3] A small army of consultants exists to help hospitals digest it, and specialized software is used to ensure that Medicare is billed maximum rates. Despite their complexity, the rules have never been clear and cannot be made so. This is because the diagnosis of an illness by a physician is somewhat subjective. Moreover, the maladies of patients and the treatments they need often defy standard definitions. So no set of codes can ever neatly classify all illnesses and the range of their severities. This shortcoming leads to a cat and mouse game between hospitals and the federal government in which hospitals routinely engage in *upcoding,* or interpreting the illnesses of patients in such a way that they fall into higher-paying DRG codes. Upcoding is so common in the industry that for most of the 1980s and 1990s Medicare payments were adjusted downward in anticipation of inflated billings from hospitals. During this time, Medicare covered less than 90 percent of hospital costs, so hospitals made up the difference by raising charges to private patients.[4]

THE RISE OF MANAGED CARE

While the government struggled to hold down Medicare payments with its complicated billing code, insurance companies and employers tried to hold down their costs by implementing a philosophy of health care delivery that has come to be called *managed care.* Managed care reduces nonessential and marginally beneficial medical treatment by limiting reimbursement for it, causing it to be rationed.

[3] Uwe E. Reinhardt, "Medicare Can Turn Anyone Into a Crook," *The Wall Street Journal,* January 21, 2000, p. A18.
[4] Holman W. Jenkins Jr., "A Hospital Chain's Lemonade Man," *The Wall Street Journal,* May 24, 2000, p. A27.

Although managed care takes many forms, the primary form is the *health management organization,* or HMO. An HMO is an organization that includes an insurer and a network of physicians, hospitals, and services such as labs. Corporations enter contracts with HMOs under which they pay a fixed monthly or annual fee per employee in return for a full range of medical care. To compete for the business of employers, HMOs must control their costs, and they do so by limiting access to expensive specialists and treatments. The idea of managed care swiftly carried the day. As recently as the late 1980s, about 70 percent of insured employees were in older fee-for-service plans, but by the late 1990s, almost 85 percent of them were in some kind of managed care plan.[5]

The rise of managed care and the imposition of DRGs by Medicare made cost-cutting the hammer of change. Both physicians and hospitals had to slash fees and discount services. This led to striking alterations in the medical industry. Physicians who had been solo practitioners were forced into HMOs to maintain full waiting rooms. Their traditional authority and the sanctity of the doctor–patient relationship were circumscribed in managed care where treatment decisions could be second-guessed by insurance bureaucrats who approved payments. Merger waves swept through all parts of the system, including insurers, managed care organizations such as HMOs, and hospitals. These mergers were attempts to lower per-unit costs by achieving economies of scale and to get power over pricing by controlling a larger share of the market. Both the profit and the not-for-profit entities that provide health care feel competitive forces, and both are forced to respond. Even tax-exempt hospitals must reduce their costs or risk catastrophic loss of the paying patients who subsidize their charitable work. These competitive forces in the health care industry led to the predatory incarnation of HCA known as Columbia/HCA Healthcare Corporation, a name the company recently shed in the hope of restoring its reputation with the public.

---

[5] Brian O'Reilly, "What Really Goes on in Your Doctor's Office?" *Fortune,* August 17, 1998, p. 166; and Mindy Charski, "A Healthy Trend Ends," *U.S. News & World Report,* September 28, 1998, p. 60.

THE RISE OF A PREDATOR

Columbia/HCA was the inspiration of a brilliant and hardworking entrepreneur named Richard L. Scott. In 1977 Scott graduated from law school and joined a Dallas law firm, where he worked on acquisitions and public offerings for health care corporations. After 10 years of this, Scott, who was no shrinking violet, decided that he wanted to run his own company. He soon startled the industry by lining up financing and offering $3.9 billion to buy Hospital Corporation of America, then the nation's largest hospital corporation. Its directors laughed at Scott. Here was a suitor, a relative unknown, whose only direct business experience was working at a donut shop in college, stepping up to take charge of a huge, complex company. Scott's bid failed.

Then, late in 1987 a Texas investor agreed to back Scott in starting a new hospital company. At the time, the hospital industry was ailing. Due to the introduction of DRGs by Medicare and the rise of managed care, both the number and length of hospital stays had declined. There was an oversupply of hospital beds. Many facilities could not cover costs and faced bankruptcy. Scott, however, had a penetrating vision of the industry in which he saw opportunity, not stagnation, and he got off to a running start. Setting up a Dallas office for the new company he named Columbia Hospital Corporation, he wrote 1,000 letters to hospitals around the country offering to buy them. Mostly, the answer was no, but eventually he bought two weak-performing El Paso hospitals.

With the two hospitals in hand, Scott began to inject the strategies that he would use to revolutionize the industry. First, he gave local physicians part ownership of the hospitals. Physicians are the source of patients for a hospital: no patient can be admitted without a doctor's signature. When physicians have an equity interest in a local hospital, they have a financial incentive to refer patients there. Second, he consolidated the El Paso market by buying a third hospital nearby and closing it. This reduced the number of beds available, raising demand for the remaining beds in Scott's hospitals. And third, he used the hospitals he owned as hubs to which he began attaching other health services, including a psychiatric hospital, diagnostic centers, and a cancer-treatment center. He planned to make money referring insured persons back and forth within a network of services owned by Columbia.[6]

Scott soon bought more hospitals. The pickings grew easier, because across the country, many independent hospitals were floundering under the twin strains of an oversupply of beds and capped payments from insurers and Medicare. Scott promised the owners and trustees of stand-alone hospitals that he would take their struggling facilities and make them efficient cogs in his Columbia system.

While Scott rapidly bought individual hospitals, Columbia also expanded by acquiring other chains. In 1990 Columbia went public, and its successful offering and rising share price gave Scott more capital with which to finance acquisitions. Between 1990 and 1994 Columbia absorbed five competing hospital chains, bringing in 199 more hospitals and 96 surgical centers.[7] One of the chains was Hospital Corporation of America (HCA), whose directors had laughed off Scott's offer only three years before. After the HCA merger in 1994, the company's name became Columbia/HCA.

HOW COLUMBIA/HCA WORKED

As Scott took over hospitals, he wrung money from them by applying a hard-nosed business discipline exceeding anything ever seen in hospital management. He was a genius at coaxing efficiencies from a corporate system. Some of his methods were praiseworthy; others danced near ethical boundaries; all of them gamed the incentives in the industry environment to maximum advantage.

Because of Columbia/HCA's size and strong balance sheet, when it took over a hospital, it refinanced the facility's debt with cheaper capital. With the savings on debt service that this created,

the corporation made the hospital more attractive by making cosmetic appearance changes, modernizing equipment, and installing a sophisticated information system. Rigorous cost-cutting then took place. Since the hospital was now in the large Columbia/HCA system, it could take advantage of the discounts and just-in-time deliveries that Scott demanded from suppliers. Columbia/HCA became the world's largest buyer of medical supplies, and Scott was an expert at squeezing vendors. Often, however, the staff had to use lower-quality items that cost less. At Good Samaritan Hospitals in Santa Clara County, California, nurses complained that the gloves the company bought were weaker and more likely to tear than those they had used previously and that the valves for chest tubes lacked open/shut indicators.[8]

Staff cuts also trimmed costs, and after Columbia/HCA takeovers there were fewer nurses and administrators and more part-time workers. This sometimes led to deteriorating patient care. At Columbia Sunrise Hospital in Las Vegas, the ratio of staff to patients fell 20 percent.[9] Nurses in critical-care units reported that it took more than six hours to get the results of urgent blood tests that should have been reported in minutes. In a poll of workers at the hospital, 44 percent believed that staffing cuts had increased medication errors and 4 percent attributed one or more patient deaths to understaffing.[10]

Scott moved in his own managers and pushed them to perform. Hospital administrators were focused on quarterly earnings and given ambitious targets, typically revenue growth of 15 percent to 40 percent per year. He used a system of "score-cards" that showed the performance of each hospital in multiple areas. For example, part of each scorecard had a "case-mix index" to track the relative proportion of patients with illnesses that were highly reimbursed under Medicare's coding system. Administrators were supposed to raise the

[6] Sandy Lutz and E. Preston Gee, *Columbia/HCA—Healthcare on Overdrive* (New York: McGraw-Hill, 1998) pp. 70–73.
[7] Robert Kuttner, "Columbia/HCA and the Resurgence of the For-Profit Hospital Business," *New England Journal of Medicine*, August 1, 1996, p. 362.

[8] Ibid.
[9] David R. Olmos, "Do Profits Come First at Vegas Hospital?" *Los Angeles Times,* September 26, 1997, p. A1.
[10] Diane Sosne, "The Truth about Hospitals That Exist to Make Money," *Seattle Times,* July 11, 1997, p. B5.

index number.[11] Much of a hospital manager's pay was based on a salary bonus plan, and 90 percent of the bonus came from meeting short-term financial goals. In the mid-1990s a typical hospital manager had an annual salary of $150,000 but could earn up to $1 million with bonus and stock options.[12] This far exceeded the compensation of managers in not-for-profit hospitals.

The Columbia/HCA system included unsparing discipline—managers who missed their targets were abruptly replaced. Some hospitals had three or four new heads in a year. Many managers resigned when the pressure became too much or when they felt they were compromising their values. One chief administrator who left a Florida hospital had been asked to put a sign in the emergency room saying that patients' green cards would be inspected. Under federal law, no patient can be released from an emergency room until his or her condition is stabilized and so anyone who comes in must be seen. The sign was an effort to scare away to some competing hospital illegal immigrants with no health insurance or ability to pay.[13]

Columbia/HCA tried to increase revenues as well as cut costs. One way was by creating incentives for doctors. Giving them equity in the hospitals was a central tactic, and many Columbia/HCA hospitals were 15 to 20 percent physician-owned. A *New York Times* investigation examined referral patterns of 62 physicians in two Columbia/HCA hospitals in Florida and found that after investing in these facilities, the doctors as a group referred more patients to them and fewer to competitors.[14] Sometimes Columbia/HCA also owned the physician's practices. During its expansion, it purchased 1,400 practices and provider networks to funnel in patients. There were other incentives. On slow weekends at Sunrise Medical Center in Las Vegas, doctors who admitted the most patients won Caribbean cruises.[15]

Another method of raising revenues was aggressive Medicare billing. As it grew, Columbia/HCA got more than 30 percent of its revenues from Medicare and became Medicare's largest single claimant. A team of *New York Times* investigative reporters studied the results of zealous billing at Cedars Medical Center in Miami.[16] Because Medicare pays a fixed amount for any patient in a given disease category, a hospital gets more if patients are coded in high-reimbursement categories. For example, in DRG 79, which is the code for upper respiratory treatments, there are four categories of pneumonia. The highest-paid category is complex respiratory infection, for which Cedars would be reimbursed $6,800 per case. The lowest-paid category is simple pneumonia, which was reimbursed at $3,150 per case.

Studying records, the *Times* reporters learned that before being taken over by Columbia in 1992, Cedars billed 31 percent of pneumonia cases as complex respiratory infections. After the takeover, complex respiratory infections rose to 93 percent of cases. Meanwhile, a county hospital across the street billed only 28 percent of its cases as complex respiratory infection. Years later, when the company was accused of illegally upcoding, or increasing payments by billing in higher categories than justified, it would argue that the billing at Cedars and other hospitals was not fraudulent; it simply reflected greater mastery of Medicare's complex coding rules than competitors could develop.

Scott introduced bold marketing. Unique to the industry was a sales force that prospected for new business. He also started a national branding campaign with television and print ads designed to fix the Columbia/HCA name and logo in the public mind so that when Americans needed a hospital they would seek out Columbia/HCA, just as when they wanted a hamburger, they looked for a McDonald's restaurant.

[11] Lucette Lagnado, "Blowing the Whistle on Columbia/HCA: An Interview with Marc Gardner," *Multinational Monitor,* April 1998, p. 18.

[12] Michele Bitoun Blecher, "Rough Crossings," *Hospitals & Health Networks,* October 5, 1997, p. 40.

[13] Ibid.

[14] Martin Gottlieb and Kurt Eichenwald, "High Stakes Investments: Health-Care Giant Offers Its Doctors a Share of Hospitals," *Sun-Sentinel,* April 13, 1997, p. 1G.

[15] Olmos, "Do Profits Come First at Vegas Hospital?" p. 1G.

[16] Martin Gottlieb, Kurt Eichenwald, and Josh Barbanel, "Health Care's Giant: Powerhouse under Scrutiny," *The New York Times,* March 28, 1997, p. A1.

RESISTANCE AND CRISIS

As time went by, Scott's strategies became widely known and discussed. His methods abraded idealistic social values, built up over many generations, in which slighting treatment to save money is wrong. Competitors spoke against him. Labor unions resented his staff cutbacks and worked to undermine him. Soon resistance to new hospital acquisitions grew. In 1995 alone, Columbia/HCA had to back out of 30 pending deals when state regulators and civic groups that Scott's opponents had lobbied rose in opposition.

Nevertheless, the company prospered. Its growth showed in the rise of annual revenues from $4.9 billion in 1990 to $20 billion in 1996. Over this time, net profits averaged 7 percent a year, an excellent return that was 15 to 20 percent higher than at competing chains. By then, Columbia/HCA was not only the largest hospital chain in the country but the largest home care operation as well, with 590 facilities in 30 states. Home care was critical in Scott's strategy to develop a continuum of services. One attraction of it was that Medicare payments for home care were more generous than were payments for hospital stays. However, when Scott required hospital administrators to capture for Columbia/HCA facilities 85 percent of discharged patients needing home care, it angered Medicare bureaucrats, who had set a figure of 62 percent referrals as the maximum permitted.[17]

While Columbia/HCA grew, Scott became wealthy. He held 9.4 million shares and by 1996 had an annual salary exceeding $2 million. At this high point, however, the fall was near. Entering 1997 Scott drove hard. He rose in the morning for 5:00 AM workouts and 6:00 AM strategy sessions. He worked frenetically and pushed those around him to do the same. Initiatives, policies, and directives spewed from him rapid-fire. Colleagues were fatigued by both his demands and the company's skyrocketing growth.

Then in March, federal authorities began a sweeping investigation into Medicare billing fraud at Columbia/HCA. Agents raided its hospitals in El Paso and removed Medicare billing documents. A federal grand jury in Florida indicted three executives for submitting false cost reports and claims. Soon federal agents served search warrants at 35 other facilities and issued subpoenas for all kinds of billing records.

These investigations punctured Columbia/HCA's stock price, stiffened resistance to acquisitions, foreshadowed friction with regulators, and threatened crippling fines. Yet Scott seemed unaware of the danger. On the day the FBI raided 35 facilities and the company's shares tumbled 12 percent, he appeared on CNN and assured listeners that "government investigations are matter-of-fact in health care."[18]

A media obsession grew. Investigative reports ran in newspapers and on television news programs, overwhelmingly built on horror stories about the effects of money incentives in Columbia/HCA hospitals. The company was strangely silent. Scott refused to respond; indeed, he seemed not to sense a crisis, but members of the Columbia/HCA board of directors did. In late July they summoned him to a meeting and forced his resignation. He got a $10 million severance package.

A NEW COURSE IN A SEA OF TROUBLES

Another board member, Thomas Frist Jr., was picked to succeed Scott. Frist quickly backed away from Scott's more aggressive strategies. He ended annual bonuses for hospital administrators, undid the equity relationships of physicians in hospitals, sold the home health care business, stopped the national branding campaign, changed billing procedures, and increased audits and compliance reports on Medicare billings. He also created the post of senior vice president of corporate ethics, compliance, and corporate responsibility. Soon a new, warm "Mission and Values" statement was adopted (see the accompanying box). And eventually, he changed the firm's name. The new name, HCA—The Healthcare Company, dropped the

---

[17] Lucette Lagnado, Anita Sharpe, and Greg Jaffe, "How Columbia/HCA Changed Health Care, for Better or Worse," *The Wall Street Journal,* August 1, 1997, p. A4.

[18] Lutz and Gee, *Columbia/HCA—Healthcare on Overdrive,* p. 135.

HCA—The Healthcare Company Mission & Vision

Above all else, we are committed to the care and improvement of human life.

In recognition of this commitment, we will strive to deliver high quality, cost-effective healthcare in the communities we serve.

In pursuit of our mission, we believe the following value statements are essential and timeless.

We recognize and affirm the unique and intrinsic worth of each individual.

We treat all those we serve with compassion and kindness.

We act with absolute honesty, integrity and fairness in the way we conduct our business and the way we live our lives.

We trust our colleagues as valuable members of our healthcare team and pledge to treat one another with loyalty, respect, and dignity.

word *Columbia*, disowning Scott's legacy by shedding this reference to the company he had created.

Downdrafts from the investigations hit the company. Patients were frightened away. With Frist's approval, 40 hospitals dropped Columbia/HCA from their name. Revenues and net income fell. Share prices fell more. The Internal Revenue Service assessed $267 million in back taxes for wrongful deductions the company had made. Lawsuits multiplied, and legal costs eventually exceeded $200 million. Hospital takeovers were shelved and new hospital construction projects canceled. New acquisitions were typically financed with stock, but with share prices falling, the pending acquisition of another health care company was canceled. Over the next several years, Frist sold more than 100 hospitals.

Late in 2000 HCA agreed to pay $840 million to resolve some Medicare fraud charges.[19] It agreed

to $745 million in civil penalties while not admitting wrongdoing. In addition, it accepted a $95 million criminal fine, pleading guilty to fraudulent pneumonia upcoding, false billing, and giving kickbacks to physicians for referring patients. HCA also agreed to an eight-year compliance program modeled after recommendations in the U.S. Sentencing Guidelines.

This did not end its legal woes. The Department of Justice has accused the company of having a "corporate culture of fraudulent cost reporting" and is pursuing additional counts of medicare fraud going back as much as 15 years. If the government prevails, liability could exceed $1.2 billion.[20] Notably absent in all the legal fireworks are prosecutions of top HCA executives. Altogether, five HCA managers in charge of regions or subsidiaries were indicted for criminal fraud, and four were either convicted by juries or entered plea agreements. One was found innocent at trial. However, no charges have been

[19] "HCA—The Health Care Company & Subsidiaries to Pay $840 Million in Criminal Fines and Civil Damages and Penalties," U.S. Department of Justice press release, December 14, 2000.

[20] Mark Taylor, "Roots of Trouble Run Deep," *Modern Healthcare*, March 19, 2001, p. 6.

leveled at Scott or other top executives. The likely meaning of this is that federal prosecutors are unable to find strong evidence of criminal intent.[21]

The slow torture by investigation and prosecution of HCA petrified the health care industry. Companies pulled back from aggressive Medicare code interpretation. The sight of HCA twisting in the wind, in the words of one observer, "scared them into underbilling."[22] Most companies also set up strong ethics and compliance programs that, at the very least, might mitigate fines if the government decided to put a microscope on their billing records as it had on those of HCA. Instead of upcoding, the industry lobbied for higher payments, and in 2000 Congress responded by raising reimbursements in the DRG codes.[23] Whereas in the past Congress squeezed payments in anticipation of upcoding, now it is making them more generous to compensate for the wave of timidity sweeping industry billing practice.

WHITHER CORPORATE HEALTH CARE?

Rick Scott's vision of corporate delivered health care lies tattered. His company goes on, rendered submissive by government. The industry abides faintheartedly. Were Scott's strategies inherently bad ones for health care delivery, or were they appropriate but simply mismanaged?

Scott applied market solutions to intractable problems that had been growing in the health care system for half a century.[24] The central problem is that health care costs are rising prohibitively. Scott imposed the for-profit corporate form on health care delivery and worked it to every advantage, ruthlessly seeking cost savings and efficiencies wherever they could be found. Often the formula succeeded, elevating hospital performance to the advantage of a range of stakeholders beyond investors. For exam-

ple, when the company took over Cape Fear Memorial Hospital in Wilmington, North Carolina, in 1995, it made $1 million in improvements. A year later, admissions were up 6 percent, babies delivered up 40 percent, unpaid care to charity patients up 12 percent, and staffing up almost 25 percent.[25] Moreover, other hospitals in the area were forced to discipline their costs or Columbia/HCA would have underbid them for the business of local employers. This dampened medical cost inflation. Story lines such as this were less newsworthy than claims that Columbia/HCA was killing patients with its miserly ways, so the public mostly heard and read about scandal, not achievement.

Nurses' unions that stood to lose members in staff cuts opposed Scott. Federal and state regulators who stood to lose power if free market forces grew stronger opposed him. Many in the public opposed him, wanting to believe that unlimited, universal health care delivered by physicians in the mold of the old-fashioned, avuncular TV doctor Marcus Welby was a realistic, affordable option. And critics with traditional values opposed him, suspicious of business methods in the vicinity of life and death decisions. Not the least among these was Pope John Paul II, who, after the El Paso raids, issued a statement saying that "the centrality and dignity of the human person are ignored and trampled on . . . when healthcare is regarded in terms of profit and not as a generous service."[26]

The result of the HCA investigations has been to push corporate methods into the background. However, the market forces they thrive on remain. Costs keep rising. Payers resist price inflation. Government still distorts health care markets by setting prices for nearly $400 billion of health care each year, more than one-third of the total, supporting its invasion with a thicket of rules forming perhaps the single most confusing body of regulation existing in any nation. Scott fearlessly dove into the regulatory thickets and made himself at home in gray areas of the law. Although companies fear exploiting these ambiguities, they continue to exist. In any case, if these industry forces continue in health care markets, and they will, aggressive strategies based on efficiency at some point must again emerge. The

[21] Ibid., p. 6.

[22] Barbara Kirchheimer, "HCA Has Point to Prove," *Modern Healthcare*, December 18–December 25, 2000, p. 14.

[23] J. D. Kleinke, *Oxymorons: The Myth of a U.S. Health Care System* (San Francisco: Jossey-Bass, 2001), p. 19.

[24] J. D. Kleinke, "Deconstructing the Columbia/HCA Investigation," *Health Affairs,* March–April 1998.

[25] Blecher, "Rough Crossings," p. 40.

[26] "News at Deadline," *Modern Healthcare*, July 7, 1997, p. 4.

alternatives are limited, but they include allowing the cost trajectory free upward movement until taxpayer revolt occurs and further restriction of access to health care beyond the 44 million Americans now uninsured—or both.

QUESTIONS

1. Is a market-driven approach valid for the health care industry? Do you support or oppose trade-offs between care quality and efficiency?

2. Is health care a basic right? Can it be limited if the cost of providing unlimited treatment is prohibitive? If so, should it be regarded as a commodity and limited by market mechanisms, or should it be rationed by government regulation? If not, how can the nation pay for it?

3. How should the strategies behind HCA's rise to prominence be assessed? Were they fundamentally flawed, ethically wrong, and unworkable? Or were they appropriate and workable in the industry environment but badly carried out?

4. On balance, did HCA use health care resources more efficiently than competitors, or did it compromise care by shifting costs to patients and staff and moving the savings to executive salaries, dividends, and acquisitions?

5. HCA experienced terrible difficulties. Could they have been prevented? If you could go back in time, replace Rick Scott, and run the company, at what point would you choose to arrive and what changes would you make to salvage the good and prevent the bad?

Part Four

Business and Government

Chapter **Nine**

Federal Regulation of Business

Lockheed Martin Skunk Works

One of the most secretive production facilities in the United States, the "Skunk Works," produced some of the most spectacular airplanes ever built. The Skunk Works was a nondescript-looking facility located at the Lockheed Airport in Burbank, California. Among the major aircraft built there were the highly respected P-38 fighter of World War II (10,000 of these planes were built); the P-80, the first U.S. jet fighter; the F-104, the first supersonic jet fighter; the unequaled, high-flying U-2 and SR-71 reconnaissance planes; and the F-117A, the stealth tactical fighter that performed so spectacularly in Desert Storm.

Clarence "Kelly" Johnson was the founder of the Skunk Works and was given a good bit of leeway from federal regulations until he turned over the management of the organization in 1975 to Ben R. Rich. Rich faced management frustrations that Johnson avoided because of new social, in contrast to military, regulations. Many of the problems he faced are chronicled in the book *Skunk Works*,[1] by Rich and Leo Janos. For instance, he was forced by law to purchase 2 percent of his materials from minority or disadvantaged businesses, but many of them, he complained, could not meet his high-security requirements. He also was required by the Equal Employment Opportunity Commission (EEOC) to employ a certain number of the disadvantaged. "I was challenged," he said, "as to why I didn't employ any Latino engineers. 'Because they didn't go to engineering school' was my reply. If I didn't comply I could lose my contract, its high priority notwithstanding. And it did no good to argue that I needed highly skilled people to do very specialized work, regardless of race, creed, or color. I tried to get a waiver on our stealth production, but it was almost impossibile."[2]

---

[1] Ben R. Rich and Leo Janos, *Skunk Works* (Boston: Little, Brown, 1994).
[2] Ibid., p. 78.

The SR-71 Blackbird, first flown in 1964, broke all speed and altitude records, setting marks that still stand. The plane flies at more than 2,000 mph (Mach 3 +, or more than three times the speed of sound) at altitudes of over 85,000 feet. At its top speed, the plane traveled about 35 miles per minute. It flew from New York to London in less than two hours. It was called the Blackbird because of a special black finish designed to withstand high heat generated on the surface of the plane by high speed. Although retired from the U.S. Air Force, several are still used today by the National Aeronautics and Space Agency. © Bettman/Corbis

Rich said that on the later airplanes, especially the F-117A, he had to work with exotic materials on the plane's outer skin. "The radar-absorbing ferrite sheeting and paints required special precautions for workers. OSHA demanded 65 different masks and dozens of types of work shoes on stealth alone. I was told by OSHA that no worker with a beard was allowed to use a mask while spray coating. Imagine if I told a union rep that the Skunk Works would not hire bearded employees—they'd have hung me in effigy."[3]

OSHA created other problems for Rich. He tells how an OSHA inspector visited the old facilities of the Skunk Works, many of them dating to World War II days. Ladders were everywhere, lots of wires, a few oil slicks, inadequate ventilation, and other disarray characteristic of a highly talented organization that knew how to avoid hazards and to produce high quality under pressure. An inspector from OSHA came, at the invitation of Rich, and fined the company $2 million for no fewer than 7,000 OSHA violations. "He socked it to me," Rich said, "for doors blocked, improper ventilation, no backup emergency lighting in a workspace, no OSHA warning label on a bottle of commercial alcohol. That latter violation cost me three grand. I felt half a victim, half a slumlord."[4]

[3] Ibid., pp. 75–76.
[4] Ibid., p. 78.

This story of the Skunk Works illustrates a serious problem with intrusive regulations that complicate business activity, sometimes unnecessarily. Experiences such as this are not unusual and are becoming more frequent in business.

In this chapter we discuss the reasons for government regulation of the private sector, the historical and current patterns of federal regulation, the scope of federal regulations, the attempts by many presidents to stem the tide of advancing regulations, ways regulations change business management, the legal basis for regulations, how regulations are made, the overall costs and benefits of regulations, and the likelihood that regulations will continue to expand.

UNDERLYING REASONS FOR GOVERNMENT REGULATION OF THE PRIVATE SECTOR

Government regulation of the private sector is justified under two circumstances: when flaws appear in the marketplace that produce undesirable consequences; and when adequate social, political, and other reasons for government regulations exist. For the first century and a half of U.S. history, regulations were introduced mostly in response to flaws in the market mechanism; thereafter, regulations were increasingly introduced for broad social reasons.

Flaws in the Market

When functioning perfectly, the competitive market mechanism determines which of society's resources can be used most efficiently in producing the goods and services that people want. It yields the "best" answer to the questions of what should be produced and when and how the product will be distributed. The market mechanism has great appeal in democratic societies because, through it, social welfare can be advanced without central government control. Although highly efficient, the free market competitive model is not flawless. Some of the more important market failures that have justified government action are as follows.

Natural Monopoly

When a firm can supply the entire market for a good or service more cheaply than any combination of smaller firms, it is said to have a natural monopoly. Under such circumstances, competition would be wasteful of resources. The typical examples of such monopolies are local public utilities, and state commissions have long regulated them. Today, however, many local utilities have been deregulated and face competition.

Natural Resource Regulation

Exploitation of a natural resource can result in monopolistic practices that should be regulated. For example, the total volume of oil that can be produced in a single field is a function of the number of wells drilled and the rate of pumping. Too many wells and too rapid pumping reduce the field pressure and the quality of recoverable oil. That is avoided by government regulation. Government allocation of limited wavelengths in the electro-magnetic spectrum is another example of natural resource regulation.

Destructive Competition

When companies dominate an industry, they may engage in unfair or destructive competition. For example, they may cut prices enough to force competitors from the market and then raise prices. Several large firms may conspire to fix prices. This is illegal, and the Department of Justice consistently prosecutes such practices.

Externalities

Externalities are costs of production that are borne not by the enterprise that causes them but by society. For example, a factory that dumps toxic waste into a river may pollute it. It costs the factory nothing, but the community may have to pay dearly to clean up the mess. Why does the factory not invest in equipment to avoid the waste? Competition inhibits it. Suppose one steel mill tries to eliminate water pollution, but competing mills avoid the expense. Costs of the first mill will rise and, if high enough, could bankrupt the company. So society either pays for cleanup or forces all factories to bear the costs. The principle applies to industrial safety practices, health hazards, and jet noise, to give just a few examples.

Inadequate Information

Competitive markets operate more efficiently when everyone associated with them has enough information to make informed choices. To the extent that such information is not available, government finds justification for regulating the knowledge in question. This category covers a very wide range of information, including information for consumers about product quality, warranty, content, and so on; information to workers about work hazards; and disclosure of financial information for investors.

Social, Political, and Other Reasons for Regulation

Socially Desirable Goods and Services

Many socially beneficial goods and services will not be produced under free market conditions, and governments act to supply them. In this category are highways, clean air, clean water, and toxic-waste disposal. Other goods and services might be exploited in free market conditions, and if they are important, the government regulates their use. Examples are grazing lands, groundwater, rivers, ocean fishing grounds, and scarce water resources.

Protecting Individual Rights and Privacy

This concern has always been a cause of federal regulation. Unethical and immoral actions of business are, of course, a reason for restrictive regulations. The first Congress passed legislation to help poor and indigent sailors. Help to individuals has expanded to include programs for safe working conditions, better and safer products for consumers, elimination of discrimination in employment, provision for improved health care, and investor protection from misinformation and fraud. The Internet has stimulated strong demands for government regulations to secure privacy for individuals.

Resolution of National and Global Problems

As the nation has grown, the federal government has taken on more and more responsibilities to resolve national problems not effectively resolvable by state and local governments or individuals. Examples are regulation of railroads, banks, pollution, discrimination, safe foods, and so on. In the global economy are fierce and competent competitors for U.S. goods and services. The federal government helps American firms compete more effectively in that market. Actions to protect American farmers and steelworkers from foreign companies selling products under cost in U.S. markets have been continuous for many years. The government has acted to correct unfair trade practices in foreign countries that restrict U.S. exports.

Regulation to Benefit Special Groups

It is possible for regulations to be passed largely as a result of legislative pressures by individuals or groups to pass measures for their own benefit. The expressed justification for such legislation, however, is not based on that objective but on more lofty goals. Nevertheless, much regulation does protect the interests of special groups, such as manufacturers of steel and producers of peanuts.

Conservation of Resources

Federal regulations seek to conserve our natural resources, such as agricultural land, pristine forests, lakes and mountains, clean air, and endangered species.

HISTORICAL PATTERNS OF FEDERAL REGULATION OF BUSINESS

The volume of government regulations historically has moved in a wave-like pattern, as shown in Figure 9.1. Each wave has been triggered by the rise of popular demand for government to solve particular prob-

FIGURE 9.1 **Historical Waves of Government Regulations of Business**

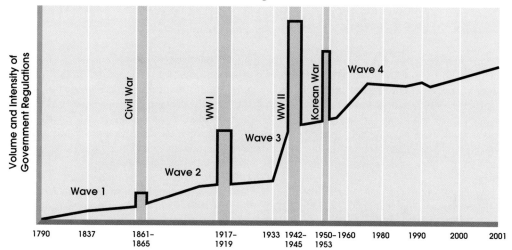

lems. After each burst of activity, the rate of new regulation has leveled off or declined. Except after wartime, the declines have been minimal. Most of the controls imposed during wartime have been lifted following the end of hostilities.

The "scale" to the left of Figure 9.1 is our estimate of relative volume and impact of federal regulations of business. Though it is only an estimate with all the limitations of such a measure, we offer it to sharpen the reader's perspective on regulatory growth. Following are highlights of a few major events in each wave.

The First Wave

This wave of government regulation took place from 1790 to 1837. During this period, regulations were predominantly promotional for business. The government gave vast financial subsidies and huge grants of land (to be sold) to private interests for the building of turnpikes, canals, and railroads. Through these actions, the federal government facilitated the building of a much-needed infrastructure. There were also tariffs to protect "infant" industries.

The Second Wave

This era of regulation was dominated by demands of the progressives and Supreme Court decisions giving the federal government power to act. At the same time, states were restrained by the Court in regulating business. Prominent in this wave were railroad regulations and the antitrust laws.

The Scope of Government Relations with Business

Following, briefly, are the many ways in which the federal government is involved with business.

Government prescribes rules of the game. Government sets broad rules of business behavior within which individuals are comparatively free to act in conformity with their self-interest. The regulations vary in the extent to which they restrain an individual business, but they serve to establish the "rules of the game."

Government is a major purchaser of the output of business. Out of a gross domestic product (GDP; of $10.6 trillion in 2002, the federal government is expected to spend $638 billion. State and local governments are expected to spend $1.3 billion.[5] Few companies do not benefit directly or indirectly from such procurement.

Government uses its contracting power to get business to do things the government wants. Businesses that want government contracts must subcontract to minority businesses, pay prevailing minimum wages, comply with safety and sanitary work regulations, refrain from discrimination in hiring, and meet pollution standards. It is a case of "no compliance, no contract."

Government promotes and subsidizes business. The government has a complex and powerful network of programs to aid business. Promotion ranges from tariff protections to loans, loan guarantees, maintenance of high levels of economic activity and direct subsidies.

Government owns vast quantities of productive equipment and wealth. The government is an important producer of goods and services, such as ammunition, guns, ships, atomic energy, postal services, weather-reporting services, and dams. The federal government owns vast stockpiles of raw materials and most of the land in many western states.

Government is an architect of economic growth. It has assumed responsibility for achieving an acceptable rate of stable economic growth, as set forth in the Employment Act of 1946.

Government protects interests in society against business exploitation. For instance, many laws protect the interests of investors, customers, employees, and the competitors of a business.

Government directly manages large areas of private business. "Manages" here means that government dictates certain decisions through regulation and joint decision making.

Government is the repository of the social conscience and redistributes resources to meet social ends. Government increasingly redirects resources by transfer payments, research and development expenditures, tax incentives, and subsidies. In mind here, among other things, are Social Security, Medicare, and Medicaid. The government also exerts moral pressure on business to conform with generally accepted social goals.

Government is our national security protector. This includes, of course, maintenance of our national military forces.

Government is the arbiter of disputes. This function cuts across a number of those noted above. In mind, for example, are laws governing labor disputes in which the government can step in to either decide an issue or determine how it can be resolved. Many laws enacted by Congress grow out of disputes among interest groups. Pending legislation on health management organizations (HMOs) is directly related to disputes among patients, administrators, and insurers.

[5] *The UCLA Business Forecast for the Nation and California* (Los Angeles: The Anderson School, UCLA, August 2001).

The Third Wave

The burst of activity in this wave was the result of the many New Deal laws designed to deal with the ravages of the Great Depression of the 1930s.

The Fourth Wave

A groundswell of interest in improving the quality of life in the 1960s and 1970s led to the fourth wave of government regulations. The result was the development of new controls that involved government more deeply in managerial decisions, enormously increased the volume of regulations, and expanded government's control over business. As a result, government regulatory agencies today are involved in decisions in major functional and operational areas of a typical large firm.

War Blips

As Figure 9.1 shows, wars have brought sudden increases in government controls. During the Civil War, there was little control over production and prices, but the North created the National Banking System to help finance the war, and this had lasting impact on the financial system. World War I witnessed the introduction of substantial controls over industry, but the war ended before the controls began to bite. The federal government exercised complete control over the economic system during World War II and to a lesser but still substantial extent during the Korean War. After both wars, the wartime controls were completely abandoned. There was no comparable increase in regulation during the Vietnam War or the Gulf War.

ATTEMPTS TO STEM THE TIDE

For more than 50 years, major efforts have been made to restrain the growth of federal regulations, reverse the trend, and reform the system. The first was the Hoover Commission, chaired by former president Hoover and completed in 1949. Since then, each president has campaigned against excessive regulation (some established commissions like the Hoover Commission) and, like King Canute, tried in vain to stem the tidal wave. Each succeeded in creating some reforms, but the trend of expansion has proceeded.

Here are a few highlights of such efforts in recent years. In the Carter administration (1976–1980), there was important deregulation of many industries. The most widely known effort was the airline industry following passage of the Airline Deregulation Act of 1978. The Natural Gas Policy Act of 1978 provided partial decontrol of natural gas by 1987. Partial decontrol of railroads (Staggers Rail Act of 1980) and trucking (Motor Carrier Act of 1980) also occurred.

© Chicago Sun-Times: cartoon by John Fischetti. Reprinted with permission.

President Reagan (1980–1988), upon taking office, named Vice President Bush to head a new Task Force on Regulatory Relief, and issued Executive Order 12291, which gave the Office of Management and Budget (OMB) strong powers and set up a new agency, the Office of Information and Regulatory Affairs (OIRA), with authority to review regulations. This executive order mandated that agencies make cost–benefit analyses of their proposed new rules and gave the OMB and the OIRA power to ensure that benefits were greater than costs before issuances. Thus, cost–benefit screening became a new and important strategy in federal regulations.

There was a sharp decline in the imposition of new regulations in the early Reagan years. However, by the end of Reagan's second term, the trend of regulatory growth resumed.

The record of the Bush administration (1988–1992) was mixed. On the one hand, the administration tried to control the imposition of new regulations. For example, President Bush appointed Vice President Quayle to head a new Council on Competitiveness. This council had overall authority to review new proposed regulations and was successful in stopping many that were perceived by business to be "unfair" or too costly. On the other hand, two new regulations were passed that have had significant impacts on industry: the Clean Air Act Amendments of 1990 and the Americans with Disabilities Act of 1990. Both have required substantial new business spending for compliance.

President Clinton in September 1993 issued Executive Order 12866, "Regulatory Planning and Review." This order reinforced President Reagan's order for cost and benefit analysis, as noted above. It also established a new planning process that required agencies to prepare plans each year for the most important actions they anticipate. These are then reviewed by OIRA, circulated among affected agencies, and returned to the originating agency for revision or action.[6]

President Clinton also asked Vice President Gore to head a commission called the National Performance Review. The commission set out "to make government *work better* and *cost less*." The final report made hundreds of specific suggestions for cutting red tape and costs, many of which were implemented.[7]

Immediately on taking office in 2001, President Bush rescinded many orders that had been signed by President Clinton and set about naming heads of regulatory agencies who were sympathetic with his intention to reduce the burdens of federal regulation. For example, one of the first laws signed by the new president was a measure revoking OSHA rules concerning the prevention of carpal tunnel syndrome, tendinitis and other maladies suffered by people engaged in repetitive motions. He cited excessive costs by industry to comply with the new regulations. Strict rules of the EPA regarding arsenic in drinking water were rescinded but were quickly reinstated after public uproar. New agency heads began to soften rules on industry. For example, the EPA delayed enforcement of stricter clean air rules. These actions are only pinpricks, however, in the mountain of federal regulations, most of which are extremely difficult if not impossible to rescind or weaken.

THE SECOND MANAGERIAL REVOLUTION

The massive accumulation of regulatory powers has brought a virtual revolution in the way corporations are managed. We contrast it with the first managerial revolution, when the old entrepreneurial class of managers was replaced by corporate professional managers. This change took place over a long period of time, but it gained public attention in the classic study of Berle and Means called *The Modern Corporation and Private Property*, published in 1932.[8] The second managerial revolution is characterized by a massive transfer of power from the managerial class to a new class of public servants in the federal, state, and local governments,

---

[6] For details of this Executive Order, see Susan E. Dudley and Angela Antonelli, "Congress and the Clinton OMB," *Regulation,* Fall 1997.

[7] Vice President Al Gore, *Creating a Government That Works Better & Costs Less,* Report of the National Performance Review (Washington, DC: Government Printing Office, 1993), p. i.

[8] Adolph A. Berle, Jr., and Gardner C. Means, *The Modern Corporation and Private Property* (New York: Macmillan, 1932).

armed with authority to make decisions formerly reserved for managers in privately owned businesses.

Traditional Industry versus Functional Regulation

The managerial revolution introduced a "new model" of regulation that contrasts with the "old model." The old style of regulation was concerned with one industry, such as railroads, airlines, or pharmaceuticals. The principal purposes of the older-type regulations (of agencies such as the Interstate Commerce Commission [ICC], FTC, and FCC) (see Table 9.1 for agency titles) were to prevent monopoly; to increase competition; to establish uniform standards of safety, security, communications, and financial practice; and to prevent abuses of managerial power.

The main focus of the newer model is on functions that cut across all industries. The principal purposes of the newer agencies (e.g., CPSC, OSHA, EEOC, EPA) are to improve the quality of life by securing cleaner air and clearer water, protecting consumers from shoddy products, ensuring more information to consumers, preventing discrimination in the workplace, and so on.

Older agency policies and regulations generally applied to entire companies in an industry. The newer agencies limit rules to specific business functions to implement their policies. For example, automobile seat belt

TABLE 9.1
Major Federal Regulatory Agencies Classified by Dominant Orientation

Agency	Date Established
Predominantly Industry	
Food and Drug Administration (FDA)	1906
Federal Reserve Board (FRB)	1913
Federal Trade Commission (FTC)	1914
Federal Home Loan Bank Board (FHLBB)	1932
Federal Deposit Insurance Corporation (FDIC)	1933
Federal Communications Commission (FCC)	1934
Federal Aviation Administration (FAA)	1958
Federal Maritime Commission (FMC)	1961
Nuclear Regulatory Commission (NRC)	1975
Federal Energy Regulatory Commission (FERC)	1977
Predominantly Functional	
Securities and Exchange Commission (SEC)	1934
National Labor Relations Board (NLRB)	1935
Equal Employment Opportunity Commission (EEOC)	1964
Environmental Protection Agency (EPA)	1970
National Highway Traffic Safety Administration (NHTSA)	1970
Occupational Safety and Health Administration (OSHA)	1971
Consumer Product Safety Commission (CPSC)	1972
Mine Safety and Health Administration (MSHA)	1977

rules established by NHTSA are directed at design engineers, OSHA workers safety rules are focused on safety engineers, and the EEOC sets standards for hiring and firing workers that concern directors of human resources. Regulators of these agencies are concerned with their particular functional area and not the total company. Indeed, in pursuit of their narrow mandate, they may even insist on regulations that adversely affect other areas. This is in contrast to older agencies that, like the ICC, were more concerned about a whole company and industry.

These are broad generalizations to make a point. In fact, many regulatory agencies are mixtures of both models. The SEC, for example, regulates the securities industry but also sets rules concerning content of financial statements prepared by corporations and how securities will be traded. The FTC, an older agency, is concerned with ensuring fair competition but also specifies rules for a company's advertising.

As late as the 1950s, aside from World War II, the federal government assumed major regulatory responsibility in only four areas: antitrust, financial institutions, transportation, and communication. Today at least one federal agency regulates something in virtually every department of an individual business.[9]

Impact of Newer Regulations on Managerial Decisions

Newer regulations make government officials active managerial partners with business executives. Government has always been a partner with business, but it has never before been so directly active in management. It is involved in decisions made by the highest corporate managers, from specific ways in which products are made and distributed, to what takes place between producer and customer after products are sold. Managers today in fact act as unofficial agents of government.

THE LEGAL BASIS OF GOVERNMENT REGULATION OF BUSINESS

The fundamental authority for federal regulation of business is the Constitution of the United States. In the Constitution, most of the economic powers exercised by the federal government are contained in Article 1, Section 8. This section gives Congress wide powers. Included is the power "to regulate commerce." This is the *commerce clause,* and upon its authority the federal government has extended its reach widely over business. There are, however, other powers in Article 1, Section 8, that also provide a base for the exercise of business regulatory powers. Included, for example, is the power to levy and collect taxes, to provide for the common defense and general welfare, to borrow money, to establish

[9] Murray Weidenbaum, *Business and Government in the Global Marketplace,* 6th ed. (Upper Saddle River, NJ: Prentice Hall, 1999), pp. 38–39.

bankruptcy laws, to promote science and useful arts by granting patents and exclusive rights over writings and discoveries, and "[t]o make all Laws which be necessary and proper for carrying into Execution the foregoing Powers, and all other Powers vested by this Constitution in the Government of the United States, or in any Department or Officer thereof."

The Constitution also is designed to "promote the general Welfare." Broadly interpreted, this clause plus the powers granted in Article 1, Section 8, now provides a broad legal authority for advancing government regulation of economic and social affairs. In contemplating this significant grant of power to the federal government, it must be kept in mind that the convention drafting the Constitution was specifically convened to give power to the central government, not to take it away.

The federal government's ability to exercise these powers to regulate business depends on the interpretation of them by the Supreme Court of the United States. As a result of liberal interpretations by the Court, the federal government today is able to impose on business just about any regulation that can be passed through the congressional law-making machinery.

SUPREME COURT INTERPRETATIONS OF CONSTITUTIONAL POWERS

Chief Justice Charles Evans Hughes is reported to have observed (when governor of New York), "we are under a Constitution, but the Constitution is what the judges say it is." This is true. Therefore, it is important to look briefly at the major themes of Court decisions about government regulation of business.

Early History

For a century and a half, the Court took two major paths so far as legal authority over business is concerned. On the one hand, it protected business from government regulation, both federal and state. On the other hand, it opened the door to new regulations. We briefly look at landmarks in these paths.

For example, in 1819 the Supreme Court gave business a strong protective shield against arbitrary state power in the *Dartmouth College* case. The New Hampshire legislature amended the charter of Dartmouth College, a private institution, to make it a public institution. The Supreme Court ruled that state legislatures could not impair a contract, and that the charter "is a contract, the obligation of which cannot be impaired without violating the Constitution of the United States.[10]

---

[10] *Dartmouth College* v. *Woodward,* 4 Wheaton 519 (1819).

In other cases, the Supreme Court firmly established the legal foundation for the supremacy of federal law over state law. In *McCulloch* v. *Maryland*, also in 1819, the Court outlawed a tax levied by Maryland on the Bank of the United States, a federally chartered bank.[11] In another famous case in this period, the Court expanded federal legal power to control interstate commerce. The state of New York sought to regulate steamboats on the Hudson River. In *Gibbons* v. *Ogden*, the Court struck down such laws on the grounds that they interfered with federal powers over commerce granted in the Constitution.[12]

But then, in 1837, the Supreme Court entered the second path in the *Charles River Bridge* case. The Charles River Bridge Corporation was chartered by the Massachusetts legislature in 1785 to build and operate for 75 years a bridge aross the Charles River between Charleston and Boston. In 1828 the legislature authorized another company to build a bridge a few yards from the first span. The property was to be surrendered to the state and be free of tolls after a period of time not exceeding six years. The Charles River Bridge Corporation sued, charging it had been granted exclusive rights for 75 years. The Supreme Court ruled that the state had a right to exercise its power over private property unless it said in "plain words" that it intended to surrender its power.[13]

Milestone Decisions: Post–Civil War to 1911

The progressive movement, described in Chapter 4, led to state laws regulating railroads after the Civil War. The Supreme Court said these laws were constitutional in *Munn* v. *Illinois* (1877) and declared that "When private property is devoted to a public use, it is subject to public regulation.[14] It becomes "affected with a public interest." This case provided a new foundation for broad regulation of industry. It supported the creation of the Interstate Commerce Commission in 1887 to control railroads, the Sherman Antitrust Act in 1890, the Food and Drug Act of 1905, the Meat Inspection Act of 1905, and other major pieces of legislation. The thrust of these new laws was to curb the abuses of an ebullient, aggressive, and often irresponsible business world.

There were, however, some positive developments for business. The Supreme Court said in the *Santa Clara* case in 1886 that corporations are cloaked in the mantle of the Fourteenth Amendment to the Constitution.[15] This amendment had been passed in 1868 to protect freed slaves and forbade states to abridge the "privileges and immunities" of citizens; to "deprive any person of life, liberty, or property without due process of

---

[11] *McCulloch* v. *Maryland*, 4 Wheaton 316 (1819).
[12] *Gibbons* v. *Ogden*, 9 Wheaton 1 (1824).
[13] *Charles River Bridge* v. *Warren Bridge*, 11 Peters 420 (1837).
[14] *Munn* v. *Illinois*, 94 U.S. 113 (1876).
[15] *Santa Clara County* v. *Southern Pac. RR.* 118 U.S. 394 (1886).

law;" or to "deny to any person within its jurisdiction the equal protection of the laws." The Court upheld the idea that a corporation is a person and that therefore the benefits of the amendment extend to it. In effect, states could regulate corporations, but the regulations had to be developed through accepted legal procedures and be nondiscriminatory. This armor proved to be highly protective to business in the legal jungles of regulation.

Efforts by federal, state, and local governments to introduce social reforms, such as permitting workers to strike and improving working conditions, met with repeated rebuffs by the Supreme Court. For example, the state of New York attempted to reduce the hours of work in bakeries to 10 a day. But this attempt, said the Court in *Lockner* v. *New York* in 1905, was an unreasonable, unnecessary, arbitrary, illegal, and "meddlesome interference with the rights of the individual" and contrary to the Fourteenth Amendment.[16]

On the other hand, the Court did permit state and local regulations over business for certain purposes falling within state powers. Generally, the Court permitted state regulations where they were believed to promote the morals, peace and good order, or health and safety of the public. For example, a Minnesota law prohibiting the sale of habit-forming drugs was permitted in *Hodge* v. *Muscatine Co.* (1905).[17]

The ruling of the Supreme Court in the first antitrust case brought by the federal government under the Sherman Antitrust Act of 1890 was not promising for those interested in breaking up monopolies. In *U.S.* v. *Knight* (1895),[18] the Court decided that a sugar-refining company that controlled 98 percent of the market had not violated the act. In a series of later cases, the Court reversed itself. Illustrative were *U.S.* v. *Standard Oil* (1911)[19] and *U.S.* v. *American Tobacco* (1911).[20] Both companies controlled about 95 percent of their respective markets, and the Court declared this percentage contrary to the law.

The Court Invalidates New Deal Laws

When President Franklin Roosevelt was elected in 1932, he faced the most devastating economic depression the country had ever suffered. A few statistics reveal the extraordinary tragedy. For instance, the gross national product dropped (in current dollars) from $103.1 billion in 1929 to $58 billion in 1932. Industrial production was almost halved between these two dates. Durable goods production in 1932 was one-third the 1929 level. Steel production in 1932 was at 20 percent capacity. The un-

[16] *Lockner* v. *New York*, 198 U.S. 45 (1905).
[17] *Hodge* v. *Muscatine Co.*, 198 U.S. 276 (1905).
[18] *U.S.* v. *E. C. Knight Co.*, 156 U.S. 1 (1895).
[19] *U.S.* v. *Standard Oil Co.*, 221 U.S. 1 (1911).
[20] *U.S.* v. *American Tobacco Co.*, 211 U.S. 106 (1911).

employment rate rose in 1933 to 25 percent of the labor force and stayed at that level for months. Thousands of businesses and farmers went bankrupt, and millions of investors lost their life savings.

To deal with this economic catastrophe, President Roosevelt's New Deal broke new federal regulatory ground. The federal government for the first time assumed responsibility for stimulating business activity out of an economic depression. It undertook to correct a wide range of abuses in the economic machinery of the nation, particularly business, and amassed more far-reaching laws to this end in a shorter period of time than ever before or since. It assumed responsibility on a large scale for relieving the distress of businesses, farmers, workers, homeowners, consumers, investors, and others.

The new laws were quickly challenged in the courts and received harsh treatment. In one day, May 27, 1935, the Court declared three laws to be unconstitutional! The most celebrated was the *Schechter* case, which struck down the National Industrial Recovery Act (NIRA). The NIRA was a major enactment that established "codes of fair competition" for all industries. The codes included minimum wage scales, maximum hours of work, collective bargaining by labor unions, prohibitions against employing child labor, fair prices, and boycotts for nonsigners of each code. The codes were agreements hammered out by trade associations and organized labor. When federal officials approved the codes, they became law.

The Schechter Poultry Corporation was a New York City firm that slaughtered chickens and resold them to local retail dealers. The government said the company violated several provisions of the Live Poultry Code, including a ban on the sale of sick chickens. The government argued that the chickens sold in New York City were from out of state and substantially affected the stream of interstate commerce. This, said the government, fell within the powers granted by the commerce clause to regulate interstate commerce: the NIRA was therefore constitutional, argued the government.

In a unanimous decision, the Supreme Court declared the NIRA to be unconstitutional. First, it stated that Congress could not delegate so much power to the president. Second, the chickens became commingled with the mass of property within the state of New York and the flow of commerce stopped. Thus, the commerce clause did not apply to federal regulatory powers and the chicken transaction fell within the domain of state power. To conclude otherwise, said the Court, "there would be virtually no limit to federal power, and for all practical purposes we should have a completely centralized government."[21]

---

[21] *Schechter Poultry Corp.* v. *United States*, 225 U.S. 495 (1935).

The Court Reverses Itself

President Roosevelt was outraged and tried, but was repulsed by the Senate, to "pack" the Court by adding six new justices to the existing nine so that he could get a majority to approve the constitutionality of his legislation. Four days after President Roosevelt submitted his court-packing plan to Congress, the Supreme Court began consideration of a few other cases, especially the constitutionality and powers of the National Labor Relations Act. One year after Roosevelt's attack, the Court, in a 5–4 decision, reversed itself in the *Jones & Laughlin* case.[22] In this case, the federal government had ordered the Jones and Laughlin Steel Corporation, the fourth-largest steel company in the United States at the time, to cease and desist engaging in unfair labor practices at its Aliquippa, Pennsylvania, plant. The complaint was about the company firing union leaders for trivial violations of company rules and refusing to bargain collectively with the labor union. The corporation said the government had no power to issue such an order because the corporation was engaged in production at a local facility and not interstate commerce.

The Court found that since the company shipped steel out of state, the case fell within the commerce clause. Therefore, Congress had the power to delegate authority to the president and the NLRB was acting upon legitimate constitutional authority.

Significance of the Decision

The complete reversal in the *Jones & Laughlin* decision from the *Schechter* case opened wide the door for federal regulation of individual businesses.

With other contemporary cases, it constituted one of the most important legal foundations supporting the flood of federal regulation that has been enacted since then. It also illustrates that the Supreme Court's interpretation of the Constitution reflects changes in the political and economic environments.

HOW GOVERNMENT REGULATIONS ARE MADE

It is a very complex process to create a regulatory policy and, subsequently, to craft the specific rules needed to impose it. In this section we explain this process.

Defining the Word *Regulation*

Regulation has been defined as "any attempt by the government to control the behavior of citizens, corporations, or subgovernments."[23] Among the many synonyms of regulation are control, intervention, influence,

---

[22] *National Labor Relations Board* v. *Jones & Laughlin Steel Corp.*, 201 U.S. 1 (1937).
[23] Attributed to Kenneth Meier and printed in *Federal Regulatory Directory,* 8th ed. (Washington, DC: Congressional Quarterly, Inc., 1997), p. 2.

power, laws, and interference. It is important to note that every regulation has both negative as well as positive aspects, and they are seldom in balance. Government subsidies to farmers, for example, are positive because they increase an individual farmer's income. They are also negative because the general population is taxed to pay for them. Whether a regulation is more positive than negative, or vice versa, depends upon the specific circumstances of each situation.

Congressional Legislation

All federal regulations originate in an act of Congress. Proposals for laws are called bills and are formulated by senators and representatives who are influenced by the demands of constituents, lobbyists, other legislators, and the president. The process is complicated and often entangled in compromises as different sides of an issue battle to influence a particular bill. Otto von Bismarck, when chancellor of Germany, once remarked: "Laws are like sausages, it is better not to see them being made." When a bill is passed by both houses of Congress and signed by the president, the proposed legislation becomes law.

Rules, Rule Making, and Regulation

Rules are decisions made by regulatory agencies to implement laws enacted by Congress. The process by which they are made is called *rule making,* and the result is a specific *regulation.* This is the most important function of government regulatory agencies. These regulations are laws with the same power as congressional legislation, presidential executive orders, or decisions of the Supreme Court.

There are many different types of rules. For example, some rules command a business to do something or stop doing something, some rules ask only for information, some set prices, some set specific standards for business to meet, some license business to do something, some establish procedures for business to follow, some prescribe how standards set by government shall be met, and some subsidize business.

Many believe that federal regulations are made by bureaucrats in isolated offices. Politicians run campaigns against the "mindless" and autocratic bureaucracy blindly exceeding authority to burden industry with unnecessary regulations. That is far from reality. All rules are based on statutes passed by Congress with powers delegated to executive branch agencies.

In implementing statutes, agencies may have narrow or broad grants of authority. Here are a few broad grants of authority. The Federal Reserve Board has complete authority to set interest rates. The Federal Trade Commission has authority to determine what is and what is not unfair advertising. The EPA can set standards that limit polluting discharges in air, in water, and on land.

On the other hand, some legislation contains specific instructions to agencies. The Clean Air Act Amendments of 1990 charge the EPA with establishing standards for 188 hazardous air pollutants. The Pollution Prevention Act of 1990 requires that each manufacturing facility that uses one or more of 329 listed chemicals must prepare an annual report.

The trend in recent years has been for the Congress to be more specific in its legislative enactments. However, the great bulk of federal regulations today are established by staffs in agencies based on broad grants of authority in many statutes passed over the years.

The fundamental process of rule making is established by the Administrative Procedures Act (APA) passed in 1946. This act sets forth in detail how the process must operate. The APA identifies two different ways in which federal agencies formulate and then enforce their regulations. The first is rule making. In this approach, the agency writes a rule to be followed by companies. This is a legislative function and the result is a law. The second is adjudication. This is a judicial function that deals with specific disputes with companies; the agency follows quasi-judicial procedures to settle the dispute.

There are two types of adjudication procedures. One is formal, where the agency holds hearings before an administrative law judge, evidence is presented, witnesses called, and a decision reached. Formal records are kept and the decision may be appealed to a federal court. The second type is informal, where an agency will determine the rights or duties of parties in question in less formal proceedings. Most adjudicatory procedures are informal.

Steps in Rule Making

The APA still stands as the fundamental guide to rule making. Since its passage, however, many laws have been enacted to add additional screens to rule making. For example, the OMB was created by President Nixon in 1970 and given the power to coordinate executive branch budgets. Later the agency was given authority to approve or disapprove specific agency-proposed regulations. For example, Executive Order 12606 directs federal agencies to determine whether proposed regulations will have a significant impact on family formation, the stability of the family, or marital commitment. Executive Order 12611 says that agencies must determine if regulatory actions will have a significant impact on the distribution of power and responsibilities among various levels of state and federal governments. Other executive orders direct agencies to be concerned about ensuring that if private property is taken and a loss incurred by the owner, the proposed regulation is justified by the public safety protected. Other orders concern potential impacts on the environment, public health, economic activity, and so on. The Congress also has required specific screens before regulations are implemented. For example, the Regulatory Flexibility Act of 1980 directs that agencies certify that a new rule will not have a significant adverse impact on small business. This act, together with the Unfunded Mandates Reform Act (1995) and Executive Order 12866, directs agencies to assess costs and benefits of regulatory alternatives and then to select regulations that will maximize benefits. Agencies must also examine a reasonable number of alternatives. These requirements are imposed for all expenditures over $100 million likely to be incurred by the regulations. Thus, agencies must go through a thicket of thorns before entering the process of implementation.

No single path is followed in all agencies for all regulations. The following sequence of activities is adapted from Cornelius M. Kerwin and James O'Reilly.[24]

1. *Origin of Authority.* The basic authority derives from Congress, as noted above.

2. *Origin of Individual Rules.* Although all rules can be traced to statutes, the origin of specific rules may arise in many sources. The head of the agency may have ideas from his or her policy agenda. Some agencies have organized systems for analyzing legislation to determine the details of rules needed to implement the statute. Some agencies have advisory committees composed of the legal counsel, technical experts, and others in the agency who can contribute to the rule-making process. Agency staff in the field who are administering rules also are sources of ideas for new regulations or modification of old ones. Agency staff often follow legislation as it weaves through Congress to determine what specific rules are needed to implement the final enactment. There are also many outside sources of ideas for rules. This includes other interested agencies, the OMB, the White House, and individuals in the private sector. Any citizen may petition an agency to make a rule.

3. *Drafting the Regulation.* The agency administering the statute must prepare the content of the new rule and show that it follows congressional authority. Extensive consultation within and outside an agency may be used in this process. This step may be done in a few days for a very simple rule, or it can take years if it is extremely complex and controversial. Some major rules of the EPA have taken a decade to prepare and issue.

4. *Office of Management and Budget Review.* The draft regulation may be reviewed by people within and outside the agency, but the most important review is that of the OMB. The OMB has broad oversight responsibilities and can return draft rules to agencies for revision.

---

[24] Cornelius M. Kerwin, *Rulemaking: How Government Agencies Write Law and Make Policy* (Washington DC: CQ Press, 1994); and James O'Reilly, *Administrative Rulemaking* (Colorado Springs: Shepard's/McGraw-Hill, 1983), pp. 90 and 131.

5. *Public Response.* When the draft is completed, it must be published in the *Federal Register.* This is the official government means of communicating proposed and completed rules and regulations to the public. Public comments are invited. Agencies can and do, of course, prepare other documents for public information and to solicit comments. The agency may conduct hearings, meet with members of Congress interested in the rule, or discuss the regulation with other interested agencies.

6. *Action on the Draft Regulation.* When the draft rule has been evaluated and revised, it is submitted to the OMB for final clearance and then again published in the *Federal Register.* If the agency decides to modify or drop the proposed rule, that decision will also be published.

7. *Post–Rule Making.* If the regulation works well and there is no difficulty with it, there is no need to tinker further with it. If there is great controversy, the agency may prepare for litigation. It may meet with business managers who are puzzled about precisely what to do, or are unhappy with the rule. The agency may issue explanations or technical corrections.

If an appeal is made to the courts by a company dissatisfied with a ruling the Supreme Court has long recognized that if Congress is very clear and precise in its intent, that governs. If, however, a statute leaves a gap to be filled by a regulatory agency, the Court will not intervene unless the agency's rule is arbitrary, capricious, or manifestly contrary to the statute. This judgment was strongly expressed in a well-known case involving Chevron and is recognized today as the *Chevron doctrine.*[25]

COSTS AND BENEFITS OF COMPLYING WITH FEDERAL REGULATIONS

The sheer volume of federal regulation of business is a growing burden and of increasing concern to managers. Each year thousands of new rules are written, and their accumulation has significant impact on everyone, especially business, that would be hard to exaggerate. Reliable data are not available to measure this impact, so we must rely on a few indicators and anecdotes to help understand complaints about regulatory burden and costs. It must be kept in mind that added to federal regulations are thousands of state and local laws with which business must comply. Since space does not permit discussion of them, the following relates only to the federal government.

---

[25] *Chevron U.S.A. v. Natural Resources Defense Council, Inc.,* 467 U.S. 843 (1984).

The Burden of Complying with Regulations

We can measure or characterize the burden of regulations in many ways. Some analysts count the number of pages in the *Federal Register*. As the pages add up, so presumably do the costs and burdens of regulation. The *Federal Register* is a fine-print, three-columns-per-page, mind-numbing, detailed volume. It reached 67,695 pages in 2001. A new number is published every working day with proposed and final regulations of federal agencies. Let us look at an average day. August 2, 2001, was perhaps typical. By this date there were already 40,154 pages for the year. Number 149 added 316 more pages containing 392,472 words, or the equivalent of 853 pages of the book you are reading.

Its contents illustrate the steady outpouring of rules from the federal bureaucracy. A number of new rules were proposed. For example, the Federal Communications Commission set out proposed assignments for digital television stations in New Mexico. The National Highway Traffic Safety Administration proposed a safety standard for radiator caps in new cars and trucks. The National Oceanic and Atmospheric Administration set forth a review of porpoises in the Gulf of Maine preparatory to listing them as endangered. And the Environmental Protection Agency proposed limits on air emissions of toxic chemicals from industries that make reinforced plastic composites. The EPA estimated that complying with this rule would cost companies $690,385 per year. However, the bulk of Number 149 was filled by a proposed rule from the Centers for Medicare and Medicaid Services setting forth physician fee schedules for 2002. This rule occupied 195 pages, including 158 pages of tiny print listing fees for everything doctors do, from "drainage of pilonidal cyst" to "sperm evaluation test."

There were also final rules. For example, the Consumer Product Safety Commission required child-resistant packaging for over-the-counter products containing ingredients that had previously been in prescription drugs. An EPA rule set legal levels of residue for the pesticide isoxadifen-ethyl in rice that winds up in animal feed, produce, or processed foods. It allowed 0.80 ppm (parts per million) in bran rice, 0.10 ppm in grain rice, and 0.50 ppm in rice hulls. The Federal Aviation Administration required modification of the software for engine controls in Eurocopter France helicopters operating in the United States. The Federal Trade Commission required manufacturers of eight kinds of household appliances such as room air conditioners and pool filters to disclose energy consumption in a comparable way. Finally, the volume contained the text of Executive Order 13221 from President George W. Bush, requiring that federal agencies buy only electronic equipment on which standby power devices used less than 1 watt.

These are just a few of the entries in Number 149. All these and other proposed and final rules, of course, are intended to benefit our society.

FIGURE 9.2

Summary of Staffing of Federal Regulatory Activity (fiscal years, full-time-equivalent employment)

Note: Social regulations include those for consumer safety and health, job safety and other working conditions, environment and energy. The economic regulations include those for finance and banking, industry-specific regulation, and general business. Source: Melinda Warren and William F. Lauber, *Regulatory Changes and Trends: An Analysis of the 1999 Federal Budget,* Center for the Study of American Business, Washington University, Regulatory Budget Report 23, June 2000, p. 3.

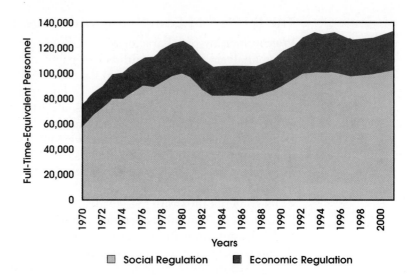

However, they also have consequences for business. As they drip out of regulatory agencies day after day, year after year, they impose a steady stream of new burdens and costs.

The number of employees of regulatory agencies is another measure of the regulatory burden. Figure 9-2 presents data for this standard. Two points stand out. First, the upward trend continues. Second, staff of agencies concerned with social programs is substantially larger than staff of agencies engaged in economic regulation.

The present mass of regulations is so huge that no corporation can faithfully comply with all the laws and rules to which it is subject. This generalization is supported by the results of a 1996 General Accounting Office (GAO) study. The agency sought to learn the costs of regulations on individual companies, but not one of the 15 companies it studied could provide total cost data nor identify all the regulations with which it was supposed to comply.

Benefits of Government Regulations

In assessing the burden of regulations on business, it is necessary to measure benefits. Such measurement is far more difficult than calculating costs. At an aggregate level, business could not operate and society could not prosper without certain types of regulation. Regulation has helped improve the position of minorities, clean the air, clean our waters, prevent monopoly, strengthen free competition, reduce industrial accidents, provide resources for the elderly, ensure health services not otherwise available, control communicable diseases, and so on.

The GAO said that most of the companies surveyed recognized that regulations provide benefits to society as a whole, to their industries, and even to them. For example, a paper company said federal regulations helped to improve its manufacturing process. A hospital said that

OSHA's blood-borne pathogens standards helped reduce needlestick injuries. Others commented that regulations benefitted them by ensuring a level playing field of uniform requirements for all businesses.[26]

Generous subsidies also benefit specific companies and industries. For example, the federal government subsidizes loans to small business (e.g., restaurants, builders), provides subsidies to companies to make international sales and purchases, provides insurance to multinational companies for foreign investment risks, provides loans and subsidies for agricultural sales, subsidizes road construction for timber removal by private companies, subsidizes minority businesses, aids the United States shipping industry, and so on.

GROWING DEMANDS FOR NEW REGULATIONS

Pressures for new regulations are strong, numerous, and likely to continue in the future. For example, uncertainties about global warming, disposal of nuclear and other toxic wastes, new demands for increased internal security, and the introduction of new genetically engineered plants and animals are today raising demands for federal regulations from the public and sometimes from business managers.

Business interests will exert great pressure for federal help in reducing costs of regulation. But individual businesses will pressure the federal government to throw hand grenades at their competitors, both domestic and foreign. For example, for years butter producers lobbied the Congress to tax oleomargarine, a competitive product to butter. Congress eventually passed a law taxing margarine in response to these pressures, but it was repealed. Businesses have petitioned the federal government to set uniform standards in some areas, such as insurance, banking, and advertising, to avoid having to deal with 50 individual state regulatory laws. One business executive explained it this way: "I would rather deal with one 800-pound gorilla than 50 state monkeys."

The Mixed Economy

Regulation has evolved to the point that virtually no aspect of economic activity is closed to government action. Despite this comparative open door to intervention, the remarkable fact about the American economy is not how much of economic life the government controls but how much it does not. Although the federal government directly controls or indirectly influences economic activity to a significant degree, the economy is in no way centrally administered or controlled. People are rather free to pursue their economic interests as they see fit. Ours is a mixed economy in which individuals enjoy much economic freedom and the free market mechanism is still a

[26] General Accounting Office, *Regulatory Burden: Measurement Challenges and Concerns Raised by Selected Companies* (Washington, DC: General Accounting Office, November 1996).

powerful allocator of resources, but governments, especially the federal government, exercise pervasive and strong controls.

A NOTE ON REGULATION IN OTHER COUNTRIES

In other countries there are different patterns of specific types of control than in the United States, but, overall, the United States is economically the freest in the world. Here are a few examples of foreign regulations.

In European countries, businesses are much more constrained than in the United States, especially with respect to relationships with labor. For example, in Germany, regulations inhibit labor mobility and raise unit labor costs to the point where wage rates are among the highest in the world. This has led companies like BMW and Mercedes to locate plants in the United States, where wage rates are lower. It is difficult to discharge unneeded workers in France and Italy. German air pollution controls cover fewer substances and processes than in the United States, but the standards of those controlled are comparable to ours. European countries today are faced with a new regulatory authority—the agencies of the European Union. Member-nations need to comply with regulations from a central European Commission, that is causing some significant changes in the business regulations in individual member-countries.

Japan is a nation with massive regulations, but implementation differs from that in the United States. Government agencies, for example, have substantial direct influence over business operations, but there is also close collaboration between business and government agencies. Regulations are focused more on helping business than on protecting consumers and other stakeholders. Laws concerning insider trading are weak. Companies are not required to report as much information about their financial condition as in the United States. The United States has exerted strong pressure on Japan to reduce its extensive import controls, with only limited success.

CONCLUDING OBSERVATIONS

In this chapter we have described how federal regulation of business has expanded over time. There have been ups and downs in the trend of regulations, but the basic direction has been up, with respect to both total volume and complexity. Successive efforts of presidents during the past 50 years have not succeeded in slowing the expansion despite the fact that some of them ran their campaigns on the promise that, if elected, they would reduce the size of government. J. M. Clark, one of the great economists of the twentieth century, astutely observed in 1932.

The frontiers of control . . . are expanding . . . they are expanding in the range of things covered and the minuteness of regulation. . . . Whether one believes government control to be desirable or undesirable, it appears fairly obvious that the increasing interdependence of all parts of the economic system . . . will force more control in the future than has been attempted in normal times in the past.[27]

As we have seen, the cost of federal regulations is huge, but the cost is offset in significant degree by the many benefits of regulation to society as a whole, individuals, companies, and industries. Analysis of both costs and benefits suggests that costs can be reduced and benefits increased by reforms in the regulatory system. That is the subject of the next chapter.

[27]J. M. Clark, "Government Regulation of Industry," *Encyclopedia of the Social Sciences,* vol. 3 (New York: The Macmillan Company, 1932), p. 129.

The FDA and Tobacco Regulation

On August 10, 1995, President Bill Clinton held a White House media event to announce a new regulatory initiative. As was his custom, he exercised a little showmanship by walking in through a red-carpeted hallway that ran behind the podium in the East Room. He then spoke to the press corps and to a group of children assembled for the occasion.

> Today I am announcing broad executive action to protect the young people of the United States from the awful dangers of tobacco. Today, and every day this year, 3,000 young people will begin to smoke; 1,000 of them ultimately will die of cancer, emphysema, heart disease and other diseases caused by smoking. That's more than a million vulnerable young people a year being hooked on nicotine that ultimately could kill them.
>
> Therefore, by executive authority, I will restrict sharply the advertising, promotion, distribution and marketing of cigarettes to teen-agers. . . . We need to act, and we must act now, before another generation of Americans is condemned to fight a difficult and grueling personal battle.[1]

The president's announcement came because the Food and Drug Administration (FDA), reversing a long-held position, had decided to regulate nicotine as a drug. This is the story of that reversal and of the subsequent effort to get the regulations implemented.

THE FOOD AND DRUG ADMINISTRATION

The Food and Drug Administration is a federal regulatory agency with headquarters in Washington, D.C., and field offices around the country. Its origins lie in the progressive era of the early 1900s when reformers agitated to protect the public from adulterated foods and unsafe drugs. In those days, manufacturers of foods tried all kinds of chicanery. For instance, they freely adulterated products to increase their quantity. Sand was mixed in sugar. Dairies watered down milk, then added chalk or plaster of paris to restore its color. Coffee and tea were sometimes bulked up with dust.[2] Dangerous

[1] Reuters, "Teen-agers and Tobacco: Excerpts from Clinton News Conference on His Tobacco Order," *The New York Times,* August 11, 1995, p. A18.

[2] These examples are from an article in *Puck* on March 12, 1884, cited in Thomas B. Allen, ed., *We Americans* (Washington, DC: National Geographic Society, 1975), p. 293.

substances were sold as drugs. Patent medicines contained opiates and morphine. False claims abounded. Dr. Rose's Arsenic Complexion Wafers sold by Sears Roebuck & Co. were said to transform "[e]ven the coarsest and most repulsive skin and complexion . . . into the perfection of womanly grace and beauty."[3] Another Sears item was a Bust Cream or Food with vegetable oils providing "nourishment for the bust glands." Sears reported size increases of two to six inches when the cream was used in combination with a suction device called the Princess Bust Developer. Using the proper regimen, any hopeful could be transformed from "a thin, awkward, unattractive girl or woman into an exquisitely formed, graceful, fascinating lady."[4]

Public pressure for regulation of foods and drugs began to build in the 1880s, when Harvey W. Wiley, a chemist in the Department of Agriculture, conducted experiments over many years revealing widespread adulteration of canned and prepared foods. Muckraking journalists wrote exposés of harmful medications. In 1905 President Theodore Roosevelt called for federal regulation in his annual message to Congress, but conservative lawmakers who rejected any role for government in consumer markets blocked action. However, their resistance was soon overcome. After Roosevelt's speech, irate physicians in the American Medical Association threatened to turn their patients against legislators who refused to act.[5] Then Upton Sinclair published *The Jungle,* a novel about immigrants working in Chicago's meat-packing plants. Before writing the book, Sinclair lived with stockyard workers, learning about disgusting and alarming practices. Then he used fictional license to make them vivid. Here is his description of meat storage rooms at a Chicago sausage plant:

> There would be meat stored in great piles in
> rooms; and the water from leaky roofs would drip
> over it, and thousands of rats would race about on

it. It was too dark in these storage places to see well, but a man could run his hand over these piles of meat and sweep off handfuls of the dried dung of rats. These rats were nuisances, and the packers would put poisoned bread out for them, they would die, and then rats, bread, and meat would go into the hoppers together. . . . [T]he meat would be shoveled into carts, and the man who did the shoveling would not trouble to lift out a rat even when he saw one. . . . There was no place for the men to wash their hands before they ate their dinner, and so they made a practice of washing them in the water that was to be ladled into the sausage.[6]

Sinclair's prose further inflamed opinion, and Congress passed the Pure Food and Drug Act of 1906 to ban adulterated or misbranded foods, drinks, and drugs from interstate commerce. The new law was sent to the Department of Agriculture, where Wiley's Bureau of Chemistry enforced it. In 1927 the Bureau of Chemistry changed its name to the Food Drug and Insecticide Administration; after another name change in 1931, it became the Food and Drug Administration.

In 1937 the nation was again aroused when more than 100 people died from a patent medicine called elixir of sulfanilamide. Congress then passed the Food, Drug, and Cosmetic Act of 1938, greatly extending the FDA's authority. Now it had the power to regulate medical devices and cosmetics, to require that manufacturers prove the safety of new drugs, and to inspect production facilities of regulated products. Since then its statutory powers have been steadily expanded by more than 30 additional laws and amendments.[7] Because it regulates products accounting for about $0.25 of every dollar consumers spend it is one of the largest and most powerful federal agencies.

---

[3] The 1902 Edition of the Sears, Roebuck Catalogue (New York: Bounty Books, 1986), p. 447. Sears, Roebuck and Co., The price was $0.35 per box of 50.

[4] Ibid., p. 459. The price was $1.50 each for the developer and the cream or food.

[5] Nathan Miller, *Theodore Roosevelt: A Life* (New York: William Morrow, 1992), pp. 459–62.

[6] Upton Sinclair, *The Jungle* (New York: New American Library, 1960), p. 136; originally published in 1905.

[7] Jon Preimesberger, ed., *Federal Regulatory Directory,* 7th ed. (Washington, DC: Congressional Quarterly Inc., 1994), pp. 301–30.

THE QUESTION OF AUTHORITY TO REGULATE TOBACCO

In early America, smoking was mostly confined to southern states, but during the Civil War, Union troops occupying the South picked up the habit and brought it home with them, creating national demand for smoking tobacco. In the century following the Civil War, smoking became widely accepted, and by the 1950s, the majority of men and about one-third of women smoked.

From the beginning, however, suspicion of adverse health effects hung over cigarettes. Suspicion turned into realization in 1964, when the surgeon general of the United States published a report on accumulated medical research. The report warned of a strong association between smoking and lung cancer.[8] It stated, for example, that death rates for male smokers were 170 percent those of male non-smokers, and that mortality increased with the number of cigarettes smoked. There was no longer any question that smoking was deadly.

Following the surgeon general's landmark report, damning medical evidence continued to accumulate. As it did, pressure was put on the FDA to regulate tobacco. Many people wondered why an agency set up to protect public health from dangerous products failed to ban a product that killed 400,000 Americans a year. Because of the Delaney Amendment of 1953, the FDA was required to ban any food containing a substance that caused cancer in humans or animals, no matter how small the amount or danger. As a result, the agency at one time banned saccharine, though the substance posed only a slight theoretical risk with ingestion of massive amounts requiring superhuman gluttony. Yet it never outlawed cigarettes filled with strong carcinogens.

In 1977 a coalition of groups led by Action on Smoking and Health filed a citizens' petition with the FDA requesting the agency to assert jurisdiction over tobacco. The petition was based on the statutory authority given to the FDA by the Food, Drug, and Cosmetics Act of 1938. Nowhere does the act mention tobacco. Instead, it sets forth general definitions of "drug" and "device" and empowers the agency to decide which substances and objects fall into those categories. In the statute, the term "drug" means:

> (A) articles recognized in the official United States Pharmacopoeia, official Homoeopathic Pharmacopoeia of the United States, or official National Formulary, or any supplement to any of them; and (B) articles intended for use in the diagnosis, cure, mitigation, treatment, or prevention of disease in man or other animals; and (C) articles (other than food) intended to affect the structure or any function of the body of man or other animals; and (D) articles intended for use as a component of any article specified in clause (A), (B), or (C).[9]

The statute defines a "device" as:

> [A]n instrument, apparatus, implement, machine, contrivance, implant, in vitro reagent, or other similar or related article, including any component, part, or accessory, which is . . . intended to affect the structure or any function of the body of man or other animals, and which does not achieve its primary intended purposes through chemical action within or on the body of man or other animals and which is not dependent upon being metabolized for the achievement of its primary intended purposes.[10]

Action on Smoking and Health requested that the FDA define cigarettes as a "device" containing the "drug" nicotine, thereby giving it the authority to restrict their sale. It also requested that cigarettes be sold only through pharmacies. The FDA rejected the petition. It argued that the law allowed classifying a substance as a drug only when the manufacturer

---

[8] Department of Health, Education, and Welfare, *Smoking and Health: Report of the Advisory Committee to the Surgeon General of the Public Health Service* (Washington, DC: Government Printing Office, 1964).

[9] 21 U.S.C. 321(g)(1). This citation references Title 21 of the *Code of Federal Regulations,* where all statutes that give the FDA its authority are codified along with the rules and regulations the agency has adopted. Section 321 is found in Chapter 9, Subchapter II.

[10] 21 U.S.C. 321(h)(3).

made a health claim for the product or intended it to be used as a drug. Since the tobacco companies did not make health claims for cigarettes or state an intent that nicotine be used for its pharmacological effects in the body, the agency had no statutory authority. In addition, it argued that Congress had known for many years that the FDA did not classify tobacco as a drug. If Congress had wanted to, it could have amended the law to clarify that tobacco fell under the agency's jurisdiction. However, it never did so, although it had regulated tobacco in other ways, for example, by requiring warning labels on cigarette packs.

Action on Smoking and Health was disappointed. The group strongly believed that nicotine was a drug under any literal or commonsense reading of the 1938 law. It appealed the rejection of its petition but lost when a federal court agreed with the FDA, holding that a regulatory agency was entitled to "substantial deference" in the reading of those laws it is in charge of administering.[11] There matters stood for many years.

NEW LEADERSHIP UNDER DAVID KESSLER

The FDA, bred of nineteenth century progressive outrage, is a reformist creation that thrives in an atmosphere of correction. While the consumer movement rode high in the 1960s and 1970s, the agency's powers steadily expanded. Then, following the election of President Ronald Reagan in 1980, the political atmosphere changed. Like other federal agencies, the FDA found its budget squeezed and its staff cut as the Reagan administration tried to reduce regulation of business. With fewer resources, it grew less aggressive, and its staff felt deflated. Business criticized it as a sluggish bureaucracy. Consumer advocates were disappointed by its loss of zeal. Its reputation hit a low in 1989 when, to speed drug approvals, a department head accepted gifts of fur coats and video equipment from a manufacturer.

However, in 1990 a new era dawned when President George Bush appointed David Kessler as commissioner. Kessler, then 39, was a Republican with a JD from the University of Chicago Law School and an MD from Harvard Medical School. He was dynamic, and he intended a new regime of vigorous enforcement. Immediately, he set to the task by confiscating 24,000 cartons of Procter & Gamble's Citrus Hill orange juice, which the company had labeled as "fresh" even though it was made from concentrate. The business community soon learned that it once again faced an energetic watchdog.

One day Jeff Nesbit, associate commissioner for public relations, approached Kessler to suggest that the time was right for regulating tobacco. Although Kessler did not know it then, Nesbit's father, a smoker, was in the hospital dying of cancer. Kessler was noncommittal, but he called a staff meeting to discuss the idea. Intense debate broke out. Some staffers thought that taking on the tobacco industry was a losing game. It invited reprisals from Congress and from conservative elements in the Bush White House. Others saw tobacco regulation as a righteous cause. How could anyone say with a straight face that the agency upheld its mission to protect public health when it pounced on mislabeled orange juice and ignored cigarettes? One attorney said that cigarette regulation was so important she was willing to devote the rest of her career to the cause if necessary.[12]

STUDY AND RESEARCH

The meeting revealed that the agency was divided, and Kessler remained noncommittal. A small interdepartmental group was formed to give the idea more study. Eventually, a member of this group, an attorney named David Adams, approached Kessler with an idea. Adams pointed out that tobacco companies could vary nicotine levels in cigarettes. Their manipulation of nicotine might be evidence that cigarettes were a product intended to have a drug-like effect on the body. If so, the

---

[11] *Action on Smoking and Health* v. *Harris*, 655 F.2d 237 (1980).

[12] This was Catherine Lorraine of the general counsel's office. David Kessler, *A Question of Intent* (New York: Public Affairs, 2001), p. 34.

David A. Kessler (1951–), commissioner of the Food and Drug Administration from October 1990 to February 1997. © AP/Wide World Photos

agency could satisfy legal criteria for regulating the nicotine in tobacco as a drug. Kessler now saw a way to bring cigarettes within the agency's jurisdiction. Under the definition of a drug in the 1938 law, a manufacturer had to intend that its product "affect the structure or any function of the body." The FDA had always rejected cigarette regulation because the tobacco companies made no health claims in their ads. However, if the agency could prove that the companies knew nicotine was addictive and supplied it to satisfy smokers' cravings, then the criteria of intent in the 1938 act's definition of a drug could be met.

The immediate problem for Kessler was that no one in the agency knew much about cigarettes. Did the tobacco industry intentionally manipulate nicotine levels? The manufacturing processes of many industries are well known, but the tobacco industry had a history of secrecy about its methods. Lawsuits by smokers had made companies wary. Departing employees were asked to sign confidentiality agreements subjecting them to adverse consequences if they revealed information about research or production. Cleverly, the companies put lawyers in charge of operations, then claimed that information and documents were protected by the attorney-client privilege. Further-

more, since the FDA had no jurisdiction over tobacco, it had no legal authority to inspect cigarette factories or to require disclosure of data about tobacco products.

By this time, the tobacco companies were aware that the FDA intended to pursue tobacco regulation. They were not about to help. Therefore, the agency started an investigation on its own to prove that nicotine levels were being manipulated, first to addict smokers, then to satisfy their cravings. One avenue of inquiry was library research. Kessler and staff members immersed themselves in literature about smoking and tobacco. When the agency tried to get articles from a tobacco collection at North Carolina State University, it ran into resistance from a librarian who felt that the FDA was going to hurt the southern economy. Kessler sent a young intern to the campus with instructions to carry a backpack and look like a student. The intern subsequently found valuable material.

Informants were critical sources of information. The agency's Office of Criminal Investigations was soon in touch with "Deep Cough," a former R. J. Reynolds manager who described how the company created a slurry from old tobacco scraps, added nicotine, and then put this reconstituted tobacco into cigarettes. There were many informants. "Philip," a former research director at Philip Morris, told FDA investigators that a process to remove all nicotine from tobacco existed. "Cigarette" had done lab research with rats at Philip Morris, once writing a paper about how the animals became addicted to nicotine and pushed levers in their cages to get more. "Saint," a chemical engineer at Philip Morris described a technique she had developed that removed carcinogens from tobacco. The company had abruptly and without explanation stopped her research. The identities of these informants were concealed to protect them from reprisals by their former employers for violating confidentiality agreements. Contacts with them were often bizarre and frequently involved clandestine meetings. Once Kessler even borrowed a voice synthesizer from the Central Intelligence Agency to disguise his identity in phone conversations with informants, but it sounded so strange that he elected not to use it.

Information from informants had to be verified before it could be taken as factual. For example,

"Macon," an employee of Brown & Williamson, revealed that the company had genetically engineered a high-nicotine tobacco plant known as Y–I. FDA investigators searched for a patent on the plant but could not find one. "Macon" remembered that Y–I had been field tested by a "Farmer Jones" in North Carolina. Investigators laughed at the name "Farmer Jones," but they eventually found a small farm owned by an L. V. Jones and verified its use for an experimental tobacco crop. "Macon" also believed that large quantities of Y–I were growing in Brazil. An investigator was assigned to examine customs forms stored in large warehouses and after considerable searching came upon an invoice showing that Brown & Williamson had imported almost 500,000 pounds of Y–I from Brazil.

A team from the FDA also visited cigarette plants owned by Philip Morris, R. J. Reynolds, and Brown & Williamson. It received carefully scripted briefings and facility tours. The visit to Brown & Williamson's manufacturing plant in Macon, Georgia, was particularly frosty. The team's hosts had received information about its two prior visits to the other companies, including information that one team member was a "bully," another was "aggressive" and "underhanded," and a third a "zealot."[13] As the team questioned Brown & Williamson representatives during the morning, the atmosphere became hostile. A lengthy lunch break was called during which the FDA team was separated from its hosts for lunch. After lunch, the team was rushed through the cigarette factory and in the end had little to show for the day.

However, after more than three years, the investigative, legal, and scientific research done by the tobacco working group had uncovered extensive evidence of intent by manufacturers to manipulate nicotine as a drug. They now knew that tobacco firms had conducted research into the addictive qualities of nicotine, that they blended tobacco to manipulate nicotine content in cigarettes, and that cigarette paper and filter material was engineered to control nicotine doses to the smoker. Moreover, informants and documents from tobacco companies made publicly available by disgruntled employees suggested that tobacco advertising had been designed to attract new smokers. Kessler felt that the time had come to compose tobacco regulations.

WRITING REGULATIONS

Although the tobacco investigation had produced enough data to justify writing new regulations, the consequences of such regulations were disturbing. In Kessler's words: "Once the FDA classified nicotine as a drug, the tobacco companies would be required to file an application that showed cigarettes to be safe and effective; since they would be unable to do so, we would have to ban them."[14] However, with 50 million addicted smokers, a ban was politically untenable. The cigarette companies would tell smokers that government prohibition had robbed them of their freedom. A black market for cigarettes was inevitable. The agency would put itself on a collision course with elected officials and a powerful, vindictive tobacco lobby.

To escape the dilemma, Kessler elected to classify cigarettes as medical devices. The FDA had the authority to regulate a wide range of medical products such as tongue depressors, breast implants, and X-ray equipment. It could put restrictions on the sale and advertising of cigarettes if they were classified as devices made with the intention of delivering the drug nicotine to users. Kessler believed that this way the agency could regulate cigarettes without banning them, as it did with medical devices that posed risks. It could start with limited restrictions and tighten them in the future.

Kessler also believed that nicotine addiction began as a pediatric disease. Children and teenagers who experimented with tobacco got hooked. They continued smoking over many years, often a lifetime. Adults who smoked did so not because of measured decisions they made—what the industry called free choice—but because of unthinking, impulsive decisions made by a teenager years before. Therefore, he elected to design regulations to reduce the incidence of this pediatric disease. Adult smoking would not be affected. The

13 Ibid., p. 180.

14 Ibid., p. 266.

FDA would only restrict the industry's ability to target youth in its advertising and marketing.

In the summer of 1995, Kessler set up a rule-making team to draft text for publication as a proposed rule in the *Federal Register*. After four months of hard work, a draft regulation was ready.

PLAYING POLITICS

Since the FDA is housed in the Department of Health and Human Services, Kessler needed the approval of Secretary Donna Shalala before going further. At a meeting in late November 1994, he outlined key provisions in the draft to Shalala and her staff.

- Advertising in publications with more than 15 percent or more than 2 million under-18 readers would be limited to black-and-white text only and include warnings such as: "ABOUT 1 OUT OF 3 KIDS WHO BECOME SMOKERS WILL DIE FROM THEIR SMOKING." Pictures and cartoon figures would be prohibited.

- Outdoor advertising within 1,000 feet of a school would be banned.

- The use of cigarette brand names on nontobacco items such as T-shirts and hats would be prohibited.

- Cigarette brand names could no longer be used to sponsor sports events.

- Vending machines would be banned. Tobacco could only be sold in face-to-face transactions.

- Tobacco companies would be made to conduct FDA-approved public education campaigns to counteract their image advertising among those under 18.

- If underage smoking had not declined by 50 percent five years after the rules went into effect, additional restrictions would be invoked.

Shalala was favorably impressed with the general content and told Kessler to work with her staff on a final draft. But Kessler soon discovered that her staff thought the regulations were a political blunder. Believing that he had Shalala's support, he decided to circumvent the staff and take the next step, which was getting White House approval.

Even though he was a Republican, Kessler had been reappointed as FDA head in 1992 by President Bill Clinton, a Democrat. This was probably political expediency on Clinton's part, since Kessler's activist approach was popular with the American public. Yet Kessler was barely acquainted with Clinton, having talked to him only once at a White House dinner. He did not have enough weight to call and schedule a meeting on his own. In fact, Clinton was worried about tobacco regulation. He believed that the two issues of tobacco and gun control had cost the Democrats control of the House of Representatives in the 1994 midterm elections. He and powerful members of his staff thought that reaction against tobacco regulation in key southern states might cost him a second term in the upcoming 1996 election.

Kessler approached Abner Mikva, an old law school acquaintance, who was an attorney on Clinton's staff. He asked Mikva to discuss with Clinton the potential public health benefits of restricting tobacco advertising and marketing. From Mikva he learned that the tobacco companies were also lobbying the White House to forestall FDA regulation. Next, working through another acquaintance, he got an appointment with Vice President Al Gore, who was widely known to support tobacco regulation. Kessler's meeting with Gore lasted only five minutes, but the vice president made a strong appeal to Clinton on behalf of the FDA.

Ultimately, the breakthrough in the battle for Clinton's support came because of Dick Morris, a shadowy figure who gave Clinton political advice based on public opinion polls. It was due to the presence and influence of Morris that Clinton had gotten the reputation of taking policy positions based on polling rather than principle. With tobacco, that reputation would prove accurate. Morris took polls in five southern states that were key to Clinton's reelection. The results showed large majorities were enthusiastic about regulations to reduce youth smoking. Morris advised the president that support of the FDA regulation was a winning position.

Soon Clinton met with Secretary Shalala and Kessler to discuss the proposed regulations. Kessler found the president supportive but unwilling to give the FDA a green light just yet. However, a month later, Kessler was back in the East

Room listening to Clinton announce that tobacco regulation would go forward. The next day, Friday, August 11, 1995, the FDA published its proposed rule in the *Federal Register*. It was a massive entry in number 155 starting on page 44,314 and ending 473 pages later on page 44,787. The proposed rule, entitled "Regulations Restricting the Sale and Distribution of Cigarettes and Smokeless Tobacco Products to Protect Children and Adolescents," covered 139 typical pages of small type in triple columns. The rest of the entry was a reproduction of the document the FDA had written to justify regulating cigarettes as a device containing the drug nicotine.[15] This part covered the remaining 334 pages.

In the proposed rule, the FDA estimated that its regulations would prevent more than 60,000 deaths and produce monetary benefits of $28 to $43 billion in lower medical costs, productivity gains, and hedonic values. It estimated an annual record-keeping burden on the industry of 1.2 million hours, increased annual costs of $227 million per year, and a revenue decline of 4 percent in 10 years.

After a proposed rule is published in the *Federal Register*, there is by law a comment period during which the agency must consider and respond to substantive comments from the public. The tobacco industry chose to take advantage of this requirement by swamping the FDA with more than 710,000 comments, a number far exceeding the previous record of 45,000. The tobacco companies submitted a 2,000-page comment with 45,000 pages of supporting documents. Many of the other comments were generated by form letters sent out by the industry.[16] Working from a rented warehouse, the FDA staff painstakingly answered each one. It took 12 months, but on August 28, 1996, the final rule appeared in the *Federal Register*. Although no major changes were made in the regulations, the agency responded to various written comments, swelling the entry to 922 pages.[17] More than four years had passed since Kessler first convened a staff meeting to discuss the prospects of regulating tobacco.

TO THE COURTS

Immediately the tobacco industry, joined by advertisers and tobacco retailers, filed suit in a federal district court in North Carolina to stop implementation of the rule. It challenged the FDA with three main arguments. The first was that the agency lacked jurisdiction over tobacco products because Congress had never given it a specific grant of authority. FDA attorneys responded that as a point of law it was wrong to claim a product was excluded because it had not been named in the Food, Drug, and Cosmetics Act of 1938. Congress had defined drugs and devices, leaving it up to the agency to determine what products fit these definitions. Under the *Chevron* doctrine, the agency was entitled to deference in its reading of the statute.[18] The second was that cigarettes did not fit the definition of a drug or device because manufacturers made no health claims about them. The FDA responded that its research on nicotine manipulation confirmed the classification was appropriate. The third was that the proposed restraints on advertising violated the industry's First Amendment guarantee of free speech. The FDA argued that the restrictions met legal guidelines for advertising restrictions as set forth previously by the U.S. Supreme Court.[19]

In its decision, the district court rejected the industry's first two arguments, upholding the restrictions on sales in the FDA rule. However, it concluded that the advertising restrictions were unconstitutional.[20] This was a win for the FDA. It left intact the agency's power to regulate tobacco. Both sides appealed the decision, hoping for a

[15] The title of this document is *Nicotine in Cigarettes and Smokeless Tobacco Products Is a Drug and These Products Are Nicotine Delivery Devices under the Federal Food, Drug, and Cosmetic Act*.
[16] Kessler, *A Question of Intent*, pp. 336–37.
[17] 61 FR 44396–45318 (1996).

[18] *Chevron U.S.A. Inc.* v. *Natural Resources Defense Council*, 467 U.S. 837 (1984).
[19] The definitive test of the constitutionality of commercial speech restraints imposed by government is set forth in *Central Hudson Gas & Electric Corp.* v. *Public Service Commission*, 447 U.S. 557 (1980).
[20] *Coyne Beahm, Inc.* v. *Food and Drug Administration*, 966 F.Supp. 1374 (1997).

complete victory. The appeals court reversed the district court, and the tobacco industry emerged triumphant. In a 2–1 decision, the court ruled that Congress had never intended to give the FDA jurisdiction over tobacco. Therefore, the agency had exceeded its powers.[21] The FDA appealed to the U.S. Supreme Court.

ENDGAME IN THE SUPREME COURT

On March 21, 2000, the Supreme Court, in a 5–4 decision, invalidated the FDA's tobacco rule. The justices divided into the conservative and liberal groups that have characterized many of the Court's decisions related to government regulation of business.[22] Associate Justice Sandra Day O'Connor, often regarded as a swing vote because she sometimes joins with the Court's liberals, joined with conservatives William Rehnquist, Antonin Scalia, Clarence Thomas, and Anthony Kennedy to build a five-member majority. She also wrote for the majority.

In her opinion, Justice O'Connor stated that although tobacco was one of the nation's most troubling public health problems, the FDA had no jurisdiction over it. She argued that if the FDA held that nicotine was a drug and cigarettes were a device to deliver that drug to the body, it would have to ban them. The Food, Drug, and Cosmetics Act of 1938 required that any drug or device regulated by the FDA had to be, in the language of the law, "safe" and "effective." Since the FDA had shown cigarettes to be an extremely dangerous health risk in its final rule, it would be required by law to prohibit tobacco companies from marketing them. However, said O'Connor, a cigarette ban would violate the clear intent of Congress. She pointed out that in 1929 and in 1963 bills were introduced in Congress to give the FDA authority over tobacco. They were not passed. Instead, the lawmakers had

passed six statutes regulating tobacco since 1965.[23] Collectively, these laws established a framework of regulation and showed that Congress rejected prohibition in favor of more limited regulation. O'Connor summed up the majority opinion this way.

> By no means do we question the seriousness of the problem that the FDA has sought to address. The agency has amply demonstrated that tobacco use, particularly among children and adolescents, poses perhaps the single most significant threat to public health in the United States. Nonetheless, no matter how "important, conspicuous, and controversial" the issue . . . an administrative agency's power to regulate in the public interest must always be grounded in a valid grant of authority from Congress.[24]

The dissenting opinion was written by Justice Stephen G. Breyer, who was joined by Justices John Paul Stevens, David Souter, and Ruth Bader Ginsburg. Justice Breyer began the dissent by pointing out that the purpose of the Food, Drug, and Cosmetic Act of 1938 was to protect public health. Since cigarettes posed a clear danger to public health, the statute had to be interpreted in a way that was "consistent with [this] overriding purpose."[25] Breyer thought the literal wording of the law gave the FDA authority to classify cigarettes as "devices" that delivered the "drug" nicotine and then to regulate their sale and use.

Rejecting the reasoning of the majority that Congress had chosen not to ban tobacco, he pointed out that nowhere in any law was there specific language denying the FDA authority over tobacco or denying the agency a right to ban tobacco products. "[O]ne can just as easily infer," he wrote, "that Congress did not intend to affect the FDA's tobacco-related

---

[21] *Brown & Williamson* v. *Food and Drug Administration,* 153 F.3d 155 (1998).

[22] See, for example, *Adarand* v. *Pena,* the case study in Chapter 18.

[23] These are the Federal Cigarette Labeling and Advertising Act of 1965, the Public Health Cigarette Smoking Act of 1969, the Alcohol and Drug Abuse Amendments of 1983, the Comprehensive Smoking Education Act of 1984, the Comprehensive Smokeless Tobacco Health Education Act of 1986, and the Alcohol, Drug Abuse, and Mental Health Administration Reorganization Act of 1992.

[24] *Food and Drug Administration* v. *Brown & Williamson,* 529 U.S. 120, at 152.

[25] 529 U.S. 162.

authority at all."[26] Breyer believed that the FDA had made a reasonable interpretation of the 1938 law in light of its "overall health-protecting purpose" and that, under the *Chevron* doctrine, the agency was entitled to broad deference. He concluded by observing that since a policy of tobacco regulation was of great import to the nation, the public could, and would, hold the president and elected representatives in Congress accountable for it. Therefore, implicitly, the Court should defer to the public rather than surmise the intent of Congress in the absence of any direct statement.

POSTSCRIPT

Early in 1997 David Kessler resigned as FDA administrator to become dean of the Yale University School of Medicine. Even after leaving, he still had an obsessive interest in tobacco regulation. He often sat late at night poring over tobacco company documents in his garage, still working out the issues. The Court's holding pained him. In his own words: "The decision that could have saved hundreds of thousands of lives had been lost by a single vote."[27]

Although the tobacco industry staved off FDA regulation, it did not escape restrictions. In 1998 tobacco companies agreed to pay $246 billion over 25 years to settle suits by state attorneys general seeking to recover billions of Medicaid dollars paid out to treat smokers' illnesses. As a condition of settlement, they also agreed to many advertising restrictions, most notably bans on billboards, cartoon figures, event sponsorships, and the use of logos on promotional items. In addition, the industry must pay for $25 million of antismoking ads each year for 10 years.

Supporters of tobacco regulation in Congress responded to the Court's decision by introducing bills to give the FDA precisely that authority denied it by the Court, including the power of an eventual ban.[28] Lawmakers friendly to Philip Morris introduced a bill giving limited regulatory authority to the FDA while prohibiting it from classifying nicotine as a drug and banning cigarettes.[29] Other tobacco companies refused to back the Philip Morris initiative. Observers suggest that Philip Morris sees some regulation as inevitable and seeks to shape it to the company's advantage.[30] Regulation could make smokers' lawsuits more difficult by seeming to confer government sanction on smoking. Philip Morris is the leading tobacco company with more than 50 percent of market share in cigarette sales. Since regulation would have some restricting effects on competition, it might lock in the company's industry leadership. Passage of any legislation is uncertain at this time.

QUESTIONS

1. Do you agree with the Food and Drug Administration that nicotine can be classified as a drug and that cigarettes can be classified as devices under the definitions in the Food, Drug, and Cosmetics Act?

2. Did the FDA make any legal or political errors that defeated its efforts to regulate tobacco?

3. Do you agree with the decision of the U.S. Supreme Court? Why or why not?

4. Do you believe that the story reveals flaws in American government and the regulatory process, or do you believe that the story reveals a system that, despite faults, is ultimately responsive and just?

[26] 529 U.S. 163.
[27] Kessler, *A Question of Intent*, p. 384.
[28] For example, the FDA Tobacco Authorities Act, H.R. 1097 (2001).
[29] The National Youth Smoking Reduction Act, H.R. 2180 (2001).
[30] See James Flanigan, "Philip Morris' Tactic: FDA Regulation," *Los Angeles Times*, March 22, 2001, p. C1; and Jeffrey H. Birnbaum, "Philip Morris to FDA: Get on Our Backs," *Fortune*, April 30, 2001, p. 32.

Chapter Ten

Reforming the Regulatory Process

California Deregulates Electricity

California governor Pete Wilson signed a bill in September 1996 to "deregulate" the electric utilities in the state. The bill had the approval of just about everyone connected with the subject because it was designed to benefit everybody.

The plan of Governor Wilson provided incentives for the utilities to sell their power plants to independent energy generators that were considered more efficient producers of energy than the utilities. The utilities were expected to buy power from these producers and other sources in a free competitive market. When the utilities sold their energy producing plants, they could use the proceeds to pay off about $3 billion in debts accumulated to pay for their nuclear plants. Competition among electricity suppliers was expected to provide energy to consumers at lower prices. Consumers were assured that by 2000 their rates would be 25 percent lower, after adjustment for inflation. As part of the 1996 deregulation plan, electricity rates were rolled back 10 percent and frozen there. By 1999 wholesale prices averaged a bit over 2 cents per kilowatt-hour, and the frozen rate was 6 to 7 cents per kilowatt-hour. The utilities could use the difference to lower rates to consumers and pay off the debt accumulated to build nuclear plants.

The Wilson plan was based on three important assumptions: (1) competition would result in the building of new energy plants, (2) consumer demand would rise at past rates, and (3) a balance would be struck between demand and supply at a low price level. The plan worked reasonably well until mid-2000, when disaster struck. Then the first of many blackouts took place. The new owners of generating plants that had been sold by the utilities began to raise prices of their electricity that was desperately needed. Demand for power had almost doubled, but supply had declined. This demand-supply imbalance resulted in a substantial increase in rates of electricity bought by the utilities, as much as seven times the legal rate fixed by the

Public Utilities Commission. The result, of course, was that the two largest utilities to be deregulated—Southern California Edison (SCE) and Pacific Gas and Electric (PG&E)—lost billions of dollars. By January 2000 the utilities had lost so much money that they threatened bankruptcy. (PG&E did declare bankruptcy in 2001, but SCE managed to avoid it.) Because of the utilities' financial problems, suppliers began to refuse to sell to them for fear they would not be paid.

The utilities were unable to find enough electric power to satisfy all demands. The result was repeated blackouts. The interruptions to energy flow created problems throughout the state and beyond its borders. For example, California Steel Industries in Fontana had been shut down for lack of energy only once in 15 years, but in 2000 it was forced to shut down 18 times for lack of power. The president of the company lamented, "We cannot run a business like this."[1] Many small businesses were forced to close, and others survived by cutting payrolls or borrowing. Residential users of electric power paid substantially more.

The State of California stepped in to buy electricity for the utilities and in the process incurred huge debts. A $12 billion bond issue was approved to permit the state to pay for the costs of electricity it incurred while helping the utilities. The state also made $43 billion long-term contracts with suppliers to supply power in the future.

California petitioned the Federal Energy Regulatory Commission to place a cap on energy wholesale prices to provide some financial relief, which it finally did in June 2001 after much hesitancy, and it ordered wholesalers to sell to California. This order resulted in moderate declines in the cost of purchased energy but still left the utilities with losses since the rates the California Public Utility Commission permitted them to charge were still below their costs of energy.

A comparatively cool 2001 summer in California and new energy supplies resulted in a reasonably satisfactory electricity demand-supply balance. But the state and the two utilities were left with huge debts. California will feel the impact of this deregulation mismanagement for many years. It has learned important lessons about what not to do that other states, in the process of electric utility deregulation, are studying carefully.

While this story concerns regulatory reform in a state, the lessons are equally applicable to the federal government, which is the principle concern of this chapter. It is, therefore, a fitting introduction. In this chapter we first set forth a few outstanding principles that should govern reform. Then recommendations are divided into two categories: statutory reforms by Congress and administrative reforms. We then make a few comments comparing regulatory reform in the United States with that in selected foreign countries. This is followed with a discussion of the antitrust laws and their reform.

[1] Mark Gimein, "Who Turned the Lights Out?" *Fortune,* February 5, 2001, p. 110.

CONGRESSIONAL AND EXECUTIVE BRANCH REFORMS

> It is almost as if federal programs were *designed* not to work. In truth, few
> are "designed" at all; the legislative process simply churns them out, one
> after another, year after year. It's little wonder that when asked if
> "government always manages to mess things up," two-thirds of Americans
> say "yes."

So wrote then–Vice President Al Gore in a massive study of ways to improve the regulatory process.[2]

Major shortcomings of federal regulation are rooted in many causes. Examples are insufficient budgets for proper implementation, contradictory laws and regulations, lax administration and incompetent managers, concentration of special interests on regulatory matters in both the Congress and executive agencies, and poorly drafted basic legislation. Among them, congressional ineptitude in drafting basic legislation is by far the most important.

Shortly after his inauguration, President Bush issued a report on ways to improve the performance of government agencies. Here is what he said:

> The need for reform is urgent. . . . New programs are frequently created
> with little review or assessment of the already-existing programs to
> address the same perceived problem. Over time, many programs with
> overlapping missions and competing agendas grow up alongside one
> another—wasting money and baffling citizens.[3]

He was wise to add:

> Though reform is badly needed, the obstacles are daunting—as previous
> generations of would-be reformers have repeatedly discovered. The work
> of reform is continually overwhelmed by the constant multiplication of
> hopeful new programs, each of whose authors is certain that this idea will
> avoid the managerial problems to which all previous government
> programs have succumbed.[4]

These generalizations, largely true, should not lead to the conclusion that the federal administrative agencies are staffed with brain-dead personnel. Both authors of this book have served in the federal government, one as a top administrative officer and the other as staff in a major agency. We attest to the fact that there are in the bureaucracy extremely talented and hardworking people who are dedicated to improving the way government operates. This point of view is corroborated by John D. Donahue of

---

[2] Al Gore, *Creating a Government That Works Better & Costs Less* (Washington, DC: Government Printing Office, 1993), p. 1.
[3] *The President's Management Agenda* (Washington, DC: Executive Office of the President, Office of Management and Budget, Fiscal Year 2002), p. 3.
[4] Ibid.

Harvard University's John F. Kennedy School of Government in his book *Making Washington Work.*[5] A survey of 8,179 customers of 27 federal agencies involved in more than 90 percent of the government's interactions with the public recorded an overall score of 68.6 on the American Customer Satisfaction Index. This compared with 71.2 received by the private sector, which shows, of course, that the public sector was as good or nearly as good as the private sector in satisfying consumer interests.[6]

Reforming the federal regulatory process is a formidable task. As noted above and in other chapters presidents of the United States have tackled the task with but limited success. So, we approach this subject with humility. At any rate, here are a few principles to guide regulatory reform which, if followed, could be helpful.

STRESS THE COMPARATIVE ADVANTAGES OF GOVERNMENT AND BUSINESS

An effort should always be made to decide whether business or government can best perform an activity needed by society. Each has strengths and weaknesses. There clearly are certain activities that government can perform more efficiently and effectively than individuals in the private sector. For example, only government can set national goals for resolving major problems facing the nation, provide for national defense, make and administer tax laws, establish the ground rules under which private enterprise functions, print money, reconcile conflicting interests in the formation of congressional laws, and formulate foreign policy.

Business has many advantages over government in the performance of other functions necessary in this society. For example, costs of government management of productive facilities are likely to be higher than those of the private sector because of a requirement for accounting for "the last penny," because equal attention must be given to unimportant and important elements of the activity, because in government personal loyalty is often more valued than efficiency, and because any activity assumed by government becomes part of a huge bureaucracy with inherent inefficiencies. Furthermore, the motives of those in the public sector are more likely to be driven by political considerations at odds with objectivity. Finally, when compared with government, business generally enjoys an advantage in flexibility and adaptability.

[5] John D. Donahue, *Making Washington Work: Tales of Innovation in the Federal Government* (Washington, DC: The Brookings Institution, 2001).
[6] Jason Peckenpaugh, "Government Narrows Gap on Customer Service," *Daily Briefing*, GovExec.com, December 22, 2000.

Business and government often work together to blend the unique characteristics that drive each. For example, government has been a partner with business in the production of national defense goods and services. Government has also used the free market as an instrument to accomplish its purposes. For example, if the government wants to protect an industry from foreign competition, it can do so by erecting a tariff. If it wishes to speed the development of automobile emissions free of pollution, it can do so by subsidizing research of the automobile companies. As Charles E. Lindblom, an eminent emeritus professor from Yale University, so cogently observed: "Many of us have been on the wrong track in identifying the market system with individualism, as though it could not serve collective purposes or could do so only exceptionally and badly."[7]

RELY MORE ON THE FREE MARKET

In recent years, there has been a worldwide movement for governments to rely more on market forces and less on regulations to achieve desired benefits to society. It has many dimensions, ranging from almost complete deregulation of industries to fostering competition through application of the antitrust laws. Here we discuss briefly privatization, deregulation, and substitution of command regulations with incentives. There is no clear demarcation among the three, for each has aspects of the others.

Privatize Government-Owned Property and Services

"Privatization is commonly defined as any process aimed at shifting functions and responsibilities, in whole or in part, from the government to the private sector."[8] Privatization jokingly has been called "a little yard sale" of government assets. But it is far more than that.

Much has been done at the federal level. For example, many military bases have been returned to private ownership. The private United Space Alliance is a joint venture between Boeing Company and Lockheed Martin Corporation. It is one of the world's largest space operations companies. The National Aeronautics and Space Agency (NASA) contracted with the company to prepare space shuttles for flight, conduct astronaut training, aid in mission control operations, maintain some of its bases, and launch satellites. The Elk Hills Naval Petroleum Reserve and a small Helium Reserve have been sold to private companies. The Federal Aviation Administration (FAA) has for years been under pressure to privatize its air traffic control operations.

---

[7] Charles E. Lindblom, *The Market System* (New Haven: Yale University Press, 2001), pp. 258–59.
[8] General Accounting Office, *Privatization: Lessons Learned by State and Local Governments,* GAO/GGD-97-48, March 1997, p. 1.

Some federal impetus toward privatization arises from the widespread policy of state and municipal governments to contract out public services to private firms. Most states are contracting with private enterprise to do much of the work of the welfare system. States are also contracting with private companies to run prisons. Pennsylvania has outsourced its data centers to Unisys Corp. Municipal governments have been privatizing for many years. Local governments have contracted vehicle towing, legal services, streetlight operations, solid-waste disposal, street repair, hospital operations, ambulance service, data processing, zoos, fire fighting, and many other functions. The claim is made that private enterprise can do these things more cheaply and efficiently than local governments, but that is not always true.[9]

Privatization in other countries is proceeding rapidly. Under the leadership of Margaret Thatcher, Great Britain deregulated most industries that had been government-owned and -operated under previous administrations. Another example is Russia, where privatization has been accomplished on a massive scale (and often accompanied by corruption).

Deregulate Selected Industries

Deregulation, as the term implies, refers to the removal or substantial reduction of government regulations of entire industries. Beginning in the 1970s, the United States deregulated one major industry after another. Examples are trucking, banking, airlines, railroads, shipping, telecommunications, and electricity. This development reversed a previous century of growing regulation of these industries. Deregulation of these industries represents reform, but at the same time, as noted in the preceding chapter, the trend for the total volume of new regulations is up.

Deregulation has produced significant benefits to society, but it has also created problems. For example, consumers have saved billions of dollars a year on air travel. However, many consumers found ticket prices rising on some routes, deteriorating services, and significant delays and cancellations of flights. Deregulation was supposed to stimulate competition in the industry, but instead the airline industry is dominated by an oligopoly of five carriers. The result has been less competition and more predatory behavior by these companies. Alfred Kahn, a professor at Cornell University, as chairman of the Civil Aviation Board (now abolished) was instrumental in deregulating the airline industry in the 1970s. He laments that he favored deregulation of the industry but not the antitrust laws! He meant, of course, that he certainly favored deregulation, since he played a significant part in it, but the antitrust agencies failed to restrain the concentration of the airlines after deregulation.

---

[9] "Privatization on a Roll," *The American Enterprise,* November–December 1997.

Reduce Command Controls in Favor of Incentive Controls

A significant route to harnessing the benefits of the free market is to replace command controls with incentives. Command controls require firms and individuals to meet specific standards or behaviors, and they are enforced by civil and, in some cases, criminal penalties, or loss of government contracts. Incentive controls seek to achieve desired regulatory ends by permitting affected firms or individuals flexibility in choosing methods to meet goals. If this is done, the presumption is that innovation will be inspired in technology, service, pricing, management, or organization. In turn this will lead to more efficiency, government standards will be met, and consumers will benefit.

Government agencies increasingly are looking for ways to replace command-and-control regulations with those that harness the power of economic motives. For example, the EPA issues permits for allowable sulfur dioxide emission levels to companies. A firm that has created more effective and cheaper pollution control measures can sell not only its unused permits but the new technology. In another area, the government has exempted automobile companies from the antitrust laws so that they can form a consortium to develop new engines. These and other efforts to replace command controls with incentive regulations are helpful. However, the net reduction to the total pyramid of command controls built over the past quarter century is not large.

Incentives to stimulate individual initiative in free markets can be an effective method to replace command controls and achieve social goals more effectively. Charles Schultze, former chair of the President's Council of Economic Advisers, evaluated this force as follows: "Harnessing the base motive of material self-interest to promote the common good is perhaps the most important social invention mankind has yet achieved."[10]

STATUTORY REFORM

The most fundamental type of regulatory reform is statutory reform by Congress, because it is Congress that grants authority to regulatory agencies. "The underlying statutes," editorialized the *Washington Post*, "are not a coherent body of law but a kind of archeological pile, each layer a reflection of the headlines and political impulses of its day."[11] Congress passes statutes with admirable goals and broad grants of authority, then denounces agencies for aggressive and costly regulations to implement them.

[10] Charles L. Schultze, *The Public Use of Private Interest* (Washington, DC: The Brookings Institution, 1977), p. 18.
[11] *Washington Post,* March 26, 1995, p. C6.

Some statutes mandate or forbid specific actions by regulatory agencies. For example, the basic OSHA legislation prohibits the use of cost–benefit analysis in regulation, said the Supreme Court in a decision made when the agency wanted to use the cost–benefit tool.[12] Congress directed the Consumer Product Safety Commission, in the Child Safety Protection Act (1994), to require labeling on toys intended for children aged three to six.

Recommendations for Congressional Regulatory Reform

A major recommendation of most critics of federal regulation is reform in the legislative process in Congress. They point to the need for revising parts of old enactments and change in the formation and enactment of new statutes. Following are a few reforms considered important by critics.

- Revise major existing legislation in the areas of environment, consumer safety, and workplace safety to require cost–benefit analysis where appropriate.

- Require regulatory agencies to report annually to the public on the quantifiable and nonquantifiable costs and benefits of their new rules.

- Legislate more authority and more funds to the Office of Management and Budget (OMB) to review new rules promulgated by the agencies.

- Attempt some rough approximations of costs and benefits for proposed legislation. It is difficult to make a convincing cost–benefit analysis of new legislation in a new field, but the discipline involved might prevent ill-conceived statutes.

- Direct the OMB and each regulatory agency to review annually 10 major regulations to evaluate whether they are being implemented with the least cost and maximum benefit.

- Provide Congress with independent analysis of proposed legislation. One critic recommends the creation of an independent office staffed with experienced analysts to evaluate costs and benefits of new legislation. Another critic recommends an independent office to give Congress high-quality counsel on technical matters.[13]

Besides statutory reform, Congress can help in reforming the administrative structure of the executive branch in many ways. For example, it

---

[12] *American Textile Manufacturers Institute* v. *Donovan,* 452 U.S. 490 (1981).

[13] These were derived from recommendations of Robert W. Crandall, Christopher DeMuth, Robert W. Hahn, Robert E. Litan, Pietro S. Nivola, and Paul R. Portney, *An Agenda for Federal Regulatory Reform,* Washington, D.C.: American Enterprise Institute for Public Policy Research and The Brookings Institution, 1997; Christopher H. Foreman Jr., "Congress & Regulatory Reform," *Brookings Review,* Winter 1998; and Murray Weidenbaum and Carol Tucker Foreman, *Regulation: Benefit or Bane* (Washington University in St. Louis, Center for the Study of American Business, July 1999).

can actively support government management reforms, use its oversight powers to insist that agencies fix their problems, and provide the investments and the tools necessary for substantial reform.

Improve Administration of the Regulatory Process

Reform of the regulatory apparatus in the executive branch is a formidable task, but it has not deterred past presidents when they first entered office to attempt such reforms. President Bush followed that tradition and formulated a comprehensive 64-page document.[14] In this report, he set five major goals and implementation steps cutting across all regulatory agencies, and seven goals and implementation steps for specific programs. For example, he identified these agency wide goals: better strategic management of human capital, better and more use of expanded information technology, and elimination of billions of dollars of waste in government programs. Among the specific programs is privatization of military housing, larger research and development funds, and reform of food aid programs. To start the process of implementing these goals and programs, the president in July 2001 directed his cabinet secretaries and agency heads to designate a "chief operating officer" to be responsible for day-to-day operations of the agency. At the same time, he established the President's Management Council (PMC), consisting of the chief operating officers. A major responsibility of the PMC is to integrate implementing systems within each agency and across agencies.

Everyone applauds such efforts and hopes they will make a difference in improving the federal regulatory programs. It is sobering to realize, however, that previous presidents have tried with minimum success.

It seems that Congress likes to make new laws rather than revising old ones. A classic illustration concerns a law passed in 1872 called the Mining Act. Under the provisions of this act, it is possible to buy public lands for $2.50 to $5.00 an acre when ore is discovered. Secretary of the Interior Bruce Babbitt in September 1995 signed over title to federal land containing more than $1 billion in minerals to a Danish mining company for $275 under the terms of the this law. He called the signing a "tawdry process" and a "flagrant abuse of the public interest," but the law mandated his action. In 1994 he signed title to land containing about $10 billion in gold to a Canadian firm for about $10,000 and called it "the biggest gold heist since the days of Butch Cassidy."[15] President Clinton and others at the time tried to persuade Congress to revise this law to prevent such lavish gifts, but without success.

[14] *The President's Management Agenda, Fiscal Year 2002* (Washington, DC: Executive Office of the President, Office of Management and Budget, August 2001).
[15] See Mark Zepezauer and Arthur Naiman, *Take the Rich Off Welfare;* excerpt at www.thirdworldtraveler.com/Corporate-Welfare/Mining_Subsidies.html.

Other Recommendations for Reform

The above recommendations for reform would, if implemented, produce an enormous improvement in the efficiency and effectiveness of the regulatory agencies. At the risk of overdoing the reform list, we note a few others.

Coordinate Regulatory Mandates

There are many instances where regulatory requirements among numerous agencies conflict. For example, there are 50 programs for the homeless administered in eight federal agencies. There are 26 programs administered by six agencies involved in food and nutrition services. One small businessman complained that one agency required him to complete a form with information on the ethnic background of applicants. A form from another agency, however, prohibited him from asking questions about race, age, and other characteristics. Conflicts among policies are endemic. Restrictive trade policies conflict with free trade policy. Export controls over weapons and advanced technologies (for national security purposes) may conflict with promoting global competitiveness. A safety inspector from OSHA at a meat-packing firm told the managers that it was contrary to regulations for floors to be wet and slippery; but Department of Agriculture rules require that floors be hosed down for sanitary reasons.

Reduce Paperwork

Congress passed the Paperwork Reduction Act in 1995, but it did not result in the reductions of paperwork envisioned. The General Accounting Office concluded that between the passage of the act and 1999, paperwork actually increased![16] Reducing paperwork refers not only to cutting the requirements for business reporting to an agency but the simplification of the data demanded by the form.

Remove Flapdoodle Standards and Specifications

Among the massive volumes of federal regulations there exist some that are absurd, trivial, or nonsensical. Classic examples are found in early OSHA regulations, many of which now have been expunged. They are, however, amusing. For instance, "Jacks which are out of order shall be tagged accordingly, and shall not be used until repairs are made." The Department of Agriculture under pressure from Pickle Packers International Inc., a trade group, defined standards for making the perfect pickle in eight mind-numbing pages of fine print. Among the standards

[16] J. Christopher Mihm, *Management Reform,* Testimony before the Subcommittee on Oversight of Government Management, Restructuring, and the District of Columbia, Committee on Governmental Affairs, U.S. Senate, May 4, 2000.

is this definition: "The diameter in whole style means the shortest diameter measured transversely to the longitudinal axis at the greatest circumference of the pickle."[17]

REGULATORY REFORM IN FOREIGN COUNTRIES

The Organisation for Economic Co-operation and Development (OECD) has studied in detail the regulatory reforms in 16 countries. It concluded that governments throughout the world are finding that detailed regulation and excessive paperwork impose unnecessary costs on business and citizens. As a result they are reforming their systems. For example, Spain privatized most state-owned enterprises, loosened state controls, and strengthened competition policies. South Korea has made substantial regulatory reforms but still, according to the OECD, is far from finished. Hungary is close to completing substantial reforms of its legal and economic system. Mexico today enjoys the benefits of a free market that in the past was centrally controlled. None of the 16 countries studied by the OECD, however, have approached the degree to which the United States has reformed its regulatory system.[18]

PATTERNS OF CHANGE IN THE ANTITRUST LAWS

Fundamental to the effective operation of the individual enterprise system is the idea of competing economic units that perform to benefit consumers. From the beginning of the American nation, this idea was written into law. Throughout its history, these laws have been redefined and reformulated by the Supreme Court and the antitrust regulatory agencies. The antitrust laws were so named because of the method of corporate consolidation in the late nineteenth century called the *trust*. Briefly, owners of stock of competing organizations transferred legal title to a group of trustees and received certificates in return. The trustees then exercised control of the firms as a single company. There are four major antitrust laws, and we briefly explain each one.

The Sherman Antitrust Act (1890)

During the nineteenth century, the states regulated local monopolistic practices but ran into difficulty in exercising control over the giant trusts that were being formed. For example, the Standard Oil Trust formed by

---

[17] Bridget O'Brian, "Government Sets New Standards for Ways to Get Properly Pickled," *The Wall Street Journal,* September 25, 1991, p. B1.
[18] "OECD Reviews of Regulatory Reform," at www.oecd.org/subject/regreform/Products/oecd_ reviews.htm.

John D. Rockefeller and many of its imitators in the 1880s provoked formidable opposition among small-business owners, farmers, and the public. So widespread and strong was the opposition to the trust movement that the Sherman Act of 1890, designed to curb the trusts, passed the Senate with but one dissenting vote and passed the House without opposition. This law is still the foundation of antitrust enforcement today.

The two most significant sections of the Sherman Act are 1 and 2. Section 1 reads: "Every contract, combination in the form of trust or otherwise, or conspiracy in restraint of trade or commerce . . . is hereby declared to be illegal." Section 2 says: "Every person who shall monopolize, or attempt to monopolize . . . trade or commerce . . . shall be deemed guilty."

The Supreme Court refused to use the Sherman Act until 1911. Demands arose for more precise definitions of illegal monopolistic practices, and Congress responded in 1914 by passing the Clayton Act and the Federal Trade Commission Act.

The Clayton Act (1914)

The Clayton Act named and outlawed specific practices when, in the words of the act, "the effect . . . may be to substantially lessen competition or tend to create a monopoly." For example, the act outlaws *price discrimination* when it substantially lessens competition or tends to create a monopoly. To sell a product at a low cost with the purpose of driving a competitor out of business is illegal. If several companies had the same directors who conspired to control a market, that would be called *interlocking directors* and would be illegal. Another practice the act specified as illegal was the use of *tying contracts.* If a supplier company sold one product to a customer only if the customer also bought other products sold by the supplier, that would be illegal tying. Many other anticompetitive practices were defined in this act.

The Federal Trade Commission Act (1914)

This act established an agency, the Federal Trade Commission, to continuously supervise and administer the antitrust laws, to stop "unfair methods of competition in commerce, and unfair or deceptive acts or practices in commerce." The act was amended in 1938 by the Wheeler-Lea Act, which gave the FTC power to regulate deceptive advertising.

The Department of Justice has authority to enforce the Sherman Act and shares jurisdiction with the FTC in Clayton Act cases. The Supreme Court, of course, has the final word in interpreting both laws and various statutes reinforcing them.

Through the years, exceptions to the antitrust laws have been granted. For example, excepted are labor unions, agricultural cooperatives, the insurance industry, baseball, certain joint export trading activities, and certain joint research efforts in some industries.

The Hart-Scott-Rodino Antitrust Improvement Act (1976)

This law requires companies to notify the FTC and DOJ of an intention to merge if their valuations exceed specified amounts. The act provides for a 30-day waiting period after the information is submitted. It also expands the powers of state attorneys general to institute triple damage suits on behalf of those injured by any violations of the Sherman Act. Some observers consider this act of equal importance to the Sherman Act.

Theories of Antitrust Enforcement

Much has been written about the purpose of the antitrust laws. One of the best statements is that given in a Supreme Court opinion made in a Sherman Act case:

> The Sherman Act was designed to be a comprehensive charter of economic liberty aimed at preserving free and unfettered competition as the rule of trade. It rests on the premise that the unrestrained interaction of competitive forces will yield the best allocation of our economic resources, the lowest prices, the highest quality, and the greatest material progress, while at the same time providing an environment conducive to the preservation of our democratic political and social institutions. But even were that premise open to question, the policy unequivocally laid down by the Act is competition.[19]

Antitrust policy is not solely an economic policy. It has social as well as political implications. Socially it means greater welfare for individuals. Politically it supports democracy by preventing concentrated economic power able to distort popular impulses.

In seeking to achieve this fundamental objective, two major theories of enforcement have developed, namely the *structure* and the *performance* theories. Until recently, the Supreme Court, as well as government regulators and academic economists, leaned toward the structure theory in deciding antitrust cases, as supported by most of the scholarly studies on concentration and merger. In the late 1960s, however, an increasing body of impressive evidence emerged that contradicted this view and supported the performance theory.

The Structure Theory

Until recently, the main view of the Court was that corporate size and large market share are a reliable index of monopoly power. The typical measure of power is concentration of assets or sales of one or a few companies in an industry. (Concentration is calculated as the ratio of sales

[19] *U.S. v. Northern Pacific R.R. Co.*, 356 U.S. 1 (1958).

and/or assets of one or a few companies in an industry to total sales and/or assets of the entire industry.) The structure theory argues that excessive concentration of market power gives corporate managers discretionary power to fix prices, determine which products come to market and in what volume, and make huge profits. Extraordinary market power produces price inflation, inefficiencies in production, and, of course, a decline in competition. Adherents of this theory argue that the way to ensure competitive markets is to break up concentrations of economic power or prevent such concentration from developing. This is the essence of the structure theory. It was supported for decades by economists and expounded in their scholarly research.[20]

The Performance Theory

This theory argues that public policy should seek efficient business performance as well as appropriate market structures. Efficient performance ensures product and process innovation, reduced costs that benefit consumers with lower prices, productive capacity in balance with product demand, profits not out of line with other industries, and emphasis on service to consumers. Furthermore, any assertion that concentration inhibits competition is seriously challenged when world markets are considered. Today more than ever, American industry is faced with powerful global competitors. The concentration numbers tend to shrink substantially when foreign competition is considered. For example, there is high concentration in the United States in jet engine production, but when sales of foreign producers are considered, the ratio drops significantly.[21]

Research Findings

These assertions have been supported by economists and scholarly research. For example, studies show a lack of correlation between measures of concentration and excessive profits.[22] Research concludes that substantial price flexibility exists in concentrated industries and that price increases during inflationary periods have been lower in industries dominated by "super concentrations" than in those less concentrated. Productivity also has risen faster in industries that are concentrated than in other industries. If high profits are found in large firms, say performance theorist, this may be due more to efficiency than to any market power they possess.[23]

---

[20] For example, see John M. Blair, *Economic Concentration, Structure, Behavior and Public Policy* (New York: Harcourt Brace, 1973).

[21] J. Fred Weston, *Concentration and Efficiency: The Other Side of the Monopoly Issue* (Croton-on-Hudson, NY: Hudson Institute, 1978).

[22] Ibid.

[23] Ibid.

Such research does not refute completely every assertion by structural theorists. Some concentrations at some times and places may result in excessive profits, price inflexibility, inhibitions to innovation, and so forth. They do show, however, that for most cases of concentration, structure theory describes the opposite of reality.

The Theories in Practice

Up to the 1970s, decisions of the Supreme Court and Department of Justice concerning monopolistic practices were based largely on the structure theory. In 1974 the Supreme Court held that the calculation of the effects of a merger should not rely exclusively on structural tests but should take into account a much broader range of economic information.[24] In 1986 a decision of a lower court based strictly on the structure theory was rejected by the Supreme Court in a decision reflecting the performance theory.[25]

The Supreme Court and the Department of Justice have not abandoned the structure theory. Rather, there has been a noticeable shift in theory and policy toward favoring efficiencies in markets over formal criteria of structure. Antitrust decisions, therefore, face a major challenge in balancing the two theories.

CHALLENGES TO ANTITRUST ENFORCEMENT AGENCIES

New major challenges confront enforcement agencies. They arise from the current merger movement, high-technology industries, and globalization.

Mergers

Proposed and actual mergers have achieved record levels in both numbers and assets. The explosive growth of the numbers of mergers and their dollar values is evident in Figure 10.1. In 1991 the total value of assets of mergers was less than $200 billion. By the end of 2000 it was over $1.6 trillion. The largest deal in 2000 was the $166 billion merger of AOL and Time Warner. The FTC agreed to this merger only if the two companies acceded to conditions that would permit competition. The 10 largest mergers in a recent 18 month period are shown in Table 10.1.

In evaluating proposed mergers and deciding which ones to challenge, the enforcement agencies face difficult choices. For example, a merger may yield significant cost savings by eliminating duplications and creating other efficiencies. However, at the same time, the merger may leave fewer companies in the industry, which increases concentration and could lead later to price increases as a result of collusion among the remaining companies.

[24] *U.S. v. General Dynamics Corp.*, 415 U.S. 486 (1974).
[25] *Cargill, Inc., and Excell Corporation v. Montford of Colorado, Inc.*, 55 L. W. 4027 (1986).

FIGURE 10.1 Mergers and Acquisitions Involving U.S. Firms

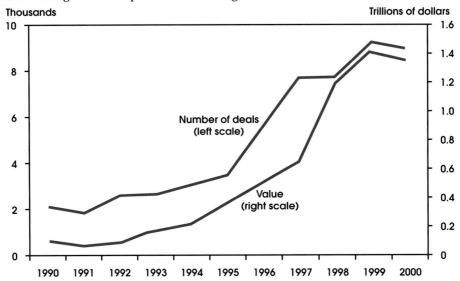

Note: Data for 2000 are through December 11.

Sources: Mergerstat; and *Economic Report of the President* (Washington, DC: Government Printing Office, January 2001), p. 41.

TABLE 10.1 Top 10 Mergers from July 1998 to January 2000

Rank	Acquirer	Acquired	Announcement Date	Amount ($ billions)	Industry
1	AOL	Time Warner	January 2000	$165.9	Internet/media
2	Exxon	Mobil	December 1998	78.9	Oil
3	Travelers Group	Citicorp	April 1998	72.6	Financial services
4	SBC Comm.	Ameritech	May 1998	62.6	Telecommunications
5	Nations Bank	BankAmerica	April 1998	61.6	Financial services
6	Vodafone Group	AirTouch Comm.	January 1999	60.3	Telecommunications
7	AT&T	MediaOne Group	April 1999	56.0	Telecommunications
8	AT&T	Telecommunications	June 1998	53.6	Telecommunications
9	Total Fina	Elf Acquitaine	July 1999	53.5	Oil
10	Bell Atlantic	GTE	July 1998	53.4	Telecommunications

Source: J. Fred Weston and Samuel C. Weaver, *Mergers and Acquisitions* (New York: McGraw-Hill, 2001), p. 3. Reproduced with permission.

Guidelines for Antitrust Action

To facilitate evaluation of mergers, in 1992 the Department of Justice jointly with the FTC established "Horizontal Merger Guidelines." The guidelines have been modified periodically since then. The most important are as follows:

- Define the relevant market, and calculate its concentration before and after the merger.

- Assess whether the merger raises concerns about adverse competitive effects.

- Determine whether entry by other firms into the market would counteract those effects.

- Consider any expected efficiency gains.[26]

Market Definition

The first step is to define the market where the merger is to take place. Then the impact on concentration is evaluated. The relevant market is generally specific products and geographic areas where a merger is likely to raise prices significantly. For example, the FTC challenged the proposed merger of Staples Inc. and Office Depot Inc. in 1997 on these grounds. It said the relevant market was "the sale of consumable office supplies through office superstores," and these were the largest firms in that market. Staples countered that the combined firms would account for less than 6 percent of the broad market for office products, including sales by discount stores, drug stores, and wholesale clubs. The FTC said the products of the two stores were much less inclusive of products in these other stores and, in the relevant market of the two stores, the merger would significantly increase concentration and be anticompetitive.[27]

Competitive Effects

The guidelines recognize that two merged firms can so concentrate an industry that collusion will result in price increases and other anticompetitive practices. Analysis of such effects is a major step in evaluation. Sometimes the antitrust authorities will permit a merger to proceed if the merged companies agree to divest certain divisions and products or agree to another arrangement to prevent anticompetitive behavior. For example, in the merger of Time Warner Inc. and Turner Broadcasting System Inc. in 1995, the FTC agreed to the merger only if the two companies separated their cable operations.

[26] *Economic Report of the President* (Washington, DC: Government Printing Office, 1998); p. 98.
[27] *FTC* v. *Staples, Inc.*, 970 F. Supp. 1066 (D.D.C. 1997).

Entry

If other firms can enter a market, it will be more difficult for merged companies to engage in anticompetitive practices. The guidelines say entry must be timely and able to counter potential anticompetitive merger practices. For example, the AOL–Time Warner merger conditions assured free entry of competitors.

Expected Efficiency Gains

Potential merger partners usually exaggerate the efficiencies to be gained through the merger and also the savings that will be passed on to consumers in lower prices and better service. Even though savings may be verifiable, a remaining question is whether they will be passed on to consumers. The Staples and Office Depot case was partly challenged on the grounds that while there undoubtedly would be savings, there was a serious question in the minds of the regulators as to whether the savings would be passed on to consumers in lower prices.

Nonhorizontal Mergers

Most mergers are of the horizontal type and these are more likely to create competitive problems than other types. The above guidelines are completely applicable to nonhorizontal mergers.[28] But there are special features of the nonhorizontal type of merger for which other guidelines are prepared. For example, the FTC stopped a proposed merger of a small company by a large firm because, said the agency, the large company could be a "deep pocket" or a "rich parent" that could open all sorts of possibilities for the small company to undersell or otherwise "ravage the less affluent competition."[29]

High-Technology Industries

Many of the fastest-growing companies are found in high-technology industries such as computer software and hardware, telecommunications, computer chips, genetic engineering, and wireless communications.

---

[28] *A horizontal merger* is one that combines the activities of companies within the same industry, such as two steel mills. A *vertical merger* takes place when a company acquires other firms, either back in the production chain, toward raw materials, or forward, toward consumers of final products and services. For example, a merger of a company producing fabricated steel shapes and forms with one mining iron ore and one building steel bridges is a vertical merger. A *conglomerate merger* is neither horizontal nor vertical and involves two firms that are engaged in unrelated lines of business. A simple illustration would be the merger of a producer of wooden office furniture with a company owning and mining coal. Conglomerate mergers can be of different varieties. For example, the acquired firms may be completely unrelated, or they may associate with a basic company purpose. Conglomerates may merge with firms that are not directly competitive, such as those with common production or distribution characteristics, or companies in the same general product line but making sales in different geographic regions.
[29] *FTC v. Reynolds Metal Company,* Trade Cases ¶70,741 (U.S. S.Ct. 1962).

Some observers wonder whether the antitrust laws are capable of dealing with the issues they create. Companies like Microsoft, Cisco, Dell, and Intel have dominant positions in the markets they serve. Their products and services are intellectual properties. A question arises for antitrust regulators about how to deal with such intellectual monopoly power while at the same time assuring innovation. Innovation clearly is squashed if companies that dominate a segment of an industry can stop new entries. Antitrust laws traditionally have been concerned with competition that adversely affects consumers. But these companies have produced products and services that clearly have benefited consumers in lower-priced and higher-quality products. Antitrust regulators in dealing with such issues tend to focus more on innovation than on competition.[30] More will be said about this subject in the Microsoft case at the end of this chapter.

The Global Market and Antitrust

American corporations face different antitrust laws and enforcement practices in other nations. Also, antitrust authorities face new issues in the spread and power of cartels created solely by foreign companies as well as cartels formed by U.S. and foreign companies. In the last few years, the DOJ has aggressively pursued companies at home and abroad for price-fixing arrangements. For example, in 1999 the DOJ fined a number of Japanese paper manufacturers and U.S. importers $6.5 million for conspiring to fix the price of thermal fax paper. In the same year, F. Hoffman–La Roche Ltd. of Switzerland and BASF of Germany paid fines of $500 million and $250 million, respectively, for a conspiracy to fix the price of vitamins. Several executives of these companies also paid fines for their part in the conspiracy. Mitsubishi Corp. of Tokyo agreed to pay a fine of $134 million for its involvement in a cartel composed of seven companies to fix the price of graphite electrodes used in steel production. The total fines levied in this case added up to $437 million.[31]

U.S. courts have held that U.S. laws apply when an alleged violation of antitrust laws has an intended and significant domestic impact on the United States. However, it may be difficult to bring a case against individuals or firms located in foreign countries. To deal with this situation, Congress in 1994 passed the International Antitrust Enforcement Assistance

---

[30] Robert Pitofsky, "Antitrust and Intellectual Property: Unresolved Issues at the Heart of the New Economy," keynote address, Symposium Beyond Microsoft, *Technology Law Journal*, Spring 2001.

[31] Steven L. Katz, Jerrold E. Fink, and Yoshiaki Tsuchitani, "Extraterritorial Enforcement of the United States Antitrust Laws," *Masuda Funai*, undated, www.masudafunai.com/English/articles/sales/sales 1.asp.

Act. This law authorizes U.S. enforcement agencies to make cooperative agreements with foreign antitrust officials.

U.S. corporations see Europe as a minefield blocking mergers not only with European companies but with other U.S. companies. The most recently publicized case is that of General Electric's proposed $45 billion merger with Honeywell International Inc. The merger was approved by the DOJ but rejected in 2001 by Mario Monti, European Union (EU) Competition Commissioner, unless GE would sell some of its assets. GE refused, and the merger was abandoned. This was the first time the EU had rejected a merger of two U.S. companies that was accepted by the DOJ. Why?

The EU official statement blocking the merger said that the merger would give GE a dominant position in Europe in the supply of avionics, nonavionics, and corporate jet engines. It would also expand GE's financial power in financing and leasing jet planes. The EU concluded that individual European companies could not compete against such "portfolio power." This decision reflected a different philosophy of mergers than in the United States. The EU focuses on protecting competitors, whereas U.S. antitrust officials focus on benefiting consumers. In Europe the emphasis is on not hurting competitors, and in the United States the emphasis is on not hurting consumers. In Europe, as a consequence, it is much easier for competitors to bring lawsuits against mergers than in the United States.

The EU has forced a number of U.S. companies proposing mergers with European firms to make important concessions before approval. This was the case with Microsoft's proposed acquisition of Telewest, a British firm.

CONCLUDING OBSERVATIONS

Reform of government regulations is clearly needed. In undertaking regulatory reforms, two important considerations must not be neglected. First, care should be taken to avoid eliminating needed regulations. Second, we probably should not expect too much.

The Tolchins remind us in the following words that no right-minded person wants to get rid of *all* regulations.

> Regulation is the connective tissue, the price we pay for an industrialized society. It is our major protection against the excesses of technology, whose rapid advances threaten man's genes, privacy, air, water, bloodstream, lifestyle, and virtual existence. It is a guard against the callous entrepreneur, who would have his workers breathe coal dust and cotton dust, who would send children into the mines and factories, who would offer jobs in exchange for health and safety, and leave the victims as public charges in hospitals and on welfare lines. . . . Regulations provide

protection against the avarice of the marketplace, against shoddy products and unscrupulous marketing practices from Wall Street to Main Street.[32]

In the future we can expect some regulatory reform. But how much? The answer is not too much because reform has a weak political base. One reason for this is that the public is not excited about it. Aside from business, the ultimate beneficiaries are generally unaware of their stake in reform. Because the benefits of reform to one person are very small in relation to the costs involved in bringing it about, there is a lack of initiative by individuals, except those in business. The result is a coalition of congressional committees, bureaucrats who administer the laws, and interest groups, constituting political power that resists quick and substantial regulatory reform. There is no comparable opposing political coalition.[33]

[32] Susan J. Tolchin and Martin Tolchin, *Dismantling America. The Risk to Deregulation* (New York: Oxford University Press, 1983), pp. 22–23.
[33] James Q. Wilson, ed., *The Politics of Regulation* (New York: Basic Books, 1980).

Microsoft Corporation and Antitrust

The rapid growth and dominance of Microsoft in the computer industry is one of the most, if not the most, spectacular success stories in the history of American business. From a two-man shoestring operation in 1975, revenues of the small firm leaped to over $25 billion in 2001. The dominance of Microsoft in PC operating systems attracted the attention of the Antitrust Division of the Department of Justice, which sued Microsoft for antitrust violations. Microsoft denied the allegations. This case focuses on that issue.

JOEL KLEIN AND BILL GATES JOIN IN COMBAT

On October 20, 1998, Joel I. Klein, assistant attorney general in charge of the Department of Justice (DOJ) Antitrust Division; 20 state attorneys general; and William Gates, chairman and chief executive officer of the Microsoft Corporation, joined in

an epic struggle before Judge Thomas Penfield Jackson in the U.S. District Court for the District of Columbia. The issues before the court were serious charges against the Microsoft Corporation set forth in briefs presented to the court. Attorney General of the United States Janet Reno, in a press release announcing the action, said:

> The Justice Department today charged Microsoft with engaging in anticompetitive and exclusionary practices designed to maintain its monopoly in personal computer operating systems and to extend that monopoly to internet browsing software.

Microsoft denied the charges.

The following discussion sets forth briefly the main arguments of the government and Microsoft and raises the question: Who is right? Is Microsoft a monopolistic predator that uses illegal means to stifle competition? Or is Microsoft acting legally in the context of a market driven by rapid technological change?

DOJ AND STATE ATTORNEYS GENERAL CHARGES

The complaints of the DOJ and attorneys general are similar and, except as noted, will be attributed to the DOJ.[1]

MICROSOFT HAS MONOPOLY POWERS

Microsoft has a monopoly in its PC Windows operating system, which enjoys 90 percent of the market. It uses that monopoly power to engage in unfair competitive practices. The exercise of this power inhibits innovation, restricts consumer and manufacturer's choices, and restrains new entry into the market. The attorneys general add that the anticompetitive practices of Microsoft threaten loss or damage to the general welfare and economies of the states.

To protect its Windows monopoly against potential competitive threats, the company has engaged in a pattern of anticompetitive activities. Included are

> agreements tying other Microsoft software products to Microsoft's Windows operating system; exclusionary agreements precluding companies from distributing, promoting, buying or using products of Microsoft's software competitors or potential competitors; and exclusionary agreements restricting the right of companies to provide services or resources to Microsoft's software competitors or potential competitors.

The prosecution says that attempting to maintain its monopoly in the market, unreasonably restraining trade, and unfairly competing are all in violation of Sections 1 and 2 of the Sherman Antitrust Act.

Franklin M. Fisher, an MIT economist, both in his written and oral testimony at the trial, strongly supported the DOJs allegations that Microsoft had monopoly power and used it.[2] A number of executives from firms such as Intel, IBM, and Sun Microsystems portrayed Microsoft in their testimony as a bullying monopolist.[3]

MICROSOFT AND NETSCAPE COMMUNICATIONS CORPORATION

Both the DOJ and attorneys general said that Microsoft's response to Internet browsers is a prominent and immediate example of the pattern of anticompetitive behavior taken to maintain and extend its monopoly. In May 1995 Gates said the Internet was "the most important single development to come along since the IBM PC was introduced in 1981." At that time, Netscape had developed an Internet browser that had 70 percent of the market. Gates saw in the Internet browser, and specifically Netscape's browser, a significant competitive threat to his Windows operating system. On January 5, 1996, he said: "Winning Internet browser share is a very, very important goal for us." On August 20, 1996, he directed: "Internet Explorer (IE) [the Microsoft browser] will be distributed every way we can . . . Bundled with Windows 95 upgrade and included by OEMs [original equipment manufacturers]."

What is the threat of Netscape's browser? The browser is software for viewing and navigating the Internet. It has the potential of offering consumers an alternative platform for software applications in competition with Windows. Java (described later) is a program language used in developing software applications. When connected with an Internet browser such as Netscape's, the two can be a serious threat to the Windows monopoly.

[1] *United States of America* v. *Microsoft Corporation*, Civil Action No. 98–1232, complaint filed in the United States District Court for the District of Columbia, May 18, 1998; and *Attorneys General, States of New York, California, Connecticut, District of Columbia, Florida, Illinois, Iowa, Kansas, Kentucky, Louisiana, Maryland, Massachusetts, Michigan, Minnesota, New Mexico, North Carolina, Ohio, South Carolina, Utah, West Virginia, Wisconsin* v. *Microsoft Corporation*, No. 1:98CVO12333, complaint filed in the United States District Court for the District of Columbia, May 18, 1998. The Department of Justice press release and complaint can be found at www.usdoj.gov/atr.

[2] Declaration of Franklin M. Fisher, in the United States District Court for the District of Columbia, *United States of America, Plaintiff,* v. *Microsoft Corporation, Defendant*, Civil Action No. 98–1232, filed May 18, 1998.
[3] Steve Lohr, "The Prosecution Almost Rests: Government Paints Microsoft as Monopolist and Bully," *The New York Times*, January 8, 1999.

In May 1995, not long before Microsoft introduced its first version of IE, the company's executives visited with Netscape executives. The government's charge is that at this meeting Microsoft attempted to persuade Netscape not to compete with Microsoft but to divide the browser market, with Microsoft the sole supplier of the browser for use with Windows 95 operating systems. This proposition, said the DOJ, "was a blatant and illegal attempt to monopolize the Internet browser market." Netscape declined the offer.

The Netscape browser continued to serve all computer users who worked on Windows 95 as well as other operating systems. It continued to have potential to become an alternative platform to Windows and, of course, a major threat to Microsoft. So Microsoft embarked on a series of moves aimed at eliminating the threat. The company developed and introduced its own browser, the IE, and used its monopoly power to drive competing Internet browsers from the market. Here are some of the actions Microsoft took that the government said were illegal and anticompetitive practices.

BUNDLING

This is a marketing strategy by which a weaker product is attached to a more popular one. Microsoft bundled its IE in its Windows operating system and said it was free to consumers, as a strategy to induce consumers to use it in favor of any other browser. Once incorporated in Windows, it could not easily be separated. This was confirmed by Professor David Farber of the University of Pennsylvania, a longtime expert in Internet technology, in testimony at the trial.[4] This was an attempt, said the DOJ, to exclude Netscape in favor of IE.

EXCLUSIONARY AGREEMENTS WITH INTERNET SERVICE PROVIDERS (ISPs) AND ONLINE SERVICES (OLSs)

Microsoft entered into anticompetitive agreements with virtually all the major and most popular ISPs and OLSs. These firms (such as AT&T Worldnet,

[4] Software Expert Criticizes Microsoft," *Los Angeles Times,* December 9, 1998, p. C3.

MCI, and Earthlink) provide communications links between PC users and the Internet. They are sometimes called Internet access providers. The agreements with these firms commit them to offer Microsoft's IE primarily or exclusively through all the channels they employ to distribute their services. They cannot promote or mention to their subscribers the existence of competing browsers. They must eliminate links on their websites by means of which subscribers can download a competing browser. They are to use the Internet sites in such a way as to ensure that Microsoft's browser is more effective than any competing system when using the service.

Why did these companies agree to do this? Microsoft agreed to place icons (notices of services) on the Windows desktop (the computer screen first seen when the computer is turned on) in a prominent place. This is an important advantage. Once the desktop position is established, it will remain because original equipment manufacturers are obliged to use the screen designed by Microsoft and not modify it without permission. As a result, these service providers are assured a position in the location where users first look when they make a decision about which service to use. If the agreements are not met, the contracts permit Microsoft to delete the mention of the service on the desktop.

EXCLUSIONARY AGREEMENTS WITH INTERNET CONTENT PROVIDERS (ICPs)

Firms such as Disney, Hollywood Online, and CBS Sportsline are ICPs that provide news, entertainment, and other information from sites on the Web. Microsoft also made exclusionary agreements with them similar to but not the same as those noted.

RESTRICTIONS ON ORIGINAL EQUIPMENT MANUFACTURERS

Around August 1996, Microsoft imposed restrictions on OEMs that were anticompetitive and illegal. They were enjoined from modifying or obscuring the sequence of any desktop screen displays unless the user initiated action to change the sequence. They cannot include any display, sound, or welcome screens until after the Windows desktop screen first appears.

With such restrictions, Microsoft, among other things, can reward firms with which it has agreements with preferred positions on the desktop screen. The restrictions provide Microsoft leverage to ensure that Microsoft-designed applications or other software reaches Windows users. For example, it ensures a preferred position on the desktop screen for its IE and a more obscure placement for competitors.

OEMs have objected to these restrictions, but Microsoft has refused to change them and threatened to deny Windows licenses to those who violate the agreement.

AMERICA ONLINE INC. (AOL)

Stephen M. Case, chairman of AOL, testified that he was approached in the spring of 1996 to make Microsoft's IE the main browser for his subscribers, which at the time were in the millions. For this, Microsoft agreed to give AOL a prominent position on the Windows desktop. However, Case complained to the DOJ that Microsoft planned to introduce its own online server in August 1996 and place it in a prominent position on the desktop of Windows. He argued that this bundling of Microsoft's online service to its operating system gave the company an unfair competitive advantage over AOL.

JAVA

Java is a programming language developed by Sun Microsystems Inc. that produces programs capable of running on almost any computer or operating system. Functioning through browsers, it can link on the Internet many computers at the same time. For example, it permits a person to play a game of poker with others on separate computers, or collect sales figures from many sources simultaneously.

The government charges that Microsoft executives saw in Java a serious threat to its operating system and took action to "neutralize" it. At the trial, the government presented e-mail and other documents purportedly showing how concerned Microsoft was. For example, in September 1996, Gates wrote an e-mail saying: "This scares the hell out of me," and called on Microsoft staff to make it a top priority to stop Java.

Sun made an agreement in March 1997 whereby it would license Java technology to Microsoft in exchange for Microsoft's ability to distribute the technology. In October 1997 Sun filed a lawsuit against Microsoft for breach of contract. Sun alleged that Microsoft was "polluting" the technology to weaken Java's use and developing its own technology to replace it. In March 1998 Judge Whyte of the U.S. District Court in San Jose, California, granted Sun an injunction enforcing the provision of the agreement that prevented Microsoft from altering Java.

BROWSER MARKET SHARES

Netscape's Navigator browser was introduced in December 1994. Within two months, it captured 60 percent of the market and reached 90 percent in early 1996. Then it began to decline and reached less than 50 percent by mid-1998. In the meantime, Microsoft's IE share rose from 5 percent after its introduction to almost 50 percent in mid-1998. There were many practitioners who asserted that Netscape's browser was superior to Microsoft's. Why, therefore, did these market shares move as they did? The primary cause, said the government, was Microsoft's anticompetitive behavior.

MICROSOFT'S RESPONSE

Microsoft replied point by point to the charges of both the DOJ and the state attorneys general.[5] The company denied it was a monopoly and had engaged in uncompetitive practices. It said, "computer software is one of the fastest moving, most innovative and most competitive businesses in history." At the trial, Microsoft's lead attorney, John Warden, said, "everything Microsoft has done is standard competitive behavior; its actions don't even come close to violating antitrust law."[6]

---

[5] *Defendant Microsoft Corporation's Answer to the Complaint Filed by the U.S. Department of Justice, United States of America* v. *Microsoft Corporation,* United States District Court for the District of Columbia, No. 98–1232 (TPJ), July 28, 1998; and *Defendant Microsoft Corporation's Answer to Plaintiff States' First Amended Complaint and Counterclaim, State of New York, ex. rel.* v. *Microsoft Corporation,* United States District Court for the District of Columbia, No. 98–1232 (TPJ), July 18, 1998.
[6] Quoted in Joseph Nocera, "High Noon," *Fortune,* November 23, 1998, p. 166.

Warden caustically assailed the government's case. He said the case was "not really an antitrust case, but a return of the Luddites, the nineteenth century reactionaries who . . . went around smashing machines with sledgehammers." Admittedly, Microsoft is a tough competitor, he said, but such behavior is legal: "the antitrust laws are not a code of civility."[7]

COMPETITION IN THE COMPUTER INDUSTRY

In a comprehensive white paper, Microsoft described in detail why it was not a monopoly and why it was not in violation of the antitrust laws. "Antitrust policy," said the company, "seeks to promote low prices, high output, and rapid innovation. On all three measures, the personal computer software industry generally—and Microsoft in particular—is a model of competitiveness."[8] The high market share of Microsoft in operating systems today may easily be gone tomorrow.

Microsoft claims that personal computer hardware and software prices are constantly falling and that, in important degree, is due to Microsoft's development of its standard operating system. Furthermore, Microsoft has substantially reduced prices on its own products.

Innovation in the computer industry has been dazzling. Product life cycles are very short, typically 12 to 18 months. Microsoft and other software producers are shipping products that were nonexistent a few years ago. Microsoft has been a major catalyst in innovation, and this will continue. Its research budget for 1998 amounts to $2.6 billion. The rapidity of innovation, of course, contributes to the intense competition in the industry. There is always the threat of new technology completely obsoleting existing products.

RELATIONS WITH NETSCAPE

Unless otherwise specified, the following is from Microsoft's response to the government's charges.

One of the reasons Netscape lost market share is because consumers believed Microsoft's IE was a superior product. At the beginning, Microsoft admits Netscape's Navigator was a better product than IE. When IE was developed, however, many reviewers said that it was the superior product. Actually, it was only after IE began beating Navigator on its merits that it started gaining users. Microsoft admits, however, that Netscape continues as a vigorous competitor to Microsoft with new successful versions of its Navigator.

BUNDLING

Microsoft has often used free software as a competitive strategy. Wrapping IE into Windows is just another application of that strategy. Not only is Microsoft giving consumers what they want, but it benefits them in terms of price. If consumers do not want to use IE, they can delete it from the operating system. Furthermore, consumers can use Netscape if they choose because it can be introduced into Windows. So they have a choice. "It takes no more than a few mouse-clicks or keystrokes to install, say, Netscape's browser and display it prominently on the PC desktop. Given that Netscape's share of browser usage remains at more than 50 percent, many Windows users clearly do just that."[9]

The government wants Microsoft to include Netscape's browser with Windows. Microsoft says that Netscape has consistently said it planned to use its browser technology as a basis for a new computing platform to make Windows obsolete. The DOJ, therefore, is asking Microsoft to incorporate a competitor's product that is intended to undermine and destroy Windows. That is unprecedented and unreasonable. Microsoft should not be asked to distribute its competitor's products along with its own. In response to allegations that Microsoft bundled its browser into Windows to thwart competition, James E. Allchin, a senior vice president of Microsoft, testified that the decision to give away free the IE "was a straightforward product-design decision that benefits consumers."[10]

[7] Quoted in John R. Wilke, "Microsoft Blasts Prosecution as 'Return of the Luddites,' " *The Wall Street Journal,* October 21, 1998.
[8] Microsoft PressPass, "Competition in the Software Industry," January 1998, www.microsoft.com/presspass/doj/1-98whitepaper.htm, p. 5.
[9] Microsoft PressPass, "Fact vs. Fiction," www.microsoft.com/presspass/fvsf.htm. December 18, 1998, p. 3.
[10] Steve Lohr and Amy Harmon, "Microsoft Executive Defends Folding Browser into Windows," *The New York Times,* January 18, 1999, p. C1.

CONTRACTS WITH OEMs

The licensing agreements Microsoft has made with OEMs have been standard in the industry. It is common practice that these contracts contain a provision not to modify or delete any part of Microsoft's copyrighted Windows software without license from the company to do so. Microsoft rightfully insists that the first time an end user turns on the computer, the system is permitted to go through the sequence as designed. OEMs, as well as users, can add icons on the Windows desktop. Such agreements are widespread in industry and are both legal and pro-competitive.

CONTRACTS WITH ISPs AND ICPs

Microsoft responded as follows to the government's charges that these contracts included unfair competitive practices:

> In attacking Microsoft's cross-marketing agreements with other firms, the Complaint seeks to deny to Microsoft the use of ordinary competitive arrangements. The challenged contracts (i) foreclose no one from full and complete access to the many available channels for the distribution of software providing web browsing functionality and (ii) are contracts for the promotion of commerce.

These contracts are commonplace in the industry and work to the mutual benefit of both parties. Microsoft helps to promote and distribute its products and the providers help to promote and distribute Microsoft's. There is nothing wrong with that. It is legal and pro-competitive.

JAVA

Microsoft claimed its "tweaking" of Java was within the contractual agreement. At the trial, Microsoft's lawyers said many consumers were frustrated with Java's shortcomings and Microsoft was trying to improve the language. In the meantime, the company said, it had developed its own technology that was much faster than Java and better designed.

WHO WAS HARMED?

A reporter at the trial observed that Microsoft's defense "boils down to one question: Where's the harm?"[11] While Warden never used these words, the question was put in hundreds of ways to the witnesses. As noted above, the DOJ and some of its witnesses claim that Microsoft's monopoly and behavior have harmed consumers. Franklin Fisher, in his written testimony said: "There is substantial probability that these anti-competitive actions will permit MS to retain its power over price in operating systems and will inhibit development of MS-independent innovations. Both would harm consumer welfare."[12]

Microsoft has repeatedly taken the position that consumers have benefited. Richard Schmalensee in his written testimony concluded: "Consumers have benefited from lower prices, greater output, better software and higher rates of innovation as a result of the actions taken by Microsoft that Plaintiffs seek to enjoin."[13]

FINDINGS OF FACT

At the end of the year-long trial in early 1999, each side had an opportunity to present its case in writing to Judge Jackson. Each did so in book-size documents, fundamentally summarizing the positions taken in court testimony. Following Judge Jackson's review of these documents, he issued his conclusions in a document called *Findings of Fact*

---

[11] Steve Lohr, "Microsoft Refrain: Who Was Harmed? *The New York Times*, October 26, 1998, p. 4.
[12] Franklin M. Fisher, Direct Testimony in the United States District Court for the District of Columbia, *United States of America, Plaintiff,* v. *Microsoft Corporation, Defendant,* Civil Action No. 98–1232, filed May 18, 1998, p. 11.
[13] Richard L. Schmalensee, Direct Testimony in the United States District Court for the District of Columbia, *United States of America Plaintiffs* v. *Microsoft Corporation Defendant,* Civil Action No. 98–1232 (TPJ), January 13, 1999, p. E–2.

on November 5, 1999. It contains his evaluation of which side presented the most believable and compelling case. Here are a few highlights of this 206-page document.[14]

First, Microsoft's share of the market for Intel-compatible PC operating systems is extremely large and stable. Second, Microsoft's dominant market share is protected by a high barrier to entry. Third, and largely as a result of that barrier, Microsoft's customers lack a commercially viable alternative to Windows. Microsoft possesses a dominant, persistent, and increasing share of the worldwide market for Intel-compatible PC operating systems. Every year for the last decade, Microsoft's share of the market for Intel-compatible PC operating systems has stood above 90 percent.

Microsoft's dominant market share is protected by barriers that prevent an aspiring entrant into the relevant market from drawing a significant number of customers away from Microsoft, even if Microsoft priced its products substantially above competitive levels for a significant period of time. "Because Microsoft's market share is so dominant, the barrier has a similar effect within the market: It prevents Intel-compatible PC operating systems other than Windows from attracting significant consumer demand, and it would continue to do so even if Microsoft held its prices substantially above the competitive level."

Judge Jackson proceeded to specify exactly how he saw Microsoft exercising its monopoly power. For example, "Microsoft attaches to a Windows license conditions that restrict the ability of OEMs to promote software that Microsoft believes could weaken the applications barrier to entry." In great detail Judge Jackson explained how he saw Microsoft's success in advancing it's Internet Explorer at the expense of Netscape's Navigator until the latter was no longer a viable threat. He mentioned how Microsoft pressured OEMs not to install Nav-

igator; how Microsoft spent $100 million a year to upgrade its IE to the point where it enjoyed, in the minds of many observers, technical superiority over Navigator; how Microsoft bundled its IE into Windows to entice customers; and how Microsoft gave valuable inducements at no cost to Internet access providers (IAPs) to exclude Navigator from their distribution channels. The net result is that Navigator's share of the browser market fell drastically after early 1996 while IE's share significantly increased in the same period. "These interactions," said the judge, "demonstrate that it is Microsoft's corporate practice to pressure other firms to halt software development that either shows the potential to weaken the applications barrier to entry or competes directly with Microsoft's most cherished software products."

Judge Jackson's key decision was that Microsoft was a monopoly and used its monopoly power aggressively. He said:

> Microsoft has demonstrated that it will use its prodigious market power and immense profits to harm any firm that insists on pursuing initiatives that could intensify competition against one of Microsoft's core products. Microsoft's past success in hurting such companies and stifling innovation deters investment in technologies and business that exhibit the potential to threaten Microsoft.

Judge Jackson apparently was determined to establish without question the facts in the case so that when he issued his final recommendations, the appellate court, where the case would go if Microsoft appealed, would not overturn them. His findings could be overturned only if they were clearly in error or if he had abused his discretion.

RESPONSES TO JUDGE JACKSON'S *FINDINGS OF FACTS*

Representatives of Microsoft looked at the same information as Judge Jackson and came to opposite conclusions. In a 70-page document issued on January 18, 2000, Microsoft gave its response to Judge

---

[14] *United States of America* v. *Microsoft Corporation; State of New York, et al.,* v. *Microsoft Corporation, Findings of Fact,* Civil Action No. 98–1232 (TPJ), undated but issued November 5, 1999.

Jackson's *Findings of Fact.* Here are a few excerpts from this document.[15]

"Plaintiffs" (throughout these excerpts Microsoft referred to the Department of Justice and the state attorneys general as plaintiffs and did not refer specifically to Judge Jackson) "failed to prove that Microsoft unlawfully maintained a monopoly in 'Intel-compatible PC operating systems' in violation of Section 2 of the Sherman Act." Microsoft contended that the offense of unlawful monopolization had two elements. One was the possession of monopoly power in the relevant market, and the second was "the willful acquisition or maintenance of that power as distinguished from growth or development as a consequence of a superior product, business acumen, or historical accident."

> Although the Court concluded in its findings of fact that Microsoft possesses monopoly power in the market for "Intel-compatible PC operating systems . . . the individual *facts* found by the Court do not establish monopoly power in a relevant antitrust market: (i) under the governing legal principles, the arena of competition relevant to decision of this case extends beyond "Intel-compatible PC operating systems" to encompass all platforms competing for the attention of software developers and users, and (ii) Microsoft does not have monopoly power within the meaning of Section 2 in the market defined by the Court or any other market at issue.
>
> On the demand side, consumers looking for computing solutions have an increasing array of alternatives, including, among other options, an Apple Macintosh running the Mac 05 or a workstation running some variant of the UNIX operating system.

In the future, said Microsoft, consumers who have simplified computers will have many more choices. "On the supply side . . . developers of mainframe and server operating systems such as IBM, Hewlett-Packard and Sun have the technical resources to develop operating systems for a vari-

ety of hardware platforms and to supply the entire market for such operating systems."

"Microsoft does not have durable monopoly power in any relevant antitrust market because it cannot control prices or exclude competition for a substantial period of time." Microsoft noted that the plaintiffs had argued that it had monopoly power because it had a large share of the market for operating systems. That was a specious argument, said Microsoft. To begin with, "today's sales do not always indicate power over sales and price tomorrow." Innovation is sure to change Microsoft's share tomorrow. Also, market share indicates monopoly power "only when sales reflect control of the productive assets (i.e., capacity to supply) in the business. . . . There is no finding, nor could there be, that Microsoft controls a significant percentage of the productive assets in the software business or any part thereof."

On the price issue, Microsoft contended that according to a court decision, monopoly power "comes from the ability to cut back the market's total output and so raise price."

> There is no finding that Microsoft could restrict the total market output of operating systems and thereby raise prices. In fact, existing operating system competitors . . . could readily expand their "output" to meet the entire demand for operating systems without acquiring new productive assets. It is simply a matter of signing new license agreements.

On the ability of Microsoft to establish "applications barriers to entry," Microsoft described the rapid technological advances in the industry. It then quoted from another court decision that "it would be difficult to design a market less susceptible to monopolization."

"Having an extremely popular product does not make a company a monopolist," said Microsoft.

> Microsoft has successfully competed with vigorous companies like IBM and Sun and maintained the popularity of its operating systems by improving its own products to the greater satisfaction of consumers. . . . Microsoft also has kept the price of its operating systems low—in fact, lower than the price of competing operating systems such as IBM's OS/2 Warp and Apple's Mac OS.

---

[15] *United States of America v. Microsoft Corporation, Defendant Microsoft Corporation's Proposed Conclusions of Law,* Civil Action No. 98–1232 (TPJ), January 18, 2000.

Microsoft then quoted a court decision as follows:

When a producer deters competitors by supplying a better product at a lower price, when he eschews monopoly profits, when he operates his business so as to meet consumer demand and increase consumer satisfaction, the goals of competition are served, even if no actual competitors see fit to enter the market at a particular time. . . . If a dominant supplier acts consistent with a competitive market—out of fear perhaps that potential competitors are ready and able to step in—the purpose of the antitrust laws is amply served.[16]

Microsoft denied wrongdoing with respect to every conclusion of Judge Jackson. Here are a few examples other than the monopoly charge. Both the Department of Justice and Judge Jackson portrayed the bundling of the IE with Windows as part of a scheme to thwart Netscape's Navigator. Microsoft saw the practice as making its products user-friendly and not a violation of the Sherman Act. The Department of Justice and Judge Jackson cited Microsoft for unlawful exclusive agreements with various Internet servers, but Microsoft said they failed to prove the charge. In another area, Microsoft said there was no proof it had license agreements with OEMs to restrain others from Windows desktop displays. What this amounts to is revisiting the arguments pro and con made in the trial.

JUDGE JACKSON'S FINAL DECISION

Following the *Findings of Fact,* the next step in the legal process was the decision, which was given by Judge Jackson on November 5, 1999. In a 12-page statement the judge ordered divestiture. He said that not later than four months after the *Final Judgment* is issued, "Microsoft shall submit to the Court and the Plaintiffs a proposed plan of divestiture. The Plaintiffs shall submit any objections to the proposed plan of divestiture to the Court within 60 days of receipt of the plan, and Microsoft shall submit its response within 30 days of receipt of the plaintiffs' objections."[17] Following approval of a final plan, and after any delays pending appeals, "Microsoft shall implement such Plan."

The *Final Judgment* prescribes a number of actions to implement the plan and prohibits certain actions. For example, within 12 months Microsoft will complete the separation of the Operating Systems Business from the Applications Business and the transfer of assets and personnel, distribution of intellectual property used in product development, and transfer of ownership of stock. After implementing the plan, the Operating Systems Business and the Applications Business are prohibited from merging or entering into agreements with one another, or other enterprises, on terms more favorable than available to third parties. Threats, exclusive agreements, or restrictions with OEMs are prohibited. Microsoft is ordered to disclose technical information and communications interfaces used in its software operating systems. Within 90 days after the effective date of the *Final Judgment,* Microsoft is ordered to establish a Compliance Committee of its corporate board of directors of no fewer than three members who are not present or former employees of Microsoft. The Compliance Committee is ordered to hire a chief compliance officer who will report to the Compliance Committee and the CEO of Microsoft. It will be this officer's responsibility to supervise Microsoft's internal programs to ensure compliance with antitrust laws and the *Final Judgment.*

RESPONSES TO THE *FINAL JUDGMENT*

Microsoft said that

the government's requested relief is extreme and unprecedented. . . . Draconian measures like breaking Microsoft into two companies, confiscating Microsoft's intellectual property (by forcing Microsoft to disclose proprietary information about its operating systems to

---

[16] *United States* v. *Syufy Enters.*, 903 F.2d 976 (2d Cir. 1984) at 668–69.

[17] *United States of America* v. *Microsoft Corporation, Final Judgment,* Civil Action No. 98–1232 (TPJ), undated.

competitors) and interfering with the design of Microsoft's products far exceed any reasonable remedy for the antitrust violations found by the Court, and are punitive in concept and effect.[18]

Microsoft then explained in detail the harm that the proposed remedy would cause the company and consumers. The company then petitioned the District of Columbia Circuit Court of Appeals for a review of the case. The Court took the case, and here are some highlights of its June 2001 opinion.

THE COURT OF APPEALS DECISION

The Appeals Court concluded that "Microsoft possesses monopoly power in a relevant market."[19] Defining the market as Intel-compatible PC operating systems, the District Court had found that Microsoft has a greater than 95 percent share. It also found the company's market position protected by a substantial entry barrier. "We uphold the District Court's finding of monopoly power in its entirety," said the Appeals Court. However, it added, the District Court "failed to provide an adequate explanation for the relief it ordered." The Court then sent the case back to the District Court to decide whether the remedy of divestiture was appropriate. "The District Court also should consider whether plaintiffs have established a sufficient causal connection between Microsoft's anticompetitive conduct and its dominant position in the OS market." On the charge that Microsoft illegally tied its browser to its operating system, the Court said the government must prove, in a new trial, that the anticompetitive effect outweighed its improved efficiency. Again, this issue should be settled in a new trial.

The Court considered other allegations of anticompetitive behaviors. For example, it concluded that license restrictions Microsoft imposed on OEMs are anticompetitive. Microsoft's conduct that destroyed incipient threats to its operating system from Netscape, Navigator, and Java is exclusionary, said the Court, and in violation of the Sherman Act.

Microsoft wanted to have the Court reject the District Court's decision on the grounds that Judge Jackson violated the code of conduct for United States judges and showed a bias against the defendant. Judge Jackson out of court had made a number of injudicious remarks about William Gates and Microsoft. For example, he said that Gates's "testimony is inherently without credibility." Gates, he said, "has a Napoleonic concept of himself and his company, an arrogance that derives from power and unalloyed success, with no leavening hard experiences, no reverses."[20] The Court sharply rebuked Judge Jackson for such remarks but also said it could find no bias in the judge's documents and that such remarks, therefore, had no bearing on the case at hand.

THE DEPARTMENT OF JUSTICE AND MICROSOFT REACH AGREEMENT

The attorney general of the United States on November 2, 2001, said, "Today we are announcing a strong, historic settlement reached by the Department of Justice and the Microsoft Corporation that will put an end to Microsoft's unlawful conduct, bring effective relief to the marketplace, and ensure that consumers will have more choices in meeting their needs of computing and working with their computers."[21] On the same day, Microsoft signed a consent decree with the government. Here are highlights of the agreement:

- Microsoft must disclose technical information such as licenses, patents, copyrights, and other intellectual property to permit systems

---

[18] *United States of America* v. *Microsoft Corporation, Defendant Microsoft Corporation's Summary Response to Plaintiffs' Proposed Final Judgment,* Civil Action No. 98–1232 (TPJ), May 10, 2000.
[19] *United States of America* v. *Microsoft Corporation,* No. 00–5212, June 28, 2001.

[20] Reported by John Schwartz, "A Judge Overturned by an Appearance of Bias, *The New York Times,* June 29, 2001.
[21] Attorney General John Ashcroft, transcript of news conference, November 2, 2001.

of software competitor's to operate smoothly on Microsoft's operating system.

- OEMs will have flexibility to contract freely with competing software developers. They can place on Microsoft's operating system their middleware products such as browsers, instant messaging software, and media players.

- Microsoft is prohibited from retaliating against PC makers and competing software developers for producing computers with competing software.

- Microsoft will be prohibited from making certain types of exclusive contracts supporting Microsoft's products.

- A full-time, on-site enforcement team of independent computer experts will be created and have broad powers and complete access to Microsoft soft-source code, records, facilities, and personnel. The team, composed of one member chosen by DOJ, a second by Microsoft, and a third by the first two team members will serve for 30 months and have offices at Microsoft headquarters. It will monitor compliance and have power to resolve disputes.

- The agreement will be in force for five years when the District Court judge approves it.

ARE MICROSOFT'S ANTITRUST PROBLEMS OVER?

Microsoft faces a new trial in the U.S. District Court as prescribed by the Appellate Court. The trial was scheduled for March 2002. Nine state attorneys general considered the agreement too liberal and said it would not change significantly the

behavior of Microsoft. So they prepared a remedy plan that Microsoft said was far too harsh but would be considered at the trail. In addition, individuals who believe they have been injured by Microsoft can bring civil suits. Corporations also can sue. Top executives of Sun Microsystems, AOL, and Netscape, for example, voiced strong dissatisfaction with the agreement. If they file suits, their cases will be strengthened by the Appellate Court decision, especially its determination that Microsoft has a monopoly. The agreement received bipartisan criticism in Congress. Senator Patrick J. Leahy, a Democrat and chair of the Senate Judiciary Committee said he would schedule hearings on the agreement. Senator Orrin G. Hatch, a Republican, voiced concern. Finally, European Union regulators are investigating Microsoft's behavior and could impose fines or restrictions or both on the company's activities. In sum, Microsoft is likely to continue to be confronted with potentially serious legal challenges.

QUESTIONS

1. Do you believe Microsoft has a monopoly?

2. Should Microsoft be split into two companies?

3. Do you believe Microsoft used its power in the market to prevent potential competitors from challenging its dominant market position in operating systems?

4. Do you believe Judge Jackson's *Final Judgment* contained appropriate remedies for violations of law he found in his *Findings of Fact?*

5. Many observers believe the Department of Justice was not severe enough in its final agreement with Microsoft. Argue the issue pro and con.

Chapter **Eleven**

Business in Politics

Carl Lindner and Chiquita Brands International

Carl H. Lindner is an 82-year-old business mogul living in Cincinnati, Ohio. He is described as a devout Baptist who disdains alcohol and never curses. For two decades he has been on the *Forbes* 400 list, making him one of the wealthiest persons in the world. The source of Lindner's wealth is American Financial Group, a $3.8 billion holding company that controls four insurance companies and Chiquita Brands International.

In the early 1980s Lindner sat on the board of Chiquita, which at the time was named United Brands. United Brands started as United Fruit Company in 1899, when bananas were first shipped from plantations in Central and South America to markets in Europe and the United States. In the early 1900s the company had as much as 75 percent of the world banana market. Over the years it expanded its plantations and built railroads, highways, ports, schools, hospitals, and housing in underdeveloped areas. There was plenty of political intrigue and chicanery in its dealings with host governments, including corporate-inspired overthrows of regimes in Nicaragua and Guatemala. In 1944 it started using the "Chiquita Banana Song" in ad campaigns that made its Chiquita brand universally recognized.[1]

When the company fell into disarray after a bribery scandal and the suicide of its chief executive, Lindner began buying its shares. In 1984 he took control, naming himself chairman and CEO, making his son president, changing the company's name to Chiquita Brands, and moving its headquarters from New York to his hometown of Cincinnati. Over the next few years, Lindner committed the fortunes of the firm to an expansion of the European market for bananas.

For many years, Europe had imposed trade limits on Chiquita bananas. These arose after World War II, when European nations decided to help former colonies—about 70 nations in Africa, the Carribean, and Asia—by favoring their banana exports. Thus, quotas and tariffs were imposed on bananas imported by Chiquita from Central and South America. Through all

[1] Nicholas Stein, "Yes We Have No Profits," *Fortune,* November 26, 2001, pp. 184–86.

the years of this restrictive trade regime, Chiquita had still prospered in the European market. Its huge, efficient plantations grew bananas at far lower cost than the operations in ex-colonies, which were mostly family businesses and small cooperatives.

Lindner believed that the already lucrative European market would expand because of growing trade with newly opened Eastern European economies and because the new European Union, when it forged an all-Europe trade policy, would reduce or eliminate banana controls. He was wrong. In the early 1990s Eastern Europe wallowed in a prolonged economic slump. Worse, in 1993 the European Union applied a new and more restrictive policy on banana imports. When it did, Chiquita's 40 percent market share in the 15 countries was reduced to 11 percent.[2]

Lindner wanted to fight the new banana restrictions. However, the government agency that represents American companies in trade disputes, the Office of the United States Trade Representative in Washington, D.C., was unresponsive. Its tiny staff had to pick battles carefully. At the time, it had higher priorities than fighting for a company that still had a dominant share of the world market and employed most of its workers outside the United States. And the newly elected Clinton administration had no interest in starting a trade war with European allies—especially for a business owner who contributed almost exclusively to Republicans.

Getting no response from his government to a straightforward request for action, Lindner, like a dreamer jolted from the pages of a high school civics book, had a sudden revelation of how Washington really works. He hired four public relations and lobbying firms and started making larger political contributions. The year before he had given $67,500 to candidates and political party committees, most of it to the GOP. In 1993 he raised his contributions to $484,000, including a check for $250,000 to a Democratic party fund.

Early in 1994, Lindner got to discuss his case at a breakfast with Mickey Kantor, the head of the trade agency. He was accompanied by then Senate Majority Leader Bob Dole (R-Kan.). Lindner had given $100,000 to a committee set up by Dole. Later in the year, Dole and 11 other senators who had received campaign contributions from Lindner wrote to Kantor supporting intervention in the banana dispute. This was followed by a note to President Clinton from Dole, Speaker of the House Newt Gingrich (R-Georgia), and House minority leader Richard Gephardt (D-Missouri) urging "an aggressive strategy . . . to prevent irreparable harm to U.S. commercial interests." Lindner had given $50,000 to a political action committee set up by Gingrich.

Over the next two years, Lindner gave $2.8 million to recipients in both parties. There were two more meetings with trade representative Kantor, and Dole introduced several bills related to banana trade in the Senate.

---

[2] James Toedtman, "Mogul Plays, Wins," *Newsday,* May 12, 1997, p. A6.

Lindner was an early supporter of Dole's 1996 presidential candidacy. In fact, Dole frequently used Lindner's corporate jet for campaigning. However, when Dole faltered in the polls, Lindner became one of Bill Clinton's 10 biggest financial supporters. "He's an operator," noted one Republican politician. "He uses his money to get access. He's totally practical. This has very little to do with philosophy."[3] After the election, he was invited to attend a coffee with the president and sleep overnight at the White House. Finally, the Clinton administration filed a formal dispute over banana protectionism with the World Trade Organization (WTO). The day of the filing, Lindner sent $10,000 checks to seven state Democratic Party committees.

In WTO proceedings, the issue was hotly disputed, but ultimately the WTO ruled against the European Union, holding that the banana trade barriers violated international trade law and harmed U.S. economic interests in the amount of $191 million a year. In response, the EU modified its system, but in a way that continued unfair discrimination.

Meanwhile, Lindner had continued his flow of large political contributions. So in 1998 the United States sought WTO approval to retaliate against Europe. Under WTO rules, when a trade impediment is ruled unfair, the injured nation is allowed to put up trade barriers of its own that punish industries in the offending countries. Retaliation is calibrated to impose costs roughly equal to the hurt born by the injured nation. Where would the retaliation hit Europe? The Clinton administration hesitated to slap big tariffs on products such as Volkswagens, French wines, or Italian shoes because the American public would be angered at the sudden price increases. Therefore, the trade agency staff proposed adding 100 percent duties to a list of less visible products. When the list was made public, companies and trade associations lobbied against the inclusion of items they imported. Mattel demanded that dolls be deleted. Gillette wanted ballpoint pens removed. The Fur Information Council of America objected to the inclusion of fur coats. Ultimately, the list was pared down to the nine items in Table 11.1.

When the duties were slapped on, small businesses that had never heard of the banana dispute were surprised when their U.S. Customs bills skyrocketed. A tiny South Carolina company that sold German bath oils and soaps saw its bill go from $1,851 to $37,783 for a six-month period. An art store in New York was forced to drop a popular line of English lithographs. An industrial battery business in Wisconsin was badly affected.[4] The main cause of the distress was, of course, that their owners had failed to write five- and six-figure checks to politicians.

[3] An anonymous "lawmaker" quoted in James Toedtman, "Turning Green to Gold," *Newsday,* May 25, 1997, p. F8.
[4] Laura Karmatz and Andrew Goldstein, "How to Become a Top Banana," *Time,* February 7, 2000, pp. 50–56.

TABLE 11.1   **Final List of Products Imported from Europe Picked for Retaliation against European Union Export Barriers to Central and South American Bananas**
The tariff in each case is a tax equal to 100 percent of the item's value.

Source: Office of the United States Trade Representative, 64 FR 19211 (1999).

Tariff Number	Product Description	Rate
3307.30.50	Bath preparations, other than bath salts	100%
4202.22.15	Handbags, with or without shoulder straps or without handle, with outer surface of sheeting of plastics	100%
4202.32.10	Articles of a kind normally carried in the pocket or handbag, with outer surface of reinforced or laminated plastics	100%
4805.50.00	Uncoated felt paper and paperboard in rolls or sheets	100%
4819.20.00	Folding cartons, boxes and cases of noncorrugated paper or paperboard	100%
4911.91.20	Lithographs on paper or paperboard, not over 0.51 mm in thickness, printed not over 20 years at time of importation	100%
6302.21.90	Bed linen, not knit or crochet, printed, of cotton, not containing any embroidery, lace, braid, edging, trimming, piping or applique work, not napped	100%
8507.20.80	Lead-acid storage batteries other than of a kind used for starting piston engines or as the primary source of power for certain electric vehicles principally designed for the transport of up to nine persons	100%
8516.71.00	Electrothermic coffee or tea makers, for domestic purposes	100%

Lindner continued to disperse the boodle, a sum exceeding $2.3 million between 1997 and 2000. In the opinion of one newspaper columnist, he was "a contributor to nearly every political candidate with a pulse."[5] For the 1999–2000 election cycle, he ranked sixth among individual contributors for giving $1.1 million. After Clinton left office, he became one of George W. Bush's biggest financial supporters. The retaliatory U.S. tariffs were suspended in July 2001 when the European Union finally agreed to give Chiquita more access to markets and phase out quotas by 2006. Until then, Lindner continued to spread cash around the nation's capitol. Unfortunately, Chiquita carried too much debt to weather the long battle and was forced into a Chapter 11 bankruptcy late in 2001. Lindner had won the international banana war, but his company faltered anyway.

The story of Carl Lindner and Chiquita Brands shows how money converts to power and how power is used to get tangible benefits. In this chapter we discuss the historical domination of business in politics, how business money enters politics, the methods business uses to exert its influence, and the issues raised by business power. As a beginning, it is important to know how the Constitution shapes American government.

[5] Steve Stephens, "Banana Protectionism Isn't an Appealing Way to Promote Free Trade," *The Columbus Dispatch,* February 1, 1999, p. B1.

HOW THE STRUCTURE OF AMERICAN GOVERNMENT AFFECTS BUSINESS

Throughout American history, business has sought and exercised political power in a government that is extraordinarily open to influence. This power, whether used for good or ill, is exercised on constitutional terrain created by the Founding Fathers over 200 years ago. The Constitution of the United States, as elaborated by judicial interpretation since its adoption in 1789, establishes the formal structure and broad rules of political activity. Its formal provisions predispose a certain pragmatic, freewheeling political culture in day-to-day political life.

Several basic features of the Constitution shape the political system. Each stands as a barrier to the concentrated power that the Founders feared would lead to tyranny. Each has consequences for corporate political activity.

First, the Constitution sets up a *federal* system, or a government in which powers are divided between a national government and fifty state governments. This structure has great significance for business, particularly for large corporations with national operations. These corporations are affected by political actions at different levels and in many places.

The *supremacy clause* in the Constitution stipulates that when the federal government passes a law, it preempts, or takes precedence over, state laws on the same subject. For example, after the *Exxon Valdez* oil spill, the State of Washington enacted oil tanker regulations designed to protect its miles of seacoast and fisheries from a catastrophic accident. Specific rules mandated special training, weekly on-ship drills, and staffing bridges with English-speaking crew members. However, the Supreme Court struck them down because they exceeded requirements legislated by Congress.[6]

The federal system has many implications for the regulation of business. Sometimes business prefers federal regulation. It has to follow one law instead of as many as 50 different state laws. In the 1960s, for instance, several states tried to pass laws requiring health-warning labels on cigarette packs. If states had been allowed one by one to require labels, the tobacco companies would have had to print specially worded cigarette packs for sale in each state. Therefore, they supported a bill in Congress that, when passed, preempted that area of regulation and required a uniform warning label across the country. The insurance industry, on the other hand, fights federal regulation, preferring instead oversight by state insurance commissions. Insurance companies are big employers and heavy campaign contributors in many states. They tend to receive gentle treatment from these commissions and fight all efforts to pass national regulations.

[6] *United States* v. *Locke,* 529 U.S. 89 (2000).

Second, the Constitution establishes a system of *separation of powers*, whereby the three branches of the federal government—legislative, executive, and judicial—have checks and balances over each other. The states mimic these power-sharing arrangements in their governments. For business, this means that the actions of one branch do not fully define public policy. For example, after Congress passes a law, corporations lobby regulatory agencies in the executive branch to get favorable implementation of its provisions.

Third, the Constitution provides for *judicial review.* This is the power of judges, ultimately those of the Supreme Court, to review actions of government officials and to refuse to uphold those that conflict with their interpretation of the Constitution. A classic example of judicial review occurred in the spring of 1952 when U.S. military forces in Korea were hard-pressed and a strike by the steelworkers' union threatened to shut down steel production. President Harry Truman ordered his Secretary of Commerce to take possession of and run the steel industry. However, the Supreme Court held that Truman had exceeded his constitutional powers, and the steel companies were returned to private hands.[7] This case is also an example of the relative independence of business from government authority that is permitted in the American system.

The government structure created by the Constitution is open. It diffuses power, creates many points of access, and invites business and other interests to attempt influence. Because no single, central authority exists, significant government action often requires widespread cooperation among levels and branches of government that share power. The system also is particularly vulnerable to blockage and delay. Because significant actions require the combined authority of several elements in the political arena, special interests can block action by getting a favorable hearing at only one juncture. To get action, on the other hand, an interest like business must successfully pressure many actors in the political equation. Thus, there has developed a style in the American system, in which interests are willing to bargain, compromise, and form temporary alliances to achieve their goals rather than stand firm on rigid ideological positions.

The First Amendment is an additional feature of the Constitution critical to business. It protects the right of business to organize and press its agenda on government. In its elegantly archaic language is stated the right "to petition the Government for a redress of grievances." The First Amendment also protects rights of free speech, freedom of the press, and freedom of assembly—all critical for pressuring government. Without these guarantees, the letter-writing campaigns, speeches, editorials, and

---

[7] *Youngstown Sheet & Tube Co.* v. *Sawyer,* 343 U.S. 579. The basis for the Court's ruling was that Congress had once considered giving presidents the power to seize industries in similar circumstances but had not done so.

advertisements that business orchestrates might be banned. Imagine how undesirably different our system would be if the public, angered by "windfall" profits, pressured Congress to restrict the lobbying rights of some industry. While the corporate right of free speech is expansive, it is restricted in one area. The Supreme Court has defined monetary campaign contributions as a form of speech[8] and, as will be explained later in this chapter, these contributions are restricted because of fears that corporate money will corrupt elections.

A HISTORY OF POLITICAL DOMINANCE BY BUSINESS

Though not ordained in the Constitution, the preeminence of business in politics is an enduring fact in America. The Revolutionary War of 1775–1783 that created the nation was, according to some historians, fought to free colonial business interests from smothering British mercantile policies.[9] The Founders who later drafted the Constitution adopted in 1789 were an economic elite. John Jay and Robert Morris, for example, were among the wealthiest men in the colonies. It comes as no surprise that the government they fabricated was conducive to domination by business interests. The prominent historian Charles Beard argued that the Constitution was an "economic document" drawn up and ratified by propertied interests, for their own benefit.[10] His thesis has been controversial, in part because it trivializes the importance of philosophical, social, and cultural forces in the politics of constitutional adoption.[11] Yet the record since adoption of the Constitution in 1789 is one of virtually unbroken business ascendancy.

Laying the Groundwork

Business interests were important in the new nation but did not dominate to the extent that they soon would. There were few large companies. The economy was 90 percent agricultural, so farmers and planters were a major part of the political elite. Their interests balanced and checked those of infant industry. The fledgling government was a tiny presence. Economic regulation was virtually nonexistent. Nevertheless, under the leadership of the first Secretary of the Treasury, Alexander Hamilton, the new government was soon turned toward the promotion of industry.

---

[8] In *Buckley* v. *Valeo,* 424 U.S. 1 (1976).

[9] See, for example, Clarence L. Ver Steeg, "The American Revolution Considered as an Economic Movement," *Huntington Library Quarterly,* August 1957.

[10] Charles Beard, *An Economic Interpretation of the Constitution of the United States* (New York: Macmillan, 1913).

[11] See, for example, Robert E. Brown, *Charles Beard and the Constitution* (Princeton: Princeton University Press, 1956); and Forrest McDonald, *We the People: The Economic Origins of the Constitution* (Chicago: University of Chicago Press, 1963).

Hamilton mistrusted the common citizen, having once said that "the people is a great beast"; he favored rule by an economic elite.[12] He was opposed by Thomas Jefferson, then secretary of state, who advocated policies to preserve a nation of small farmers. However, with the support of business leaders, Hamilton carried out a visionary program to stimulate the growth of manufacturing. His actions laid the groundwork for the unexampled industrial growth that roared through the next century. He so angered Jefferson that the two rarely spoke even as they served together in George Washington's cabinet.

Economic development was rapid. Although Jefferson served as president from 1800 to 1808, it was already too late to reverse Hamilton's probusiness policies. As the young nation's economy expanded, so also did the political power of business.

Ascendance, Corruption, and Reform

During the nineteenth century, commercial interests grew in strength. When the Civil War between 1860 and 1865 decimated the power base of southern agriculture, a major counterweight to the power of northern industry vanished. In the period following the war, big business dominated state governments and the federal government in a way never seen before or since. It was a time of great imbalance, in which economic interests faced only frail obstacles. Companies commonly manipulated the politics of whole states. West Virginia and Kentucky were dominated by coal companies. New York, a number of midwestern states, and California were controlled by railroads. Montana politics was engineered by the Anaconda Copper Mining Company. In Ohio, Texas, and Pennsylvania, oil companies predominated; the great critic of Standard Oil, Henry Demarest Lloyd, wrote that "the Standard has done everything with the Pennsylvania legislature, except refine it."[13]

Business was also predominant in Washington, D.C. Through ascendancy in the Republican party, corporations had decisive influence over the nomination and election of a string of probusiness Republican presidents from Ulysses S. Grant in 1868 to William McKinley in 1900.[14] In the Congress, senators were suborned by business money; some even openly represented companies and industries. One observer noted that in 1889,

> a United States senator . . . represented something more than a state, more even than a region. He represented principalities and powers in business. One senator, for instance, represented the Union Pacific Railway

[12] Quoted in Vernon Louis Parrington, *Main Currents in American Thought,* vol. 1 (New York: Harcourt, Brace, 1958), p. 300; originally published in 1927.

[13] "The Story of a Great Monopoly," *The Atlantic,* March 1881, p. 322.

[14] The exception was the election of the Democrat and reformer Grover Cleveland in 1884. But even Cleveland had strong business supporters, Andrew Carnegie and James J. Hill among them. His administration never threatened business interests.

Nineteenth century political cartoonist Joseph Keppler (1838–1894) was a critic of big business who particularly resented the ascendancy of moneyed interests in politics. This cartoon appeared in the magazine *Puck* on January 23, 1889.

System, another the New York Central, still another the insurance interests of New York and New Jersey. . . . Coal and iron owned a coterie from the Middle and Eastern seaport states. Cotton had half a dozen senators. And so it went.[15]

Under these circumstances, corruption was rampant. Grant's first term, for example, was stained by the famous "whiskey ring" scandals in which liquor companies cheated on their taxes and a member of Grant's cabinet solicited bribes in exchange for licenses to sell liquor to Indian tribes. In Grant's second term, the Crédit Mobilier Company gave members of Congress shares of its stock to avoid investigation of its fraudulent railroad construction work.

The soaring political fortunes of business in the post–Civil War era invited reaction. A counterbalancing of corporate power began that continues to this day. Late in the century, farmers tried to reassert agrarian values through the Populist party. They foundered, but not before wresting

[15] William Allen White, *Masks in a Pageant* (New York: Macmillan, 1928), p. 79.

control of several state legislatures from corporations and forcing through legislation to control the railroads, the biggest companies of that day. More important, the populist movement was the beginning of a long-lived democratic reform tradition opposed to big business power. Two other formidable business adversaries emerged. One was organized labor, which was destined to be the strongest single element opposing industry over the following century. The other was the powerful Anti-Saloon League, which advocated prohibition of alcohol. Like labor, the Anti-Saloon League became a strong national adversary of business. Brewers and distillers were not its only adversaries. Big corporations in many industries worked against prohibition because they opposed the principle and onset of more government regulation.

After 1900, reforms of the progressive movement curtailed overweening corporate power. For example, the Seventeenth Amendment in 1913 instituted the direct election of senators by voters in each state. Corporations fought the amendment. Before, state legislatures had chosen senators, a practice that invited corrupting influence by big companies. For example, in 1884 representatives of Standard Oil called members of the Ohio legislature one by one into a back room where $65,000 in bribes was handed out to obtain the election of Henry B. Payne to the Senate. One witness saw "canvas bags and coin bags and cases for greenbacks littered and scattered around the room and on the table and on the floor . . . with something green sticking out."[16]

Big business also fought suffrage for women. The battle was led by liquor companies that feared women would vote for prohibition. However, there was broader fear of women voters. It was widely believed by businessmen that women would vote for radical and socialist measures. The powerful Women's Christian Temperance Union, which had as many as 10,000 local chapters by 1890, frightened business by standing against liquor, child labor, and income inequality. Yet after adoption of the Nineteenth Amendment giving women the vote in 1920, no strong shifts in voting patterns appeared.

The great political reforms of the progressive era were reactions to corruption in a political system dominated by business. It would be a mistake, however, to conclude that because of reforms and newly emerged opponents, the primacy of economic interests had been eclipsed. While business was more often checked after the turn of the century, it remained preeminent. Corruption continued. In 1920 Warren G. Harding, a backroom candidate picked by powerful business interests at a deadlocked Republican nominating convention, was elected president. His vice president was Calvin Coolidge, the rabidly antilabor ex-governor of Massachusetts. Harding's administration was so beset by

[16] Quoted in Henry Demarest Lloyd, *Wealth Against Commonwealth* (New York: Harper, 1898), pp. 377–78.

scandals in which officials accepted money for granting favors to corporations that Congress was considering impeaching him when he died of a stroke in 1923. The worst scandal involved Secretary of the Interior Albert B. Fall, who accepted bribes from oil company executives in return for the right to pump oil from government reserves in Teapot Dome, Wyoming. The Teapot Dome affair came to light only after Harding's death, but so besmirched his reputation that it was eight years before his grand tomb in Marion, Ohio, could be dedicated.

Business Falls Back under the New Deal

By the time that Harding had been officially laid to rest, the stock market had crashed and catastrophic economic depression racked the country. Conservative business executives argued that the depression would correct itself without government action. After the election of Franklin D. Roosevelt in 1932, corporations fought his efforts to regulate banking and industry, strengthen labor unions, and enact social security. Du Pont, General Motors, and other firms supported the anti-Roosevelt Liberty Lobby, which opposed New Deal measures. Against social security, for example, business lobbyists argued that children would no longer support aging parents, that the required payroll tax would discourage workers and they would quit their jobs, and that its protection would remove the "romance of life."

Many executives hated Roosevelt. They said that he was bringing communism to the United States and called him names such as "Stalin Delano Roosevelt."[17] But business had lost its way. Corporate opposition to New Deal measures ran counter to public sentiment. It became ineffective and was sometimes disgraceful. In 1935, for example, utility lobbyists sent Congress 250,000 fake letters and telegrams in a losing effort to stop a bill. Subsequently they ran a whispering campaign saying Roosevelt was insane.

Much New Deal legislation was profoundly egalitarian and humanitarian and reasserted the tradition of agrarian idealism. Because business lacked a positive philosophy for change, its political power was greatly diminished. According to Edwin M. Epstein, "corporate political influence reached its nadir during the New Deal."[18] Roosevelt was hurt by all the hate and felt that through his major New Deal programs, he had saved capitalism in spite of the capitalists.

The New Deal was a political sea change born out of the Great Depression. One lasting legacy of the era was the philosophy that government should be used to correct the flaws of capitalism and control the economy so that prosperity would no longer depend solely on unbridled market

---

[17] William Manchester, *The Glory and the Dream,* vol. 1 (Boston: Little, Brown, 1973), p. 126.
[18] *The Corporation in American Politics* (Englewood Cliffs, NJ: Prentice Hall, 1969), p. 31.

forces.[19] Government would also be used to create a "welfare state" to protect citizens from want. Whereas, in the past, government had kept its hands off corporations, now it would actively use interest rates, regulation, taxes, subsidies, and other policy instruments to control them. Whereas, in the past, most domestic spending had been for infrastructure programs that promoted business, spending would increasingly focus on social programs such as social security. These changes laid the groundwork for an increasingly large, powerful, and activist federal government.

Postwar Politics and Winds of Change

In the 1940s, industry's patriotic World War II production record and subsequent postwar prosperity quieted lingering public restiveness about corporate political activity. During the 1950s, corporations once again predominated in a very hospitable political environment. In the years between 1952 and 1960, Dwight D. Eisenhower was a probusiness president with a cabinet dominated by political appointees from business. A probusiness conservative coalition of southern Democrats and Republicans in Congress ensured legislative support. Corporations could promote their policy agendas by influencing a small number of leaders. Charls E. Walker, an official in the Eisenhower administration and currently a business lobbyist, recalls how only four men shaped economic policy.

> These four officials were President Eisenhower, Treasury Secretary Robert Anderson, Speaker of the House Sam Rayburn, and Senate majority leader Lyndon B. Johnson. These four men would get together every week over a drink at the White House and the President would say, "I think we ought to do this or that." Then Mr. Sam or LBJ might say, "Well, that's a real good idea; send it up and we'll get it through." And they would. They could deliver because at that time they had great influence in Congress, partly because of the seniority system.[20]

However, changing political trends soon led business into more sophisticated methods of political intervention. During the 1960s and 1970s, national politics became dominated by a liberal reform agenda. New groups rose to defy corporations, internal reforms made Congress more openly democratic and responsive to business's foes, business was bridled with massive new regulatory schemes, and government swelled with new tiers of authority.[21] Business suffered unaccustomed defeats at the hands of public interest groups and agency staffs in government, defeats that encouraged more aggression from companies.

---

[19] For the story of how this philosophy developed during the New Deal years, see Alan Brinkley, *The End of Reform: New Deal Liberalism in Recession and War* (New York: Knopf, 1995).
[20] Quoted in Gene E. Bradley, "How to Work in Washington: Building Understanding for Your Business," *Columbia Journal of World Business*, Spring 1994, p. 53.
[21] These factors are analyzed by David Vogel in *Fluctuating Fortunes: The Political Power of Business in America* (New York: Basic Books, 1989), chaps. 3–6.

THE RISE OF ANTAGONISTIC GROUPS

During the late 1960s, the climate of pressure politics changed with the rise of new groups focused on consumer, environmental, taxpayer, civil rights, and other issues. Some, including Ralph Nader's Public Citizen, the Natural Resources Defense Council, and the Consumer Federation of America, grew to have many members and enough power to push an agenda of restricting and regulating corporations.

The presence of these groups changed the political arena for business. A decade earlier, corporations had dominated Washington politics with quiet, behind-the-scenes influence over key leaders. Now they faced an array of hostile groups that used a favorable climate of public opinion to wrest control of the policy agenda away from business. The result was a remarkable period, lasting roughly from the late 1960s to the late 1970s, during which the antagonists of business pressured Congress to enact one massive regulatory program after another.

The rise of groups hostile to business is part of a broader trend in which new groups of all kinds, including business groups, have been stimulated by growth of government. Government growth is reflected by fast-rising federal spending. In 1960 the federal budget was $92 billion. By 1980 it reached $591 billion, an increase of more than 600 percent, and by 2000 it was $2 trillion.[22] As government grows, interest groups proliferate around policy areas. One estimate is that there are around 23,000 organized interest groups, roughly 400 percent more than in the 1950s.[23]

The heyday of the public interest movement was short-lived. Citizen lobbies have some advantages. They can focus on dramatic, emotional, or confrontational issues and get media coverage. They also get the support of public opinion by identifying themselves with the lofty idea of a public interest in opposition to the so-called special interests of business. GM, Ford, and their suppliers employ more than one million workers, and big oil companies have millions of shareholders. Yet public interest groups, even those with tiny memberships, often succeed in painting such corporations and industries as selfish entities seeking special political favors.

However, citizen lobbies are unable to match the financial resources of business. They cannot make as large political contributions and cannot afford to hire as many lobbyists. Over a recent two and one-half years, for

[22] Bureau of the Census, *Statistical Abstract of the United States: 2000,* 120th ed. (Washington, DC: U.S. Government Printing Office, 2000), table 532. This figure is a rounding of the $1.956 trillion estimate.
[23] Burdett A. Loomis and Allan J. Cigler, "Introduction: The Changing Nature of Interest Group Politics," in Cigler and Loomis, *Interest Group Politics,* 5th ed. (Washington, DC: Congressional Quarterly Press, 1998), p. 11.

example, the four big American tobacco companies spent $44.2 million just on lobbyists, an average of $106,415 for each day that Congress was in session.[24] No antitobacco group can match this. By the late 1970s, business interests had mobilized to fight the public interest movement in more sophisticated ways, and never again would the movement win great victories, although it remains as an institutionalized foe of business.

DIFFUSION OF POWER IN GOVERNMENT

A second change in the climate of politics, besides new groups, has been the diffusion and decentralization of power in Washington, D.C. Three major reasons for this are (1) reforms in Congress, (2) the decline of political parties, and (3) increased complexity of government.

Traditionally, the House and Senate were run autocratically by a few party leaders and powerful committee chairs. But the stubborn resistance of southern Democrats to civil rights legislation in the 1960s eventually led in 1974 to an uprising of junior legislators, who passed procedural reforms that democratized Congress by taking power from the party leaders and spreading it widely. After 1974, subcommittees could hold hearings on any subject they wished; they developed large staffs and often became small fiefdoms of independent action. Instead of an institution dominated by a few leaders, Congress was described by one observer as "like a log floating down a river with 535 giant ants aboard, and each one thinks he or she is steering."[25]

After the reforms, business lobbyists had to contact nearly every member of a committee or subcommittee to get support for a measure, rather than just the chair. Veteran lobbyist Charls E. Walker muses about the old days. "On a tax issue if you had the agreement of the chairman of Ways and Means, you could go out and play golf," but "these days you can't rest easy unless you've worked all the members."[26]

Changes outside Congress further undermined party leaders. One change was the rise of political action committees (PACs) formed by interest groups and corporations to contribute campaign money. Previously, Senate and House members who were loyal to party leaders could count on substantial campaign funds from the Republican and Democratic parties. After 1974, however, special-interest PACs began contributing such large amounts that legislators could act more independently of party leaders and still raise enough money to be reelected.

[24] Kirsten B. Mitchell, "Cigarette Companies Continue Lobbying in Washington," *Winston-Salem Journal,* October 21, 2001, p. 1.
[25] Bradley, "How to Work in Washington," p. 55.
[26] Quoted in Jill Abramson, "The Business of Persuasion Thrives in Nation's Capital," *The New York Times,* September 29, 1998, p. A23.

Other factors also eroded party authority. The media, particularly television, have replaced to some extent the parties as a source of information about candidates. Using television, politicians can bypass their parties and speak directly to voters. Also, the electorate is more highly educated and independent than it was in past eras and many voters identify only weakly with parties. Increasingly, they split their ballots and use decision cues other than party labels. In the 1990s, changes in campaign finance laws allowed parties to gorge themselves with soft money. This restored much of their influence. However, new reforms imposing limits on soft money may once again deflate the role of parties.

An additional cause of power diffusion is the growth in size and complexity of the federal government. Washington today is a maze of competing power centers, including elected officials, congressional committees, cabinet departments, regulatory agencies, political parties, courts, and interest groups. Relations among these power centers continuously shift as partisan tides, personal ambitions, power struggles, and emerging issues glide across the political landscape.

The sum total of government activity has a much greater impact on business than in the past, and because of this, corporations are far more politically active than in past eras. The expanded size and scope of government mean that its actions can be critical to company operations. Many bills passed by Congress directly affect earnings. Legislation affects taxes, interest rates, import/export rules, antitrust policy, defense spending, regulatory compliance costs, health care costs, the dollar exchange rate, uses of information, and much more.

THE UNIVERSE OF ORGANIZED BUSINESS INTERESTS

Literally thousands of groups represent business. What follows is a summary of this universe.

The most prominent groups are *peak associations* that represent many different companies and industries. The largest is the U.S. Chamber of Commerce, which was founded in 1912. The Chamber is a federation of 3,000 local and state chapters, 830 trade associations, and 3 million businesses, 96 percent of which have fewer than 100 employees. The next largest is the National Association of Manufacturers (NAM), founded in 1895, which, as the name suggests, represents manufacturers. It has a membership of 14,000 companies and trade associations.

Both the Chamber and the NAM carry a conservative business agenda to Congress and the American public. Because both have large memberships diversified in size and interests, they focus their efforts on broad issues that improve the business climate. For example, the Chamber has recently campaigned for election of business-friendly judges in states. The NAM lobbies for policies that promote economic growth, including free trade measures and an assortment of tax cuts.

Another prominent peak association is the National Federation of Independent Businesses (NFIB), representing 645,000 small businesses. The NFIB is the most conservative and least bipartisan of these three powerful groups. It pursues a lobbying agenda of rolling back government rules, reducing taxes, and keeping a lid on the minimum wage. In the 2000 elections, 96 percent of its campaign contributions went to Republican candidates. It does little work with Democrats. The president of the Chamber once said, "I love the NFIB, the way they get out there on the edge, like when they said, 'Get rid of the IRS.' They make us sound reasonable."[27]

The Business Roundtable is the organization that speaks for the largest corporations. It was founded in 1972 and consists of 200 CEOs whose companies pay membership dues to support it. Each year it focuses on a few issues critical to big business. In 2001, for example, it spent almost $22 million in a victorious lobbying campaign for normalized trade relations with China.[28] The great strength of the Roundtable is that its member CEOs are its lobbyists. They go to Washington carrying its message directly to members of Congress.

Besides these peak associations, more than 6,000 *trade associations* represent companies grouped by industry. Virtually every industry has one or more such associations. Illustrative are the American Boiler Manufacturers Association, the Compressed Gas Association, the Oxygenated Fuels Association, the National Turkey Federation, and the Institute of Makers of Explosives. Beyond lobbying for the industries they represent, trade groups also act as early warning systems in Washington for companies, hold training conferences, and publish data. Trade associations such as the American Petroleum Institute have large staffs and deep financial resources and are among the most powerful players in Washington. Corporations with diversified business lines often belong to many trade associations.

More than 700 corporations now have staffs of government relations experts in Washington. These *Washington offices* are set up mainly by big companies. General Electric, for example, has a staff of 12 lobbyists organized into teams that specialize in lobbying for the needs of separate business segments. Some specialize in contacting Republicans; others work more with Democrats. The office also gives GE managers information about how events in Washington may affect their operations. Most firms supplement their Washington offices by hiring outside lobbyists. In 2001 Boeing had almost three dozen lobbying firms on retainers in addition to a Washington office staffed with former Department of Defense officials and members of Congress.[29] Few small firms can afford to have Washington outposts. They rely on trade associations or hired lobbyists.

[27] Quoted in Jeffrey H. Birnbaum, "Power Player," *Fortune Small Business,* October 2001, p. 56.
[28] Shawn Zeller, "Deep Pockets for China Trade," *National Journal,* May 26, 2001, p. 1586.
[29] Brody Mullins, "The Wind Beneath Boeing's Wings," *National Journal,* November 17, 2001, p. 3607.

Business interests also form *coalitions* to create broader support. There are dozens of business coalitions in Washington at any given time. These groupings of instant allies can be ephemeral. Most form around a single issue and break up when that issue loses urgency. The advantage of membership in a coalition is that lobbying by a range of diverse allies can get support from more legislators and officials than would the efforts of any single entity. Frequently, coalition allies on one issue find themselves opposing each other on another issue.

Business gains strength when it is united, but there is chronic disunity. Long-standing tensions exist between domestic and foreign firms, truckers and railroads, manufacturers and retailers, and raw material producers and end-product manufacturers. To illustrate, for many years the American Sugar Alliance, which represents sugar growers and refiners, has fought to preserve federal price supports on raw cane and beet sugar. It is opposed by big corporations such as RJR Nabisco and Coca-Cola, which argue that higher sugar prices raise the cost of manufacturing cookies, candy, and soft drinks.

A powerful Coalition for Sugar Reform was formed in 1997 in an attempt to repeal these price supports. Members include trade groups, such as the American Bakers Association and the Chocolate Manufacturers Association; public interest groups, such as the Consumer Federation of America; and environmental groups, such as Friends of the Earth, that think the subsidies encourage cane-growing in the Florida everglades. The coalition has hired top Washington lobbyists to work on Congress. Some of its tactics are theatrical, as when it sent lollipops to congressional staff with a note saying, "it's time to lick big sugar," and hired child actors dressed as newsboys of the 1800s to hand out a paper called *Bittersweet Times* containing its policy views.[30] Yet, so far, the sugar growers have prevailed and subsidies continue.

LOBBYING

There are two broad areas of business involvement in politics. The first is government relations, or lobbying, in which business influences policy by contacting government officials. The second is the electoral process, in which business influence is exercised to elect or defeat candidates, primarily by contributing money. Naturally, the two areas are closely related.

Lobbying is advocating a viewpoint to government. A lobbyist presents the position of a corporation, interest group, or trade association to a government official. The word lobbyist entered the language in the early 1800s to describe people who stood in the lobbies of legislative halls trying to intercept lawmakers on their way in and out.

---

[30] Jerry Hagstrom, "From the K Street Corridor," *National Journal,* May 3, 1997, p. 880.

Lobbying has negative connotations for many, and business lobbyists are caricatured as pleading selfish interests, ignoring the public interest, and corrupting officials. However, lobbyists perform two valuable functions. First, they give lawmakers useful technical information about bills, and second, they give them politically crucial information about how constituents and special interests stand. These briefings are valuable because legislators cannot possibly investigate each issue and provision in roughly 12,000 bills before Congress each year. Every industry has quirks and problems about which that industry's lobbyists have special knowledge.

Lobbyists can mislead a lawmaker with bias and falsehood, but this is counterproductive. A former member of Congress explains the consequences.

> There is a proper term for a lobbyist who lies or misleads or distorts, and that proper term is *former lobbyist.* When you are dealing with each other . . . the truth is your . . . real capital. Once you mislead, once you exaggerate, once you fail to give an accurate picture, you'll never be allowed in the office again.[31]

A lobbyist who lacks integrity loses access to the very people he or she earns a living from influencing. In addition, effective business lobbyists must defend their proposals based on public benefit, since legislators and regulators, as a rule, cannot justify acting simply to promote corporate self-interest.

However, some of the most effective lobbying focuses on matters that are out of the public eye. Obscure changes in wording or small amendments made in committee meetings can mean enormous advantage for an industry or a company. For many years, the law permitted the Immigration and Naturalization Service to collect a $6 per passenger fee from cruise ships to cover inspection costs when they docked in U.S. ports. Lobbying by the cruise lines' trade association succeeded in getting a senator to amend immigration law, adding just one word, through an amendment buried in a budget act. The change ended the fee for any cruise from U.S. ports, saving the industry about $20 million a year. An investigation by *The New York Times* was unable even to discover which senator wrote the amendment. Senator Ted Stevens (R-Alaska), who chairs the committee that produced the budget bill, said he knew who the legislator was, but due to confidentiality rules of the Senate he would not reveal the name.[32] Even when they can be identified, legislators who support such changes are rarely questioned about them by voters while reaping the rewards of support from industries that benefit.

---

[31] Quoted in Michael Watkins, Mickey Edwards, and Usha Thakrar, *Winning the Influence Game: What Every Business Leader Should Know About Government* (New York: Wiley, 2001), p. 173; emphasis in original.
[32] Douglas Frantz, "Cruise Lines Profit From Friends in Congress," *The New York Times*, February 19, 1999, p. A16.

Business lobbyists often cooperate closely with elected representatives. Usually, there is little effort by the lawmakers to keep them at arm's length. Recently, the Republican leadership in the Senate invited business lobbyists to join with it in "working groups" to shape strategy for pending legislation. The lobbyists get a chance to convey the wishes of corporations and trade associations directly to these powerful lawmakers. In return, the senators seek their help in getting the bills passed by, for example, pressuring other members of the Senate for support. Much the same kind of semiformal liaison occurs in the House, where Republican leaders set strategy with a few key lobbyists in what is called the "Thursday Group."[33] In addition, House leaders organize coalitions of industry lobbyists around specific pieces of legislation and meet regularly with them while these bills are pending.[34]

Lobbyists are loosely regulated. Restricting them is hard because the First Amendment protects the right of citizens to contact government officials. Advocacy by lobbyists is speech; therefore, limiting it is constitutionally suspect. Beyond antibribery laws and some limits on the value of gifts, there are few legal restrictions on lobbying.[35] Congress did, however, adopt some gift-giving rules in 1995 to prevent the appearance of impropriety. The House prohibits lobbyists from giving gifts of any size to members, including, for example, meals. The Senate prohibits any gift over $50 or any series of gifts over $10 that add up to $100 per year.

Inevitably, gaping loopholes have opened. Although lobbyists cannot take a member to a restaurant, every evening in House office buildings, lobbyists and trade associations sponsor lavish receptions overflowing with food. These are permitted if there are no forks! According to rule interpretations of the House Ethics Committee, if forks were present, the receptions would be meals. Small groups of lobbyists also regularly dine with House members in private rooms at Washington restaurants. These occasions are defined as fund-raising dinners, which are allowed under House rules and federal election law. Instead of simply taking the representative out for a forbidden meal, the lobbyist sends out invitations beforehand to a few colleagues. The attending lobbyists all pay from $50 or

[33] Louis Jacobson and Brody Mullins, "The GOP's New Bridge to K Street," *National Journal,* May 5, 2001, p. 1330.
[34] Louis Jacobson, "Speak Bluntly and Carry a Soft Stick," *National Journal,* June 16, 2001, p. 1818.
[35] The Lobbying Disclosure Act of 1995 requires lobbyists to register with Congress if, over six months, they spend more than 20 percent of their time engaged in lobbying Congress or any on a list of 4,600 executive branch officials on behalf of a client. A lobbying firm must register if it has both an employee who is registered and lobbying expenditures of $20,500 over six months. Approximately 17,000 lobbyists registered under the law in 1999, but its definition of lobbying is narrow and many others did not have to register. For more information, see General Accounting Office, *Federal Lobbying: Differences in Lobbying Definitions and Their Impact,* GAO/GGD–99–38, Washington, DC, April 1999.

$100 up to the legal limit of $1,000 each to "attend," and instead of leaving with just a full stomach, the representative also receives contributions to his or her campaign from the "fund-raiser."

Lobbying Methods and Tactics

Business uses many lobbying techniques. In-person contact with officials is the gold standard, but direct contact, however critical, occupies only a minor portion of a lobbyist's time. Members of Congress typically have appointments booked all day at five- to ten-minute intervals. So for many lobbyists, most contacts are with assistants and staff. They also attend committee meetings in the House and Senate, and it is common practice for them to catch a representative's eye and give a thumbs-up or thumbs-down signal as various provisions come to a vote. Unless they are former senators or representatives, they are not allowed on the floor of either chamber, but they may stand in hallways and confer with lawmakers. Lobbyists in hallways with laptops draft debating points and legislative language that they send to lawmakers on the floor.

Outside legislative chambers, they do research and write promotional material. They organize and attend parties, fund-raisers, and other events. The Motion Picture Association of America capitalizes on the glamour of Hollywood with a private theater in Washington, D.C., in which senators and representatives see films before public release. They serve in political campaigns for the advantage it gives them in later working with elected officials. And they set up charity events, seminars, and speaking engagements for members of Congress and regulatory agencies.

Many corporations also hire advocacy firms, where top lobbyists make as much as $550 an hour to press their cases. The most prominent of these firms employ former administration officials, ex-legislators, and knowledgeable insiders of both political parties to offer a potent mix of access, influence, and advice. Lobbying firms may serve many clients at once. Recently, the biggest accounts at one leading firm, Patton Boggs, were AOL Time Warner, United Airlines, Hoffman–La Roche, Dole Food Co., and a Dutch telephone company. Pragmatism reigns. Another large firm, Washington Council Ernst & Young, represents both tobacco-maker R. J. Reynolds and Aetna, a company that insures smokers and their health plans. There are hundreds of lobbying firms in the nation's capitol. The biggest full-service firms book annual fees of more than $30 million.[36] Some tiny firms are set up to lobby just one committee or representative. Their lobbyists are invariably former members of the committee or legislator's staff, although a former mistress is said to run one such firm.[37]

[36] Shawn Zeller, "For the Big 10, Income Keeps Rising, *National Journal,* April 14, 2001, p. 1112; and Shawn Zeller, "K Street's Top 10: The Shifting Lineup," *National Journal,* October 20, 2001, p. 3270.
[37] Elizabeth Drew, *The Corruption of American Politics* (Woodstock, NY: Overlook Press, 1999), p. 63.

Many lobbyists are former elected officials, congressional staffers, or employees of regulatory agencies. This is illustrated by the roster of lobbyists for the pharmaceutical industry, the largest and best-funded industry lobby in recent years. Of 625 lobbyists employed by drug companies, trade associations, and 134 lobby firms under contract, about half are former legislators or employees of agencies such as the Food and Drug Administration.[38] Former officials and employees are legally prohibited from lobbying Congress or the agencies where they worked for one year after they leave, but they may still run lobby campaigns by setting strategy.

Direct-contact lobbying is only one method in the industry arsenal. Business lobbyists may try to influence a decision by having customers, employees, or other constituents, including the public, pressure government officials for action. These efforts are called *grassroots lobbying*. There are many ways to create grassroots support. Specialized firms cultivate mass mail, phone calls, faxes, and e-mail to a lawmaker. Typically, they charge from $25 to $75 for each letter generated. During its antitrust case, Microsoft hired such a firm to orchestrate a nationwide letter-writing campaign on its behalf. The firm called people on the phone, saying the call was for a survey. Its operators asked people who supported Microsoft's position if they were willing to send a letter to a state attorney general. If so, the firm wrote the letter and sent it to them for a signature and mailing in a pre-stamped, pre-addressed envelope. Hundreds of letters containing identical or similar phrasing poured in from these citizens, giving the appearance of support for Microsoft.[39]

Some of this kind of lobbying is directed at getting just a few influential friends or constituents of a representative to call him or her and ask for support on an issue—in the vernacular of Washington, this is "grasstops" lobbying. Advertising campaigns also generate grassroots support. Many companies spend millions of dollars for ads that present their point of view to the public. In the end, grassroots lobbying is one of the most effective methods for influencing Congress.[40] Lawmakers are very attentive to the thinking of voters.

THE CORPORATE ROLE IN ELECTIONS

In the first presidential campaign, George Washington did little campaigning and spent only £39 on "treats" for the voters.[41] Since then, the length and cost of campaigns for federal offices—president, vice president,

---

[38] Leslie Wayne and Melody Petersen, "A Muscular Lobby Rolls Up Its Sleeves," *The New York Times,* November 4, 2001, sec. 3, p. 13.
[39] Joseph Menn and Edmund Sanders, "Lobbyists Tied to Microsoft Wrote Citizens' Letters," *Los Angeles Times,* July 23, 2001, p. A1.
[40] See Michael D. Lord, "Corporate Political Strategy and Legislative Decision Making," *Business & Society,* March 2000.
[41] James V. DeLong, "Free Money," *Reason,* August–September 2000, p. 42.

senator, and representative—have soared. In the 1999–2000 election cycle, total campaign spending for federal races was $3.8 billion, a large sum, but one that should be kept in perspective. It was less than the cost of an aircraft carrier and less than the nation spent on video games.

Efforts to Limit Corporate Influence

Throughout the nineteenth century, companies made direct contributions from their treasuries to candidates, a practice that reached its zenith in William McKinley's campaigns. The election of 1896 matched the probusiness Republican McKinley against the radical Populist William Jennings Bryan. Bryan, a spellbinder on the stump, scared the eastern financial establishment by advocating the silver standard, a basic and unwelcome change in the currency system. McKinley's campaign manager, Marcus Hanna, capitalized on their fright. He established recommended levels of contribution to the McKinley campaign. For example, he assessed .25 percent of the assets of each bank from the trembling financiers and, overall, raised about $3.5 million.[42] This inflated McKinley's campaign funding to double that of any prior election, which was sufficient to elect him. In 1900 Bryan again opposed McKinley, this time on a platform of breaking up trusts. So Hanna assessed giant trusts such as Standard Oil and U.S. Steel amounts based on their assets. He raised a new record sum, and McKinley won by an even larger margin. Hanna believed his assessment scheme had elevated the ethics of campaign finance above the borderline bribery and petty extortion that had long characterized it, but progressive reformers sought to derail the business juggernaut. In 1907 they passed the Tillman Act to prohibit banks and corporations from making direct contributions to federal candidates, and this is still the law today.

Egalitarian ideals heavily influence American political culture. Huge campaign contributions by business strain popular belief in a rough equality among interests. The Tillman Act was the first of many efforts to protect the electoral system from lopsided contributions by business. But money, especially corporate money, plays an essential role in funding elections. It is a resource that can be converted to power. Candidates use it to persuade voters. Contributors use it to buy access, influence, and favors. Because money is elemental, new sources and methods of giving arise when old loopholes are closed.

After 1907 the Tillman Act, a sweeping reform in its day, was quickly and continuously skirted. Companies found clever, indirect ways to funnel dollars into campaigns. They gave salary bonuses to managers for use as campaign contributions, loaned money to candidates and later forgave the debts, payed for expensive postage-stamp-size ads in political party

---

[42] See Herbert Croly, *Marcus Alonzo Hanna: His Life and Work* (New York: Macmillan, 1912), p. 220. A grateful McKinley engineered the appointment of Hanna to the U.S. Senate.

booklets, loaned employees to campaigns, and provided free services such as air travel or rental cars. Also, since the Tillman Act did not limit individual contributions, wealthy donors stepped in. These "fat cats," who included many corporate executives, legally gave unlimited sums.

In response to growing appearances of impropriety, Congress eventually passed the Federal Election Campaign Act (FECA) in 1971, which required public disclosure of campaign contributions and expenditures. However, immediately after its passage, the election of 1972 again made corporate money in politics a major reform issue. It was in 1972 that a record for known contributions was set when W. Clement Stone, an insurance company executive, gave $2 million to the Nixon campaign. Then, investigations related to the Watergate scandals revealed that 21 corporations had violated the Tillman Act by making direct contributions totaling $842,000, also to the Nixon campaign.

In reaction to this illegality and to the appearance of influence buying that was created by large fat-cat contributions, Congress extensively amended the FECA in 1974 (the first of five amending acts over a decade). As revised, the FECA curbed wealthy donors by placing ceilings on both campaign contributions and expenditures. It continued the Tillman Act's prohibition on direct corporate contributions. Congress also established public financing for presidential candidates and created the Federal Election Commission to enforce the law.

The 1974 FECA amendments set up a regulatory framework designed to limit contributions by business. However, 30 years later, it is evident that federal election law has failed to control as intended large corporate, special-interest, and individual contributions. The reason is that FECA regulations were soon undermined by three developments, dooming the FECA, like the Tillman Act years before, to failure in its primary mission of restraining corporate influence.

First, in 1976 the Supreme Court severely compromised the FECA's design for controlling campaign money. In *Buckley* v. *Valeo*, the Court held that giving and spending money in political campaigns are a form of expression protected by the guarantee of free speech in the First Amendment.[43] The Court upheld the FECA's *contribution* limits, saying that the government had a legitimate interest in avoiding corruption and the appearance of corruption that unlimited contributions invited. But it invalidated *expenditure* limits as too great a restraint on political speech. This badly compromised the law's ability to limit campaign spending.

The Federal Election Campaign Act as it now stands attempts to limit contributions from wealthy contributors and special interests by restricting contributions to federal candidates. Figure 11.1 shows the overall legal scheme in more detail. The dollar limits set in 1974 were not changed until 2002, when some individual limits were raised (as shown

[43] 421 U.S. 1.

FIGURE 11.1
Federal Election Campaign Act Contribution and Expenditure Limits. The intent of the law is to prevent corporations and wealthy donors from corrupting office holders.

Source	Legal Prohibitions and Limits

Corporations

- Prohibited from contributing to federal candidates* from corporate accounts
- ($10,000 to state political party committees where permitted by state law for registering and turning out voters)**
- May set up and contribute through a "separate, segregated fund," known as a political action committee

Individuals

- $1,000 ($2,000)**per election† to candidates
- $5,000 per year to political action committees
- $5,000 ($10,000) per year to state party committees
- $20,000 ($25,000) per year to national party committees
- $25,000 per year combined to the four sources above ($37,500 per year to candidates and up to $57,500 including political action committees and state and national party committees)
- Unlimited expenditures to own campaign if running for office†
- Unlimited independent expenditures on behalf of or against candidates or causes

Political Action Committees

- $5,000 per election to candidates and their committees
- $15,000 per year to national party committees
- $5,000 per year to other committees
- Unlimited independent expenditures

*Federal candidates include president, vice president, senator, and member of the House of Representatives.
**Amounts in parentheses are new or raised limits set by the Bipartisan Campaign Reform Act of 2002 scheduled to take effect January 1, 2003.
†Primary elections, general elections, special elections, and nominating conventions or caucuses are all separate elections, and individuals or committees may contribute up to the legal limit in each.
‡Presidential and vice presidential candidates are limited to $50,000 if federal funding is accepted.

in parentheses). During this 28-year period inflation reduced the value of maximum contributions by more than two-thirds. Meanwhile, the growing size of the electorate and the increasing use of television made campaigns far more expensive. This encouraged efforts to dodge the law's contribution limits. These limits now are indexed to inflation.

Second, the proliferation of interest groups caused by the growth of government created more organized interests to fund campaigns. Because the FECA—even after the *Buckley* decision—limited individual contributions, the era of fat cats seemed to be over, though, as we will see, only temporarily. So corporations raced to set up devices called political action committees (PACs), which could legally contribute to candidates on their behalf. The number of PACs grew rapidly, and with them the sums of money entering elections.

Third, corporations and lobbyists adapted to the new FECA regime by learning how to exploit, avoid, and live with its regulations. Their machinations over 30 years parallel those that followed the reforms of the Tillman Act in 1907 and show again that political money is like water in a stream: dammed up in one place, it flows around and over in another.

What follows is a discussion of some ways that corporations now funnel money to politicians and government officials.

POLITICAL ACTION COMMITTEES

When Congress limited individual contributions, it left open a loophole permitting organizations to establish *political action committees*, or committees of organization members who receive money from other members and contribute it to candidates. Although corporations previously had not formed PACs, unions had used them since the 1940s to support prolabor candidates and already had more than 200. The FECA limits went into effect in 1974, and by the end of the year there were 89 corporate PACS. The number rose steadily, peaking at 1,816 in 1988, then slowly declined to 1,525 in 2001. Leveling off and decline came as corporations' experience with PACs diminished expectations of what they could accomplish. Other interests also use PACs, and in 2001 there were 3,835 of them, including 318 labor union and 872 trade association and other membership-group PACs.[44] As Figure 11.2 shows, contributions by corporate PACs continue to rise even as their numbers decline, and business PACs far outspend those of labor unions.

How PACs Work

To start a PAC, a corporation must set up an account for contributions, a "separate segregated fund," to which it cannot legally donate 1 cent (because of the prohibition since 1907 of direct corporate giving). The money in the PAC is disbursed to candidates based on decisions made by PAC officers, who must be corporate employees. There are no dollar limits on the overall total of PAC expenditures each year, though each individual PAC contribution must comply with FECA limits. Corporations may, and typically do, pay the administrative costs of PACs.

Corporate PACs get their funds primarily from contributions by employees. The law spells out the solicitation procedure and divides those eligible to contribute into two groups. Group 1, or stockholders, executives, managers, and their families, can be solicited as often as desired in person or by mail. They can contribute by check or through monthly payroll deductions. Many corporations suggest amounts based on a percentage of salary, usually .25 to 1 percent of annual salary. Group 2, or hourly paid employees and their families, can be solicited only twice a year, and then only by mail to the home. It is illegal for companies to require or

---

[44] Federal Election Commission news release, "FEC Issues Semi-Annual Federal PAC Count," August 21, 2001. FEC data cited in this chapter can be found on the FEC website at www.fec.gov.

FIGURE 11.2   Total Contribution Trend for Corporate and Labor PACs, 1986–2000

Source: Federal Election Commission.

apply pressure for PAC contributions, but many employees resent the solicitations and feel subtle pressure to contribute.

The majority of PACs raise and contribute less than $50,000 during a two-year election cycle, although four gave more than $1 million during 1999–2000. The biggest was United Parcel Service PAC, which gave candidates $1,755,065. It was followed by FED EXPAC, at $1,206,680, and Ernst & Young PAC at $1,041,386.

Corporate PACs coordinate their spending with company lobbyists, who know that contributions create an expectation of access, or a hearing of the corporation's position, after the candidate is elected. Overall, corporate PACs give more to Republicans than to Democrats; however, big company PACs usually pursue a strategy of giving contributions to many House and Senate candidates of both parties, favoring incumbents (who are usually reelected) but often giving also to their opponents. This pattern of giving ensures access to office holders of both parties. Although PACs can give up to $5,000 to candidates, most contributions are relatively small ones of only $500 to $2,000. In 2000 a $2,000 contribution was less than one one-thousandth of 1 percent of the $5,750,000 cost of an average Senate race and less than one-tenth of 1 percent of the $656,000 cost of an average House race.

Some corporations elect not to have PACs. One survey of more than 500 of the largest corporations found that only 43 percent had one.[45] The main reason that companies forgo a PAC is to avoid incessant pressure from candidates for contributions. A recent survey of corporate PACs found that 70 percent of their contributions were made due to candidate requests.[46] Public perception is that corporations push money on politicians, but politicians are also persistent and systematic in asking for it. For instance, some staff members of congressional committees, as part of their duties, find corporations affected by provisions in pending bills so that committee members can request contributions from them. Many business executives are repelled by the implications of such a solicitation. However, the rising costs of elections, particularly television ads, fixate politicians on campaign funding. Senator Harry Reid (D-Nevada) describes the ordeal he faces raising the $4 million he needs to run in a smaller state:

> To raise that much money, you have to raise about $13,000 or $14,000 a week every year. You don't take a week off for Christmas. If you do, you have to raise more money. If you do that 52 weeks a year for six years, you can raise enough to be competitive in a race. . . . In some states . . . you have to raise twice that much or three or four times that much. Instead of raising $13,000 or $14,000 a week, people have to raise $50,000 a week.[47]

CIRCUMVENTING CONTRIBUTIONS LIMITS

Although federal law prohibits corporate contributions and imposes strict contribution limits on individuals and political committees, there are many ways to go around it.

A time-honored fund-raising technique that is unregulated by the FECA is *brokering*. Brokering takes place when a lobbyist or corporate executive acts as an intermediary between candidates and contributors. For example, a Washington lobbying firm might sponsor a $1,000-a-plate dinner for a senator. Buying such a meal counts as a campaign contribution under the law. If 400 people attend, the firm has brokered a $400,000 contribution (minus expenses) to the senator.

A second technique for evading contribution limits is *bundling*. It is legal for any individual (even a nonemployee) to contribute to a corporate PAC and to earmark the contribution, or stipulate which candidate is to receive it. The PAC then acts as a conduit for these earmarked funds, which do *not* count against contribution limits. Bundling is used to pass on a collection of "bundled" checks to a politician. A PAC may

[45] Ralph Vartabedian, "Many Top Firms Say No to Political Contributions," *Los Angeles Times,* September 22, 1997, p. A1.

[46] Eliza Newlin Carney, Donor Fatigue," *National Journal,* February 22, 1997, p. 366.

[47] Quoted in Derek Willis, "Debating McCain-Feingold," *CQ Weekly,* March 10, 2001, p. 524.

legally give only $10,000 per election to a congressional candidate, but there is no limit to the amount of earmarked contributions for which a PAC may act as a conduit.

A third way that business money enters politics in excess of FECA limits is through the use of *soft money,* or money given to political parties that is unregulated under federal law. Soft money giving arose after a 1979 amendment to the FECA put contributions for state and local party-building activities outside the limits and prohibitions of the statute. This money could be given directly to the parties where it was supposed to be used for such things as yard signs, posters, brochures, newsletters, and mailings. Soon, however, the national parties began to collect large sums and transfer them to state parties where they were used in inventive ways, not to buy lawn signs, but to further the election of federal candidates.

Although corporations are barred from contributing to federal campaigns, a series of advisory opinions by the Federal Election Commission opened the door for them to give soft-money contributions to national party committees. As a result, corporations and executives began to give colossal and rising sums to the Democratic and Republican parties. In the 1999–2000 election cycle, for example, AT&T, the largest soft-money donor, contributed totals of $2.3 million to the Republican party and $1.5 million to the Democratic party in payments from subsidiaries and executives.[48]

In 1996 the Supreme Court permitted the use of soft money for political ads.[49] The Court made a distinction between "issue advocacy," which presents a political view or comment on an electoral race, and "express advocacy," which specifically suggests the election or defeat of a candidate using words such as "vote for," "defeat," or "support." Soft money, therefore, could be used for issue advertising that tiptoed around direct electioneering by avoiding the use of certain phrases, although the intent to support or oppose a candidate for federal office was clear. Within a few years more than 90 percent of soft money was buying television ads, not lawn signs and bumper stickers for local candidates.[50]

By the late 1990s, the amount of soft money in elections made a mockery of the post-Watergate campaign spending limits. Its rapid rise is suggested by Figure 11.3, which shows its receipt by the national committees of both political parties. Since large sums of soft money were being raised and spent outside federal election law, it is not clear what percentage of the total is shown in Figure 11.3. One consequence of this uncertainty is that the total amount of money in elections cannot be calculated with accuracy over the time period in the figure.

---

[48] Common Cause, "Top Soft Money Donors," www.commoncause.org.
[49] *Colorado Republican Federal Campaign Committee* v. *FEC,* 116 S.Ct. 2390 (1996).
[50] Norman Ornstein, "Reformers Bloodied But Not Bowed," *Los Angeles Times,* July 22, 2001, p. M6.

FIGURE 11.3 Soft Money Raised by Democratic and Republican National Party Committees during Two-Year Election Cycles since 1992

Source: Federal Election Committee.

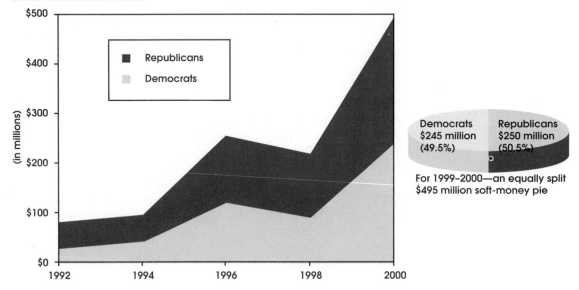

For 1999–2000—an equally split $495 million soft-money pie

Democrats $245 million (49.5%)

Republicans $250 million (50.5%)

Individuals and PACs can make unlimited *independent expenditures* for or against candidates in addition to direct contributions. An independent expenditure is money spent to promote the election of a candidate, buying a radio ad or billboard, for example, that is not coordinated in any way with the candidate. So while it is illegal for a corporate PAC to give more than $5,000 to Jones, a candidate for Congress, the PAC can spend an unlimited amount buying media ads to "elect Jones," provided that the Jones campaign is not informed or consulted. The Supreme Court, in the *Buckley* decision, protected independent expenditures as free speech that cannot be limited. In practice, corporate PACs do not make significant independent expenditures—less than 1 percent of their contributions—but the potential still exists.

There are many more methods for burrowing around the spirit of election law to convert money into political influence. For example, companies regularly contribute to charity foundations set up by lawmakers and their wives, honor them by endowing chaired professorships at universities in their names, subsidize their travel, and pay honoraria—typically about $2,000—for brief speeches at breakfasts and luncheons.

In sum, using a variety of tactics, corporations have been able to get around the prohibitions and limits shown in Figure 11.1 to push enormous sums of money at politicians. A PAC wishing to influence a Senate candidate, for example, can give $5,000 in the primary, $5,000 in the general election, and $5,000 each to trade association PACs that are supporting the candidate. And it can make unlimited independent expenditures in the race.

REFORM LEGISLATION IN 2002

The spectacle of individuals, companies, and PACs giving soft money in unlimited amounts mocked the spirit of the strict contribution and spending limits in the law. As Americans grew increasingly cynical of a political system fueled by millionaires and big corporations, Senator John McCain (R-Arizona) waged an uphill, seven-year battle in Congress to pass reform legislation. Finally, after unfavorable public reaction to news that Enron Corporation manipulated government officials with large campaign contributions, McCain's bill was enacted as the Bipartisan Campaign Reform Act of 2002.

The new law amends the Federal Election Campaign Act in many ways. The most important changes are these.

- Corporations are barred from making soft money contributions, except donations of up to $10,000 to state parties in states that permit soft money. These funds can only be used for voter registration and get-out-the-vote drives.

- Some individual contribution limits are raised (see figures in parentheses in Figure 11.1). Contribution limits are raised even higher for a candidate running against a wealthy opponent who is spending large amounts of his or her own money.

- Advocacy groups are barred from broadcasting ads that advocate the election or defeat of a candidate within 30 days of a primary and 60 days of a general election (a fallback provision that would remain in effect if the overall ban is held unconstitutional, permits such ads only if the groups register as political action committees and pay for them entirely with individual contributions).

- Contributions and expenditures must be more promptly and fully disclosed. Penalties for violating the law are increased.

Eliminating nonregulated soft money reduces the reliance of politicians on big business and a few super-rich donors. More generous individual contribution limits make it easier to raise funds from a larger number of less affluent sources. The ban on broadcast ads by citizen's groups in the months lending up to elections is intended to prevent corporations from turning to electioneering through groups as a substitute for soft money gifts to the national parties.

THE INFLUENCE PROCESS

In America, there is a historic fear that business money will corrupt officeholders. Because of this fear, even where business's influence efforts are legal, the large sums involved raise apprehensions.

Critics believe that corporate money creates unwholesome obligations to special interests. Business contributions are seen as blatant efforts to buy action; they are investments from which donors expect a return. Charles Keating, the owner of Lincoln Savings and Loan and a large campaign donor, once confirmed the critics' worst fears when he said, "One question, among many, has had to do with whether my financial support in any way influenced several political figures to take up my cause. I want to say in the most forceful way I can: I certainly hope so."[51]

Bribery is illegal. If lawmakers or regulators accept money as a condition for official action, they commit a crime. This does not mean that contributions associated with lobbying are made without the expectation of a return. Large contributions create a debt on the part of legislators who receive them. However, because of bribery laws, the etiquette of legislator–lobbyist relations requires that collection of the debt be discrete. To avoid suspicion of bribery, financial contributions are not mentioned in connection with requests for action. Former Senator Tom Eagleton (D-Missouri) explains how it works.

> I've never had . . . a guy come into this office or over the phone say,
> "Tom, such-and-such vote's coming up next week. You remember I gave X
> in your last campaign, and I'm certainly expecting you to vote that way."
> I've never had anything that direct, blunt, or obscene. However, let's
> change the phraseology to this: "Tom, this is so-and-so. You know next
> week an important vote's coming up on such-and-such. I just want to
> remind you, Tom, I feel very strongly about that issue. Okay, my friend,
> good to hear from you." Now a senator receives "gentle" calls of that sort.[52]

Proof or measurement of business influence in politics is elusive. Often there is a correlation between contribution and action, that is, one occurs followed by the other. Did the contribution cause the lawmaker to vote a certain way? Or did the contribution reward earlier support by a like-thinking representative? There are other strong influences on representatives apart from money, including party loyalty, ideological disposition, and the opinions of voters back home. What, then, caused the vote or action to occur?

Sometimes the influence of business money is barely visible to researchers. A lobbyist is alleged to have said that figuring out political

---

[51] In Herbert E. Alexander, *Financing Politics,* 4th ed. (Washington, DC: Congressional Quarterly Press, 1992), p. 68.
[52] Quoted in Hedrick Smith, *The Power Game* (New York: Ballantine Books, 1988), p. 255.

influence is like finding a black cat in the coal bin at midnight. Former U.S. Senator William Proxmire (D-Wisconsin), who throughout his career declined to accept campaign contributions, once said this:

> The payoff may be as obvious and overt as a floor vote in favor of a contributor's desired tax loophole or appropriation. Or it may be subtle . . . a floor speech not delivered . . . a bill pigeonholed in subcommittee . . . an amendment not offered. . . . Or the payoff can come in a private conversation with four or five key colleagues in the privacy of the cloakroom.[53]

Debate is perennial over whether too much corporate money enters politics. Beginning with the 1907 Tillman Act, efforts to eliminate it have been ineffective. Most recently, the ban on corporate campaign contributions in the FECA, though still on the books, was rendered nearly meaningless by the soft-money loophole. More than a century after the McKinley elections radiated with corporate financial power, the nation has made little progress in controlling the spectacle. Why not more?

One reason is that silencing speech, including corporate speech, goes against the grain in a political system that regards unlimited debate and free expression as supreme virtues. In *Buckley,* the Supreme Court held that a monetary contribution is a form of speech protected by the First Amendment. Therefore, suppression of the contributions of any group or interest is constitutionally suspect. Yet since 1907, legal restraints on corporate giving have been permitted. The Supreme Court has held that speech restrictions on corporations, in the form of contribution limits, are constitutional for two reasons. First, the corporate form, which allows the accumulation of immense wealth based on success in economic markets, is an unfair advantage in the political arena.

> [T]he resources in the treasury of a business corporation . . . are not an indication of popular support for the corporation's political ideas. They reflect instead the economically motivated decisions of investors and customers. The availability of these resources may make a corporation a formidable political presence, even though the power of the corporation may be no reflection on the power of its ideas.[54]

Second, the Court recognizes a "compelling governmental interest" in preventing corruption or the appearance of corruption in elections."[55] The presence of unlimited corporate cash, even if there is no overt corruption, undermines perceptions of integrity on which democratic elections

[53] Quoted in Center for Responsive Politics, "Ten Myths about Money in Politics," in Anthony Corrado et al., *Campaign Finance Reform: A Sourcebook* (Washington, DC: Brookings Institution Press, 1997), p. 155.
[54] *Federal Election Commission* v. *Massachusetts Citizens for Life,* 479 U.S. 257 (1986), from the opinion by Justice William J. Brennan, Jr.
[55] *Austin* v. *Michigan Chamber of Commerce,* 58 LW 4373 (1990).

FIGURE 11.4 **The Fundamental Vision of Election Law**
The challenge to the courts and to Congress with respect to election law is to balance the guarantee of free speech in the First Amendment against an implied duty to maintain elections free of corruption and the appearance of corruption.

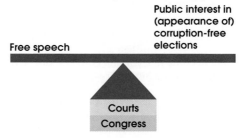

depend for their legitimacy. So the Court finds it permissible to balance the right of free speech against the importance of maintaining elections free of both the appearance and reality of corruption. Figure 11.4 illustrates this fundamental vision of election law.

However, not everyone agrees. Conservative dissenters on the court refuse to accept this balancing. Justice Antonin Scalia argues that corporations should have the right to unlimited free speech, that they should be able to make campaign contributions and spend as much money as they wish. Prohibiting corporate funds in elections is, he writes, "incompatible with the absolutely central truth of the First Amendment: that government cannot be trusted to assure, through censorship, the 'fairness' of political debate."[56] He trusts the ability of the public to judge the validity of corporate arguments and to withdraw support from politicians who succumb to corporate influence and sell out the public interest. Justice Clarence Thomas has also dissented, taking to task those justices who restrict corporate speech by upholding contribution limits. "I remain baffled," he writes, "that this Court has extended the most generous First Amendment safeguards to filing lawsuits, wearing profane jackets, and exhibiting drive-in movies with nudity, but has offered only tepid protection to the core speech and associational rights that our Founders sought to defend."[57] And Justice Anthony Kennedy believes that contributions limits suppress "speech on which democracy depends."[58]

The Bipartisan Campaign Reform Act of 2002 has been challenged by business and advocacy groups arguing that some of its provisions are unconstitutional. They believe that bans on soft money and pre-election blackouts of group ads suppress political speech protected under the First

---

[56] Dissenting in *Austin,* 58 LW 4379.
[57] *Federal Election Commission* v. *Colorado Republican Federal Campaign Committee,* 121 S.Ct. 2372 (2001).
[58] Dissenting in *Nixon* v. *Shrink Missouri Government PAC,* No. 98–963 (2000), slip opinion, p. 1.

Amendment. It is indisputable that these bans limit the extent to which some interests can voice partisan ideas. However, defenders of the reforms believe that they simply refine certain restrictions that the Supreme Court has consistently upheld as justified to preserve corruption-free elections. Some provisions in the new law may be struck down. Those that survive legal challenge will be eroded like past reforms as business money finds new channels into politics.

CONCLUDING OBSERVATIONS

Clearly, business retains its historically dominant position among interests. There is a significant imbalance of resources between corporate interests and other interests such as poor people, small farmers, environmentalists, and consumer advocates. Labor can sometimes match the political muscle of business, but often not. However, an equal or greater imbalance has existed since the end of the colonial era, and business is today forced to deal with more, and stronger, opposing interests than in the past.

The rise of soft money and refinements in lobbying methods create a perception that corporate money is undermining the independence of officials. However, specific evidence of deep corruption, as opposed to periodic and healthy exposures of lawbreaking, is not forthcoming. In part because of disclosure rules, American politics is cleaner than the politics of most other nations and cleaner than in past eras.

The challenge for American society is to balance the First Amendment right of corporations to free political expression against the societal interest of maintaining corruption-free elections and government decisions. So far, our society has successfully maintained a rough, if not perfect, balance.

A Win for Federal Express

In the waning hours of the second session of the 104th Congress, lawmakers witnessed heated, partisan debate over an amendment to an aviation bill. Republicans, who introduced it at the request of Federal Express Corporation, argued that it simply corrected a minor error in a previous bill. Pro-labor Democrats, however, portrayed it as an all-out corporate and Republican assault on the working people of America.

What follows is the story of this amendment. It requires patience to penetrate the arcana of law and bureaucracy to see the flash of money and power at work. Yet it is worth the effort to learn how government determines the fortunes of corporations and how corporations flex political muscle.

FEDERAL EXPRESS

Federal Express, also called FedEx, was started in 1971 by an entrepreneur named Frederick W. Smith. Since then, Smith has built it into one of America's largest corporations. With revenues of $19.6 billion it ranked 103 on the *Fortune* 500 list in 2001. Federal Express offers rapid transport and delivery of documents, packages, and freight in 211 countries. Its 144,000 employees operate 640 aircraft and 53,000 vehicles.[1]

The mail, package, and freight delivery industry is highly competitive in price and service. FedEx battles for customers with firms such as DHL Worldwide Express, passenger airlines that carry freight, airfreight companies, and the U.S. Postal Service, but its biggest competitor is United Parcel Service of America, Inc. (UPS). UPS, with $29.7 billion in revenues in 2000, is twice the size of FedEx and its operations are similar. It delivers in 200 countries, about the same as FedEx; it operates 622 aircraft, slightly fewer than FedEx; but it has a fleet of 150,000 vehicles, almost three times as many as FedEx.[2]

One difference between these two rivals is that UPS's employees are unionized, while FedEx's are not. Although 3,500 FedEx pilots are in a pilot's union, its remaining employees are nonunion. UPS, on the other hand, is heavily unionized. The International Brotherhood of Teamsters represents 214,000 of its 359,000 employees, and its pilots are also in a union.

Management culture at Federal Express is opposed to unions. The company uses a range of tactics to keep organizers at bay, including a Guaranteed Fair Treatment program in which any worker can appeal a supervisor's decision all the way up to CEO Smith. Some hourly FedEx employees have sought to bring in unions.[3] Both the Teamsters and the United Automobile Workers of America have been trying for years to organize union elections. However, despite strenuous efforts, they have failed. This gives FedEx a labor cost advantage over UPS.

TWO LABOR LAWS, TWO APPROACHES TO LABOR RELATIONS

The success that Federal Express has had in preventing unionization of its employees, besides the pilots, is due in large part to the way union activity

is regulated by the federal government. Two main laws guide organizing, and they are very different in philosophy.

THE RAILWAY LABOR ACT

The first law is the Railway Labor Act of 1926. Early in this century, labor law favored managers of companies and discouraged union activity. The Railway Labor Act was the first major statute to encourage and protect unions. In it Congress required that railroad managers bargain in good faith with workers about union contracts and created an agency called the Labor Mediation Board to settle union–management disputes. The law applied only to railroads, but, unlike today, these were among the largest and most visible businesses of that era, and so it was very significant.

With the growth of the airlines, the law was extended to include air carriers. It was then further extended to cover express companies. However, there was only one express company in existence, Railway Express Agency (REA), which was a unique company. The story of this firm begins during World War I when the government nationalized all the railroads, including four express companies that shipped packages by railroad. After the war, the assets of all four companies were transferred to a newly created entity named Railway Express Agency, which was owned by 86 railroad companies in proportion to the amount of express business carried over their tracks.[4] Since REA was an outgrowth of existing railroads, the Railway Labor Act was extended to cover its employees. In the 1950s REA began using trucks, and in the 1960s it also began using planes; but as rail traffic dropped, its revenues declined and it was liquidated in 1975.

Only four years earlier, Federal Express had emerged with a new express service model based on bringing packages to a central hub from where they were flown to customers. Under Smith, FedEx created a new market for fast door-to-door delivery. FedEx started with a fleet of Falcon 20 aircraft and soon bought larger cargo jets. From the beginning, it was classified as an "air carrier" under the Railway Labor Act.

[1] Figures in this paragraph are from the company's Form 10K405, filed on August 21, 2001.
[2] Form 10K, United Parcel Service, Inc., April 2, 2001, p. 12.
[3] See, for example, the "FED UP" website at http://ourworld.compusever.com/homepages/kevin_osiowy.

[4] George Drury, "Yesterday's FedEx: Railway Express Agency," *Trains Magazine*, August 1996, p. 75.

THE NATIONAL LABOR RELATIONS ACT

A second law that oversees management–union interactions is the National Labor Relations Act (NLRA) of 1935. The NLRA gives much more extensive protection to workers and unions than did the Railway Labor Act. It prohibited tactics that companies commonly used to stop unions, including, for example, firing union members and refusing to bargain, and it set up a powerful new agency, the National Labor Relations Board (NLRB), with strong powers to remedy unfair practices. The NLRB has jurisdiction over employees at all companies other than railroads, airlines, and express companies covered in the less stringent Railway Labor Act.[5]

It is much more difficult for a union to organize employees under the Railway Labor Act than under the NLRA. The fundamental purposes of the laws are different. The main goal of the former is to protect against labor disharmony that could disrupt the flow of interstate commerce. Thus, enforcement focuses on mediating disputes and avoiding strikes. Bargaining agreements are not allowed to expire, and negotiations simply continue until a new agreement is reached. In short, it strengthens the hand of management.

The goal of the NLRA, on the other hand, is to fortify the rights of workers to organize and bargain and to protect them from management abuses. One other key difference between the two laws is that the Railway Labor Act only allows workers to organize a national union, whereas the NLRA permits organizing local unions city by city. It is, of course, much easier for the union to win elections one location at a time. Winning a vote of the national workforce of a large corporation is a daunting task.

Although UPS and FedEx have similar operations today, UPS began as a trucking and courier company. Therefore, its workers fall under the NLRA. This explains why UPS workers are unionized and Federal Express workers are not. As long as FedEx workers remain under the Railway Labor Act, a successful union drive is unlikely.

UNION EFFORTS TO ORGANIZE FEDEX

Labor union membership in the United States is falling. In 1983, 20 percent of all wage and salary workers were union members, but that fell to 14 percent in 1999.[6] The decline has been steep for the two unions that have tried hardest to organize FedEx workers. In the late 1960s the United Auto Workers (UAW) had 1.5 million members; today it has a little more than half that number. The Teamsters, which had more than two million members in the 1970s, lost almost one-third of them because of trucking deregulation. So it would be a welcome gain for either one to grab the wage earners at Federal Express. Both unions have tried. FedEx CEO Smith once wrote in the company newsletter that if all these hourly workers were unionized, they would pay $20 million in annual dues.[7]

In 1990 the United Auto Workers started a big campaign to organize FedEx workers on the East Coast. It sponsored rallies and organizing drives in Pennsylvania, New Jersey, and Delaware, but it faced a stiff task. Under the Railway Labor Act, the union had to get 35 percent of all FedEx workers nationwide to sign organizing petitions or no election could be held. It would be much easier if the workers could be organized city by city under the NLRA.

Since FedEx had far more truck drivers than pilots, the UAW petitioned the National Labor Relations Board to place the drivers under the NLRA. It argued that although FedEx was classified as an "air carrier" subject to the Railway Labor Act, most of its workers had nothing to do with airplanes. Instead, they worked at pick-up counters, sorted packages, and dispatched and drove trucks; therefore, they should be reclassified as covered under the National Labor Relations Act.

In mid-1995, after a hearing on the union's petition, the National Labor Relations Board decided that the case was ambiguous and decided to submit both sides' arguments to the National Mediation Board, the body that resolves disputes under

---

[5] In addition to employees of rail, air, and express companies, the NLRA also excludes agricultural and government workers.

[6] U.S. Census Bureau, *Statistical Abstract of the United States: 2000,* 120th ed. (Washington, DC: Hoover's Business Press, 2000), table 712.
[7] John H. White and Brian Jackson, "Rival Unions Vie for FedEx," *Chicago Sun-Times,* May 13, 1997, p. 43.

the Railway Labor Act, for an advisory opinion.[8] One board member, William B. Gould IV, the chairman of the NLRB, wrote a dissenting opinion in which he agreed with the union and stated that FedEx workers outside its air operations should fall under NLRA jurisdiction. His dissent was unsettling for Federal Express.

In November 1995, however, the National Mediation Board issued its opinion, holding that all Federal Express employees were covered under the Railway Labor Act and stating in part:

> Federal Express is an air express delivery service which holds itself out for hire to transport packages, both domestically and internationally. . . . [T]here is no dispute over whether Federal Express is a common carrier by air. . . . The [Railway Labor] Act's definition of an employee of an air carrier includes, "every air pilot or other person who performs any work as an employee or subordinate official of such carrier or carriers, subject to its or their continuing authority to supervise and direct the manner of rendition of his service." The Railway Labor Act does not limit its coverage to air carrier employees who fly or maintain aircraft. Rather, its coverage extends to virtually all employees engaged in performing a service for the carrier so that the carrier may transport passengers or freight.
>
> Employees working in the . . . positions sought by the UAW perform functions equally crucial to Federal Express' mission as an integrated air express delivery service. As the record demonstrates, without the functions performed by the employees at issue, Federal Express could not provide the on-time express delivery required of an air express delivery service.[9]

The board suggested that ruling otherwise would break off parts of labor forces at railroads and airlines around the country and "drastically alter labor relations" at all these companies. Even if some employees do not work with airplanes, if a company is classified as an "air carrier," all its workers should be covered by the Railway Labor Act, not just some of them.

The National Mediation Board opinion was sent to the National Labor Relations Board, which took it under consideration and continued to deliberate. The situation now was that the NLRB could still reject the National Mediation Board's opinion to allow the UAW to organize FedEx employees under the NLRA. This was a threat to the antiunion stance of FedEx management.

This opinion was sent to the National Labor Relations Board, which took it under consideration. Although it favored the FedEx position, the Board could still reject it and place the company's workers under the union-friendly NLRA. FedEx saw this as a threat.

Quickly, another threat arose for Federal Express when, a month later, Congress passed the Interstate Commerce Commission Termination Act of 1995, ending the existence of the nation's first independent regulatory commission 108 years after its creation. The Interstate Commerce Commission (ICC) was set up in 1887 to regulate railroads, and over the years its reach was expanded to trucking companies, bus lines, moving companies, freight forwarders, and pipelines. However, recent deregulation of these industries had considerably reduced its duties. Congress acted to shut down the withered agency, moving its remaining powers into the Department of Transportation.

Terminating the ICC was a complex legislative process because, over the years, Congress had passed 22 major statutes for the agency to administer. A bill had to be written in which all these laws were rescinded, rewritten, or amended. The intricate process of drafting the bill went forward, and, in due course, both the House and the Senate passed it.

Then, during the House–Senate conference committee proceedings that take place to reconcile different versions of bills passed in each chamber, ICC staff members recommended dropping the words "express company" from the Interstate Commerce Act because they thought that the language was obsolete. After all, the only company ever classified as an express company was the defunct Railway Express Agency, then 20 years in its grave. So when the conference version was sent back to both chambers and passed in 1995, it eliminated the words "express company" from the original ICC Act and, in a conforming amendment, also dropped them

[8] *Federal Express Corp.,* 317 NLRB 1155 (1995).
[9] *Federal Express Corporation,* 23 NMB 32, November 22, 1995.

from the Railway Labor Act. Nobody paid attention to this detail. Republicans later claimed that it was only a mistake, fixable with a technical amendment. Democrats would balk, arguing that adding the words again was a substantive change for the benefit of one corporation.

Once alerted, Federal Express badly wanted the words "express company" put back. They were added assurance that its truck drivers were covered by the Railway Labor Act.[10] If the National Labor Relations Board, in its pending decision, held that some of its employees were exposed to union-friendly organizing because they worked for an "air carrier," then FedEx could petition for reclassification as an "express company." For years, FedEx had argued to the National Mediation Board that it was both an "air carrier" and an "express company." The Board had never agreed, but it might in the future. The company resolved to get the words back into the law.

FEDERAL EXPRESS MOBILIZES

Federal Express is adroit with political influence in Washington, D.C. It does not shrink from pressing government for special favors. For example, in 1990 it got Congress to exempt its aircraft from local noise abatement rules. In 1994 it got a bill ending the authority of states to regulate the routes of its planes and trucks. In 1995 it succeeded in scrapping federal safety rules for trucks in the 10,001-to-26,000-pound range, the category for most of its delivery trucks.[11] In 1996 the Transportation Department gave it exclusive air cargo rights to China. And in the same year, a White House meeting between Smith and President Clinton led to pressure on Japan to drop restrictions on FedEx cargo flights, which it did.

Federal Express lobbyists approached Republican lawmakers at the start of the second session of the 104th Congress in 1996, requesting amendment of the Railway Labor Act to restore the words "express company." They stressed that

omission of the words was just a mistake, because elsewhere the ICC Act stated that "the enactment of the ICC Termination Act of 1995 shall neither expand or contract coverage of the employees and employers by the Railway Labor Act." Therefore, putting the words back was a necessary and legitimate correction.

When organized labor discovered what Federal Express was up to, its lobbyists called on labor-friendly House members of both parties to fight the change. It did not see the change as a minor matter; it saw instead the end of an opportunity to organize FedEx employees.

Five attempts to reinsert the words during the session failed. The Republicans never took the open route of sending the amendment to a committee for discussion. No public hearings were held. Instead, they went in the back door, hooking it on as a rider to unrelated legislation. In the House, they attached it to the fiscal year 1996 appropriations bill and it was voted down. They attached it to the National Transportation Safety Board reauthorization bill and it failed. They attached it to a bill amending the Railroad Unemployment Act and it failed. They attached it to the Department of Transportation appropriation bill and it failed. In the Senate, they attached it to a Department of Labor appropriations bill and it failed again.

Five defeats might have discouraged another company, but not Federal Express. The company knows how to orchestrate a range of tactics to sway politicians. It uses its fleet of seven corporate jets to fly members of the House and Senate to fundraising dinners around the country. Two former senators sat on the company's board of directors, former Republican leader Howard H. Baker Jr. and former Democratic leader George J. Mitchell.

Federal Express lobbies aggressively because CEO Smith understands the importance of government to the company's fortunes. Unlike many top executives who avoid what they consider an unseemly morass of shakedowns and deals, Smith frequently visits Capitol Hill to see members of Congress. The company has a Washington office with four registered lobbyists, including the son of former Senator David H. Pryor (D-Arkansas).[12] It

[10] Frank Swoboda, "Labor Wants to End FedEx's Railway Act Protection," *Washington Post,* October 2, 1996, p. C1.
[11] Public Citizen press release of October 2, 1996, cited in the *Congressional Record,* October 2, 1996, p. S12189.

[12] Michael Steel, "FedEx Flies High," *National Journal,* February 24, 2001, p. 555.

Washington Law Firms Hired by Federal Express

Here is a list of the firms hired by Federal Express in the first six months of 1996 and the fees paid to them. Firms hired to work on the Railway Labor Act are shown with an asterisk.

Oldsker, Ryan, Phillips & Utrecht	$80,000
The Dutko Group*	60,000
O'Brien Calio	60,000
Cassidy & Associates	42,000
Aun Eppard Associates	40,000
Washington Counsel, P.C.	40,000
Cliff Madison Government Relations*	20,000
Bill Simpson & Associates	15,000
James E. Boland*	10,000

Source: Public Citizen from Senate records and printed in Neil A. Lewis, "This Mr. Smith Gets His Way in Washington," *New York Times,* October 12, 1996, p. B1. Reprinted with permission of The New York Times.

also hires Washington lobbying firms for special jobs. In just the first six months of 1996, it had spent $1.2 million on lobbying, and $367,000 of this went to nine outside firms, some of which were hired for work on the Railway Labor Act amendment.[13] Its heavy involvement is not surprising, however, because its business is heavily regulated. By editing the Railway Labor Act, the hand of government was poised to shape its labor market.

Federal Express also makes large campaign contributions. In the 1996 election cycle, its political action committee gave $980,000 to senators and representatives of both parties, and the company itself gave $400,000 in soft money to the Republican party and $250,000 to the Democratic party.[14]

[13] Neil A. Lewis, "This Mr. Smith Gets His Way in Washington," *New York Times,* October 12, 1996, p. B1.
[14] Contribution figures are from Federal Election Commission reports and Bob Woodward and Ann Devroy, "When Mr. Smith Came to Washington," *Washington Post National Weekly Edition,* August 25, 1997, p. 12.

THE FINAL PUSH

As the end of the legislative session approached, an ideal opportunity for inserting the "express company" rider arrived. Both the House and Senate had passed a Federal Aviation Authorization bill with broad, bipartisan support. Besides $19 billion in funding for the Federal Aviation Administration and increased airport security, the bill ladled out $4.6 billion for airport construction in many legislators' districts and states. This spending would translate into votes in the upcoming elections.

A House–Senate conference committee composed of the principal sponsors from each chamber met to iron out differences and create a uniform version for final approval by each chamber. One committee member, Senator Earnest Hollings (D-South Carolina), was picked to propose the FedEx amendment. Hollings was indebted to Federal Express because during a recent drought in South Carolina, FedEx planes had flown in hay for starving cattle. Also, the company's PAC had given $4,000 to his

Laws Bearing on the FedEx Amendment

Railway Labor Act of 1926. This law contains labor relations rules for employees of railroads, air carriers, and express companies. Federal Express is classified as an air carrier under this law.

National Labor Relations Act of 1935. This law contains labor relations rules for all workers not covered by the Railway Labor Act (except those in agriculture and government). It goes further in protecting workers' rights and makes it easier to organize unions.

Interstate Commerce Commission Termination Act of 1995. This act abolished the Interstate Commerce Commission and transferred its remaining powers elsewhere. A passage in it took out the words "express company" from the original ICC Act and, through a conforming amendment, from the Railway Labor Act as well.

Federal Aviation Reauthorization Act of 1996. This act authorized funds for airport construction and aviation safety. For Federal Express, Senator Earnest Hollings attached an amendment to the conference report of this bill to reinsert the words "express company" in the Railway Labor Act.

A Scorecard of Federal Agencies

National Mediation Board. This agency mediates disputes over wages, hours, and working conditions that arise under the Railway Labor Act. It is a small entity with three board members and a handful of employees.

National Labor Relations Board. This is an independent agency given responsibility to enforce the National Labor Relations Act. It conducts union elections and is empowered to investigate and remedy a wide range of unfair labor practices.

Interstate Commerce Commission. This was the first independent regulatory agency in American history. It had extensive powers to regulate railroads and other forms of surface transportation. Its existence ended in 1995.

Surface Transportation Board. The agency Congress created to receive residual powers once exercised by the Interstate Commerce Commission. It is in the Federal Highway Administration, which is, in turn, part of the Department of Transportation.

Federal Aviation Administration. This is another agency within the Department of Transportation. It sets and enforces rules for airline safety and operation.

campaign. The conference committee approved Hollings' amendment by a vote of 8–6. Thus, when the enormously popular bill was reported back to the House and Senate for enactment, it contained the amendment FedEx wanted.

DEBATE IN THE HOUSE

On September 27, the conference report came up in the House. Immediately, cries of objection to the Hollings amendment were heard from enraged prolabor Democrats. Representative Joe Moakley (D-Massachusetts) took the lead.

> This bill contains a direct attack on working Americans. This bill contains a provision that was not part of either the House or Senate bill. This provision will resurrect the term "express carrier" solely on behalf of the Federal Express Co. . . . [T]his bill pulls that term out of the trash heap, and in doing so will effectively prohibit the employees of Federal Express from unionizing.

The supporters of this provision, this blatant attack on American workers, call it a technical correction. The person testifying before the committee said it was inadvertently left out of the House bill. It was inadvertently left out of the Senate bill. But somehow it showed up in the conference committee report.

I would argue that for the 130,000 employees of Federal Express this change is hardly a correction, it is more like a misdirection.

If Federal Express employees cannot unionize locally, Mr. Speaker, they cannot unionize at all, and the powerful people at the top of Federal Express know it.

So I urge my colleagues to stand up for those 130,000 employees of this company and defeat . . . the bill. Despite all of the progress this bill will make towards improving air travel and airline safety, it should be defeated because of that one provision.[15]

One by one, other Democrats rose to fight the amendment. Representative William O. Lipinski (D-Illinois) called it a "horrible extraneous provision" designed "to aid and assist one giant corporation against the American middle class."[16] Representative Peter A. DeFazio (D-Oregon) remarked that "the working people of this country are going to be screwed by a large corporation, screwed behind the closed doors of a conference committee."[17] Representative Jerrold Nadler (D-New York) called the change "a union-busting provision, pure and simple."[18] Others rose as well; perhaps the most colorful rhetoric was that of Representative Harold L. Volkmer (D-Missouri):

I love flowers and flowers are very beautiful, and what I saw developing as this bill passed through the House, passed through the Senate, started in the conference up to Wednesday was a beautiful bouquet of flowers that smelled just beautifully. And then Wednesday night, something happened. Wednesday night, a skunk snuck in a beautiful flower garden and smelled up the whole thing, and this bill now just smells, smells, smells terribly.

Why? Because of one special interest provision that was put in there for Federal Express. . . .

I think somebody should take a look at the Federal Election Commission reports and let us see where FedEx money is going to. How much is the Republican National Committee getting from FedEx? How much are the members of the leadership on that side getting from FedEx?

I think there is our answer right there, Members. That is what this is all about. It is a payoff; that is all it is, a payoff.[19]

Republican leaders spoke to defend the amendment. They argued that it was indeed a "technical" correction. They pointed out that there had been no intent to expand or contract coverage of workers under the Railway Labor Act. In the end, they prevailed, and in a vote that hewed closely to party lines, the Federal Aviation Authorization Act of 1996 passed the House.

FILIBUSTER IN THE SENATE

Three days later, the conference report came to the floor in the Senate. At the time, the Senate was ready to adjourn so members could get home to campaign before the November elections. However, Democrats planned a fight. Senator Ted Kennedy (D-Massachusetts) led the charge by starting a filibuster on Monday, September 30, when the conference report came to the floor.

Unlike the House, the rules of the Senate permit each senator unlimited time to speak unless he or she voluntarily yields. A senator who is against legislation can tie up the Senate and prevent action on a bill simply by keeping the floor and refusing to yield. This is called a filibuster. The only way to get the agenda moving again when a filibuster is in progress is to invoke Senate Rule XXII. Under Rule XXII, a senator can be forced to give up the floor if 16 other senators sign a petition calling for a vote of cloture (KLO-chur). Then, if two-thirds plus one of the senators present vote in favor of cloture, the motion passes and the filibuster must end. Absent a successful cloture motion, Senator Kennedy would hold the floor and the Senate could not finish its business and adjourn.

---

[15] *Congressional Record,* September 27, 1996, p. H11453.
[16] Ibid.
[17] Ibid., p. H11457.
[18] Ibid., p. H11458.

[19] Ibid., pp. H11460–61.

Kennedy strongly condemned Federal Express and the Republicans for "denying some fundamental justice to scores of American workers who have been playing by the rules."[20] He said that FedEx truck drivers had not had a raise in seven years. He read letters from FedEx employees who wanted a union. One complained that FedEx drivers are subject to stressful and dangerous policies. To meet guaranteed 10:30 A.M. delivery times they have to rush and sometimes drive unsafely. One driver in Chicago hit a 70-year-old woman at 10:28 or 10:29 while looking for an address. Other complaints were aired.

Then Kennedy attacked the Republicans.

Few things more vividly illustrate the antiworker bias of the Republican Congress than this shameful antiworker rider. Republicans say, "Who cares about a handful of truck drivers in Pennsylvania?"

We reply, "We do. Democrats do. Democrats are on their side."

It has placed a spotlight on a cynical Republican attempt to help one of their corporate friends at the expense of that company's employees.

They had hoped to carry out their scheme in the shadows, so that no one would recognize the injustice that was being done. That part of the Republican plan has already failed. The entire country now knows that the Republican Congress is ending as it began, with an assault on working men and women and their families. Key Republicans in Congress have conspired with Federal Express to . . . deprive Federal Express workers of their right to form a local union.[21]

Senator Hollings soon rose to defend his amendment. It was, he said, simply a "technical correction" that did not change coverage of FedEx employees under the law. He accused Kennedy of grandstanding and making a partisan issue of the matter to hurt Republicans in the elections only a month away.

[I]t is not a question of one company succeeds. It is the question of one Congress can succeed. Congress made the error, not Federal Express. Federal

Express had nothing to do with the dropping of the language when we passed the ICC termination bill last December. We made a mistake. We are on trial. And this distortion: coming in here and flyblowing a wonderful company—"antiworker," "a Republican attack" . . .—none of that has anything to do with it.

. . . I have been a Democrat since 1948. I think you were just learning to drive at that time. So you can't define who is a Democrat, we will see how the Democrats vote.

We know this is a partisan onslaught. We know this [is] nonsense about working people and working families.[22]

Senator Kennedy's filibuster continued for three days. Finally, a petition signed by 16 senators forced a roll-call vote on a motion for cloture, which passed 66–31. In the majority, 49 Republicans were joined by 17 Democrats. Many of these Democrats would have voted with Kennedy, but they believed that the aviation bill was too important to kill because of this rider. Voting against were 29 Democrats and two Republicans. This was a very close vote. If only two senators had switched sides, the motion would have failed, Kennedy's opponents would have had to concede defeat, and Federal Express would have lost.

Now, however, there was no way for prolabor forces to stop the Federal Aviation Authorization Act, and it passed with 92 "yeas" and only two "nays." The two no votes were cast by Senator Arlen Specter (R-Pennsylvania) and Senator Paul Simon (D-Illinois), both of whom dissented in principle because of the Hollings amendment. Surprisingly, they were not joined by Senator Kennedy, who, having failed in his primary objective, decided to vote for the rest of the act, which everyone agreed had great merit.

POSTSCRIPT

President Clinton signed the aviation act into law five days later. After the Senate debate, John Sweeney, president of the AFL-CIO, refused to take phone calls from Senate Democrats and

---

[20] *Congressional Record,* October 2, 1996, p. S12178.
[21] *Congressional Record,* October 3, 1996, pp. S12219 and S12182.

[22] Ibid., pp. S12221 and 12223.

threatened to cut off campaign contributions to the Democratic party. He relented after a visit from an apologetic Ted Kennedy.[23]

The term "express company" remains in Section 151 of the Railway Labor Act. Eight months after the battle in Congress, the National Labor Relations Board denied the UAW's request to reclassify trucking employees at Federal Express under the National Labor Relations Act. Its decision was based on the argument that more than 85 percent of FedEx shipments travel by air at some point, so the trucking employees who handle them are an integral part of the air operation. The decision also said that the Hollings amendment to the aviation act showed a congressional intent to classify Federal Express under the Railway Labor Act.[24]

Federal Express keeps up its political efforts. According to Federal Election Commission disclosure data, since 1997 the company has given $1.5 million in soft money, 70 percent of it to the Republicans. Its PAC, which contributes on top of the company's soft-money checks, gave $1.2 million to candidates in the 2000 elections alone. Frederick Smith has himself given $94,000. Because of its reputation as a big money-giver, Federal Express is often solicited by politicians and party leaders. "[Y]ou better be responsive," Smith once told the *Washington Post*. "Whether you use the language of the street and call it a shakedown or whether you just call it our system, however you put it, it's a messy system."[25] Smith might

have been saying that with as much influence as Federal Express has, he believes that it is also a victim.

QUESTIONS

1. Was the FedEx amendment a technical fix or a substantive change in the Railway Labor Act?

2. Do you agree with Federal Express? Based on your knowledge of its business and the way it operates, is there a logical argument for classifying it as an "express company"?

3. Do you agree with the United Auto Workers? Should trucking employees of Federal Express be reclassified as non–air carrier employees, so that they can organize and bargain collectively under the National Labor Relations Act?

4. Was the decision in Congress on the amendment based on merit or politics or both? Were Republicans doing an unwarranted favor for Federal Express? Were Democrats unfairly using the amendment as a pretext for painting Republicans as antilabor?

5. Did Federal Express buy the victory with money spent on lobbying and campaign contributions? Would the result have been the same without this effort?

6. What is the lesson of this story? Does it teach that the public should be cynical about the political process in Washington, D.C., because it favors special interests with money? Or does it illustrate a political process open to many interests that produced a reasonable outcome in a situation where no party had a monopoly on truth and logic?

[23] Robert Novak, "Senate Democrats' Betrayal of Labor Is Telling Tale of How Washington Works," *Buffalo News,* October 17, 1996, p. 3B.

[24] *Federal Express Corporation and International Union, United Automobile, Aerospace and Agricultural Implement Workers of America, UAW, Petitioner,* 33 NLRB No. 157, May 30, 1997.

[25] Woodward and Devroy, "When Mr. Smith Came to Washington," p. 12.

Part Five

Global
Management
Issues

Chapter Twelve

Multinational Corporations and Government Relationships

The Coca-Cola Company

Coca-Cola was invented in 1886 by a Civil War officer named John S. Pemberton. After the war, he opened a drug store in Atlanta that was not successful. As a graduate pharmacist he experimented with a variety of concoctions and eventually focused on soft drinks. He finally developed a formula that pleased him and decided to give it a name. His friend F. M. Robinson suggested Coca-Cola based on two ingredients, namely, "coca" a dried leaf of a South American shrub, and "cola" an extract of the kola nut. Pemberton persuaded an owner of soda fountains in Atlanta to try selling the drink. He did, and it immediately became popular with the public. On Pemberton's death in 1888 the ownership of and all rights to the formula were acquired by Asa G. Candler for $2,300. Candler eventually formed the Coca-Cola Company in 1892 to produce a drink that the public soon began calling "Coke."[1]

The Coca-Cola Company today is the world's largest manufacturer, distributor, and marketer of soft-drink concentrates and syrups. Its products are sold in nearly 200 countries, and its brands are the leading soft drinks in most of them. The company also sells juice and juice-drink products. Sales in 2001 were $20.1 billion, of which 62 percent came from outside the United States. Its net profit for the year was $3.9 billion. It had 38,000 employees; only 9,800 of them worked in the United States.

---

[1] Hannah Campbell, *Why Did They Name It?* (New York: Ace Books, 1964), pp. 63–64.

The company has relationships with three types of bottlers to which it sells its secret concentrates and syrups. First are independent bottlers in which the company has no ownership interest. Second are bottlers in which the company has a minority equity position. Third are bottlers in which the company holds a controlling interest. In 2000 the first group sold 25 percent of the worldwide case volume; the second, 59 percent; and the third, the remaining 16 percent.

The company divided the world into five major marketing areas. They are, with their share of net operating revenues, as follows: North America, 39 percent; Africa and Middle East, 4 percent; Europe and Eurasia, 21 percent; Latin America, 11 percent; and Asia Pacific, 25 percent. The company's principal markets outside the United States, as measured by gallon sales, are Mexico, Brazil, Japan, and Germany. These countries reported 26 percent of global sales. The fastest 10-year annual growth rates were China, 29 percent; Eurasia, 19 percent; Middle East and North Africa, 12 percent; and Chile, 10 percent.

In its 10-K report for the year 2000 to the SEC the company said:

> Our Company believes that its success ultimately depends on its ability to build and nurture relationships with others: consumers, customers, bottlers, partners, governmental authorities and other constituencies touched by our business. To this end, the Company has adopted an overriding business strategy of "Think local, act local," applicable to virtually all aspects of its business. This strategy is designed to put the responsibility and accountability for ensuring local relevance and maximizing business performance in the hands of those closest to the market, locale by locale.[2]

Associated with this strategy is an expanding portfolio of products from tea to plain water. The company, in effect, has transformed itself from a single-product firm into a producer and marketer of beverages favored by local consumers. The result is 230 different products designed to meet consumer preferences in various markets. Besides carbonated drinks, Coca-Cola is selling more bottled water, tea, and other noncarbonated beverages. In Germany, for instance, the company is expanding consumer choices with such products as caffeine-free Coca-Cola and Fanta Sunny Melon. In the Asia Pacific area, the company developed 35 new brands to satisfy different consumer tastes. In Japan, its Georgia Coffee is drunk by traditional tea drinkers. In Africa and the Middle East, Fanta Strawberry, Fanta Apple, lemon-flavored Limca, and Hi-C juices are big sellers.

The company has vocal and sometimes violent critics in foreign lands. Coca-Cola is a dominant worldwide brand, and its commercial activity cannot be separated from foreign political attitudes about the power and presence of the United States. Like other American companies such as Nike, McDonalds, and Kentucky Fried Chicken, Coca-Cola is a target for critics who are angry

---

[2] The Coca-Cola Company, *Form 10-K Annual Report to the Securities and Exchange Commission, 2000.*

with the United States. For example, hours after the U.S. bombing raids in Afghanistan, demonstrators targeted high-profile American companies, including Coca-Cola. Activist groups complained about "Coca-Colonization" of the planet. In India, the People's War Group blew up the Hindustan Coca-Cola bottling plant and trucks in the Günthur district.[3]

Coca-Cola's top management stumbled diplomatically in Europe in 1999 when Cokes were found contaminated in Belgium. In June 1999 several dozen school children became ill after drinking Coke bottled in an Antwerp plant. They complained of headaches, upset stomachs, nausea, diarrhea, and other maladies. Several days later, more people complained of the same symptoms from drinking Coke bottled in Dunkirk, France. A few were hospitalized, but none died. The company's managers did not deal with the problem with the same skill that they merchandised Coke. Two days passed before the cans containing health risks were publicly identified. Meanwhile, the Belgian government banned the sale of all Coca-Cola drinks, and the European Commission alerted member nations of possible threats to consumers. Douglas Ivester, CEO of the company, was in Paris at the time; but instead of going to Belgium to deal with the situation, he flew home to Atlanta and for several days made no public statements. If Ivester had acted quickly, he might have controlled the flow of events to prevent serious damage to the company's image. He was roundly criticized for his apparent poor diplomacy in the matter.[4]

It did not take long to identify what went wrong. In Belgium, the cause was the misuse of carbon dioxide that put fizz in soft drinks. In France, a few pallets used to transport soft-drink cans had become contaminated with fungicide. Once these problems were resolved, Coca-Cola products were pronounced safe by independent analysts and reappeared on store shelves.[5]

A different hazard occurred in 1999 in Uzbekistan. In the mid-1990s Coca-Cola and Pepsi were battling for supremacy in Uzbekistan, and Coca-Cola emerged the winner. Some thought it might have been due to the marriage of the daughter of the president of Uzbekistan to the president of Coke's bottling company. In July 2001 the two were separated, and the situation of Coke in Uzbekistan deteriorated. Government inspectors questioned employees and searched tax records and other documents at Coke's main plants. They left with the company's computers. It is not clear whether there is a connection between the marital separation and the decline of Coke's fortunes in Uzbekistan.[6]

---

[3] "India: Naxals Blast Coke Plant in Günthur," *The Hindu,* October 22, 2001.
[4] Michael Watkins, Mickey Edwards, and Usha Thakbar, *Winning the Influence Game* (New York: John Wiley & Sons, Inc., 2001), pp. 200–1.
[5] BBC News, "World: Europe, Belgium Ban Coca-Cola," June 14,1999; BBC, "Business: The Company File, European Warning over Coca-Cola," June 16, 1999; and Environment News Service, "Coca-Cola Ban Widens in Europe," June 16, 1999.
[6] Steve LeVine and Betsy McKay, "Coke Finds Mixing Marriage and Business Is Tricky in Tashkent, Daughter of Uzbek President Splits with Bottler, and Now His Firm Is Being Probed," *The Wall Street Journal,* August, 21, 2001, p. A1.

Coca-Cola faces other challenges in foreign countries. In Mexico, the company is trying to stop a plan to levy a 20 percent tax on soft drinks. In Costa Rica, it is battling antitrust allegations that it entered exclusive agreements with retailers to stop competition. If found guilty, it could be fined 10 percent of its annual sales in that country. In Angola, the company battles demands for bribes but refuses to pay them, apparently with some success.[7] In several other African countries, Coca-Cola continues operations despite war conditions.

In 2001 Coca-Cola signed a three-year partnership with UNAIDS, the United Nations agency coordinating activities fighting HIV and AIDS. Coca-Cola will provide multiple services throughout Africa to support AIDS education; distribute preventive measures, such as AIDS testing kits and condoms; and publicize treatment programs. The company's distribution system will extend these services to the far corners of the continent.[8] Natalie Rule, a representative of the company said: "We want to use our infrastructure, our presence in local communities. We want to help in providing our marketing expertise to develop public awareness and information campaigns. And we're looking more internally at our human resources policies in Africa."[9]

The Coca-Cola story illustrates the development, strategy, and unique problems of a large multinational corporation. In this chapter we first define the multinational corporation (MNC), then we examine the power of large MNCs and their critics. This is followed by analysis of relationships between governments and MNCs. Trade protectionism creates problems for MNCs, and that is discussed next. Finally, the chapter closes with a discussion of corruption in business and government transactions.

THE MULTINATIONAL CORPORATION DEFINED

The River Rouge plant of the Ford Motor Company was renowned throughout the world for decades after it was built in the 1920s in Dearborn, Michigan. In one huge complex, the company produced virtually everything needed to manufacture its Model A. Iron ore entered the factory at one end, and a shiny new black Ford car drove out the other end.

A new model of production has replaced this one. It is epitomized in this label attached to an electronic device sold by a U.S. company: "Made in one or more of the following countries: Korea, Hong Kong, Malaysia, Singapore, Taiwan, Thailand, Indonesia, or the Philippines. The exact country of origin is unknown."[10] This is a bit dramatic but makes the

[7] Henri E. Cauvin, "Braving War and Graft, Coke Goes Back to Angola," *The New York Times,* April 22, 2001, sec. 3, p. 1.
[8] John Donnelly, "Activists Hope Firms' Involvement Boosts Battle Against Aids in Africa," *The Boston Globe,* September 4, 2001, p. D1.
[9] Ibid.
[10] Robert J. Eaton, when chairman of DaimlerChrysler, in a speech delivered at the Alfred Herrhausen Society Colloquium in Berlin, Germany, July 2, 1999.

point that today's multinational corporation is a far different enterprise than the typical company of the past.

The MNC is an organization engaged in doing business in foreign countries. It is not always incorporated or private. It can be a cooperative, a private company, or a state-owned entity. Almost every large business today has some direct or indirect involvement with foreign countries, but only when it performs one or more of the functions of designing, producing, marketing, staffing, or financing its products or services for foreign operations does it become truly multinational. Many MNCs progress through the following stages:

1. Exports products to foreign countries.

2. Establishes sales organizations abroad.

3. Licenses use of patents and technology to foreign firms that make and sell the MNC's products.

4. Establishes foreign manufacturing facilities, but important decisions about such matters as product design, marketing, and finance are made at the home office.

5. Gives foreign production facilities substantial autonomy but still reserves some important decisions for the home office.

6. Decentralizes authority throughout the company so that functions at home and abroad are done by executives from different countries.

There are, of course, many models for the operation of companies as they move through these steps. Some companies give foreign subsidiaries substantial authority to make their own decisions. Others prefer to retain important decision making at home. The mix varies considerably. Companies in the later stages noted above have been given different names, such as transnational, global, international, multinational, and worldwide. There is no consensus on the meaning of any of these names, although some observers do distinguish different characteristics among them. For simplicity, we choose to use MNC interchangeably with the others.

Becoming a mature multinational corporation involves much more than rearranging the functions of a business. Managers and staffs who think in global dimensions are found throughout the enterprise. They are sensitive to and comfortable with the thinking of those from different cultures. They search for and accept best practices wherever they are found. Status is determined by merit rather than nationality. These are a few characteristics of what might be called a global mind-set.[11] Today there are not many companies that illustrate this idea, but they are growing in number.

---

[11] For a fuller discussion of this point, see Gail Dutton, "Building a Global Brain," *Management Review*, May 1999.

Some MNCs are said to be stateless or borderless, meaning that if they choose, they can with impunity, move their world headquarters anywhere. This distinction, however, is more theoretical than operational. They are national firms with international operations. Even a company such as Switzerland's Nestlé, although 99 percent of its sales and 89 percent of its assets are outside the home country, is not likely to move its headquarters for many reasons. The common stock ownership and control of the typical MNC remains national rather than international. Most employees at company headquarters are nationals of the home nation. The company keeps its records in the home currency and is subject to its tax and other laws. These ties are part of the culture of the company, which is not easily modified.[12] Finally, each U.S. company must get a charter from a state. The charter grants a company the right to do specific things in defined ways. The authority given can be modified or withdrawn by the state. The state, therefore, has legal authority over the actions of the MNC.[13]

THE SIGNIFICANCE AND POWER OF MNCs

The largest MNCs in the world are ranked in the accompanying tables. Table 12.1 lists companies by size of foreign assets. Table 12.2 ranks them according to their score on the Transnationality Index, or TNA, a measure calculated by the U.N. The U.N. prefers the word *transnational* to *multinational*, and the index is calculated as the average of three ratios: foreign assets to total assets, foreign sales to total sales, and foreign employment to total employment. Each ranking reveals a different dimension of the large MNCs.

The U.N. calculates that there are 60,000 MNCs in the world, and they have 820,000 foreign affiliates.[14] Most of the parent firms of the large MNCs are in a few developed countries (the United States, Japan, and the European Union) called the Triad by the UN. Each of the top five companies in Table 12.1 has larger sales than the GDPs of all but seven of the nations of the world. The largest 500 U.S. MNCs, according to *Forbes*, were responsible for $7 trillion of sales in 2000 and had assets of $12.9 trillion.[15] They directly employed 24.9 million people.

The international operations of these corporations have grown dramatically in recent years. For example, between 1989 and 1975 world foreign direct investment (FDI) averaged about $200 billion a year. But by 2000

[12] Yao-Su Ha, "Global Corporations Are National Firms with International Operations," *California Management Review,* Winter 1992.
[13] Paul N. Doremus, William W. Keller, Louis W. Pauly, and Simon Reich, *The Myth of the Global Corporation* (Princeton, NJ: Princeton University Press, 1998).
[14] United Nations, *World Investment Report 2001. Promoting Linkages* (New York: United Nations, 1999), p. 9.
[15] "Forbes 500," *Forbes,* April 16, 2001, p. 238.

TABLE 12.1   The World's 10 Largest Transnational Corporations, Ranked by Foreign Assets, 1999 (billions of dollars and number of employees)

Source: United Nations, *World Investment Report 2001*, p. 90. Reprinted with permission.

Corporation	Country	Industry	Assets		Sales		Employment	
			Foreign	Total	Foreign	Total	Foreign	Total
General Electric	United States	Electronics	141.1	405.2	32.7	111.6	143,000	310,000
Exxon Mobil Corporation	United States	Petroleum expl./ref./distr.	99.4	144.5	115.5	160.9	68,000	107,000
Royal Dutch/ Shell Group	The Netherlands/ United Kingdom	Petroleum expl./ref./distr.	68.7	113.9	53.5	105.4	57,367	99,310
General Motors	United States	Motor vehicles	68.5	274.7	46.5	176.6	162,300	398,000
Ford Motor Company	United States	Motor vehicles	—	273.4	50.1	162.6	191,486	364,550
Toyota Motor Corporation	Japan	Motor vehicles	56.3	154.9	60.0	119.7	13,500	214,631
Daimler- Chrysler AG	Germany	Motor vehicles	55.7	175.9	122.4	151.0	225,705	466,938
TotalFina SA	France	Petroleum expl./ref./distr.	—	77.6	31.6	39.6	50,538	74,437
IBM	United States	Computers	44.7	87.5	50.4	87.6	161,612	307,401
BP	United Kingdom	Petroleum expl./ref./distr.	39.3	52.6	57.7	83.5	62,150	80,400

TABLE 12.2   The World's 10 Largest Corporations in Terms of Transnationality, 1999

Source: UNCTAD/Erasmus University database. Adapted from United Nations, *World Investment Report 2001*, p. 101. Reprinted with permission.

Ranking 1999 by					
TNI*	Foreign assets	Corporation	Country	Industry	TNI
1	57	Thomson Corporation	Canada	Media/publishing	95.4
2	11	Nestlé SA	Switzerland	Food/beverages	95.2
3	21	ABB	Switzerland	Electrical equipment	94.1
4	80	Electrolux AB	Sweden	Electrical equipment/electronics	93.2
5	59	Holcim (ex Holderbank)	Switzerland	Construction materials	91.8
6	27	Roche Group	Switzerland	Pharmaceuticals	91.5
7	35	British American Tobacco Plc	United Kingdom	Food/tobacco	90.7
8	24	Unilever	United Kingdom/ The Netherlands	Food/beverages	89.3
9	23	Seagram Company	Canada	Beverages/media	88.6
10	75	Akzo Nobel NV	Netherlands	Chemicals	82.6

*TNI is the abbreviation for "transnationality index," which is calculated as the average of three ratios: foreign assets to total assets, foreign sales to total sales and foreign employment to total employment.

this had jumped to $1.3 trillion.[16] Cross-border mergers and acquisitions accounted for most of the FDI. Most of the FDI flowed between developed countries, with the greatest amounts moving between the United States, the European Union, and Japan. This group was responsible for 71 percent of world inflows and 82 percent of outflows in 2000. The 49 least developed countries got only 0.3 percent of the FDI inflows. The U.N. estimated that 91.6 percent of total FDI outflow went to developed countries in 1998. Only 8.1 percent went to the developing countries. The remainder went to central and eastern Europe.[17] Although this investment in developing nations was not a large piece of the world's total outflow of FDI in 1998 (estimated at $649 billion and raised to $800 billion in 1999), it strongly promoted their economic growth. The largest inflow of FDI to the United States came from Europe, especially the United Kingdom. The largest outflow from the United States went to Europe.

The economic and political clout of the MNCs is not defined solely by these numbers. They have other powers. For example, they can move their foreign assets around to favor some countries at the expense of others. They can "persuade" a country's leaders to adopt policies favorable to them by increasing or decreasing their investments, employees, and use of technology in the country. Professor Thomas Donaldson of Georgetown University correctly observes that "with the exception of a handful of nation-states, multinationals are alone in possessing the size, technology, and economic reach necessary to influence human affairs on a global basis."[18] Supporters of the MNCs see them as constructive forces bringing poorer nations new technology, new products at low cost, new jobs and income, and financial investments. Critics have a very different view.

Critics of MNC Power

Critics of MNCs range from host governments to organized activist groups. Among the latter are well-known groups such as Ralph Nader's organizations, the Sierra Club, Greenpeace, and Friends of the Earth. These groups have worldwide influence, and the Internet has been of enormous help to them in strengthening it. The Internet has provided virtually instantaneous communication with a vast audience at very little cost. It is much easier than in the past for them to form coalitions across national boundaries to pressure MNCs to meet their demands.

---

[16] Foreign direct investment is the acquisition of physical assets by an MNC in a foreign country to be controlled by the acquiring enterprise. An investor must have 10 percent of the equity in a facility before the U.S. Department of Commerce acknowledges control and concludes it is an FDI. Data cited from *World Investment Report,* p. 291.

[17] *World Investment Report 1999,* p. 20.

[18] Thomas Donaldson, *The Ethics of International Business* (New York: Oxford University Press, 1989), p. 31.

For instance, the organization of thousands of demonstrators from all over the world at the meeting of the World Trade Organization (WTO) in Seattle in December 2000 was significantly helped by the Internet.

Critics see MNCs as powerful despoilers of the ecological, political, and social systems where they operate. As one critic observes: "In effect, what has taken place is a massive shift in power, out of the hands of nation-states and democratic governments and into the hands of MNCs and banks. It is now the MNCs that effectively govern the lives of the vast majority of the people on Earth."[19] Critics see the MNCs as greedy global bullies interested only in profits and detached from human interests. Some see the MNCs as more powerful than nation-states.

Even friends of MNCs have concerns about their power. For example, Jeffrey E. Garten, dean of the Yale School of Management and staunch defender of business, wrote: "The big problem with these gigantic mergers [he had in mind some huge mergers in recent years, such as Daimler and Chrysler, British Petroleum and Amoco, Exxon and Mobil] is the growing imbalance between public and private power in our society."[20]

Critics of MNCs have been effective in influencing corporations around the world to meet their demands. For example, they pressured corporations to get out of South Africa when that nation was practicing apartheid and to get out of Myanmar because of the human rights abuses of that government. Many companies responded and left these countries. Demonstrations of activists have forced changed policies of many companies, such as Royal Dutch/Shell, Monsanto, Nike, and McDonald's. A major impact of these activist groups has been to pressure MNCs to develop codes of ethics and social responsibility and to accept codes prepared by others, as described in Chapters 4 and 5.

CONFLICTS BETWEEN GOVERNMENT AND MNC OBJECTIVES

Following is a list of the fundamental goals of MNCs and host governments. These will vary in importance, of course, between countries and MNCs. It is clear from the list that sometimes the goals of MNCs can conflict with the goals of nations.

Fundamental Goals of MNCs

The fundamental motive of going abroad is, of course, profit. Besides making a satisfactory profit, the typical large MNC may also have in mind many goals. For example, it may want to

[19] Tony Clark, "Mechanisms of Corporate Rule," in Jerry Mander and Edward Goldsmith, eds., *The Case Against the Global Economy* (San Francisco: Sierra Club Books, 1996), chap. 26. This book presents a detailed statement of the many specific criticisms leveled at MNCs.
[20] Jeffrey E. Garten, "Megamergers Are a Clear and Present Danger," *Business Week,* January 25, 1999.

- Manufacture in those countries where it finds the greatest competitive advantage.
- Buy and sell anywhere in the world to take advantage of the most favorable price to the company.
- Take advantage throughout the world of changes in labor costs, productivity, trade agreements, and currency fluctuations.
- Expand or contract based on worldwide competitive advantages.
- Obtain a high and rising return on invested capital.
- Achieve greater sales.
- Hold risks within reasonable limits in relation to profits.
- Maintain and improve technological and other company strengths.
- Maintain control of important decisions.
- Encounter fewer barriers in host countries.

Fundamental Goals of Host Governments

Individual countries have different goals they wish to achieve. Their differences are wider than variations of goals of individual MNCs. However, most countries, developed and less developed, want to

- Achieve economic growth.
- Achieve full employment of people and resources.
- Improve managerial and worker skills.
- Maintain price stability.
- Develop a favorable balance of trade.
- Achieve a more equitable distribution of income among the population.
- Retain a fair share of profits made by MNCs in their country.
- Improve technological development.
- Improve worker productivity.
- Increase local ownership of the means of production.
- Retain hegemony over the economic system.
- Control national security decisions.
- Develop and maintain social and political stability.
- Advance the quality of life of the people of the country.
- Protect the nation's physical environment.

MNCs have been and can be of enormous help to governments trying to achieve most of these goals, especially the economic ones. Of course, many critics do not accept this view. From either perspective, it is clear that conflicts between the two sets of goals are inevitable.

MNCs AND LESS DEVELOPED COUNTRIES (LDCs)

Relationships between MNCs and LDCs have changed dramatically during the past two decades. Former resentments and deep suspicion have given way to the welcome mat as the LDCs have seen the benefits that infusion of MNC capital and technology bring to their and other countries. Indeed, LDCs offer generous inducements to MNCs to place plants in their countries. Included are tax holidays, exemptions from import duties, construction of infrastructure, low-interest loans, cheap labor, and relaxation of environmental restrictions. Rubens Ricupero, the secretary-general, United Nations Conference on Trade and Development, said, "all countries in the world, with no exceptions that I know of, are trying to attract foreign direct investment, which is an important condition for development."[21] For example, Ford was offered a package of free land, lower taxes, and infrastructure worth about $300 million to build a plant outside Salvador, Brazil. In return, Ford was expected to provide 5,000 jobs and to jump-start industrialization of the area.[22] Indonesia exempts exporters from its value-added tax to encourage local affiliates of foreign-owned MNCs. Some countries have established official agencies to help MNCs in their development of affiliates. Examples are the Economic Development Board of Singapore, the Welsh Development Agency of Wales, and the National Linkage Programme of Ireland. The latter was established in 1998 to help foreign MNCs match their sourcing requirements with local companies. Many LDCs today have similar government organizations that work in partnership with private enterprises at home and abroad to facilitate FDI.[23]

Such positive efforts to induce FDI inflows do not mean, of course, that there is universal harmony between the goals of MNCs and host governments. Both have serious complaints. For example, many LDCs seethe with resentment at their obligation to give up some power and independence in exchange for the wealth an MNC may bring. They complain they are struggling to meet standards agreed upon as members of the World Trade Organization concerning such issues as working conditions,

[21] Transcript of press conference by Kofi Annan and leadership of the International Chamber of Commerce, July 7, 1999, M2 Communications, Ltd.
[22] Chris Kraul, "Brazil Debates High Cost of Car Plant in Poor State," *Los Angeles Times*, December 5, 1999, p. C1.
[23] *World Investment Report*, pp. 141–52.

human rights, unions, tariffs, finance, and environment. They believe such standards have benefited the wealthy nations more than the LDCs. They want reductions of agricultural tariffs in developed countries to admit more of their exports. Many of them depend upon exports of textiles and want advanced countries to reduce tariffs on such products. They want cheaper medicines and the right to reproduce or buy them at lower costs, despite patents, to alleviate urgent medical problems. They see disadvantages to inviting into their country powerful foreign companies whose policies are determined by a group of managers in the far-off home country. The strength of these firms sometimes overpowers smaller local companies that cannot compete with them. Some LDCs deplore the social values that an MNC may bring and watch with anger when those values change the culture of their society.

On the other hand, the MNCs claim there are many prized assets they can bring to a country. For example, they

- Provide employment.

- Improve technical skills of workers and managers.

- Provide products and services that raise the standard of living.

- Introduce and develop new technology and technical skills.

- Provide greater access to international markets.

- Raise the gross national product.

- Increase productivity.

- Help build foreign exchange reserves.

- Encourage the development of new industries.

- Assume investment risk for projects that might not otherwise be undertaken.

In many countries, there is a love-hate relationship with MNCs. Even in the developed countries this is present. In France, for instance, there is widespread resistance to American influences that range from ubiquitous use of the English language to the introduction of genetically engineered foods. A poll taken in France revealed that 12 percent of the people said they admired the United States, 46 percent either were critical of or worried by it, and 75 percent wanted less American influence on "economic and financial globalization."[24] Yet they devour McDonald's hamburgers and enjoy Hollywood movies.

---

[24] "The force of globalisation is a fact of modern life, French leaders accept. But they feel it needs to be kept in check," *The Economist,* August 4, 2001, p. 43.

MNC managers have their own litany of complaints. For example, the International Finance Corporation, an affiliate of the World Bank, polled 3,685 managers from 69 countries about 15 obstacles they encountered doing business in different regions of the world. There were variations, of course, between countries and regions, but most managers said these were the dominant obstacles in LDCs: poor infrastructure, corruption, crime and theft, inflation, and taxes.[25]

MNCs AND INDUSTRIALIZED NATIONS

LDCs are not alone in seeking advantages offered by MNCs. For example, California, Tennessee, and other states brought in Japanese automobile plants with various inducements. European countries have offered inducements to semiconductor companies to locate there. This has existed for years in the developed countries. Indeed, it was the inducement of capital from England in the 1800s that helped build the railroad system in the United States.

Industrialized countries may impose barriers of various types that disgruntle foreign investors. For example, foreign company investments in the United States are restricted in many areas: national defense, nuclear energy, coastal shipping, and broadcasting. Industrial countries also impose barriers to protect some industries from foreign competition. Examples are automobile companies in the 1980s, peanuts, and steel. Foreign managers, like those in the United States, chafe at government rules they must obey. All business managers have a long litany of complaints about government regulations.

U.S. MNC–Government Relations

A policy of the United States for many decades has been, and still is, to foster worldwide economic progress. The government has always viewed the MNC as an instrument of this global development effort. Sometimes, however, the goals of MNCs and U.S. foreign policy conflict. In addition, as noted in Chapters 9 and 10, corporations based in the United States have strong complaints about regulatory restrictions.

While the basic business–government relationship can be adversarial, there is still plenty of cooperation between MNCs and government agencies. Remember, too, there are thousands of lobbyists in Washington and state capitals who successfully pressure government to favor the interests of the companies and industries they represent.

Examples of specific aids to the MNCs provided by governments abound. Substantial subsidies are made to encourage agricultural exports, and special measures help companies that explore for scarce resources,

---

[25] Aymo Brunetti, Gregory Kisunko, and Beatrice Weder, *How Businesses See Government,* Discussion Paper 33 (Washington, DC: World Bank, 1998).

such as oil. The government provides abundant information without cost about foreign business opportunities. The Export-Import Bank, created in 1934, is a government-owned corporation that promotes U.S. foreign trade in the form of direct and guaranteed loans to foreign buyers of U.S. export products. The U.S. Trade Representative stands ready to negotiate with foreign countries for agreements that benefit U.S. exporters.

The federal government, on the other hand, also restrains MNCs. For instance, the Clinton administration, because of tensions with China over human rights, told the Export-Import Bank it should not help American MNCs participate in China's mammoth $30 billion Three Gorges dam project. For national security reasons, U.S. manufacturers of sophisticated electronics equipment are forbidden to sell these products abroad. The United States has invoked economic sanctions for many countries that, of course, limit U.S. export business with them.

Raymond Vernon, a prominent scholar of the MNC and professor at Harvard University, sees increasing conflict in the future between MNCs and their home governments. He writes: "My concern . . . is that some of the most important political struggles which multinational enterprises face in the future will originate within the home countries of the multinationals."[26] He predicts heightened conflict between those who advocate free markets and those who feel disadvantaged by the MNCs. That is happening now. For instance, labor unions attack the MNCs for exporting jobs. Activist critics, such as Ralph Nader, denounce MNCs, alleging that in foreign operations they abuse human rights, exploit workers, pollute, and in general fail to act responsibly. These groups are becoming more vocal and organized in their attacks. On the other hand are groups that believe the world will benefit from free markets left to operate comparatively unfettered.

MNC–Government Relations in Other Industrialized Countries

The United States is not the only country encouraging or inhibiting home-based MNCs. A good illustration is Europe's Airbus Industries four-nation consortium. Since 1970 this group has received billions of dollars in government aid to finance the development of commercial airliners. The consortium was formed and supported by France, Great Britain, Germany, and Spain as a direct challenge to American dominance in the civilian jet airliner business. It has worked. At the time Airbus was started, three U.S. companies (Boeing, Lockheed, and McDonnell Douglas) dominated the world's commercial jet market. Airbus today has captured a large piece of the market and is a strong challenger to Boeing, the only current U.S. producer of these airplanes.

[26] Raymond Vernon, *In the Hurricane's Eye* (Cambridge, MA: Harvard University Press, 1998), p. 109.

The relationships between business and government in European countries are much more cooperative than in the United States, except Great Britain, where the link is similar to that in the United States. The French government owns a number of large companies. In countries such as the Netherlands, Sweden, Norway, and Denmark, there are close relationships between government and large companies. There are intimate relationships between large companies and the Japanese government. The government there is deeply involved in helping Japanese companies penetrate foreign markets and protect their turf at home from foreign competition. In China, South Korea, and in many countries in Southeast Asia, the relationship is very close, with companies owned and operated by officers in the military (as in China) or by family members (as in Indonesia).

FREE TRADE VERSUS PROTECTIONISM

Free trade has been the policy throughout most of the history of the United States. However, there have been significant deviations from that policy. In recent years, the United States has taken the lead in creating international agencies to advance free trade throughout the world. At the same time, protectionist pressures have increased in the United States and in most other nations. Why free trade? Why protectionism?

Why Free Trade?

The case for free trade is comparatively simple. By virtue of climate, labor conditions, raw materials, capital, management, or other considerations, some nations have an advantage over others in the production of particular goods. For example, Brazil can produce coffee beans at a much lower cost than the United States. Coffee beans could be grown in hothouses in the United States, but not at a price equal to that which Brazilians can charge and make a profit. But the United States has a distinct advantage over Brazil in producing computers. Resources will be used most efficiently when each country produces that for which it enjoys a cost advantage. Gain will be maximized when each nation specializes in producing those products for which it has the greatest economic edge. This is what economists call the *law of comparative advantage*. It follows that maximum gain on a worldwide basis will be realized if there are no impediments to trade, if there is free competition in pricing, and if capital flows are unrestricted.

It is not always easy, however, to see just where a nation has a comparative advantage. At the extremes the case is clear, but not in the middle range. Differences in monetary units, rates of productivity of capital and labor, changes in markets, or elasticities of demand, for instance, obscure the degree of advantage one nation may have over another at any time. Nevertheless, it is argued that free trade will stimulate competition, reward individual initiative, increase productivity, and improve national well-being. It will enlarge job opportunities and produce for consumers a wider variety of goods and services at minimum prices and with higher quality.

This is the theory. In practice, all countries have erected restraints on imports to protect their industries. We now discuss pressures for and against free trade around the world.

The United States Moves toward Free Trade

Because of international negotiations, global trade is far freer and more open and efficient that in years past, leading to an extraordinary leap in world trade, as shown in Figure 12.1. A significant milestone in world trade was the ratification of the General Agreement on Tariffs and Trade (GATT) in 1947 among the nations of the world to begin negotiations to lower tariffs. A series of so-called rounds, eight in all, took place, and each resulted in reductions of trade barriers. The last round reduced tariff barriers by more than 30 percent overall and by a higher percentage among highly industrialized countries. For some items (e.g., some pharmaceuticals, construction equipment, and paper) tariffs were eliminated.

FIGURE 12.1   **World Merchandise Trade by Major Product Group**

Source: *World Trade Statistics,* WTO, 2001.

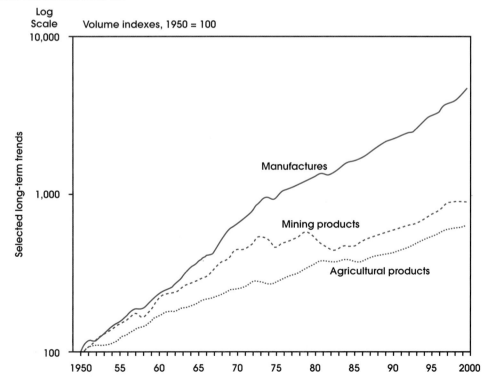

The participants in the last Round agreed that a faster method of tariff negotiations than GATT was essential, and as a result, they approved a new dispute settlement process to be known as the World Trade Organization (WTO) and located in Geneva, Switzerland. Since its formation in 1995, the United States and other nations have used the WTO dispute settlement procedure to resolve trade questions. The United States has formulated and carried out with other nations many treaties, tariff eliminations, and tariff reductions. For example, a milestone was reached in U.S. trade policy with the creation of the Canada–United States Free Trade agreement signed in 1987. Another significant step in free trade was made in 1992 when the United States, Canada, and Mexico signed the North American Free Trade Agreement (NAFTA). Area free trade agreements are being formed around the world. The most important one, in terms of scope, is the European Union (EU). These treaties will be discussed in detail in the next chapter.

Pressures for Protectionism

Most domestic businesses, whether engaged in foreign trade or not, feel pressures from foreign competitors with better products and lower prices. Many seek and get protection from the government. This is protectionism, and it exists in the trade history of all nations.

In the early history of the United States, the motivation for protectionism was to protect infant industries. Recently, there have been powerful pressures on government to protect some mature industries (e.g., automobiles, steel, textiles) from foreign competition. Here are three justifications often given for protectionist measures.

First, the United States has large trade deficits that must be reduced. In 1975 the United States enjoyed a small trade surplus (the difference between total exports and total imports of goods and services). Each year since there have been large annual deficits. In 1999 total exports were $1.033 trillion, imports were $1.355 trillion, and the deficit was $322 billion. Protectionists are concerned about the persistence and size of these deficits, believing they are detrimental to the United States and should be corrected. One way, they assert, is to discourage excessive imports and encourage more exports.

Second, protectionists want to shield industries from "unfair" foreign competition. For example, foreign competitors have penetrated the U.S. market with products such as textiles, steel, shoes, motorcycles, dolls, luggage, automobiles, and television sets. A significant result, say protectionists, is loss of jobs.

Third, unfair trade barriers in foreign countries restrict American imports. Examples are nontariff barriers such as excessive and delayed inspection of imported products; unreasonable requirements for products to meet technical standards for product characteristics, such as size, quality, health, and safety; customs and practices that inhibit consumer purchases of foreign goods and services; and quotas. These practices cost American jobs and should be stopped or retaliated against.

The Politics of Protectionism

President Bush has said often that expanding free trade is one of his highest priorities. In a speech before the Council of the Americas, he said: "When we negotiate for open markets we are providing new hope for the world's poor . . . and when we promote open trade we are promoting political freedom."[27] Why then did he support substantial restrictions on imports of steel in his first major trade initiative? His staff explained that the decision followed a thorough examination of the problems of the steel industry and help was justified. For example, the industry today employs one-fifth the number of steelworkers it did in 1980, production has slumped, steel mills have closed, and the financial strength of the industry has weakened. This is a result, the industry claims, of lower-priced imports from many different countries. Another reason for the president's decision is that the industry and its unions have political strength. They are major financial contributors to political campaigns, and their workers' votes can spell the difference between election and defeat in several critical electoral states where steelworkers are concentrated, such as Pennsylvania, Ohio, and West Virginia. The administration brought the steel issue before the International Trade Commission, and the Commission sided with the industry in a decision in late 2001. The president has until the summer of 2002 to decide import restrictions, and creditable observers believe they will be substantial.[28] The political calculus concerning other import restrictions on such products as sugar, peanuts, motorcycles, and textiles varies from case to case.

Free Trader Responses to Protectionists

Free traders advance many arguments against protectionism. One main argument, of course, is the logic for free trade. Another is that the exceptional rise in world trade, as shown in Figure 12.1, is due in no small degree to lowered tariff barriers throughout the world negotiated in the GATT rounds. Senator Phil Gramm argues that impediments or hindrances to free trade are "immoral." "They limit my freedom," he said. "If I want to buy a shirt in China, who has the right to tell me as a free person that I can't do it?"[29]

---

[27] Reported by Joseph Kahn, "Bush Moves against Steel Imports; Trade Tensions Are Likely to Rise," *The New York Times,* June 6, 2001, p. 1.

[28] Joseph Kahn, "Trade Panel Backs Steel Makers, Enabling Broad Sanctions," *The New York Times,* October 23, 2001, p. 1.

[29] Reported by Gerald F. Seib and John Harwood, "Disparate Groups on Right Join Forces to Make Opposition to China's Trade Status a Key Issue," *The Wall Street Journal,* June 10, 1997, p. A20.

Laura D'Andrea Tyson, former chair of the President's Council of Economic Advisers, takes issue with those advocating protectionism to reduce deficits. She says the dire implications advanced by people concerned about the deficits are overstated. While large, the deficits are only a little more than 1 percent of U.S. GDP. Furthermore, about 40 percent of U.S. imports are intracompany transactions of American MNCs.[30]

U.S. Deviation from Free Trade Policy

Despite strong free trade rhetoric and the steady lowering of tariff and other trade barriers, the United States protects industries from foreign competition. Over the years, it has raised tariffs, imposed quotas, and prohibited the import of various products. There are hundreds of examples of deviation from free trade theory and policy that have added to the crazy quilt of world trade impediments. Here are some examples.

Trade records are marbled with "buy American" laws. The Federal Buy American Act of 1933, still in force, requires federal agencies to pay up to a 6 percent differential for domestically produced goods. Many states have similar laws covering a wide range of products. The Merchant Marine Act prohibits foreign vessels from plying domestic waterways. The Passenger Vessel Services Act requires ships going from one U.S. port to another to be U.S. flagged, U.S. built, and U.S. crewed.

U.S. tariffs have declined significantly in recent years, but there are many exceptions. For example, we have high tariffs on imports of sugar, peanuts, certain types of glassware, textiles, motorcycles, and steel. At the same time, we have given duty-free status to hundreds of products under a Generalized System of Preferences (GSP). The purpose of this system is to foster economic development for many LDCs by increasing their trade with the United States. While the total value of products involved is not great in terms of total U.S. trade, it can be very important to developing countries.[31]

The hodgepodge of quotas has fostered strange movements of international trade. For example, textile and clothing manufacturers have created complex systems to evade quotas. Esquel, a family-owned business in Hong Kong, is the largest men's cotton shirt manufacturer in the world, with annual sales of about $500 million and 43,000 employees. The company was shipping 12 million garments a year from plants in China when the United States and the EU put quotas on Chinese exports of these items. So, Esquel moved to Penang, Malaysia. Soon, quotas were placed on shipments from that country. The company then built plants in Sri Lanka.[32] This type of cat-and-mouse game is being played with many foreign producers.

---

[30] Laura D'Andrea Tyson, "Trade Deficits Won't Ruin Us," *The New York Times,* November 24, 1997.
[31] General Accounting Office, *International Trade, Comparison of U.S. and European Union Preference Programs* (Washington, DC: General Accounting Office, June 2001).
[32] Andrew Tanzer, "The Great Quota Hustle," *Forbes,* March 6, 2000.

Compared with the total trade of the United States, such restraints are not significant. Barriers imposed on U.S. imports by major trading partners are relatively much more important. Briefly, here are illustrative barriers on imports in Japan, Europe, and China.[33]

Japanese Trade Barriers

Japan is the third-largest export market for U.S. products. Total merchandise exports to Japan in 2000 were $81 billion, and U.S. imports from Japan were $147 billion, creating a sizable deficit. Part of the reason for the deficit was barriers established in Japan against imports. In recent years, under pressure from the United States and other nations, Japan has reduced tariff and quota restrictions. However, there remain formidable import barriers.

While Japan has reduced tariffs and quotas on some agricultural products, importers still face a set of high and complex barriers. Tariffs ranging from 10 percent to 40 percent exist for products such as beef, oranges, apples, ice cream, citrus fruit juices, and tomatoes. Rice imports are restricted through a quota system. Even comparatively small imports of rice are either blended with Japanese domestically grown rice or exported as food aid. In either case, Japanese consumers have little opportunity to taste higher-quality and lower-priced rice from the United States. Fresh potatoes from the United States are banned on the grounds that they may carry a disease called potato wart. Fresh apples from the United States must go through quarantine to prevent transmission of fire blight.

Japan has many nontariff barriers, for example, paperwork that delays moving imports to consumers. The story of the flat glass industry provides another example. The flat glass industry in the United States has tried for years to penetrate the Japanese market with no success. Even with what appeared to be firm commitments made in the U.S.–Japan Flat Glass Agreement to permit foreign flat glass sales in Japan, total foreign glass imports have been only about 7 percent of the market. The main reason is that the industry is dominated by three companies—Asahi Flat Glass (with 40 percent of the market), Nippon Sheet (with about 30 percent), and Central Glass (with about 20 percent). These three companies act in unison with respect to price, deliveries, purchasing quotas, and other restraints. One major restraint is the power they exercise over the market that makes users reluctant to buy outside this oligopoly. In testimony before Congress, a vice president of Guardian Industries Corporation, a U.S. company that for years tried to penetrate the market, said: "Foreign suppliers clearly are not part of the club. Any distributors tempted to purchase imported glass are pressured in a variety of ways, including threats that their domestic sources of supply would be cut off."[34]

---

[33] The following on trade barriers in Japan, the European Union, and the People's Republic of China were derived from the U.S. Trade Representative (www.ustr.gov) unless otherwise specified.
[34] Testimony of Peter S. Walters before the House Ways and Means Trade Subcommittee, U.S. House of Representatives, July 15, 1998.

European Union Trade Barriers

The EU and the United States share the largest two-way trade and investment relationship in the world. In 2000 the U.S. merchandise exports to the 15 members of the EU were $164.8 billion. U.S. imports from the EU were $220.4, recording a sizable deficit of $55.6 billion. Importers into the EU face many restrictions imposed by the European Commission that apply to all member-nations. The EU is moving steadily to harmonize the regulations of members, but many differences persist in areas of trade, investment, intellectual property, services, and laws.

An example is treatment of genetically modified food and crops. Austria, Luxembourg, and Italy impose marketing bans on some genentically engineered products despite EU approval of them. U.S. exports of corn to Spain and Portugal have stopped. Italy suspended import of four genentically engineered corn varieties already authorized for sale in processed foods. The EU prohibits antimicrobial treatments in poultry imported from the United States. As in other nations, the EU and member-states have varying testing, labeling, and certification requirements for imports. For instance, in France a veterinary certificate is required for pet foods. Greece has its own standards for processed meat and other foods. Finland has unique standards for navigation lights on recreational craft. Member-states differ concerning intellectual property protection. Banking and investment regulations vary among the nations. Some European countries are touchy about wines, and there are EU regulations protecting domestic wine growers. The regulations permit only importation of those wines produced in conformance with oenological practices authorized for the production of EU wines. The EU member-states heavily subsidize agriculture and protect a range of other industries from foreign competition.

The People's Republic of China

The U.S. trade deficit with China reached $83.8 billion in 2000. U.S. merchandise exports were $16.3 billion, and U.S. imports from China were $100.1 billion, up 22.4 percent from 1999. It is the eleventh largest export market for U.S. products. China has far more stringent controls than any nation. Overall tariffs on imports, however, have fallen from 42 percent in 1996 to about 17 percent today. Nontariff barriers have gradually been reduced, but they are still formidable. In anticipation of its membership in the WTO, the government has recently undertaken extensive modification of its laws to be consistent with WTO regulations. There has been widespread resistance to many reforms by provincial and local governments, especially measures that would reduce protection of their local enterprises. Here are a few examples of the network of trade rules in China.

Tariffs are high on many products—for wine and spirits (65 percent), motorcycles (60 percent), raisins (40 percent), canned fruits (from 25 to

30 percent), potato and potato products (13 to 45 percent), and some motor vehicles (100 percent or more). On the other hand, tariffs are very low or nonexistent for other products, such as high-tech electronics, considered necessary for the development of key industries.

Importers face hundreds of formidable nontariff barriers. For example, there are quotas for more than 40 categories of commodities, such as watches, automobiles, fertilizers, steel, and textiles. Demanding regulations concerning quarantines, inspection requirements, product standards, and import approvals frustrate importers. It is often difficult for importers to find out precisely what are the inspection requirements for their products, and different standards for the same product vary among ports of entry.

Classical Free Trade Theory Versus Reality

The reality is that the global economy is a mixture of free trade and protectionism. It always has been. Furthermore, classical free trade theory based on comparative advantage, explained above, has lost much validity for a large part of world trade. Many of the assumptions of the seventeenth and eighteenth centuries, upon which the theory is based, no longer are valid in today's world.

Professor Michael Porter of the Harvard Business School has formulated a major modification to classical theory to fit the modern world. He calls it *competitive advantage of nations.* Porter asks: Why does a nation achieve global superiority in one industry? He answers that it is because "industrial clusters" are formed in the nation. These clusters are composed of firms and industries that are mutually supporting, innovative, competitive, low-cost producers, and committed to meeting demanding consumer tastes.

Why is it, he asks, that Switzerland, a landlocked country with few natural resources, is a world leader in the production of chocolates? Why is it that Italy is a world leader in producing quality shoes? Why is it that Japan, a country whose economy was in shambles after World War II, is a global leader in making low-cost, mass-produced, quality, high-technology products?

Porter's answer lies in a congeries of factors that go beyond natural resources. Among the factors are a sizable demand from sophisticated consumers, an educated and skilled workforce, intense competition in the industry, and the existence of related and supporting suppliers. Government plays a part, but not a major one. Porter's theory is convincingly and amply illustrated in a major research project on the subject.[35] Classical theory is still valid for many products. However, Porter's work modernizes it to better fit the current reality of trade among nations in a vast range of products.

---

[35] Michael E. Porter, *The Comparative Advantage of Nations* (New York: Free Press, 1990).

Classical economic doctrine postulates that when industries are granted relief from foreign competition, they fail to make needed capital investments, grow lazy, forget product quality, lose incentives, fail to innovate, raise prices, and enjoy excess profits from captive markets. Recent experiences in five protected industries in the United States contradict this theory. Indeed, relief from predatory foreign trade practices in the automobile, steel, textile, semiconductor, and machine tool industries has produced just the reverse results. In each of these industries, foreign competitive practices have had serious adverse impacts. But in each case, federal protective measures from foreign imports have had remarkably beneficial results.[36]

The experience in these industries does not mean, of course, that protectionism is a good policy. It means, rather, that a government can help an industry recover from predatory foreign trade when it chooses the appropriate means, on a limited scale, for a limited period of time, for a few industries, and for the right reasons. Free trade should be the policy, but with some exceptions.

CORRUPTION IN BUSINESS AND GOVERNMENT TRANSACTIONS

Cultural differences, practices, and laws among the many countries where MNCs do business create extremely difficult moral, ethical, and legal problems for MNCs. The way in which business is conducted around the world sometimes entangles U.S. companies in a complex web of influence, politics, customs, and subtle business arrangements. Companies have found in many LDCs, and even in some highly industrialized countries, that to do business it is necessary to make a variety of payments. This is not new. It has been going on for centuries. What is new is the widespread and often intense publicity given to instances of corruption involving high government officials. In today's age of instantaneous communications and investigative journalism, it is much more difficult to keep corruption out of the limelight.

For example, public attention was riveted on a series of reports of corruption at the top levels of governments and corporations in the 1970s. The Watergate scandals of the Nixon administration led to the resignation of the president. Among corrupt practices discovered were widespread illegal contributions of corporations to the administration's political fund-raising. Public attention a few years later was directed to a series of payoffs to foreign public officials to capture aircraft contracts. One was an illicit payment of $25 million by the Lockheed Aircraft Corporation to Prime Minister Kakuei Tanaka of Japan, which led to Tanaka's criminal conviction. At the same time, a high-level party official

---

[36] Alan Tonelson, "Beating Back Predatory Trade," *Foreign Affairs*, July–August 1994.

in South Korea threatened the $300 million refinery investment of Gulf Oil Corporation if Bob Dorsey, CEO of Gulf, did not make a contribution of $10 million to the party. Dorsey haggled the threat down to $3 million.[37] Such incidents revealed a need for new laws and corporate codes of conduct to deal with such corruption.

Transparency International (TI), organized in Berlin, Germany, in 1993, is an organization on a mission to fight international corruption. Since 1996 TI has published periodically a "corruption perceptions index" for individual countries. The 2001 index for the 10 least corrupt and the 10 most corrupt from a total of 91 countries is shown in Table 12.3. The index for each country is based on a poll of subjective assessments of managers, academics, and analysis.[38] There are many weaknesses in this methodology, but the indexes do reflect opinions of competent observers on important, but not all, types of corruption. When the 2001 index was issued, Peter Eigen, chair of Transparency International, concluded: "There is no end in sight to the misuse of power by those in public office—and corruption levels are perceived to be as high as ever in both the developed and developing worlds."[39]

What Is Corruption?

There is no consensus about a definition of corruption; there is more agreement about types of corruption. At one end of a spectrum is what might be called petty corruption or "grease" payments. These are bribes involving small amounts of money made to facilitate action by a low-level employee. They range from tips for services rendered to "requests" for money to get someone to do their regular duties, such as unloading articles off ships or clearing incoming products through customs. These small bribes are often called "lubrication bribes," "honest graft," "tokens of appreciation," "contributions," and so on. The practice is accepted around the world as legitimate for services rendered. These payments are often justified as offsets to low salaries in foreign countries. At the other end of the spectrum are extortion and outrageous bribery. This type of corruption is illustrated by the involvement of high-level political office holders in a country. Examples are the cases of Lockheed and Gulf Oil Corporation noted above. Paying a top-level official to help a company win a contract would also be at this end of the spectrum.

Between the extremes are a variety of payoffs where the lines of demarcation between the legitimate and unethical are not always clear.

[37] Peter Nehemkis, "Business Payoffs Abroad: Rhetoric and Reality," *California Management Review,* Winter 1975. See also, Neil H. Jacoby, Peter Nehemkis, and Richard Eells, *Bribery and Extortion in World Business* (New York: Macmillan, 1977).
[38] "The Corruption Perception Index 2001," June 17, 2001, Paris, France, www.transparency.org/documents/cpi/2001/cpi2001.html.
[39] Ibid.

TABLE 12.3
The Corruption Perceptions Index 2001

Source: Transparency International, "New Index Highlights Worldwide Corruption Crisis," Paris, June 27, 2001, www.transparency. org/documents/cpi/2001/ cpi2001.html. Copyright Transparency International. Reprinted with permission.

10 Highest		10 Lowest	
Country	**Score**	**Country**	**Score**
Finland	9.9	Tanzania	2.2
Denmark	9.5	Ukraine	2.1
New Zealand	9.4	Azerbaijan	2.0
Iceland	9.2	Bolivia	2.0
Singapore	9.2	Cameroon	2.0
Sweden	9.0	Kenya	2.0
Canada	8.9	Indonesia	1.9
Netherlands	8.8	Uganda	1.9
Luxembourg	8.7	Nigeria	1.0
Norway	8.6	Bangladesh	0.4

Suppose, for example, the normal practice in a country is for an import expediter to charge a moderate commission for services. However, the person involved not only charges a somewhat higher than customary fee, but also has close ties to a government agency buying the imported item. When is the payment "normal," and when does it become tainted with bribery? Paying a tax collector to reduce a company's tax load would be a clear example of bribery. Expensive jewelry given to an official's spouse would be considered bribery if the official could grant important favors to the giver. Paid vacations and free air travel, lavish entertainment, and, of course, cash given to a high political official would be forms of bribery. These types of corruption, depending partly on their size, have different degrees of importance.

Consequences of Corruption

Kimberly Ann Elliott, research fellow of the Institute for International Economics, points out in her book *Corruption* that "widespread corruption threatens the very basis of an open, multilateral world economy."[40] Corruption raises the costs of doing business; it distorts government allocation of expenditures; it can, as with present-day Russia, slow the development of a free market; it can have a corrosive impact on both government service and business efficiency; it distorts competition; and it can undermine political legitimacy. Evaluation of the TI index ratings show a correlation between a high level of corruption in a country and a poor economic performance.

Laws and Codes to Control Corruption

Following the Watergate scandals, the Securities and Exchange Commission (SEC) began an investigation in 1974 to find out to what extent corporations had been illegally involved in making corporate contributions to

---

[40] Kimberly Ann Elliott, *Corruption and the Global Economy* (Washington, DC: Institute for International Economics, June 1997), p. 13.

former President Nixon's 1972 reelection campaign. The SEC investigations revealed both illegal contributions to the Nixon campaign and deceptive accounting practices intended to cover up illegal foreign payments. Many of these payments were legal under U.S. law, but withholding material information from shareholders was not. The SEC "invited" corporations to make voluntary disclosures of this activity. More than 400 responded and disclosed they had made almost $1 billion in questionable payments, mostly foreign. This disclosure immediately opened a Pandora's box of complex and troublesome questions concerning international investment methods of MNCs, U.S. foreign policy, applicable laws, and morality. The need for some legislative action to curb corruption became obvious, and in 1977 the first major anticorruption law in the world, the Foreign Corrupt Practices Act (FCPA), was passed by Congress.

This act makes it a criminal offense to offer a bribe to a foreign government official. For unlawful acts, companies may be fined $2 million and individual managers may face fines of up to $1 million and five years in jail. The law does not apply to facilitating or "grease" payments intended only to expedite normal business affairs. The law prohibits offering money or anything of value to any person (foreign or domestic) if it is known that any or all of the money or value offered will be used to influence a foreign official, politician, or political party. This means, of course, that a corporation or an individual manager may run afoul of the law if it is known that commission payments are used to induce government officials to do something for the company. The law also requires companies to keep accounting records in reasonable detail that accurately and fairly reflect transactions.

In response to complaints of business, Congress amended this law in 1988 to clarify some ambiguities in the original version. Also important was a "sense of Congress" that urged the president to initiate discussions about prohibitions of bribery in the Organisation for Economic Co-operation and Development (OECD) countries. But not much pressure was exerted on the OECD, largely because of quiet opposition by some European countries. Eventually, however, the OECD formulated the Convention Combating Bribery of Foreign Public Officials in International Business Transactions in 1997. This multinational treaty committed OECD members to have their legislative bodies pass measures to criminalize bribery by public officials. It was ratified by most of the OECD member-nations. This was a major step in the battle over corruption and for the first time committed the OECD's 40 members to outlawing the most significant types of corruption.

These commitments were paralleled by initiatives of the United Nations, organizations of countries throughout the world, and corporations. Prosecutions of U.S. companies for violating the FCPA, however, were few. Between 1977 and 1995 the DOJ prosecuted only 16 cases. After that, the pace of prosecutions quickened and many more were prosecuted. For example, Litton Industries in 1999 pleaded guilty to charges stemming from illegal payments to secure contracts in Greece and Taiwan and paid a fine of $18.5 million. A Lockheed vice president was sent to jail for violating the law. Two top executives of Triton Energy Corporation were charged with making improper payments to Triton's Indonesia business agent who allegedly passed the payments on to the Indonesian government for favorable treatment of Triton's Indonesian business. The two officers were also charged with falsifying records. Revelations such as these caused some companies to develop improved systems to train their employees with specific instructions about what they needed to know to avoid violating the law.[41]

Has the FCPA Hurt U.S. Companies in Foreign Trade?

American companies have complained for years about losing contracts to MNCs from foreign countries and to U.S. rivals that tolerate bribes. Are the complaints justified? Some studies say "yes" and some say "no." A 1996 study by the Department of Commerce concluded that American firms lost $11 billion worth of business in the previous two years to companies that paid bribes.[42] Generally, the studies made since then suggest that the FCPA has had a negative effect on some companies but not on others. Some executives, such as Jack Welch, former CEO of General Electric, believe a company can win without bribes if it produces high-quality products at low prices.[43]

CONCLUDING OBSERVATIONS

MNCs are extremely powerful institutions roaming the globe. They have major impacts on markets, social systems, and political institutions. Consequently, they are obliged to act responsibly to society as well as to their shareholders. Most of the large MNCs appear to have discharged their power reasonably well, but not well enough to meet and help resolve some major problems of today and tomorrow. On their behalf, we observe that complexities of doing global business raise serious economic, ethical, political, social, and moral issues for their managements. We believe more top managers of U.S. corporations, with help and prodding from government and strong activist critics, are exercising power responsibly. We continue this discussion of MNCs in the next chapter.

---

[41] A good example is *FCPA Guidelines,* prepared by Raytheon Company's Office of Business & Compliance for all employees. This is a clear, reasonably short, but thorough analysis of what every employee should know and do.

[42] Trade Promotion Coordinating Committee, *Toward the Next American Century: A U.S. Strategic Response to Foreign Competitive Practices* (Washington, DC: U.S. Government Printing Office, October 1996.

[43] Elliott, *Corruption,* pp. 18–19.

Union Carbide Corporation and Bhopal

On December 3, 1984, tragic events occurred at a Union Carbide pesticide plant in Bhopal, India. Water entered a large tank where a volatile chemical was stored, starting a violent reaction. Rapidly, a sequence of safety procedures and devices failed. Fugitive vapors sailed over plant boundaries, forming a lethal cloud that moved with the south wind, enveloping slum dwellings, searing lungs and eyes, asphyxiating fated souls, scarring the unlucky.

Bhopal is the worst sudden industrial accident ever in terms of human life lost. Death and injury estimates vary widely. The official death toll set forth by the Indian government for that night is 4,037, with an additional 60,000 serious injuries. Greenpeace has put the death toll at 16,000, with an estimated 500,000 injured.[1] The incredible event galvanized industry critics. "Like Auschwitz and Hiroshima," wrote one, "the catastrophe at Bhopal is a manifestation of something fundamentally wrong in our stewardship of the earth."[2] Union Carbide was debilitated and slowly declined as a company after the incident. The government of India earned mixed reviews for its response. The chemical industry changed, but according to some, not enough. And the gas victims endure a continuing struggle to get compensation and medical care.[3]

UNION CARBIDE IN INDIA

Union Carbide established an Indian subsidiary named Union Carbide India Ltd. (UCIL) in 1934. At first the company owned a 60 percent majority interest, but over the years this was reduced to 50.9 percent. Shares in the ownership of the other 49.1 percent traded on the Bombay Stock Exchange. This ownership scheme was significant because although UCIL operated with a great deal

[1] "Has the World Forgotten Bhopal?" *The Lancet,* December 2, 2000, p. 1863.
[2] David Weir, *The Bhopal Syndrome* (San Francisco: Sierra Club Books, 1987), p. xii.
[3] Kim Fortun, *Advocacy After Bhopal* (Chicago: University of Chicago Press, 2001).

of autonomy, it gave the appearance that Union Carbide was in control of its operations. By itself, UCIL was one of India's largest firms. In 1984, the year of the incident, it had 14 plants and 9,000 employees, including 500 at Bhopal. Most of its revenues came from selling Eveready batteries.

Union Carbide decided to build a pesticide plant at Bhopal in 1969. The plant formulated pesticides from chemical ingredients imported to the site. At that time, there was a growing demand in India and throughout Asia for pesticides because of the "green revolution," a type of planned agriculture that requires intensive use of pesticides and fertilizers on special strains of food crops such as wheat, rice, and corn. Although pesticides may be misused and pose some risk, they also have great social value. Without pesticides, damage to crops, losses in food storage, and toxic mold growth in food supplies would cause much loss of life from starvation and food poisoning, especially in countries such as India. Exhibit 1 shows a Union Carbide advertisement from the 1960s that describes the company's activities in India.

The Bhopal plant would supply these pesticides and serve a market anticipated to expand rapidly. The plant's location in Bhopal was encouraged by tax incentives from the city and the surrounding state of Madhya Pradesh. After a few years, however, the Indian government pressured UCIL to stop importing chemical ingredients. The company then proposed to manufacture methyl isocyanate (MIC) at the plant rather than ship it in from Carbide facilities outside the country. This was a fateful decision.

Methyl isocyanate, CH_3NCO, is a colorless, odorless liquid. Its presence can be detected by tearing and the burning sensation it causes in the eyes and noses of exposed individuals. At the Bhopal plant it was used as an intermediate chemical in pesticide manufacture. It was not the final product; rather, MIC molecules were created, then pumped into a vessel where they reacted with other chemicals. The reaction created unique molecules with qualities that disrupted insect nervous systems, causing convulsions and death. The plant

EXHIBIT 1   Union Carbide Advertisement
This ad appeared in *Fortune* magazine in April 1962.
Photo courtesy of the Union Carbide Corporation.

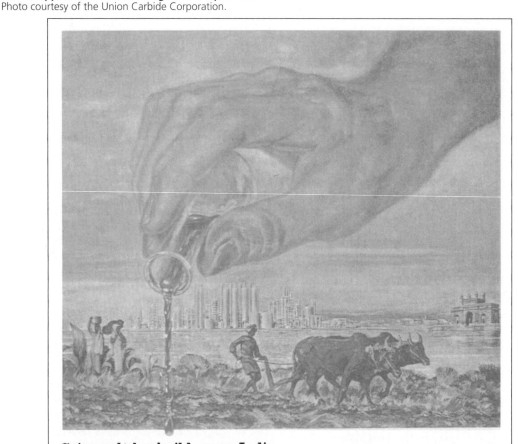

Science helps build a new India

Oxen working the fields . . . the eternal river Ganges . . . jeweled elephants on parade. Today these symbols of ancient India exist side by side with a new sight—modern industry. India has developed bold new plans to build its economy and bring the promise of a bright future to its more than 400,000,000 people. ▷ But India needs the technical knowledge of the western world. For example, working with Indian engineers and technicians, Union Carbide recently made available its vast scientific resources to help build a major chemicals and plastics plant near Bombay. ▷ Throughout the free world, Union Carbide has been actively engaged in building plants for the manufacture of chemicals, plastics, carbons, gases, and metals. The people of Union Carbide welcome the opportunity to use their knowledge and skills in partnership with the citizens of so many great countries.

A HAND IN THINGS TO COME   **UNION CARBIDE**

WRITE *for booklet B-3 "The Exciting Universe of Union Carbide", which tells how research in the fields of carbons, chemicals, gases, metals, plastics and nuclear energy keeps bringing new wonders into your life.*
Union Carbide Corporation, 270 Park Avenue, New York 17, N.Y.

turned out two similar pesticides marketed under the names Sevin and Temik.

In 1975 UCIL received a permit from the Ministry of Industry in New Delhi to build an MIC production unit at the Bhopal plant. Two months before the issuance of this permit, the city of Bhopal had enacted a development plan requiring dangerous industries to relocate in an industrial zone 15 miles away. Pursuant to the plan, M. N. Buch, the Bhopal city administrator, tried to move the UCIL pesticide plant and convert the site to housing and light commercial use. For reasons that are unclear, his effort failed, and Buch was soon transferred to forestry duties elsewhere.

The MIC unit was based on a process design provided by Union Carbide's engineers in the United States and elaborated by engineers in India. The design required storage of MIC in big tanks. An alternative used at most other pesticide plants would have been to produce small amounts of MIC only as they were consumed in pesticide production. The decision to use large storage tanks was based on an optimistic projection that pesticide sales would grow dramatically. Since an Indian law, the Foreign Exchange Regulation Act of 1973, requires foreign multinationals to share technology and use Indian resources, detailed design work was done by an Indian subsidiary of a British firm. Local labor using Indian equipment and materials built the unit.

In 1980 the MIC unit began operation under UCIL's management. During the five years of design and construction, densely populated shantytowns sprang up nearby, inhabited mainly by impoverished, unemployed people who had left rural areas seeking their fortunes in the city. A childlike faith that the facility was a benevolent presence turning out miraculous substances to make plants grow was widespread among them. In fact, when the MIC unit came on line the plant began to pose higher risk to its neighbors; it now made the basic chemicals used in pesticides rather than using shipped-in ingredients. One step in the manufacture of MIC, for example, creates phosgene, the lethal "mustard gas" used in World War I. The benighted crowd by the plant abided unaware.

In 1981 a phosgene leak killed one worker, and a crusading Indian journalist wrote articles about dangers to the population. No one acted. A year later, a second phosgene leak forced temporary evacuation of some surrounding neighborhoods. Worker safety and environmental inspections of the plant were done by the state Department of Labor, an agency with only 15 factory inspectors to cover 8,000 plants and a record of lax enforcement.[4] Oversight was not vigorous.

Meanwhile, the Indian economy had turned down, and stiff competition from other pesticide firms marketing new, less expensive products reduced demand for Sevin and Temik. As revenues fell, so did the plant's budget, and it was necessary to defer some maintenance, lessen the rigor of training, and lay off workers. By the time of the incident, the MIC unit was operating with six workers per shift, half the number anticipated by its designers.

UNION CARBIDE'S RELATIONSHIP WITH THE BHOPAL PLANT

What was the organizational relationship of Union Carbide Corporation in the United States to its subsidiary, Union Carbide India Ltd., and ultimately to the Bhopal plant? How much direction and control did the corporate parent half a world away in Danbury, Connecticut, exercise over the facility?

The Bhopal plant fit into the Union Carbide management hierarchy as shown in the chart in Exhibit 2. Although Carbide employees from the United States managed the plant in its early years, in 1982, under pressure from the government, it was turned over to Indian managers. The experience of colonial rule in India created a strong political need for leaders to put on shows of strength with foreign investors. Indians felt a burning desire to avoid any appearance of subjugation and

[4] Sheila Jasanoff, "Managing India's Environment," *Environment,* October 1986, p. 33.

EXHIBIT 2
Union Carbide's
Organization
Structure as Related
to the Bhopal Plant

```
                        ┌─────────────────────┐
                        │  Board of Directors  │
                        └─────────────────────┘
                                   │
                        ┌─────────────────────┐
                        │  Warren M. Anderson  │
                        │   Chairman and CEO   │
                        └─────────────────────┘
                                   │
                        ┌─────────────────────┐
                        │     Alec Flamm       │
                        │     President        │
                        └─────────────────────┘
                                   │
                        ┌─────────────────────┐
                        │ Technology, Services │
                        │ & Specialty Products │
                        │        Group         │
                        │                      │
                        │        USA           │
┌──────────────────┐    └─────────────────────┘    ┌──────────────────┐
│  Union Carbide   │               │                │  Union Carbide   │
│ Agricultural     │───────────────┼────────────────│  Eastern, Inc.   │
│ Products         │               │                │                  │
│ Company, Inc.    │               │                │   Hong Kong      │
│                  │    ┌─────────────────────┐     │                  │
│      USA         │    │  Board of Directors  │    └──────────────────┘
└──────────────────┘    └─────────────────────┘
                                   │
                        ┌─────────────────────┐
                        │   Union Carbide      │
                        │   India Ltd.         │
                        │                      │
                        │     Bombay           │
                        └─────────────────────┘
                                   │
                        ┌─────────────────────┐
                        │  Bhopal Pesticide    │
                        │      Plant           │
                        └─────────────────────┘
```

demanded self-sufficiency. This is what had led to passage of the law requiring foreign investors to use Indian firms and workers in certain ways—and to put pressure on Union Carbide to turn the plant completely over to its Indian subsidiary.

The Bhopal plant was but one of 500 facilities in 34 countries in the Union Carbide Corporation universe. There was no regular or direct reporting relationship between it and Union Carbide's headquarters in Danbury, Connecticut. At the request of UCIL, employees of Union Carbide had gone to India twice to perform safety inspections on the plant. Other than those occasions, managers in the United States had received information or reporting about the plant only infrequently and irregularly when major changes or capital expenditures

were requested. Thus, the Bhopal plant was run with near total independence from the American corporation. In litigation to determine where victim's lawsuits should be tried, a U.S. court described its autonomy in these words:

> . . . [Union Carbide Corporation's] participation [in the design and construction of the plant] was limited and its involvement in plant operations terminated long before the accident . . . [It] was constructed and managed by Indians in India. No Americans were employed at the plant at the time of the accident. In the five years from 1980 to 1984, although more than 1,000 Indians were employed at the plant, only one American was employed there and he left in 1982. No Americans visited the

plant for more than one year prior to the accident, and during the 5-year period before the accident the communications between the plant and the United States were almost nonexistent.[5]

Thus, the Bhopal plant was run by UCIL with near total independence from the American corporation. Despite this, shortly after the gas leak Chairman Warren M. Anderson said that Carbide accepted "moral responsibility" for the tragedy.

THE GAS LEAK

On the eve of the disaster, tank 610, one of three storage tanks in the MIC unit, sat filled with 11,290 gallons of MIC. The tank, having a capacity of 15,000 gallons, was a partly buried, stainless steel, pressurized vessel. Its purpose was to take in MIC made elsewhere in the plant and hold it for some time until it was sent to the pesticide production area through a transfer pipe, there to be converted into Sevin or Temik.

At about 9:30 P.M. a supervisor ordered an operator, R. Khan, to unclog four filter valves near the MIC production area by washing them out with water. Khan connected a water hose to the piping above the clogged valves but neglected to insert a slip blind, a device that seals lines to prevent water leaks into adjacent pipes. Khan's omission, if it occurred, would have violated established procedure.

Because of either this careless washing method or the introduction of water elsewhere, 120 to 240 gallons of water entered tank 610, starting a powerful exothermic (heat building) reaction. At first, operators were unaware of the danger, and for two hours pressure in the tank rose unnoticed. At 10:20 P.M. they logged tank pressure at 2 pounds per square inch (ppsi). At 11:30 P.M. a new operator in the MIC control room noticed that the pressure was 10 ppsi, but he was unconcerned because this was within tolerable limits, gauges were often wrong, and he had not read the log to learn that the pressure was now five times what it had been an hour earlier.

Unfortunately, refrigeration units that cooled the tanks had been shut down for five months to save electricity costs. Had they been running, as the MIC processing manual required, the heat from the reaction with the water might have taken place over days instead of hours.

As pressure built, leaks developed. Soon workers sensed the presence of MIC. Their eyes watered. At 11:45 someone spotted a small, yellowish drip from overhead piping. The supervisor suggested fixing the leak after the regular 12:15 A.M. tea break. At 12:40 the tea break ended. By now the control room gauge showed the pressure in tank 610 was 40 ppsi. In a short time it rose to 55 ppsi, the top of the scale. A glance at the tank temperature gauge brought more bad news: The MIC was 77°F, 36° higher than the specified safety limit and hot enough to vaporize. Startled by readings on the gauges, the control room operator ran out to tank 610. He felt radiating heat and heard the concrete over it cracking. Within seconds, a pressure-release valve opened and a white cloud of deadly MIC vapor shot into the atmosphere with a high-decibel screech.

Back in the control room, operators turned a switch to activate the vent gas scrubber, a safety device designed to neutralize escaping toxic gases by circulating them through caustic soda. It was down for maintenance and inoperable. Even if it had been on line, it was too small to handle the explosive volume of MIC shooting from the tank. A flare tower designed to burn off toxic gases before they reached the atmosphere was also off line; it had been dismantled for maintenance and an elbow joint was missing. Another emergency measure, transferring MIC from tank 610 to one of the other storage tanks, was foreclosed because both were too full. This situation also violated the processing manual, which called for leaving one tank empty as a safeguard.

At about 1:00 A.M. an operator triggered an alarm to warn workers of danger. The plant superintendent, entering the control room, ordered a water spraying device be directed on the venting gas, but this last-resort measure had little effect. Now most workers ran in panic, ignoring four emergency buses they were supposed to drive through the surrounding area to evacuate residents. Two intrepid operators stayed at the control panel, sharing the only available oxygen mask

[5] *In re Union Carbide Corporation Gas Plant Disaster at Bhopal,* 809 F.2d 195 (1987), at 200.

when the room filled with MIC vapor. Finally, at 2:30, the pressure in tank 610 dropped, the leaking safety valve resealed, and the venting ceased. Roughly 10,000 gallons of MIC, about 90 percent of the tank's contents, was now settling over the city.

That night the wind was calm, the temperature about 60°, and the dense chemical mist lingered just above the ground. Animals died. The gas attacked people in the streets and seeped into their bedrooms. Those who panicked and ran into the night air suffered higher exposures.

As the poisonous cloud enveloped victims, MIC reacted with water in their eyes. This reaction, like the reaction in tank 610, created heat that burned corneal cells, rendering them opaque. Residents with cloudy, burning eyes staggered about. Many victims suffered shortness of breath, coughing fits, inflammation of the respiratory tract, and chemical pneumonia. In the lungs, MIC molecules reacted with moisture, causing chemical burns. Fluid oozed from seared tissue and pooled, a condition called pulmonary edema, and its victims literally drowned in their own secretions. Burned lung tissue eventually healed over with a tough protein substance called fibrin, creating areas of fibrosis that diminished breathing capacity. Because MIC is so reactive with water, simply breathing through a wet cloth would have saved many lives. However, people lacked this simple knowledge.

UNION CARBIDE REACTS

Awakened early in the morning, CEO Warren M. Anderson rushed to Carbide's Danbury, Connecticut, headquarters and learned of the rising death toll. When the extent of the disaster was evident, a senior management committee held an emergency meeting. They decided to send emergency medical supplies, respirators, oxygen (all Carbide products), and an American doctor with knowledge of MIC to Bhopal.

The next day, Tuesday, December 5, Carbide dispatched a team of technical experts to examine the plant. On Thursday, Anderson himself left for India. However, after arriving in Bhopal, he was charged with criminal negligence, placed under house arrest, and then asked to leave the country.

With worldwide attention focused on Bhopal, Carbide held daily press conferences. Christmas parties were canceled. Flags at Carbide facilities flew at half-mast. All of its nearly 100,000 employees observed a moment of silence for the victims. It gave $1 million to an emergency relief fund and offered to turn its guest house in Bhopal into an orphanage. Months later, the company offered another $5 million, but the money was refused because Indian politicians trembled in fear that they would be seen cooperating with the company. The Indian public reviled anything associated with Carbide. Later, when the state government learned that Carbide had set up a training school for the unemployed in Bhopal, it flattened the facility with bulldozers.

CARBIDE FIGHTS LAWSUITS AND A TAKEOVER BID

No sooner had the mists cleared than American attorneys arrived in Bhopal seeking litigants for damage claims. They walked the streets signing up plaintiffs. Just four days after the gas leak, the first suit was filed in a U.S. court; soon cases seeking $40 billion in damages for 200,000 Indians were filed against Carbide.

However, the Indian Parliament passed a law giving the Indian government exclusive right to represent victims. Then India sued in the United States. Union Carbide offered $350 million to settle existing claims (an offer rejected by the Indian government) and brought a motion to have the cases heard in India. Both Indian and American lawyers claiming to represent victims opposed the motion, knowing that wrongful death awards in India were small compared with those in the United States. However, in 1986 a federal court ruled that the cases should be heard in India, noting that "to retain the litigation in [the United States] . . . would be yet another example of imperialism, another situation in which an established sovereign inflicted its rules, its standards and values on a developing nation."[6] This was a victory for Carbide and a de-

---

[6] *In re Union Carbide Corporation Gas Plant Disaster,* 634 F.Supp. 867 (S.D.N.Y. 1986).

feat for American lawyers, who could not carry their cases to India in defiance of the government.

In late 1986 the Indian government filed a $3.3 billion civil suit against Carbide in an Indian court.[7] The suit alleged that Union Carbide Corporation, in addition to being majority shareholder in Union Carbide India Ltd., had exercised policy control over the establishment and design of the Bhopal plant. The Bhopal plant was defective in design because its safety standards were lower than similar Carbide plants in the United States. Carbide had consciously permitted inadequate safety standards to exist. The suit also alleged that Carbide was conducting an "ultrahazardous activity" at the Bhopal plant and had strict and absolute liability for compensating victims regardless of whether the plant was operating carefully or not.

Carbide countered with the defense that it had a holding company relationship with UCIL and never had exercised direct control over the Bhopal plant; it was prohibited from doing so by Indian laws that required management by Indian nationals. In addition to the civil suit, Carbide's chairman, Warren Anderson, and several UCIL executives were charged with homicide in a Bhopal court. This apparently was a pressure tactic, since no attempt to arrest them was made. The Indian court had no power to extradite and try Anderson, a United States citizen.

On top of its legal battle, Carbide had to fight for its independence. In December 1985, GAF Corporation, which had been accumulating Carbide's shares, made a takeover bid. After a suspenseful month-long battle, Carbide fought off GAF, but only at the cost of taking on enormous new debt to buy back 55 percent of its outstanding shares. This huge debt had to be reduced because interest payments were crippling. So in 1986 Carbide sold $3.5 billion of assets, including its most popular consumer brands—Eveready batteries, Glad bags, and Prestone antifreeze. It had sacrificed stable sources of revenue and was now a smaller, weaker company more exposed to cyclical economic trends.

---

[7] *Union of India* v. *Union Carbide Corp. and Union Carbide India Ltd.*, Bhopal District Court, No. 1113 (1986).

INVESTIGATING THE CAUSE OF THE MIC LEAK

In the days following the gas leak, there was worldwide interest in pinning down its precise cause. A team of reporters from *The New York Times* interviewed plant workers in Bhopal. Their six-week investigation concluded that a large volume of water entered tank 610, causing the accident.[8] The *Times* reporters thought that water had entered when R. Khan failed to use a slip blind as he washed out piping. Water from his hose simply backed up and eventually flowed about 400 feet into the tank. Their account was widely accepted as authoritative, and this theory, called the "water washing theory," gained currency. However, it was not to be the only theory of the accident's cause.

Immediately after the disaster, Union Carbide also rushed a team of investigators to Bhopal. But the team got little cooperation from Indian authorities operating in a climate of anti-Carbide popular protest. It was denied access to plant records and workers. Yet the investigators got to look at tank 610 and took core samples from the bottom residue. These samples went back to the United States, where more than 500 experimental chemical reactions were undertaken to explain their chemical composition. In March 1985 Carbide finally released its first report on the accident. It stated that entry of water into the tank caused the accident, but it rejected the water washing theory.

Instead, Carbide scientists felt the only way that an amount of water sufficient to cause the observed reaction could have entered the tank was through accidental or deliberate connection of a water hose to piping that led directly into the tank.

---

[8] The team wrote a series of articles. See Stuart Diamond, "The Bhopal Disaster: How It Happened," *The New York Times,* January 28, 1985; Thomas J. Lueck, "Carbide Says Inquiry Showed Errors but Is Incomplete," *The New York Times,* January 28, 1985; Stuart Diamond, "The Disaster in Bhopal: Workers Recall Horror," *The New York Times,* January 30, 1985; and Robert Reinhold, "Disaster in Bhopal: Where Does Blame Lie?" *The New York Times,* January 31, 1985.

This was possible, because outlets for compressed air, nitrogen, steam, and water were stationed throughout the plant. The investigators rejected the water washing hypothesis for several reasons. The piping system was designed to prevent water contamination even without a slip blind. Valves between the piping being washed and tank 610 were found closed after the accident. And the volume of water required to create the reaction—1,000 to 2,000 pounds—was far too much to be explained by valve leakage.

The Carbide report gave a plausible alternative to the water washing theory, but within months an investigation by the Indian government rejected it. This study, made by Indian scientists and engineers, confirmed that the entry of water into the MIC tank caused the reaction but concluded that the improper washing procedure was to blame (see Exhibit 3).

There matters stood until late 1985, when the Indian government allowed Carbide more access to plant records and employees. Carbide investigators sought out the plant's employees. More than 70 interviews, and careful examination of plant records and physical evidence, led them to conclude that the cause of the gas leak was sabotage

EXHIBIT 3 **Two Theories Clash on Water Entry into MIC Tank**
Source: Courtesy of Union Carbide.

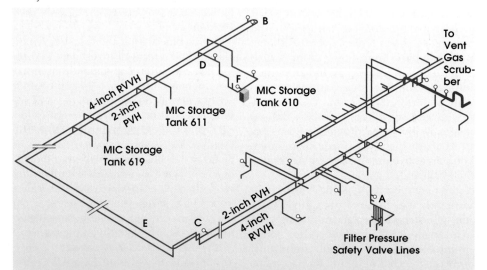

According to the water washing theory of Indian government, water was introduced through a hose into bleeder A at filter pressure safety valve lines. As hose kept running, water proceeded through leaking valve in that area and rose up into the relief valve vent header line (RVVH). It took a turn at the jumper line, B, and moved into the process vent header line (PVH), filling it in the reverse direction all the way to the slip blind, C. When PVH was completely filled, water rose at line D and proceeded into MIC storage tank 610.

On Feb. 8, 1985, two months after the leak, India's Central Bureau of Investigation drilled a hole in the PVH line at point E to drain any water left in the line. No water emerged. Carbide says this fact alone disproves the water washing theory. The fact various valves in the pathway to the tank were closed also disproves the theory, according to Carbide.

Carbide espouses an alternate theory: The company says it has proof that water was introduced by a "disgruntled employee" who removed pressure gauge F, attached a hose to the open piping, and ran water into the MIC tank. Gas then escaped through a rupture disk and proceeded through the RVVH and out the vent gas scrubber.

by a disgruntled employee who intentionally hooked a water hose to the tank.

Here is the sequence of events on the night of December 2–3 that Carbide set forth. At 10:20 P.M. the pressure gauge on tank 610 read 2 ppsi. This meant that no water had yet entered the tank and no reaction had begun. At 10:45 the regular shift change occurred. Shift changes take half an hour, and the MIC storage area would have been deserted. At this time, an operator who had been angry for days about his failure to get a promotion stole into the area. He unscrewed the local pressure indicator gauge on tank 610, hooked up a rubber water hose, and turned the water on. Five minutes would have sufficed to do this.

Carbide claimed to know the name of this person, but it has never been made public. Its investigative team speculated that his intention was simply to ruin the MIC batch in the tank; it is doubtful that this worker realized all that might happen. The interviews revealed that the workers thought of MIC chiefly as a lacrimator, a chemical that causes tearing; they did not regard it as a lethal hazard.

Now the plot thickens. A few minutes after midnight, MIC operators noted the fast pressure rise in tank 610. Walking to the tank, they found the water hose connected and removed it, then informed their supervisors. The supervisors tried to prevent a catastrophic pressure rise by draining water from tank 610. Between 12:15 and 12:30 A.M., just minutes before the explosive release, they transferred about 1 metric ton of the contents from tank 610 to a holding tank. Water is heavier than MIC, and the transfer was made through a drain in the tank's bottom; thus, the supervisors hoped to remove the water. They failed, and within 15 minutes the relief valve blew.

The investigators had physical evidence to support this scenario. After the accident, the local pressure gauge hole on tank 610 was still open and no plug had been inserted, as would have been normal for routine maintenance. When the MIC unit was examined, a crude drawing of the hose connection was found on the back of one page from that night's log book. Also, operators outside the MIC unit told the investigation team that MIC operators had told them about the hose connection that night. In addition, log entries had been falsi-

fied, revealing a crude cover-up effort. The major falsification was an attempt to hide the transfer of contents from tank 610.

Why did the supervisors and operators attempt a cover-up? The Carbide investigators gave this explanation.

> Not knowing if the attempted transfer had exacerbated the incident, or whether they could have otherwise prevented it, or whether they would be blamed for not having notified plant management earlier, those involved decided on a cover-up. They altered logs that morning to disguise their involvement. As is common in many such incidents, the reflexive tendency to cover up simply took over.[9]

A SETTLEMENT IS REACHED

The theory of deliberate sabotage became the centerpiece of Carbide's legal defense. However, the case never came to trial. In 1989 a settlement was reached in which Carbide agreed to pay $470 million to the Indian government, which would distribute the money to victims (see Exhibit 4). In return, India agreed to stop all legal action against Carbide, UCIL, and their executives. India agreed to this settlement, which was far less than the $3.3 billion it was asking for, because a trial and subsequent appeals in the Indian court system would likely have taken 20 years.

Carbide paid the settlement using $200 million in insurance and taking a charge of $.43 per share against 1988 net earnings of $5.31 per share. Victims' groups were upset because they thought the settlement too small, and they challenged it. In 1991 the Indian Supreme Court rejected these appeals but permitted reinstatement of criminal proceedings against Warren Anderson and top managers at UCIL.[10] An arrest warrant for Anderson on manslaughter charges was issued in India in

[9] Ashok S. Kalelkar, "Investigation of Large-Magnitude Incidents: Bhopal as a Case Study," paper presented at the Instititution of Chemical Engineers conference on Preventing Major Chemical Accidents, London, England, May 1988, p. 27.
[10] *Union Carbide Corp.* v. *Union of India*, AIR 1992 (S.C.) 248.

EXHIBIT 4
Calculating the $470 Million Settlement
Source: Kim Fortun, *Advocacy after Bhopal* (Chicago: University of Chicago Press, 2001), p. 38.

Amount	Medical Categorization
$ 43,500,000	$14,500 payments for 3,000 deaths
$ 50,000,000	$25,000 payments for up to 2,000 victims with injuries of "utmost severity"
$156,000,000	$5,200 payments to 30,000 permanently disabled
$ 64,300,000	$3,215 payments to 20,000 temporarily disabled
$140,600,000	Amount to cover 150,000 minor injuries, future injuries, property damage, commercial loss, and other claims.
$ 15,600,000	Medical treatment and rehabilitation of victims
$470,000,000	Total settlement

1992, but it has never been served. A trial of several UCIL managers has dragged on for years with no end in sight.

The Indian government was slow and inefficient in distributing settlement funds to gas victims. In 1993, 40 special courts began processing claims, but the activity was riddled with corruption. Healthy people bribed physicians for false medical records with which they could get compensation. Twelve court officials were fired for soliciting bribes from gas victims who sought payments. More than 600,000 claims have been filed, and the payout is now largely complete. By 2001, 14,824 death claims were approved, but compensation averaged only $1,300. Ninety percent of all claims were settled for $550, the minimum allowed.[11]

POSTSCRIPT

In 1994 Union Carbide sold for $90 million its 50.9 percent equity in UCIL to the Indian subsidiary of a British company. Much of the money from the sale funded a hospital in Bhopal. In 1991, at the request of the Indian Supreme Court, Union Carbide and UCIL had agreed to provide up to $17 million for a hospital to be built by the Indian government in fulfillment of an offer made in 1986. Meanwhile, this commitment had increased to $20 million. An additional $54 million from the sale of Union Carbide's shares of UCIL went to the hospital and local clinics. This ended Carbide's involvement in India.

Activist groups representing victims keep demanding further justice from the company and its officers, but Indian courts refuse to oblige. In 1999 lawyers for victims sought more compensation by filing a case in the United States under new charges that Union Carbide had violated a 1789 law passed to remedy injuries to foreign citizens caused by pirates. The case was dismissed.[12]

Though charges remain open, the Indian government has never tried to serve a warrant on Warren Anderson, who retired in Florida and is now in his 80s. Victims' groups say that this is because the government caters to big multinational corporations. Pursuing a vendetta against Carbide would frighten foreign investors.

After Bhopal, Union Carbide became a smaller, less resilient company. It was forced to sell or spin-off its most lucrative businesses. In 1984, the year of the gas leak, Carbide had 98,400 employees and sales of $9.5 billion; by 2000 it had only $5.9 billion in sales and 11,000 employees. The end for Union Carbide came in 2001 when it merged with a much larger Dow Chemical Co. and its workforce suffered the bulk of cost-reduction layoffs.[13]

The Bhopal plant never reopened. It was dismantled and some of its equipment sold. Each year on the anniversary of the gas leak, activists return to repaint graffiti on plant walls that still stand.

[11] Paul Watson, "Cloud of Despair in Bhopal," *Los Angeles Times,* August 30, 2001, p. A6.

[12] The law is the Alien Tort Claims Act, and the case is *Bano* v. *Union Carbide Corp.,* QDS:02762952 (S.D.N.Y. 2000).
[13] Susan Warren, "Cost-Cutting Effort at Dow Chemical to Take 4,500 Jobs," *The Wall Street Journal,* May 2, 2001, p. A6.

"HANG ANDERSON" is an example.[14] Recently the state government considered plans to convert the site into an amusement park.

In the wake of Bhopal, Congress passed legislation requiring chemical companies to disclose the presence of dangerous chemicals to surrounding populations and to create emergency plans. The industry adopted the Responsible Care initiative (discussed in Chapter 5) to improve both its safety and its public image. However, in the United States alone between 1994 and 1999, chemical plants reported 1,913 accidents that killed 33 workers, injured almost 1,900 more, and hospitalized 217 nearby residents.[15]

Despite the passage of years, Bhopal does not fade away. It is the subject of at least four documentary films, and in 2000 a dramatized feature film, *Bhopal Express*, was a box office hit in India. More than a dozen books have dissected Bhopal. One notable recent publication is *Five Past Midnight in Bhopal*, a tendentious piece of reality fiction by noted French author Dominique Lapierre and a co-author that appeared in 2001.[16] It climbed best-seller lists in France and Spain. According to Lapierre, film director Oliver Stone is negotiating for movie rights. So Bhopal may come to a theater near you.

QUESTIONS

1. Who is responsible for the Bhopal accident? How should blame be apportioned among parties involved, including Union Carbide Corporation, UCIL, plant workers, governments in India, or others?

2. What principles of corporate social responsibility and business ethics are applicable to the actions of the parties in question?

3. How well did the legal system work? Do you agree with the decision to try the lawsuits in India? Were victims fairly compensated? Was Union Carbide sufficiently punished?

4. Did Union Carbide handle the crisis well? How would you grade its performance in facing uniquely difficult circumstances?

5. What lessons can other corporations and countries learn from this story?

---

[14] Daniel Pearl, "An Indian City Poisoned by Union Carbide Gas Forgets the Past," *The Wall Street Journal,* February 12, 2001, p. A17.

[15] Susan Warren, "Chemical Companies Keep Lessons of Bhopal Spill Fresh," *The Wall Street Journal,* February 13, 2001, p. B4.

[16] Dominique Lapierre and Javier Moro, *Five Past Midnight in Bhopal* (New York: Warner Books, 2002).

Chapter Thirteen

Globalization and BGS Relationships

DaimlerChrysler

On May 8, 1998, the supervisory board of Daimler-Benz AG, Germany's largest corporation, gave its unanimous approval for a merger with Chrysler Corporation, an American firm. When completed in 1999, the combination formed the world's third largest auto company as measured by revenues (after General Motors and Ford) and the fifth-largest in terms of unit sales. Together, the companies sold cars and trucks in more than 200 countries. It was also the largest acquisition of an American company by a foreign firm. The new DaimlerChrysler had total sales in 2000 of $146 billion. However, by 2001 total sales declined to $135 billion and operating profits dropped from $6.8 billion in 2000 to $4.6 billion. These disappointing results were mainly due to declines in the Chrysler business segment.

Daimler is best known in the United States for making the prestigious Mercedes-Benz, but it is also involved in aerospace, diesel engines, finance, railway systems, and automotive electronics. Chrysler produces the well-known Chrysler, Dodge, and Jeep vehicle brands and is known for bringing innovative new products such as the PT Cruiser to market. Jurgen E. Schrempp, CEO of Daimler, set forth a vision for the new company. It was to be "Number one worldwide in the premium car segment, a world market leader with sport-utility vehicles and minivans, and the world's largest producer of commercial vehicles.[1]

Why Merge?

Observers and managers of the two companies saw the merger as a perfect fit driven by clear strategic motives. For example, the global auto industry was becoming more and more competitive, mainly because world production

[1] "Birth of a Global Company," www.daimlerchrysler.com/specials/8111birth/sr81117._e.htm.

capacity for cars and trucks was greater than market demand. Companies were forced to combine to provide the capital and technical skills to lower production and design costs and bring products to market more quickly. This reality stimulated global thinking. Chrysler was basically an American car company and needed the reach of Daimler to become a global presence. It also gained access to Daimler's superior production technology. Daimler, on the other hand, got access to mass-production methods developed by Chrysler, and it extended its product line by adding Chrysler's light trucks, vans, and utility vehicles. Both companies gained by increasing production volumes, thereby lowering cost per unit. The merger created a truly multinational business, not simply a bigger German or U.S. firm.

Cross-Border Merger Failures

In the euphoria that followed the merger stockholders, Wall Street analysts, workers, and managers of the two companies gave the combination rave reviews. It was forgotten that most cross-border mergers, especially of auto companies, either failed or did not run smoothly. A few high-profile mergers illustrate the point. Ford bought Jaguar and Aston Martin and sank huge investments in them to modernize their production lines, but it is still struggling to find profits. Renault's acquisition of American Motors Corporation was a failure. On the other hand, General Motor's acquisition of Germany's Adam Opel A.G. turned out to be a success.[2] Outside the automobile industry there have been many significant failures or continuing problems. For example, Merrill Lynch acquired branch offices in Japan and ran into severe cultural problems training Japanese brokers to U.S. standards. Sony's acquisition of Columbia Pictures Entertainment Inc. did not turn out to be a good investment.[3]

Chrysler was highly profitable at the time of the merger, but it failed to meet expectations after that. In the second half of 2000 it lost $1.8 billion. Its market share dropped from 15.1 percent for the first three months of 2000 to 14.2 percent in the same period in 2001. This sent shock waves through Dusseldorf, the headquarters of DaimlerChrysler. Schrempp sent Dieter Zetsche, a problem-solving executive at Daimler, to replace Chrysler's top executive. Zetsche brought with him a group of Daimler executives, who replaced top managers of Chrysler who had already left or were soon fired by Zetsche. There were two main reasons for Chrysler's difficulties. One was the deteriorating U.S. economy, and the other was a clash of corporate cultures.

[2] Edmund L. Andrews and Laura M. Holson, "Shaping a Global Giant: The Overview," *The New York Times,* May 7, 1998.
[3] Louis Uchitelle, "Shaping a Global Giant: The Multinationals," *The New York Times,* May 8, 1998.

Blending Cultures

Daimler's management style was stodgy and formal. Decisions were slow and procedures ponderous. Subordinates prepared carefully drawn papers to support their recommendations, which managers considered before eventually reaching a decision. This contrasted starkly with the habit in Chrysler, where staffs made verbal recommendations and got prompt answers from management. Chrysler managers were aggressive and imaginative. They felt that the merger had injected a rigidly conservative system into their free-wheeling culture. The managers at Daimler thought the merger jeopardized their world-class car design and quality production capability by combining it with a system that mass-produced lower-quality vehicles. The wide pay differentials between top managers of the two companies exacerbated differences. Daimler managers were envious of Chrysler managers, who made two to three times what they did. Daimler managers, on the other hand, enjoyed generous travel expenses and other perquisites that the Chrysler managers disdained as German profligacy.[4]

Zetsche recognized these problems and set out to improve profitability and smooth the cultural differences that were sapping morale. He fired the manager of sales and marketing and quickly prepared a plan to cut costs, revive sales of Chrysler vehicles, and boost morale.[5] The plan projected profitability by 2003.

The story of the Daimler-Benz-Chrysler merger illustrates pressures on corporations to think globally and the cultural problems they often face in cross-border mergers. Managers of companies in many countries and industries face problems very similar to those faced by the leaders of these two auto companies. In this chapter we will discuss these and other aspects of globalization in more depth, including the growth of trading agreements, the importance of the international financial system, global varieties of capitalism, and the erosion of nation-state sovereignty.

WHAT IS GLOBALIZATION?

Globalization is an idea that rose to great prominence in the last years of the twentieth century. Barry Bosworth and Philip H. Gordon of the Brookings Institution define globalization broadly as follows: "globalization is the expansion and intensification of linkages and flows—of people, goods, capital, ideas, and cultures—across national borders."[6] There is no consensus about this definition because globalization is many-

---

[4] *The Economist,* "Merger Brief: The DaimlerChrysler Emulsion," July 29, 2000.
[5] Stephen Grahm, "Daimler Expects to Meet Profit Target," *Los Angeles Times,* January 5, 2002.
[6] Barry Bosworth and Philip H. Gordon, "Managing a Globalizing World," *Brookings Review,* Fall 2001, p. 3.

faceted and observers see different elements in it. For example, some economists define it as the integration of economic systems. Political scientists may see it is a process that creates diffusion of national political authority through large trade blocks and the power of MNCs. Sociologists may see it as a process that erodes national cultures. Globalization is a controversial term for such reasons as these.

One source of controversy over the word globalization is wide differences between views about its impact on the world. Champions of globalization see it as creating enormous riches, wealth, and higher standards of living for millions of people. Critics see it differently. Ralph Nader said, "The essence of globalization is a subordination of human rights, of labor rights, consumer, environmental rights, democracy rights, to the imperatives of global trade and investment."[7]

Some observers see today's globalization as nothing new. It has its roots, they correctly point out, in the growth of huge trading companies in the sixteenth century. Other observers say today's globalization is far different from anything in the past. Bosworth and Gordon observe that global integration in recent years far exceeds that of the past "in degree, intensity, speed, volume, and geographic reach."[8] So rapid has been the change that some analysts speak of it as a revolution.

Major Forces in Expanding Globalization

There have been many forces behind the growth of globalization. The following are the major ones.

- Technological advances have significantly increased the speed and reduced the costs of communications. In 1930, for example, the cost of a one minute telephone call to London from New York was about $244.65. In 1990 it was $3.32. Today a comparable communication over the Internet via e-mail is virtually instantaneous and costless not only to London but around the world.

- World trade has risen spectacularly over the past several decades, as shown in Figure 12.1, and foreign trade has become a larger proportion of GDP for many nations. In the United States, for example, trade has increased from about 5 percent of GDP in the 1930s to 25 percent today.

- MNCs, as noted in the last chapter, have grown significantly in numbers, foreign investments, sales, employees, and worldwide influence.

- There has been an explosive growth in the amount of money floating around the world to finance trade and acquire foreign assets. Speculative money has also become abundant.

[7] Ralph Nader, transcript of "Globalization and Human Rights," a PBS program, www.pbs.org./globalization/prologue.html.
[8] Bosworth and Gordon, "Managing a Globalizing World," p. 3.

- Many countries have been receptive to free market ideas and have implemented them.

- Transportation costs and delivery schedules of goods have been substantially reduced.

- Standardized products of similar quality, such as cameras, soft drinks, watches, computers, chemicals, and drugs, have become popular around the world with but minor modifications to fit local situations.

- Relative peace has prevailed in the world. However, the impact on globalization of the current battle with terrorism remains to be determined.

- A number of multilateral organizations have facilitated globalization, including the World Trade Organization (WTO), the United Nations, the World Bank, and the International Monetary Fund (IMF).

- It should be mentioned that many nongovernment organizations (NGOs) have pressured MNCs to be more concerned with environmental issues, human rights, and social responsibilities.

Pros and Cons of Globalization: An Overview

The primary benefits of globalization as seen by its supporters are the following.

- It has lifted millions of people out of poverty into middle-class status.

- Consumers have benefited with more variety, lower costs, and higher quality of products.

- Working conditions have improved for millions of workers.

- Human rights, especially in developing countries, have improved.

- Per capita income has grown for millions of people, especially in developing countries.

- Globalization has spurred the spread of capitalism.

- Globalization has stimulated more nations to adopt democratic governance.

Globalization, however, has attracted many critics with a multitude of complaints. Here are a few of the more significant ones.

- Workers in developed countries are displaced as companies employ more workers paid lower-wages in developing countries.

- Millions of people in the developing countries remain in poverty.

- The gap between per capita incomes of developed and developing countries has widened.

- Globalization has resulted in growing environmental degradation.

- Globalization has contaminated the cultures of both developed and undeveloped countries.

- Globalization has undermined the sovereignty of developing countries.

- Globalization has produced world financial instability.

In this chapter space limits prevent an extended examination of many of these dimensions of globalization. This chapter is an extension of Chapter 12, which discussed two great forces driving globalization, namely, trade and the MNC. Our intent is to discuss in this chapter other major trends of globalization that have an important impact on the BGS relationship.

INCREASING FOREIGN COMPETITION

The pace and intensity of economic competition have accelerated with globalization. Before the 1980s, foreign trade was such a small part of total U.S. output (about 5 percent) that it received little attention. Then, increasingly, foreign producers successfully challenged American corporations both at home and abroad. In some major industries and important products, foreign companies were able to penetrate the U.S. market with higher quality and lower prices than comparable American products. This awakened the United States and its corporations to the comparatively weak competitive position of some industries. For example, consumer electronics virtually disappeared in the United States. Radios and television sets were clear examples. By the end of the 1980s, only one company, Zenith, was making TV sets in the United States, and that company stopped production in 1995. Semiconductors, invented in the United States, were dominated by Japanese companies. In steel, automobiles, machine tools, and other industries, statistics of decline were compelling. The United States once was the world leader in robotics, structural ceramics, and flexible manufacturing, but it lost those positions to foreign businesses.

However, the United States did have strengths. Then, as now, the United States was the world leader in supercomputers, software engineering, artificial intelligence, computer-aided design and engineering, telecommunications, genetic engineering, rocket propulsion, and new drug development. Many products were then and are now the finest in the world. In mind, for example, are satellite navigation systems, fiber optics, communications satellites, pacemakers, oil drill bits, motion pictures, and locomotives, to mention but a few.[9]

---

[9] See Michael Dertouzos et al., *Made in America: Regaining the Productive Edge* (Cambridge, MA: MIT Press, 1998); and "What America Makes Best," *Fortune*, March 28, 1988.

[T]here appear to be no serious rivals to U.S. economic preeminence on the horizon. Ironically, the greatest danger we now face stems from unwarranted complacence about the future. The rapid pace of globalization is changing and intensifying the competitive challenge. The technological capabilities of many advanced economies are steadily improving while a new wave of emerging economies is producing fast followers in some key areas and potential leaders in a few. The reality of the global economy is that companies have many choices about where to invest—capital, technology, and talent are available globally.

Source: William R. Hambrecht, William C. Steere, Jr., and William R. Brody, "Chairmen's Forward," *Going Global* (Washington, DC: Council on Competitiveness, 1988), p. 6.

How Did U.S. Corporations Respond to This Competitive Threat?

Important objectives of the response of American managers have been to reduce costs, improve product quality, stay ahead of competition technically, exploit new markets, raise market share, and, of course, enhance profits. A few of the important strategies employed to achieve these objectives are as follows.

Partnerships with Suppliers

Forming partnerships with suppliers has been one approach to achieving reduced costs. This contrasts with the old system where companies negotiated as adversaries (often under severe pressure) with the lowest-cost suppliers. In the new system, companies arrange long-term relationships with suppliers, cooperate with them in engineering design, and give them a voice in quality improvement. Companies also arrange just-in-time (JIT) delivery schedules with suppliers. JIT systems integrate the flow of components from suppliers into production schedules so that the part is delivered at the precise moment it is needed in production. This eliminates the need for inventories and lowers production cost. Experience of many companies has shown that closer relationships with suppliers will unleash innovation, improve quality, and lower cost of production.

Coordinating Functional Departments

Functional departments in the past often acted independently of other departments. Now there is more integration of basic functions such as product development, research, product design, manufacturing, communications, human resources, and marketing. Top priority is given to product quality control and flexible manufacturing. The result is a reduction in product development time, lower costs, and quicker accommodation to changes in consumer demand.

Outsourcing

Outsourcing occurs when a company moves work out of the enterprise, both at home and abroad, to reduce costs. Sometimes outsourcing is done because a company believes others can do the work at lower costs. Sometimes outsourcing is done to take advantage of lower labor costs in foreign lands. Foreign companies do the same. Japanese firms, for example, outsource to Southeast Asia. German companies have gone to lower-wage areas in Poland.

This practice has led to severe criticism of many companies, alleging they are exploiting foreign workers. Sometimes there is truth to these allegations, but many responsible companies seek to avoid exploitation. (See the Levi Strauss case at the end of Chapter 6.) A positive result of outsourcing to low-wage countries is not only that jobs are provided, but manufacturing technology moves there and workers are trained in new skills.

Increasing Foreign Direct Investment (FDI)

FDI, as noted in the last chapter, refers to investments for building a plant, purchasing all of the stock of a company, or acquiring a controlling interest in a foreign company. There has been a surge of FDI in the past decade. In 2000 total FDI outflow from the United States amounted to $139 billion (slightly below the 1999 high for the decade). About half went to Europe, mostly to the United Kingdom. Most of the investment was for mergers and acquisitions.[10]

There are many motives for establishing manufacturing plants abroad, for example, reducing production and distribution costs, reducing taxes, jumping tariff barriers, creating alternative suppliers, acquiring needed foreign technical skills, and getting closer to customers. Kasra Ferdows, a professor of Georgetown University, says a company can gain a competitive advantage by methodically upgrading its foreign plants. He illustrates this with examples of Hewlett-Packard Company's factory in Guadalajara, Mexico, which not only assembles computers but designs computer memory boards. 3M's plant in Bangalore, India, manufactures software but also writes software.[11]

FDI also aids in the economic development of LDCs by introducing new technology, managerial styles, worker skills, market access to other countries, and competition. As noted in Chapter 12, these are among the reasons why LDCs welcome MNCs.

---

[10] United Nations Development Programme, *World Investment Report, 2001, Promoting Linkages* (New York: United Nations, 2001), p. 12.
[11] Kassra Ferdows, "Making the Most of Foreign Factories," *Harvard Business Review,* March–April, 1997, p. 74.

Improving Productivity

Productivity, the index of production output per unit of labor input, is an important measure of the economic strength of a country, its competitive advantage, and its standard of living. For example, if productivity is expanding, business can and does raise wages without increasing prices. When it is rising, the goods and services available to consumers are increasing. Unfortunately, despite a massive effort by the U.S. Bureau of Labor Statistics to develop accurate measures of productivity, the numbers are hardly precise. This is not so much a fault of experts who calculate the subject but of the complexity of the measurement problem.[12]

Figure 13.1 displays the rate of productivity growth from 1973 to 1999. It is clear that productivity accelerated in the 1990s. The average annual growth rate of 3.1 percent in this period is more than double the long-term historical rate for the United States. This is one reason for the exceptional boom in economic growth during the decade. Alan Greenspan, chairman of the Federal Reserve Board, attributes this trend to advances in technology and its application.

Forming Combinations with Other Companies

The growth of foreign operations of American companies has been facilitated by arranging combinations with other companies through mergers, acquisitions, and alliances. Mergers take place when one company is

FIGURE 13.1
Output Per Hour in the Nonfarm Business Sector

Sources: Department of Commerce (Bureau of Economic Analysis) and Department of Labor (Bureau of Labor Statistics).

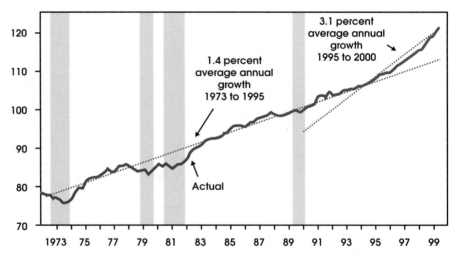

Note: Productivity is the average of income- and product-side measures. Productivity for 2000 is inferred from the first three quarters. Shading indicates recessions.

[12] For a discussion of the problems of measuring productivity, see "Expanding the Nation's Productive Capacity," *Economic Report of the President* (Washington, DC: U.S. Government Printing Office, 1995), chap. 3.

formed from one or more other companies. Acquisitions take place when one firm acquires a controlling interest in another, generally with an offer to buy enough shares of stock to gain control. An alliance is a cooperative arrangement between two or more companies to achieve a specific purpose.

Mergers and Acquisitions (M&As)

Globalization has stimulated M&As both in the United States and in foreign countries. The fundamental reason for this trend, of course, is the assumption that merged companies will be more efficient and more competitive, an assumption not always realized. Both numbers and values of M&As have soared during the past decade. As shown in Figure 13.2, the total value of mergers in the United States rose from $71 billion in 1991 to $1.3 trillion in 2000. The number of M&As increased from 1,877 in 1991 to 9,566 in 2000.[13] The largest M&A in the United States in 2000 was America Online Inc.–Time Warner, the total value of which was $101 billion.

U.S. companies are increasingly active in foreign countries. Acquisitions of foreign companies rose from a value of $5.6 billion in 1991 to $136.7 billion in 2000. At the same time, foreign companies have been active in acquiring U.S. companies. Foreign buyers of U.S. businesses (including U.S.-owned plants in foreign countries) totaled 188 in 1991 and

FIGURE 13.2   **Trends in Mergers and Acquisitions, 1981–2000**

Source: *Mergerstat Review, 2001* (Los Angeles: Mergerstat, 2001), p. 1. www.mergerstat.com

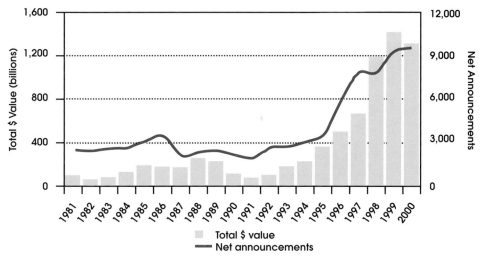

[13] These numbers and those that follow are from *Mergerstat Review, 2001* (Los Angeles: Mergerstat, 2001).

1,248 in 2001. The largest acquisition of a U.S. company by a foreign company in 2000 was Deutsche Telekom AG–Germany's purchase of VoiceStream Wireless Corp., for $41.6 billion.

M&As between European firms have been growing rapidly as the EU becomes more integrated. A recent decision of the European Commission is likely to accelerate M&As. In June 2000 the Commission passed a law that makes it easier for hostile takeovers to occur and more difficult for companies to defend themselves by selling stock to a so-called white knight, or a friendly buyer. EU rules require member-countries to conform their national statutes to the Commission's provisions by 2006.[14]

Alliances

Companies seek to grow mainly by internal expansion or merger and acquisition, or both. Today more companies are expanding through alliances. Peter Pekar, Jr., a consultant on alliances, calculates that alliances have recently been growing about 25 percent a year and numbered more than 10,000 in 2000.[15]

Among all types of alliances, joint ventures are most prominent. These are partnerships by which two or more firms create an organization to achieve specific objectives. Joint ventures are much less expensive than building factories from scratch or buying companies. They make it possible for a company to meet shifting market demands quicker than by building new marketing and distribution systems. Through joint ventures, companies can share risks and costs in developing emerging technologies or new products. They can defend strategic positions against forces too strong for one firm to resist. They can penetrate trade barriers. They help a company coordinate resources in a global market system, accumulate more capital, and pool technical skills in developing technologies.

American companies have formed alliances for years with foreign partners. For instance, Ford formed one with Mazda in 1978 that still exists. Fuji Photo and Xerox formed a joint venture more than a quarter century ago with 12 employees; it now has thousands. Hewlett-Packard formed a joint venture with Yokogawa more than 25 years ago. U.S. companies, of course, also form alliances with other U.S. companies.

Failure rates of both M&As and alliances are high—in the 50 percent area. M&As often fail because of difficulties in meshing the cultures of the merged firms. Often, the foreseen cost and efficiency improvements have not materialized. Alliances fail for these reasons plus others, such as mismatched personal characteristics, poor communications between partners, unclear management responsibilities, or an ambiguous agreement.

---

[14] Edmund L. Andrews, "Europeans Open Door for Hostile Takeovers," *The New York Times*, June 7, 2001.
[15] Peter Pekar, Jr., *Alliances Take Center Stage: Powerful Growth & Earnings Engine for All Companies* (Los Angeles: Houlihan Lokey Howard & Capital, 2001).

For success with these forms of organization, it is essential that skillful preparation be done. If done well, the results can be beneficial.

Consortiums

Consortiums are a different type of alliance. In 1984 Congress passed the National Cooperative Research Act, permitting two or more competitors to form a consortium for a specific purpose. An outstanding example is SEMATECH (Semiconductor Manufacturing Technology). It was formed at a time when American companies were losing world market share for computer chips because of the superiority of Japanese producers. The mission of the consortium is to develop new technologies to achieve world leadership. The consortium has developed low-cost methods to manufacture specialized high-value computer chips. This gives the industry new competitive power in the global market, not only in selling sophisticated chips but also in exporting the chip-making machines. Other industries have taken advantage of the National Cooperative Research Act.

EXPANDING REGIONAL TRADING AGREEMENTS

Rapid increase in the number of regional trading arrangements has been a major force in globalization. So numerous have they been that nearly all countries now belong to at least one trading club.[16] According to the Council of Economic Advisers, the United States has been a partner in more than 300 of these trade agreements, ranging from the huge, three-nation North American Free Trade Agreement (NAFTA), to much more simple bilateral agreements with single countries.[17] These agreements, of course, increase global competition. They also expand trade and give further impetus to globalization. The four largest are the EU, NAFTA, the Mercado Comun del Sur (Mercosur), and the Asia-Pacific Economic Cooperation (APEC) forum.

The European Union On January 1, 1993, the EU became a unified regional market. On that date, a long list of customs, tariffs, and nontariff barriers were removed between the 12 European nations comprising the union at that time. Also removed were many national laws and policies affecting trade. They were replaced with hundreds of new rules and regulations concerning such matters as health, environment, and quality standards that were to be consistent among member-states. Since 1993, three more nations have joined, making 15 in all, and now 16 more countries are seeking entry, as shown in Figure 13.3.

---

[16] See Jeffrey A. Frankel, *Regional Trading Blocs in the World Economic System* (Washington, DC: Institute for International Economics, October 1997).
[17] *Economic Report of the President* (Washington, DC: U.S. Government Printing Office, 2001), p. 250.

FIGURE 13.3 **Current and Prospective Members of the EU**

Source: "Survey of Europe," *The Economist*, October 23, 1999, p. 4.

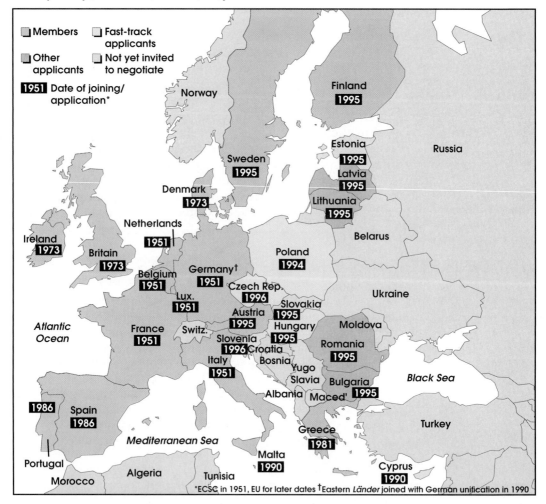

Today the EU offers great opportunities for American companies, but it also poses serious competitive threats. This vast market of more than 350 million people with a gross domestic product more than $9 trillion, about equal to that of the United States, is a lucrative market. It is the largest purchaser of U.S.-produced goods and services and the biggest foreign investor in the United States. There are in Europe today companies clearly the equal in competitiveness with the best American companies.

The fundamental objective of the EU is to form a union among member-nations that will assure political and economic stability among the dominant nations of Europe. A milestone step in this direction took place on

January 1, 1999, when the EU adopted a uniform currency—the euro. The European Central Bank (ECB), established in 1998, arranged the conversion of the currencies of the members of the European Monetary Union (EMU), which took place on January 1, 2002.[18] Jeffrey Garten, dean of the Yale School of Management, predicts that the euro "will be the most important change in the global economy well into the next century."[19]

Some futurists see great promise for the EU in stabilizing Europe to achieve economic growth and a political stability that prevents the type of wars that in the past periodically devastated the continent. There are skeptics, however, who see serious internal problems. They predict that individual countries will become frustrated by the loss of financial sovereignty that comes with the creation of the ECB. Some think countries will be so pressured by business to change policies concerning working conditions, hours of work, and social contributions that the result will be political turmoil. Some observers believe the EMU can exist in the long term only with complete political union, and they are skeptical that European nationalists will accept the necessary loss of sovereignty such a union entails.

There are deep divisions among member nations about further enlargement of the union. France, for example, opposes much further expansion. Other nations fear the results of the free movement of people permitted on entrance to the union and the availability of such rights as welfare benefits. Granting membership to some poorer nations in Eastern Europe will undoubtedly generate difficult problems, not the least of which will be the technical difficulty faced by new members of conforming their national statutes to some 80,000 pages of EU law.

At a summit in Lisbon in 2000, EU leaders "vowed to make the EU the world's most competitive and dynamic economy by 2010."[20] Cynics said this was nothing more than rhetorical hyperbole. Which view to accept is unclear at this time.

The North American Free Trade Agreement   NAFTA created a free trade block consisting of the United States, Canada, and Mexico. The first step in its formation was taken in 1987 when the United States and Canada signed the Canada–United States Free Trade Agreement (CFTA). In 1994 the agreement was extended to Mexico. By linking the United States, Canada, and Mexico, NAFTA created the largest trading block in the world with more than 400 million customers in countries with a combined annual gross domestic product in 2001 of more than $12 trillion.

---

[18] At the time of conversion, three countries had declined to join the EMU—Great Britain, Denmark, and Sweden.

[19] Jeffrey E. Garten, "The Euro Will Turn Europe into a Superpower," *Business Week,* May 4, 1998, p. 30.

[20] "European Liberalisation," *The Economist,* November 3, 2001, p. 68.

NAFTA is a massive, detailed, mind-numbing, nearly 2,000-page treaty of thousands of specific agreements. Here are a few highlights.

- One-half the products the United States exports to Mexico became duty-free the day after the treaty was implemented. Other tariffs have been eliminated in phases as specified in the treaty.

- Major nontariff barriers, such as quotas on pharmaceuticals, were removed.

- Restrictions on foreign investment in Mexico were removed except for oil exploration.

- U.S. and Canadian banks were permitted to acquire Mexican banks.

- Various restrictions on intellectual property, agricultural products, and automobiles were removed.

NAFTA has generated many benefits and also problems for both the United States and Mexico. For example, trade between the two countries has increased significantly. U.S. exports to Mexico increased from $57 billion in 1996 to $112 billion in 2000. U.S. imports from Mexico jumped from $74 billion in 1996 to $136 billion in 2000. Precisely how much of this increase was due to NAFTA is impossible to say, but it has been substantial.

Labor unions in the United States opposed NAFTA from its beginning. They are concerned about the movement of American industry to Mexico to take advantage of the lower wages paid Mexican workers. Particularly hard hit has been the textile industry in the United States. There is no doubt that this movement of jobs has been significant, but studies show that the net impact on American workers has been positive. Far more jobs in the United States have been created by NAFTA than have been lost.[21]

Some important problems have arisen in the operation of NAFTA. One example concerns trucking. The treaty specifies that Mexican trucks will have free access to American markets, but from the beginning there have been restrictions put on this provision largely because too many Mexican trucks do not meet U.S. domestic standards. The Teamsters Union has been especially strong in opposing it. Mexico, of course, wants the provision implemented. Before 2001, Mexican trucks could cross the border and drive no more than 20 miles before transferring cargo to American trucks. However, under a new agreement they now have full access to American highways if certain rules are followed. For example, Mexican truckers must be licensed to meet U.S. standards and electronic verification must be available at border crossings. Rigorous inspections

[21] *Study on the Operation and Effects of the North American Free Trade Agreement,* submitted to Congress, July 1997.

are required before Mexican trucks are permitted on U.S. highways. Trucks can cross the border only at stations with full truck inspection capacity.

Important issues have arisen about the environment. There has been a large increase in employment along the border of the United States and Mexico. In 1994 there were approximately 600,000 people in the area, and by 2001 that had more than doubled to about 1.6 million. One result has been serious environmental degradation. According to an assessment completed in 1999, 12 percent of the population did not have access to potable water, 30 percent lacked wastewater treatment facilities, and 25 percent needed access to solid-waste disposal facilities. Since 1994 the two countries have provided about $3.1 billion to address such problems, with the United States contributing 80 percent of it.[22]

Finally, we note a lengthy report from Public Citizen, a progressive reform group, purporting to be a "report card" assessing the performance of NAFTA. The evaluation was F for all areas: U.S. job creation and quality, agriculture, environment, public health (food safety), wage levels, Mexican economic development and living standards, sovereignty and democratic governance, highway safety, drug enforcement, smuggling, labor issues, environmental agreements, and training programs. "Under NAFTA, conditions not only have not improved, they have deteriorated in many areas. As a result, on each of the issues examined, the only fair grade for NAFTA is a failing one."[23]

The treaty provides that current members can admit additional members. From the beginning of NAFTA, discussions have continued about its extension, first to Chile, then to all of South America. Chile and other South American countries have expressed interest in joining. Thirty-four leaders of Western Hemisphere countries met in Quebec in April 2001 to examine the possibilities of a free trade area for the entire region. This was the third such meeting, and this, like the others, failed to reach any conclusions. Labor unions are strongly opposed. Their main concerns are the same as with NAFTA—environmental degradation, loss of jobs in the United States, and lower wage rates. In addition, some countries, especially Brazil, are opposed because they fear loss of sovereignty.

Mercosur In March 1991, Argentina, Brazil, Paraguay, and Uruguay signed the Mercosur accord to establish a preferential trading area. Later, Chile and Bolivia became associated members. This is a large trading area with approximately 240 million people and a combined GDP more than $1 trillion, which is half that of all Latin America. One objective of

---

[22] General Accounting Office, *U.S.–Mexico Border* (Washington, DC: General Accounting Office, March 2000), p. 4.
[23] Public Citizen Global Trade Watch, *Report Card,* December 1998, www.citizen.org/pctrade/nafta/reports/5years.htm.

the agreement is eventually to install a common currency. Today, however, the accord is far from this goal. Argentina is suffering a serious economic and financial crisis that is disrupting trade in the area. Economists Sebastian Edwards, a professor at UCLA's Anderson School, believes that "Mercosur is going to be one more chapter in a long history of failed attempts at Latin American integration."[24] But there may be hope. Roberto Bouzas, an Argentine economist, said that Mercosur could drift into irrelevance but that would be a shame since cooperation among its members has "bolstered stability, democracy and economic reform in the region over the past 10 years. All would benefit if the integration continued."[25]

APEC APEC was established in 1989. Today it includes 21 countries with a GDP of $18 trillion. Included in its membership is the United States, China, and Japan. This organization is primarily a forum for discussion of many different problems in the area, apart from trade. For example, it has discussion groups concerned with energy, fisheries, human resource development, transportation, tourism, and so on. It is understandable that no action other than talk has occurred. There are wide differences among the nations with respect to GDP, political organization, culture, and national objectives. Leaders in the group, including the United States, have met to discuss plans for an eventual free trade area covering the APEC nations. Because of wide diversity among them, cynics conclude that is a vision not likely to occur. However, as a forum for discussion it performs a useful purpose.

GLOBALIZATION AND INTERNATIONAL FINANCIAL STABILITY

Today the forces of globalization have produced a large and rapid movement of trillions of dollars across national boundaries. These funds have been immensely important in the world's prosperity of the last decade. At the same time, they have been a dominant force in financial crises of many countries. The statistical data presented in this and the last chapter demonstrate positive results of cross-border financial flows. The most serious manifestation of negative results was the crisis in Southeast Asia beginning in 1997. Starting in Thailand, the crisis spread almost immediately to Indonesia, Malaysia, the Philippines, and South Korea. In 1998 the Russian financial system collapsed and countries in Latin America also came under intense pressure. For a decade, the Southeast Asian countries had been increasing their GDP at 6 percent or more a year. Mil-

---

[24] Quoted in Chris Kraul, "Argentina Crisis Puts Trade Block at Risk," *Los Angeles Times,* July, 16, 2001, p. C1.
[25] Quoted in "Another Blow to Mercosur," *The Economist,* March 31, 2001, p. 33.

lions of people rose from poverty to middle-income levels. Then a financial crisis reversed these trends. What happened?

Forces at play in these crises differed among the nations. But there is general agreement on the most important factors. Of great significance were huge inflows of money into these countries. One reasonable estimate is that $1.5 trillion were involved in daily foreign exchange transactions. In addition, foreign banks loaned generously to these countries, and domestic banks freely used the money to make loans. Billions if not trillions of dollars generated by speculators in foreign currencies and securities added to the volume. Hundreds of billions of dollars of this money could be transferred instantly by the touch of a computer keyboard.

The banking systems of many countries lagged the expansion of financial transactions. There was insufficient bank regulation and weak supervision. Banks borrowed money with short-term maturities and loaned it with long maturities to borrowers with political connections who often employed it unwisely. Important information about banks and private corporations was not available to investors, so they could not make appropriate risk assessments. Such practices led to excessive construction of factories and office buildings, a real estate boom with accompanying inflated prices, and soaring stock markets. Laws, ideas, and institutions needed to accompany vibrant capitalism were weak or absent.

Eventually, borrowers were unable to repay loans, export markets weakened, and a few banks and companies became insolvent. Foreign investors and speculators lost confidence and withdrew their funds. The result, of course, was financial disaster. This was a pattern started in Thailand and then developed in other South Asian countries. The same pattern appeared in Russia, Mexico, and Brazil. Thailand asked the International Monetary Fund (IMF) for help, and the agency responded with $17.2 billion. Rescue packages amounting to billions of dollars were also sent to other nations.

The International Monetary Fund was created in 1945 when 29 countries at a conference in Bretton Woods, New Hampshire, agreed to its mission and responsibilities. Currently, 182 member-countries contribute to its reserve, which amounts to about $300 million. The statutory purposes of the IMF are fundamentally to promote international monetary cooperation among its members, promote financial stability, and extend credits and loans to members who are experiencing problems in meeting their financial obligations. As of April 30, 2000, the IMF had credits and loans outstanding to 92 countries of about $66 billion. The IMF has no authority over its members but provides financial aid when needed. When making loans, it can and does prescribe various measures and policies that should be taken to resolve the financial problems of the borrower. The IMF works closely with the World Bank, a sister institution concerned with the economic development of poorer nations and their efforts to resolve financial problems and create economic growth.

Bitter controversy has developed over the prescriptions the IMF recommends when it extends financial aid. Specifically, with the Southeast Asia crisis reputable economists—such as Martin Feldstein, former chairman of the President's Council of Economic Advisers and professor of economics at Harvard, and Joseph Stiglitz, former chief economist of the World Bank and now a professor of economics at Stanford—were extremely critical of the medicine the IMF prescribed for Thailand and other nations, including Russia. In Thailand, the IMF prescribed a balanced budget, higher interest rates, the closing of insolvent banks, closer supervision of financial institutions, and support of the exchange value of the baht (the local currency). Feldstein and Stiglitz said such austerity measures were mostly the reverse of what should have been applied in these countries.[26]

Lawrence Summers, then deputy secretary of the treasury and now president of Harvard University, and Stanley Fischer, the IMF's first deputy managing director and former professor of the Massachusetts Institute of Technology, came to the defense of the IMF. Secretary Summers said the IMF has bailed out and strengthened many countries, such as Russia and Poland, and has advanced trade liberalization around the world. It has not had a major default in 50 years. He added that the agency is indispensable.

Arguments about the policies of IMF are part of a larger issue of international financial governance. The forces of globalization have acted with extraordinary power and are changing financial structures, capital flows, and monetary policies throughout the world. What is absent is a global governance system accepted by all nations to harmonize these forces. There are some, but far from enough, institutions in place to help manage disruptions and harmonize changes. One agency, of course, is the IMF. There are no others at this level. The so-called Group of Seven (G7) is composed of finance ministers of seven countries—the United States, Canada, Great Britain, Germany, France, Italy, and Japan. They meet regularly but have not yet agreed to any organized global integrating agency. There are many nongovernment groups, however, working in this area. For example, there is the International Forum on Globalization (IFG), "an alliance of 60 leading activists, scholars, economists, researchers and writers formed to stimulate new thinking, joint activity, and public education in response to economic globalization."[27] It was established in 1994, represents 60 organizations in 25 countries, and issues special reports. The Financial Stability Forum (FSF) was formed by

---

[26] See Joseph Stiglitz, "What I Learned at the World Economic Crisis," *The New Republic,* April 17/24, 2000; and Martin Feldstein, "Focus on Crisis Management," *The Wall Street Journal,* October 6, 1998.

[27] The International Forum on Globalization, www.ifg.org.

the finance ministers and central bank governors of the G7 countries in 1999. Its purpose is to promote international financial stability.[28] Think tanks and activist groups are busy prescribing what the financial architecture of the world should be. In sum, students can find different positions on what should be done to secure global financial stability in the future.

SPREADING CAPITALISM

The global spread of capitalism is one of the most significant trends in recent history. This development resulted from many forces. Highly important was the defeat of authoritarian governments in World War II and the imposition by the victorious powers of democratic free market principles and institutions. The model was American capitalism. Following the war, a major foreign policy of the United States was to foster democracy and free market economies throughout the world. The rapid economic growth of the United States after the war also attracted admirers. The heady burst of economic activity confirmed the notion that the American model of capitalism was the best approach to wealth and national power. The extraordinary rise of Japan to become the world's second-largest economy was seen as a striking illustration of this dogma.

Deviations from the American Capitalistic Model

The classical capitalism model has been the foundation of the free market economy of the United States. As amply illustrated throughout this book, however, there have been substantial deviations from this model in the United States. There is no country today with the same democratic free market structure as the United States. The most economically advanced countries, however, display most of the basic features of the American economy. But there are significant differences.

To oversimplify, for example, while the Japanese economy fundamentally is free market, it is dominated by an interlacing of companies in massive aggregations called *keiretsu*. So dominant a feature is this system that one author calls it *alliance capitalism*.[29] South Korea has adopted the Japanese model of gigantic alliances of companies in comparatively few conglomerates, called *chaebols*. In some Southeast Asian countries, popular leaders give close friends and family members control of state enterprises. This has been called *crony capitalism*. The Chinese model features government by the Communist Party and much central planning and

---

[28] See its website at www.fsforum.org.
[29] Michael I. Gerlach, *Alliance Capitalism: The Social Organization of Japanese Business* (Berkeley: University of California Press, 1992).

control over the economy. However, it has established free market zones, loosened the reins over banking, and ended the control of military leaders over state enterprises. It is toe deep into capitalism and slowly moving deeper. Most countries of the world have embraced free markets and other forms of capitalism, but each has adopted variations in political controls, state ownership of productive enterprises, government relationships with corporate enterprises (both public, and private), protectionism, and financial structures. There are obviously many different brands of capitalism around the world, but the central point is that globalization and capitalism have expanded together in recent years.

Critics of Global Capitalism

Jeffrey E. Garten wrote an article entitled, "Can the World Survive the Triumph of Capitalism?"[30] This was a review of a book by William Greider, a thoughtful and incisive critic of global capitalism. Garten answers his question in the affirmative, but, he says, we must take seriously the critics of global capitalism. Greider points out in his book that the global economy has made possible the accumulation of great wealth but at the same time has serious flaws.[31] Among them, first, is that global capitalism is repeating some of the shortcomings of capitalism experienced 100 years ago in the United States; for example, exploitation of workers, including children, and inequality of income distribution. Second, uncontrolled investments lead to excessive productive capacity and overproduction of many products. Third, the exuberant growth of global capitalism leads to degradation of the environment. Fourth, the extraordinary growth of money and its free flow inevitably will result in destabilizing the world's financial systems. Greider wrote his book before the 1997–1998 world financial crisis. He was, therefore, prescient.

Greider, and many other critics, see fallacies in some fundamental assumptions of capitalism. For example, rising incomes created by vigorous global capitalism will raise all boats. That demonstrably has not happened. Throughout the world, including the major industrial nations such as the United States, the income gap between the rich and poor has widened. "In sub-Saharan Africa the global development effort has not succeeded," said Lawrence Summers when secretary of the treasury. He continued, "Per capita incomes in Africa in the late 1990s were lower than they were 30 years ago. Average incomes for a region of 600 million are now only 65 cents a day. And across large parts of the continent, children are more likely to die before their first birthday than to learn to read."[32]

---

[30] Jeffrey E. Garten, "Can the World Survive the Triumph of Capitalism?" *Harvard Business Review*, January–February 1997.
[31] William Greider, *One World, Ready or Not: The Manic Logic of Global Capitalism* (New York: Simon & Schuster, 1997).
[32] Lawrence H. Summers, "Rising to the Challenge of Global Economic Integration," in a speech to the School of Advanced International Studies, Washington, DC, September 20, 2000.

Another assumption is that if left alone from government interference the free market system will function efficiently and effectively to resolve a nation's economic problems. This assumption is flawed, say critics, because history shows that if left to its own forces, the free market system can lead to serious social and also economic problems.

Another assumption is that free markets and political democracy go together. Without democracy, free markets will wither and fade away. That is demonstrably not true say critics. They point to many nations where this has not happened. In the fascist societies of Italy, Germany, and Spain in the 1940s, for example, there were free markets but no democracy. Today in China, as noted above, there are a few free market areas, and they are growing, but there is no political democracy. Indeed, the Chinese government has been diligent in stifling praise for democracy. The free market has thrived under authoritarian rule in Singapore.

Most of the critics of capitalism do not wish to abolish it but only to reform it. They accept the view that there has never been an invention in the history of the world as capable of improving the general welfare of society as capitalism. But it does exhibit defects that in the political democracies are gradually being corrected to meet the needs of the times.

Institutions and Ideas of Capitalism

There is also growing realization that for capitalism to produce its potential advantages there must be certain fundamental structural arrangements. Toward the end of the twentieth century, conventional wisdom among many observers was that if a nation embraced the free market philosophy it would reap the same benefits as the advanced democracies with strong capitalistic systems. When this did not work too well, in Russia, for example, more observers saw that for capitalism to work there had to be many fundamental institutional arrangements in place. What they had in mind, for example, was a trustworthy financial system with general transparency, bankruptcy courts, antitrust laws, a minimum social security net, limited government regulation, an efficient tax system, an acceptance of the idea of private property and a legal system to protect it, an understanding and acceptance of the profit motive in private enterprise, and an assumption of private enterprise responsibilities to workers and communities.

These institutions and ideas cannot be installed overnight. Most are either absent or slowly evolving in many developing countries. The failure of global capitalism to benefit and transform many less developed countries is due to the absence of some of these requirements. For example, most of the less developed countries know that they must have capital to grow. Sources of capital do not exist in their countries, so they must depend upon foreign investment. But foreign investors will not deploy their capital in the absence of institutions to protect it.

Jeffrey Sachs, director of the Institute for International Development at Harvard, says that even when these institutions are developing in a nation, other factors may be decisive. For example, difficult geography, poor public health, and skewed demographics can inhibit economic development. Disease in the tropics, illiteracy, or internal wars have also kept countries, from prosperity.[33]

GLOBALIZATION ERODES NATION-STATE SOVEREIGNTY

Market forces have eroded the sovereignty of nations, and yet the nation-state still retains unlimited authority within its own borders. How is this paradox explained?

As demonstrated in the above discussion of the financial crisis in Southeast Asia, governments felt helpless to prevent the wreckage created by abrupt and voluminous capital withdrawals. To make their industries competitive in global markets, governments must attract capital and technology. This cannot be done, they know, if too much restraint is placed on the free flow of money. The competitiveness imperative amounts to an infringement on state authority.

Another type of erosion on sovereignty flows from agreements that governments make with international institutions that supplant decisions heretofore made by governments. In mind are decisions of the WTO about trade rules that bind members. Similarly, NAFTA ties Canada, the United States, and Mexico to its provisions. The European Commission has issued hundreds of economic rules that bind its members. We explained how the IMF imposes decisions on countries receiving its financial aid. The ECB makes important monetary decisions formerly made by central banks of individual countries of Europe.

At a different level, governments in both industrialized and developing countries are held hostage to the power of large multinational corporations. A case in point is DaimlerChrysler. This third-largest car maker in the world in sales, and the biggest industrial company in Europe after Royal Dutch/Shell, has exceptional clout. The German government will be receptive to its pressures for tax and social reforms that improve the firm's competitive position. If costs of production in Germany are prohibitively high, the company can move its headquarters to the United States, close plants in Germany, and build assembly plants elsewhere. LDCs can be expected to respond faster to pressures of giant MNCs than large industrial states.

---

[33] Peter Passell, "Capitalism Doesn't Always Take. Location Is Destiny," *The New York Times,* June 12, 1997.

Such erosion of sovereignty is expected by many analysts of the subject to continue as globalization expands. For example, Kenichi Ohmae, a well-known Japanese management consultant, believes we are witnessing the end of the nation-state.[34] This view, or slight modifications of it, have been expressed by many other observers.[35] The argument is that the market is becoming much more powerful than the nation-states in determining economic, political, cultural, and social affairs. This is inevitable as globalization expands.[36] It is not a bad thing, this side argues. Free and open markets, integrated in a world economy, will secure the greatest prosperity for all.

Opposed to this view are those who acknowledge that some powers of government have been yielded to the market. But, they argue, free markets have not been particularly effective in providing a social net for people, environmental quality, or human rights. Government remains the solution of last resort to meet these needs. Sometimes, in France and Germany, for example, market forces have forced moderate retrenchment in social programs. However, worldwide the trend is toward more rather than less concern about social demands. Robert Gilpin, emeritus professor from Princeton University, points out that "despite the significance of globalization, it has not replaced the state, national differences, and politics as the really important determinants of domestic and international affairs."[37] The same point is made by John Micklethwait and Adrian Wooldridge, two reporters for *The Economist*. They write:

> In general, the people who herald the end of the nation-state do so in tones of triumph. However, even as they celebrate the removal of the old order, many, particularly on the left, are struck by a nasty second thought: The end of the nation-state could mean the end of the welfare state. Governments will have no choice but to cut taxes, reduce social benefits, and lighten regulations if they are to have any chance of attracting mobile capital. Globalization is threatening not just the nation-state but also the benefits that it provides.[38]

---

[34] Kenichi Ohmae, *The End of the Nation State* (New York: Free Press, 1995).

[35] See, for example, Walter B. Wriston, *The Twilight of Sovereignty: How the Information Revolution Is Transforming Our World* (New York: Scribners, 1992); and Susan Strange, *The Retreat of the State: The Diffusion of Power in the World Economy* (New York: Cambridge University Press, 1996).

[36] Thomas L. Friedman, *The Lexus and the Olive Tree: Understanding Globalization* (New York: Farrar, Straus, Giroux, 1999).

[37] Robert Gilpin, *The Challenge of Global Capitalism* (Princeton, NJ: Princeton University Press, 2000), p. 312.

[38] John Micklethwait and Adrian Wooldridge, *A Future Perfect: The Challenge and Hidden Promise of Globalization* (New York: Crown Business, 2000), p. 147.

Peter Drucker, an eminent professor at Claremont College, looks at this issue with a historian's perspective:

> Since the early Industrial Revolution, it has been argued that economic interdependence would prove stronger than nationalist passions. Kant was the first to say so. The "moderates" of 1860 believed it until the first shots were fired at Fort Sumter. The Liberals of Austria-Hungary believed to the very end that their economy was far too integrated to be split into separate countries. So, quite clearly, did Mikhail Gorbachev. But whenever in the last 200 years political passions and nation-state politics have collided with economic rationality, political passions and the nation-state have won.[39]

EROSION OF CULTURES

Officials from 19 countries met in Ottawa, Canada, in 1998 to discuss the growing impact throughout the world of U.S.-produced movies, television shows, music, and other entertainment. Their purpose was to decide what to do to protect their cultures from this infusion of American values. In Canada, for instance, the vast majority of movies, CDs, and magazines are American and, of course, the Internet is predominantly U.S. generated. Regulatory proposals were made to the Canadian government to limit television time devoted to U.S.-made programs. "Market forces, left to their own devices," said Sheila Copps, the minister of Canadian heritage, "would have made the entire Canadian broadcasting system a U.S. subsidiary."[40] This raises a question, of course: Is the issue the alteration of culture or commercial self-interest?

The rapid and explosive spread of American culture throughout the world is one significant trend within globalization. Coca-Cola is consumed worldwide. American movies are shown even in remote corners of the world in preference to other films. Baseball caps of American teams and American blue jeans are worn by teenagers everywhere. Kentucky Fried Chicken and McDonald's can be found the world over. The American databases on the Internet, some with information despised by people in the United States, are available wherever a computer can be found. All this is conveyed in English, a language used universally.

Throughout the world there is resentment about the transmission of certain Western cultural values. The French for years have sought to reject entry of English words and phrases into their language. Members of the French Académie Française cringe at the use by the general population of such expressions as *le hotdog*. The French government identified 3,000 En-

---

[39] Peter Drucker, "The Global Economy and the Nation-State," *Foreign Affairs,* September–October 1997, p. 172.
[40] Roge Ricklefs, "Canada Fights to Fend off American Tastes and Tunes," *The Wall Street Journal,* September 24, 1998, p. B1.

glish words that should be expunged from their language. It did not happen. A poll taken by the U.S. State Department in the fall of 2000 asked people in Europe and the United States, "How much of a threat do you think American popular culture such as music, televison and films is to the cultures of other countries in the world?" The most responses of "threats" came from France, where 8 percent said "very serious threat" and 30 percent said "serious threat." In the United States, the corresponding figures were 7 and 17 percent. But a more favorable response was given to this question: "In general, what is your opinion of American popular culture, such as music, television and films?" Nine percent of the French said "very favorable" and 43 percent said "somewhat favorable." Corresponding figures for Great Britain were 20 and 47 percent. People in Germany and Italy responded about the same as the British. Americans did not see their culture as a threat to foreign cultures.[41]

There is much ambivalence about the impact of the U.S. exports on other cultures. Around the world, shrill rhetoric from activists and intellectuals damns the United States, while ordinary people flock to see the violence and sexuality in American-made films. French critics blast McDonald's for the pernicious impact of its fast-food philosophy on the country's traditional leisurely way of eating, while they watch French citizens, indifferent to the menace, fill its restaurants.

Communications and the sale of American products are not the only forces spreading new cultural values around the world. Economic forces of globalization have encouraged massive migrations of peoples. In Germany, for example, the demand for workers brought a large influx of Turkish workers who, of course, brought with them their cultures, some aspects of which infiltrated into German society. In the United States, recent Latin American and Asian immigrants have influenced American language and music. Throughout the world, globalization has stirred migrations of workers, leading to the diffusion of many different ethnic, religious, and commercial values.

A major question, of course, is: How much of the spread of cultures around the world really changes the core values of peoples? This was addressed by Samuel P. Huntington in his seminal book on civilizations.[42] He points out that much of the cultural diffusion may be faddish and does not alter underlying values. There are core cultural values in societies that are not easily changed. For example, he says, use of the English language in the world is more a convenient means of intercultural communication than a force to change core values.

[41] Reported by Steven Kull, "Culture Wars? How Americans and Europeans View Globalization," *Brookings Review,* Fall 2001, p. 20.
[42] Samuel P. Huntington, *The Clash of Civilizations and the Remaking of World Order* (New York: Simon & Schuster, 1996).

FIGURE 13.4 **Main Forces in Globalization**

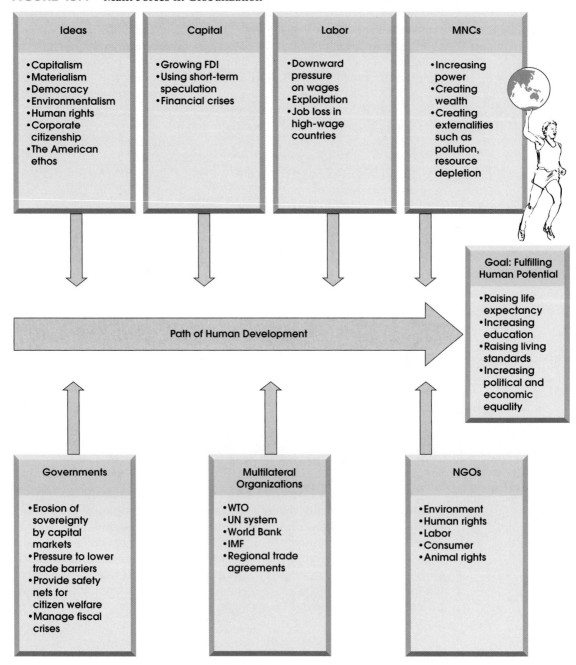

There seems little doubt that globalization has significantly influenced the flow of values. Some forces, such as types of entertainment, may have temporary impact. Other forces, such as technological innovations (e.g., computers, biotechnology, pharmaceuticals, motor vehicles), may have more lasting impact. However, it is difficult to reject the thesis of Huntington and others that the core cultures of peoples are not easily and significantly changed.

CONCLUDING OBSERVATIONS

In this and the preceding chapter we have examined a range of ideas and entities that interact in complex ways in the phenomenon of globalization. Figure 13.4 shows the main forces discussed and suggests that, in one way or another, all have an influence on the movement of humanity toward its destiny, which, optimistically, we show as moving in the direction of fulfilling human potential.

Globalization is a revolutionary phenomenon. It has created enormous wealth for people all over the world. At the same time, it has led to exploitation, dislocation, and suffering for some who have yet to experience its benefits. It has changed business–government–society relationships in profound and fundamental ways. On balance, there seems to be little question that the forces of globalization are beneficial to the peoples of the world and promise even greater benefits in the future. To achieve this promise, however, important reforms are necessary.

The World Trade Organization and Its Critics

The WTO was relatively unknown to the world's public until a meeting of the organization's ministers in Seattle in 1999 scheduled for November 30–December 3. At that meeting, the WTO dramatically gained worldwide recognition as a result of the tens of thousands of activists who demonstrated against the organization and forcefully advanced their demands. Activist groups are not the only critics of the WTO. Responsible voices of countries around the world, members of the U.S. Congress, academics, lawyers, and others have voiced specific criticisms of the organization. This case presents important criticisms leveled at the WTO and responses of supporters of the organization. Before examining these complaints, we

describe briefly the origin, organization, and functions of the WTO.

WHAT IS THE WTO?

The WTO was established in 1994 at the last meeting of GATT (General Agreement on Tariff and Trade). GATT was created in 1947 by 23 nations to stabilize and advance free trade around the world. World trade had been devastated by high tariffs in the 1930s and World War II. GATT was successful in achieving its objectives after eight rounds of meetings extending over five decades. Tariffs were dramatically reduced and world trade exploded sixteenfold. As noted in the chapter, trade has been one significant driving force in the expansion of globalization. However, GATT was narrowly focused on tariffs, and national representatives believed its reach should be expanded. In addition, they believed that further trade liberalization was needed and new rules were necessary to stiffen the spines of politicians to thwart special interest drives for tariff protections.[1] For these reasons, delegates decided to create a new agency, which they did on January 1, 1995. There were 90 member-nations at the birth of the WTO. Today there are 144 nations, which, together, generate most of the world's trade.

The most important function of the WTO is to administer the implementation of several trade agreements and trade rules built over a 50-year period under the operation of GATT. In addition to administering the GATT agreements, which focus principally on trade, the WTO administers other agreements. Different agreements, for example, have been negotiated concerned with food safety laws, product standards, telecommunications, finance, and intellectual properties. Aside from administering these agreements, there are other functions of the WTO, including being a forum for trade negotiations, adjudicating trade disputes, monitoring national trade policies, providing technical assistance to developing countries, and cooperating with other international organizations. The WTO says a major function is to assure that "trading conditions are stable, predictable, and transparent."[2]

Exhibit 1 is the organization chart of the WTO. The highest decision-making body, as shown in the chart, is the *Ministerial Conference*. It is composed of representatives from all WTO members and meets at least once every two years. This body tries to decide important policy by consensus. Each member-country has one vote. At the next level is the *General Council,* which normally is composed of ambassadors and heads of delegations in Geneva, the home of the WTO. Representatives of countries may on occasion join the Council. It meets several times a year in Geneva. This Council also meets as the Trade Policy

Review Body, which, as the name implies, reviews trade policies. It also meets as a Dispute Settlement Body, which examines and generally approves panel decisions concerning trade disputes. Under the General Council are special committees and working groups that deal with individual agreements and general operating problems. The range of activities of the WTO is identified in the chart.

Exhibit 2 is a flow chart of the dispute settlement process called the *Dispute Settlement Understanding (DSU)*. This process is a core function of the WTO in settling member disputes. It is a more formal process than that of GATT but is still based upon principles of negotiation, conciliation, mediation, and arbitration laid down by GATT. The first step in the dispute process is the *consultation stage*, in which members are given 60 days to seek a resolution of their dispute through discussions among themselves. If the parties in the dispute cannot resolve their differences, an impartial panel of experts meets to adjudicate the dispute. Deliberations of the panel are confidential, and minutes of its meetings are not made public. Panels are composed of three people, or more if the parties so desire. Panel members vary depending on the issue to be adjudicated. They may be government or nongovernment personnel, but they are to be experts in the substantive fields relevant to the issue at hand. Panel members are chosen by agreement among the parties, and once chosen, they act as individuals in their deliberations and not as government officials. There are rules concerning these panelists. For example, they are charged with avoiding conflicts of interest and must notify the WTO of any question concerning their independence and impartiality. If the panel concludes that a nation has violated a WTO agreement, it can recommend that the nation should withdraw the offending measure.

Countries involved in a dispute can appeal a panel decision to a seven-member *Standing Appellate Body (SAB)*. Members of this body are appointed by the WTO for four-year terms and each person may be reappointed once. Members of the SAB must not be affiliated with any government but be "broadly representative" of the WTO membership. The SAB reviews the panel findings, which are binding according to a "reverse consensus" rule. This rule binds the parties unless a consensus (a unanimous vote) develops *against* the report

[1] "Who Needs the WTO," *The Economist,* December 4, 1999.
[2] WTO, "10 Common Misunderstandings about the WTO," www.wto.gov, undated.

EXHIBIT 1
WTO Structure
All WTO members may participate in all councils, committees, and so forth, except the Appellate Body, Dispute Settlement panels, Textiles Monitoring Body, and plurilateral committees.

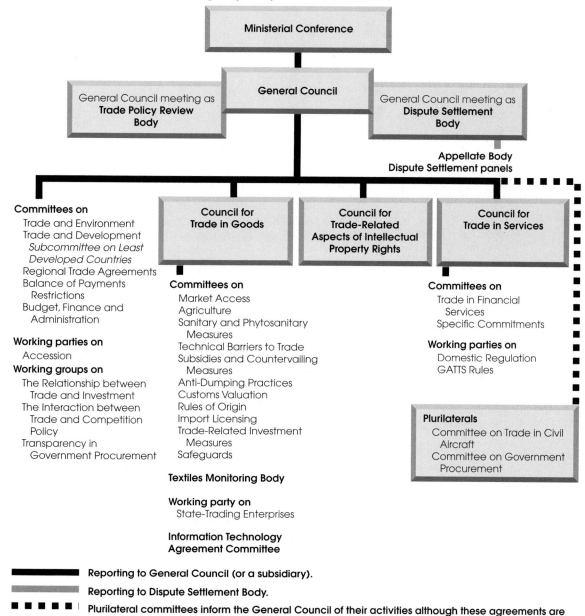

Reporting to General Council (or a subsidiary).

Reporting to Dispute Settlement Body.

Plurilateral committees inform the General Council of their activities although these agreements are not signed by all WTO members.

The General Council also meets as the Trade Policy Review Body and Dispute Settlement Body.

For the current negotiations, the Services Council and Agriculture Committee meet in "special sessions" and report directly to the General Council.

Source: World Trade Organization.

EXHIBIT 2
Flow Chart of WTO's Dispute Settlement Process

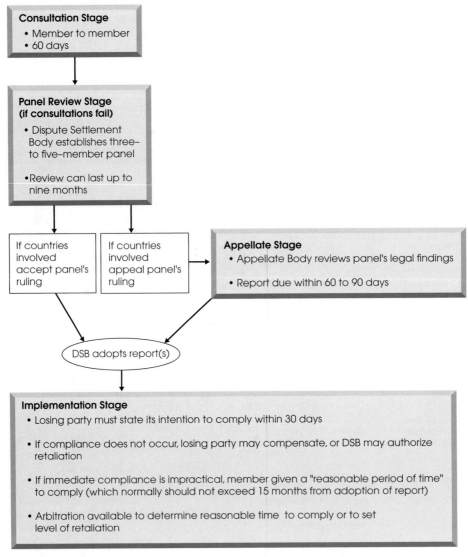

Consultation Stage
- Member to member
- 60 days

Panel Review Stage (if consultations fail)
- Dispute Settlement Body establishes three- to five-member panel
- Review can last up to nine months

If countries involved accept panel's ruling

If countries involved appeal panel's ruling

Appellate Stage
- Appellate Body reviews panel's legal findings
- Report due within 60 to 90 days

DSB adopts report(s)

Implementation Stage
- Losing party must state its intention to comply within 30 days
- If compliance does not occur, losing party may compensate, or DSB may authorize retaliation
- If immediate compliance is impractical, member given a "reasonable period of time" to comply (which normally should not exceed 15 months from adoption of report)
- Arbitration available to determine reasonable time to comply or to set level of retaliation

Source: General Accounting Office.

among the WTO membership. This will not happen because the winning party is not likely to vote against a ruling in its favor.[3]

[3] John O. McGinnis and Mark L. Movsesian, "The World Trade Constitution," *Harvard Law Review*, December 2000, pp. 530–36.

If the losing party does not accept the SAB decision, it may accept retaliation or offer compensation to the aggrieved party. If implementation of the ruling is immediately impractical, an extension of a reasonable period of time, not to exceed 15 months, may be accepted. If the losing party does not conform to the ruling within the implementation period, the complaining party may ask the WTO for permission to retaliate. Retaliation can take the form of raising a tariff on the noncomplying country's goods, or taking trade actions equivalent to the amount of harm suffered by the complaining country.[4] For example, the United States took this kind of action in the case of banana restrictions imposed by the European Union in 1995. In that case, the EU granted duty-free quotas for bananas grown in former colonies of some EU members while imports from Latin America were restricted. The United States and Latin American countries complained that this violated WTO rules. The claim was upheld in the DSU, and the EU modified its restrictions, but this too was ruled as violating rules. The United States was then permitted by the WTO rules to retaliate by imposing import restrictions on specified products from the EU amounting each year to $191.4 million, an amount calculated as equaling the harm done to U.S. economic interests.[5] The details of this retaliation are set forth in the story about Chiquita Brands International at the beginning of Chapter 11.

CRITICS OF THE WTO

Critics of the WTO cover a wide spectrum of ideologies and complaints. At one extreme are those who are strong supporters of the WTO but see flaws in the organization and want them corrected. At the other extreme are those who want the WTO abolished. At this end of the spectrum are an ill-defined group of environmentalists, human rights activists, anarchists, and an assortment of malcontents who loathe the current economic order and object to about everything in it. For the first time, these groups came together at the WTO meeting in Seattle in a more organized way and in greater numbers than in past demonstrations. Their targets included not only the WTO but the World Bank, the International Monetary Fund, capitalism and globalism, and the world economic, social, and political systems. The complaints ranged from reasoned positions to simple slogans. Exhibit 3 lists a

sampling of criticisms of different activist groups. Many of the complaints expressed in Seattle have been reflected in corporate, government, and nongovernment policy-making bodies. *The Economist* editorialized that "This new kind of protest is more than a mere nuisance: It is getting its way."[6] Following are pros and cons of more important criticisms of the WTO.

LOSS OF NATIONAL SOVEREIGNTY

The WTO has been accused of intruding on national sovereignty because of the binding nature of the organization's decision-making authority in trade disputes. Developing countries are particularly concerned because they fear that the WTO will formulate rules that impinge on their authority over the environment, working conditions, and other national prerogatives. National sovereignty has three important facets: economic, social, and political. It is important to note that the WTO has limited power over governments if they do not choose to abide by WTO decisions. The major decisions of the Ministerial Conference may require ratification of each nation's legislative body before they can be implemented. The WTO has no enforcement powers. It cannot overturn national laws or levy fines on violators. Judge Robert H. Bork, a well-known constitutional authority, said the sovereignty issue "is merely a scarecrow."[7] The WTO cannot bind any nation if it does not wish to be bound. However, the WTO can strengthen sovereignty by developing a world trading system that lessens the ability of special interest groups to force protectionism in a nation.

The WTO can impinge on sovereignty but only if a nation accepts it. As noted in Chapter 13, nations are willing to accept this intrusion for various gains. Nations are less willing to accept impingement on social and political elements of national sovereignty than of economic elements. This explains in part why some developing nations may warmly embrace free trade engendered by WTO rules but at the same time strongly oppose them because of impacts on their social and political sovereignty.

---

[4] General Accounting Office, *World Trade Organization: Issues in Dispute Settlement* (Washington, DC: GAO/NSIAD–00–210, August 2000), p. 8.
[5] Ibid., pp. 41–42.

[6] "Anti-Capitalist Protests," *The Economist*, September 23, 2000, p. 85.
[7] McGinnis and Movsesion, pp. 373–74.

EXHIBIT 3 Who They Are, What They Want
A look at some of the groups protesting the World Trade Organization in Seattle.

Group/Description	Position on the WTO
Alliance for Sustainable Jobs & the Environment Alliance formed between locked-out Kaiser Steel workers and environmental groups in Northern California.	Believes that the WTO subverts the labor and environmental laws of this country.
American Federation of Labor and Congress of Industrial Organizations AFL-CIO is a federation of 68 unions—13 million members.	Persuade the WTO to incorporate rules to enforce worker rights and environmental and consumer protections.
Direct Action Network Coalition of grassroots and street theater groups from the western United States and Canada.	Persuade public that WTO represents the next step in multinational corporate control.
Global Exchange International human rights group based in San Francisco.	Charges that among other things the WTO serves only the interests of multinational corporations, tramples over labor and human rights, and is destroying the environment.
Humane Society of the United States Promotes the protection of all animals	Wants the WTO to become animal-friendly. Some members of these groups dressed as sea turtles in the protest to highlight the importance of turtle-exclusion devices.
Institute for Agriculture and Trade Policy Research and advocacy group working for change in agriculture and natural resources.	Seeks to educate people about the implications of the WTO's actions on issues of agriculture, food safety, food security, dumping, and so on.
International Forum on Globalization U.S. based think tank of intellectuals and activist from 20 countries.	Seeks to provide as much information as possible to the public and activists so they are aware of the issues that drive the WTO.
People's Assembly International group representing 13 nations; came together specifically to protest the WTO	Educate people about the impact of the WTO and expand the linkages among anti-imperialist groups.
Rainforest Action Network Works to protect the Earth's rainforests.	Contends the WTO is fundamentally flawed, because trade provisions come before the laws of nations and power is shifted away from local communities and governments and given to corporations.

This was complied from interviews, news releases, and websites.
Source: Lynn Marshall, *Los Angeles Times,* December 3, 1999, p. A22.

THE WTO IS UNDEMOCRATIC

The WTO lacks the checks and balances of democracy and as a result is arbitrary and biased in favor of the rich and powerful countries, claim the critics. There is no place where representatives of workers, farmers, consumers, communities, environmentalists, and human rights groups can be heard. Furthermore, the most important policies made at the Ministerial Conference are decided by each member-country having but one vote. The result is a powerful organization that can establish international trade standards, operate in a nondemocratic manner, and be biased toward trade that overrides other values, such as environmental damage and human rights.

Defenders of the WTO point out that the agency's decisions are based upon an established body of laws (which fill 700 pages) developed over a period of 50 years. Decisions of the WTO are generally by consensus. This means that every country accepts the decision. Basic trade rules negotiated by governments are ratified by parliaments or other legislative bodies of member-nations. In negotiations among countries, issues other than tariffs can be addressed under various agreements administered by the WTO. There are, however, rules governing such inclusions. For example, some agreements provide that "technical regulations shall not be more trade-restrictive than necessary to fulfil a legitimate objective, taking account of the risks nonfulfillment would create."[8] Precisely what this means depends upon decisions of the Appellate Body concerned with specific cases.

ENVIRONMENTAL IMPERIALISM

Some activist groups accuse developed countries of environmental imperialism, which is using economic power to ignore or downgrade environmental factors in trade decisions. The World Wildlife Fund (WWF), for example, is seeking levies on imported goods produced by methods it does not approve. The failure of the WTO to protect turtles in one of its decisions was criticized by some Seattle activists not only in words but by costumes that made them look like turtles. In the case, the United States placed an embargo on the import of certain shrimp and shrimp products from countries that did not adopt fishing regulations to protect endangered sea turtles from drowning in shrimp nets. Countries affected by the embargo took the issue to the WTO. Both the WTO panel and the Appellate Body ruled against the United States on grounds such as the United States did not engage seriously in negotiations with the countries affected, the U.S. decision was applied in an arbi-

trary and discriminatory manner, and the United States did not have a right to take unilateral measures to protect a resource not in its territory.[9] The WTO rulings were based strictly on legal grounds.

The environment, working conditions, food safety, and human rights, for example, are factors critics say the WTO neglects and should do more about. Fundamentally, they want the WTO to impose sanctions on countries that do not meet their standards. While the WTO should study these factors, says William H. Lash III, a recognized expert in these matters, the goal of the WTO should be to remove barriers to trade, not add new ones. He says, "Those who advocate linking trade and labor or the environment at the WTO are not interested in promoting world trade. They are interested in the leverage of trade to promote their often statist views. They seek not the spirit of the WTO but its perceived power and prestige."[10]

LACK OF TRANSPARENCY

Critics complain that the proceedings of the panels and the Appellate Body are confidential. The public cannot attend and proceedings are not made public. However, parties may disclose their own submissions to these groups but must not make public the submissions of the other party. Opinions of individual panelists remain anonymous.

Some agreements endorse transparency. For example, "The Sanitary and Phytosanitary Standards (SPS) and the Technical Barriers to Trade (TBT) agreements require members to publish measures `promptly' and in a manner accessible to interested members."[11] Activities of the WTO, aside from panel and Appellate Body decisions, are made public. McGinnis and Movsesian recommend that greater transparency rules be adopted in dispute settlements. They say "if the decisions of the WTO adjudicative system are to enjoy public confidence, the process must be as transparent to the public as possible."[12]

---

[8] Ibid., pp. 598–99.

[9] General Accounting Office, *World Trade Organization*, p. 70; and McGinnis and Movsesion, pp. 591–94.
[10] William H. Lash III, "The Limited but Important Role of the WTO," *The Cato Journal,* Winter 2000, p. 372.
[11] McGinnis and Movsesion, p. 597.
[12] Ibid., p. 603.

COMPLAINTS OF EMERGING NATIONS

Two journalists observing the WTO summit meeting in Seattle reported numerous complaints voiced by poor and emerging nations. They reported that these nations are bitter that they have not received the promised rewards of previous trade accords. They believe most accords are for the benefit of the large developed countries, such as the United States. The accords in mind, particularly those involving the United States, concern lifting import restrictions on clothing, textiles, and agricultural products. Industrial nations, like Japan, have joined the less developed countries in pushing for modification of antidumping agreements. As noted in Chapter 12, the U.S. government faces strong pressures, for example, from steel, textile, agriculture, and chemical interests. These groups want protections from foreign imports. Some groups want import restrictions to curtail what they perceive as dumping products priced below cost on U.S. markets. Others want to protect jobs where their industry cannot compete with foreign producers.

Former U.S. trade representative Charlene Barshefsky said that she realized there were many trade problems of poorer countries. "The least-developed countries, the poorest, are of greatest concern because they are falling behind," she told reporters. Helping such nations, she said, "is very important, in and of itself—no strings attached." She also noted that those countries that were most open to the global economy had been benefited by it.[13]

ABOLISH THE WTO?

Many critics want to abolish the WTO. One powerful voice is that of Ralph Nader's Public Citizen. In an editorial, the organization based its recommendation to abolish the organization on three grounds:

First, the WTO's trade rules intentionally prioritize trade and commercial considerations over all other values. Never does the WTO say, "Trade should be undertaken in such a way as to promote values that the international community has agreed are important in their own right such as protection of human rights, the environment or labor rights." WTO rules generally require domestic laws, rules and regulations designed to further worker, consumer, environmental, health, safety, human rights, animal protection or other non-commercial interests to be undertaken in the "least trade restrictive" fashion possible.

Second the WTO intentionally overrides domestic decisions about how economies should be organized and corporations controlled. Its rules drastically shrink the choices available to democratically controlled governments, with violations potentially punished with harsh penalties.

Third, the WTO does not just regulate, it actively promotes, global trade. Its rules are biased to facilitate global commerce at the expense of efforts to promote local economic development and policies that move communities, countries and regions in the direction of greater self-reliance—a direction necessary to move towards a world of ecological sustainability and democratic governments.[14]

These quotes are not the full text of the recommendation, which can be found in a special issue of Ralph Nader's *Multinational Monitor*. Placards were present at the Seattle WTO summit meeting supporting this recommendation. On the other hand, many supporters of the WTO see it, and its predecessor organizations, as an important force behind a broad increase in the world's general welfare in the past 50 years. It must be maintained and strengthened, they say.

The WTO set forth arguments of its value in a document entitled "10 Benefits of the WTO Trading System."[15] Here are a few quotes from this document.

[13] Quotes and observations from Jonathan Peterson and Evelyn Iritani, "Rich-Poor Tensions Divide WTO," *Los Angeles Times,* November 30, 1999, p. C1.

[14] "Dismantle the WTO," *Multinational Monitor,* October–November 1999, p. 5.
[15] "10 Benefits of the WTO Trading System," www.wto.gov, 1999.

The System Helps Promote Peace

Peace is partly an outcome of two of the most fundamental principles of the trading system: *helping trade to flow smoothly,* and providing countries with a constructive and fair outlet for *dealing with disputes over trade issues.* It is also an outcome of the *international confidence and cooperation* that the system creates and reinforces.

. . . [I]f trade flows smoothly and both sides enjoy a healthy commercial relationship, political conflict is less likely. What's more, smoothly-flowing trade also helps people all over the world become better off. People who are more prosperous and contented are also less likely to fight.

Smaller Countries Are Helped with WTO

Without a multilateral regime such as the WTO system, the more powerful countries would be freer to impose their will unilateral on their smaller trading partners. Smaller countries would have to deal with each of the major economic powers individually, and would be much less able to resist unwanted pressure.

Freer Trade Cuts Costs of Living

Protectionism is expensive: it raises prices. The WTO's global system lowers trade barriers through negotiation and applies the principle of non-discrimination. The result is reduced costs of production (because imports used in production are cheaper) and reduced prices of finished goods and services, and ultimately a lower cost of living.

Trade Stimulates Economic Growth, Including Jobs

Trade clearly has the potential to create jobs. In practice there is often factual evidence that lower trade barriers have been good for employment. But the picture is complicated by a number of factors. Nevertheless, the alternative—protectionism—is not the way to tackle employment problems.

Governments Are Shielded from Lobbying

One of the lessons of the protectionism that dominated the early decades of the twentieth century was the damage that can be caused if narrow sectoral interests gain an unbalanced share of political influence. The result was increasingly restrictive policy which turned into a trade war that no one won and everyone lost.

Protectionism can also escalate as other countries retaliate. . . . That's exactly what happened in the 1920s and 30s with disastrous effects. Even the sectors demanding protection ended up losing.

Governments need to be armed against pressure from narrow interest groups, and the WTO system can help.

CONCLUDING OBSERVATIONS

An organization such as the WTO, dealing with world trade, seeking to harmonize trade relations among the many nations of the world, and making decisions that affect nations and people, is bound to be highly controversial. In this case study, after presenting the nature and operations of the WTO, we succinctly presented the more important criticisms of the WTO and responses in its support.

QUESTIONS

1. What is the WTO and how is it organized?

2. Describe the WTO decision-making process for trade disputes. Do you think it is an effective system?

3. Who are the dominant critics of the WTO? What do they complain about?

4. What major positive responses to these criticisms are made in the WTO's behalf?

5. Should the WTO be abolished, as suggested by some critics?

Part Six

Pollution Control and Environmental Management

Chapter **Fourteen**

Industrial Pollution and Environmental Policy

The Indian Health Service Solves a Mystery

Daniel Schultz, a surgeon at the Santa Fe Indian Hospital in New Mexico, was puzzled and alarmed when, in an 18-month period in 1984 and 1985, he diagnosed three cases of malignant mesothelioma in Indians from a nearby pueblo. An investigation of a state tumor registry revealed two more cases from this pueblo in 1970 and 1982, for a total of five cases over 15 years. On average, the victims were 65 years old and lived only 3.8 months after diagnosis.[1]

Malignant mesothelioma is an incurable tumor in the lining of the chest cavity that is virtually always caused by exposure to asbestos. It has a latency period of 40 to 50 years. Five cases of this unusual cancer in a pueblo of 2,000 Indians was roughly 1,000 times the number predicted over 15 years by standard mortality tables. Normally, five cases could be expected in a city of two million, not such a tiny Indian pueblo. Samples of lung tissue from the three cases in the Indian Hospital revealed the presence of all three types of asbestos used in commerce—chrysotile, amosite, and crocidolite. The Indians had been exposed to airborne asbestos fibers. But how? Schultz called in Richard J. Driscoll, an environmental health officer with the Indian Health Service (IHS), a small agency in the Department of Health and Human Services. Driscoll, along with colleagues from the IHS, set out to do some detective work to learn how asbestos exposure was occurring.

[1] Richard J. Driscoll, Wallace J. Mulligan, Daniel Schultz, and Anthony Candelaria, "Malignant Mesothelioma: A Cluster in a Native American Pueblo," *The New England Journal of Medicine*, June 2, 1988, p. 1437.

Immediately, the investigators ran into a problem. The Indians were reluctant subjects. They had a superstitious belief that fatal illness was explained by the presence of evil in its victims. They believed that people who discussed disease were wishing it on others and inviting additional sickness. The Indians also disliked attention and interference from outsiders because they wanted to keep their native culture and ways intact. Tribal elders finally agreed to discuss possible causes of asbestos exposure. Here is the story that emerged.

In the 1930s, a brick-manufacturing plant was built in the vicinity of the pueblo. A small private railroad was started to shuttle between the plant and a nearby main line of the Santa Fe Railroad, and a steam locomotive operated on it. When the boiler and pipe insulation on the locomotive needed replacement, workers discarded the old asbestos insulation near the tracks, where it was found by members of the tribe and brought back to the pueblo. It was put to many uses. Asbestos pads were used for worktable insulation by silversmiths making Indian jewelry. Dancers at religious festivals scraped and pounded their deer-hide leggings with crumbling wads of pipe insulation to whiten them, releasing clouds of floating asbestos fibers. Gradually the Indians found more and more uses for asbestos, and the trackside scrap was supplemented by tribe members in construction work who scavenged at their job sites for more.

The investigators discovered that four of the five mesothelioma victims had been silversmiths and that all five had been active participants in ceremonial dances. The Indians were reluctant to give up their asbestos; selling it had become a cottage industry in the pueblo. When the investigators went door to door, they found that Indian families were hoarding asbestos in bags, pots, and jars. It was hard to get them to part with it, but they found that by emphasizing the harm it could cause to children, most of it could be removed.

The story of what happened to the Indians in the pueblo is analogous to what has happened to large populations in industrial societies. In both cases, dangerous substances with useful qualities promised better living. In both cases, elevated exposure to these substances predated adequate knowledge of their harmful effects. And in both cases, it was only after substantial exposures had occurred and sickness began to appear that government agencies mobilized to protect public health.

In this chapter we discuss the nature of industrial pollutants and the practices and social philosophies that allowed them to darken skies, poison waters, and despoil land. We then discuss how, in the United States beginning in the 1970s, massive regulatory programs developed to control industrial pollution. We explain the current operation of these programs, how they affect corporations, and how well they work.

POLLUTION

Pollution refers to substances in the environment that endanger human welfare. Much of it comes from natural sources. Forest fires give off particles and toxic metals such as mercury. Water picks up asbestos as it flows over rocks, gravel, and sand. Natural background radiation in North America is about 300 millirem a year, the equivalent of 50 chest X rays. Tons of oil seep from fissures in the ocean floor.

Human activity adds more contaminants. For millions of years, hunter-gatherer bands generated little pollution. However, a gradual revolution in agricultural methods beginning about 10,000 years ago led to more settled societies in which populations grew and people gathered in cities. Wherever they lived, the primary pollution problem people faced was gases and particles from indoor fuel combustion for cooking and heating. Significant death and disease rates are associated with exposure to the smoke of animal dung, wood, and charcoal, although this was unknown in those days.[2]

Eventually, cities filled with workers showing up as a result of the industrial revolution, and population densities increased markedly. The pollution problem this created, on top of haze from the smoke of many indoor fires, was the concentration of huge amounts of human and animal waste. Few homes had lavatories. Primitive sewers were not flushed with water. Dead animals, dung from beasts of burden, and entrails from butcher shops littered streets. A sewage engineer described London in 1847 this way.

> There are . . . thousands of houses in the metropolis which have no drainage whatever, and the greater part of them have stinking overflowing cesspools. And there are hundreds of streets, courts and alleys that have no sewers. . . . I have visited many places where filth was lying scattered about the rooms, vaults, cellar areas and yards, so thick and so deep that it was hardly possible to move for it.[3]

Water treatment plant technology, widely introduced only in the late 1800s, eventually resolved this problem by ensuring sanitary water supplies, but not in time to prevent an enormous death toll from waterborne disease. By this time, contaminants from fossil-fuel combustion and manufacturing activity had become a serious problem.

Most industrial pollution simply adds to background levels of naturally occurring substances, so that human exposures to metals, carbon compounds, radiation, and other substances reach artificially high levels. It is estimated, for example, that because of environmental exposure, the average American carries a tissue concentration of lead at least 1,000 times

---

[2] Nigel Bruce et al., "Indoor Air Pollution in Developing Countries: A Major Environmental and Public Health Challenge," *Bulletin of the World Health Organization,* September 2000.

[3] Quoted in Clive Ponting, *A Green History of the World* (New York: St. Martin's Press, 1992), p. 354.

greater than prehistoric people.[4] Some industrial pollutants, however, are not found in nature. The rise of synthetic chemical production since the 1940s led to the creation and dispersal of persistent, complex artificial molecules used in plastics, fumigants, and pesticides.

Industrial activity both harms human health and disturbs natural ecology. We will briefly discuss its impact in each area.

Human Health

Disease caused by industrial pollution is significant, but it is far less significant than disease caused by older, nonindustrial forms of pollution. Table 14.1 shows the estimated burden of disease caused by air, water, and land pollution. The total burden of disease caused by pollution is calculated in disability-adjusted life years, or DALYs. DALYs combine in a single measure years of life lost due to premature death and years of life lived with disabilities.[5]

As the table shows, exposure to pollution is estimated to produce 18 percent of the disease burden in less developed nations but only 4.5 percent in developed ones. Most of the burden in developing nations is attributable to the age-old risks of unsanitary water and indoor combustion of wood and coal. Urban air pollution from factories and vehicles plus pesticides and toxic waste—the by-products of modern industry—is responsible for only 3 percent of DALYs in developing nations and 3.5 percent in developed ones. Clearly, when nations industrialize, far from creating a deadly blizzard of pollution, they instead greatly reduce the overall burden of disease by reducing

TABLE 14.1
Health Risks Posed by Major Sources of Environmental Pollution

	Percent of DALYs	
Environmental Health Risk	**Less Developed Countries**	**Developed Countries**
Water supply and sanitation	7	1
Indoor air pollution	4	0
Urban air pollution	2	1
Agricultural chemicals and industrial waste	1	2.5
All pollution-related causes	**18**	**4.5**

Source: Kseniya Lvovsky, "Health and Environment," World Bank, draft working paper, Washington, DC, April 2000, p. 4.

[4] Joel Schwartz and Ronnie Levin, "Lead: Example of the Job Ahead," *EPA Journal*, March–April 1992, p. 42.
[5] Calculation of DALYs is based on estimates of life expectancy, subjective quantification of disability weights by expert panels, and age-based discounting techniques in which years of life in the most productive years have higher value. The use of DALYs has been controversial. See, for example, Ruth Bonita Kasturi, "Global Health Status: Two Steps Forward, One Step Back," *The Lancet*, August 12, 2000.

exposures to lethal nonindustrial pollutants. The main advances are access to water unpolluted by feces and the transition from dirty fuels to cleaner ones such as gasoline, electricity, and nuclear energy.

The Biosphere

Beyond harming human health, industrial activity also impinges on the biosphere, the slender margin atop the earth's surface that supports life, a space "so thin it cannot be seen edgewise from an orbiting spacecraft."[6] Among the unintended effects of global economic growth within this delicate space are these:

- *Disruption of natural chemistry.* The carbon cycle is overwhelmed by carbon released in fossil fuel combustion and from soil and vegetation as land is cleared. Unabsorbed carbon dioxide is building up in the atmosphere, raising concerns about climate change. The nitrogen cycle is overwhelmed by nitrogen releases during fossil fuel combustion, tilling of soil, and application of fertilizers. Airborne nitrogen oxides create acid rain. Waterborne nitrogen causes eutrophication in water bodies. The fresh-water cycle is strained by diversion of large quantities of water for agricultural and industrial uses that returns to water bodies polluted by chemicals and fertilizers.

- *Land conversion.* Humans have converted 25 percent of land area to agriculture and another 4 percent to cities.[7] This adds up to 29 percent of the world's land surface that has been changed from its pristine state. Biodiversity in converted areas has been reduced. Reflectivity of incoming solar radiation is altered.

- *Degradation of broad ecosystems.* Over the past 10,000 years, global forests have been reduced by 20 to 50 percent. Rain forests are still shrinking; however, there has been no net global forest loss since 1980. Grasslands are shrinking. Polar systems show signs of climate warming. Coastal ecosystems are overfished, and more than a quarter of the world's coral reefs are damaged from human activity. The number of plant and animal species is declining, though the rate of species decline is unclear because statistics are highly speculative estimates. Ozone in the upper atmosphere is besieged by a murderous family of molecules having no counterpart in nature.

Full consequences of these disruptions within the biosphere are unknown. However, they raise serious concerns and imply broad ethical duties for businesses and industrial societies.

[6] E. O. Wilson, "Hotspots: Preserving Pieces of a Fragile Biosphere," *National Geographic,* January 2002, p. 86.
[7] United Nations Development Programme et al., *World Resources 2000–2001* (Washington, DC: World Resources Institute, 2000), p. 24.

INDUSTRIAL GROWTH, POLLUTION, AND THE ENVIRONMENT

There is no question that economic activity, broadly defined, is the source of enduring pollution problems. And world economic activity is greater than in the past. As noted in Chapter 2, global output of goods and services since 1950 exceeds that for all preceding human history. The world economy continues to become more integrated and to accelerate because of faster communications, lowering trade barriers, and free flows of direct foreign investment.

Today there are nations on every continent with ambitious development plans that put industry before environmental protection. Poor nations house the vast majority of the 4 billion people with purchasing power of less than two U.S. dollars per day.[8] Their leaders see industrial growth as the only practical way of raising living standards and building national power. If these populous, underdeveloped nations take the path of the environmentally destructive eighteenth and nineteenth century industrial revolution in Europe, the United States, and Japan, the resulting pollution and resource depletion could lead to ecological disaster.

During the first industrial revolution, there was little concern for protecting nature or human health. Each wave of technological development created a new pollution nightmare. By the early 1800s, great forests had been toppled to get wood to power steam engines. Then, with the rise of iron and steel manufacturing, smoky fumes poured from metallurgic complexes. In the late 1800s, the introduction of electricity created insatiable demand for copper to make wire, leading to destructive mining and smelting. The Anaconda Copper Mining Company, for example, began operating in 1882 and eventually dug 10,000 miles of passageways in ore-bearing hills surrounding what is now Butte, Montana. Copper ore roasting in open pits belched fumes of sulfur and arsenic in smoke so thick that streetlamps burned at midday. The teeth of cows grazing nearby were coated with fugitive copper fallen from the air. Isaac Edinger, a nearby rancher of that time, said:

> I used to carry a few of those gold-colored teeth in my pocket all the time because no one would believe me, and I'd have to show 'em. When they were shown they always wanted to keep the evidence, and I'd have to get a new supply every time I went back to the slaughterhouse.[9]

The mining eventually contaminated the area's underground aquifer and stunted vegetation for miles. Today a 600-acre open pit mine filled with 28 billion gallons of poisoned water sits near the city of Butte. The

---

[8] United Nations Development Programme, *Human Development Report 2001* (New York: Oxford University Press, 2001), p. 9.

[9] C. B. Glasscock, *The War of the Copper Kings: Builders of Butte and Wolves of Wall Street* (New York: Grosset & Dunlap, 1935), p. 86.

water is so acidic that it liquefies boat propellers. When a flock of snow geese migrating from the Canadian arctic happened to land there a few years back, 342 of them died. Autopsies found burns in their necks and intestines.[10]

Industrial takeoff eras in other countries were just as destructive. Half a world away from Butte, in the mountains north of Tokyo, the giant Ashio copper-mining complex caused ecological damage equaling or exceeding that in Butte. Mining operations left gaping holes in the landscape. Fallout from smelter emissions blackened hundreds of square miles of forests and suffocated fish in nearby rivers. In 1883 a sulfurous gas release shriveled the leaves of mulberry trees in a nearby town. Silkworms that fed on the leaves and supported a thriving local silk industry spat out greenish fluid and died. Their livelihood destroyed, the silk farmers abandoned the area. Copper fallout also contaminated wide swathes of other farmland, igniting a farmer's political movement to shut down the smelter. However, the movement was doomed to defeat. The mine had great importance to the government because exported copper brought in foreign currency and strengthened Japan's drive to become a world power.

With the rise of the synthetic chemical industry in the twentieth century, a new range of toxic emissions entered the environment. And so it went as industry after industry piled on its characteristic load. For more than 150 years pollutants flowed freely. Not until the second half of the twentieth century did industrialized nations do much to control their emissions. However, today the United States, Europe, and Japan have such stringent regulation that most forms of pollution are declining significantly, even as their populations and economies grow. Subsequently, we will describe this regulation in the United States.

Much interest today is focused on the notion of *sustainable development*, that is, nonpolluting economic growth that raises standards of living without depleting the net resources of the earth. However, the modern industrial revolution, as it is currently unfolding in developing nations, bears little resemblance to this ideal. In fact, at least in its early stages, it promises to exceed the old-time industrial revolutions in generating pollution and depleting resources. First, the new industrialization is faster. Economic growth rates in countries such as Korea, Thailand, and China have compressed the transformation into less than two decades rather than the 100 years and more it took England and the United States. As growth skyrockets, a range of modern industries quickly appears, creating more varied and dangerous pollutants than were typical of eighteenth and nineteenth century factories. Occasionally, developed nations aggravate this situation by sending their dirty and dangerous businesses

---

[10] Edwin Dobb, "Pennies from Hell," *Harper's Magazine*, October 1996, p. 39.

to the developing world. Asbestos manufacturing, now virtually nonexistent in the United States, flourishes as an export industry in Brazil, Pakistan, India, and Korea. Urban population density in developing countries is typically much higher than it was in the nations of the West when they industrialized, so larger numbers of people are exposed to deadly pollutants.

However, there is evidence that environmental quality in growing economies does not follow a path of steady deterioration as in the old industrial revolution model. Studies suggest that developing economies now follow a sequence in which pollution rises rapidly in the early stages of growth when incomes are low. As per capita gross domestic product continues to rise, pollution reaches a peak and eventually decreases, even as GDP continues to rise. This phenomenon can be represented as an inverted U-shaped curve, known as an *environmental Kuznets curve,*[11] illustrated in Figure 14.1.

Researchers studying more than 50 countries found, for example, that there was a rapid rise of sulfur dioxide emissions in the cities of countries undergoing economic development. Sulfur dioxide, a by-product of coal and oil combustion, is closely associated with industrialization. But this rise slowed and eventually leveled off when per capita GDP, measured as purchasing power parity with U.S. dollars, reached about $4,000. After that, emissions began to decline even as incomes continued to rise.

FIGURE 14.1
The Environmental Kuznets Curve

Source: Adapted from Håkan Nordström and Scott Vaughan, *Trade and Environment* (Geneva: WTO Publications, 1999), p. 48.

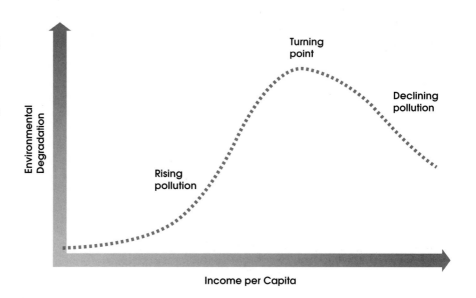

[11] Simon Kuznets won the 1971 Nobel Prize in economics for his studies of economic growth. He also said that, in addition to environmental quality, income inequality followed an inverted U-shaped relationship during development, first worsening, then leveling off, then declining.

Particle emissions leveled off somewhat later, at a per capita GDP of around $8,000, and three measures of water quality based on oxygen demand caused by organic pollutants leveled off at a per capita GDP of $7,500. Waterborne concentrations of the heavy metal arsenic stabilized at $4,900 and began to decline at $10,000.[12] These findings support the existence of an inverted U pattern for these pollutants. Although not all studies have arrived at the same figures and not all pollutants studied trace an inverted U pattern, there is general support for the theory.[13]

A number of factors explain the environmental Kuznets curve. To begin, as countries industrialize, their economies change in composition. During the early stages, less capital-intensive agricultural and food processing sectors are dominant. Pollution from agriculturally based industries is quantitatively less and less toxic than from industries that come later. In the middle stages of industrialization, enough capital has accumulated to bring the rise of more heavily polluting industries such as cement-making, chemicals, and rubber. Later stages characteristically see the growth of industries that require both capital and technical skill, including basic metals, paper and printing, and machinery.[14] Then, in the last structural shifts, much cleaner technology and service industries rise.

While the advent of heavily polluting industries increases degradation, growth brings other changes. With greater affluence there is more education. Changes in values occur as the population ascends from poverty even as the environment deteriorates. Preserving environmental quality and protecting public health assume more importance. Corporations, particularly highly visible MNCs, may be pressured to use cleaner technologies. Governments grow stronger and may become more responsive to citizen demands for pollution reduction. Regulatory agencies strengthen with an influx of technically skilled personnel. These factors all underlie the observed pollution reductions coming with continued GDP growth.

If the environmental Kuznets curve predicts the future, economic growth does not necessarily lead to steadily increasing levels of pollution. The view that development inevitably brings ruinous buildups of pollutants is rooted in the historical experience of the West. However, modern growth may be much cleaner. In fact, growth may be a solution to environmental damage, not the cause. However, while the inverted U pattern is characteristic of nations, it is not necessarily predictive of the global ex-

[12] Gene M. Grossman and Alan B. Krueger, "Economic Growth and the Environment," *Quarterly Journal of Economics,* May 1995 p. 353. Data are from the Global Environmental Monitoring System, a joint project of the World Health Organization and the United Nations Environmental Programme.
[13] Håkan Nordström and Scott Vaughan, *Trade and Environment,* Special Studies 4 (Geneva: WTO Publications, 1999), chap. 5.
[14] Richard M. Auty, "Pollution Patterns during the Industrial Transition," *The Geographic Journal,* July 1997 p. 206.

perience. Some natural systems continue to deteriorate with increasing economic activity. Although sustainable development is a useful philosophy, and as we will see, some nations and corporations attempt to approach it in practice, the broad global reality bears little resemblance to the sustainable ideal. Still, current fascination with sustainability suggests a shift in thinking about the relationship between industry and ecology. In the next section we discuss ideas that arose to support industrialization and then explain how they are now being challenged.

IDEAS SHAPE ATTITUDES TOWARD THE ENVIRONMENT

What is the proper relationship between business and nature? In the past, and to some extent still, Western values that regard nature as an adversary to be conquered have legitimized industrial activity. These values were incubated in ancient Mediterranean society. Eventually they appeared in biblical text, giving them religious sanction and magnifying their influence. In the story of creation in Genesis, God creates first nature and then man and afterward instructs man on how to relate to nature.

> Be fruitful and multiply, and replenish the earth and subdue it; and have dominion over the fish of the sea, and over the fowl of the air, and over every living thing that moveth upon the earth. (1:28)

This Judeo-Christian view laid the foundation for the conviction in Western civilization that humans were both separate from and superior to the natural world. The Judeo-Christian heritage also incorporated the idea that humans must exercise wise stewardship over their dominion, but until recently the stewardship idea languished as a minor theme.

When Church dogma began to lose its primacy during the Renaissance in Europe, secular philosophers did not reject the biblical doctrine of human superiority to nature but reinforced it with their own worldly thinking. Within the comparatively short span of 150 years, four new ideas appeared that, combined, determined how nature would be regarded and treated during the coming industrial revolution.

The theory of *dualism* held that humans were separate from nature. The French philosopher René Descartes (1596–1650) believed that nature operated like a machine, according to fixed laws that humans could study and understand. Humans were separate from nature and other living organisms because they alone had the power of reason and, unlike plants and animals, had souls. Descartes's perspective laid the foundation for modern experimental science but also established a dualism reinforcing the Judeo-Christian idea that humans were superior to and apart from nature.

The Renaissance brought improved living conditions, growth of cities, inventions, and the birth of industries. Such events kindled great optimism in European intellectuals who wrote about the idea of *progress,* or the belief that history was a narrative of improvement in which humanity moved from lower to higher levels on an inevitable march to perfection. This idea rejected the pessimism of previous civilizations that had looked back on past golden eras. Charles Darwin's theory of evolution supported the idea of progress in the popular mind. As industry expanded, the exploitation of nature for human welfare was soon entwined with the notion of progress.

Then, during the early years of the industrial revolution in England, powerful doctrines of economics and ethics arose, which in additional ways justified the exploitation of nature. The theory of *capitalism,* based on principles set forth by Adam Smith in 1776, valued nature primarily as a commodity to be used in wealth-creating activity that increased the vigor, welfare, and comfort of society. As a practical matter, early capitalism in action largely ignored environmental damage. This tendency still exists. For example, the gross domestic product, the accounting system of capitalism, rises when goods and services are produced but does not fall when pollution damage occurs. Thus, the GDP rose because of the *Exxon Valdez* oil spill, adding the millions of dollars spent by Exxon on the cleanup but not subtracting the costs of dead animals and degraded shoreline.

Finally, the doctrine of *utilitarianism,* or "the greatest good for the greatest number," arrived in England simultaneously with the rise of capitalism. It also was used to justify economic activity that assaulted nature. Industry made the utilitarian argument that, although pollution was noxious, the economic benefits of jobs, products, taxes, and growth outweighed environmental costs and were the "greatest good." Utilitarianism was an ethical worldview that rationalized the destructive side effects of commerce. It blinded Western societies to alternative, but less exploitive, views of nature.

In Eastern civilization, the values of Buddhism, Confucianism, and Taoism placed stronger emphasis on the interconnection of people and nature. They supported a more humble, less domineering role for humanity. However, their main impact was on interpersonal relations. Industrialization in Asia has been as destructive of the environment as in the West.[15]

New Ideas Challenge the Old

In the second half of the twentieth century, an alternative, nonexploitive environmental ethic emerged. Naturalist Aldo Leopold pioneered the revised worldview. His seminal statement of a new "land ethic" in a 1949

---

[15] Ponting, *A Green History of the World,* chap. 2.

book, *A Sand County Almanac,* inspired other ethicists to rethink traditional ideas about the man–nature relationship. He wrote:

> All ethics so far evolved rest upon a single premise: that the individual is a member of a community of interdependent parts. . . . The land ethic simply enlarges the boundaries of the community to include soils, waters, plants, and animals, or collectively: the land. . . . In short, a land ethic changes the role of *Homo sapiens* from conqueror of the land-community to plain member and citizen of it. It implies respect for his fellow members and also respect for the community as such.[16]

For Leopold, the conventional boundaries of ethical duty were too narrow. Expansion was merited to include not only duties toward fellow humans but also duties to nonhuman entities in nature, both living and nonliving.

In the early 1970s, a more radical form of this land ethic came from Norwegian philosopher Arne Naess. Naess argued that Leopold and mainstream environmentalists were too shallow in their thinking because they were conciliatory with the industrial-age worldview. Naess said there were "deeper concerns" than how to compromise the protection of nature with ongoing economic activity. His position came to be called *deep ecology.* Naess argued that human domination of nature should cease. Philosophies of domination should be replaced by notions of biospheric egalitarianism in which all species had equal rights to live and flourish. Nature should no longer be valued only as inputs for factories as in capitalist economics because it has an intrinsic value that must not be compromised. In short, Naess rejected the four traditional ideas about the man–nature relationship that support industrial activity. He concluded that the present level of human interference in nature was excessive and detrimental and that drastic changes were needed.[17]

The views of Naess and other philosophers who share his thinking have inspired anticorporate environmental groups. Some, such as Earth First! and the Environmental Liberation Front, believe that extreme measures, including lawlessness, are warranted by the moral obligation to end the destruction of nature.

Other new philosophies justify the expansion of rights to nonhuman entities. For example, philosopher Peter Singer popularized the idea of *speciesism,* or "a prejudice or attitude of bias toward the members of one's own species and against those of members of other species," that is analogous to racism or sexism.[18] The racist and sexist believe that skin

[16] Aldo Leopold, *A Sand County Almanac* (New York: Ballantine, 1970), pp. 239–40.
[17] Naess's basic arguments are in "The Shallow and the Deep, Long-Range Ecology Movement: A Summary," *Inquiry,* Spring 1973; and "A Defense of the Deep Ecology Movement," *Environmental Economics,* Fall 1984.
[18] Peter Singer, *Animal Liberation* (New York: Avon, 1975), p. 7.

color and sex determine people's worth; the speciesist believes that the number of one's legs or whether one lives in trees, the sea, or a condominium determines one's rights. Traditionally, when *Homo sapiens* compete for rights with plants and animals, the latter have lost. Singer argues that humans, though superior in important ways, are simply one species among many. And the others have intrinsic value independent of any economic usefulness to *Homo sapiens.*

Singer's arguments, like those of Naess, challenge the age-old view of human dominance and undermine the human-centered morality of industrial development—at least until such development occurs in a way that respects nature. Without a practical technique of sustainability, therefore, adopting this new ethic would curtail global industrial growth, perhaps consigning hundreds of millions of humans to a condition of permanent poverty. On the other hand, it would prevent further ecosystem deterioration.

ENVIRONMENTAL REGULATION IN THE UNITED STATES

The dominant approach to industrial pollution control in the United States has been to pass laws that strictly regulate emissions, effluents, and wastes. Before the 1970s there was little environmental regulation; but by the 1960s the public had became frightened of pollution, and a strong popular mandate for controlling it emerged. As a result, during what came to be called the "environmental decade" of the 1970s, Congress passed a remarkable string of new laws, creating a broad statutory base for regulating industry.

Although more laws have been passed since the 1970s, the ones from that decade still form the basic regulatory framework. Most have been reauthorized and amended, some several times, and some of these revisions, such as the Clean Air Act Amendments of 1990, were so extensive that they fundamentally altered the statute, always by making it more complex and requiring more expensive regulation.

The Environmental Protection Agency

The Environmental Protection Agency (EPA) is the nation's largest regulatory agency. Its mission is to protect human health and to preserve the natural environment. Although many agencies administer environmental laws, the EPA enforces more than 30 statutes making up the overwhelming bulk of regulation in this area. In 2001 it had more than 18,000 employees and a budget of $7 billion, making it larger and better funded than the Department of State.

When Congress passes an environmental law, EPA employees write detailed, specific rules to carry out its general directives. According to one study, between 1981 and 1999 the agency issued more than 2,700 regulations, 115 of which had an impact on the economy of $100 million or more.[19] The EPA can enforce these rules directly on corporations, but laws permit delegating enforcement to the states. State regulators, acting with federal funding and following EPA guidelines, now do most of the enforcement of the nation's environmental laws.

The EPA was created in 1970 by President Richard Nixon. At the time, it had a tiny budget and most of the laws it would one day administer had yet to be passed; but it quickly flexed its muscles. During its first two years, it took more than 1,000 enforcement actions, handing out $9 million in fines to startled companies. In late 1971 it drove home to industry the extent of its powers with a dramatic demonstration. When a temperature inversion in Birmingham, Alabama, caused the buildup of air contaminants to high levels, the agency shut down every factory in the heavily industrialized city for 24 hours. To this day, the EPA retains an aggressive enforcement philosophy.

Throughout the 1970s the agency had an excellent reputation for effectiveness, but it soon bogged down. Some indigestion was inevitable as passage of new laws piled up work. In addition, Congress responded to public pressure by filling some of these laws with unrealistic goals and impossible timetables. For instance, the goal of the Federal Water Pollution Control Act of 1972 to eliminate all polluting discharges into waterways by 1985 was sheer fantasy. The technology required to purify all effluents did not exist at the time (and still does not exist). By the end of the decade, the agency was being criticized for paperwork backlogs, rule-making delays, and inadequate enforcement.

The election of President Ronald Reagan in 1980 worsened the EPA's problems. While campaigning, Reagan called EPA regulators "environmental extremists," and after his election, the agency's budget was so severely butchered that not until 1992 did it return to its pre-Reagan level. Notwithstanding, during these years the EPA faced a continuing avalanche of new statutory duties as Congress revamped basic laws, each time expanding them. To illustrate, the Clean Air Act passed in 1970 was 50 pages long, but when Congress amended it in 1990 it ballooned to 800 pages.[20] These 800 pages rolled out 538 specific requirements for new rules, standards, and reports, imposing rigid deadlines on 361 of them.[21]

---

[19] General Accounting Office, *Environmental Protection: Assessing the Impacts of EPA's Regulations through Retrospective Studies,* GAO/RCED–99–250, September, 1999, p. 3 and fn. 4.

[20] Kenneth Chilton, *Environmental Dialogue: Setting Priorities for Environmental Protection,* Policy Study No. 108 (St. Louis: Center for the Study of American Business, Washington University, October 1991), p. 19.

[21] General Accounting Office, *Air Pollution: Status of Implementation and Issues of the Clean Air Act Amendments of 1990,* GAO/RCED–00–72, April 2000, p. 3.

Although the EPA remains an aggressive agency, its work overload continues. Moreover, since the early 1990s its budget has been under constant pressure from Republicans in Congress wanting to reduce the regulatory burden it imposes on corporations.

PRINCIPAL AREAS OF ENVIRONMENTAL POLICY

There are three media for pollution: air, water, and land. Here we give a brief overview of regulations that protect them from degradation. In each area, we describe laws, basic problems, central concerns for business, and progress.

Air

Air pollution is best described as a set of complex interrelated problems, each requiring different control measures. The Clean Air Act, most recently amended in 1990, is the primary air quality statute. Although this law permits the use of some market incentives, these provisions depart from its core philosophy, which is to impose inflexible, draconian, command controls. We now discuss regulation of different air pollution problems.

National Air Quality

The Clean Air Act requires the EPA to set National Ambient Air Quality Standards that limit pollution from substances harmful to public health and the environment. These standards are supposed to be set without regard for cost and must provide an "adequate margin of safety" that protects even the most sensitive people. To do this, the EPA has set standards to curb emissions of six substances, called *criteria pollutants,* that are the primary threat to air quality because they are emitted in large quantities:

- *Carbon monoxide* (CO) is a gas produced from incomplete combustion of carbon in fuels such as gasoline. Its largest source is vehicle emissions. High concentrations of CO reduce the oxygen carrying capacity of the blood and may aggravate cardiovascular disease.

- *Nitrogen dioxide* (NO_2) is a gas resulting from oxidation in the atmosphere of nitrogen oxide (NO), a pollutant formed during high temperature combustion. It comes mainly from vehicle exhaust and fuel combustion in industry. It is a lung irritant and aggravates respiratory disease.

- *Sulfur dioxide* (SO_2) is a gas that comes almost entirely from the burning of coal and oil, which releases trapped sulfur compounds into the atmosphere. Electric utilities are the biggest source. It also is a lung irritant.

- *Ozone* (O_3) molecules are not directly emitted from vehicles or industrial processes. Instead, they form in the air by chemical reactions between nitrogen dioxide and molecules known as *volatile organic compounds* (VOCs), which are essentially vapors from substances such as gasoline, paint, floor waxes, and similar petroleum-based compounds. These airborne reactions are promoted by the energy in sunlight, which is why urban smog is often worse on sunny days. Industry accounts for about half of all VOC emissions and vehicles for the other half. Ozone is a gas that irritates the lungs, and high concentrations damage lung tissue. Near ground level, ozone is considered a pollutant. High in the atmosphere, ozone absorbs solar radiation, making life possible on earth.

- *Particulates* (PM, or particulate matter) are dust particles raised primarily by industrial activity and vehicles traveling over roads. Coal-burning power plants, for example, emit massive numbers of particles because fly ash cannot be completely removed from stack gases by existing control methods. The EPA regulates particles as small as 10 micrometers (about one-tenth the diameter of a human hair) or less. Industry is responsible for less than 5 percent of particulate emissions. Most particles come from dust raised by the wind. However, particles from industrial processes can contain harmful substances. Recently, the agency tried to introduce standards for particles as small as 2.5 micrometers. Particulates are the most dangerous health risk among the criteria pollutants. They are associated with respiratory and cardiovascular disease and heavy exposures raise near-term death rates for infants and for the aged and infirm.

- *Lead* (Pb) is a metal that causes significant health problems such as seizures and mental retardation. With the elimination of leaded gasoline, the problem of lead in urban air has ended. Airborne lead is now a problem only in areas around lead processing sources such as lead smelters and battery plants.

With each criteria pollutant, the EPA sets standards for maximum concentrations. The CO standard, for example, is 9 parts per million (ppm) averaged over eight hours, or 35 ppm in one hour. Industrial activity is the source of only about one-quarter of aggregate criteria pollutant emissions. Note, however, that industry is the only major source of both SO_2 and Pb. As shown in Table 14.2, in 1998 industry was responsible for about 49 million tons of the 190.2 million tons emitted. By far the largest industrial sources of criteria pollutants are coal-fired power plants.

To suppress criteria pollutants, the Clean Air Act mandates a range of expensive actions including, most importantly, emission controls on power plants, factories, smelters, and vehicles. Since controls began in 1970, emissions have dropped nearly one-third. Figure 14.2 shows how remarkable this reduction is, since it was achieved in an uphill battle against

TABLE 14.2
Estimated Emissions by Source of Six Criteria Pollutants, 1998 (in thousands of tons)

Criteria Pollutant	Industry*	Vehicles	Other†	Total
Carbon monoxide	6,375	70,300	12,779	89,454
Nitrogen oxides	10,340	13,044	1,070	24,454
Sulfur dioxide	18,098	1,410	139	19,647
Volatile organic compounds	8,667	7,786	1,464	17,917
Particulates (PM10)	1,563	718	32,460	34,741
Lead	3,481	522	30	3,973
Totals	48,524	93,062	47,942	190,186
Percentages	**26%**	**49%**	**25%**	**100%**

*Includes industrial fuel combustion and industrial processes.
†Includes residential, agricultural, and natural emissions.
Source: Environmental Protection Agency, *National Air Quality and Emissions Trends Report, 1998,* Appendix A, tables A–2 to A–8.

FIGURE 14.2
Declining Emissions of Six Criteria Pollutants, 1970–1999

Source: Adapted from Environmental Protection Agency, *FY 2000 Annual Report* (Washington, DC: EPA, 2001), p. II–2.

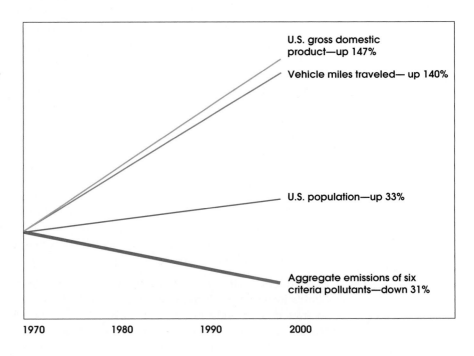

U.S. gross domestic product—up 147%

Vehicle miles traveled— up 140%

U.S. population—up 33%

Aggregate emissions of six criteria pollutants—down 31%

1970   1980   1990   2000

a growing economy and rising use of vehicles. Nevertheless, in 1970 Congress had set a national goal of achieving clean and healthy air by 1975. Thirty years later, in 2000, the EPA estimated that 62 million Americans still lived in counties where the air quality violated national standards for one or more of the criteria pollutants.[22] Thus, much work remains.

[22]Environmental Protection Agency, *FY 2000 Annual Report* (Washington, DC: EPA, 2001), p. II–2.

Hazardous Air Pollutants

Besides controlling the six criteria pollutants, the Clean Air Act mandates control of hazardous air pollutants, also called air toxics. Air toxics pose health risks in smaller amounts than criteria pollutants. The EPA has identified 329 air toxics and estimates overall releases total more than 45 million tons annually, about one-fourth the amount of criteria pollutants. Examples are arsenic, asbestos, benzine, chromium, dioxins, radionuclides, and vinyl chloride. Exposure can lead to premature death from a range of illnesses, including cancer. Cars and trucks are the major source of air toxics. Reformulation of gasoline in the 1950s reduced these emissions. Benzene emissions, for example, have dropped by almost 40 percent since reformulation began in the early 1990s.[23] However, about 50 percent of air toxics come from vehicle exhausts.

Only 26 percent of aggregate air toxics come from large industrial plants, and, again, electric utilities are by far the biggest culprits. They release more air toxics than the four other major industry sources combined, that is, petroleum refineries, pulp and paper mills, metal coating facilities, and chemical plants.[24] The Clean Air Act requires the EPA to set emission standards for 188 air toxics at levels that prevent disease and requires industry to use the "maximum achievable control technology" to comply. Significant reductions have been encouraged by the requirement that corporations publicly reveal the amount of these chemicals they release. Since this disclosure requirement went into effect, corporations have significantly reduced emissions. The EPA reports downward trends for all air toxics.

Acid Precipitation

Acid precipitation is caused primarily by releases of two criteria pollutants, sulfur dioxide and nitrogen oxide. In the atmosphere, these gases undergo chemical reactions and return to earth as acids that alter the pH of water, degrading lakes and forests and causing deterioration of human structures. When Congress amended the Clean Air Act in 1990, it responded to public alarm about acid rain by requiring the EPA to reduce emissions of the two precursor substances that cause it, primarily by lowering emissions of electric utilities.

When the amendments were passed in 1990, sulfur dioxide emissions totaled 23.7 million tons per year and nitrogen oxide 24 million tons per year. Large amounts of these substances coming from coal-fired electric

---

[23] Environmental Protection Agency, *National Air Quality and Emissions Trends Report* (Washington DC: EPA, 1998), p. 3.

[24] General Accounting Office, *Environmental Protection: Wider Use of Advanced Technologies Can Improve Emissions Monitoring,* GAO–01–313, p. 20. Air toxics figures in this paragraph are for 1996.

utility boilers in the Northeast and Midwest were blamed for degrading sensitive eastern lakes and forests that are downwind of their emission plumes. Coal combustion releases large amounts of SO_2 and NO. About 70 percent of the SO_2 in the United States comes from electric utilities, and there are effective, though extremely expensive, methods for removing it from boiler exhaust streams. About 30 percent of the nation's NO comes from electric utilities, but control equipment is much less effective.[25]

To fight acid rain, Congress set up a program to roll back electric utility emissions of SO_2 and NO below levels found before 1980. To reduce SO_2, the program allocates emission allowances to utilities. Each allowance entitles the utility to emit one ton of SO_2. At the end of the year, the utility must own enough allowances to cover its emissions, otherwise it is fined $2,000 for each ton of emissions it cannot cover. The trading program gives utilities considerable flexibility to find the least expensive way of eliminating SO_2. They can install control equipment, use coal with lower sulfur content, or produce more electricity with cleaner boilers and less with more polluting ones, and then sell extra allowances they no longer need to other utilities. Or they can save allowances for future use. In 2000 a permanent cap was placed on the number of allowances to force emission reductions. No allowances are sold for NO. The program achieves NO cuts by setting emissions limits that require installation of control devices.

Table 14.3 shows that SO_2 emissions have fallen below 1980 levels and are moving in the direction of the 2010 goal. NO emissions, on the other hand, have held steady for the past 20 years, and there is no progress toward reduction. In eastern woodlands studied, sulfur deposition has fallen and nitrogen deposition has changed little. Some studies suggest that pollution reduction is insufficient to restore the natural pH of soils and lakes in the east.[26]

TABLE 14.3
Annual Emissions of Acid Rain Pollutants and Reduction Goals

	Annual Emissions (in millions of tons per year)			
	1980	1990	1998	2010 (Goals)
SO_2	25.9	23.7	19.7	15.9
NO	24.8	24	24.5	22.8

Sources: Environmental Protection Agency, *National Air Quality and Emissions Trends Report*, 1988, p. 125; and General Acounting Office, *Acid Rain*, GAO/RCED–00–47, March 2000, p. 5.

[25] General Accounting Office, *Acid Rain: Emissions Trends and Effects in the Eastern United States*, GAO/RCED–00–47, March 9, 2000, p. 5.
[26] Antonio Regalado, "Northeast Isn't Rebounding Completely from Effects of Acid Rain, Study Finds," *The Wall Street Journal*, March 26, 2001, p. B8.

Indoor Air Pollution

Indoor air in developed nations is contaminated by a mixture of harmful substances. These include asbestos, radon, tobacco smoke, combustion by-products from cooking, chlorine gas released from chlorinated water, biological contaminants such as mite dust, and vapors from household insecticides, glues, and paints. They pose serious health problems because Americans spend 80 to 90 percent of their lives indoors, where concentrations of air pollutants can be two- to five-times greater than in outdoor air. Radon, for example, is a colorless, odorless, radioactive gas commonly found in soils. It seeps up from the ground into homes, building up to dangerous concentrations in still air. Radon causes an estimated 21,800 lung cancer deaths yearly.[27] This is more than 10 times the estimated number of cancer deaths from all toxic chemical emissions by industry.

In 1987 the EPA ranked indoor air as one of the top five human health risks, but the agency has done little about the problem. Congress is reluctant to let EPA inspectors invade homes and offices with air sampling equipment, forms, and ticket books. Beyond spending on research that is very modest in relation to the risks posed, the agency has a voluntary radon measurement program and publishes information to educate the public. Meanwhile, the health problem grows worse as more tightly sealed, energy-efficient buildings trap pollutants. It is estimated that indoor air pollution annually causes 85,000 to 150,000 deaths, compared to between 65,000 and 200,000 deaths from outdoor air pollution.[28]

Ozone Destroying Chemicals

While ozone in urban smog is unwanted, ozone in the upper atmosphere screens out ultraviolet energy harmful to living tissue. Emissions of long-lived chlorine-containing molecules such as chlorofluorocarbons (CFCs) and similar compounds pose a threat to the ozone layer. In the presence of a chlorine atom, a chain reaction occurs that destroys thousands of ozone molecules. In high latitudes, the ozone layer has thinned as much as 30 percent due to the presence of industrial chemicals. The thinning ozone layer exposes humans to stronger ultraviolet radiation, causing skin cancers and eye cataracts. High levels of ozone in urban smog are insufficient to protect humans from radiation damage. Ninety percent of ozone resides in the stratosphere.

[27] Susan Baily, "New Report: Radon Blamed for Cancer Deaths," *Nuclear News,* November 1998, p. 61. See also, R. W. Field et al., "Residential Radon Gas Exposure and Lung Cancer," *American Journal of Epidemiology,* June 2000.
[28] Bjørn Lomborg, *The Skeptical Environmentalist* (Cambridge: Cambridge University Press, 2001), p. 184, citing Centers for Disease Control figures.

In 1987 a treaty called the Montreal Protocol was signed to phase out the use of CFCs and other ozone-depleting substances. It sets timetables for phasing out 95 chemicals, including a large family of CFCs. Since its signing, world production of these substances has dropped 86 percent and the ozone layer has stopped thinning and stabilized.[29] CFCs are large, tough molecules that persist until they reach the upper atmosphere, where ultraviolet radiation breaks them down. This gives them extremely long lifetimes, typically 50 to 100 years and in one case more than 1,000 years, and although emissions of them have dramatically fallen, concentrations are still rising in the stratosphere. However, if the Montreal Protocol is fully implemented, scientists estimate that the ozone layer will fully restore itself by 2050.

The United States and other developed nations ceased all CFC production by 1996 as required by the treaty, but elsewhere in the world there are problems. Developing nations, given until 2010, have cut production by only 13 percent. Substitutes for CFCs used as aerosols, refrigerants, and flame retardants have been developed, but they are more expensive than CFCs, and many businesses in poor countries cannot pay the price of conversion. A thriving black market for CFCs delays their elimination. Despite such problems, progress is substantial. The United Nations estimates that without the Montreal Protocol, by 2050 only 30 percent of the ozone layer would be left above some parts of the earth. High levels of radiation would cause more than 20 million additional skin cancers and 130 million more eye cataracts.[30]

Greenhouse Gases

The industrial revolution set off a continuing rise in the emission of a group of gases, called *greenhouse gases,* that trap heat in the atmosphere instead of allowing it to radiate into space.[31] The most important among them is carbon dioxide, which makes up about 60 percent of greenhouse gas emissions. Between 1850 and 2000, CO_2 resident in the earth's atmosphere rose from about 280 to 370 parts per million by volume.[32] Wood and fossil fuel combustion release such huge amounts of carbon that natural processes of carbon absorption by forests and oceans are overwhelmed, allowing more carbon to remain in the atmosphere in CO_2 molecules. Over the last century, the global mean surface air temperature warmed an estimated 0.7° to 1.5°, leading to speculation that copious greenhouse gas emissions have caused global warming. The fear is that

[29] United Nations Environment Programme, *Backgrounder: Basic Facts and Data on the Science and Politics of Ozone Protection,* Nairobe, Kenya: UNEP, October 5, 2001, p. 5.
[30] Ibid., p. 4.
[31] The six main greenhouse gases are carbon dioxide (CO_2), methane (CH_4), nitrous oxide (N_2O), hydrofluorocarbons (HFCs), perfluorocarbons (PFCs), and sulphur hexafluoride (SF_6).
[32] National Academy of Sciences, *Climate Change Science: An Analysis of Some Key Questions* (Washington, DC: National Academy Press, 2001), p. 2.

this warming will lead to ruinous alternations of climate. Scientific consensus is building that climate change is occurring, but great uncertainty remains about its extent and its consequences.

The major effort to slow global warming is an international treaty, the Kyoto Protocol, agreed to in principle in 1997 but not yet in effect. It requires industrial nations to cut their greenhouse gas emissions an average of 5.2 percent below 1990 levels by 2012. The United States, with the highest emissions of any nation, was given a 7 percent reduction target. However, the Kyoto Protocol has turned out to be flawed and inadequate as a precautionary step. Its main flaw is that it excludes developing nations from emission cuts. Even if the industrial nations with the highest emissions achieve their mandated cuts, global carbon emissions might still rise because growing nations such as China, Mexico, and Brazil are not committed to reductions. Moreover, scientists believe that the planned cuts would result in only a marginal reduction of climate warming. One projection is that temperature increases and sea level rises predicted for 2100 would be delayed only six years, until 2106, if Kyoto were implemented.[33]

Great economic sacrifice in the developed world would be required to achieve even Kyoto's small goals. The 7 percent emissions cut in the United States is actually far more, because it is from a baseline of 1990 emissions. Since 1990, CO_2 emissions have grown along with the U.S. economy. In 2000 alone, CO_2 emissions jumped more than 3 percent.[34] A 7 percent reduction from 1990 levels, therefore, becomes an estimated 30 percent reduction from emissions levels that would have prevailed in the U.S. economy in 2012, the year that reduction targets are to be met. Changes required to achieve this reduction would ripple through the economy and lead to as much as a 4 percent GDP decline.[35] Energy costs would soar as government regulated and taxed energy use and electric utilities spent billions converting from coal- and oil-fired generation to natural gas. Manufacturers might move to developing nations to reduce costs, shifting jobs overseas. For these reasons, the United States has rejected the Kyoto Protocol, although other developed nations continue negotiations.

The EPA has only voluntary programs to cut greenhouse emissions. One example is Green Lights, a slight project that encourages companies to install low-energy lighting. These EPA programs produce only infinitesimal reductions in CO_2 emissions. Overall, no regulatory authority exists to limit greenhouse emissions significantly. The only foreseeable effort, the Kyoto Protocol, is unsound because it promises to create economic disruptions far out of proportion to the marginal environmental improvements it can produce.

---

[33] Lomborg, *The Skeptical Environmentalist,* p. 304.
[34] "U.S. Carbon Dioxide Emissions Jump in 2000," *Los Angeles Times,* November 11, 2001, p. A36.
[35] "Emissions Impossible?" *The Wall Street Journal,* July 23, 2001, p. A14.

Water

The basic statute for fighting water pollution is the Federal Water Pollution Control Act Amendments of 1972, usually called the Clean Water Act. Congress intended it to be a powerful measure that would stop the deterioration of the nation's lakes, rivers, streams, and estuaries. The act set a goal of eliminating *all* polluting discharges into these waters by 1985. However, the goal was not met and will not soon be met.

The Clean Water Act is effective in reducing, but not eliminating, polluted factory outflows, or effluents. Every industrial plant uses water, and sources of pollution are numerous. In production processes, water is used as a washing, scrubbing, cooling, or mixing medium. It becomes contaminated with a variety of particles and dissolved chemicals. Years ago, untreated effluents were directly discharged into water bodies or sewers, but the Clean Water Act prohibits any polluted factory discharge without a permit.

Permits are issued by either the EPA or state regulators and cover three categories of pollutants. *Conventional* pollutants are contaminants found in household wastewater, including biological oxygen demand,[36] suspended solids, oil and grease, pH, and fecal coliform bacteria. *Toxic* pollutants are 126 organic industrial wastes that are dangerous in very small amounts, such as asbestos, organic compounds, pesticides, and metals such as cadmium and zinc. *Nonconventional* pollutants are other pollutants that can be measured, for instance, ammonia, sulfides, phosphorus, and nitrogen.

The EPA regulates industrial effluents from "point sources," that is, sites that discharge from a single location, using a permit system called the National Pollution Discharge Elimination System (NPDES). Under the NPDES, each industrial facility must get a permit specifying the volume of one or more substances it can pour into a water body. Effluent limits are based on scientific estimates of how much of a substance the water body can absorb before deteriorating unacceptably and on the ability of available equipment to remove a particular pollutant. The EPA sets water quality criteria for pollutants. Usually there are two standards, one for protecting human health and the other for aquatic life. To give examples, the chloroform standard prohibits chronic exposure of aquatic life to concentrations of more than 1,240 µg/l (micrograms per cubic liter) and exposure of humans to more than 470 µg/l. As noted, permit limits are also based on how much pollution the best control devices can remove from wastewater. These devices range from simple screens for

---

[36] Biological oxygen demand encompasses a variety of organic materials that, when discharged into surface waters, are broken down by protozoa and bacteria. If large quantities of such material are present, the level of dissolved oxygen in the water is lowered, causing odors and threatening the respiration of aquatic life.

large particles to intricate chemical and biological treatment systems. For example, plants that make paperboard out of wastepaper have small amounts of the wood preservative pentachlorophenol (C_6HCl_5O) in their wastewater streams. C_6HCl_5O is so poisonous that swallowing one-tenth of an ounce, about a teaspoon, can be lethal. However, for this substance the EPA has defined the best control technology standard as effluent containing no more than 0.87 pound of C_6HCl_5O for each 1 million pounds of paperboard produced because the best control technology cannot remove more of it. In other words, a paperboard factory can drain almost 14 ounces of C_6HCl_5O into a river or stream every time it makes a million pounds of paperboard. Currently, about 96,000 facilities operate under an NPDES permit.

While the EPA has limited factory discharges, "nonpoint" effluent, or runoff that enters surface waters from diffuse sources, is largely uncontrolled. Runoff from agriculture—animal wastes, pesticides, and fertilizers—is now the primary cause of impaired water bodies. Although general language in the Clean Water Act permits the EPA to act against any source of water pollution, the law avoided specific language aimed at farmers because of their political power. However, growing pollution from big animal feedlots and poultry farms led the EPA to place several thousand factory farms under permits. Urban runoff is another major contributor to poor water quality. As urban areas increase in size, more water flows over their impermeable surfaces, collecting pollutants and carrying them to water bodies. The Clean Air Act empowers the EPA to require control measures by cities, including detention ponds, street sweeping, and public education programs.[37] Nonpoint sources are now the biggest contributors to water pollution and efforts to control them are just beginning.

Overall, the quality of surface waters is much improved from 1972 when the Clean Water Act was passed. Then, it was estimated that only 30 to 40 percent of the nation's waters met the law's water quality goals.[38] Today, 60 to 90 percent do.[39] However, progress from now on will be difficult. The current Clean Water Act emphasizes control of point source pollution by industry using end-of-the-pipe equipment. Yet the biggest source of pollution now is copious and little-controlled runoff from farms and cities. Adequate regulation of runoff requires a revision of the law to give the EPA new tools and powers. The existing permit system is ill-suited to control nonpoint pollution.

[37] General Accounting Office, *Water Quality: Better Data and Evaluation of Urban Runoff Programs Needed to Assess Effectiveness,* GAO–01–679, June 2001, p. 5.
[38] Kevin Kane, *How's the Water? The State of the Nation's Water Quality* Working Paper 171 (St. Louis: Center for the Study of American Business, January 2000), p. 3.
[39] Environmental Protection Agency, *FY 2002 Annual Plan,* p. II–1.

Land

After Congress passed air and water pollution control laws early in the 1970s, it became apparent that poor handling and disposal of solid hazardous wastes was a major problem. Also, devices that removed air- and waterborne poisons from industrial processes under the new laws produced tons of poisoned sludge, slime, and dust that ended up in poorly contained landfills. Authority over the handling of hazardous waste was inadequate to prevent mismanagement. Responding to the menace, Congress passed two laws.

The Resource Conservation and Recovery Act of 1976 (RCRA) gave the EPA authority to manage hazardous waste "from cradle to grave," that is, from the moment it is created to the moment it is destroyed or interred. Firms must now label, handle, store, treat, and discard hazardous waste under strict guidelines, keeping meticulous records all the while.

The RCRA is a difficult statute to administer and with which to comply. It demands that regulators keep track of literally all hazardous waste produced anywhere in the country—an exhausting job. It relies on smothering command-and-control regulation and prohibits balancing costs against benefits. One indication of the regulatory burden it imposes is that when it was first implemented, nearly half the nation's waste disposal facilities elected to close rather than comply with it. Figure 14.3 illustrates a typical installation of wells required to monitor groundwater quality under a solid-waste disposal site.

The RCRA is, in the words of one observer, "an amazingly inflexible law with extraordinarily detailed regulations, demanding controls, and a glacially slow permitting system [that] entails almost astronomically high costs."[40] If, for example, a factory wants to install a treatment tank for waste, it can take up to nine months and cost $80,000 to get the permit. One steel company had to wait seven months simply for a permit to put a fence around its waste pit and use propane-powered cannons to scare animals away.[41] A permit for a landfill takes more than five years and costs as much as $1 million. Although costs are high, there is no question that hazardous waste is much better handled than before the RCRA.

While the RCRA ensured that existing facilities would operate at a high standard, it did nothing about thousands of abandoned toxic waste sites around the country. So Congress passed another law to clean them up. This law is the Comprehensive Environmental Response, Compensation, and Liability Act of 1980, better known as Superfund, so-named after the large trust fund it sets up to pay for cleanups. This trust fund was originally generated from special taxes on oil and chemical companies and a small—0.12 percent—addition to the general corporate income

---

[40] Robert J. Smith, "RCRA Lives, Alas," *Regulation*, Summer 1991, p. 14.
[41] General Accounting Office, *Hazardous Waste: Progress under the Corrective Action Program is Limited*, GAO/RCED–98–3, October 1997, p. 9.

FIGURE 14.3 RCRA Landfill Groundwater Monitoring Requirements

The EPA grants permits to all operators of hazardous waste dumps that comply with standards for physical layout, groundwater monitoring, and emergency planning. The drawing is a cross section of ground below a landfill illustrating minimal RCRA monitoring requirements. Water samples drawn from downgradient wells can detect chemical contamination seeping into the groundwater (saturated zone) from the landfill above. Today, approximately 3,700 hazardous waste landfills are in operation.

Source: Environmental Protection Agency.

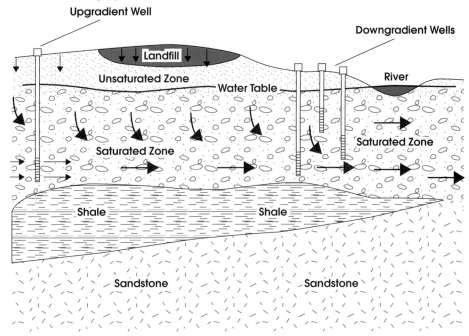

tax. However, these taxes expired in 1995, and now funding comes only from congressional appropriations and payments companies must make to clean up their old wastes.

Congress set up Superfund as a temporary measure that would be phased out when hazardous sites were all cleaned. However, the number of sites is higher than predicted and the cleaning process more difficult and expensive than envisioned in 1980. After passage of the law, the EPA set up a shortlist of 1,200 sites that posed the greatest risk to human health and the environment, usually because of groundwater or drinking-water contamination. Since then, 233 of these sites have been fully restored and cleaning is in progress on another 540.[42] The priority list still contains about 1,200 heavily contaminated sites. As completed sites depart the list, new ones rotate on from a waiting list of another 3,000 heavily contaminated sites.

[42] "Congress Seeks Superfunding," *Waste Treatment Technology News,* October 2001.

Superfund sites are complicated and expensive to restore. An average project takes a decade and costs $20 to $30 million. Methods of decontamination and containment differ from site to site. In San Bernardino, California, two plumes of groundwater contaminated by chemicals used in metal plating have moved as far as eight miles under the city. At a cost of more than $100 million so far, the EPA dug seven wells that extract water from the leading edge of the underground stream. The wells pump 14,000 gallons per minute through four miles of large water mains laid under city streets for the project. The water goes to a treatment plant, where toxic chemicals are removed using activated charcoal. In Midvale, Utah, a milling plant that extracted lead, zinc, and copper from ore closed in 1971, leaving mounds of tailings up to 50 feet high. High winds blew particles of lead, cadmium, and arsenic from the piles into the surrounding community, where they contaminated soils.[43] The EPA is building a cap made of soil mixed with a stabilizing chemical to prevent wind erosion. Sometimes, for example, when dirt is contaminated by dioxins from herbicide manufacturing, EPA rules require that it be dug up and incinerated at high temperatures. Figure 14.4 shows a diagram of an incinerator. At a rate of 20 tons per

FIGURE 14.4   **Typical Rotary Kiln Incinerator at a Superfund Site**

Source: EPA. From: General Accounting Office, *Superfund: EPA Could Further Ensure the Safe Operation of On-Site Incinerators*, GAO/RCED–97–43, March 1997, p. 4.

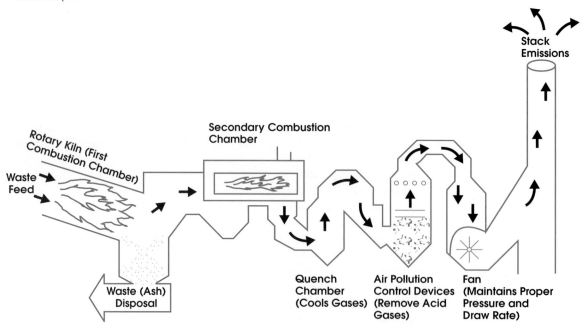

[43] These examples are in General Accounting Office, *Superfund: Analysis of Costs at Five Superfund Sites*, GAO/RCED–00–22, January 2000, apps. I and IV.

hour and a cost of about \$1,200 per ton, excavated soil is trucked to a giant revolving kiln, where it is heated to 1,800° F to break down the hazardous organic compounds into simple molecules of CO_2 and H_2O. The dirt is then backfilled.

Superfund cleanups must conform to strict RCRA standards. In incineration, for example, the standard for dioxins requires 99.9999 percent destruction efficiency, that is, for every 1 million molecules entering the incinerator, only 1 can emerge. Waste ash is treated and disposed of as hazardous waste. Incinerators are surrounded by air pollution monitors that set off alarms if stack emissions fail to meet standards.

Who pays for all this? The law establishes harsh rules of liability for any company that has ever dumped hazardous waste in a Superfund site. In legal terminology, this liability is strict, retroactive, and joint and several. In practical terms, this means that any company that ever dumped hazardous waste on a site can be responsible for the full cleanup cost even if it obeyed the law of years past, was not negligent, and dumped only a small part of the total waste. So far, the EPA has spent almost \$18 billion fixing contaminated sites, but it has recovered more than \$16 billion from companies to cover costs. The job is far from over. It is estimated that another \$15 billion will be spent by 2010.

ASSESSING THE NATION'S ENVIRONMENTAL LAWS

How well do the laws work? A fair overall assessment is that while they have forced industry to cut emissions and have reduced hazards to public health and the environment, they are flawed in important ways. Basic statutes were passed in the 1970s, before the nation had much experience with the complex task of environmental regulation. The laws of the 1970s are now called "first generation" laws in anticipation of a second generation of laws in which Congress incorporates lessons of experience. The great strength of these early laws is that they set very high standards, enforcement of which is strict. Their weaknesses, however, are multiple and include the following.

- *Inconsistent philosophy.* The costs of environmental protection are high, yet major statutes differ in allowing money to be taken into consideration. The Toxic Substances Control Act permits balancing public health benefits against pollution control costs. The Clean Air Act, however, forbids considering costs and mandates air quality standards that protect against "any adverse health effects," presumably at any cost. A central lesson from more than three decades of environmental enforcement is that the costs of absolute purity and total risk elimination are usually prohibitive.

- *Rigidity.* The laws most often rely on a command-and-control philosophy of regulation that allows little leeway in compliance. In enforcing the Clean Water Act, for example, the EPA specifies the procedures for testing water samples down to the capacity of laboratory glassware. If a test requires a 100–milliliter beaker, the lab cannot deviate from this size without submitting a formal application for modification.

- *Bureaucratic sluggishness.* The EPA is a massive, complex bureaucracy under constant budget constraints and its mechanisms grind slowly. While the agency tries to improve its administrative efficiency, its actions are delayed by bureaucratic tendencies such as the need for multiple approvals, a predilection for undertaking lengthy reviews, and fear of deviation from procedures. One study found that it took an average of 1.4 years to act on minor modifications such as changing the size of a glass beaker. Formal rule changes took up to three years.[44]

- *Complexity.* Air emissions at large industrial plants such as petroleum refineries, chemical plants, and electric power stations are often controlled under multiple laws and regulatory programs. Chemical plants, for example, are subject to as many as 16 different emission-control programs, including, among others, those for ozone reduction, limitation of toxic air pollutants, improving visibility, reducing particle emissions, and controlling acid rain. These programs can have different goals, timetables, permits, rules, and paperwork, imposing a confusing burden of duties on management. Overlap, duplication, and inconsistency in standards and enforcement create difficult compliance problems for management.[45]

- *Focus on compliance, not results.* Large bakeries are required to reduce emissions of ethanol, a by-product of yeast fermentation. The EPA mandates 80 to 95 percent reduction and a high-energy catalytic oxidation process that uses toxic metals is the only way to achieve this. Alternative technologies for reducing ethanol emissions now exist, but although they eliminate the need for toxic metals and use far less energy, the EPA rejects them because they allow ethanol emissions slightly over the 80 percent minimum. The environment suffers from this focus on strict compliance. The environmental costs of electricity production and of using poisonous metals likely exceed the benefits achieved from getting small increments of ethanol reduction to the 80 percent level.[46] Innovation is stifled by such an inflexible focus on compliance. The underlying problem is that "first generation" laws tend to focus on treat-

[44] General Accounting Office, *Environmental Protection: Wider Use of Advanced Technologies Can Improve Emissions Monitoring,* GAO–01–313, June 2001, pp. 44–47.
[45] General Accounting Office, *Air Pollution: Emission Sources Regulated by Multiple Clean Air Act Provisions,* GAO/RCED–00–155, May 2000, pp. 7–10.
[46] The Business Roundtable, *Unleashing Innovation: The Right Approach to Global Climate Change* (Washington, DC: The Business Roundtable, April 2001), p. 16.

ing pollution after it has been created rather than on the causes of its generation.

- *Adversarial approach.* The EPA's inflexible manner of regulation lends itself to a combative style in which there is heavy emphasis on penalizing violators. The fate of advanced technologies developed for monitoring industrial air and water emissions illustrates this. In one case, new equipment can test wastewater for the presence of multiple chemicals simultaneously and register amounts in parts per trillion. This apparatus is less expensive to use than EPA-approved devices that test for just one chemical at a time and detect pollutants only in parts per billion. However, companies that make the new testing equipment cannot sell it. Corporations, fearful that more accurate test results will be seen by the EPA as evidence of noncompliance, will not buy it.[47]

- *Transmedia pollution.* The basic laws are inadequate to deal with pollution that moves between water, air, and/or land. When pollutants are caught in control devices, they are not destroyed but merely trapped and eventually transferred elsewhere in the environment (one exception is high-temperature incineration that breaks down dangerous molecules into harmless water vapor, oxygen, and simple organic compounds). For example, devices that remove small particles from coal boiler exhaust create a sludge containing impurities found in coal, including mercury, arsenic, and radioactive particles. The sludge is dumped in landfills that then become hazardous waste sites. At these landfills, aromatic compounds from the sludge can evaporate back into the atmosphere, and other pollutants can bind with soil particles or seep into groundwater. Typically, older statutes direct that a pollutant be controlled in one medium without full consideration of its migration to another, reflecting the more limited scientific understanding of the 1970s. The EPA and state environmental agencies are organized along media lines, which contributes to a fragmenting of enforcement efforts.

For many years, business has advocated major changes in environmental laws. Industrial companies facing heavy compliance requirements would like to see much more flexibility. The Business Roundtable, which represents the largest corporations, recently issued a reform agenda. It suggests setting targets, then letting corporations achieve emission cuts in innovative and cost-effective ways. It wants more market-oriented enforcement such as the emissions trading regime set up to reduce pollutants

[47] General Accounting Office, *Environmental Protection: Wider Use of Advanced Technologies Can Improve Emissions Monitoring,* pp. 27–28, 40.

that cause acid rain. And it wants more flexibility in compliance rules for corporations that set up voluntary pollution-reduction programs.[48] These proposals have a wide following, even in the EPA, and the agency runs a series of pilot and experimental programs incorporating such ideas. However, until environmental statutes are rewritten based on a changed regulatory philosophy, the future application of such experiments is limited.

CONCLUDING OBSERVATIONS

Industrial processes damage the environment and cause serious local and global deterioration. A first wave of environmental statutes in the United States has reduced pollution and deterioration, primarily through rigid and expensive regulations. Now that experience has been gained with these laws, their high cost, inflexibility, and adversarial nature are seen as short-comings. There are many suggestions for more cost-effective and flexible regulation. In the next chapter we discuss methods for determining how regulatory programs can become more efficient and effective and also what corporations are doing to reduce pollution and protect the environment.

[48] The Business Roundtable, *Blueprint 2001: Drafting Environmental Policy for the Future,* www.brtable.org.

Owls, Loggers, and Old-Growth Forests

On May 25, 2001, John Shelk, the great grandson of the founder of the Ochoco Lumber Co., reluctantly closed the company's Prineville, Oregon, sawmill after 63 years of operation. It was a bad day, but the people of Oregon are used to such news. In the previous 10 years, 89 sawmills had closed in the state.

For the small logging community of Prineville, it was a disaster. One-hundred and eighty jobs and a payroll of nearly $5 million a year evaporated. Another $8 to $10 million a year paid to contract loggers and truck drivers disappeared. The $15 million or so a year that the company paid into the United States Treasury for timber purchases on federal lands vanished.[1] Under current revenue sharing policy, 25 percent of money generated on federal lands is shared with local government to support local schools and road construction—a loss to Prineville of about $3.75 million a year. Also, the City of Prineville Railway lost 40 percent of its business. Built to carry lumber from sawmills in the town to a main line 18 miles away, the small operation brought in $800,000 to $1 million a year in municipal revenue. The little railroad now projects an annual deficit of about $23,000.[2]

Beyond the economic toll, Prineville lost a socially responsible citizen. The Ochoco Lumbermill gave scholarships to 50 college students. Along with other firms, it had helped built the high school stadium and a local museum. Dislocated

[1] Statement of Bruce Daucsavage, prepared for the Subcommittee on Public Lands and Forests, Energy and Natural Resources Committee, U.S. Senate, October 2, 2001, p. 4.

[2] Steve Lundgren, "End of the Line," *The Oregonian,* July 29, 2001, p. A17.

mill workers lacked opportunities. The Viles family, for instance, lost two salaries. Dan Viles, 51, a skilled lumber grader, was out of a job after 19 years at the mill. His wife Teena, a planer lead person, had worked there for 15 years. The Viles are eligible for federally funded retraining. Dan took some aptitude tests that showed he would be a good short-order cook or brewmaster. However, there is little prospect of finding such jobs in Prineville now.

The Prineville sawmill took felled trees from surrounding forests, mostly ponderosa pine, and turned them into boards and molding. Its output was in high demand. Consumption of lumber in the United States is rising. Prineville is also home to several manufacturing companies that took the high-quality pine lumber and turned it into products such as doors, windows, and cabinets. Thus, lack of demand did not shutter the mill.

Lack of raw timber did. Until the late 1970s the sawmill used large logs from the surrounding forests of central and eastern Oregon. The U.S. Forest Service conducted frequent timber sales. Ochoco Lumber Co. bid on stands of trees, and if the bid was accepted, the company sent a check to the agency, hired loggers to cut the trees, and engaged independent truck drivers to bring the raw logs to the mill's pond. Then, growing national debate about the uses of wilderness areas caused the Forest Service to impose restrictive new rules. Some ancient forests were closed to timber sales. Clear-cutting, the common practice of felling every tree in an area, was forbidden. Many timber sales allowed only the thinning of stands in younger forests, resulting in harvests of smaller diameter logs.

The Ochoco Lumbermill adjusted to these changes. It bought 60,000 acres of forests to supply part of its sawtimber needs, about 20 percent. By the late 1980s it had spent more than $15 million on new machinery that was more efficient for small-log milling. However, almost as soon as this capital investment was made, the Forest Service again cut back on timber sales, this time because of lawsuits by environmental groups to protect the northern spotted owl. Lacking the needed flow of sawtimber, the mill closed.

The northern spotted owl (*Strix occidentalis caurina*) is a reclusive, nocturnal bird that lives deep in the forests of Washington, Oregon, and northern California. Since the 1800s timber cutting and land development have reduced the owl's habitat by as much as 80 percent, threatening its extinction. Congress passed the Endangered Species Act in 1973 to prevent the demise of such creatures, and in 1990 the owl was added to the list of species entitled to special protection. Unfortunately for the wood products industry, the owls live in the most productive timber lands of the Pacific Northwest. Their predicament has caused federal timber harvests to decline more than 90 percent. It is this decline that starved the saws in Prineville—and in many other small mill towns in the forested regions of the West coast. An industry and a way of life are moribund. This is the story.

THE NORTHERN SPOTTED OWL

The northern spotted owl is a perch-and-dive predator with a wingspan of 2 feet and a weight of about 1 1/2 pounds. Its body is mottled brown with patches of white. Its habitat ranges from British Columbia in the north to the redwood stands above San Francisco in the south.

Like other owls, the northern spotted owl is anatomically adapted to nighttime activity. It has a large head and a large brain, compared with other birds, and big round eyes. "Indeed," notes one biologist, "the heads of owls are basically little more than brains with raptorial beaks and the largest possible eyes and ears attached."[3] Spotted owls' eyes have rod-rich retinas, endowing them with exceptionally acute black-and-white vision in low-light conditions. They can locate and dive on scampering mice in illuminations as much as 30 times below the lowest reported human visual threshold.

Their hearing is similarly acute. Without benefit of vision, they can locate tree squirrels or mice that make small rustling noises in frequency ranges inaudible to humans. Their brains calculate time lags of microseconds in the arrival of sounds at each ear, enabling them to fly unerringly through darkness to a sound source. The spotted owl, despite its sedentary daytime roosting, has a high metabolism

[3] Paul A. Johnsgard, *North American Owls: Biology and Natural History* (Washington, DC: Smithsonian Institution Press, 1988), p. 42.

The northern spotted owl.
Source: U.S. Fish and Wildlife Service.

and hunts actively through the night. Its prey is mainly small mammals such as flying squirrels, wood rats, rabbits, mice, and tree voles, but it also kills reptiles and small birds.

Northern spotted owls exhibit a wide range of social behavior. They have courtship rituals, and pairs bond for extended periods. They communicate with postural signals, displays of aggression, and a variety of hoots and calls. They are territorial and announce their presence with a series of four

hoots (described phonetically as "hooo hoo hoo hooo").[4] These low hoots have long wavelengths especially suited for penetrating dense foliage. The territory of a mated spotted owl pair is huge; obser-

[4] This is what ornithologists refer to as its "four-note location call." It has other vocalizations as well, including "barks" and whistles. U.S. Department of the Interior, *Recovery Plan for the Northern Spotted Owl—Draft* (Washington, DC: U.S. Government Printing Office, April 1992), p. 15.

vation with radiotelemetry reveals foraging ranges from 1,000 to 27,000 acres.[5] Reproduction occurs in spring and summer, when females lay an average of two eggs. After hatching, the young owls are cared for by the parents for only a month before flying away to establish their own territories.

OLD GROWTH

Spotted owls prefer old-growth forests. Forests develop in stages, during which they undergo changes in composition. Although the definition of an old-growth forest is not precise, it is generally held to be a forest that is 200 or more years old. Such ancient forests are more structurally and biologically complex than younger forests. Snags and logs, for example, provide habitat niches for a variety of plant and animal life. During the 200 to 500 years it takes a large log to disintegrate, it may nurse an expansive population of bacteria, insects, lichens, plants, and small animals that use the stored moisture and nutrients in the deadwood. First come boring insects that open pathways into the log. Then microorganisms such as fungi invade the wood, followed by mites, spiders, and beetles feeding on them. Birds come to catch the insects. As the wood fragments, ferns and small hemlocks force their roots in and tap stored moisture. Soon mice and wood rats find homes, attracting predators such as the northern spotted owl. Eventually, scavengers that feed on dead vegetation and animal feces show up. Put poetically, in the downed tree, "decay is merely a counterpoint, life and death a single process, like a mirror fugue conceived by a composer even better than Bach."[6]

Old-growth forests achieve great natural beauty and inspire comparisons with cathedrals. They have much richer biotic communities than younger forests and are repositories for species that have adapted to ecological niches created under old-growth conditions. The spotted owl is one such species. The dense vegetation protects them from predators such as the red-tailed hawk. A thick, mul-

tilayered forest canopy also provides thermal cover, insulating them from extremes of heat and cold. Owls nest in the cavities of standing snags, and fallen snags create conditions that support abundant prey to satisfy their voracious appetites. The spotted owl plays a role in the old-growth ecosystem by culling small mammal and bird populations.

Early studies of northern spotted owls suggested that they lived only in old-growth stands.[7] Environmentalists claimed that the owl was like a canary in a coal mine. If the owl at the top of the forest food chain was in danger of extinction, this was a warning that other species and the old-growth habitat itself were also endangered. Subsequent studies have shown that some northern spotted owls live and breed in younger forests and forests that have been logged. Occasionally they go far astray. Recently, a juvenile spotted owl flew into a suburb of Seattle, roosting in a maple tree between Fitness World and Jimmy Z's bar. People gathered with cameras and binoculars. Newspapers reported on its activities.[8] Eventually, a wildlife biologist climbed the tree as the owl slept, lassoed it by the neck with a wire noose at the end of a pole, and drove it to an old-growth forest.

Such stories seem to cast doubt on the belief that spotted owls need old-growth to survive. Yet they clearly prefer old-growth, and population densities are highest in mature forests. Where they live in younger forests, they seek out areas of high structural diversity. Some owls do try to nest, roost, and forage in early-succession forests, but ornithologists believe that these are juvenile owls dispersing from old-growth stands. Spotted owls are territorial, live 10 to 15 years, and maintain large domains in diminishing stands of old growth. This makes it difficult for juvenile owls to stake out territories in the fewer and fewer remaining stands of high structural complexity. Therefore, some young owls leaving nests after breeding season are pushed into

---

[5] Ibid., p. 23.
[6] David Kelly and Gary Braasch, *Secrets of the Old Growth Forest* (Salt Lake City: Peregrine Smith Books, 1988), p. 39.

[7] A study in Washington, for example, found that 97 percent of spotted owls lived in old growth, with no known reproductive pairs in second-growth areas. "Proposed Threatened Status for the Northern Spotted Owl," 54 FR 26668, June 23, 1989.
[8] Diane Brooks, "Rare Owl Roosts in Everett," *Seattle Times*, November 19, 1998, p. B1.

younger forests. They forage and breed there, but scientists believe that reproductive success in young forests is insufficient to balance higher death rates from predation by the great horned owl, a natural enemy foraging in more open areas that accommodate its larger wingspan.[9]

LOSS OF OLD GROWTH IMPERILS THE SPOTTED OWL

The expansion of America came at the expense of wilderness. When pilgrims landed at Plymouth Rock, the landmass destined to become the continental United States had 850 million acres of forest. By the 1920s only 138 million acres of virgin forest remained, roughly 16 percent of what had existed.[10] The rest had been burned, grazed, cut, radically disturbed, or converted to other uses. Reduction of forest area stopped in the 1870s, and, on balance, regrowth now exceeds losses.

The northwest coastal forest inhabited by spotted owls covered about 94 million acres in the 1860s when settlers and loggers first arrived. Today only about 30 million acres of this coastal forest remain, including just 7.7 million acres of old growth. Much of this old growth is not contiguous; rather, it is a checkerboard of old stands mixed with bare timber-harvest areas, young growth, and tree farms. Of these 7.7 million acres, 2.8 million acres are in national parks or wilderness areas closed forever to logging. By the late 1980s about 2 percent of the remaining 4.9 million acres of old growth was being cut each year, largely for timber sales on federal lands. At this rate, nearly all old-growth habitat outside national parks would have been gone in 50 years.

Little remaining old growth is on private land; most is on federal land managed by the Forest Service and the Bureau of Land Management. These agencies are required by law to open forests for "multiple use" activities such as logging, mining, and recreation. So they hold timber auctions in which logging companies bid for the right to fell selected stands of timber. Once the winning bids are picked, timber harvesting proceeds based on precise regulations describing boundaries, logging techniques, and the restoration and replanting that is necessary. In 60 years a replanted forest can be reharvested; a high-density replanting will yield more timber than the original old growth.

In 1989 government biologists estimated that there were only 1,550 breeding pairs of the owls in the Pacific Northwest.[11] This low count worried scientists who believed that the owl was on the margin of survival as a species.[12] When species decline to very low numbers, there is danger that even if human impacts are reduced or removed, events in nature, such as random fluctuations of climate or food supply, cannot be overcome. When numbers fall, the reproductive pattern of the species is critical. Unfortunately, the spotted owl has a very low reproductive efficiency. A mated pair produces an average of .50 young per year. Then juvenile owls suffer an 88 percent morality rate in their first year.[13]

[9] See, for example, remarks of ecologist H. Ronald Pullium cited by Paul R. Ehrlich and Anne H. Ehrlich in *Betrayal of Science and Reason* (Washington, DC: Island Press, 1998), p. 118.
[10] Figures for forest size are from Michael Williams, *Americans and Their Forests: A Historical Geography* (New York: Cambridge University Press, 1989), pp. 3–4.

[11] "Protected Status Proposed for the Northern Spotted Owl," *Endangered Species Technical Bulletin,* July 1989, p. 1.
[12] Two subspecies of spotted owl, the northern spotted owl (*Strix occidentalis caurina*) and the California spotted owl (*Strix occidentalis occidentalis*) mix together at the extremes of their ranges in northern California. Although the California spotted owl is more plentiful, environmental groups have sued the U.S. Fish and Wildlife Service demanding that it also be listed as threatened or endangered. A third subspecies, the Mexican spotted owl (*Strix occidentalis lucida*), lives in the forests of Arizona, Utah, Colorado, Texas, and Mexico. It was listed as threatened in 1993; see "Final Rule to List the Mexican Spotted Owl as a Threatened Species," 58 FR 14248, March 16, 1993. Scientific debate exists about whether the California and northern spotted owls are, in fact genetically distinct subspecies.
[13] Daniel Simberloff, "The Spotted Owl Fracas: Mixing Academic, Applied, and Political Ecology," *Ecology,* August 1987, p. 768.

ENVIRONMENTALIST CAMPAIGN TO PROTECT THE OWL

In the 1980s environmental groups took up the cause of the northern spotted owl. They believed that the owl had intrinsic, unlimited value as a species; its extinction would be an irrevocable mistake. Equally important, they knew that the owl's use of old growth as habitat made saving owls a convenient pretext for saving ancient forests from the logger's ax. Using the owl, they could invoke the Endangered Species Act and elevate the goal of forest preservation above the economic interests of timber companies, lumber mills, and loggers.

The Endangered Species Act is an exceptionally strong statute. Passed in 1973, it set forth procedures for designating, or "listing," such species. The act defines an *endangered* species as one that is "in danger of extinction throughout all or a significant portion of its range." It also permits listing of a *threatened* species that is "likely to become an endangered species in the future throughout all or a significant portion of its range." Once a species is listed in either category, it is entitled to a great deal of protection. Under threat of civil or criminal penalties, it is illegal to "take"—that is, "to harass, harm, pursue, hunt, shoot, wound, kill, trap, capture, or collect"—any individual of the listed species on public or private lands. The law also protects geographically defined "critical habitat" of listed species. And it requires that listings be based solely on scientific evidence about species survival needs; consideration of economic and political consequences is generally prohibited. The law is enforced by two agencies. The Fish and Wildlife Service within the Department of the Interior is responsible for plants and animals found on land and in freshwater environments and for migratory birds. The National Marine Fisheries Service within the Department of Commerce enforces the law with respect to marine species. In 2001 there were 1,246 species, 507 animals and 736 plants, listed as threatened or endangered.[14]

At first, the Fish and Wildlife Service declined to list the northern spotted owl as endangered. Its biologists believed that evidence of a long-term threat to its survival was insufficient. Angry environmentalists sued the agency. In 1990, bowing to the pressure, it listed the spotted owl as a "threatened" species.[15] This set the powerful devices of the Endangered Species Act in motion, and soon an entire region of the country felt the consequences. The Fish and Wildlife Service adopted protective rules that remain in force today. Logging is banned within 70 acres of a known spotted owl nest and is sharply restricted within a 2,000-acre radius. Even when a nest is found empty, there is a three-year moratorium on logging to ensure that it is abandoned. Before activities such as forestry or road maintenance and construction can take place in owl habitat, the agency must issue a clearance, called a "biological opinion."

In 1991 a federal district court in Seattle issued an injunction virtually halting timber sales in the government-owned old-growth forests of the Pacific Northwest until the Fish and Wildlife Service developed a species recovery plan for the owl. The Endangered Species Act requires a written plan to serve as a road map for the eventual recovery and delisting of a species. This was a boon for the owls, which could sleep during the day without the annoying buzz of chainsaws, but it was a disaster for the forest products industry, which depended on timber harvests. In 1990, the year before the injunction, 10.6 billion board feet of timber were cut on federal lands.[16] In 1991 only 4.4 billion board feet were harvested before the injunction took hold. And the next year only 0.7 billion board feet were sold.[17]

[14] "The Species Litigation Act," *The Wall Street Journal,* April 20, 2001, p. A20.

[15] "Determination of Threatened Status for the Northern Spotted Owl," 55 FR 21623, June 26, 1990.
[16] A board foot is a measure of timber volume. One board foot equals a volume of 12 × 12 × 1 inches.
[17] Department of the Interior memorandum in *The Administration's Response to the Spotted Owl Crisis: Joint Oversight Hearing before the Subcommittee on National Parks and Public Lands of the Committee on Interior and Insular Affairs,* U.S. House of Representatives, March 24, 1992, p. 167.

HARD TIMES IN THE PACIFIC NORTHWEST

Halted timber sales brought hardship. Hundreds of small-town economies built on jobs created by logging, milling, and related trucking and shipping spiraled downward. The owl injunction came on the heels of a prolonged recession in the Pacific Northwest in the early 1980s. Thousands of loggers and mill workers had already lost jobs. Now, because of the Endangered Species Act, many more would be jobless.

Despair and anger permeated logging towns. In Forks, Washington, where unemployment rose to 20 percent, someone shot a spotted owl and nailed it to a sign (risking a $20,000 fine and one year in prison). In Oregon, loggers had bumper stickers that read: "IF IT'S HOOTIN', I'M SHOOTIN'," "SAVE A LOGGER/EAT AN OWL," and "I LIKE SPOTTED OWLS . . . FRIED." Northern California suffered too. In Happy Camp, all four sawmills closed and the town collapsed as area timber harvests declined from 50 million board feet to 8 million. The population fell from 2,500 to 1,100, and more than half those remaining were on public assistance.[18]

In 1992 the Fish and Wildlife Service finally prepared a recovery plan for the spotted owl, but it failed to satisfy environmental groups. They went to court, alleging it was inadequate, and won. Their victory extended the injunction against logging until the agency came up with a new recovery plan. Of course, environmentalists were likely to challenge any new plan because as long as the injunction remained in effect, old growth in the Pacific Northwest was protected. By this time, those trying to save the spotted owl and its old-growth habitat were locked in bitter scientific, legal, political, and personal conflict with those whose livelihood depended on the productivity of national forests.

In 1993 then newly elected President Clinton fulfilled a campaign promise by presiding over a "timber summit" in Portland Oregon, where he listened to the strong and polarized views of scientists, environmentalists, and timber industry representatives.

As a result, early in 1994 the Clinton administration introduced the Northwest Forest Plan (NWFP) designed to resolve the impasse and move forward. The NWFP attempted to appease both environmentalists and industry. It covered 24.4 million forest acres. Logging was proscribed in 80 percent of this area. This was thought to be sufficient to permit recovery of the spotted owl; therefore, the NWFP also became the official owl recovery plan. The remaining 20 percent of the area in the NWFP was to be managed for timber production based on guidelines set up to protect the owl and other endangered species. For example, no logging would be permitted in "owl circles" having a radius of 2.7 miles extending from known owl nests. The plan permitted logging 1.2 billion board feet annually in mature and old-growth forests.[19] This harvest level was nearly double that of years since the injunction but was still almost 90 percent less than the year before the injunction. The NWFP spelled permanent loss of tens of thousands of timber jobs, so it committed $1.2 billion over five years to retrain workers, help small businesses, and compensate for lost tax revenues in timber towns.

Despite the broad recovery plan and paltry timber harvest authorized by the NWFP, environmentalists sued to block it. However, it was upheld by a federal court. Even so, little timber cutting took place. At first, delay was caused by convoluted, bureaucratic Forest Service procedures for setting up timber auctions. Later, environmentalists began to challenge timber auctions, suing the agency at every turn to block action.

The political climate in this battle over the forests changed after the midterm elections of 1994 in which Republicans gained a congressional majority. They attacked environmental laws, including the Endangered Species Act, which they regarded as a prime example of runaway government power. By this time, a storm of protest swirled around the statute, much of it generated by the rising property rights movement. This movement represents property owners hurt by regulations that reduce the value of their land. Both corporations

---

[18] Richard C. Paddock, "Town's Decline Rivals That of the Spotted Owl," *Los Angeles Times,* October 23, 1995, p. A3.

[19] Report of the Forest Ecosystem Management Assessment Team, *Forest Ecosystem Management: An Ecological, Economic, and Social Assessment* (Washington, DC: U.S. Department of Agriculture et al., July 1993)

that owned expanses of timber and small landowners with only a few acres were hurt when they could not harvest the trees they owned. They demanded compensation by government when this occurred.

A clause in the Fifth Amendment, known as the *takings clause,* protects property owners. It reads: "nor shall private property be taken for public use without just compensation." In the past, the takings clause has been interpreted as requiring compensation only when government takes over property through eminent domain or when the owner is wholly deprived of its use. Except in unusual circumstances, it has never been held to require payment for land-use restrictions incidental to enforcement of environmental laws. However, opponents of heavy-handed regulation seized on the takings clause to argue that landowners deserved compensation when regulators reduced property values. Eventually, this position achieved some success in the courtroom. In 1997 an Oregon jury awarded Boise Cascade Corp. more than $2 million for the value of 56 acres of timberland that it was unable to harvest because of a spotted owl nest.[20] However, this precedent never took hold. Other courts held that endangered species restrictions were not a taking for public use in the same sense as when the government seized entire properties using eminent domain.

Many forest products companies began negotiating *habitat conservation plans* with the government. A habitat conservation plan is a binding agreement, permitted under the Endangered Species Act and entered into voluntarily, in which a landowner agrees to take conservation measures, usually beyond the letter of the law, and in return receives permission to log or otherwise use property, even if it means harm to endangered species or critical habitat in the process. These plans were little used, because previously the government had preferred an inflexible enforcement of the Endangered Species Act. However, as anger about the statute's role in reducing timber harvests rose, sentiment in Congress for changing it grew. Suddenly,

the Clinton administration discovered the virtues of habitat conservation plans.

An early example of one of the plans came in 1995 when the Murray Pacific Company, which owned a 53,000-acre tree farm in Washington populated by spotted owls, agreed to preserve 43 percent of the property as habitat for the owl and four other endangered species. The agreement was detailed and specific; for example, the company was to leave trees outside five cave openings to protect a bat species and had to monitor the temperature of streams and leave more trees standing on their banks to shade them if readings began to rise. In exchange, Murray Pacific received an "incidental take permit" absolving it from blame if, in logging the rest of the property, any members of an endangered species were harassed or killed. A similar plan was negotiated with Weyerhaeuser Co., permitting it to log parts of 209,000 acres of owl habitat it owns in Oregon. In return, Weyerhaeuser agreed to leave corridors of old growth for spotted owls. Without the plans, both Murray Pacific and Weyerhaeuser probably would have been denied the right to log their land at all.

By 2000 there were more than 300 habitat conservation plans.[21] The agreements have "no-surprise" clauses, guarantees that even if new evidence about an endangered species emerges years later, no additional conservation measures will be required.[22] They also include a "baseline" policy so that if the numbers of an endangered species increase, the landowner is not required to take additional measures to protect them. This removes an incentive for private landowners to drive out or kill endangered species before their presence can be reported and the land rendered useless for development or timber harvest.

Environmental groups oppose habitat conservation plans, incidental take permits, and the no-surprises policy, all of which they see as compromising the survival chances of species on the borderline. Incidental take permits allow logging companies to destroy some owl habitat. And the no-surprises policy may turn out to be foolish.

---

[20] Kate Freedlander, "Timber Firm Wins Judgment on State's Logging Limits," *The Oregonian,* November 23, 1997, p. 1.

[21] Standford Law Society, *The Endangered Species Act* (Stanford, CA: Stanford University Press, 2001), p. 133.
[22] "Habitat Conservation Plan Assurances ('No Surprises') Rule," 63 FR 8859, February 23, 1998.

Science is just beginning to understand certain species and complex ecosystems. Yet habitat conservation plans are locked into place for decades—some for as long as 100 years. Even if new information about causes of extinction is discovered, landowners cannot be forced to alter their activities. They can volunteer to do so, and government must pick up the cost. However, although habitat conservation plans may have compromised species protection, they also relieved industry pressure for emasculation of the Endangered Species Act.

ENVIRONMENTALISTS BLOCK TIMBER HARVESTS

Habitat conservation plans have facilitated logging on some timberland owned by individuals and forest products companies, but logging in federal forests covered by the NWFP has fallen far short of the promised 1.2 billion board feet annually. Timber harvests never reached that level, and in 2000 only 62 million board feet came out of the woods, just 5 percent of what had been promised. The main roadblocks are set by environmentalists, who use both the law and tactics of civil disobedience to stop logging.

The Endangered Species Act allows citizen suits to prod federal agencies when they fail to meet statutory obligations. Environmental activists have brought hundreds of citizen suits over the last decade challenging timber harvests. Most of these actions are based on the presence of endangered species in areas to be logged. Others claim that timber auctions have been inadequately surveyed for the presence of species. Still others press for listing of new species or compliance with legal deadlines to complete recovery plans for previously listed species. Several environmental groups specialize in this litigation. The Center for Biological Diversity, for example, averaged one new lawsuit every 32 days for years following the adoption of the NWFP.[23] The lawsuits tie down government agencies, forcing them to put more resources into litigation and leaving less energy for managing species. The overworked agencies miss so many

deadlines that one environmental lawyer says bringing "[a] missed deadline case is like shooting fish in a barrel."[24] When environmental lawyers win the suits, they are entitled to bill their hours to a government fund that pays them $150 to $350 per hour. This keeps the suits coming.

The purpose of the lawsuits is to preserve the forests. Zero cutting is the goal. After a forest fire in the Ochoco National Forest near Prineville, Oregon, environmental litigators filed a 104-page appeal when the Forest Service tried to sell 54 trees that had been cut to create a fire break—even though the trees had been lying on the ground for almost a year.[25] They argued that the trees should be allowed to decay on the forest floor, returning their nutrients to the soil. A California environmental group developed software enabling it to create so many timber sale appeals that it blocked or slowed the sale of almost 500 million board feet.[26]

Activists also use a wide range of protest tactics. In the national forests, they sit in trees, lie in front of logging trucks, and put metal spikes in trees scheduled for harvest so that saw blades will shatter if the logs are milled. On private timberland, they trespass and occupy sites slated for logging. All this is illegal once a stand of trees is clear of appeals and ready for logging under government rules. However, activists feel justified by the ethical duty to protect species and forests. "It's against the law to trespass," says one, "but we feel there's a higher law."[27] In some cases, activists take it upon themselves to survey potential timber harvests for endangered species. In the Willamette National Forest, logging protestors documented 20 red tree vole nests. Though not endangered themselves, these small mammals are prey for spotted owls. The discovery of the nests led Forest Service biologists to take 51 acres out of a 94-acre timber sale.[28]

[23] Tom Knudson, "A Flood of Costly Lawsuits Raises Questions About Motive," *Sacramento Bee,* April 24, 2001, p. A1.

[24] Ibid., p. A1.
[25] Steve Lundgren, "End of the Line," *The Oregonian,* July 29, 2001, p. A17.
[26] William Wade Keye, "Mill Towns Subsist on Logs from Afar," *Sacramento Bee,* October 28, 2001, p. B6.
[27] Eric Bailey, "Two Sides Firmly Rooted over Logging Battle," *Los Angeles Times,* May 29, 2001, p. B8.
[28] Kim Murphy, "Logging Protesters Sit to Conquer," *Los Angeles Times,* September 26, 2001, p. A24.

STALEMATE

The battle between loggers and environmentalists is stalemated. However, in this stalemate the environmentalists win because old forest is left standing. Their victory is not total. The northern spotted owl population continues to decline, although its numbers are so small that reliable estimates are elusive. In addition, secondary manufacturers in the Pacific Northwest, unable to supply their need for wood locally, increasingly rely on imported timber from countries such as Canada, Brazil, and Chile. Logs, planks, and chips arrive by ship and are trucked to the region's small factories. There, within sight of some of the world's great forests, they substitute for locally grown wood in porch posts, door frames, and garden furniture. The irony would be no greater if Saudi Arabian refineries depended on imported oil or Hawaiian canneries on pineapples from the mainland. There is a second irony. Because there are fewer environmental safeguards on wood production in other countries than in the United States environmentalists have, in effect, made species extinction and damage to forest ecosystems an export item.

Logging interests in the Pacific Northwest are defeated. The government promise of sustained timber yields has been broken. Federal agencies that once managed forests to get maximum productivity have now shifted their orientation to biological research and species protection. Timber auctions are snarled in protracted litigation. Logging leads to confrontation with ideologues who regard each stand of gnarled snags as an exquisite masterwork of creation.

Neither party can rectify the underlying cause of the owl's tenuous grip on the future. Human settlement has tattered the broad ocean of green canopy that once stretched over the Pacific Northwest, leaving only islands of the original natural expanse. After passage of the Endangered Species Act it was, in retrospect, inevitable that the load of species preservation would fall on federal land holding almost all of the last ancient forests. Unless this statute is amended to add flexibility, it will increasingly dictate that land now used for logging, mining, and recreation must be managed solely as species habitat. Environmental groups

clearly see this potential. They have, for example, stopped some oil production in Alaska by suing to have a sea duck, the spectacled eider, listed as endangered. Large expanses of spectacled eider habitat are now off limits to drilling rigs.

In a recent editorial, *The Wall Street Journal* commented that "most people have no concept of how much it costs to protect natural resources, and so feel there's nothing to lose from more regulations."[29] The exact price of protecting the spotted owl is elusive, but high. One study looked at projections of wood prices, consumption and production trends in the United States, and estimated changes in wood products revenues, incomes, and costs to consumers due to owl protection. The authors concluded that measures to raise the survival odds of the owl to 91 percent would lead to a $33 billion reduction in economic welfare, most of which would come out of the pockets of workers and businesses in the Pacific Northwest. Enforcing the Endangered Species Act in a way that would raise the owl's survival odds to 95 percent would push the economic sacrifice up to $46 billion.[30] If this is the case, assuming a spotted owl population of 5,000, a number in the high range of recent estimates, the price tag on each owl is $6.6 to $9.9 million.

The timber conflict is also rooted in opposing values. Environmentalists want to save species. A species such as the northern spotted owl takes millions of years to evolve. Its loss would be irretrievable in the span of time that constitutes human historical consciousness. One more element would be removed from the profusion of life on earth. And humanity would be impoverished for that subtraction from its biological inheritance, a subtraction made all the worse because perhaps avoidable. On the other side, there is no more eloquent exponent than Neal Korpela, a forklift driver who is jobless after 25 years at the Ochoco Lumbermill in Prineville. "Tough decisions have to be made . . . about how we're going to value people over animals and plants," he says. "Most

[29] "The Earth Rebalanced," July 10, 2001, p. A18.
[30] C. Montgomery et al., "The Marginal Cost of Species Preservation: The Northern Spotted Owl," *Journal of Environmental Economics and Management* 26 (1994), p. 11.

of the economy of Crook County is an endangered species, and no one seems to have a habitat recovery program for us."[31]

QUESTIONS

1. Are you in favor of using the national forests of the Pacific Northwest to preserve the northern spotted owl, even if it means catastrophic loss of jobs, mill closures, depleted tax revenues, underfunded schools, and growing reliance on imported lumber?

[31] Quoted in "Machines Quiet at Newly Closed MIll," Associated Press, August 1, 2001.

2. When government prohibits logging near spotted owl nests, does this violate rights given the landowners by the takings clause of the Fifth Amendment? Should owners of private timberland be compensated by the government for their losses? Would it be fair to shift the burden of species protection to taxpayers?

3. Evaluate the actions of environmental groups. Are the values of activists correct? Do they have an ethical duty to natural law? Are environmental litigators abusing the privilege of citizen suits?

4. Should enforcement of the Endangered Species Act continue to become more flexible? Or should it tighten to protect spotted owls and other endangered species more? What changes, if any, should be made in the Endangered Species Act?

Chapter **Fifteen**

Managing Environmental Quality

Louisiana-Pacific Corporation

In 1973, Arthur and Margaret Orjias settled on 50 acres of land in an eastern Colorado valley. They had almost finished building their house in 1984, when a new Louisiana-Pacific Corporation (LP) plant started operating nearby. The Montrose Plant, as it was called, turned out waferboard, a type of paneling made by mixing aspen chips in a glue-like resin, pressing them into wafers, and baking them in an oven. The oven was heated by burning wood. Inside it, hot exhaust gases from the fire cured the board. These gases emerged from the oven containing formaldehyde, isocyanates, and tiny wood particles.

Immediately after production began, nearby residents were bothered by smoke so dense that cars going through the valley sometimes turned on their headlights during the day. The Orjias suffered from coughing, headaches, earaches, swollen glands, and nausea. After three years of medical problems and unresolved complaints to the company, the couple abandoned their home and moved.

A year later, Colorado regulators finally issued a permit to the Montrose Plant mandating the use of air pollution controls and setting emission levels. A continuous monitor that recorded an opacity reading on a graph every six minutes was also required (see Figure 15.1).

For the next two years, the plant repeatedly violated its permit and, in 1990, it was fined $80,000 by the Colorado Department of Public Health. A new and more stringent permit was then issued, placing an hourly limit on wood fuel for the oven and limiting the plant to production of 210,000 square board feet of finished panels per 12-hour shift. These limits were intended to improve air quality in the valley.

FIGURE 15.1 An Opacity Monitor

Factories and power plants are given permits by the EPA or state regulators mandating the use of mechanical or chemical devices to remove gases, particles, and odors. To reduce smoke, the Montrose Plant was required to run exhaust gases through an electrified filter. Positively charged soot particles in the oven exhaust smoke were run through negatively charged filters that attracted and retained them. Filtered exhaust streams were to have an opacity reading of 20 percent or less, that is, no more than 20 percent of the light passing through the air in the exhaust stream could be reflected by particles. This 20 percent opacity limit was to be achieved 95 percent of the time. The diagram illustrates how an opacity monitor works. A light beam from the left passes through exhaust gases and any loss of light is measured by the detector at right.

Source: General Accounting Office

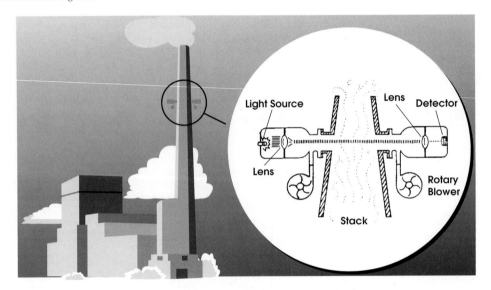

The plant manager, however, ordered employees to tamper with the opacity monitor. When permit limits were likely to be exceeded, the workers placed adhesive tape with reflective backing near the light beam to trick the device, and they wedged wood chips in the recording pen to prevent it from going over the 20 percent limit. After a fired employee revealed what was going on, the EPA raided the plant, seizing 23 boxes of records. It took investigators three years to figure out how the scheme worked.

Meanwhile, the Montrose Plant documents so alarmed the EPA that even before their full review, it launched an investigation of LP facilities nationwide. What it found was a corporate culture of disrespect for environmental rules. "[I]n the structure of an organization like this you don't need to tell people to violate the law," said a federal prosecutor. "You tell them 'we need so much production' and people know what they're going to have to do."[1] As a preliminary move, the EPA barred LP from buying timber from the U.S. Forest Service. Then in 1993, the agency culminated its na-

---

[1] Quoted in Mark Eddy, "Judge Fines Timber Firm $37 Million," *Denver Post,* May 28, 1998, p. A1.

tionwide investigation, fining LP $11 million and forcing it to install $70 million of new pollution control equipment.

In 1995 the EPA brought a criminal indictment against LP and two employees in the Montrose Plant matter.[2] The firm's top three executives resigned and a new management team came in, determined to improve environmental performance. The Montrose Plant case was settled in 1998 when the company agreed to a $37 million fine and five years' probation. The plant superintendent was fined $10,000 and given six months' home detention, and a supervisor was sentenced to five months in prison, both for criminal conspiracy to violate the Clean Air Act. LP's new CEO Mark A. Suwyn appeared in the courtroom to apologize for the corporation. He announced that the Montrose Plant would be a "model of environmental compliance."[3]

Louisiana-Pacific is a large building materials maker with 80 mills and manufacturing plants. Strict enforcement of environmental laws taught the company a lesson, so it is now "greening" itself. It adopted a new "Corporate Policy on Protection of the Environment" and set up special management systems at each of its facilities focused on meeting (and exceeding) environmental rules. It spent hundreds of millions of dollars on new pollution control devices. At waferboard mills, for example, it put in costly ceramic thermal units that reduce formaldehyde emissions by heating exhaust gases rising through stacks to high temperatures. And it is moving beyond pollution control to think more in terms of zero emissions and resource conservation.

The company may be making progress. It incurred losses from 1995 to 1997 due to legal costs and fines, but since then it has been profitable. In 1999 it paid a $100,000 fine when a California particleboard plant polluted a stream. However, one of its plants won an environmental award from the State of Oregon, and the company was lauded as one of 20 environmental success stories in a recent book.[4]

Command-and-control enforcement is critical in environmental regulation. It forced Louisiana-Pacific to move beyond an obsession with maximum output to a focus on protecting the environment. Yet, as important as strict regulation is, further progress in reducing pollution requires more corporate initiative. Strict enforcement will always be necessary, but a more flexible approach to the rules benefits companies that are not miscreants.

In this chapter we will explain the process of assessing and choosing which pollution risks are most important to regulate. We then discuss alternative approaches to regulation with emphasis on new, more flexible, initiatives. Finally, we show how companies are now managed differently so they can move beyond simple legal compliance.

[2] *United States* v. *Louisiana Pacific Corp.,* 908 F.Supp 835 (1995); 925 F.Supp. 1484 (1995); and 106 F.34d 345 (1997).
[3] Quoted in Nina Siegal, "If I Believed in Hell, This Could Be No Worse," *The Progressive,* December 1998, p. 30.
[4] Pamela J. Gordon, *Lean and Green: Profit for Your Workplace and the Environment* (San Francisco: Berrett-Koehler, 2001).

REGULATING ENVIRONMENTAL RISK

Environmental regulation is very expensive. The cost to the nation of complying with environmental regulations is greater than the cost of complying with all other forms of social and economic regulation combined.[5] In 2000 total environmental compliance costs were estimated at $148 billion.[6] This is a large sum, greater than the GDP of Indonesia but also less than 2 percent of U.S. GDP. Is the money well spent? It seems to be. Recent estimates of yearly monetized benefits accruing to the nation have ranged from $162 billion to $3.3 trillion.[7]

If the nation's environmental expenditures are to have maximum benefit, they must be focused on the highest risks to human health and the natural environment. *Risk* is a probability existing somewhere between zero and absolute certainty that a harm will occur. The probability of any pollution risk can be studied scientifically; then regulators, politicians, and the public must decide what, if anything, should be done to mitigate it.

Congress, in recent years, has added about 30 provisions in environmental laws requiring that regulatory decisions be based on risk assessments. The goal of these provisions is to focus limited dollars on the greatest hazards. The EPA does many risk assessments, and they have great significance for business. If they show that a pollutant or activity poses relatively high risks, laws can require enormous expenditures to reduce it.

ANALYZING HUMAN HEALTH RISKS

The basic model for analyzing human health risks is shown in Figure 15.2. It separates risk analysis into two parts represented by two ovals. In the left oval are the elements of *risk assessment,* the largely scientific process of discovering and weighing the dangers posed by a contaminant or activity. In the right oval are the elements of *risk management,* the process of deciding what action to take (or not take) regarding specific risks. We will explain the nature and interaction of these elements.

Risk Assessment

There are four basic steps in the risk assessment oval. These steps have become standard at the EPA and other agencies that sometimes evaluate the dangers of pollutants. In fact, they are now the standard worldwide.

[5] Based on the Congressional Budget Office's 1997 estimate that environmental compliance costs were 52 percent of overall compliance costs and its 1998 estimate of between 70 to 74 percent. See General Accounting Office, *Regulatory Accounting: Analysis of OMB's Reports on the Costs and Benefits of Federal Regulation,* GAO/GGD–99–59, April 20, 1999, pp. 32–33.
[6] See General Accounting Office, *Environmental Protection Agency: Status of Achieving Key Outcomes,* GAO–01–774, June 2001, p. 5.
[7] General Accounting Office, *Regulatory Accounting,* pp. 32–33.

FIGURE 15.2
Elements of Risk Assessment and Risk Management and Their Sequence

Source: Environmental Protection Agency, Office of Research and Development

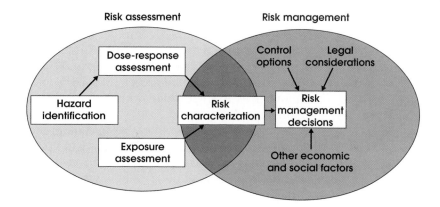

In theory, risk assessment is a scientific process leading to an objective, quantitative measure of the risks posed by any substance. As we will see, however, science is not fully up to the job. So the EPA and other agencies make a series of precautionary assumptions based on the fear that scientific data, which are often flimsy or ambiguous, might understate risks to human health. As the precautionary assumptions are piled one on top of another, the process grows less rigorous and, in the view of some critics, begins to overstate risks. When risks are overstated, of course, regulation of business becomes more expensive and the nation's environmental regulation dollars are not well spent. Nevertheless, risks are often overstated to ensure that public health is protected with a margin of safety.

Hazard Identification

Hazard identification establishes a link between a substance, such as a chemical, and human disease. When a substance is thought to pose a risk, there are two basic methods of proving it dangerous.

The first is *animal tests,* in which animals such as mice and rats are exposed to high levels of the substance through diet, inhalation, or other means for an appreciable part of their life span. In a cancer study, as many as 1,000 animals may be divided into three groups with different exposure levels. One group is exposed to the maximum dose that the animals can tolerate without dying. The second group receives half this dose. The third group is a control group receiving no exposure. At the end of the test, the animals are dissected and tumors and other abnormalities in organs are counted. If the exposed animals have many tumors, the assumption is that the chemical is an animal carcinogen, and regulators tend then to make the precautionary assumption that it is a human carcinogen as well.

Several problems cast doubt on the validity of animal tests. First, scientists rely heavily on strains of rats and mice genetically disposed to high rates of tumor production.[8] This predisposition raises doubts about whether a substance is a complete carcinogen or simply a tumor promoter in an otherwise susceptible species. EPA guidelines call for adding benign and malignant tumors and basing the assumption of carcinogenicity on the total rather than only on the number of malignant tumors. This is an additional precautionary assumption that may exaggerate risk.

Second, in animals exposed to large amounts of a chemical, tumors can arise from tissue irritation rather than normal carcinogenesis. For example, rats forced to breathe extreme concentrations of formaldehyde exhibit nasal inflammation. Tumors appear in their noses, but some or all of them result from abnormally rapid cell division that magnifies chromosomal abnormalities, not from the carcinogenic properties of formaldehyde. It is scientifically uncertain if a substance that promotes cancer in high doses also promotes it in low doses. Humans, of course, have lower environmental exposures to chemicals than the prodigious doses given to test animals.

And third, animal physiology can be so different from that of humans that disease processes are unique. For example, gasoline vapor causes kidney tumors in male rats, but the biological mechanism causing these tumors is unique to rats; humans lack one protein involved. Even animals differ in their susceptibility to disease. Inhalation of cadmium dust, to which workers in battery factories are exposed, causes high levels of cancer in rats but no cancer in mice. Which result is appropriate for assessing risk to workers? Here EPA guidelines call for making the precautionary assumption that human risk calculations should be based on the reaction of the most sensitive species.

A second method of identifying hazards is the *epidemiological study,* a statistical survey of human mortality (death) and morbidity (sickness) in a sample population. Epidemiological studies can establish a link between industrial pollutants and health problems. To illustrate, recent studies show the following associations.

- Elevated risk of loss of color vision among workers exposed to styrene in factories producing fiberglass-reinforced plastics.[9]

- Elevated mortality from lymphatic cancers among workers at synthetic rubber plants.[10]

[8] Tracy Lyon, "Carcinogenesis in Transgenic Mouse Models," *Environmental Health Perspectives,* September 1997, pp. 912–13.

[9] Fabriziomaria Gobba et al., "Acquired Dyschromatopsia among Styrene-Exposed Workers," *Journal of Occupational Medicine,* July 1991.

[10] Elizabeth Ward et al., "Mortality Study of Workers in 1,3-Butadiene Production Units Identified from a Chemical Workers Cohort," *Environmental Health Perspectives,* June 1995, pp. 598–603.

- Lower birth weight in children born to mothers living near a landfill containing organic chemical wastes such as benzene, methyl chloride, and toluene.[11]

Epidemiological studies have the advantage of measuring real human illness, but they have low statistical power and are riddled with uncertainties. In particular, people are exposed to literally thousands of substances, and individual exposures vary. For example, the study of synthetic rubber plant workers, noted above, showed four lymphatic cancers among 364 workers, more in a group that size than the 0.69 predicted by mortality tables for the general population. All 364 workers had been exposed to the chemical 1,3-butadiene (bue-ta-DIE-een) by working for at least six months in butadiene production units at three Union Carbide synthetic rubber plants in West Virginia. The four lymphatic cancers are statistically significant but still a small number. Could exposure to multiple chemicals over the 39-year period covered by the study have caused these cancers?

There are difficulties with epidemiological studies beyond multiple, confounding exposures. Because lung tumors and other cancers have latency periods of up to 40 years, these studies may not detect harm done by recent exposures. Death certificates and diagnoses of disease are frequently inaccurate. Multiple diseases contribute to many deaths. In addition, data from one population may not predict risk for another population. For example, worker populations, on which many epidemiological studies are based, are healthier than the general population, which contains more sensitive older and younger people. In the study at the Union Carbide butadiene units, for example, only 185 of the 365 workers died over the 39 years, compared with 202 deaths that would have been expected in the general population. However, though their accuracy is subject to doubt, the results of epidemiological tests can be valuable. Arsenic, for instance, does not cause cancer in lab animals; only epidemiological tests show it to be a human carcinogen.

Dose-Response Assessment

A dose-response assessment is a quantitative estimate of how toxic a substance is to humans or animals at increasing levels of exposure. The potency of carcinogens, for example, varies widely. Formaldehyde is a strong carcinogen that causes tumors in 50 percent of exposed lab animals at a dose of 15 parts per million (ppm). Vinyl chloride, on the other hand, is a very weak carcinogen that is benign at less than 50 ppm and, even at the much higher dose of 600 ppm, causes tumors in less than 25 percent of animals.[12]

---

[11] Michael Berry and Frank Bove, "Birth Weight Reduction Associated with Residence Near a Hazardous Waste Landfill," *Environmental Health Perspectives,* August 1997, pp. 856–61.
[12] Louis A. Cox Jr. and Paolo F. Ricci, "Dealing with Uncertainty: From Health Risk Assessment to Environmental Decision Making," *Journal of Energy Engineering,* August 1992, p. 79.

Public exposures to toxic substances are usually well below the exposures of workers. And the exposures of both workers and the public are far lower than the extreme exposures of animals in high-dose tests. For most chemicals, in fact, regulators have to extrapolate from high doses to predict the effects on human populations at much lower doses. For many years, the EPA has used a model that assumes a linear dose-response rate—that is, that there will be a proportionate decrease in cancers from large exposures to small ones (if, for example, exposure decreases by 25 percent, then cancers will decrease by 25 percent).

Figure 15.3 illustrates the theory of extrapolation from high to low doses with respect to carcinogens. The shaded area covers an observed range of responses at relatively high doses. Epidemiological studies on workers and laboratory experiments with rodents typically produce such data in high-dose ranges. The linear extension from the observed range is a prediction made in the absence of experimental data, one that is conservative in protecting public health. It suggests that risks rise substantially over the range of exposure to a human population such as the public. Many carcinogens, on the other hand, are less dangerous at low doses, as represented by the *sublinear* curve extending from the observed range. And still other carcinogens have a *threshold,* that is, they do not produce tumors at very low exposure levels and pose no risk until some threshold exposure amount is exceeded. If the hypothetical substance in Figure 15.3 responded based on the threshold curve as illustrated, there would be little risk of harm to public health within the exposure range shown.

FIGURE 15.3
**Alternative
Assumptions for
Extrapolating the
Effects of High
Doses to Lower
Dose Levels**

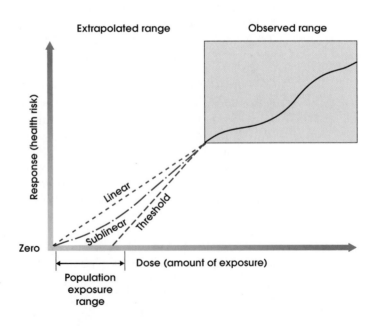

The EPA makes the precautionary assumption that, in the absence of rigorous low-dose data, risk estimates in high-to-low-dose extrapolation should be based on the linear curve. This leads to risk figures suggesting that more needs to be done to protect the public from exposures. This necessitates higher expenditures for controlling smaller releases of carcinogens. Threshold assumptions, on the other hand, would show less justification for high expenditures to control low levels of pollution. Environmentalists who favor more regulation approve of the linear model. However, industry, which dislikes the expensive regulations it spawns, favors the use of sublinear and threshold models that lead to less regulation. The EPA has recently suggested willingness to depart from the linear model when rigorous evidence supports the validity of an alternative assumption. Since many toxic chemicals are as yet incompletely studied, such evidence is frequently lacking. For example, data on human exposure are available on only 6 percent of 1,456 toxic chemicals of concern to the EPA.[13]

Exposure Assessment

Exposure assessment is the study of how much of a substance humans absorb through inhalation, ingestion, or skin absorption. The level of a substance in one of the three media—air, water, and land—does not indicate how much of that substance is taken in by humans. Further study is needed to verify intake and concentrations in the bodies of humans or animals. An example is a study of people putting gas in their tanks. Gasoline contains five toxic organic compounds that evaporate easily.[14] Pumping gas displaces air in fuel tanks, exposing people to them. To measure this exposure, researchers took blood samples of 60 motorists, both before and after they filled their tanks. They found that blood concentrations of all five compounds rose after gas pumping. Benzene, for instance, rose from 0.19 parts per billion (ppb) to 0.54 ppb and toluene (TOL-you-een) from 0.38 ppb to 0.74 ppb. The higher concentrations lasted no longer than 10 minutes. This study confirms that motorists have short-term exposure to carcinogens when they pump gas.

To make exposure assessments, researchers measure activities that bring individuals in contact with toxic substances, including such things as how much water people drink, their length of skin contact with water, amounts of soil eaten by children at play, inhalation rates, and consumption of various foods. Because movements and activities differ among

---

[13] General Accounting Office, *Environmental Information: EPA Needs Better Information to Manage Risks and Measure Results,* GAO–01–97T, October 3, 2000, p. 4.

[14] These are benzene, ethyl benzene, *m-/p*-xylene, *o*-oxylene, and toluene. Lorraine C. Backer et al., "Exposure to Regular Gasoline and Ethanol Oxyfuel during Refueling in Alaska," *Environmental Health Perspectives,* August 1997, p. 850.

people in studied populations, regulators present their estimates as a distribution of individual exposures. The estimates include both a central estimate (based on mean or median exposure) of the average person's exposure and an upper-end estimate for the most highly exposed persons.[15]

Risk Characterization

Risk characterization is an overall conclusion about the dangers of a substance. It is a detailed, written narrative describing the scientific evidence, including areas of ambiguity. A risk characterization for a carcinogen, for example, discusses the kinds of tumors promoted, human and animal data that suggest cancer causation for pertinent routes of exposure (oral, inhalation, skin absorption), and dose-response levels. Based on the discussion, the narrative ultimately characterizes the risks in quantitative terms. For example, the EPA estimates the lifetime risk of leukemia from inhalation of benzene in a range from 2.2 to 7.8 in one million for a person exposed to 1 $\mu g/m^3$ (one microgram per cubic meter). That is, in a population of one million people exposed to very low levels of airborne benzene over the 75 years that the EPA calculates as an average lifetime, there will be two to eight extra cases of leukemia.

Such quantitative risk estimates then help to decide what level of abatement should be required of industry. There is no agreement about how high a risk should be before regulators must act to reduce it. In 1980 the Supreme Court, in a case that required OSHA to establish significant health risks to workers before requiring expensive worker protective measures, addressed the subject of "significant" risk.

> Some risks are plainly acceptable and others are plainly unacceptable. If, for example, the odds are one in a billion that a person will die from cancer by taking a drink of chlorinated water, the risk clearly could not be considered significant. On the other hand, if the odds are one in a thousand that regular inhalation of gasoline vapors that are 2 percent benzene will be fatal, a reasonable person might well consider the risk significant and take the appropriate steps to decrease or eliminate it.[16]

At the EPA, a lifetime risk of contracting cancer from a chemical substance or radiation source greater than 1 in 10,000 is generally considered excessive and subject to regulation. The goal of regulation is to reduce such risks to 1 in a million or lower. However, risks that fall between 1 in 10,000 and 1 in a million are usually considered acceptable.[17] With ben-

[15] For the EPA, the highest exposed groups are those above the 90th percentile. General Accounting Office, *Chemical Risk Assessment: Selected Federal Agencies' Procedures, Assumptions, and Policies,* GAO–01–810, August 2001, p. 80.

[16] *Industrial Union Department, AFL-CIO* v. *American Petroleum Institute,* 488 U.S. 655 (1989).

[17] General Accounting Office, *Radiation Standards: Scientific Basis Inconclusive,* GAO/RCED–00–152, p. 9 and fn. 23.

zene, the EPA estimates that long-term exposures to air concentrations of 0.13 to 0.45 $\mu g/m^3$ pose a 1 in 1,000,000 risk, but when concentrations rise to 13 to 45 $\mu g/m^3$ exposed individuals face a 1 in 10,000 risk.[18] Therefore, if populations living near an oil refinery or a chemical plant were exposed to concentrations above 45 $\mu g/m^3$ the EPA would be inclined to force the facility to reduce air emissions.

Policy guidelines developed from quantitative risk estimates enrage some environmental activists. Asks one: "Would you let me shoot into a crowd of 100,000 people and kill one of them? No? Well, how come Dow chemical can do it? It's okay for the corporations to do it, but the little guy with a gun goes to jail."[19] However, the alternative to a policy of accepting pollution risks between 1 in 10,000 and 1 in 1,000,000 is to decide that virtually no level of risk is acceptable. Eliminating infinitesimal risks from chemicals in an industrial society is not possible. Efforts to reduce them much below the EPA's acceptable range are often prohibitively expensive. Law enforcement to protect citizens from killers costs far less.

Risk characterizations are built on a series of calculations about toxicity, potency, and exposure that, as we have noted, are made using scientific method. Yet because of the limits of science in this area, research findings are adulterated by a series of precautionary assumptions. So risk characterizations may not be accurate, and when they are not they tend to overestimate risks, requiring more expensive pollution controls. With benzene, for example, the EPA's risk estimates are based on linear extrapolation to low doses because there is no data on human exposures in the range of 1 to 45 $\mu g/m^3$. The resulting 1 in 10,000 to 1 in 1,000,000 risk estimates are, therefore, conservative, likely to overstate risk, and likely to impose higher than necessary control costs on business.

Risk Management

Risk management, the right oval in Figure 15.2, encompasses regulation of pollutants and health risks. Whereas risk assessment in the left oval is nominally hard science, risk management decisions are based on the social sciences—law, economics, politics, and ethics. We will discuss the elements of risk management.

Control Options

These are alternative methods for reducing most risks. For example, hazardous wastes can be stored in a landfill or broken down into harmless substances by high-temperature incineration. A spectrum of regulatory options also exists, ranging from strict enforcement to voluntary request. Later in the chapter these options are discussed at more length.

---

[18] IRIS Summary, II.C.1.2, January 19, 2000.
[19] Quoted in John A. Hird, *Superfund: The Political Economy of Environmental Risk* (Baltimore: Johns Hopkins University Press, 1994), p. 200.

Legal Considerations

Many environmental laws are specific about risk reduction required and methods of achieving it. The Clean Air Act directs the EPA to set standards for control of hazardous air pollutants based on levels that can be achieved by the best control devices on the market. The Food Quality Protection Act of 1996 directs the EPA to set standards for pesticide residues in fruits and vegetables at levels where "there is a reasonable certainty of no harm." Then, because Congress considered children especially vulnerable to pesticides, it required that the EPA further reduce the risk by a multiple of 10. The Endangered Species Act prohibits consideration of economic factors in the decision to list a species as endangered. In general, environmental laws so often dictate regulatory decisions that one observer calls them "Congressional handcuffs."[20] However, there is always some latitude for regulators when they set up the specific rules to carry out congressional requirements. For example, the EPA defined the best technology standard for hazardous air pollutant emissions as the level of control achieved by the best-controlled 12 percent of industry sites. This percentage does not appear in the statute, only in the rule developed by the EPA.

Other Economic and Social Factors

Risk decisions cannot always be based solely on scientific findings. Technical data, such as control device engineering, may open or limit options. Public opinion polls or interviews may define politically acceptable options. Cost–benefit studies can illuminate economic consequences of alternative regulatory approaches. We will now discuss cost–benefit analysis at greater length.

COST–BENEFIT ANALYSIS

Cost–benefit analysis is the systematic calculation and comparison of the costs and benefits of a proposed action. If benefits exceed costs, the action is desirable, other things being equal. Rigorous cost–benefit studies assign common values, such as dollar amounts, to all costs and benefits so that they can be compared using a common denominator.

Both Congress and the executive branch require environmental regulators to submit cost–benefit figures justifying any rule that imposes compliance costs of $100 million or more on the U.S. economy.[21] These studies are lengthy and expensive to prepare. Although they may lead to

[20] Kenneth W. Chilton, *Enhancing Environmental Protection While Fostering Economic Growth*, Policy Study No. 151 (St. Louis: Washington University, Center for the Study of American Business, March 1999), p. 22.
[21] Cost–benefit studies are required by President Clinton's Executive Order 12866 and by several statutes, for example, the Unfunded Mandates Reform Act of 1995.

more cost-effective decisions, the requirement that they be done complicates and slows regulation. Cost calculations may include capital costs to industry, inflation, plant closures, and lost jobs. Benefits can include increases in aesthetic appeal, rising property values, increased tourism, reduced medical expenses, and the value of lives saved. The accounting can be detailed. For example, the expected number of cancers avoided by abating pollution is calculated from risk data. They are then described by age distribution, disabilities likely to result, their length, medical costs, lost productivity, foregone wages, and amounts of compensable pain and suffering. The money value of a statistical life can be estimated in several ways, but it is usually calculated with a formula based on wage premiums demanded by workers in high-risk occupations.

Advantages of Cost–Benefit Analysis

Cost–benefit analysis has several advantages. First, it forces methodical consideration of each economic impact a policy will have on society. It disciplines thinking, though it does not always result in clear choices. Cost–benefit studies show which alternative is optimal in economic terms, but they do not show which alternative is best in terms of noneconomic criteria such as ethical duty or political consequences.

A second advantage is that it can inject rational calculation into emotional arguments. When the public is fired up over a new menace, politicians, responding to the alarm, can be hasty to legislate. Already some of the nation's biggest environmental programs, for example, Superfund and the Acid Rain Program in the Clean Air Act, set forth in the wake of extensive frights, are criticized for imposing costs on society greater than benefits.[22] Passionate decisions are not necessarily wrong, but dispassionate ones may be better.

And third, cost–benefit analysis that reveals marginal abatement costs can help regulators find the most efficient level of regulation. Figure 15.4 illustrates the typical relationship between environmental regulation and changes in costs and benefits. Initially, at or near zero, pollution controls are very cost-effective. Control equipment rapidly cuts emissions and reduces risks to public health, creating rising benefits. However, as higher levels of control are reached, it is increasingly expensive to remove each additional increment. More complex control equipment must be purchased. More energy will be consumed by its operation. New control technologies may have to be invented. Yet even as this money is spent, the risk to public health is reduced less and less because falling concentrations of toxics pose fewer dangers. Costs begin to rise more rapidly than benefits, ultimately

[22] In 1998, however, the EPA estimated benefits of NO_x emission reduction at $430 million to $2 billion a year as opposed to costs of $190 million. General Accounting Office, *Regulatory Accounting: Analysis of OMB's Reports on the Costs and Benefits of Federal Regulation,* GAO/GGD–99–59, April 1999, p. 70.

FIGURE 15.4
Relationship between Extent of Regulation, Costs, and Benefits in Environmental Regulation

Source: Adapted from Kenneth W. Chilton, *Enhancing Environmental Protection while Fostering Economic Growth,* Policy Study No. 151 (St. Louis: Washington University, Center for the Study of American Business, March 1999), p. 8.

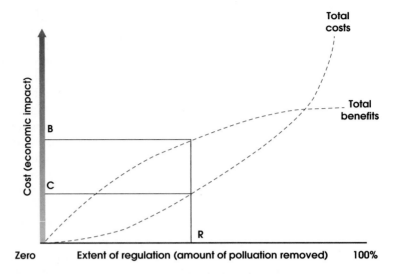

exceeding them and eventually rising exponentially as 100 percent cleanup, a quixotic goal, is neared. The ideal level of regulation is at point R, the point where benefits most exceed costs (B minus C). At this point, each dollar spent produces maximum benefit. In theory, dollars spent for regulation after point R could be better spent on reducing other, less-regulated environmental risks. In cases such as this, cost–benefit analysis can identify efficient regulatory goals to prevent skyrocketing expenditures for trivial benefits. It provides an artificial but a valuable test of efficient resource allocation for regulators not subject to a market mechanism.

Criticisms of Cost–Benefit Analysis

As attractive a method as cost–benefit analysis is, it has critics. Here are a few of their concerns.

First, fixing precise values of costs and benefits is difficult and controversial. Where benefits are measured in dollars, how can the value of a clear sky, fish in a stream, fragrant air, or extra years of life be priced? Their worth is subjective. Assigning dollar amounts to untraded goods such as beauty or human life invites discord. There are ways to do it, but they require disputable judgments.

One method of measuring the monetary worth of natural features is *contingent valuation,* a polling process in which people are asked to put a dollar amount on nature. The EPA recently issued a rule requiring that the gargantuan Navajo Generating Station, a coal-burning power plant in Arizona, cut sulfur dioxide emissions by 90 percent at an annual cost of $89.6 million. The plant is only 12 miles to the north of Grand Canyon National Park. The ecological benefit of the rule is a 7 percent improvement of winter visibility in the Grand Canyon, meaning that a person can see about 133 miles instead of only 124. Is this worth $89.6 million annually? Yes, said the EPA, based on a survey in which a sample of the public was asked how much money their households would be willing to pay each year for cleaner Grand Canyon air. This turned out to be from $1.30 to $2.50 per year per household. The EPA multiplied these figures by the number of American households, making the visibility improvement worth $90 million to $200 million.[23]

Methods of calculating the value of human life are controversial because they clash with public values of fairness and equity. If life value is based on wages earned over a lifetime, an objection is that the lives of workers in low-wage jobs are worth less than the lives of people in high-paying jobs. One critic notes that such calculations run "directly contrary to the egalitarian principle, with origins deep in the Judeo-Christian heritage, that all persons are equal before the law and God."[24] Because of such criticisms, EPA valuations of life are now based on earnings surveys that measure wage premiums paid in dangerous occupations. Some critics of life valuation reject all approaches, arguing that the very process of pricing human life mocks its extraordinary and sacred dignity.

Related criticisms come from environmentalists who dislike cost–benefit approaches because they invite trade-off of environmental quality. To them, pristine nature has an intrinsic value transcending money. In American history, the Bill of Rights and the Emancipation Proclamation were never subject to cost–benefit study; the moral rights they set forth were considered absolute.[25] Now we have a duty to respect nature as we respect humanity, apart from money considerations. Such objections reject the importance of efficiency in policy decisions. For many, maximum efficiency is not a test of the Good Society. Although cost–benefit analysis seems objective and neutral, it implies that ethical duties can be balanced against utilitarian benefits to society.

Another difficulty with cost–benefit analysis is that the benefits and costs of a program often fall to separate parties. Purifying factory wastewater raises costs to the business and to consumers of its product. Yet benefits from clean water accrue to shoreline property owners, realtors, individuals with lower medical bills, and fish. In such cases, weighing diverse cost–benefit effects raises questions of justice.

In sum, there is validity in criticisms of cost–benefit analysis, but it may nonetheless bring better regulation. It is a hard reality that dollars for pollution abatement are limited. Decisions about where to spend

---

[23] General Accounting Office, *Navajo Generating Station's Emissions Limit,* GAO/RCED–98–28, January 1998, pp. 1–3 and app. III.

[24] Thomas O. McGarity, "Health Benefits Analysis for Air Pollution Control: An Overview," in John Blodgett, ed., *Health Benefits of Air Pollution Control: A Discussion* (Washington, DC: Library of Congress, Congressional Research Service, February 27, 1989), p. 55.

[25] Steven Kelman, "Cost–Benefit Analysis: An Ethical Critique," *Regulation,* January–February 1981, p. 31.

them are required. No society can afford reduction of pollution to the no-risk level. Expenditures below this level suggest policies that compromise otherwise priceless values to maintain a healthy living standard.

REGULATORY OPTIONS FOR MANAGING ENVIRONMENTAL RISKS

Regulators and legislators have many options for reducing risks to health and the environment. Figure 15.5 illustrates the range of choices. Most regulatory activity takes place on the far left of the spectrum. However, there is growing use of options to the right based on evidence that some balance between control and freedom is often more effective.

FIGURE 15.5

A Spectrum of Regulatory Options

Command-and-Control Regulation

One cause of high pollution-abatement costs is heavy reliance on command-and-control regulation. Most federal statutes ask regulators to set uniform standards across industries, apply rigid rules to individual pollution sources, specify cleanup technology, set strict timetables for action, issue permits, and enforce compliance, all with limited or no consideration of costs. There are advantages to command-and-control regulation. It enforces predictable and uniform standards. There is great equity in applying the same rules to all firms in an industry. The record proves that it produces abatements and it comforts the public to know that the EPA is there like an old-fashioned schoolmarm, watching companies like a hawk, slapping wrists, and putting unregenerate polluters in the dunce's chair.

However, this approach can be inefficient and increase costs without commensurate increases in benefits. One example is a study done by the EPA and Amoco Corporation of how typical regulation worked at a single Amoco refinery. A key finding was that under the EPA's command-and-control regimen, cuts in air emissions cost an average $2,100 per ton, but if the refinery were given more flexibility, 90 percent of reductions would cost only $500 per ton.[26] This study was a major stimulus for the introduction of new methods for controlling pollution either by using market incentives or by making regulation more flexible.

[26] Caleb Solomon, "What Really Pollutes? Study of a Refinery Proves an Eye-Opener," *The Wall Street Journal*, March 29, 1993, p. A1.

Market Incentive Regulation

Market mechanisms give polluters financial motives to control pollution while also giving them flexibility in how reductions are to be achieved. They are all simply variations on tax and quota schemes. However, the market forces they unleash usually bring on abatement more efficiently and creatively than traditional command-and-control regulation. In the past decade, they have grown tremendously in popularity around the world, mainly in Europe, much less in the United States. There are many varieties of market incentives.

Taxes and fees can be imposed on polluting emissions or products. They are widely used in Europe. Italy, for example, puts a tax of 53 euros per ton per year on SO_2 emissions and 105 euros on NO_x emissions.[27] The United States has some similar taxes. Most states charge an annual fee of about $35 a ton, authorized in the Clean Air Act, for permits to emit criteria pollutants.[28] Product taxes are a variant. An Austrian tax on fertilizers and pesticides reduced their use by 30 percent within two years. All taxes and fees are unpopular with those who must pay, and politicians hesitate to enact them. The United States has the lowest revenue as a percent of GDP from so-called green taxes of any developed nation.[29]

Deposit-and-refund laws require consumers of products that degrade the environment to pay an extra, refundable charge at the time of purchase, giving them an incentive to recycle the products after use. Only 10 states have laws providing redemption values for beverage containers, and the number is not growing. A similar device, the *product take-back program,* is designed to shift responsibility for pollution or waste creation from the end user to the manufacturer. These programs are most widespread in Europe. Manufacturers are required to take back or recycle their products, for example, car batteries and heavy applicances such as refrigerators, at the end of their lives. Sometimes the manufacturer is charged a fee for future disposal costs.

Emission trading programs, sometimes called cap-and-trade programs, work by setting an overall limit on emissions of a pollutant. Then total emissions are divided among individual sources by giving each source permits allowing the amount of pollution currently emitted. After that, sources are allowed to release only amounts they can cover with permits

---

[27] Organization for Economic Cooperation and Development, *Economic Instruments for Pollution Control and Natural Resources Management in OECD Countries: A Survey* (Paris: OECD, October 1999), p. 16.

[28] Environmental Protection Agency, *The United States Experience with Economic Incentives for Protecting the Environment,* 240–R–01–001, January 2001, pp. 37–38.

[29] "Guess Who Taxes Pollution Least," *Business Week,* September 17, 2001, p. 36.

or suffer heavy fines. Each permit equals a unit of pollution, for example, one pound or one ton, and sources are allowed to trade them at a market price. Total emission reduction comes when, at scheduled intervals, the government retires permits from the market. Companies have a financial incentive to reduce emissions. By lowering emissions faster than required by permit reductions they can sell unused permits to other firms. And they must lower emissions as permits are retired or face the cost of buying additional ones at market rates.

Emission trading results in sources with low abatement costs taking out more of the pollution than sources with higher costs. It costs some companies less to abate pollution for many reasons, including the kind of fuel used, type of industrial process, age of equipment, and level of control already reached. Thus, the same net reduction is achieved at much lower cost than under a command-and-control system that ignores differences in marginal abatement costs from firm to firm.

The premier example of emission trading is the sulfur emissions trading program among coal-burning utilities in the United States. National emissions have been capped. On an auction market, or with each other, utilities now buy and sell one-ton permits to release SO_2. To reduce pollution, the EPA is retiring permits, in effect, lowering the nationwide cap and clearing the nation's skies. It is estimated that the program has reduced SO_2 emissions at a cost savings of $700 million annually over traditional enforcement methods.[30] Its success has led to much imitation by other governments around the world. A provision in the Kyoto Protocol calls for CO_2 permit trading between countries. If carried out, this would be the grandest trading scheme ever.

Companies also use permit trades to achieve efficiencies in pollution reduction. British Petroleum reduces emissions of the global warming gases carbon dioxide and methane using an internal trading market. In 2000 each of its 150 business units in about 100 countries was given a quota for the number of pounds of these gases it could release, with the total adding up to the entire emissions of the company. BP's target is reduction of companywide emissions by 2010 to 10 percent less than what they were in 1990. To hit this target, every year 4 percent of the permits are retired, resulting in a 4 percent annual decline in BP's releases of the gases.[31] Royal Dutch/Shell has a similar program. Despite reducing emissions, however, the companies are criticized by environmentalists for a certain irony in their efforts. As one activist observes: "These companies come off as good corporate 'citizens,' when they are really at the core of the problem because they produce the fuel that is burned worldwide and ends up heating the climate."[32]

[30] "Emissions Impossible?" *The Wall Street Journal,* July 23, 2001, p. A14.
[31] John Carey, "A Free-Market Cure for Global Warming," *Business Week,* May 15, 2000 pp. 60–61.

Despite growing interest, market incentives so far play only a minor role in most nations. Environmental groups sometimes oppose them, concluding that when rights to buy and sell waste are legislated, the moral duty to respect nature is replaced by a calculating money scheme. "Suppose there were a $100 fine for throwing a beer can into the Grand Canyon, and a wealthy hiker decided to pay $100 for the convenience," writes a critic. "Would there be nothing wrong in his treating the fine as if it were simply an expensive dumping charge?"[33]

Information disclosure about environmental performance is a form of regulation having the potential to harness market forces by affecting consumer perceptions and equity prices. An example is the Toxics Release Inventory (TRI) compiled by the EPA. Each year, the agency requires that industrial facilities releasing any of 650 pollutants into air, water, or land report the amount of those emissions. The information is then published, and citizens can search it to find out what substances they are exposed to by nearby businesses.[34] In 1999 reported toxic releases were 7.8 billion pounds. Since the TRI started in 1987 total releases have risen, but that is because new chemicals and new industries have been added over the years. However, TRI disclosures have spurred voluntary emissions reductions. William K. Reilly, former head of the EPA, tells the story of how Monsanto's chairman told him that after looking at the company's pollution data, he realized for the first time how high the volume really was. He set a goal of reducing emissions by 90 percent over the next four years.[35] Looking at manufacturing facilities, the only sources reported by the TRI since its inception, wastes have fallen 46 percent, an amount exceeding reductions required by laws.[36]

Flexible Regulation

Market incentive approaches are growing in importance, though they remain far less important than command and control. Yet there are still other means of introducing more flexibility in regulation.

Collaboration with industry is illustrated by Project XL (eXellence and Leadership), begun in 1996. In Project XL, the EPA collaborates with a few companies, relaxing some of the most strict rules to allow innovative, lower-cost methods of reducing emissions. Participating firms agree to reduce pollution beyond levels set by existing standards. At a Weyerhaeuser

---

[32] Joshua Karliner, executive director of the Transnational Resource and Action Center, in Danielle Knight, "Environment: Corporate Giants Begin Greenhouse Gas Trading," Inter Press Service, October 18, 2000.

[33] Michael J. Sandel, "It's Immoral to Buy the Right to Pollute," *The New York Times,* December 15, 1997, p. A19.

[34] The Toxics Release Inventory home page is on the EPA website at www.epa.gov/tri.

[35] William K. Reilly, "Private Enterprises and Public Obligations: Achieving Sustainable Development," *California Management Review,* Summer 1999, p. 22.

[36] Environmental Protection Agency, "EPA Issues New Toxics Report, Improves Means of Reporting," *Environmental News,* April 11, 2001, p. 1.

pulp mill in Georgia, for example, the EPA agreed to let managers choose the most cost-effective pollution control methods and lessened their paperwork burden by letting them report just once every two years. In return, Weyerhaeuser promised that over a 10-year period it would achieve a list of specific goals exceeding what it would have done under traditional regulation. It also promised to report progress to the public twice yearly via the Internet.[37]

Project XL is one of several collaborative programs started by the EPA. Its One Stop Reporting Program aims to reform onerous reporting requirements and has a goal of reducing paperwork by 25 percent. Its National Environmental Performance Track program enrolls companies with outstanding environmental records, then reduces their reporting requirements, lessens frequency of inspections, and allows them more flexible rule compliance. Many states are also experimenting with more cooperative enforcement measures.

The EPA has approximately 20 *voluntary programs.* For example, AgSTAR promotes manure-handling practices to lower methane emissions from dairy and swine farms, WasteWise focuses on reducing trash, Green Lights encourages energy-saving lighting, and the WAVE program aims to reduce water use in buildings. When a company signs up for a voluntary program, there are often reporting requirements. The WAVE program, for example, requires firms to identify methods for reduced water use. But no enforcement actions are taken for failure to meet goals. Companies have many motives for participating. They get technical advice from the EPA, the agency freely hands out awards that have public relations value, and there can be cost savings.

MANAGING ENVIRONMENTAL QUALITY

In the 1970s corporations passed over a great divide, leaving an era of freedom in which they were subject to few environmental constraints and entering an era of strict rules and limits. At first, managers saw the new rules as cost burdens. A few resented regulators, hid problems, and resisted the laws. Most found regulation to be expensive, adversarial, and sometimes irrational, but they complied. Although resistance and grudging compliance remain, many companies have moved away from this, adopting management systems that protect the environment, often beyond regulatory requirements. This new thinking is not altruistic. As in the past, corporate alignment with social values is mainly a response to market pressures that arise. Some of the most important market and nonmarket pressures are summarized in Table 15.1.

---

[37] Kelly H. Ferguson, "EPA Regulatory Reinvention Program Offers Flexibility for Weyco Flint River," *Pulp & Paper,* August 1998, p. 65.

TABLE 15.1 Inducements to Higher Environmental Performance

Consumer demands	Consumers increasingly favor less-polluting, resource-conserving products. A recent survey found that more than 60 percent of Americans "avoided or considered avoiding a product or brand for environmental reasons."*
Insurance premiums	Insurers lower premiums for companies when they face less risk of liability for pollution damage.
Disclosure requirements	Government agencies require considerable public disclosure of environmental information. Toxics Release Inventory data is one example. Another is disclosure to investors of potential environmental liabilities in Form 10Ks required by the Securities and Exchange Commission.
Access to international markets	Nations vary in environmental requirements. European standards for recycling and packaging, for example, are often more strict than those in the United States.
Activist pressures	Environmental groups are vigilant and aggressive. They collect and distribute information about corporate environmental performance. Some groups have developed performance standards and successfully pressured companies to adopt them. For example, more than 170 banana farms in Latin America, including all those of Chiquita Brands International, are certified as environmentally sound under the Better Banana Project system developed by the Rainforest Alliance.† There are many partnerships between companies and activists.
Regulatory relief	Companies in the EPA's flexible regulation projects that reduce compliance costs and pressures must have excellent compliance records and promise to exceed legal requirements in the future.
Legal liabilities	The law now has a tight grip on polluters. The EPA fines companies for violating laws. Managers have been imprisoned for criminal violations.
U.S. Sentencing Commission Guidelines	When criminal offenses occur, sentencing guidelines reduce penalties for companies and their managers if management controls to ensure compliance with environmental laws were in place.
Profit and cost reduction potential	Many companies find ways to convert former wastes into salable products or raw material for production processes. Changing production processes to reduce emissions often lowers costs. And studies suggest that firms with better environmental performance tend to be more profitable.‡
Industry standards	Many industries, sometimes in cooperation with environmental groups, have created environmental management codes and systems. Responsible Care imposes rules on chemical companies if they wish to join the industry trade association. Twenty-one companies in the Semiconductor Industry Association work in a program to reduce emissions of compounds that cause global warming. Most industry codes require auditing to certify companies as in compliance.
Cross-industry standards	A set of standards named ISO 14000, developed by the International Standards Organization, sets up universal standards for managing environmental aspects of manufacturing. To be certified under these standards, companies must go through a rigorous inspection and auditing process. The Global Reporting Initiative requires reporting of a "triple bottom line" that includes information about environmental impacts. Increasingly, companies and governments around the world are requiring that suppliers be certified under some of these green codes.

*"How Green Is Your Market?" *The Economist,* January 8, 2000, p. 66.
†Jim Carlton, "Chiquita to Take Part in Environmental Program," *The Wall Street Journal,* November 16, 2000, p. A3.
‡For example, Glen Dowell, Stuart Hart, and Bernard Yeung, "Do Corporate Global Environmental Standards Create or Destroy Market Value?" *Management Science,* August 2000.

Core Elements of an Environmental Management System

- An environmental policy.

- Planning and strategy that include environmental factors.

- Environmental impact assessments.

- Pollution reduction and elimination.

- Energy conservation and recycling.

- Formal collaboration with stakeholders.

- Development of performance measures.

- Environmental audits.

- Employee awards, incentives, and training.

- A philosophy of continuous improvement.

Environmental Management Systems

The most proactive companies establish an *environmental management system (EMS)*, which is a group of methods and tools for aligning corporate strategies, policies, and operations with principles that protect ecosystems. A set of standards for environmental management developed by the International Standards Organization, called *ISO 14001* (one of a broader family of standards known as ISO 14000), is considered the model for a basic EMS. Although some companies, for instance, ExxonMobil, design their own EMSs, typically firms base them on ISO 14001 and apply for certification by trained outside auditors. This is done because there is a trend for corporations to require that suppliers and vendors have a working EMS, and ISO 14001 certification verifies this. Matsushita Electrical Industrial, for instance, has a "green sourcing" policy in which it considers a supplier's environmental record along with cost, quality, and delivery and gives priority to companies certified under ISO 14001.[38] Matsushita is a high-volume exporter, and its key motive is access to European markets, where environmental standards for products are far more stringent than in Japan. To meet rising public and industry expectations, the EMS has moved from a few vanguard corporations into the mainstream. However, there is much further to go. A recent survey found that only 28 percent of 214 manufacturing plants surveyed had one.[39]

[38] Abe Hideaki, "Environmental Standard Bearers," *Look Japan,* September 1999, p. 5.
[39] Richard Florida and Derek Davison, "Gaining from Green Management: Environmental Management Systems Inside and Outside the Factory," *California Management Review,* Spring 2001, p. 66.

CAPITALISM EVOLVING

The spread of environmental management suggests that the business community is rethinking old assumptions about its relationship to nature. We cannot predict how far this rethinking will go, but a recent book, *Natural Capitalism,* offers a vision of sustainable activity that stands in contrast to the exploitation of nature in traditional industrial capitalism.[40] Its authors argue that four major shifts are required to create a new paradigm of "natural capitalism."

First, companies must become much more productive with resources and be far more conserving of energy and material.

Second, there must be a shift to biologically inspired production models in which the waste is not released as pollution but becomes an input for another process. This mimics nature where, for example, waste of one species is food for another. In fact, industrial facilities can be connected in a web of materials exchange. At Kalundborg, an industrial park in Denmark, some facilities feed off each other this way. One plant makes plasterboard using surplus gas from a refinery and gypsum from a coal-burning power plant. The power plant also sends excess steam to a pharmaceutical plant and warm water to a fish farm.

Third, strategy must move to new business models emphasizing services rather than the sale of goods. The authors illustrate this with the story of a carpet company that redefined its business from making and selling new carpet to the service of providing floor covering. After once installing carpets, it later replaces only worn areas and recycles old carpeting into new. This service and recycling approach reduces the extraction of virgin resources from nature.

Fourth, business must reinvest in natural capital by finding ways to create value from maintenance and restoration of ecosystems.

Capitalism, as practiced now, conforms little to this nature-friendly vision. Nevertheless, companies are taking a broad range of actions to reduce adverse environmental impacts. What follows are some illustrations, often from the vanguard, of these actions.

- *Precautionary action.* An idea called *the precautionary principle,* which has taken root among environmentalists, holds that when industrial activity poses a risk to human health or ecosystems, even if that threat is as yet poorly understood, prudence calls for restraint. Recently, advances in methods for detecting chemicals in living tissue led scientists to discover tiny amounts of the substance perfluorooctane sulfonate (PFO), as little as 0.5 parts per million, in human blood and animal tissue around the world. The source is 3M Co., which began using the

[40] Amory B. Lovins, L. Hunter Lovins, and Paul Hawken, *Natural Capitalism: Creating the Next Industrial Revolution* (Boston: Little Brown, 1999).

chemical in Scotchgard fabric protector in the late 1950s. Learning this, 3M scientists expressed surprise and disbelief. They examined health data on workers at Scotchgard plants exposed to PFO over many years and found no adverse effects. However, 3M decided to take the product off the market in 2000 to avert any possible harm to life. Since it had no substitute for PFO, it lost a $500 million-a-year business.[41] Of course, the company anticipated government action and it was petrified by the lawsuit potential. These pressures enforced the precautionary principle, illustrating once again that environmental responsibility by business is not usually altruism. It is more often an adaptation to compelling forces.

- *Pollution prevention.* End-of-the-pipe control technologies isolate or neutralize pollutants after they are generated. Pollution prevention is the modification of industrial processes to eliminate contaminants before they are created. For example, many companies have stopped using solvents to clean production equipment, substituting soap or isopropyl alcohol in their place. This eliminates evaporation of hazardous compounds in solvents and often works just as well and at lower cost. Simple forms of pollution prevention, such as putting a lid on a tank to stop evaporation or tightening valves to stop leaks, are used by many companies. After such easy steps, however, pollution prevention requires complex redesigns of processes and products. These projects are expensive and raise technical barriers. At many firms, pollution prevention projects will not be approved, even if they reduce harmful emissions or reduce costs, unless they will bring a return on capital invested equal to or greater than alternative investments. A government study found that only one-quarter to one-half of the firms reporting for the Toxics Release Inventory undertook one or more pollution prevention measures in an eight-year period.[42]

- *Product analysis.* Products can be examined from an environmental standpoint. Eastman Kodak uses life-cycle assessment to gauge the environmental impact of a product from manufacturing through lifetime use to disposal. The company looks at factors such as raw materials used, energy consumed, emissions, and potential for recycling. Hewlett-Packard has a network of more than 70 "product stewards," each in charge of the environmental impact of a specific product line.[43]

---

[41] Joseph Weber, "3M's Big Cleanup," *Business Week,* June 5, 2000, pp. 96–97.
[42] General Accounting Office, *Environmental Protection: EPA Should Strengthen Its Efforts to Measure and Encourage Pollution Prevention,* GAO–01–283, February 2001, p. 3.
[43] Lynelle Preston, "Sustainability at Hewlett-Packard: From Theory to Practice," *California Management Review,* Spring 2001, p. 27.

- *Environmental metrics.* Companies are innovating to find better ways of measuring environmental costs and performance. In the past, costs such as record keeping for hazardous substances or excess energy consumption have been hidden in overhead accounts. External costs that companies impose on society by damaging the environment have gone unmeasured and are not incorporated into management accounting. Some companies are experimenting with accounting methods that reveal such formerly obscured costs and are developing innovative ways to measure environmental performance. DuPont has adopted a policy of "sustainable growth." Its goal is to increase net income from those products and services that add value by using knowledge and to reduce income from more material-intensive business lines. Therefore, it adopted a new measure called *shareholder value added per pound of production,* or SVA/lb.[44] This measure falls when more natural resources such as petroleum or coal have to be used in production, because the pounds add up. It rises when more economic value is created with applied technology—that is, knowledge—because the technology milks more product from a given unit of a material resource. Using SVA/lb, top management can measure and compare the performance of business units in meeting sustainable growth goals.

CONCLUDING OBSERVATIONS

Global economic growth carries with it many threats to the thin, fragile biosphere in which human life exists. As such threats are recognized, societies adopt regulations to control the danger. However, regulation that only commands is inadequate to the ultimate task, which is the creation of industrial activity that harmonizes with natural cycles. In this chapter we explained interim progress that is making regulation more flexible and focused on the greatest risks to human health. Then we enumerated forces in the business environment that create incentives in industry to operate more sustainably. These forces have led to the adoption of more eco-efficient management styles. The trend is clearly toward less-polluting, less-resource-intensive economic activity. The reality, however, is that while leading corporations are more environmentally proactive, sustainability is as yet a remote ideal.

[44] Chad Holliday, "Sustainable Growth, the DuPont Way," *Harvard Business Review,* September 2001, p. 134.

Johns Manville Corporation and the Asbestos Nightmare

Like a cinema character who falls from glory to misfortune but eventually recovers the Good Life, Johns Manville Corporation has a story to tell. Founded in 1901, it was the world's largest asbestos company and it prospered until the 1970s, when growing fear of disease wilted demand for the substance. Then, injured workers sued the company, throwing it into bankruptcy. While sheltered in bankruptcy during the 1980s, it set up a special trust arrangement to compensate asbestos victims. It also stopped making asbestos products. Emerging from bankruptcy, the company returned to profitability and was bought by Warren Buffett in 2001. As a member of Buffett's Berkshire Hathaway family of companies, and free of all responsibility for paying asbestos victims, it now prospers again.

This is a happy ending, but only because Johns Manville escaped the turbulence in its wake, a vortex that has since pulled other companies into bankruptcy and threatens to swallow more. A major cause of the difficulties is that the pioneering trust arrangement set up by Johns Manville, which other companies copied, does not work well.

ASBESTOS

Asbestos is a generic term for a family of fibrous minerals found mainly in underground rock formations. The asbestos most widely used in industrial society is chrysotile (KRIS-ah-till); among other kinds, only amosite (AM-ah-site) and crocidolite (crow-SID-alight) have seen commercial application and only in very small amounts.[1] To get asbestos, ore is mined and put through a manufacturing process. Rocks are crushed to free asbestos fibers, and a blowing process separates them from the debris. These fibers are then combined with other materials to make commercial products. For instance, fibers longer than 1 centimeter (about 4/10 inch) can be spun with cotton into yarn for fireproof clothing. Short fibers of 5 micrometers or less can be matted with wool to create felt insulation for boiler pipes. Asbestos easily blends with other materials and has been used in a wide range of products, including ceiling tile, roofing, cement, gaskets, and plastics. It has phenomenal strength, does not burn, and resists heat conduction. So it adds these useful qualities to any material with which it is joined. Over the years, asbestos has brought great benefits to society. Its fireproofing quality has saved uncounted lives. In brake linings, it has increased motor vehicle safety. Its use in paint, roofing, and insulation has added comfort to living.

Workers are exposed to asbestos when they breathe air containing fibers the size of tiny motes of dust. Even the largest chrysotile fibers have a diameter only one-twenty-fifth that of a human hair, so they are easily inhaled. Being sharp, the fibers tend to stick in the lungs. Heavy exposures lead to asbestosis, a chronic, progressive condition marked by shortness of breath and coughing due to irreversible scarring of lung tissue. The fibers also initiate cellular changes leading to lung cancer and to mesothelioma, a rare and fatal cancer of abdominal membranes. Because of long latency periods, 10 to 40 years can pass before the onset of illness. However, X rays will reveal lung abnormalities long before symptoms appear.

Chrysotile is less dangerous than other kinds of asbestos. Within weeks to months after inhalation, the lungs expel most chrysotile fibers. Amosite and crocidolite fibers, on the other hand, remain embedded for many years. Chrysotile fibers, because of their curled shape, do not penetrate as deeply into lung tissue and, because of their chemical composition, break up more easily. Nevertheless, prolonged exposure to chrysotile dust is extremely dangerous. An epidemiological study of 17,800 insulation workers revealed that it is a potent carcinogen. In a 10-year period, these workers had 486 lung cancers,

---

[1] All types of asbestos are inorganic chemical compounds; chrysotile, for example, is composed of magnesium, silicon, oxygen, and hydrogen ($3MgO \cdot 2SiO_2 \cdot 2H_2O$).

An old photograph showing spray application of LIMPET asbestos, a product of the Keasbey and Mattison Company. The two unprotected workmen at right are feeding lumps of asbestos into mixing machines.
Source: David E. Lilienfield, "The Silence: The Asbestos Industry and Early Occupational Cancer Research—A Case Study." *American Journal of Public Health* 81, no. 6 (June 1991), p. 796. © American Journal of Public Health.

460 percent more than the 105.6 cases predicted for the general population.[2]

Even low exposures to asbestos are dangerous. Illness has been found among family members of asbestos workers whose only exposure was the dust that came into the home on the breadwinner's clothes at the end of the day.[3] Years ago, in asbestos towns, where sons followed fathers into dusty plants, the ranks of families were decimated. Because of widespread use, the general population in developed countries is exposed to asbestos. Autopsy results show that most people have less than 50 asbestos fibers per gram of dry lung, however, heavy occupational exposures can create a burden of more than four million fibers per gram of dry lung.[4]

THE ASBESTOS GIANT

Johns Manville Corporation was created in the merger of two roofing and insulating companies in 1901. It grew over the years, and by the 1960s it had 33 plants and mines and turned out more than 500 asbestos-bearing products. And it was

[2] Irving J. Selikoff et al., "Mortality Experience of Insulation Workers in the United States and Canada, 1943–1976," *Annals of the New York Academy of Sciences* 330 (1976), pp. 91–116.
[3] Henry A. Anderson et al., "Asbestosis among Household Contacts of Asbestos Factory Workers," in Irving J. Selikoff and E. Cuyler Hammond, eds., *Health Hazards of Asbestos Exposure* (New York: New York Academy of Sciences, 1979), p. 387.
[4] Hiroyuki Yamada et al., "Talc and Amosite/Crocidolite Preferentially Deposited in the Lungs of Nonoccupational Female Lung Cancer Cases in Urban areas of Japan," *Environmental Health Perspectives,* May 1997, pp. 505–6; and Andrew Churg et al., Correspondence, *The New England Journal of Medicine,* October 1, 1998, p. 999.

extremely profitable. Management applied heavy pressure on business units to make quarterly and yearly performance numbers.

Johns Manville workers and managers knew that asbestos dust caused serious illness. As early as the 1940s, the company installed advanced dust collection and filtration machinery to protect workers. But in many plants where profit pressure existed, operation of this equipment was considered a cost unrelated to productivity, and so repair and maintenance were deferred.

Bill Sells, a Johns Manville manager in the 1960s, told of acquiring a new vocabulary after taking over the Waukegan, Illinois, plant. A worker who had serious asbestosis was said to be "dusted." When the company physician took X rays and discovered workers with pathological lung changes, these "red cases" had to be assigned to lower-exposure areas. Sells installed better ventilation systems and saw improvement in companywide practice, but it came too late. "During the 1970s and 1980s," he writes, "I had to say good-bye to every member of my Waukegan administrative staff. They had become my friends and now, one by one, they contracted mesothelioma and died."[5]

Sells blames the failure to protect workers on a corporate culture that reinforced an attitude of denial. Managers believed that asbestos was a terrific product and that the company was doing what it could to reduce exposure. In fact, Johns Manville had set an exposure limit of 6 f/cm^3 (fibers per cubic centimeter) in its plants, half the standard of 12 f/cm^3 recommended in the 1960s by an industry trade association and well below the probable 100 f/cm^3 or more exposures that occurred years before in uncontrolled plants. This was commendable, but the company went no further. It did not, for example, aggressively fund research to confirm the safety of any exposure level. Today the standard set as safe by the Occupational Safety and Health Administration is 0.2 f/cm^3, only 3 percent of Johns Manville's 1960s standard.[6]

[5] Bill Sells, "What Asbestos Taught Me about Managing Risk," *Harvard Business Review*, March–April 1994, p. 82.
[6] The permissible exposure limit is a time-weighted average of 0.2 fibers >5 $\mu m/cm^3$, eight hours per day, 40 hours per week.

BANKRUPTCY

Johns Manville's culture of denial got a rude shock in the 1970s when injured workers began to sue and received large awards from juries. Two important changes in the law were responsible. First, courts permitted workers to bring tort actions, or suits alleging wrongful acts, against asbestos makers. Previously, they had been restricted to low-paying state worker-compensation claims. Second, there were major changes in products liability law, or the body of common law that requires manufacturers such as Johns Manville to compensate persons who are injured by their products.

Before the 1960s, manufacturer liability was based on the idea of *negligent conduct*. For an injured person to win in court, a manufacturer had to be proven negligent, that is, shown to have acted without reasonable care in making a product. But by the time asbestos cases arose, products liability law had begun to incorporate a theory of *strict liability*, under which manufacturers could be found legally responsible for injuring consumers even if they had not been negligent.[7] The rise of strict liability made it much harder for Johns Manville to win cases. A landmark defeat for the company came in 1982, when a court accepted the argument that it was liable for asbestos injury even without the plaintiff proving that management knew asbestos was dangerous.[8] This decision turned the tide of litigation against Johns Manville, making bankruptcy inevitable.

In other cases, attorneys proved that the firm's executives engaged in a conspiracy to hide the dangers of asbestos. They learned that in the 1920s Raybestos-Manhattan, a brake-lining manufacturer, had requested that Metropolitan Life Insur-

[7] See American Law Institute, *Restatement of the Law of Torts, 2d*, vol. 2 (Washington, DC: American Law Institute Publishers, 1965), sec. 402A, pp. 347–48. Section 402A imposes liability for damages on anyone who sells a product in defective condition unreasonably dangerous to the consumer where the product reaches the consumer without substantial change and causes the consumer injury even though the seller has exercised all possible care in the manufacture and distribution of the product.
[8] *Beshada* v. *Johns-Manville Products Corp.*, 90 N.J. 191, 447 A.2d 539 (1982).

ance Co. undertake health surveys of its workers. Metropolitan reported in 1931 that there was a high incidence of asbestosis among Raybestos-Manhattan workers and issued a strong warning about asbestos. The report was discussed at a meeting between top executives of Johns Manville and Raybestos-Manhattan, and those present agreed to keep the information secret to avoid lawsuits. The minutes of the meeting were locked in a vault at Raybestos-Manhattan until the executive keeping them died; then they were given to the man's relatives, who kept them in storage for many years. After asbestos litigation appeared, a family member chose to give the secret meeting minutes to an attorney for asbestos victims. With the conspiracy revealed, Johns Manville could no longer convince juries that management had been unaware of asbestos dangers in the past. Juries that heard about the secret meeting set records awarding punitive damages to sick workers. Punitive damages are sums awarded in excess of due compensation for injury to punish a corporation for flagrant misbehavior.

Another breakthrough was the testimony of Dr. Kenneth W. Smith, a former company doctor at a Johns Manville plant in Canada. Smith stated that in 1949 he grew concerned about employees and sent a report to management stating that of 708 workers he had X-rayed, only 4 had normal, healthy lungs. To avoid upsetting the workers and lowering their productivity, he withheld his findings from them. Dr. Smith documented the fact that top company officers—including a future Johns Manville president—had seen his report but did not act on it.

The growth curve in the number of suits was rapid. The first came in 1968, and by 1973 there were only 13; but by 1980 there were 5,000 and by 1982 there were 16,500. Most of the plaintiffs were not Johns Manville employees. They had worked at shipyards, factories, and construction companies using the company's products. Ultimately, the beleaguered firm could no longer hold back the deluge. Another 36,000 claims were predicted for a total liability of at least $2 billion and probably much more. In fact, this would turn out to be a gross underestimate. However, at the time, even the lower estimate was unaffordable.

On August 26, 1982, Johns Manville filed a voluntary petition to reorganize under Chapter 11 of the Bankruptcy Reform Act of 1978. Chapter 11 allows companies that might become bankrupt to restructure their debts before insolvency occurs.

THE BANKRUPTCY PERIOD

The day after the bankruptcy, Johns Manville published a letter in leading newspapers trying to explain its action to creditors, investors, and the public.

> To avoid Chapter 11, we would have had to strangle the company slowly, by deferring maintenance and postponing capital expenditures. We would also have had to cannibalize our good business just to keep going. If recent trends had continued, we would have had to mortgage our plants and properties and new credit would be most difficult and expensive to obtain. This is no way to go forward.

However, controversy followed. An impressionable *Fortune* magazine writer called it "a particularly daring example of the new uses of bankruptcy,"[9] and a Harvard law professor admired it as "pretty creative."[10] A former asbestos worker accused the firm of "cold-hearted profit motives" and "murder."[11]

Johns Manville continued normal business operations but was protected from creditors. Payments to suppliers, banks, and victorious plaintiffs stopped. Lawsuits were frozen. The company's assets were sequestered until it negotiated with its creditors a reorganization agreement, or a plan to pay its debts, and had the plan approved by a bankruptcy court.

Six years passed as the company negotiated such a plan with attorneys for asbestos victims and other creditors. During this time, more than 2,000 claimants died while their lawsuits were

---

[9] Anna Cifelli, "Management in Bankruptcy," *Fortune,* October 31, 1983, p.18.

[10] Quote in Clemens P. Work, "Bankruptcy: An Escape Hatch for Ailing Firms," *U.S. News & World Report,* August 22, 1983, p. 66.

[11] Quoted in Ben Sherwood, Gary Geipel, "Asbestos Lawsuits Paralyzed, House Panel Told," *Los Angeles Times,* February 11, 1983.

stalled by the bickering. A letter from a physician underscored this tragic aspect of the Chapter 11 gambit.

> Death and disease are not held in abeyance for legal writs. The victims are barred from applying for the financial help needed to ease their difficulties. Men are dying of mesothelioma or lung cancer, unable to seek medical care to ease their last days, and others are not able to afford the medical surveillance that could save their lives. Still others, short of breath, with asbestos lung scarring and no longer able to make a living, can't keep their families together.
>
> It is hard to appreciate the terror of a woman whose husband has been sent home from a hospital with a tracheostomy tube in his throat, unable to afford a nurse, resuscitating him at each emergency, until the final episode. Or widows—of shipyard workers, steam-locomotive repairmen, construction workers, power and utility plant personnel, and other craftsmen—having used slowly accumulated retirement dollars for the illness brought on by asbestos.
>
> Some have written me that they come close to begging in the streets. Others get along by visiting the children in rotation. Often, when I write a widow for scientific information, the reply comes from a trailer park: the house sold. After a lifetime of hard work, to die and to have his widow live in penury is a bitter final reward for a worker.[12]

A TRUST IS BORN

In late 1988 Johns Manville emerged from Chapter 11. The court-approved reorganization plan required putting $2.5 billion into a trust fund that would be run independently of the company and from which payments to all present and future victims would be made. To fund the Manville Personal Injury Settlement Trust, as it was officially named, the company did a one-for-eight reverse split of common shares and turned over 80 percent

of them to the trust. If, for example, you had held 800 shares of Johns Manville before the split, you owned only 100 afterward. The other 700 went to the trust to pay asbestos victims. Thus, common shareholders—including many former asbestos-plant employees—were the biggest financial losers under the reorganization plan. Ironically, Johns Manville's victims became its new owners because the trust, owning most of the common shares, had effective control of the company.

There was more. Johns Manville also had to pay into the trust 20 percent of its adjusted net earnings (a measure of profit) beginning in 1992 and for as long as needed to pay all injury claims. In return, the plan gave current and former company executives permanent immunity from lawsuits and shielded the company from further asbestos suits. Sick workers who had waited six years to resolve their cases now could only apply to the trust for compensation. Under the trust's rules, Johns Manville's payout to asbestos victims was limited and far lower than it would have been had the pre–Chapter 11 lawsuits gone forward. This was the key to the company's survival. The trust would pay scheduled amounts; there would be no more crushing punitive damages awarded.

The company's CEO, W. Thomas Stephens, argued that the reorganization plan was fair and noted that most of the managers who had made mistakes in years past were now dead. "I get a little hot under the collar when people say that [Johns] Manville entered Chapter 11 to evade its legal responsibilities," he said. "Giving up $2.5 billion, 20 percent of your profits, and 80 percent of your stock is not exactly walking away from the right solution."[13]

THE REBIRTH OF JOHNS MANVILLE

During its six years in Chapter 11, Johns Manville ended all asbestos operations. On emerging from bankruptcy, it no longer sold any asbestos-bearing

---

[12] Dr. Irving Selikoff, letter written to the *New York Times* in 1985, reprinted in Paul Brodeur, *Outrageous Misconduct: The Asbestos Industry on Trial* (New York: Pantheon Books, 1985), pp. 302–3.

[13] Quoted in George Melloan, "A Company Held Captive by the Plaintiff Bar," *The Wall Street Journal,* October 4, 1988, p. A29.

products, but it had other problems. Its reputation had suffered. Eventually, it tried to escape the asbestos stigma with a short-lived name change to Shuller Corporation in 1996.[14] However, because the Johns Manville brand name was so well established, a new CEO reversed this decision a year later.

Another major problem was making its common shares attractive again to investors. Although Johns Manville showed annual profits throughout the bankruptcy years (except for three years when extraordinary charges related to reorganization occurred) and remained profitable, investors were frightened away by its future obligation to pay 20 percent of its profits to the trust. To make the stock more attractive, the company and the trust negotiated an agreement in 1994 in which the company gave the trust an additional 32.5 million shares and, in return, the annual profit payment to the trust was eliminated.

PROBLEMS WITH THE TRUST

The goal of the trust is to pay adequate and fair compensation to all asbestos victims, both present and future. When it was created in 1988, epidemiologists and statisticians predicted about 100,000 asbestos-injury claims would be settled for an average of $25,000 each. However, both claims and settlements soon swelled far beyond expectations. By 1990 the trust had settled 23,867 claims at an average $43,231 each, and an additional 157,000 claims existed. More were predicted. Based on these numbers, the trust could not pay existing claims, let alone future ones.[15]

When this shortfall became apparent, a federal judge ordered the trust to suspend payments until revised payout guidelines could be set up. It took 4 1/2 years of legal wrangling before operations resumed. The solution was to pay only 10 percent of the value of all current and future claims and to

reduce the fees of lawyers representing victims to 25 percent of their awards. So, for example, a former shipyard worker with mesothelioma, entitled to receive $200,000 for the illness under the original payout schedule, got only $20,000 and might owe a lawyer $5,000, netting only $15,000 in the end. The bankruptcy court judged this plan fair since all present and future claimants would be equally paid.[16] But victims felt anger and disappointment.

Part of the problem was that most of the trust's assets were its holdings of Johns Manville stock. Since the stock remained under a cloud due to uncertainty about the obligations of the company to the trust, share price did not appreciate. By the mid-1990s, the trust still held approximately 80 percent of Johns Manville shares. This gave it a controlling interest, and four trust representatives sat on the company's board. Relations between the two entities were rocky. In 1996 the trust forced out CEO Stephens over his reluctance to pay a dividend. Stephens had preferred to use available cash for capital investments, while the trust wanted the cash transferred to it through dividends so it would have more money to pay claims. Under a new CEO, the company began paying dividends, but conflicts continued. At one point, the CEO asked the four trustees on the board to resign, but they refused. Eventually, the trust decided that the best way to raise cash was to sell the company.[17] In early 2001 it sold all its shares to Berkshire Hathaway, which purchased Johns Manville for approximately $1.8 billion and began to operate it as a wholly owned subsidiary.[18] The company continues to be a leading manufacturer of insulation and building materials. In 2000 it had 10,000 employees and revenues of more than $2 billion. It no longer carries any legal obligation to help asbestos victims. That burden now falls entirely on the trust.

Unfortunately for the trust, the Johns Manville sale failed to remedy its long-term underfunding. The number of claims continued to rise beyond

---

[14] Over the years, the company has had the following name changes: H. W. Johns-Manville Company (1901), Johns-Manville Corporation (1926), Manville Corporation (1981), Schuller Corporation (1996), and Johns Manville Corporation (1997).
[15] *Ocsek* v. *Manville Corp. Asbestos Compensation Fund,* 956 F.2d 152 (7th Cir. 1992) at 154.

[16] *In re Johns-Manville Corporation,* 876 F. Supp. 473 (E. & S.D.N.Y. 1995).
[17] Daniel Gross, "Recovery Lessons from an Industrial Phoenix," *The New York Times,* April 29, 2001, p. C4.
[18] Berkshire Hathaway Inc., *Form 10K,* March 30, 2001, p. 9.

EXHIBIT 1

In 1994 the Manville Personal Injury Settlement Trust set up seven claim categories.

The first three categories enumerate clinical stages of progressive lung damage commonly known as asbestosis. The first stage is asymptomatic. To be eligible for payment, injured workers in each category must prove (1) exposure to a Johns Manville asbestos product. (2) exposure sufficiently heavy to cause symptoms, (3) a latency period of at least 10 years between exposure and diagnosis, and (4) a physician's diagnosis documented by medical tests and records.

Initially, the trust intended to make settlements for the full amount stipulated in each category. But current rules permit the trust to pay only 5 percent of the fixed dollar value in each category to all present and future claimants.

Category	Scheduled Disease	Scheduled Value
1	Bilateral pleural disease	$12,000
2	Nondisabling bilateral interstitial lung disease	$25,000
3	Disabling bilateral interstitial lung disease	$50,000
4	Other cancer (colorectal; laryngeal; esophageal; or pharyngeal)	$40,000
5	Lung cancer (one)	$60,000
6	Lung cancer (two)*	$90,000
7	Malignant mesothelioma	$200,000

*Category 6 claimants must establish that they are nonsmokers.

those anticipated, and in mid-2001 the trust cut the pro rata amount it pays on claims from 10 percent to only 5 percent (see Exhibit 1). It also imposed a temporary moratorium on filing new claims. By late 2001 the trust had paid $2.7 billion to more than 441,000 asbestos victims. It had almost $2 billion in assets, but this was clearly not enough to handle a rising number of claims.[19] There were 34,000 pending claims, and new ones were arriving at a rate of 7,700 per month.

THE ASBESTOS NIGHTMARE

Asbestos liabilities now batter other companies. Almost two decades after large punitive damage awards drove Johns Manville into bankruptcy, asbestos plaintiffs still prevail in court. In 2001 a Texas jury awarded $56 million to a man with mesothelioma suing Kelly-Moore Paint Co., which had made a joint compound containing asbestos. Another Texas jury awarded $130 million to five workers with lung diseases who were exposed to asbestos more than 30 years earlier. And a Mississippi jury awarded $130 million to six laborers who had been exposed to asbestos on jobs back in the 1950s and 1960s. Although their lungs were injured, they were not yet sick.[20]

Lawsuits and claims continue to rise because there are many victims of asbestos. Although asbestos production and use declined after the 1970s and high workplace exposures ended, long latency periods mean that many workers are still just now becoming ill. In addition, inadvisable and badly managed projects to remove old asbestos insulation from buildings created many new worker exposures in the 1980s and 1990s.

New claims are encouraged by entrepreneurial attorneys. Dozens of law firms specialize in asbestos claims and litigation. They advertise in the media and on the Internet to recruit clients. Some firms sponsor mobile X-ray vans that screen large

[19] "Manville Personal Injury Settlement Trust, Consolidated Statements of Net Claimants' Equity, Changes in Net Claimants' Equity, and Cash Flows as of September 30, 2001," at www.mantrust.org/FILINGS/Q3_01.

[20] Lisa Girion, "Firms Hit Hard as Asbestos Claims Rise," *Los Angeles Times,* December 12, 2001, p. A1.

numbers of people for signs of asbestos exposure. Before X rays are given, the person being screened must sign a form agreeing to let the law firm represent him or her. These mass screenings result in a rise of claims by people who are not sick and may never get sick. The individuals are entitled to compensation if they can verify lung damage, but their claims leave less money for people who are seriously ill.

Currently, there are about 575,000 asbestos claims, and the courts are overwhelmed. In consequence, judges resort to a wholesale approach for settling cases. In so-called inventory settlements, lawyers demand that companies pay aggregate sums in the millions of dollars to large groups of claimants.[21] If the companies refuse, the attorneys threaten to take the cases before juries one by one. Most companies are unwilling to risk large punitive damage awards from juries sympathetic to sick workers, so they cave in. However, in consequence they wind up paying large sums to people who are not sick and who they may not have harmed, since exposure to any company's asbestos product decades earlier is often impossible to verify.

Since 1982, when Johns Manville went under, 41 other companies have been pushed into bankruptcy. Some of them were liquidated, but 25 firms followed the Johns Manville example by going into Chapter 11 and shifting their liabilities to a trust. In 1994 the trust arrangement was formalized by Congress when it added a provision in the U.S. Federal Bankruptcy Code allowing bankruptcy courts to immunize companies from asbestos lawsuits if they agreed to give more than 51 percent of net worth to a "qualified settlement trust" for claimants. In fact, companies have typically put 50 to 90 percent of their assets into the trusts.[22]

Asbestos compensation is an intractable problem. No satisfactory device or arrangement for compensating victims has worked well. The tort system and the courts are overwhelmed. The Johns Manville trust model is characterized by underfunding leading to inadequate and falling compensation of victims. An innovative plan in which Owens Corning agreed with more than 120 law firms to limit payments failed when attorneys from firms outside the agreement continued to press lawsuits and demand high settlements. The U.S. Supreme Court has twice refused to let lawyers consolidate asbestos cases into large class actions, because it felt that future claimants were not adequately considered.[23] Instead, the justices called on Congress to take action. In 1999 Republicans in Congress, with the support of industry, introduced the Fairness in Asbestos Compensation Act.[24] The bill would have made asbestos claims affordable by setting strict medical criteria, limiting payments to victims, and capping punitive damage awards by juries. The proposal angered attorneys' groups, which prevailed on their traditional Democratic party allies to consign it to oblivion. As long as groups representing trial attorneys can block action, a legislated change to current compensation arrangements is unlikely.

There is no end in sight to the asbestos nightmare. Nearly all former asbestos manufacturers are now in bankruptcy, and as their number dwindles, attorneys have set their sights on new targets. "The asbestos companies are going bankrupt faster than you and I can eat the food," one of them told a reporter. "We need to find someone else to pay the victims."[25] Ford Motor Co. is being sued by workers exposed to asbestos brake linings in its vehicles over the years. Sears, Roebuck & Co. is being sued by a man who claims that building materials he bought from the company in the 1940s caused a form of cancer associated with asbestos exposure. Dow Jones & Co., the publisher of *The Wall Street Journal,* is being sued by a former employee who claims exposure to asbestos while installing insulation at a printing plant. Even Campbell Soup, IBM, and Procter & Gamble have been targeted. No company may be immune.

[21] Douglas McLeod, "Claims Trust to Get Tough with Asbestos Claimants," *Business Insurance,* December 24, 2001, p. 1.
[22] Queena Sook Kim, "Firms Hit by Asbestos Litigation Take Bankruptcy Route," *The Wall Street Journal,* December 21, 2000, p. B4.
[23] *See Amchem Prods.* v. *Windsor,* 117 S. Ct. 2503 (1997), and *Ortiz* v. *Fiberboard Corp.,* 119 S. Ct. 2295 (1999).
[24] H.R. 1283, S. 758.
[25] Mark Lanier, quoted in Richard B. Schmitt, "How Plaintiffs' Lawyers Have Turned Asbestos into a Court Perennial," *The Wall Street Journal,* March 5, 2001, p. A1.

QUESTIONS

1. Did Johns Manville make responsible use of bankruptcy law? What were the advantages and disadvantages of the Chapter 11 filing?

2. Was the reorganization plan fair to the company's stakeholders, including asbestos victims, shareholders, creditors, and employees? Was the trust fund the best alternative for compensating injured asbestos workers?

3. Was Johns Manville adequately punished for its actions? Should it have been permitted to reorganize and resume normal operations? Is it fair that the company has no current obligation to asbestos victims?

4. Is there a better solution for compensating asbestos victims than the current trust fund arrangement? Are current victims, who receive only 5 percent of planned settlement amounts, being fairly treated?

Part Seven

Business and the Consumer

Chapter **Sixteen**

Consumerism

Wal-Mart Stores, Inc.

Samuel Moore Walton opened a new variety merchandise store in Rogers, Arkansas, on July 2, 1962. A sign across the front said WAL-MART. On one side of the sign was "We Sell For Less." On the other was "Satisfaction Guaranteed." These two cornerstone philosophies still guide the company. Overall, there was and still is complete dedication to the consumer.

This new store began a revolution in retailing as great as that started by J. C. Penney, F. W. Woolworth, and Sears & Roebuck at the beginning of the twentieth century. Wal-Mart's sales were about $1 million the first year, compared with $2 million for another variety store in the town. But the underlying philosophies and managerial strategies developed by Sam Walton led to fabulous growth.

In his autobiography Sam Walton succinctly stated the core philosophy of his company:

> [T]he secret of successful retailing is to give our customers what they want . . . if you think about it from your point of view as a customer, you want everything: a wide assortment of good quality merchandise; the lowest possible prices; guaranteed satisfaction with what you buy; friendly, knowledgeable service, convenient hours; free parking; a pleasant shopping experience. You love it when you visit a store that somehow exceeds your expectations, and you hate it when a store inconveniences you, or gives you a hard time, or just pretends you're invisible.[1]

The company grew to become the largest retail store in the world. In 2001 sales were more than $44 billion and profits slightly short of $7 billion. The company had 1,250,000 employees in 1,736 domestic stores and 1,072 foreign outlets in Latin America, Europe, Canada, and Asia.

Walton was charismatic. He seemed bound for success. In high school he was president of his senior class and quarterbacked the football team to the state championship. At the University of Missouri he was again pres-

---

[1] Sam Walton with John Huey, *Sam Walton: Made in America* (New York: Doubleday, 1992), p. 173.

ident of the senior class. He began his career working for a J. C. Penney store but quit after a short time to run his own department store. He settled on a Ben Franklin store in the small town of Newport, Arkansas, because his new wife refused to live in a city with more than 10,000 people. Soon, he irritated competitors by making lengthy visits to their stores during which he closely scrutinized every detail of their businesses. After achieving success in his first store, he began to open others and eventually created the Wal-Mart chain.

His empire was built on the consistent application of basic strategies. At first, he located stores in small towns to avoid competing with bigger chains. He cut costs obsessively and reduced markups. And he motivated employees by sharing profits and treating them with dignity. He called employees "associates" and shared the company's financial data with them by posting reports in every store. He also paid attention to details. He visited his stores constantly, getting involved in how products were placed on the shelves and other seemingly trivial matters. To reduce theft, he required that cashiers put dollar bills in registers face up, so that George Washington's image would quietly lecture about honesty. The original motive for having greeters at the entrances of Wal-Marts was Walton's conviction that they would cut shoplifting by scrutinizing people who were leaving the store.[2]

For years before his death from leukemia in 1992, Sam Walton was hailed as a genius, a hero, the epitome of entrepreneurship, who brought good merchandise at low prices to locations neglected by large discounters. President George Bush awarded him the nation's highest civil tribute, the Medal of Freedom, for his deeds. However, he was not universally loved.

Many small-town merchants were forced out of business when Sam Walton brought his stores to town and undersold them. For example, when Wal-Mart set up a store near tiny Pawhuska, Oklahoma, in 1983, the town's downtown soon emptied. A J. C. Penney outlet withdrew. A Western Auto store shut down. By 1986 an entire block of stores closed. Boarded shops gave the Pawhuska town square a bombed-out look. The small shopkeepers lost friends, entered bankruptcy, and moved or found other work (one or two at Wal-Mart). Remaining businesses struggled. Peters Hardware had to drop Corning dishes and Oneida silverware because its prices were uncompetitive. Customers at a drugstore in nearby Hominy, Oklahoma, waved Wal-Mart's advertised drug prices at the pharmacist.[3]

Another poignant story is that of James McConkey, owner of a hardware store in Albany, Missouri, population 2,100. On Christmas eve 1985, he looked at his stock of brand-new bicycles and the appliances filling his

[2] Bob Ortega: *In Sam We Trust: The Untold Story of Sam Walton and How Wal-Mart Is Devouring America* (New York: Times Books, 1988).
[3] Karen Blumenthal, "Arrival of Discounter Tears the Civic Fabric of Small-Town Life," *The Wall Street Journal,* April 14, 1987, p. A1.

shelves. His store and downtown Albany were festooned in Christmas decorations. All was festive except one thing: there were no customers. They all were at a Wal-Mart store in Maryville, population 9,500, and 34 miles west of Albany.[4] This is a typical experience for merchants in small towns near Wal-Mart stores. The only way they can compete is to find a niche not served by Wal-Mart and exploit it. That, however, is very difficult for the typical small-town merchant.

Wal-Mart not only has changed the facade of many downtown commercial areas but in the process has ended a way of life in many small towns. Observers maintain that Wal-Mart cannot be blamed as the sole force diminishing small-town business. Other factors have been at work, and Wal-Mart's aggressive pricing has merely speeded the inevitable. Many people have tried to keep Wal-Mart outlets out, but generally unsuccessfully. Failing to stop the chain, they have sometimes prevailed on local city councils to pass ordinances limiting the square feet allowed. In Oklahoma, five druggists filed a $1 million predatory pricing lawsuit against Wal-Mart, and eventually a court ordered it to stop selling some products below cost and to pay $288,000 in damages to the merchants.[5]

The company has stumbled and learned some painful lessons in its foreign expansion. In Germany, for example, it did not understand the culture, the type of regulations to be followed, or the nature of the competition it faced. One German merchant said Wal-Mart executives came to Germany to tell them how to operate, and they did not even speak German.[6] For example, laws enacted in the 1930s to protect German storekeepers from Jewish competitors prohibit discounts of more than 3 percent. After Wal-Mart entered the country in 1997, it sold milk, sugar, butter, flour, rice, and cooking oil at below cost. The government's Cartel Office accused it of starting a price war to drive small shopkeepers out of business. Wal-Mart countered that its lowered prices benefited consumers.[7] However, this philosophy was alien to the thinking of the German agency, which levied large fines and forced the company to raise its prices. Similar conflicts have occurred in other countries. In Seoul, South Korea, the company was seen "as a fearsome foreign invader that is disrupting a retail landscape long dominated by a small group of powerful conglomerates and a huge network of mom-and-pop stores."[8]

---

[4] Hugh Sidey, "Stack It Deep, Sell It Cheap, Stack It High and Watch It Fly!" *Time,* April 20, 1992.

[5] Ellen Neuborne, "David Beats Goliath in Wal-Mart Pricing War," *USA Today,* October 13, 1993, p. 1B.

[6] Wendy Zellner, Katherine A. Schmidt, Moon Iklwan, and Heidi Dawley, "How Well Does Wal-Mart Travel?" *Business Week,* September 3, 2001.

[7] Carol J. Williams, "Germany Refuses to Bargain on Wal-Mart's Below-Cost Sales," *Los Angeles Times,* September 9, 2000, p. C1.

[8] Evelyn Iritani, "Wal-Mart Is Changing the Country's Retail Landscape," *Los Angeles Times,* September 12, 1998, p. D1.

Almost 50 years ago, Peter Drucker wrote in *The Practice of Management,* "There is only one valid definition of business purpose: *to create a customer. . . .* The customer is the foundation of a business and keeps it in existence."[9] Sam Walton was an expert at creating customers, and the growth of Wal-Mart reflected this. Yet his compulsive drive to serve customers has imposed costs on other businesses, their owners, and small-town and foreign societies. His story illustrates the commanding priority of markets in American life, the existence of a dark aspect to even the most overwhelming success in value creation for customers, and the near futility of opposition to the march of commercialism.

In this chapter we begin by defining and discussing the idea of consumerism. Then we describe the protective shield of statutes and regulations for customers. Finally, we examine issues of food safety, products liability, false and deceptive advertising, and consumer privacy.

CONSUMERISM

A *consumer* is a person who uses products and services. *Consumerism* is a word with two meanings. In common usage it refers to a movement to promote the rights and powers of consumers in relation to the sellers of products and services. It is also an exceptionally powerful ideology that guides social conduct. We will discuss both these themes.

Consumerism as a Protective Movement

The idea of a collective interest in protecting consumers is ancient, dating back to the earliest transactions between merchants and customers. Fraud, deception, and greed are universal in consumer markets. In the United States an organized social movement to protect consumers sprang to life when Populist farmers attacked railroads for unfair charges and bad service. In the early years of the twentieth century, the Progressive movement focused on a wide range of marketplace abuses and passed laws such as the Food and Drug Act of 1906 to protect consumers. Consumer protection expanded slowly until an era of progressive activism in the 1960s and 1970s prompted a new wave of legislation to protect consumers and expand their rights.

There were several triggers for this modern movement. Popular critics accused business of manipulating consumers. In *The Waste Makers,* for example, Vance Packard attacked corporations for everything from using annual model changes to make automobiles obsolete to designing potato peelers that blended in with the peelings and got thrown away, thereby

[9] Peter Drucker, *The Practice of Management* (New York: Harper, 1954), p. 37.

creating a need for another purchase.[10] Ralph Nader incited the public about automobile safety in his book *Unsafe at Any Speed* and emerged as the leader of a national movement.[11] President John F. Kennedy responded to rising, widespread consumer discontent in a special message to Congress in March 1962. In it he said that consumers had basic rights and that these rights had been widely denied. They were the right to make intelligent choices among products and services; to have access to accurate information; to register complaints and be heard; to be offered fair prices and acceptable quality; to have safe and healthful products; and to receive adequate service.

Congress responded to President Kennedy's speech. Over the next decade it passed more than a dozen major consumer protection statutes and set up four new federal agencies—the Federal Highway Administration (1966) to set highway safety standards, the Federal Railroad Administration (1966) to regulate rail safety, the National Highway Traffic Safety Administration (1970) to protect the public from unsafe automobiles, and the Consumer Product Safety Commission (1972) to guard against unsafe products. These legislative successes marked the peak of the modern consumer movement. By the mid–1970s the business community had mobilized to block the great dream of its activists, which was to consolidate enforcement of consumer laws, then scattered among many agencies, into one superagency named the Consumer Protection Agency. The inspiration for these activists was the advent of the Environmental Protection Agency in 1970. The EPA had been set up to centralize enforcement of environmental regulations dispersed among many agencies. Its coordinated effort quickly improved and strengthened environmental regulation.

Consumer activists longed for a comparable agency in their field. By 1976, however, conservatives and business lobbies had won a battle for public opinion, convincing Americans that their government was growing too powerful. They claimed that the rising tide of regulatory red tape was creating costs out of all proportion to benefits and crippling the ability of corporations to compete in international markets. In the changed political climate shaped by these views, the Consumer Protection Agency bill was decisively defeated in 1976 and has never been seriously advanced since. In the same year, however, Congress passed the Airline Deregulation Act of 1976. This legislation was designed to help consumers by abolishing the Civil Aeronautics Board, an agency that controlled airline routes and approved ticket prices. Congress believed that government regulation in the airline industry stifled industry competition and that loosening the grip of government control would lead to lower fares. This is exactly what has happened.

---

[10] Vance Packard, *The Waste Makers* (New York: David McKay, 1960).
[11] Ralph Nader, *Unsafe at Any Speed* (New York: Pocket Books, 1966).

FIGURE 16.1
Spending on Consumer Health and Safety by Federal Regulatory Agencies: 1960–2001
Figures are current (nomial) dollars.

Source: Center for the Study of American Business, *Budget of the United States Government*, various fiscal years.

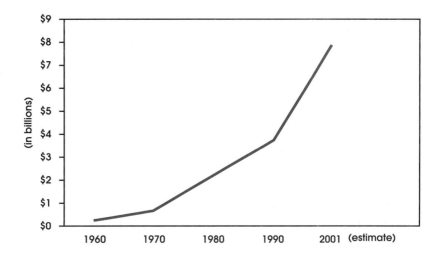

Since 1976 Congress has not been predisposed to pass many new laws and has not set up another new consumer agency. Nevertheless, there have been some new statutes and federal agencies have been minting a steady stream of new rules pursuant to existing authorities. The result is steady growth in consumer regulation. Figure 16.1 shows the expansion of spending by agencies that protect consumer health and safety. In fiscal year 1960, existing agencies spent $250 million dollars, but that rose steadily, and by 2001, 18 major consumer agencies spent an estimated $7.9 billion.[12] State and local governments have also significantly expanded their regulatory activity. Consumer protection is today a major function of government.

Consumerism as an Ideology

Gary Cross, a historian of American commercial culture, has defined consumerism as "the belief that goods give meaning to individuals and their roles in society."[13] According to Cross, consumerism, which has never been a formal philosophy, nonetheless emerged in the twentieth century as the dominant ideology in America and, increasingly, in the world. "Americans," says Cross, "define themselves and their relationships with others through the exchange and use of goods."[14]

---

[12] Melinda Warren, *2001 Regulatory Budget Report* (St. Louis: Center for the Study of American Business, June 2000), p. 8. Expenditures are in current (nominal) dollars.
[13] Gary Cross, *An All Consuming Society: Why Commercialism Won in Modern America.* (New York: Columbia University Press, 2000), p. 1.
[14] Ibid., p. 4.

The stage for an ascendency of commercial values began with a confluence of events at the turn of the twentieth century. The railroads were knitting territory together, creating national markets. The great merger wave of 1896–1904 created businesses with the reach to serve these expanded markets. Machines and assembly lines made mass production of consumer goods possible. Electricity and other new technologies led to a steady stream of new consumer products, for example, autos, watches, refrigerators, and radios. Simultaneously, in large numbers people were leaving cramped small-town societies and moving to cities with more fluid social currents. Waves of immigrants, people newly adrift from their cultural moorings, arrived in the country.

In such an open society characterized by loose social ties, high mobility, and cultural variation, people began to express role and status through the products they consumed. Immigrants, for example, joined American culture when they drank Coca-Cola. Their children declared their participation when they displayed clothing styles appropriate to the New World. Advertising facilitated this social communication through products. It created new national brands and endowed them with social significance, allowing people to declare their membership in groups, their status, and their values by the goods they displayed. The ads endowed products with meanings that were widely shared and understood, even by strangers, in a large and mobile population. Later, youth cultures grew up around automobiles. Families flaunted their social status and distanced themselves from the less successful by purchasing large homes in exclusive neighborhoods.

According to Cross, consumerism is a more powerful worldview than political ideologies, religions, or class and ethnic distinctions. We are unable to appreciate this fully because of its pervasiveness and the lack of an alternative. The alternative of simplified, utilitarian living in the mold of the Puritans, Benjamin Franklin, and Henry David Thoreau, is now an impractical vision. Ralph Nader and other leaders of the consumer movement have exhorted Americans to be practical in their expenditures, to be vigilant against advertising that tempts them into extravagance, and to prioritize function over excitement in their purchases. This appeal has had few converts.

Attempts to create sanctuaries from consumerism in our society have also been losing efforts. Blue laws prohibiting stores to open on Sundays, once pervasive, were an effort to rope off one day of the week and free it of commercialism. Such laws now have little importance. When radio was new, pioneers of broadcasting such as David Sarnoff of RCA were afraid to air commercials. For the first time, the voices and ideas of outsiders came right into the sheltered retreat of the family living room. Would commercials offend? Quickly, the answer came. They would not upset the vast majority. More recently, consumer advocates have tried to fence off childhood from the blandishments of materialism. Battles have been fought over ads on children's television programs, ads in schools, and ads for cigarettes and tobacco suspected of appealing to underage starters. Although there have been some victories with respect to specific products and policies, it is far too late to sequester children from advertising.

CONSUMERS' PROTECTIVE SHIELD

We return to an examination of the massive statutory shield that protects consumers from abuses, real and imagined, in the operation of the free competitive market. In addition to federal laws and regulations, there are other significant protections. A primary one is the legal system, which we will discuss later in the chapter. Every state and local government has extensive laws to protect consumers, ranging from uniform electrical connections to fraudulent billing. An important protection exists in the dissemination of information in the mass media and the growth of investigative reporting.

More than 50 federal agencies and bureaus are active in consumer affairs. The six most important ones are the Federal Trade Commission (FTC), the Consumer Product Safety Commission (CPSC), the National Highway Traffic Safety Administration (NHTSA), the Food and Drug Administration (FDA), the Food Safety and Inspection Service (FSIS) of the Department of Agriculture, and the Environmental Protection Agency (EPA). We shall discuss briefly activities of the first five in this chapter. The preceding two chapters dealt at length with the EPA. This list of agencies might well include the Securities and Exchange Commission (SEC), which protects investors; the Department of Energy, which is concerned with nuclear waste hazards; and the Federal Deposit Insurance Corporation (FDIC), which protects depositors of financial institutions.

To get a sense of the scope and complexity of these agencies, we have chosen three for a brief analysis, as follows.

The Consumer Product Safety Commission (CPSC)

This agency, created by Congress in 1972, is directed by six major statutes. These laws mandate it to

1. Protect the public against unreasonable risks of injury and death associated with consumer products.

2. Assist consumers to evaluate the comparative safety of products.

3. Develop uniform safety standards for consumer products and minimize conflicting state and local regulations.

4. Promote research and investigations into the causes and prevention of product-related deaths, illnesses, and injuries.

This is a formidable charge. The CPSC regulates every consumer product except guns, boats, planes, cars, trucks, foods, drugs, cosmetics, tobacco, and pesticides, which are in the province of other government agencies. Even with these exclusions, the agency's mandate is enormous, since it must oversee 15,000 classes of products, work with thousands of manufacturers, and address the complaints of millions of consumers.

Unfortunately, from the time of its creation in 1972, the CPSC has faced serious barriers in achieving its mandated goals. While it was the Nixon administration that gave it birth, the political environment was difficult. It became embroiled in political battles in both the Ford and Carter administrations. President Reagan wanted to abolish it but could not. Instead, he drastically cut its budget. Since then the budget of the agency has been increased. In 1998, for example, it was $46 billion and by 2001 it had risen to $55 billion.

By far, most of the activity of the agency concerns the development with industry of voluntary safety standards. For example, it has worked with manufacturers to set specific standards for bicycles, bunk beds, toys, lawn mowers, cigarette lighters, swimming pool covers, spas, and thousands of other products. It has also set limits on the amount of chemicals in products, such as methylene chloride in paint strippers, paint thinners, spray paints, and adhesive removers.

The CPSC has banned products that do not meet specified standards. Examples include hazardous toys, charcoal lighter fluid, bicycles, and lawn darts. It has initiated recalls of products including playground equipment, toys using lead paint, and children's furniture. Toys and children's products are a prime concern of the agency. Other product categories in which recalls were made include home electrical appliances, gas furnaces, fireworks, and smoke detectors. In addition, imported products are inspected and some have been detained. They include mostly toys, fireworks, bicycles, and children's sleepwear.

An agency with such a broad mandate, limited resources, and political embroilment has attracted many critics. Critics claim that the agency relies too much on voluntary agreements and industry self-policing. They argue that the recall program should be severely cut back or stopped because the agency expends too many resources on it, costs to manufacturers are substantial, and the program saves few lives. They say that it would be better if the agency spent its money on informing consumers about product safety rather than on regulating the products themselves. Of course, these are debatable propositions.

The National Highway Traffic Safety Administration (NHTSA)

This agency was created by Congress, in 1966, and has authority to

1. Mandate minimum safety standards for automobiles, trucks, and their accessories.

2. Establish fuel economy standards.

3. Administer state and community highway safety grant programs.

4. Conduct research, development, and demonstration of new vehicle safety techniques.

Regulations of this agency cover virtually every feature of the automobile. No other agency has such extensive controls over a single product. A short list of programs just to protect occupants of an automobile would include air bags, safety belts, energy-absorbing or collapsible steering columns, penetrating-resistance windshields, recessed door handles, breakaway rearview mirrors, padded dashboards, crushable front ends, passenger compartment designs to resist crushing, and tire standards.

The agency has power to mandate recall of defective products. A highly-publicized recall initiated by the agency was the joint announcement of Bridgestone/Firestone and Ford Motor Co., on August 9, 2000, to recall 14.4 million tires that contained safety-related defects. Most of the tires in question were original equipment on Ford vehicles, primarily the Ford Explorer. The decision was based on evidence that defects caused the tires treads to shred at high speeds and vehicles to roll over.

Automobile companies have complained about the costs of many of the agency's mandates, but there is no doubt that the regulations have saved thousands of lives. Some industry critics claim that its programs cost too much and that less expensive alternatives exist for saving lives, such as better lighting on highways, limiting highway speeds, installing breakaway traffic lights and signs, and padding abutments.

The Food and Drug Administration (FDA)

This agency evolved out of the authority established by Congress in the Food and Drug Act of 1906. The original legislation gives it power to regulate in interstate commerce misbranded and adulterated foods, drinks, and drugs. In the Food, Drug, and Cosmetic Act of 1938 the agency also received the power to make manufacturers prove that their drugs were safe before marketing them. Today, the agency operates under more than 30 enactments. Other important statutes enforced by the FDA include the Public Health Service Act of 1944, which gives it authority to ensure safety, purity, and potency of vaccines, blood, serum, and other biological products; the Nutrition Labeling and Education Act of 1990, which mandates the agency to develop uniform nutrition labeling on packaged food items; and the Generic Drug Enforcement Act of 1992, which permits it to oversee the generic drug industry.[15]

[15] Congressional Quarterly, *Federal Regulatory Directory,* 7th ed. (Washington, DC: Congressional Quarterly Inc., 1994), pp. 328–30.

The FDA is an active and powerful watchdog of the public health and it is continuously embroiled in heated controversies. For example, the agency has been constantly pressed to speed up its new drug authorizations. It has responded and has substantially reduced the time needed to approve. Congress expressed its interest in speeding the FDA's approval process and President Clinton signed legislation in 1997 to accelerate the review system for experimental medical devices and to give desperately ill patients the ability to get experimental drugs outside of clinical trials. The FDA has the difficult task of balancing vital needs with safety approval precautions. Former commissioner David Kessler lamented that people want new drugs in a hurry, but if anything goes wrong, they blame the FDA for moving too fast.

FOOD SAFETY ISSUES

Americans probably have the world's safest food supply. Food is relatively inexpensive, plentiful, and wholesome. But is the supply safe enough? The Centers for Disease Control and Prevention estimate there are 76 million foodborne illnesses annually in the United States, 325,000 hospitalizations, and 5,000 deaths.[16] The General Accounting Office (GAO) reports there are more than 200 known illnesses associated with bacteria, parasites, or viruses transmitted through food. They range from temporary maladies, such as diarrhea or vomiting, to acute and chronic illnesses, such as kidney failure, gastroenteritis, meningitis, and paralysis. Some, such as *Escherichia coli* (E. coli), can be fatal.[17]

Food safety is an increasingly complex problem. The globalization of food production has put an increasingly difficult burden on food protection agencies. Both the volume and wide dispersion of foods add to the difficulty in identifying tainted foods. Thomas Billy, former administrator of the Food Safety and Inspection Service, illustrated the extent to which products are quickly distributed. He used as an example one day's production in a commercial beef slaughter and fabrication facility: "Some 2.6 million pounds of finished product were dispersed to 87 distributors and 40 processors in 34 states and four countries. Eighty percent of the one-day's production was distributed within two days—the entire production within a week."[18]

There are many important issues in this area for consumers, but space permits discussion of only a few. We review briefly the overlapping jurisdictions of federal agencies responsible for the food supply, the food

---

[16] Reported in General Accounting Office, *Food Safety: Federal Oversight of Seafood Does Not Sufficiently Protect Consumers,* GAO-01-204, January 31, 2001.
[17] Ibid., p. 3.
[18] Thomas J. Billy, "A Subject That Affects Everybody," speech delivered to the U.S. Chamber of Commerce, Washington, DC, November 15, 1999.

safety inspection system, the Delaney clause, and the question of "how safe is safe?"

Overlapping Federal Agency Jurisdictions

The GAO has concluded that "The existing federal system to ensure a safe food supply is fragmented, characterized by a maze of often inconsistent legal and regulatory requirements carried out by 12 different federal agencies."[19] The GAO has found inconsistencies and illogical differences in inspection approaches to food safety, budgets, staffs, and authorizing laws.

Two agencies have primary responsibility for food safety—the Food Safety and Inspection Service (FSIS) of the Department of Agriculture and the FDA in the Department of Health and Human Services. The FSIS has jurisdiction over meat, poultry, and some egg products. The FDA regulates all other foods. These agencies work closely with the Customs Service, the Centers for Disease Control and Prevention, and other agencies that do research on foodborne diseases. The Environmental Protection Agency (EPA) is responsible for pesticides, fungicides, and rodenticides that may affect food safety.

In light of periodic outbreaks of diseases caused by food contamination, and a substantial increase in imported fruits and vegetables, more attention has been focused on the food inspection system. The FSIS and the FDA employ two different systems for imported foods. The FSIS has statutory authority to require exporters of meat and poultry to the United States to have food safety systems in their countries equivalent to the system in the United States. The FSIS also inspects some incoming shipments for safety. The FDA, on the other hand, relies principally on inspections of foods for safety by selecting and testing samples at ports of entry, warehouses, and businesses. In choosing samples for testing, the FDA relies heavily on the judgment of inspectors. In conducting these examinations, the inspectors have many tools, such as sampling guidance and historical data, to help them, but they rely heavily on their sense of sight, smell, and touch to assess the conditions of food shipments. To detect pathogenic contamination, however, the samples are sent to an FDA laboratory for testing. Traditionally, this testing has taken several weeks, so the agency developed what is known as "rapid tests" to identify within a day or two the potentially unsafe imported foods before they enter the U.S. food supply.

In recent years the volume of imported foods has increased significantly. Simultaneously, inspection coverage has declined—from 8 percent of shipments in 1992 to 1.7 percent in 1997. As a result, pressures have been put on the FDA to expand its rapid test system. However, important

---

[19] General Accounting Office, *Food Safety,* April 1998, p. 1.

expansion faces a number of limitations. For example, harmless bacteria in foods may mask the presence of pathogenic bacteria. The food tested may not be a reliable sample of a total shipment, because sampling is sometimes too limited. As a result, larger sampling of a shipment to assure food safety is necessary. This is not only costly but difficult to achieve in light of staffing limitations.

In 1997, to improve food inspection, the federal government introduced the Hazard Analysis and Critical Control Point (HACCP) system. This system, initiated for meats and poultry, was later expanded to include fruits, vegetable juices, and seafood. The system requires food processors to identify points during food processing where contamination can occur. Various methods are then defined by the companies and government inspectors to test for food contamination. With this system, government inspectors focus less on hands-on inspections and more on oversight of quality assurance methods.

In a 2001 report to Congress on the FDA's experience with the HACCP system for seafood imports, the GAO said the system yielded "insufficient assurance that the products are safe." Some reasons for this shortcoming were given by the GAO. For example, the FDA has been unable to increase the number of countries with a complete seafood equivalence agreement. Less than one-third of the importers showed compliance with HACCP requirements. The FDA has been unable to keep up with the growth of imported seafood. A survey in 1999 revealed that less than 1 percent of all seafood imported into the United States was tested.[20] The food inspection agencies have simply had inadequate funds to employ needed inspectors. In addition, said Caroline Smith De-Waal, director of food safety at the independent Center for Science in the Public Interest, "We are regulating the food supply today using horse-and-buggy technology."[21]

The National Academy of Sciences concluded in a study that the food safety system today provides an "acceptable" level of protection for consumers, but it could be improved. It recommended replacement of fragmented authorities with a national food law. It also suggested the appointment of a "food safety czar."[22] Senator Richard Durbin (D-Illinois) has sponsored legislation to do this since 1998. He has other supporters in Congress, but industry lobbying has blocked the bill's progress. President Bush endorsed the idea in his campaign for the presidency but it was not until the September 11 terrorist attacks on the World Trade

[20] General Accounting Office, *Food Safety,* January 2001.

[21] Edmund Sanders, "Push to Centralize Food Inspections Gets New Life," *Los Angeles Times,* November 24, 2001.

[22] Ricardo Alonzo-Zaldiver, "Panel Presses Congress on Need for 'Food-Safety Czar,' " *Los Angeles Times,* September 21, 1998.

Center and the Pentagon and the anthrax scares in early 2002 that the idea gained momentum.[23]

The Delaney Clause and Food Additives

The Delaney clause is one of the most stringent and controversial consumer protection laws. This clause, a 1958 amendment to the Food, Drug and Cosmetic Act (FDCA) of 1938, allows no flexibility in its prohibition against the addition to food of any substance known to produce cancer in any species, in any dosage, and under any circumstances. Applying this clause has raised difficult administrative problems, but strong efforts to alter it have been stopped in Congress and the courts. A fundamental problem is political. Defenders have only to accuse legislators supporting change of favoring more cancer. This is a terrifying charge for any politician.

The FDA has primary responsibility for food safety with respect to around 2,700 "direct" food additives and thousands more "indirect" additives that may get into foods through ingredients in packaging materials. The issue, therefore, is not a negligible one. For example, the Delaney clause is an open invitation for ingenious toxicologists to find cause for outlawing even the most innocuous substances. Experimenters have created tumors with hundreds of common food substances. Instruments are capable of detecting traces of substances at the level of one part in a trillion. The result is that almost everything anyone eats can be known to contain traces of carcinogens.

The FDA has sought to avoid banning substances that exist in minuscule quantities in foods and cause no harm. These efforts, however, have been rebuffed by court decisions that point to the zero tolerance wording in the legislation. The courts have said that if there is to be any change in the law, it is up to Congress, not the judiciary.[24]

To complicate matters, this clause conflicts with another law, the Federal Insecticide, Rodenticide, and Fungicide Act (FIFRA), passed in 1972. This act, among other things, gives the EPA authority to regulate pesticides. FIFRA did not embody the concept of zero tolerance since that would ban a large number of important pesticides. Concentrations of pesticides in most raw fruits and vegetables are well below allowed tolerances, and concentrations of pesticides in processed foods are also below allowances in the raw products. But Delaney permits zero tolerance, hence the "Delaney paradox." Pesticide levels acceptable to the EPA in raw fruits and vegetables cannot be legally accepted when appearing in processed foods made from the same crops.[25]

---

[23] Sanders, "Push to Centralize Food Inspections."
[24] *Kathleen E. Les* v. *William K. Reilly*, 968 F.2d 985 (1992).
[25] Daniel M. Byrd, "Goodbye Pesticides?" *Regulation*, Fall 1997, p. 59.

Widespread dissatisfaction with this situation led to passage of the Food Quality Protection Act of 1996 (FQPS) to correct the problem. Since rescinding the Delaney Clause was politically unthinkable, Congress finessed the issue in this way. The 1996 law specifies that before both raw and processed foods can be offered for sale, the pesticide safety level must be at the point where there is "a reasonable certainty that no harm will result from aggregate exposure." It directs regulators to base safety findings on risk assessment and management methods.

How Safe Is Safe?

Both in the preparation of legislation and in the bureaucracy, a troubling question arises: How safe is safe? Most scientists believe that the cancer threat from pesticides in foods, for example, is minuscule compared with many other daily risks, such as those from smoking. Professor Bruce Ames, a biochemist at the University of California Berkeley, points out that many foods contain natural toxins at higher levels than residues of dangerous pesticides. Potatoes, cabbage, broccoli, tomatoes, celery, coffee, and many fruits contain a variety of carcinogens. As they evolved, food plants developed these toxins to repel insects, fungi, and other predators. He points out that up to 10 percent of a plant's weight is made up of natural pesticides. The ordinary potato, he says, contains 150 chemicals before it is sprayed with pesticides. Most scientists affirm that by the time a food gets to market, very little pesticide residue remains.[26] Such scientific conclusions stand in stark contrast to the uncompromising standard of the Delaney Clause.

Nevertheless, there are troubling aspects to potential hazards of contaminants in the food supply. For example, there are thousands of chemicals, animal drugs, and microbiological organisms in food, some of which may be dangerous to human beings alone or in combination. But which ones, and how dangerous? Identifying and testing them is a gigantic task that has only partly been accomplished. Critics point out that restrictions in foreign countries on the use of pesticides and additives are not as strong as in this country, and we import more and more foods from abroad. According to the USDA's Economic Research Service, 62 percent of all fish, fish products, and shellfish eaten in the United States comes from abroad, as do 34 percent of fresh fruits and 10 percent of vegetables.[27] Little of this produce is tested when it arrives on our shores. These are significant concerns, and the search for an answer to What is safe? must continue.

[26] Gisela Bolte and Dick Thompson, "Do You Dare to Eat a Peach?" *Time,* March 17, 1989; and John F. Ross, "Risks, Where Do Real Dangers Lie?" *Smithsonian,* November 1995.
[27] Jeffrey P. Cohn, "The International Flow of Food," *FDA Consumer,* January–February 2001, p. 29.

The growth of imported foods is sure to expand, and since only a small fraction of imports are tested, inspiring cooperation with foreign countries in establishing food safety standards is more important than ever. A significant endeavor in establishing global standards is that of the Codex Alimentarius Commission. It was created in 1962 and is jointly run by the United Nation's Food and Agricultural Organization and the World Health Organization. The Codex sets safety standards for foods. By the end of 1999, the 165 country members of the organization agreed on maximum safe limits for 1,200 food additives, 197 pesticides, and 25 contaminants. It has also set 204 food standards.[28] Codex standards are voluntary, but countries that do not follow them have weakened positions in trade disputes before the WTO.

This area swirls with controversy and persistent problems. Not nearly enough is known about linkages between cancer and human health with specific food contaminants; doses that humans can safely tolerate; the risks to humans of adding chemicals to animal feed; which natural and human-introduced chemicals are hazardous to consumers; and how to identify sources of serious contamination in a long food production and processing chain.

PRODUCTS LIABILITY LAW

Consumers have legal recourse to compensation for injury of person, property, or reputation by individuals or corporations. This includes, of course automobile accidents, medical malpractice, professional malpractice, or defective products. An area of special concern to both consumers and business is products liability.

For most of our history, consumers had little recourse in being compensated for defective products. Today manufacturers or other sellers of products can be held liable for defective products under three fundamental theories, namely, negligence, breach of warranty, and strict liability.

Negligence

Under this theory, manufacturers have an obligation to do what a reasonable person could be expected to do. Not only the manufacturer but all those in the stream of events leading to the final sale to a customer must exercise reasonable care. They can be held liable today even for injury resulting from unintended but reasonably foreseeable misuse.

The law has not always been this generous to consumers. Until a few years ago, manufacturers were well protected from consumer liability suits. An injured consumer tried to collect damages through either contract law or caveat emptor (let the buyer beware). Under contract law,

---

[28] Ibid.

the courts would accept the defendant's argument that in the absence of a direct contract between the manufacturer and the consumer, called *privity*, the plaintiff had no case against the producer but had to go to the retailer. If retailers lost a suit, they would sue the wholesaler, and the wholesaler, in turn, the manufacturer. This chain seldom resulted in redress to consumers. This doctrine was based on an English decision in 1842.[29] Under the caveat emptor principle, the vendor was liable only when there was an agreement that provided for that liability. These views were developed at a time when consumers generally dealt face to face with manufacturers of the products they bought. As the distribution chain evolved in industrial society, that experience, of course, became rarer and rarer.

This legal protective wall for manufacturers was broken by the milestone case of *McPherson* v. *Buick Motor Company,* in 1916.[30] McPherson was injured when a wooden spoke in a wheel of his Buick collapsed. General Motors claimed that the car was bought from a dealer and the company had no liability. The court disagreed and said the company was negligent in not properly inspecting the wheel. Furthermore, the court said, General Motors was responsible irrespective of who was in the chain of events prior to the purchase.

This legal philosophy has been vastly stretched in subsequent decisions. For example, General Motors was held responsible by the court for designing products that minimized risks in collisions. If it did not do so, it was liable for damages.[31] The New Jersey Supreme Court said, in effect, that the manufacturer had the responsibility for warning of dangers that were not only undiscovered but scientifically undiscoverable at the time the products were first introduced for use in the workplace.[32] This is a puzzling rule for a company to follow. However, it may provide major protection for injured consumers, as it did for workers injured by inhaling asbestos.

Warranties

A manufacturer or seller can be held liable for a breach of warranty, either explicit or implied. An express warranty is an explicit claim made by the manufacturer to the seller. It can be stated on a card or on labels, packages, or advertising. The Magnuson-Moss Warranty Improvement Act of 1974 sets forth federal standards for written consumer product warranties.

When a product is sold, there is an automatic implied warranty that it is fit for the ordinary use to which it is intended. The landmark case

---

[29] *Winterbottom* v. *Wright,* 15 Eng. Rep. 402 (Eng. 1842), 177.

[30] 217 N.Y. 382, 111 N.E. 1040 (1916).

[31] *Larson* v. *General Motors Corporation,* 391 F.2d 495 (8th Cir. 1968).

[32] *Beshada et al.* v. *Johns-Manville Products Corporation,* 90 N.J. 191,447 A.2d 539 (1982).

about implied warranties is *Henningsen* v. *Bloomfield Motors, Inc.*[33] In this case, Henningsen bought a Plymouth automobile. A few days after purchase, the steering mechanism failed and his wife, who was driving, crashed and was injured. The dealer and the company claimed that when the purchase contract was approved by Henningsen, he had signed a disclaimer appearing on the back of the contract. (Included in eight inches of fine print was a sentence saying there was agreement that there were no warranties express or implied by either the dealer or the manufacturer on the vehicle or its parts.) The court said that the automobile company was legally responsible for making cars good enough to serve the purpose for which they were intended.

Strict Liability

This legal weapon makes it possible for injured consumers to hold all those in the chain of distribution responsible for defective products. This theory puts the focus on the product, not the reasonableness of the producer or seller. Anyone who sells any product in a defective condition that is "unreasonably" dangerous to a consumer is liable for the harm caused. If there are no defects in the design of the product, but the product is "unreasonably" dangerous, a producer will still be held liable for injury if customers are not properly warned about its use.

The landmark case in the development of strict liability was *Greenman* v. *Yuba Power Products, Inc.* The court said that "a manufacturer is strictly liable when an article he places on the market, knowing that it will be used without inspection, proves to have a defect that causes injury to a human being.[34]

This area of the law has become very complex. Paul H. Rubin, a professor at Emory University, expresses a view held by many observers: "this system has been undermined by unreasonable standards—imposed by the courts—defining parties' liability for damages."[35]

PRODUCTS LIABILITY SUITS

The number of products liability suits reached a high of more than 30,000 in 1997 then dropped sharply to about 14,000 in 2000.[36] Products liability suits in recent years have been concentrated in the areas of asbestos, breast implants, automobiles, and tobacco. A number of reasons are advanced as to why the number of suits has declined since 1997. For

[33] N.J. Supreme Court, 161 A.2d 69 (1960).
[34] 27 Cal. Reptr. 697, 377 P.2d 897 (1962).
[35] Paul H. Rubin, "Fundamental Reform of Tort Law," *Regulation,* www.cato.org/pubs/regulation/reg18v4b.html.
[36] Business Digest, "Jury Awards Rise Sharply in Defective-Product Cases," *The New York Times,* January 30, 2001.

example, rising litigation costs and legal restraints have made it less attractive for lawyers to take on small damage cases. Many small cases no longer reach juries because they are settled in mediation. Then, too, manufacturers have significantly improved the safety of their products.[37]

However, awards in individual cases have increased significantly, from about $500,000 in 1993 to $1.8 million in 1999.[38] Juries have become more willing to punish manufacturers when they perceive outrageous wrongdoing. Here are a few examples. In 2000 a Florida jury found six tobacco companies guilty of conspiracy and fraud and ordered them to pay damages of $145 billion to Florida smokers who had died or were ill. In 1999 General Motors was ordered to pay $4.9 billion to six people who were trapped and burned in a Chevy Malibu when the gas tank exploded after a rear-end collision. Then there was the highly publicized case of $2.7 million awarded to a woman who was scalded by a cup of carry-out coffee at McDonald's. Such large awards are usually reduced by judges, due in part to a 2001 Supreme Court decision holding that appellate courts must give careful scrutiny to jury awards to decide whether they are excessive. Justice John Paul Stevens, writing for the court, said there were constitutional restraints on punitive awards in the due process guarantee of the Fourteenth Amendment and the Eighth Amendment's prohibition of "excessive fines."[39]

Huge punitive awards are a fraction of 1 percent of total products liability suits. While they are few overall, a large award can be devastating to a single company. Products liability remains a potential threat for people in business from medical doctors to giant corporations.

Business Wants Products Liability Reform

The business community, stung by products liability suits, rising liability insurance costs, differing state liability laws, and high-profile business bankruptcies because of product liability awards (e.g., Dow Corning, A. H. Robins, and Johns Manville), has pressed Congress for years to reform and make uniform the nation's product liability laws. Opponents of congressional action have been powerful consumer groups and plaintiffs' lawyers.

The business community seeks a number of reforms. For example, business wants Congress to pass legislation that will establish uniform liability standards across the states. Business wants to eliminate a manufacturers' liability when products made today may cause injuries in the future that cannot be reasonably foreseen. Business wants a cap on punitive awards. Business wants judges to determine punitive damages, not

---

[37] Ted Rohrlich, "We Aren't Seeing You in Court," *Los Angeles Times,* February 1, 2001.
[38] *Business Digest,* "Jury Awards Rise Sharply in Defective-Product Cases."
[39] *Cooper Industries Inc.* v. *Leatherman Tool Group Inc.,* 531 U.S. 923 (2000).

juries. This is because judges tend to award lower punitive damages than juries. The Supreme Court, as discussed in Chapter 7, has moved in the direction of restraining damage awards.

State Activities

Some states have recently introduced reforms, such as caps on punitive damages. For example, Connecticut limits punitive damages on products liability cases to twice the compensation damages awarded. Louisiana virtually eliminates punitive damages in civil suits. A powerful protection for consumers is the way state attorneys general are banding together to file class action suits.

The Impact of Products Liability on Business

Current products liability laws have a range of impacts on companies. All manufacturers are concerned about the possibility of large liability awards. Some have dropped high-risk products, including asbestos, football helmets, off-road vehicles, and vaccines, for fear of liability suits. Others have slowed or halted the introduction of new products, depriving consumers of an unknown number of innovations. When making products, companies have learned that the following actions are important for preventing products liability suits.

- *Attention to design.* Products can be scrutinized in the design stage to identify hazards and risks that might be avoided through altering the design. Design is central in some products liability suits. For example, the manufacturer of a range hood was sued after a boy fighting with his brother in a kitchen fell and was severely injured by the hood's sharp edge. Although the boy was roughhousing with his brother when there was no adult supervision, the manufacturer lost the case because under questioning it admitted that designing a rounded edge would not have been more expensive and would not have impaired the range hood's function.[40]

- *Improving quality.* There are many marketing and cost advantages to reducing product flaws. One added advantage is liability reduction. Systematic quality programs include a chain of actions to prevent flawed products from reaching the markets, including reliability testing and inspections. One manufacturer of timing devices sold clocks that could catch on fire after only four hours of continuous operation- a product with disastrously high potential liability. It had installed the wrong electronic component in them because it looked similar to the correct component. An effective quality control program might have prevented such an error.

[40] Randall L. Goodden, *Product Liability Prevention: A Strategic Guide* (Milwaukee, WI: ASQ Quality Press, 2000), p. 100.

- *Instructions and warning labels.* Instruction are opportunities to teach consumers how to use a product safely. Warning labels are pointed advisories about potential abuses of which consumers may be unaware. Courts have held that warning labels are not necessary for such obvious, common sense dangers as putting fingers in a rotating lawn mower blade. However, in the current litigious climate many manufacturers take no chances. One company put a label on its hair dryer reading: "Do not use while sleeping." Another put a warning on a Superman costume stating: "Wearing this outfit does not enable you to fly."[41]

- *Product recalls.* When reports are received that a defect in a product poses a risk of harm, manufacturers may conduct recalls. Recalls are extremely expensive, and can be prohibitively expensive for very small manufacturers, but they eliminate or reduce liability. Large companies, such as auto companies, have recall procedures in place so that they can react quickly to news of problems.

Such actions as these reduce, but cannot eliminate products liability actions. The United States legal system makes it easier for plaintiffs to win large damage awards from product makers than the systems of other countries. In Europe, attorneys do not work on a contingency basis. It is illegal in many European nations, and otherwise against professional codes, for them to take a case and take payment out of an ultimate damage award. Except for the United Kingdom, lawyers are not permitted to advertise for clients as do American lawyers seeking litigants for tobacco, breast implant, asbestos, and other class-action products liability suits. European countries require losers to pay court costs. And in addition, awards tend to be much lower, particularly since punitive damages are usually not allowed. In Asia, products liability is a relatively new idea. Chinese products liability laws were introduced only in 1993. And in Japan, only since 1995 have consumers been allowed to sue manufacturers. In short, nowhere else in the world is there a legal system so favorable to litigation over products as in the United States.[42]

FALSE AND DECEPTIVE ADVERTISING

Advertising is ubiquitous. Consumers cannot escape it on TV, in the media, on billboards, on packaging, and on the Internet. More than $200 billion is spent each year in the United States to advertise consumer products. The states have been especially active in recent years in protecting consumers against abuses in advertising. At the federal level, the

---

[41] Ibid., p. 119.
[42] Ibid., pp. 12–23.

dominant agency concerned with advertising is the FTC. The FDA, the USDA, and the Department of Labor also deal with certain types of false and deceptive advertising. For example, the Department of Labor reviews claims of companies regarding the manufacture of their products in the United States.

Fundamentally, the purposes of advertising are to make the consumer aware of a product or service, inform the consumer of its characteristics, and then persuade the consumer to buy it. A wide range of policy issues flows from these simple purposes. For example, what should consumers be told about product contents, use, maintenance requirements, and warranties? What is the impact of advertising on social values? How should products be advertised? How far should government go in regulating advertising?

These are significant issues. We discuss here only false and deceptive advertising to illustrate but one dimension of the issues. Advertising is false when its claims are explicitly, literally untrue. A few years ago, a dishwasher manufacturer advertised that the washer would completely clean dishes, pots, and pans "without prior rinsing or scraping." That was clearly untrue, said the FTC, and the company had to stop making that claim. On the other hand, puffery is not objectionable to the FTC. If a restaurant claims that "we serve the best hamburgers in town," that is acceptable because consumers know it is an exaggeration and are not deceived. However, if an advertisement says, "Our hamburgers are the lowest price in town," the FTC wants factual evidence that the statement is true. In dealing with this subject, one is reminded of the words attributed to Mark Twain: "When in doubt, tell the truth, it will amaze most people, delight your friends, and confuse your enemies." Some American advertisers apparently have not heard or been convinced of Twain's recommendation.

Federal Trade Commission Guidelines

The FTC has developed guidelines and policy statements for advertising a variety of products in many industries. They cover, for example, foods, plants and trees, jewelry, dog and cat products, lady's handbags, wigs, law books, and tires. There are policy statements concerning deceptive pricing, bait-and-switch advertising (that which is offered to get the consumer to buy something else), deceptive warranties and guarantees, food additives, and environmental marketing claims. For instance, a joint policy statement was issued by the FTC and the Federal Communications Commission (FCC) in 2000 to protect consumers from unfair and deceptive advertising and marketing of long-distance telephone services.

The FTC has developed detailed definitions of words such as deceptive, truthful, free, and misleading. For example, in a policy statement on deceptive advertising, the FTC said: "The Commission will find deception if there is a representation, omission, or practice that is likely to mislead the consumer acting reasonably in the circumstances, to the consumer's detriment."[43] Here are two cases to illustrate FTC action.

The FTC charged Web/TV Networks, Inc. (WNI), a subsidiary of Microsoft Corp, with false and deceptive advertising of its TV set-top box and Internet service. WNI claimed that the box would permit a purchaser to access the Internet through a television set without a computer and bring "all the incredible entertainment and information of the Internet right to your TV." The FTC said these claims were deceptive. For instance, the box would not bring all the Internet's entertainment and information, nor was it equivalent to a computer in its ability to access Internet content. In October 2000 the FTC reached a settlement with the company, providing that it would stop distributing advertising and other promotional materials with such claims and educate the public about using Internet-access products.

The FTC has charged some health providers with misleading and deceptive advertising. One high-profile case in this area concerned Jenny Craig, Inc. The FTC said Jenny Craig could not prove claims made about weight loss, price, and safety. For example, the company claimed that nine out of ten customers would recommend the Jenny Craig program to a friend; and the company represented that it had surveys backing up the claim, when it did not. Jenny Craig agreed to stop that claim, to substantiate weight-loss claims in its advertising, to reveal all costs associated with its program, and to include a statement that weight loss is temporary for most dieters.[44]

States Move Aggressively

States have been more active than the federal government in reviewing false and deceptive advertising. The state attorneys general have been aggressive not only in challenging individual companies but in joining with other states in bringing multistate lawsuits against large national advertisers. Here are a few actions taken by state attorneys general.

Twenty-six state attorneys general reached an agreement with Publishers Clearing House on charges of false and deceptive advertising. In its advertising, the company made it surprisingly easy for some people to believe they had won a fabulous sweepstake prize. Thousands of people thought they had to purchase products of the company to be eligible to win. One man said he spent about $70,000 a year for 12 years to buy products of the company in hopes of winning. Such flagrant enticements as "You are a winner" and more subtle words were in millions of mailings to persuade the less discerning person that he or she was about to

[43] Federal Trade Commission, "FTC Policy Statement on Deception," www.ftc.gov/bep/policysstmt/ad-decpt.htm, December 25, 1998.
[44] Federal Trade Commission, "FTC Reaches Settlement with Jenny Craig to End Diet Program Advertising Litigation," www.ftc.gov/opa/1997/9705/jcraig-2htm.

win a prize. The company settled with the state attorneys general in 2001 and agreed to stop such false and deceptive advertising and pay $34 million in customer refunds.

Texas challenged Sara Lee for suggesting that its "light" cheesecake is a low-calorie product. Several states challenged Kellogg Co. for its advertising of the nutritional benefits of its cereals. Quaker Oats settled a challenge by the state of Texas over its claim that eating oatmeal reduces cholesterol. States have been active in challenging automobile dealers for their deceptive advertising concerning the costs of leasing an automobile.

There are many other important issues in advertising; for example, using images of sexuality, encouragement of materialism, and the impact of advertising in special problem areas such as alcohol and tobacco consumption. Charles Lindblom, an emeritus professor from Princeton University, raises a different type of question about advertising in these words: "The problem posed by the steady flow of seductive communications from market elites, then, is not that they decide for consumers what they are to buy. It is that they degrade the mind or, more precisely, degrade the human capacity to use the mind. Can that be proved? No, I think not, but it is a conclusion also hard to deny."[45]

THE FTC AND CONSUMER PRIVACY

Everyone wants privacy, but there is no consensus about its exact meaning or what constitutes a violation of it. Perceived infringements range from cameras placed at intersections to catch red-light runners, to unsolicited commercial telephone calls, to Internet pornography parents view as an invasion of their privacy and that of their children. In any regulation of such situations, important questions arise about free speech, consumer convenience, ill-advised restraints on e-commerce, and costs to business of compliance.

Dozens of Internet privacy bills have been introduced in Congress but there is considerable hesitancy in both parties to pass them. Senator Patrick Leahy (D-Vermont), a privacy legislation advocate, has long warned that simple responses to privacy issues could do more harm than good. Representative Dick Armey (R-Texas) recently sent a letter to his colleagues in the House warning them against taking any action. He wrote, "Congress is an inexperienced and amateur mechanic trying to tinker with the supercharged, high-tech engine of our economy. . . . We need to be careful not to let our good intentions get in the way of common sense."[46]

[45] Charles E. Lindblom, *The Market System; What It Is, How It Works, and What to Make of It* (New Haven: Yale University Press, 2001), p. 217.
[46] John Schwartz, "Government Is Wary of Tackling Online Privacy," *The New York Times,* September 6, 2001, p. C6.

Consumers have become increasingly concerned about the availability and use of their personal information. So dominant among consumer concerns is this issue that Timothy J. Muris, chairman of the FTC, stated that "Privacy has become a large and central part of the FTC's consumer protection mission."[47] This issue is intensified by the increased possibilities for collection and sharing of personal information on the Internet. It is easy to collect personal data when consumers use the Internet to buy something. It is also easy for the acquired information to be sold to third parties. For example, e-commerce entrepreneurs sell data about which products consumers buy, where they buy, how frequently they buy, and how much they spend. With data that track purchasing habits, a merchant can target particular consumers more precisely and less expensively.

Past Privacy Actions by the FTC

Until recently, consumer information issues were not neglected by the FTC, but neither were they the center of attention. In the 1990s the agency focused more resources on fighting a broad range of Internet frauds such as pyramid schemes, charging consumer credit cards for unauthorized purchases, bogus investment advice, medical quackery, and failure to deliver purchased products.[48] It brought more than 100 actions against Internet scams involving hundreds of businesses and individuals. It created *Consumer Sentinel,* now the largest database of consumer fraud complaints in North America. A Fraud Rapid Response Team was established to track data on the Internet to spot emerging rackets and take quick action to stop them. An Internet lab was created in the agency to keep staff abreast of new technology that could be used for fraudulent and deceptive purposes.

Although consumer privacy issues were deemphasized in favor of more attention to frauds, some actions were taken. Public forums were held to explore online privacy issues. FTC staff surveyed more than 1,400 websites to examine online information practices. Based on analysis of survey data, Congress passed the Children's Online Privacy Protection Act, a law that requires website operators to give parents notice of their information practices and to get their consent before collecting and using information about their children. Some law enforcement actions were also taken.

[47] Timothy J. Muris, "Protecting Consumers' Privacy: 2002 and Beyond," speech delivered at the Privacy 2001 Conference, Cleveland, Ohio, October 4, 2001.
[48] Federal Trade Commission, *The FTC's First Five Years Protecting Consumers* (Washington, DC: FTC, 1999): The materials in this section of the chapter came from this report.

Current FTC Actions

Recently, the commission has initiated more actions against companies for violation of its information rules. For example, Eli Lilly and Company was charged with the unauthorized disclosure of sensitive personal information when it inadvertently released the identity of Prozac users in a mass e-mail. The company and the agency reached a consent agreement. In another case, American Pop Corn Co., of Sioux City, Iowa, was forced to pay a $10,000 fine for collecting information from children on its website. American Pop Corn, which markets Jolly Time popcorn, maintained a Kid's Club page featuring games, recipes, crafts, and jokes. (A sample joke: Why did the farmer stop telling secrets in the corn field? *Because the corn was all ears*).[49] The site also contained educational lessons for teachers to use in their classrooms, including a lesson about the history of popcorn and a science lesson inviting students to measure the volume of popcorn before and after popping. Without the parental consent required under the FTC's Children's Online Privacy Protection Rule, the company collected children's names, e-mail addresses, and home addresses. It required them to give additional information if they wanted to enter contests. In addition to paying the fine, American Pop Corn agreed to post a privacy policy statement on the site requiring it to notify parents whenever a child registered.[50] It remains to be seen if the jokes will improve as much as the privacy policy. This was the fifth case under the children's privacy rule since it went into effect in 2000.

Many other actions were taken in the interest of protecting personal information about consumers. For example, in 2002 the commission published in the *Federal Register* a 54-page proposed rule for regulating telemarketing practices.[51] Among the proposals was a national "do not call" registry, a database for consumers who do not want telemarketer calls. If this rule is made final, it would be illegal for a telemarketer to call any consumer who registers. It would also be illegal for a telemarketer or anyone else to interfere with or prevent a consumer from putting his or her name on the "do not call" list. Under the provisions of the Gramm-Leach-Bliley Act of 1999, the FTC ordered banks and other financial institutions to establish policies concerning the use of financial information about customers and to mail copies of these policies to consumers. When notices about the policies were sent, however, many contained ambiguities, misrepresentations, and language that confused consumers. Finally, the FTC and the Department of Commerce joined to encourage industry

[49] At www.jollytime.com/kidsclub/kidsclub_jokes.asp.
[50] Federal Trade Commission, "Popcorn Company Settles FTC Privacy Violation Charges," press release, February 14, 2002.
[51] "Telemarketing Sales Rule," 67 FR 4492–4546, January 30, 2002.

self-regulation on the use of "cookies." These are files placed in the computers of consumers when they visit websites. Cookies facilitate online profiling, that is, gathering data about consumers, sometimes without their knowledge. This data can include information about the Internet sites that consumers visit, their purchasing preferences, their travel destinations, and their credit card numbers.

What of the Future?

FTC Chairman Muris announced in October 2001 that his agency was not preparing to ask for new legislation. Instead, it was going to focus on enforcing existing rules and accelerating educational programs. He observed that consumers were concerned about three significant consequences that can result from misuse of information about them and said that the agency would work on measures to address these concerns. The first concern is risks to physical security. Parents do not want the whereabouts of their children to be widely known, nor do women want their addresses publicly available. Second is the risk of economic injury. Identity theft plagues the information age. It can be a devastating experience for any victim. Third, consumers do not want uninvited intrusions into their privacy from telephone calls and unsolicited, disgusting spam e-mails on their computers. In focusing on these concerns, said the chairman, the agency is placing emphasis on both online and offline invasions of personal information privacy.

The following are a few programs the chairman said were to be emphasized:

- *Protecting consumers from unwanted telemarketing.* Existing protections are inadequate. The major agency initiative here is the establishment of its proposed "do not call" list.

- *Stopping abuse of "pre-acquired account information."* Consumers are sometimes asked for information connected with the actual or potential purchase of a product or service. Dishonest telemarketers can, with this information, charge credit cards although the consumer has not agreed to a purchase.

- *Attacking in-box spam.* The agency is evaluating methods of reducing unwanted junk e-mail, particularly messages such as pyramid schemes and get-rich-quick frauds that seek to swindle consumers.

- *Controlling identity theft.* The FTC has authority under the Identify Theft and Assumption Deterrence Act to combat ID theft. According to Muris, more effort is needed. He wants to expand the FTC database on the subject to make it easier to identify patterns and thieves. He also wants to prepare a universal fraud complaint form for use by all agencies involved with this threat.

- *Increasing enforcement of the Fair Credit Reporting Act.* This statute attempts to assure that consumer credit reports are accurate. It requires users of the reports to notify consumers promptly if their report is used to deny them a loan, insurance, or a job. Other provisions protect the privacy of consumer credit information.

- *Enforcing privacy policies.* The FTC has been successful in encouraging Internet sites to post privacy policies. Today, most popular sites have such policies. The job now is to ensure that these policies are followed.

- *Expanding education programs.* Consumers and businesses need education to understand fully privacy laws and FTC regulations. The agency itself needs to keep abreast of new technologies that affect consumer information privacy.

CONCLUDING OBSERVATIONS

There is no question that today business is increasingly concerned about the interests and demands of consumers, government regulators, and consumer advocacy groups. Consumer issues will become more complex as the population grows, product choices expand, technology changes the nature of products, and global competition intensifies. We expect, therefore, even more attention to consumer issues in both business and government.

Advertising Alcohol

In the 1950s and 1960s, alcoholic beverage ads were unsophisticated. Most beer ads, for instance, the Hamm's beer animations of bears at play, were low-key and simple. Ads for distilled spirits and wine were similarly unsophisticated. However, in 1970 all this changed with the injection of powerful techniques from the world of cigarette marketing. In that year, Philip Morris, the largest U.S. tobacco company, aquired Miller Brewing Company. In those days, Miller was a small brewer, with only 4.2 percent of the domestic beer market. Philip Morris quickly revolutionized beer marketing by introducing market segmentation, target marketing, and image-oriented lifestyle advertising. By 1980 Miller was the nation's second-largest brewer with a 20 percent market share. More important,

other beer, wine, and liquor marketers adopted its sophisticated methods, and the industry's advertising was transformed.

Despite spending of more than $4 billion a year to advertise alcohol, national consumption is not rising. Since the first poll was taken in 1939, the number of American adults who drink has hovered near 60 percent—the current figure is 64 percent.[1] Per capita consumption has been level for the last 20 years.[2] And despite a population increase of

[1] "Vices: Smoking, Drinking, and Gambling," *The American Enterprise,* October–November 2001, p. 62.
[2] U.S. Census Bureau, *Statistical Abstract of the United States: 2000,* 120th ed. (Washington, DC, 2000), table 238.

20 percent, total domestic production of alcoholic beverages has not risen over this time either.[3] This mature and stagnant market generates fierce competition for market share in three segments. Beer now has 59 percent, wine 12 percent, and distilled spirits 28 percent.[4] This competition is the driving force behind the industry's emphasis on clever advertising.

THE ATTACK ON ALCOHOL ADVERTISING

A strong anti-alcohol movement exists. America's brief experiment with prohibition ended in 1933, but a 2001 poll showed that 20 percent of Americans want to turn back the clock and ban alcohol again.[5] These neoprohibitionists are the backbone of the movement; its leaders are activists in church, health, consumer, and citizens' groups such as Mothers Against Drunk Driving (MADD). Its greatest successes have been getting all states to raise the legal drinking age to 21 and establishing a national drunken-driving standard of .08 blood alcohol content.[6] It also wants to ban or restrict alcoholic beverage advertising. The movement's indictment against alcohol ads is based on four beliefs.

First, advertising increases consumption. Many ads are designed to attract new drinkers and promote additional drinking. Miller Lite's classic "Tastes Great—Less Filling" spots attempted to reposition beer as a competitor to soft drinks, telling consumers that light beer is a low-calorie drink that can be consumed more often than regular beer. The Michelob beer campaign based on the slogan "Put a little weekend in your week" encouraged weekend social drinkers to think of all days of the week as drinking occasions. A recent campaign by the Wine Marketing Council suggests that wine goes with television viewing.

Studies of the effect of advertising on consumption have generated mixed evidence. Generally, national studies find no correlation between overall spending for alcohol ads and consumption. But some studies of local areas show that increased advertising does raise consumption and that advertising bans reduce it.[7] No firm conclusion is yet possible. This does not deter critics who believe that when alcohol ads saturate the media, they create a climate of undeserved social approval for drinking. George Hacker of the Center for Science in the Public Interest, a consumer organization with a leading role in the fight against alcohol ads, prefers to rely on plain, unscientific common sense.

> To pretend, as alcohol marketers do, that the advertisements do not have any effect on consumption is disingenuous at best. . . . [C]onsider that [companies] spend hundreds of millions of dollars advertising their products. One would think they have some faith in that investment. Try finding an advertising agency modest enough to confess that marketers have been wasting all (or even some of) that money. . . . [T]o suggest that it does not help bring in new consumers and encourage current users to consume more begs credulity. Trusting one's eyes and ears makes more sense.[8]

Second, ads encourage children and teenagers to start drinking. The underage audience is bombarded with ads for beer, wine, and liquor. Youths see as many as 2,000 beer and wine commercials on televison every year.[9] The cumulative mass of

[3] Ibid., table 1242, and U.S. Bureau of the Census, *Statistical Abstract of the United States:* 1990, 110th ed. (Washington, DC, 1990), table 1318.

[4] Statement of Peter Cressy, president of the Distilled Spirits Council of the United States, transcript of "NBC's Hard Sell," *The News Hour*, January 1, 2002, p. 5.

[5] International Communications Research, "Drinking and Driving Survey," July 13–17, 2001, sponsored by the Harvard School of Public Health, question 26.

[6] Mark Murray, "Unbottling the 0.8 Percent Solution," *National Journal*, November 4, 2000, p. 3488.

[7] For an overview of this research, see Henry Saffer, "Studying the Effects of Alcohol Advertising on Consumption," *Alcohol Health & Research World*, vol. 20, no. 4 (1996), and Hae-Kyong Bang, "Analyzing the Impact of the Liquor Industry's Lifting of the Ban on Broadcast Advertising," *Journal of Public Policy & Marketing*, Spring 1998.

[8] George A. Hacker, "Liquor Advertisements on Television: Just Say No," *Journal of Public Policy & Marketing*, Spring 1998, p. 139.

[9] Center for Science in the Public Interest, "Stop Liquor Ads on TV: Talking Points," at www.cspinet.org/booze/liquorads/liquor_talkingpoints.htm.

Polygamy Porter, a brand marketed by Wasatch Brewing Co., is a parody of the Mormon custom, now banned, of taking multiple wives. The ad campaign features the slogan "Why have just one!" This kind of appeal is condemned by the anti-alcohol movement for encouraging more consumption.
Photo courtesy of Wasatch Brewing Company.

alcohol ads is an irresistible lesson that drinking is fun and leads to social acceptance. Researchers report that fifth- and sixth-grade children who can describe alcohol ads have more positive attitudes toward drinking than less knowledgeable children.[10] And many ads are popular with children. For example, one survey found that Budweiser spots featuring the lizards Frankie and Louie were the favorites of children aged six to seventeen.[11] Alcohol ads seep in at very early ages. Millie Webb is president of MADD. Two of her children were killed in a drunken-driving accident. One day she noticed a frog on her patio and showed it to her three-year-old nephew, who knew its name. "He said 'Budweiser,' " she recalls. "It broke my heart."[12]

Underage consumption is significant. There are about 12 million drinkers between 12 and 20 years old, creating a market estimated at $10 billion.[13] By the eighth grade, 52 percent of children have used alcohol and 25 percent have been drunk. By the twelfth grade, 80 percent have used alcohol and 62 percent have been drunk, more than half of them once a month or more.[14] Activists claim that the alcoholic beverage industry targets underage

[10] Joel W. Grube, "Television Beer Advertising and Drinking Knowledge, Beliefs, and Intentions among Schoolchildren," *American Journal of Public Health,* February 1994. See also Erica W. Austin and Christopher Knaus, "Predicting the Potential for Risky Behavior among Those 'Too Young' to Drink as the Result of Appealing Advertising," *Journal of Health Communication,* January–March 2000.
[11] Kathy DeSalvo, "FTC Investigates Alcohol Company's Ad Practices," *SHOOT,* September 25, 1998, p. 39.

[12] Mark O'Keefe, "Critics Take Aim at NBC Plan to Air Liquor Ads," *Family Living,* January 14, 2002, p. D8.
[13] The estimate is by Joseph Califano Jr., director of the National Center on Addiction and Substance Abuse at Columbia University. Quoted by Cal Thomas, "Congress Must Ban Liquor Ads from TV," *Baltimore Sun,* December 20, 2001, p. A23.
[14] "2000 Data from In-School Surveys of 8th, 10th, and 12th Grade Students," the Monitoring the Future Study, Institute for Survey Research, University of Michigan, table 1, at http://monitoringthefuture.org/data00/data.html.

drinkers not only with advertising but with specialty products designed to attract youth. These include "alcopops," fruit-flavored malt drinks resembling sodas, "shooters," single-serving vodka and tequila cocktails with names such as Yellin Melon Balls and Blu-Dacious Kamikaze, and novelty products such as cups of strawberry gelatin containing vodka.[15] Although the industry denies targeting under-21 drinkers, it makes no difference to critics. "Whether alcohol producers intentionally target 15- and 16-year-olds is irrelevant," argues Hacker, "[t]hat they reach them with the most sophisticated means and the most seductive messages creates enough of a problem."[16]

Third, sophisticated lifestyle advertising used by alcohol makers is manipulative because it locks into inner drives. Informational advertising presents details about a product, for example, its price, availability, and quality. In contrast, lifestyle advertising positions a product to fulfill emotional needs. Pictures and copy associate alcohol with fulfillment of desires for popularity, success, sophistication, rebellion, romance, and sexual conquest. The ads endow commodity products such as vodka or lager beer with brand images. Then, by drinking that brand, the consumer adopts and projects the brand image. These ads may convey little or no objective information about the beverage, only an emotional theme. Sexual images are a staple of alcohol marketing. However, one study of alcohol ads in magazines during a 14-year period found that other appeals predominated over sexual imagery. In *Life,* for example, prestige and social acceptance were more frequent themes.[17] Whatever the image, critics believe that lifestyle ads are highly manipulative because they play on emotions. If consumers respond to them they are being tricked into fulfilling inner needs by drinking.

Fourth, alcohol advertising is targeted not only at young drinkers but, sometimes inappropriately, at other groups too. An example of objectionable targeting is the heavy advertising of malt liquors in inner-city black neighborhoods and in black media. Malt liquor has a higher alcohol content than regular beer, and advertisements for it appeal to drinkers looking for a high. Recently, United States Beverage Company introduced a malt liquor called Phat Boy. "Phat" is a slang word used by teens for something hip, cool, or exciting. Phat Boy was marketed with graffiti-style ads as "the new malt liquor with an attitude." It came in 40-ounce bottles, each having nearly as much alcohol as a six-pack of regular beer. After an outcry by activists, the company dropped the brand, although the reason it cited was poor sales.[18] Hispanics are also targeted. For example, alcohol companies stage parties, promotions, concerts, and happy hours with Cinco de Mayo themes. One critic laments that "[t]he alcohol industry has managed to erase all reference to this day as a historical event, one that Latino youth and their families should take pride in, and transformed it into a major marketing time of year."[19] Joseph E. Seagram & Sons changed the picture of the captain on bottles of Captain Morgan Spiced Rum when focus groups revealed that a less cartoon-like image attracted more male Hispanic drinkers.[20]

ALCOHOL MARKETERS DEFEND THEIR ADVERTISING

The industry defends its ads. First, it says, ads are not the cause of alcohol abuse. As noted, studies fail to show that advertising increases consumption. So commercials and billboards cannot be blamed for car accidents, teen suicides, sexual ag-

[15] Alejandro Bodipo-Memba, "'Shooters' and Other Alcoholic Novelties Face Scrutiny," *The Wall Street Journal,* April 14, 1999, p. B1.

[16] George A. Hacker, "Alcohol Advertising: Are Our Kids Collateral or Intended Targets?" speech to the Leadership to Keep Children Alcohol Free Conference, January 10, 2002, p. 3.

[17] Geng Cui, "Advertising of Alcoholic Beverages in African-American and Women's Magazines: Implications for Health Communication," *Howard Journal of Communications,* October 2000, p. 288.

[18] Melanie Wells, "Phat Boy Brew on Way Out," *USA Today,* September 14, 1998, p. 12B.

[19] Juana Mora, "A Day of Pride, Prey to an Ad Blitz," *Los Angeles Times,* April 23, 2000, p. B17.

[20] Shelly Branch, "Seagram's Captain Morgan Gets Allied Domecq's Attention," *The Wall Street Journal,* November 20, 2000, p. B4.

This ad associates Bud Dry with fun, companionship, and sexuality.
© Joel Gordon.

gression, spouse abuse, binge drinking, and alcoholism. Alcoholism, for example, is a complex disease caused by personality, family, genetic, and physiological factors rather than by viewing ads. So the main result of restraints would be to deprive moderate drinkers of product information, not to ameliorate social problems. As one advertising executive notes, trying to stop problem drinking with an ad ban "makes as little sense as trying to control the Ku Klux Klan by outlawing bed linens."[21] Ad restrictions would also muzzle a competitive weapon. Because of stagnating demand, most alcohol ads are aimed not at expanding demand but at getting consumers to switch brands. Without advertising, starting a new national brand would be almost impossible and established brands would have an insurmountable advantage. Innovative products such as ice beers would be hard to introduce.

Second, anti-alcohol groups assume that the public is too stupid to make responsible decisions. The idea of curbing ads is condescending. Consumers are intelligent and skeptical. They are not duped by the association of alcohol with attractive images. Does anyone expect brewers and vintners to associate their products with root canals, traffic congestion, or income taxes? The rejection of lifestyle advertising is also condescending. If a consumer uses an alcohol brand to feel more sophisticated, popular, or sexual, who is to say that this method of satisfying the person's inner need is wrong? No one would criticize a woman for feeling glamorous while she is wearing perfume, even though the perfume is simply a chemical, nonessential to healthy life, and the glamour was created by ad imagery. If advertising endows alcoholic beverages with a quality that satisfies emotional needs in responsible drinkers, it bestows a legitimate benefit. The critics assume there is no merit to a product beyond its utilitarian qualities. What a dull world it would be if all products were marketed and used on this basis.

Third, the beer, wine, and spirits industries have voluntary codes of advertising behavior. The policies in these codes are extensive and specific. For example, the Beer Institute's *Advertising & Marketing Code* prohibits depictions of excessive consumption, intoxication, and drinking while driving. Models in beer ads must be over 25 and "reasonably appear" to be over 21 years old. No ads should be placed in media

[21] Eric Clark, *The Want Makers,* (New York: Viking Press, 1988) p. 285.

where the audience is primarily under 21 years old, and beer ads should never show "any symbol, language, music, gesture, or cartoon character that is intended to appeal primarily to persons below the legal purchase age." No depictions of Santa Claus or sexual promiscuity are permitted.[22] The Wine Institute's *Code of Advertising Standards* has similar guidelines. It prohibits showing the Easter bunny.[23] The Distilled Spirits Council of the United States *Code of Good Practice for Distilled Spirits Advertising and Marketing* is the most detailed and in its Preamble claims to "ensure responsible, tasteful, and dignified advertising. . . to adult consumers." Its provisions are similar to the two other codes. It allows "depictions of persons in a social or romantic setting" but forbids advertisers to "depict sexual prowess as a result of beverage alcohol consumption."[24]

Fourth, alcohol makers deflect critics by broadcasting public service announcements that preach moderation and by setting up education and community-action projects such as designated-driver programs. There are many such programs. The Distilled Spirits Council of the United States sponsors college campus programs in which students teach each other about moderation, and it has a program for training bartenders to serve drinks responsibly. Anheuser-Busch, Inc., has six public service programs that promote responsible drinking. Alert Cab, for instance, gives free taxi rides to restaurant and bar patrons who have been drinking.

Finally, the industry does not deny the practice of targeting younger drinkers, minorities, women, and other groups with advertising themes. The Anheuser-Busch frogs and lizards, for example, have strong appeal to legal buyers age 21 to 29, who are the heaviest beer drinkers. Brown-Forman Corporation recently changed the Southern Comfort bottle when focus groups aged 21 to 24 said that the brand lacked a contemporary image. The bottle, originally designed in 1874, was reshaped and the words "The Grand Old Drink of the South" were dropped from the label.[25]

The puzzle faced by companies is that this critical young age group of consumers shares many interests and behaviors with teenagers below the legal drinking age. With respect to ads aimed at minorities, the industry believes this practice is legitimate. Market segmentation and the targeted advertising that makes it work are standard in many industries. When toy companies make black or Latina dolls, social critics applaud, but when alcohol companies make products that appeal to minority communities, critics argue that these consumers are too gullible and naive to withstand manipulation, implying that minority consumers are not as astute as white consumers. The real problem is that the product is alcohol, not that the ads have ethnic or racial appeal.

RESTRICTING ALCOHOL ADVERTISING

Today there is little government regulation of alcohol ads, and, in recent years, federal courts have weakened that which does exist and raised barriers to added restrictions. Two federal agencies have some power over the claims that companies make.

Under a 1935 law, the Bureau of Alcohol, Tobacco and Firearms regulates container labels to prevent false claims, obscene images, and the use of words such as "strong" and "extra strength." Originally, the law prohibited statements of alcohol content on labels so that companies could not start strength wars. However, in 1995 the Supreme Court held that censoring this information violated bottlers' speech rights, so alcohol content can now be printed on labels.[26] A second agency, the Federal Trade Commission, has the power to stop "deceptive" and "unfair" advertising claims, and now and then it flexes its muscles regarding alcohol ads. Industry critics have petitioned a third agency, the Federal Communications Commission, to allow counteradvertising with antidrinking themes, but so far the agency has refused.

Altogether, the body of government regulation covering alcohol advertising imposes few restraints. Critics want stronger measures. In the

[22] At www.beerinstitute.org/admarkcode.htm.
[23] At www.wineinstitute.org/communications/statistics/Code_of_Advertising.htm.
[24] At www.discus.org/industry/code/code.htm.
[25] Shelly Branch, "Southern Comfort Is Spirited into Present," *The Wall Street Journal,* June 15, 2001, p. B6.
[26] *Rubin* v. *Coors Brewing Company,* 514 U.S. 618 (1995).

1990s several bills were introduced in Congress to limit alcohol ads, for example, by banning them near schools and playgrounds, in publications with large youth readerships, on college campuses, and during prime-time television hours.[27] The prospect for such measures faded after a 1999 Supreme Court decision that struck down a federal ban on broadcast ads by casinos.[28] Many alcohol ad restrictions favored by critics focus on protecting impressionable children from ads. The casino ad ban was similar. It had been enacted to protect vulnerable people from gambling addiction, but the court invalidated it as an infringement of speech in those states where casino gambling was legal. It is likely that the court would look at an alcohol ad ban the same way. The court has also chipped away at other restrictions. Until 1996 Rhode Island banned price advertising for alcoholic beverages, claiming it was justified in doing so to promote temperance. However, the Supreme Court struck the ban down, saying that price advertising is protected by the First Amendment's free-speech guarantee.[29]

ARE RESTRICTIONS ON ALCOHOL AND TOBACCO ADS CONSTITUTIONAL?

Images and statements in advertising are speech. Therefore, proposals for muzzling liquor, beer, and wine companies raise constitutional issues. The First Amendment protects all speech from government-imposed curbs, but courts have distinguished *noncommercial* speech from *commercial* speech. The former is speech in the broad marketplace of ideas, encompassing political, scientific, and artistic expression. Such speech is broadly protected. The latter is speech intended to stimulate

business transactions, including advertising. This kind of speech receives less protection.

In both areas, the general principle used by courts to test restrictions is that the right to speech must be balanced against society's need to maintain the general welfare. The right of free speech is assumed to be a fundamental barrier against tyranny and is not restricted lightly. Courts will not permit censorship of noncommercial speech unless it poses an imminent threat to public welfare, as it would, for example, if a speaker incited violence or a writer tried to publish military secrets.

With respect to commercial speech, however, various restrictions are allowed. For example, ads for securities offerings can appear only in the austere format of a legal notice and tobacco ads are barred on radio and TV. Would courts approve additional restrictions on alcoholic beverage advertising?

The most important legal guidelines for weighing restraints on commercial speech are those set forth by the Supreme Court in 1980 in the *Central Hudson* case.[30] Here the Court struck down a New York regulation banning advertising by public utilities, a regulation intended to help conserve energy. Justice Lewis Powell, writing for the majority, set forth a four-part test to decide when commercial speech could be restricted.

- The ad in question should promote a lawful product and must be accurate. If an ad is misleading or suggests illegal activity, it does not merit protection.

- The government interest in restricting the particular commercial speech must be substantial, not trivial or unimportant.

- The advertising restriction must directly further the interest of the government. In other words, it should demonstrably help the government reach its public policy goal.

- The suppression of commercial speech must not be more extensive than is necessary to achieve the government's purpose.

[27] See, for example, the "Voluntary Alcohol Advertising Standards for Children Act," H.R. 1292, 105th Congress., 1st Sess. (1997), introduced by Representative Joseph P. Kennedy II (D-Massachusetts).
[28] *Greater New Orleans Broadcasting Association, Inc.* v. *U.S.,* 527 U.S. 173 (1999).
[29] *44 Liquormart* v. *Rhode Island,* 517 U.S. 484 (1996).

[30] *Central Hudson Gas & Electric Corp.* v. *Public Service Commission,* 447 U.S. 557.

All government actions to ban or restrict alcohol ads could be challenged by industry and would have to pass the four-part *Central Hudson* test to survive.

THE CURRENT FOCUS ON VOLUNTARY RESTRAINT

In the presence of constitutional obstacles to government-enacted restrictions, the most important restraints on alcohol advertising are voluntary limits adopted by companies and industry associations. A recent study by the Federal Trade Commission examined this self-regulation. It concluded that improvement was needed.[31] For example, the codes of the Beer Institute, the Distilled Spirits Council, and the Wine Institute all require that the majority of the audience in any media where an ad is placed be over 21 years old. However, only 30 percent of the population is younger than 21. Using a hypothetical example, if 45 percent of an audience is underage, that population group is overrepresented, but the placement would still meet industry guidelines. In addition, enforcement of industry codes is weak, and the FTC recommended creation of independent review boards to evaluate complaints.

Overall, voluntary advertising restrictions have tightened in recent years. One exception is the steady drive of distilled spirits makers to expand broadcast advertising. In 1948 the liquor industry voluntarily banned broadcast advertising. However, in 1996 Seagram & Sons began to air commercials on cable television and other companies followed. Brown-Forman began advertising Jack Daniels whiskey on local television stations. Liquor companies believe that limiting their messages to print media is no longer justified. For 20 years liquor sales have declined compared with sales of wine and beer. During this time liquor companies sat by watching as vintners and brewers saturated the airwaves. They do not wish to hold back any longer. They argue that the ethanol in all alcoholic drinks is the same, therefore, tying one arm behind their back in the competition for drinker's dollars makes no sense.

In 2001 NBC announced that it would be the first national network to run liquor ads. It adopted a set of voluntary guidelines requiring, among other things, that four months of public service messages about responsible drinking be run by the companies before product ads could appear. NBC thought it could tap into a new source of advertising revenue, but early in 2002 heavy criticism forced it to abort the plan after running only about 50 of the preliminary responsible drinking spots.[32] NBC executives backed off when congressional opponents scheduled hearings on the use of public airwaves for distilled spirits advertising. Their main concern was not that Congress would ban liquor ads. They saw that the hearings would open all alcohol ads to legislative scrutiny and they feared the loss of revenue from lucrative beer and wine commercials.

QUESTIONS

1. Are some beer, wine, or spirits ads misleading? What examples can you give? What is misleading in them?

2. Do alcoholic beverage companies that fight for their right to advertise also generally fulfill their corresponding ethical duty to be informative and truthful?

3. Do you support liquor ads on television and radio networks?

4. Do you believe there is a need for more restrictions on alcohol advertising? If so, what limits are needed? How could a ban or restrictions pass constitutional muster with respect to the *Central Hudson* guidelines?

[31] Federal Trade Commission, *Self Regulation in the Alcohol Industry* (Washington, DC: FTC, September 1999).

[32] Corie Brown, "NBC's Plans for Liquor Ads Have Dried Up," *Los Angeles Times,* March 21, 2002, p. C1.

Commercialism in Schools

For more than 100 years company commercials have invaded classrooms. The General Accounting Office (GAO) notes that "corporate-sponsored instructional materials can be traced back to at least 1890, when a paint company developed a handout on primary and secondary colors for schools to distribute in their art classes."[1] During the past decade, the school–business relationship has grown in visibility, in both elementary and secondary schools, to the point where children are exposed to corporate advertising from the time they get on a school bus in the morning until they finish their homework at night. This case is concerned with the causes of school commercialism, its costs and benefits to students, and recommendations for change.

ORIGINS OF THE NEW COMMERCIALISM

Two major trends in society spur increased commercial activity in schools. First, educational budgets across the nation are strained and educators are in search of new sources of money. Second, corporations have cash to market their products and services and see the younger generation as important consumers.

There are few school superintendents and teachers who do not believe more money is necessary to educate their students better. Many schools, especially in poorer districts, are in need of instruction materials such as textbooks, computers, furniture, technical knowledge, and even chalk. In many schools, teachers have less discretionary money than they had in years past. So, many of them dip into their meager earnings to help satisfy these needs. The poorer the school the more eager it is to attract corporate marketing dollars.

Almost 50 million children attend schools. They have enormous spending power. The Consumers Union estimates that elementary school children have disposable incomes of about $15 billion per year to buy food, beverages, clothes, toys, and games. Teenagers have about $57 billion to spend on such items. In addition, both groups influence the spending of their parents.[2] Corporations are aware that school is an ideal place to influence children to buy their products and to build lifetime loyalties to their brands.

THE CHANGE IN THE COMMERCIAL FOCUS

Local businesses supported schools in the past primarily with contributions of cash, time, equipment, and expertise. In exchange, business gained recognition, for example, in school papers, yearbooks, sports programs, and band uniforms. The commercial plugs generally were subtle and quiet. This arrangement was widely tolerated and abided without serious criticism. Today, however, the Consumers Union reports that

> corporate involvement in schools often goes beyond self-serving philanthropy to become commercial opportunism. Limited local promotions are overshadowed by national marketing or advocacy efforts from major companies that often put corporate logos, brand names, and other messages before school kids. Oil and utility companies, food companies, health providers, banks and credit card companies are among those who look for ways to get their messages to kids while they are a "captive audience" in school.[3]

The GAO, in a comprehensive study of this new corporate promotional activity, reports that school policies, corporate marketing techniques, state and local laws, and criticisms vary widely across the

[1] General Accounting Office, *Public Education: Commercial Activities in Schools,* GAO/HEHS–00–156, September 2000, pp. 5–6.

[2] Consumers Union, "Commercial Pressures on Kids at School," www.consumersunion.org/other/captivekids/pressures.htm.
[3] Ibid., p. 1.

United States. There is no uniformity. For example, only 19 states in 2000 had statutes or regulations concerned with commercial promotions in schools. In 14 of these states, the laws were not comprehensive and covered only specific types of activities. To illustrate, New Mexico permits advertising on and in school buses, but Virginia prohibits such advertising. Among the schools visited by GAO representatives, the visibility and types of promotional activities varied widely. In most areas, local school officials decide what commercial activities are permitted.[4]

TYPES OF COMMERCIAL ACTIVITIES IN SCHOOLS

Commercial activities can be classified into four categories, as follows: (1) the sale of products, (2) direct advertising, (3) indirect advertising, and (4) market research. Here are illustrations in each category.

Sale of Products

Every school visited by the GAO representatives had a products program to raise money. Included in this category are soft drinks, foods, class rings, school pictures, and band uniforms. Coca-Cola has arranged exclusive contracts with schools. One of the most lucrative was made with Colorado Springs School District 11. The contract entitled the district to $8.4 million over 10 years if it sold more than 70,000 cases of Coke a year.[5] Contracts have frequently been arranged for food companies to sell their products in schools or on school grounds. McDonald's, Burger King, Pizza Hut, and Taco Bell have facilities in thousands of schools.[6] Other companies sell candy bars, popcorn, and many so-called junk foods from vending machines. Schools also engage in fund-raising programs selling specific items—candy bars, cookies, magazines—to finance student activities. Schools endorse programs that give them cash based on a percentage of the sales price of a product purchased away from

school. There are many variations of such programs. For example, Hershey has a program giving schools cash for Hershey candy wrappers.

Direct Advertising

In this category are corporation logos placed in school hallways, on top of stadium scoreboards, in and outside of buses, and even on blackboards in classrooms. For example, Dr. Pepper arranged to have its logo painted on the rooftops of two high schools to be seen by passengers of planes landing at Dallas–Fort Worth International Airport.[7] Logos, brand names, and product ads are permitted by schools in all sorts of places, including student newspapers, yearbooks, equipment, uniforms, book covers, school calendars, blackboards, and buses.

Many students see commercials on Channel One, a television news program designed for broadcast into schools. Begun in 1989, Channel One claims it is viewed five days a week in 350,000 classrooms in about 12,000 schools. It is a 12-minute news program for students in grades 6 through 12 that has two minutes of commercials. Broadcasts are free to schools that make it mandatory in the curriculum. The incentive for a school to accept this arrangement is a free satellite dish, VCRs, and classroom TV monitors. For the Channel One producers, the incentive is to have two minutes of the program devoted to advertising for which Channel One is paid a fee by advertisers. The commercials are for brands such as Snickers, Pepsi, and Reebok. Schools are expected to sign a three-year contract requiring that Channel One news be broadcast on 90 percent of school days and in 80 percent of classrooms.[8]

Indirect Advertising

This category includes corporate-sponsored educational materials, contests, incentives, and corporate grants and gifts. Here is a sampling of specific programs from a collection of sponsored educational materials compiled by the Consumers Union.[9] This organization found such materials widespread among schools and in many forms. Included are

[4] General Accounting Office, *Public Education,* pp. 3–4.
[5] Steven Manning, "How Corporations Are Buying Their Way into America's Classrooms," *The Nation,* September 27, 1999 p. 12.
[6] Naomi Klein, *No Logo* (New York: Picador, 1999), p. 90.

[7] Ibid., p. 15.
[8] Consumers Union, "Evaluations," www.consumersunion.org/other/captivekids/evaluations.htm.
[9] Ibid., p. 4.

teaching packets covering classroom topics, videotapes, software, and printed materials. The subjects included solid-waste issues, nutrition lessons, health and safety issues, and lessons in economics, history, money management, and communications. The Consumers Union found that while much of this material did not contain blatant advertisements, "Nearly 80 percent contained biased or incomplete information, promoting a viewpoint that favors consumption of the sponsor's product or service or a position that favors the company or its economic agenda. A few contained significant inaccuracies."[10] For example, the American Coal Foundation said in its teaching materials that "the earth could benefit rather than be harmed from increased carbon dioxide."[11] Kellogg, in a lesson on breakfast foods, said that the sole thing to worry about was fat content, but did not mention sugar and sodium content in cereals.[12]

Covers Concepts Marketing Services, Inc., claims that more than 16 million students in almost 25,000 schools use its free book covers. Advertisers on the covers include Nike, McDonald's, and Hershey. According to Cover Concepts, most advertisers send "socially responsible" messages such as "Stay in School."[13]

Market Research

In this category are projects that conduct market research on students for commercial purposes. Techniques range from simple taste tests of soft drinks to tracking student behaviors at websites. The latter methodology is not widely employed, but it is attractive for marketers because it has potential for developing data that are helpful in targeting products to children. ZapMe, a California company that has practiced in this field since 1998, gives participating schools 15 personal computers, a high-speed Internet connection, and, sometimes, a printer and a computer lab. Each computer provides access to about 12,000 educational sites. Ads are shown on the computer screens, and schools agree to have the computers used an average of four hours each school day. In 2000 almost 1,800 schools were working with ZapMe. At these schools, the company can construct a profile of each student's Internet activity. The company says it has not used student data nor sold it to companies that customize ads for children.[14]

The GAO study reported that market research in schools is growing. Among the more traditional research techniques found in schools are taste tests, focus groups, and surveys. More recently, students have been invited to serve on Internet panels to respond to surveys.[15]

THE DEBATE ABOUT COMMERCIALISM IN SCHOOLS

The ubiquity, volume, and growth of commercial programs have created widespread controversy. The Consumers Union puts the issue in these terms: "Are the many promotional messages and commercial influences reaching kids at school undermining the integrity of education, or are they an acceptable price to pay for an infusion of materials, programs, and equipment into financially hard-pressed classrooms?"[16] Here are some arguments made by defenders and critics.

Critics of commercialism in schools make these charges.

- *Too much control of class materials is ceded to nonacademic sources.* Determination of teaching materials, curriculum, and other educational subjects should not be controlled by business interests. A self-serving business bias is inherent in most commercial arrangements. Business interests may or may not coincide with educational requirements. To prevent conflicts between the two, quid pro quo arrangements should be avoided.

[10] Ibid., p. 3.
[11] Ibid., p. 4.
[12] Ibid.
[13] Ibid., p. 23.

[14] General Accounting Office, *Public Education*, pp. 27–28.
[15] Ibid., p. 31.
[16] Consumers Union, "How Great a Problem?" *Captive Kids: A Report on Commercial Pressures on Kids at School,"* www.consumersunion.org/other/captivekids/problem.htm, July 7, 2000, p. 1. The following discussion of pros and cons, including quotations, is adapted from this publication unless otherwise specified.

- *Commercialism compromises the integrity of education.* The responsibility of teachers is to educate, not to sell candy bars, sugar water, chewing gum, or other products. Education has higher purposes. Influencing students to buy one product over another or learning biased business messages are not valid educational objectives. One teacher told of receiving many copies of a beautiful handbook on the Constitution and the Bill of Rights from the Philip Morris Company that he was to give to students but did not. The reason was that the company's logo was on the front and back covers of the books.[17] Gary Ruskin, director of Commercial Alert, a Washington, D.C., advocacy group, says there is "a mounting worry that this near-limitless expansion of ads comes at a cost: mercantile values such as advertising, marketing and profit trample other values such as those attached to home, family, religion, education and the environment."[18]

- *Ads in schools suggest endorsement.* Children are taught to trust the teacher and the integrity of the classroom. Advertisements in schools become enveloped in that ethos and give the appearance of endorsement. Products take on a credibility they would not otherwise have and may not deserve. Millions of menus for school foods are distributed carrying multiple advertisements for various products, including junk foods. Alex Molnar, professor of education at the University of Wisconsin–Milwaukee and a longtime scholar in children's education, observed that "One could argue that a person comes to the marketplace skeptical, as a consumer, but in school, everything that's going on is supposed to be good for you. When you take that venue and you exploit it for a particular special interest, you do a lot of damage to children."[19]

- *Lines between education and propaganda become blurred.* It is often easy to be blinded to the distinction between biased opinion and fact in an advertisement or in materials distributed by a corporate sponsor. Ads and materials distributed to teachers and students often omit uncomfortable facts, or fail to present an objective, complete analysis of the subject. So for example, a teacher may not be knowledgeable enough about nutrition to evaluate properly a sponsor's discussion of foods. Many programs and materials entering schools are not channeled through review boards that normally evaluate texts and other elements of curriculums.

- *Teachers may not have strong evaluation skills.* Alex Molner says "most teachers haven't been taught how to evaluate materials for commercialism and bias." "They don't see the need to," he says, and unless a teacher is knowledgeable in a topic, it many be very difficult to properly evaluate it for teaching purposes.[20]

- *In-school ads manipulate youthful, less experienced consumers.* Critics argue that people are influenced by advertising. To assume that children are not is naive. Business marketers are skilled in influencing people with their promotional materials. If they are not convinced of the benefits to their company, they are astute enough to avoid that expense. Studies are not unanimous on the influence of advertising on people. A study in Great Britain determined that even very young children could discriminate between advertising and programming on television. However, other studies draw different conclusions. And simple common sense suggests that repetitive brand messages sink in.

- *Commercial support should be replaced by pure philanthropy.* The Consumers Union comments on this point as follows: "Rather than sell students' minds to business in exchange for free programs or technology, schools need to pressure

[17] Ibid., p. 4.
[18] Gary Ruskin, "The Cost of Commercialism," *Multinational Monitor,* January–February, 1999, p. 9.
[19] Quoted in Constance L. Hays, "USA: New Report Examines Commercialism in Schools," *The New York Times,* September 14, 2000.

[20] Consumers Union, "How Great a Problem?" p. 7.

the corporate sector to live up to its nonmarketing responsibility to support schools, the institutions that are preparing the corporations' future workers, future consumers, and future citizens."[21] Corporate support for education would be more noble if it sprang from altruism. Strategic philanthropy, in which the corporation gets recognition and perhaps marketing advantage, is based on an inferior motive. And support predicated on a quid pro quo or contract is simply a business transaction that belies any respectable claim of deep concern for the well-being of education.

Defenders of the contracts and arrangements that schools make with corporations advance these arguments.

- *Corporate-sponsored programs give schools needed finances, equipment, and materials.* A fundamental reason for these programs is that state and local governments do not provide the funds educators say they need, and corporate programs help to bridge the gap. There is no question that many schools, especially in poorer counties, need financial support. More schools in such areas join in commercial contracts than do schools in richer districts. Because of these contracts, some of the neediest students are helped.

- *Commercialism is ubiquitous.* Students are exposed to commercialism everywhere, and as a result they are not unduly influenced by commercialism at school. At home television is awash in commercials, and in a short time they learn to tune them out. Brian Young, a professor at the University of Exeter in Great Britain, in a study of the impact of advertising on children found that "children as young as six can understand the purpose of commercials and can distinguish them from entertainment."[22] Thus, students are not gullible objects in a game controlled by corporate marketers.

- *Teachers can evaluate materials and handle them appropriately.* Teachers can judge commercialism and bias in the materials submitted by business, say the defenders. Indeed, they can use materials where they do detect bias as lessons on how to evaluate commercials. Teachers receiving materials in their academic subjects can determine their objectivity and accuracy. "It doesn't take the words provided by Exxon for material to be one-sided," argues one teacher, "nor should we assume that because something is sponsored by a corporate donor it is automatically bad."[23] Not all materials offered schools by business are defective for teaching young minds.

- *Business has the information and the resources to prepare effective teaching materials.* Materials concerned with a company's business may provide insightful and unique information for both teachers and students. Such materials may be especially valuable in schools that are short of textbooks. One teacher told the Consumers Union, "If it's free (and good) it's for me! Great, glossy, up to date, motivating materials . . . are a heck of a lot better than the 1966 textbooks that many teachers are refurbishing to pass out each September."[24]

- *Business has a long and continuing record of contributing to education beyond the financial support that comes from commercial arrangements.* Actually, business has been a longtime philanthropic supporter of education. Corporate charitable contributions, including cash and in-kind gifts, amounted to $10.8 billion in 2000. Over the years, approximately 30 percent of corporate charitable contributions have gone to education. Most of this has been given to higher education, but in recent years more has gone to grades K through 12. Corporate giving is driven by two motives. First, business leaders are concerned about broad problems in education and want to do something about them. Second, they see the need to train workers better. In fact, business philanthropy for education is substantial and growing.

21 Ibid., p. 6.
22 "Kid Gloves," *The Economist,* January 6, 2001, p. 60.
23 Consumers Union, "How Great a Problem?" p. 2.
24 Ibid., p. 3.

ETHICAL GUIDELINES FOR CORPORATE INVOLVEMENT IN SCHOOLS

In 1990 the Milwaukee Conference on Corporate Involvement in Schools, a project of the University of Wisconsin–Milwaukee, held a two-day conference that produced ethical guidelines for corporate activities in schools. Here are a few of the guidelines.

- Corporate involvement shall not require students to observe, listen to, or read advertising.

- Selling or providing access to a captive audience in the classroom for commercial purposes is exploitation and a violation of public trust.

- Since school property and time are publicly funded, selling or providing free access to advertising on school property outside the classroom raises ethical and legal issues.

- Corporate involvement must support the goals and objectives of the schools. Curriculum and instruction are the prerogatives of educators.

- Programs of corporate involvement must be structured to meet an identified education need, not a commercial motive, and must be evaluated for educational effectiveness by the school/district on an ongoing basis.

- Corporate involvement should not limit the discretion of schools and teachers in the use of sponsored materials.

- Sponsor recognition and corporate logos should be for identification rather than commercial purposes.[25]

QUESTIONS

1. What motivates the growth of commercialism in schools?

2. What are the principal arguments in favor of commercial activities?

3. What are the principal arguments against commercial activities?

4. Appraise the merit of the ethical guidelines for commercial activities set forth at the end of the case study.

[25] Ibid., pp. 9–10.

Part **Eight**

Human Resources

Chapter **Seventeen**

The Changing Face of Organizational Life

Ford Motor Company

Henry Ford (1863–1947) was a brilliant inventor. After incorporating the Ford Motor Company in 1903, he designed one car after another, naming each chassis after a letter of the alphabet. In 1908, he began selling the Model T, a utilitarian, crank-started auto that came only in black. An early Model T cost $850, but Ford introduced the first moving auto assembly line and, by 1924, mass output lowered the price to $290. He sold 15.5 million of them before production ended in 1927 and the Model A was introduced.

Hidden behind the success story of the Model T, and less known, is the darker side of Ford Motor Company. Henry Ford was an obstinate man, obsessed with power, iron-willed, dictatorial, and cynical about human nature. He spied on his employees in their homes to see if they smoked or drank. Believing that workers were motivated by fear, he created a tense atmosphere marked by frequent dismissals that were capricious and arbitrary. Managers arrived at work to find their desks chopped to pieces. One morning, an entire department of 84 office workers came in to find their desks gone. Many managers had no job title; this made it less likely that they would establish a power base. Sometimes two managers were given the same duties and the one failing to thrive in the competition was fired. Shy by nature, Ford hired sadistic lieutenants to carry out these petty assassinations while at a safe remove he set the tone. In his autobiography, he wrote that a "great business is really too big to be human."[1]

---

[1] Henry Ford, *My Life and Work* (Garden City, NY: Doubleday, 1923), p. 263.

As the firm grew, Henry Ford's authoritarian style became embedded in its informal culture. Independent managers left, and he was surrounded by sycophants who would have jumped into the Detroit River if he had asked. They, in turn, were ruthless and autocratic with their subordinates.[2]

This internal atmosphere left power in Ford's hands, but it hindered adaptation to external forces. Despite warnings in the form of fast-dropping market share in the mid-1920s, Ford Motor Company failed utterly to anticipate a sea change in the auto market. It clung to the spartan Model T even as consumers turned to the styling changes, closed body design, and model hierarchy offered by General Motors. Finally, in 1927, Ford had to suspend production, stilling its great River Rouge assembly plant for seven months while the Model A was hurriedly designed. It never recovered the market share it once held.

Although the company regained its footing and made successful new models over the years, authoritarianism remained firmly entrenched. In 1945 Henry Ford himself felt its sting when he was ousted in a coup engineered by family members. He was replaced by his grandson, Henry Ford II, who also proved to be an autocrat.

In the early 1980s Ford suffered three years of disastrous losses, mainly due to heightened international competition. Japanese auto companies had captured 20 percent of the domestic market. The company studied Japanese management and decided to emulate its focus on teamwork and continuous quality improvement. It set out to make an innovative world-class sedan using teams similar to those used by Japanese car makers.

In Japanese management philosophy, competing personalities and individualism are thought to hamper productivity. So Ford tried to change its corporate culture. Over the years, it had tended to select autocrats for management positions. A study of 2,000 Ford managers classified 76 percent as "noncreative types who are comfortable with strong authority" (as compared to about 38 percent of the population).[3] To facilitate change, thousands of managers went to workshops on participative management.

Ford was rewarded for its efforts when the innovative Taurus sedan appeared in 1985. It was a quick success and became the best-selling car in America between 1993 and 1995. In 1994 Ford made an extraordinary $5.3 billion in profits, a sum exceeded by only one other company in the world (Royal Dutch/Shell with $6.2 billion). Yet in that year, a new Ford chairman, Alexander Trotman, started Ford 2000, a radical change program to prepare the company for an even more competitive global car market.

Ford 2000 revised the company's organization chart, dividing it by product lines instead of by regions and countries. It tore apart bureaucracy and

[2] Anne Jardim, *The First Henry Ford: A Study in Personality and Business Leadership* (Cambridge, MA: MIT Press, 1970), pp. 114–15.
[3] Melinda G. Builes and Paul Ingrassia, "Ford's Leaders Push Radical Shift in Culture as Competition Grows," *The Wall Street Journal,* December 3, 1985, p. A1.

instilled a new teamwork philosophy. Layers of middle management disappeared. Tasks were defined in meetings instead of by superiors. Promotions and performance reviews were done by committees. To cut costs and speed timetables for new models, product design, engineering, and manufacturing, once separate divisions, merged. These changes were traumatic for workers. More than 25,000 managers left hierarchical slots and moved into teams. Jobs were eliminated and early retirements encouraged.

Although Ford's profit performance was strong, the Ford 2000 upheaval failed to make it a more dominant competitor. Its combined market share of cars and trucks in the critical U.S. and European markets slowly declined. Competition in the global automobile industry is relentless. Inroads against competitors are excruciatingly difficult due to a worldwide production overcapacity. Because of the potential for oversupply, car companies cannot easily raise output to increase revenue. For the same reason, and because brand loyalty in consumers is declining, they cannot inflate prices. The only way to create profits in this situation is to cut costs and increase net income on each car sold. Leaner organizations save money. So does new technology, and, as part of Ford 2000, the company invested in new manufacturing techniques such as computers that not only design cars but automatically cut the tools and dies used in their production and then configure assembly lines to make them.

In January 1999 a new CEO, Jacques Nasser, took over at Ford. Nasser, a man of relentless energy who functioned on three hours of sleep, harbored visions of turning Ford into a high-flying company like General Electric and, perhaps, saw himself as a legendary leader in the mold of Jack Welch. He pushed methods that paralleled those used at GE, vowing to remake Ford's culture yet again. He introduced a GE-like forced ranking system to evaluate managers. He threw out the Ford 2000 total quality management program and brought in Six Sigma, the quality method used at GE. He diversified Ford into auto-related services, buying muffler shops and auto junkyards. He launched partnership agreements with Microsoft Corp. and Yahoo! Inc. to move Ford into e-commerce. He also restitched the Ford 2000 organization chart, putting regional divisions back in and adding 14 new vice presidents.

Ford earned a record profit in 1999. However, troubles soon appeared. Introducing Six Sigma had disrupted Ford's quality program, and the company slipped into last place in quality among the seven largest automakers. Employees sued over the forced ranking system, claiming it led to age discrimination. A crisis hit in the summer of 2000, when the National Highway and Transportation Safety Administration connected Firestone tire failures on Ford Explorers to accidents causing 173 deaths and 700 injuries. Questions about the safety of the Explorer were raised. In a public spectacle, Ford traded accusations of blame with Firestone. Firestone recalled 6.5 million tires and eventually refused to sell any more tires to Ford. Ford decided to recall another 13 million Firestone tires at a cost of nearly $3 billion.

Stories appeared in the press saying that William Clay Ford, Jr., the great grandson of Henry Ford and chairman of the board, was unhappy with Nasser. The descendants of Henry Ford still own enough stock in the company to exercise a controlling interest. In October 2001 Nasser was deposed and William Clay Ford, Jr., became the new CEO. Early in 2002 he announced still another restructuring. Despite Ford 2000 and the Nasser initiatives, the company had failed to get its costs under control. Toyota, for example, made vehicles for $1,800 less than Ford. Quality problems had forced several expensive vehicle recalls apart from tire recalls. Ford would have to shrink. Factories that could have made one million cars a year had to be closed. Four car models were cut. And 35,000 positions would be pruned from the company's workforce of 345,000.

This short history of Ford Motor Company illustrates how a set of forces—a founder's example, leadership, management philosophy, international competition, and technological change—shape the workplace. In this chapter we explain how these and other forces shape working life for the 3.8 billion mortals toiling in the global economy.

EXTERNAL FORCES CHANGING THE WORKPLACE

Those who work today, especially those who work in large corporations, are swept up in turbulence caused by five environmental forces: (1) demographic change, (2) technological change, (3) structural change, (4) competition, and (5) government intervention. These forces often interact, magnifying their power. A discussion of each one follows.

Demographic Change

Population dynamics slowly but continuously alter labor forces. Out of a 2000 population of 275 million Americans, about half, or 141 million, comprise the civilian labor force as either working or unemployed (the rest are retired, disabled, students, homemakers, children under age 16, or not counted because they got unreported wages). This is the third-largest labor force in the world, though it pales in comparison to China's 751 million and India's 441 million.[4]

Historically, the American labor force has grown rapidly and continuously. It continues to grow, but more slowly, at a rate expected to be about 1.1 percent a year through 2010.[5] Amid this slower overall workforce expansion, however, the number of workers in some demographic

---

[4] Figures are from the U.S. Bureau of Labor Statistics and World Bank, *World Development Indicators 2001* (Washington, DC: World Bank, April 2001), table 2.2. Figures for China and India are for 1999.
[5] Howard N. Fullerton, Jr., and Mitra Toossi, "Labor Force Projections to 2010: Steady Growth and Changing Composition," *Monthly Labor Review,* November 2001, table 1.

TABLE 17.1 The Changing Civilian Labor Force: 2000–2010 (in Thousands)

Demographic Component	2000	Percent of Labor Force in 2000	2010	Percent of Labor Force in 2010	Percent Change in Numbers
Total labor force	140,863	100	157,721	100	11.9
Men	75,247	53.4	82,221	52.1	9.2
Women	65,616	46.6	75,500	47.9	15.1
Children 10–14	0	0	0	0	0
White	117,574	83.5	128,043	81.2	8.9
White male	63,861	45.5	68,159	43.2	6.7
Black	16,603	11.8	20,041	12.7	20.7
Hispanic origin	15,368	10.9	20,947	13.3	36.3
Asian and other*	6,687	4.7	9,636	6.1	44.1
Median age	39.3 years		40.6 years		

*Includes Pacific Islanders, American Indians, and Alaska Natives.
Source: Bureau of Labor Statistics.

categories is growing faster than in others, producing incremental but significant changes. Table 17.1 shows data for the 2000 labor force and projects current trends to the year 2010.

Table 17.1 shows that, proportionately, Hispanics and Asians are increasing their numbers faster than whites and blacks. By 2010 Hispanics will replace blacks as the second-largest ethnic group in the labor force. Asians are the fastest-growing group in terms of percentage increase, but they will remain the smallest ethnic category at a little over 6 percent. Since the 1970s women have increased participation more rapidly than men, and although this trend is slowing, it will continue until 2010.

These changes mean that the workforce continues to become more diverse in gender and ethnicity. In percentage terms, however, the change will not be great. Whites will decline by only 2.3 percent. Hispanics will increase by 2.4 percent and Asians by 1.4 percent. Blacks will increase by less than 1 percent. These are modest shifts. However, businesses in cosmopolitan areas will experience more rapid diversity increases than these national figures suggest.

The workforce is also aging. High fertility rates following World War II created a baby boom generation born between 1946 and 1964. As this generation entered the labor market in the 1970s, the median age of the workforce began to decline, reaching a low of 34.6 years in 1980. The baby boomers are now a bulge of workers in their late thirties to midfifties. As they age, the median age of the workforce rises, and it is predicted to reach 40.6 years in 2010. Because the nation's fertility rate has declined since the baby boom years, generational cohorts of workers following the baby boomers are smaller. As these aging mainstays of the labor force retire in large numbers over the next two decades, a shortage of skilled and experienced workers may arise. If this shortage becomes real, it could hurt productivity and economic growth. Employers who adopt more flexible work arrangements may entice baby boomers to stay on the job longer.[6]

Graying of the workforce is faster in other developing nations. It is caused by increases in life expectancy and by declines in fertility. Life expectancy has increased markedly in most nations. In the United States it has risen from 47 in 1900 to 77 in 2001.[7] Birthrates have fallen in more wealthy societies and are now below replacement rates in many European nations and in Japan. In Germany and Japan, for example, the fertility rate of 1.4 births per woman is below the replacement rate of 2.1 and the populations of these nations are predicted to decline after 2010. Because fewer young workers will arrive in the next 10 to 20 years, these countries face a challenge in filling entry- and lower-level jobs.

While many developed nations confront population declines and all have aging workforces, some Third World nations have explosively growing, youthful populations. Since the 1970s the United States has absorbed a huge wave of immigrants from these nations and currently takes in an estimated 980,000 persons each year.[8] The influx of immigrants has shaped the American labor force by accelerating its overall growth, increasing the number of Hispanics and Asians, and slowing the rise in average age. Since the fertility rate in the United States is 2.1, equal to the replacement rate, immigration may prevent the population declines facing Europe and Japan.[9] Immigration gives the United States a long-run competitive advantage in labor costs. Japan and some European countries have tight immigration laws. The Japanese want to preserve racial purity and have difficulty integrating non-Japanese into their workplaces. Many European nations are strongly ethnocentric and restrict immigration. However, immigration always brings an influx of younger workers who are less costly and more adaptable.

As indicated in Table 17.1 there are no children aged 10–14 in the labor force. Child labor is insignificant in the labor forces of developed nations, but elsewhere it is so common that children average about 12 percent of the total world labor force. Child labor is associated with poverty, low educational opportunity, and heavy dependence on the agricultural sector. It declines with economic development.[10] Rates are

---

[6] General Accounting Office, *Older Workers: Demographic Trends Pose Challenges for Employers and Workers,* GAO–02–85, November 2001, p. 23.

[7] Robert A. Rosenblatt, "U.S. Not as Gray as 31 Other Countries," *Los Angeles Times,* December 15, 2001, p. A17.

[8] Fullerton and Toossi, "Labor Force Projections to 2010," p. 24.

[9] Robert J. Samuelson, "The Specter of Global Aging," *Washington Post National Weekly Edition,* March 6–11, 2001, p. 17.

[10] Iftikhar Ahmed, *Getting Rid of Child Labor* (Geneva: International Labor Organization/ International Programme on the Elimination of Child Labor, 2000), pp. 25–32.

highest in sub-Saharan Africa, where children average 30 percent of labor forces. However, in sheer numbers, most child labor is found in Asia. Almost 70 percent of all working children toil in that part of the world, most of them in east Asian nations.[11] The prevalence of child labor is declining rapidly. The current estimate of 12 percent is a drop from 30 percent in 1980.[12]

Technological Change

Yellow Cab installed a new navigation system to manage its fleet of 450 taxis in Dallas. Signals from a global positioning device in each cab are relayed by satellite to dispatchers, who can see their exact street location on a monitor. When a customer calls, the system finds the closest cab and calculates the fare to a destination. This technology increases Yellow Cab's efficiency in many ways. Not only does it save gas, but, fortuitously, it stopped a payola system in which dispatchers gave more lucrative runs to drivers who kicked back some of the fare.[13]

Technological change has many impacts on work. It affects the number and type of jobs available. Invention of the airplane, for example, created new job titles such as pilot and flight attendant. Webmasters, or employees who design and update websites, emerged with the rise of the Internet. New machines are used by management to raise productivity and reduce costs. Robots in auto manufacturing made American companies more competitive in cost and quality with Japanese automakers. Automated teller machines at banks both increased daily transactions and reduced the number of employees necessary to do them.

Automation has a turbulent impact on employment because it creates jobs for the architects of the machine age while displacing traditional manufacturing and service jobs. Overall, the number of jobs available in the United States has continuously increased, absorbing new workers in the growing labor force. This is projected to continue. However, automation causes significant job loss in less-skilled manufacturing and service occupations. In the coal-mining industry, for example, mechanization has eliminated 300,000 pick-and-shovel jobs since the 1950s. The movement to robotics in the 1980s put almost 40,000 robots on U.S. assembly lines and eliminated two-thirds of all assembly-line jobs by 1990. In service industries, the blows have been softer but still telling. Between 1987 and 1998, 20 percent of telephone operators were eliminated due to au-

---

[11] Kaushik Basu, *Child Labor: Cause, Consequence and Cure, with Remarks on International Labor Standards* (Washington, DC: World Bank, December 5, 1998), p. 9.
[12] Figures in this paragraph are based on 1998 labor force statistics for 148 nations in World Bank, *World Development Indicators 2000* (Washington, DC: World Bank, April 2000), table 2.3.
[13] Art Pine, "Technology May Not Drive Nation's Productivity, but It Can Hail a Taxi," *Los Angeles Times,* December 27, 1997, p. A20.

tomation of their services, even as the average number of daily conversations increased by more than 600 percent.[14]

Structural Change

The American economy has been powerfully shaped by three long-term structural trends. Their action is similar in all industrialized nations, where they shape the economy and, with it, the job landscape.

First, the *agricultural sector* has declined from predominance to near insignificance as an occupation. In colonial America, farming occupied 95 percent of Americans, but in 2000 it employed only 2.4 percent as fewer and larger farms delivered the nation's food supply using intensive and highly automated crop and animal agriculture.[15] In the 1920s, for example, the largest poultry farm in the country had a flock of 500 chickens; today, up to 100,000 birds are raised in a single, long, narrow poultry building, and multibuilding operations raise millions of birds at once. The Bureau of Labor Statistics predicts that the number of agricultural workers will fall a little more, to 2.3 percent of the labor force, by 2010.

Second, the percentage of workers employed in the *goods-producing sector* has declined for many decades.[16] In 1950 industry jobs dominated, occupying 78 percent of workers, but by 2000 this kind of employment lost its prominence and occupied only 17.7 percent of the labor force. By 2010 these occupations are predicted to slump further to 16.1 percent. There are many reasons for the fall of manufacturing work, but the two most significant are productivity growth, primarily through automation, and relocation of assembly to lower-wage countries. In steel production, for example, foreign competition caused a steady drop in U.S. jobs from a peak of 620,400 in 1953 to only 110,000 in 1998. Since 1970, however, the amount of steel made per hour by each U.S. worker has more than doubled because of automated production methods. Goods-producing jobs have declined only as a percentage of the overall labor force. In absolute numbers, employment in this sector has held steady since 1980, and manufacturing output in the United States is prodigious, adding more than $1.5 trillion annually to the GDP, a sum that exceeds the French GDP.

[14] Stephen Franklin, "Telephone Operators Are among Those Being Displaced by Technology," *San Jose Mercury News,* September 6, 1998; U.S. Census Bureau, *Statistical Abstract of the United States:* 2000, 120th ed. (Washington, DC, 2000), table 917.

[15] Sector employment figures in this section are from Jay M. Berman, "Industry Output and Employment Projections to 2010," *Monthly Labor Review,* November 2001, tables 1 and 4; and from various editors of the *Statistical Abstract of the United States.* Sector employment percentages for 2000 do not total 100 percent; the missing increment of 7.8 percent includes private household wage and salary earners and nonagricultural self-employed.

[16] The goods-producing sector includes primarily manufacturing but also mining and construction.

TABLE 17.2

Comparative Occupational Structures of Eight Developed Nations: 1999*

	Agriculture	Industry	Services
Australia	5%	21%	74%
Canada	4	22	75
France	4	24	72
Germany	3	34	64
Italy	6	33	62
Japan	5	31	64
Sweden	3	24	73
United Kingdom†	2	26	72

*Numbers may not equal 100 percent due to rounding.
†Figures are for 1998.
Source: Bureau of Labor Statistics, *Comparative Civilian Labor Force Statistics: Ten Countries 1959–2000* (Washington, DC: U.S. Department of Labor, March 16, 2001), table 7.

Third, there is explosive growth in the *service sector*, which includes jobs in retailing, transportation, health care, and other occupations that add value to manufactured goods. Service jobs rose from 10 percent of the workforce in 1950 to 72.1 percent in 2000 and are predicted to rise to 77 percent in 2010. The nation's fastest-growing occupation, business computer services, exemplifies this explosive growth. It employed 271,000 people in 1979, then grew by 773 percent to employ 2.1 million in 2000.

The action of these three trends is remarkably similar in all developed nations. Table 17.2 shows how they have shaped the occupational structure elsewhere. The eight nations in the table have all seen long-term job losses in agriculture and industry and steep growth in service sector employment. Less developed nations that have not yet started to industrialize tend to have large agricultural sectors. Some developing nations are dominated by their industry sectors. For example, industry is 49 percent of GDP in China, 46 percent in Malaysia, and 43 percent in Indonesia.[17]

Structural change is also a major factor in the decline of labor unions. Before the wave of protective legislation passed in the 1930s, unions represented only 5 percent of industrial workers, but this tripled to 15 percent by 1940 and reached a zenith of 25 percent in the 1950s.[18] Unions raised wages and increased benefits for blue-collar workers, and these improvements rippled through the entire manufacturing sector because nonunionized companies had to approximate the welfare levels of union workers if they wished to prevent unionization.

In the 1970s, however, union membership in the private sector began a long slide as structural change eroded its base of factory workers. Employment shifted to service industries and to industries employing

[17] World Bank, *World Development Indicators,* table 4.2.
[18] Bureau of the Census, *Statistical Abstract of the United States: 1956* (Washington, DC: U.S. Government Printing Office, 1956) table 271.

knowledge workers who are difficult for industrial unions to organize and to low-wage countries where unions are illegal or weak. By 2001 unions represented only 9 percent of private sector employees in the United States. The upward push on wages and benefits that unions provide for both members and nonmembers has weakened commensurately. Today, the United States has lower union representation of the private labor force than other developed economies. In the European Union, on the other hand, although union membership declined during the 1990s in every member-nation, roughly a third to a half of all workers remain unionized, except in France, where union membership is only slightly higher than in the United States. This is one reason that labor costs are higher in some European nations than in the United States.[19]

Competitive Pressures

Recent trends have intensified competition for American companies. Customers demand higher quality, better service, and faster new-product development. Deregulation of large industries such as airlines, telecommunications, trucking, and electric utilities has stirred formerly complacent rivals. Foreign trade grew from just 9 percent of the U.S. economy in 1960 to 29 percent in 2000, with most of this growth coming in the 1990s.[20] Corporations are increasingly challenged by foreign competitors in both domestic and foreign markets. These foreign competitors have many advantages, including lower labor costs, a strong dollar, and, sometimes, higher worker productivity.

American workers, and workers in other developed nations, including Japan and those of the European Union, are exposed to a global labor market that contains pools of low-cost workers. In less affluent, less industrialized countries, wages are lower for many reasons, including oversupply of labor compared with demand, low living standards, local currency devaluations, labor policies of authoritarian regimes where workers have no political power, and wage competition among countries seeking to attract jobs.

American workers are, by global standards, extremely expensive. In 2000 the average hourly compensation for a manufacturing worker in the United States was $19.86 an hour. This was not the highest in the world; that distinction went to German workers making $24.01 an hour. Workers in Japan and seven European nations also cost more than Americans. However, because of a weakening euro, compensation costs in the highest-paying European nations have fallen much closer to American levels. And elsewhere an hour of labor costs far less, for

[19] Greg J. Bamber and Russell D. Lansbury, eds., *International & Comparative Employment Relations,* rev. ed. (London: Sage Publications, 1998), app. pp. 357–59.
[20] Betty Su, "The U.S. Economy to 2010," *Monthly Labor Review,* November 2001, table 1.

example, $5.98 in Taiwan, $4.75 in Portugal, $2.46 in Mexico, and less than $0.50 in Sri Lanka.[21]

Given this wage variation, companies in some industries can no longer afford to do low-skilled manufacturing in the United States and contract to have it done in a foreign country. Or they find ways to increase productivity of domestic labor by reducing employees to a minimum and applying technology to enlarge their output. Either way, there are generally fewer jobs for American workers in the occupation affected. Similar wage competition exists in globalizing service industries.

Government Intervention

Historically, a strong laissez-faire current in American economic philosophy made governments at all levels reluctant to interfere with the *employment contract,* or the agreement by which an employee exchanges his or her labor in return for specific pay and working conditions. Today, government intervention is extensive and growing, but this is a twentieth-century trend.

Before 1860, the number of persons employed as wage earners in factories, mines, railroads, and other workplaces was relatively small. But with industrialization, their numbers skyrocketed. Between 1860 and 1890, the number of wage earners rose from 1.33 million to 4.25 million, an increase of 320 percent.[22] This rapid growth in numbers, which would continue into the 1930s, created a new class interest, and it was an aggrieved one. In the hard-hearted wisdom of the day, employers treated workers as simply production costs to be minimized; there was relentless downward pressure on wages and reluctance to improve working conditions.

Liberty of Contract

Prior to the 1930s, there was little government intervention on behalf of workers, and what there was consisted mostly of feeble state safety regulations and laws to limit working hours. In the late nineteenth and early twentieth centuries, strong majorities on the Supreme Court adhered to the *liberty of contract doctrine.* This doctrine held that employers and workers should be free from government intervention to negotiate all aspects of the employment contract, including wages, hours, duties, and conditions.[23] For many years, the Court struck down state and federal laws that

---

[21] Department of Labor, News Release, "International Comparisons of Hourly Compensation Costs for Production Workers in Manufacturing, 2000," September 25, 2001, table 2. The figures are for total compensation cost, including wages, benefits, employer expenditures for social insurance, and, in some countries, labor taxes.

[22] Arthur M. Schlesinger, *Political and Social Growth of the United States: 1852–1933.* (New York: Macmillan, 1935), p. 203.

[23] The liberty of contract majority first emerged in *Allgeyer* v *Louisiana,* 106 U.S. 578 (1897), where Justice Rufus W. Peckham grounded it in the due process clause of the Fourteenth Amendment, which states that no state "can deprive any person of life, liberty, or property, without due process of law."

Turn-of-the-century cartoonist Art Young drew this cynical view of the lopsided employment contract in the days before labor unions and laws protecting worker rights.

interfered with this theoretical freedom. Such laws were regarded as "meddlesome interferences with the rights of the individual."[24]

The great flaw in the liberty of contract doctrine was that it assumed equal bargaining power for all parties, whereas employers unquestionably predominated. For employers, liberty of contract was the liberty to exploit. Employees could be fired at will and had to accept virtually any working conditions. Unchallenged dominion of employers opened the door to the negligent treatment of workers that fueled the labor union movement, a social movement to empower workers. Employers resisted demands for kinder treatment of workers and bitterly fought the rise of unions.

[24] Justice Peckham, writing for a 5–4 majority in *Lockner* v. *New York,* 198 U.S. 61 (1905). The decision struck down an 1897 New York State law limiting bakery employees to 60-hour weeks.

Waves of Regulation

It was not until the 1930s that government regulation of the workplace began to redress the huge power imbalance favoring employers. One major step was the Norris-LaGuardia Anti-Injunction Act of 1932, which struck down a type of employer–employee agreement called, in the colorful language of unionists, a "yellow dog contract." These were agreements that workers would not join unions. Employers virtually extorted signatures on them when workers were hired, and hapless applicants had little choice but to sign if they wanted the job—and jobs were scarce in the 1930s. If union organizing began, companies went to court, where judges enforced the agreements. The Norris-LaGuardia Act outlawed yellow dog contracts, overturning a 1908 Supreme Court decision that upheld them under the liberty of contract doctrine.[25]

The new law encouraged unions. It was soon followed by the National Labor Relations Act of 1935, which guaranteed union organizing and bargaining rights, and by other laws that fleshed out a body of rules for labor relations. After the 1930s, employers still dominated the employment contract, but company power over wages and working conditions was increasingly checked by unions.

Figure 17.1 shows how this first wave of federal workplace regulation, which established union rights, was followed by two subsequent waves. A second wave, between 1963 and 1974, moved federal law into new areas, protecting civil rights, worker health and safety, and pension rights. A third wave, between 1986 and 1996, again broadened the scope of federal law to address additional, and somewhat narrower, employment issues. During this period, Congress enacted the following laws.

- A provision in the Comprehensive Omnibus Budget Reconciliation Act of 1986 allows separated workers to continue in group health plans for up to 18 months at their own expense.

- The Immigrant Reform and Control Act of 1986 protects work rights of legal aliens and prohibits hiring illegal aliens.

- The Worker Adjustment and Retraining Act of 1988 requires companies with more than 100 workers to give 60 days' notice prior to plant closings or large layoffs.

- The Employee Polygraph Protection Act of 1988 prohibits the use of lie detectors to screen job applicants and narrows grounds for using the tests to detect employee theft or sabotage.

- The Drug-Free Workplace Act of 1988 requires companies with federal contracts to take measures against drug abuse.

---

[25] *Adair* v. *United States,* 291 U.S. 293 (1908).

FIGURE 17.1 **A Chronology of Major Workplace Regulations**

This figure shows the historical march of major statutes (and one executive order) regulating labor–management and employer–employee relations. Note the existence of three rough clusters or waves of intervention.

Source: Adapted from General Accounting Office, "Testimony: Rethinking the Federal Role in Worker Protection and Workforce Development," 1995, p. 5.

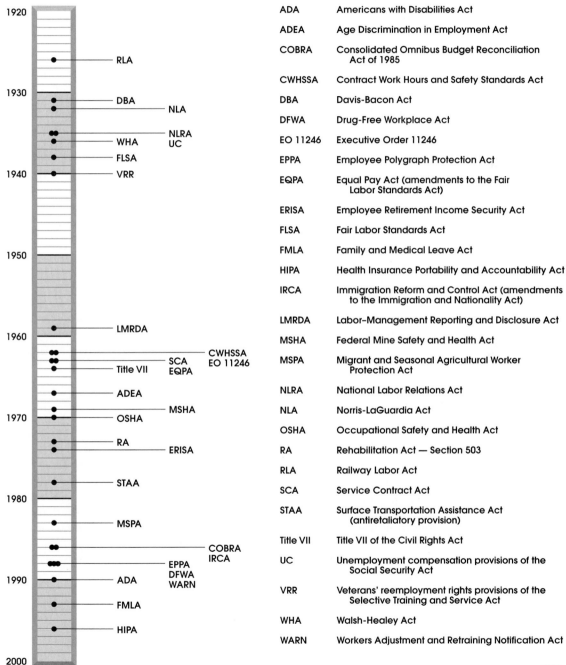

ADA	Americans with Disabilities Act
ADEA	Age Discrimination in Employment Act
COBRA	Consolidated Omnibus Budget Reconciliation Act of 1985
CWHSSA	Contract Work Hours and Safety Standards Act
DBA	Davis-Bacon Act
DFWA	Drug-Free Workplace Act
EO 11246	Executive Order 11246
EPPA	Employee Polygraph Protection Act
EQPA	Equal Pay Act (amendments to the Fair Labor Standards Act)
ERISA	Employee Retirement Income Security Act
FLSA	Fair Labor Standards Act
FMLA	Family and Medical Leave Act
HIPA	Health Insurance Portability and Accountability Act
IRCA	Immigration Reform and Control Act (amendments to the Immigration and Nationality Act)
LMRDA	Labor-Management Reporting and Disclosure Act
MSHA	Federal Mine Safety and Health Act
MSPA	Migrant and Seasonal Agricultural Worker Protection Act
NLRA	National Labor Relations Act
NLA	Norris-LaGuardia Act
OSHA	Occupational Safety and Health Act
RA	Rehabilitation Act — Section 503
RLA	Railway Labor Act
SCA	Service Contract Act
STAA	Surface Transportation Assistance Act (antiretaliatory provision)
Title VII	Title VII of the Civil Rights Act
UC	Unemployment compensation provisions of the Social Security Act
VRR	Veterans' reemployment rights provisions of the Selective Training and Service Act
WHA	Walsh-Healey Act
WARN	Workers Adjustment and Retraining Notification Act

- The Americans with Disabilities Act of 1990 prohibits discrimination against the disabled and requires employers to make reasonable accommodations for people with substantial physical or mental impairments.

- The Family and Medical Leave Act of 1993 gives workers the right to take up to 12 weeks of unpaid leave for family reasons such as childbirth or illness.

- The Health Insurance Portability and Accountability Act of 1996 guarantees that preexisting medical problems will continue to be covered by health insurance when workers switch jobs.

Altogether, approximately 200 federal laws have been enacted since the 1930s, including amendments to original statutes, so only the major ones are shown in Figure 17.1. These laws have been based on the dominant perspective of 1930s reformers that the relationship between labor and management is antagonistic. Based on this model, a broad and complex regulatory structure has been created over more than 70 years to counterbalance the perceived weakness of workers in the employment contract with corporations.

Federal regulations are only part of the growing web of regulation that fetters employers. State courts and legislatures have created additional rules that employers must follow. Legislatures in many states have enacted laws that go beyond federal requirements, turning the states into "policy laboratories" that experiment with the cutting edges of employment law.[26] For example, Vermont gives workers 24 hours of leave to attend school functions and go to medical appointments. Texas bars suits against former employers who write recommendation letters. Louisiana bans employment discrimination due to the sickle cell trait, and each year more states are adopting laws to ban discrimination based on genetic test results.

Federal laws typically apply only to firms with more than a specified number of employees—often as many as 50 or 100. Many states enact laws that extend the same employee protections to smaller firms. The federal Family and Medical Leave Act, for example, entitles employees of firms with 50 or more workers to take as long as 12 weeks of unpaid leave for family matters such as adoption, illness, or birth. But Oregon lowers the size of the company to 25 workers and Vermont to 15. The federal law requiring 60-day advance notification of plant closings applies only to companies with 100 or more workers, but in Hawaii, employers with 50 or more workers must give 45-day notice. These state actions enhance worker protections.

[26] Kirstin Downey Grimsley, "Where Congress Fears to Tread," *Washington Post National Weekly Edition,* August 21, 2000, p. 18.

State courts have added additional worker protections. While federal courts often decide issues of constitutionality and statutory interpretation, they have not expanded workplace rights beyond the statutes. State courts, on the other hand, have used doctrines of common law to establish new employee rights in the absence of legislation. A leading example of the power of state courts is how, in recent years, they have revised the doctrine of employment-at-will, shriveling perhaps the most fundamental right of an employer—the right to hire and fire.

Erosion of the Employment-at-Will Doctrine

In the United States, there is a body of common law, or law derived from judicial decisions, that governs employer–employee relationships. In general, this law holds that employers and employees may enter voluntary employment contracts and that either party may freely end these agreements anytime.

While employed, an employee must act "solely and entirely" for the employer's benefit in all work-related matters or be liable for termination and damages. Furthermore, when a conflict arises between an employee and an employer, the employee must conform to the employer's rules. The common law in this area is derived from paternalistic English common law that, in turn, was influenced by Roman law that framed employment in terms of a master–servant relationship. Under this body of law, employers have had extensive rights to restrict employee freedom and arbitrarily fire workers.

Unit recently, an extreme interpretation of the employment contract prevailed. It resounds in the oft-quoted statement by a Tennessee judge in 1884: "All may dismiss their employees at will be they many or few, for good cause, for no cause, or even for cause morally wrong without being thereby guilty of legal wrong."[27] *Employment-at-will,* therefore, was traditionally defined as an employment contract that could be ended by either party without notice and for any reason—or for no reason.

With the rise of government intervention since the 1930s, absolute discharge rights have been eroded. Federal and state laws take away the right to fire employees for many reasons, including union activity, pregnancy, physical disability, race, sex, national origin, and religious belief. In addition, state courts have introduced three common-law exceptions to firing at will.

First, employees cannot be fired for complying with public policy. In *Petermann* v. *International Brotherhood of Teamsters,* a supervisor requested a California worker to dissemble in testimony before a legislative committee probing unions.[28] The worker answered questions honestly anyway and was fired. The court struck down the firing, declaring an overriding public

[27] *Payne* v. *Western & Atlantic R.R. Co.,* 81 Tenn. 507 (1884).
[28] 344 Cal. App. 2d 25 (1959).

interest in ensuring truthful testimony to lawmakers. In another case, *Sabine Pilot Service, Inc.* v. *Hauck,* a deck hand was ordered to pump oily bilge water into the ocean off the Texas coast. The worker read a placard posted on the ship stating that this was illegal, phoned the Coast Guard for confirmation, and refused to do it any more. He was fired. A Texas court held that an employer could not fire a worker for refusing to disobey the law.[29] This exception to firing at will is recognized in 43 states.[30]

A second check on freedom to fire is recognized where an implied contract exists. Daniel Foley worked at Chase Manhattan Bank, and his superiors made oral statements that his job was secure. For seven years he got regular promotions and raises. One day, Foley learned that the FBI was investigating his supervisor for embezzling money at a former job, so he told a vice president. Shortly, the supervisor fired Foley. However, a California court ruled that Foley had been promised permanent employment if his performance was satisfactory. It held, in *Foley* v. *Interactive Data Corp.,* that the company had violated an implied contract.[31] Following this decision, companies began to avoid hinted promises of job tenure, such as references to "permanent" employees in brochures and handbooks. Courts in 38 states have adopted this exception.

Third, courts in 11 states limit the employer's ability to fire when an implied covenant of good faith is breached. These courts accept that such a covenant is present in all employer–employee relations. The test of any firing is whether it meets an implied duty to be fair and just. Unfair and malicious dismissals fail to pass. In *Cleary* v. *American Airlines,* for example, the company fired an 18-year employee, giving no reason.[32] Although company policy contained a statement that the firm reserved the right to fire an employee for any reason, a California court was convinced that the purpose of the firing was to avoid paying Cleary a sales commission. It awarded him punitive damages.

Of the three exceptions to employment-at-will, the implied covenant of good faith exception departs most from the vision of unrestricted dismissal. Indeed, it defies the amoral core of employment-at-will. Those courts adopting it reject the old notion of employer–employee equality, believing that employers overmatch the power of employees and have a duty of fairness in actions that determine the livelihoods of their workers. In a case where Kmart Corporation fired an employee to avoid paying retirement benefits, a Nevada court, holding the firing in "bad faith," noted that:

> We have become a nation of employees. We are dependent upon others for our means of livelihood, and most of our people have become completely

[29] 687 S.W.2d 733 (Tex. 1985).
[30] Charles J. Muhl, "The Employment-at-Will Doctrine: Three Major Exceptions," *Monthly Labor Review,* January 2001, p. 4.
[31] 205 Cal. App. 3d 344 (1985).
[32] 168 Cal. Reptr. 722 (1980).

dependent upon wages. If they lose their jobs they lose every resource except for the relief supplied by the various forms of social security. Such dependence of the mass of the people upon others for all of their income is something new in the world. For our generation, the substance of life is in another man's hands.[33]

Only three states fail to take up any of the new exceptions, and only six states embrace all of them. The great majority have adopted one or two, and the overall trend is toward greater restriction on the employer's ability to fire. One state, Montana, now has a law that permits employers to discharge workers only for "good cause."

Work and Worker Protection in Other Industrialized Nations

The level of benefits and protections in the United States is high but not exceptional. Elsewhere in the developed world, workers benefit from similar and even greater welfare guarantees. Cultural differences are evident in how worker rights are supported, but in every nation where strong welfare measures are in place, labor costs are high.

Japanese workers are among the world's most expensive. In 1997 average hourly compensation for a manufacturing worker in Japan was $22, or $1.14 more than an American counterpart. The fringe benefits of regular employees in the large companies that employ about 40 percent of the Japanese workforce typically include company housing, family allowances, meals, child education expenses, and paid vacations. Japanese males, called salarymen, enjoy virtual lifetime employment in major firms. Protection against job loss is not, however, extended to women. When salarymen die, they are often buried in corporate cemeteries. These benefits are provided voluntarily by paternalistic Japanese companies.

Japanese history and culture in part explain why companies are so generous. Japan's long feudal period shaped cultural patterns based on values derived from the spread of ancient Chinese culture to the islands, including belief in rigid status hierarchies, strong duties of loyalty owed to rulers, emphasis on group rather than individual welfare, and the belief that a paternalistic government should provide for citizen welfare. Later, these values molded the relationship between modern workers and the industrial corporation. Just as the feudal Japanese vassal owed fealty to a lord, workers were asked to give loyalty to their company and place work group interests above individual interests.

Japanese workers are very committed. They work long hours. Vacations are rarely taken, even as holiday credits accumulate. Sick leave is seldom used. Many workers save the bulk of their entitlements to time off until they are bought out at retirement around age 60. Foreign observers

---

[33] Quoted in Charles J. Muhl, "The Employment-at-Will Doctrine: Three Major Exceptions," p. 10, citing 103 Nev. 49, 732 P.2d 1364 (1987).

believe that Japanese salarymen sometimes work themselves to illness or death. One explanation for this hard work is that career ladders in large corporations have frequent small promotion and salary steps.[34] A stereotypical case is that of Kazumi Kanaya, a Toyota Motors manager who crumpled at the office one day and lapsed into a permanent coma. Kanaya worked 12 hours a day every day, seldom taking a day off in spite of gout so painful that he needed a cane to walk. Although his wife pushed him to get medical attention, he argued that his work schedule precluded it. Near the end, he was in charge of an important sales office at Toyota, and the company culture dictated extraordinary efforts. He worked seven days a week, often staying until after 10:00 P.M. His collapse was due to untreated meningitis.[35]

It is estimated that every year 10,000 salarymen die from working too hard. Such deaths are so common that a word, *karoshi*, appeared in the Japanese language to denote death from the stress of overwork.[36] However, overwork is not seen as a problem caused by unreasonable employers. Rather, they see exceptional dedication as a duty called forth by the beneficence of the company toward its workers. Moreover, the Japanese are not the world's hardest workers. A 2001 International Labor Organization survey showed that Americans, Australians, and Mexicans worked longer hours. Americans worked, on average, about 140 more hours than the Japanese each year.[37]

In the United States, worker rights and social protections were wrested from employers by pugnacious and politically active labor unions. In Japan, however, the centuries-old Confucian tradition of harmony in relationships prevented a similar labor–management fissure from developing. Unions never grew strong and unified. Most today are company unions, and they rarely strike or make strident demands. Likewise, there is no adversarial relationship between companies and government agencies enforcing worker rights in Japan as there often is in the United States. Japanese workers have far fewer legislated rights than U.S. and European workers.

Industrialized nations in northern Europe also give high wages and comprehensive benefits to workers. This is reflected in average hourly compensation for manufacturing workers of $16.38 in France, $20.14 in Sweden, $20.44 in Denmark, $21.11 in Belgium, $21.24 in Switzerland,

---

[34] Toyohiro Kono and Stewart Clegg, *Trends in Japanese Management: Continuing Strengths, Current Problems and Changing Priorities* (New York: Palgrave, 2001), p. 280.

[35] Darius Mehri, "Death by Overwork: Corporate Pressure on Employees Takes a Fatal Toll in Japan," *Multinational Monitor,* June 2000, p. 26.

[36] Sonni Efron, "Jobs Take a Deadly Toll on Japanese," *Los Angeles Times,* April 12, 2000, p. A1.

[37] Cynthia L. Webb, "The Workweek Gets Longer," *Washington Post National Weekly Edition,* September 10–16, 2001, p. 21.

$22.05 in Norway, and, highest of all, $24.01 in Germany. In the aftermath of World War II, these countries adopted, in similar versions, a *social welfare model* of industrial relations to protect their populations against the ravages of depression and unemployment experienced in the 1930s. Governments took over major industries and ran them to ensure full employment. Lavish welfare packages for workers were legislated in European parliaments. Socialist parties supported the creation of powerful unions that could negotiate wages and benefits over entire industries.

Forces of global competitiveness now strain this social welfare model. European workers are so expensive to employ that job-creating investments go elsewhere. In Germany, for example, the benefits and protections achieved by German workers are unmatched, which is why Germany has the highest labor costs in the world and has struggled for more than a decade to get unemployment below 10 percent. A complex network of laws, union agreements, and customs makes its labor market relatively inflexible. Workers are entitled to generous government pensions, health insurance, sick leave, unemployment, 30 days of paid vacations, and a six-month notice before termination. This is much more generous than worker benefits and protections in the United States. When Chrysler Corp. merged with Daimler-Benz, Chrysler workers were amazed to learn that the German autoworkers had a union contract giving them a 35-hour workweek, a medical plan with no deductible that allowed them to choose their own physicians, and paid sick leave for up to four weeks.[38]

Employers fund much of this. German companies must pay taxes and contributions equaling 49 percent of each worker's direct wages, including 27 percent in employment taxes, 12 percent for pensions, and 10 percent for health insurance.[39] In addition, German laws tightly regulate much business activity, for example, by prescribing the hours when factory machines can run and prohibiting most labor during an official Sunday "pause." The average German works 12.5 weeks less each year than the average American.[40]

Such expensive labor discourages investments that create more jobs, and unemployment was high in Europe through the 1990s. As a result, there are many proposals for reform. European governments have reprivatized most industries, but they have had less success rolling back social supports for workers in the face of opposition by powerful unions and socialist parties. Recently, German unions have experimented with more flexible arrangements, and the German government has proposed scaling back social benefits, including pensions and sick pay. In 2001, for

[38] Harry Kelber, "One Carmaker, Two Unions," *Progressive Populist,* July 1998, p. 9.
[39] Grace Sung, "Europe's Job Woes Bogged Down by Reform Inaction," *The Straits Times,* January 22, 2002, p. 4.
[40] Webb, "The Workweek Gets Longer," p. 21.

example, it ended the practice of allowing older workers to collect unemployment compensation even when they were not looking for a job. However, Italian unions recently called nationwide strikes when the government announced proposals to weaken workers' social protections.

Despite industry opposition, some European governments continue to take actions that make their labor costs even higher. France, like Germany, suffers from chronic unemployment near 10 percent. In 2000 its socialist government, over the objections of employers, implemented a 35-hour workweek law. The purpose of this law was to create more jobs by mandating shorter hours, assuming that companies would be forced to hire more people to maintain output. Like their German counterparts, French employees are expensive. Employers have to pay similarly high social taxes to provide for their security and benefits. And the new law made them even more expensive by requiring that laid-off workers be paid for nine months while they sought new jobs. The unintended, but logical, result of the 35-hour law has been rising productivity in French industry as employers choose to invest in new machinery instead of new workers.

Throughout Europe, the results of lavish social safety nets and protections for workers are persistent, high unemployment and slowed economic growth. In Germany and other affluent European nations, only gradual and modest rollbacks of entitlements for workers are likely.

THE TURBULENT WORKPLACE

The combined impact of the five major forces changing the workplace creates uncertainty and anxiety. For some workers, opportunities are greater; for others, there are fewer rewards. The vicissitudes of work life are illustrated by corporate downsizing. And a new employment contract between workers and companies may be emerging.

Corporate Downsizing

There are many ways a firm can restructure to improve the fit between its organization and its strategy. These include buying and selling assets, revising capital structure, changing organization charts, and casting off significant numbers of employees.[41] All these methods can be effective in improving market performance, particularly if they are part of a careful plan. For workers, however, the most disruptive form of restructuring is the mass layoff or downsizing.

---

[41] Edward H. Bowman, Harbir Singh, Michael Useem, and Raja Bhadury, "When Does Restructuring Improve Economic Performance?" *California Management Review*, Winter 1999, pp. 33–35.

Downsizing occurs for many reasons. When IBM announced layoffs of 60,000 workers in 1993, it was reacting to technology shifts in computing that reduced revenues from its traditional mainframe business. When AT&T made 34,000 layoffs in 1996, it was responding to deregulation that opened its long-distance business to regional phone company competitors. When Boeing announced 30,000 layoffs in 2001, it did so because new orders for airplanes evaporated after the September 11 terrorist attacks.

Some companies have been shrinking for years. Since 1978 General Motor's North American workforce has steadily declined from 520,000 to 212,000. To reduce costs, GM has moved more than 20 percent of its manufacturing from the United States to Mexico. The average Mexican production worker earns $2.46 per hour and does not belong to a union. The average United Auto Workers member at GM's Flint Metal Center makes almost $100,000 a year in wages and benefits, and union rules allow machines to run fewer hours and at slower speeds than in Mexico.[42] Like Ford, GM has fallen behind its competitors in the global race to reduce the cost of making an automobile. The logic of closing American plants and sending work to Mexico will remain compelling.

Critics say that making workers bear the burden of adjustment to the vicissitudes of business cycles and global competition is unfair. Historically, mass layoffs were used only as a last resort and were embarrassing signs of management failure. Today, layoffs are no longer a source of shame, at least in the United States, where downsizing is now a routine option. Top executives sometimes make record salaries in downsizing years, and stockholders are often enriched by short-term price jumps in their shares after big job cuts.

Lavish executive compensation can look obscene in contrast to the real pain of economic adjustment passed on to workers. Their suffering is illustrated in a story about a secretary named Linda, told by a manager conducting a mass layoff in which workers were called without notice to a conference room and read a prepared statement that terminated them.

> We avoided looking at each other as I spoke. When I finished, she didn't move for several long seconds; then she stood up and paced the length of the room and started wringing her hands. "What am I supposed to do?" she pleaded, not waiting for the answer that we couldn't give. "I am a single mother, my parents are gone, and I just closed on a house two weeks ago. I *need* my job," she said as the tears started to flow. My reaction was to offer some comfort, at least offer some words of encouragement, but we had been strictly warned by the company attorney not to do anything of the sort. It was for the good of the company that we restrain ourselves, lest

---

[42] Warren Brown and Frank Swoboda, "At GM, a Stalled Revolution," *Washington Post National Weekly Edition,* July 20–27, 1998, p. 20.

we make some passing promise that would end up in court later. We all just sat there until she gathered her papers and walked out.[43]

This portrait of suffering at the hands of a heartless corporation is like many that make their way into the news. This woman received more individual attention than the 75 employees caught in the net of a 1,700-worker downsizing at Dell Computer. Like sheep, they went on a one-hour notice to a nearby hotel, there to be terminated by managers who never bothered to introduce themselves during an eight-minute presentation.[44] However, to generalize from these sad stories about the fortunes of American workers is misleading. The pain of losing a job can be terrible. However, the long-term trend in the economy is that more jobs are being created than lost. Approximately 55 million jobs in the United States were permanently lost between 1979 and 2001, but more than 88 million jobs were created—a net gain of 33 million.[45] And after the recession of 1981–1982, the unemployment rate declined from a high of 11 percent to a low of 4.3 percent in early 1999 before rising back over 5 percent in 2001.

Downsizing is a complex response to global forces. Transnational firms in all countries feel pressure to make cost-cutting workforce reductions to meet the competition. American firms operate in a more flexible labor environment than their European and Japanese competitors, and they are better able to reduce employment, so in the last two decades, American firms have shed the most employees. European firms have to contend with powerful unions and laws that protect job security and make outsourcing to foreign countries more difficult. They have been slower and less sweeping in their workforce adjustments.

Large Japanese firms, because of the principle of lifetime employment, have the most difficult time of all. Case law in Japanese courts makes it hard to dismiss workers in lifetime employment systems for any reason. The courts have held that terminations are legal only under certain circumstances. The firm must be in acute financial distress. It must have made and documented efforts to avoid the dismissals. Then it must have "sincerely explained" these efforts to the workers and attempted to get their consent in the process. Finally, it must have used objective standards in choosing which employees to separate.[46]

In addition to legal barriers, the Japanese business ideology also opposes layoffs. Recently, Okuda Hiroshi, chairman of Toyota Motor Corp.,

[43] Alan Downs, *Corporate Executions* (New York: Amacom, 1995), p. 76.
[44] Adam Cohen and Cathy Booth Thomas, "Inside a Layoff," *Time,* April 16, 2001, p. 38.
[45] Estimate calculated using Bureau of Labor Statistics historical data on employment, mass layoffs, and displaced workers.
[46] Charles J. Tackney, "Changing Approaches to Employment Relations in Japan," in Gregg J. Bamber et al., *Employment Relations in the Asia-Pacific: Changing Approaches* (London: Business Press, 2000), p. 68.

said that managers should explore every possible alternative before fir- ing extra people on the payroll, otherwise, they were not worthy of being called managers. "The only way I would lay people off," he said, "is if I were prepared to resign my own job to take responsibility."[47] The shame of layoffs leads Japanese managers to try other methods of lowering labor costs, including offering early retirement incentives, slowing re- cruitment, using part-time workers, transferring workers to other units or to supplier firms, reducing executive bonuses, cutting dividends, and even using surplus workers to start a new business.

Some commentators have concluded that these moves, particularly growing reliance on temporary, outsourced, and nonregular employees, show that the principle of lifetime employment is collapsing. On the con- trary, it is being protected. Though global forces have put pressure on Japanese firms to reduce labor costs, few have done so by mass layoffs. The other methods are preferred. Recently, Isuzu Motors, Nissan Motor, and Matsushita Electric have cut their workforces significantly, however, all were pushed by major foreign shareholders. More typical is Fujitsu Ltd. Forced by enormous losses to shed as many as 15,000 workers, or 10 percent of its employees, the company planned to cut most of them from operations outside Japan.[48]

Downsizing is a complex phenomenon of workforce restructuring, in which some firms are cutting workers, others are adding them, and many are doing both. It is more difficult to restructure workforces in some nations than in others, but global companies in every nation see their staffs shriveled by winds of economic change. Corporations cannot control structural and technological forces that define markets, and they cannot compete if locked into outmoded, excessively labor-intensive practices to avoid hurting workers.

When Daewoo Motor Co. of South Korea became insolvent in 2001 it had to lay off 7,000 workers. Its paternalistic approach to employees based on the Japanese model could not save the jobs. All that remained was an empathy that eludes American managers. As part of a voluntary trial of humiliation and atonement, Chairman Lee Jong Dae spoke to the fated employees. One day, he dropped to his knees in front of a factory worker and said: "My deepest apologies to you and your family for lay- ing you off. I am determined to find you a job. Please forgive me."[49]

A strength of the American economy compared to, for example, the German and Japanese economies, is the relative ease with which labor is shifted from declining sectors to rising ones. It would be hardest on workers in the end if American firms, bloated with highly paid and

---

[47] "Respecting Human Beings," *LOOK JAPAN,* January 2000, p. 26.
[48] "Report Says Fujitsu to Fire Up to 15,000," *Los Angeles Times,* August 20, 2001, p. C2.
[49] Hae Won Choi, "After Massive Layoff, Daewoo's CEO Begs a Thousand Pardons," *The Wall Street Journal,* June 26, 2001, p. A1.

aging personnel, grew uncompetitive with global rivals. Yet this is no consolation to individuals who suffer callous managers trained to handle them impersonally, as if they were debt or raw materials.

A Revised Employment Contract

The turbulence in the workplace caused by environmental forces is bringing fundamental change to the nature of jobs. Not so long ago work was done in eight-hour days on rising trajectories of pay and power within hierarchical, pyramid-shaped, corporate organizations. The largest of these organizations, firms such as Mitsubishi Corporation in Japan; Unilever, Siemens, and Nestlé in Europe; and AT&T, General Motors, and IBM in the United States; were insulated in domestic markets or protected by their market power from fierce international competition. They could offer unwritten promises of lifetime employment and did so.

The unwritten employment contract was an exchange of the worker's time, skill, and loyalty for a career of growing compensation, status, and security within the company. Now, though, this contract equation is less sacrosanct. Competitive and global forces have altered the assumptions on which it was based. Technological changes have torn down the barriers that insulated large companies from global competition. Workers in developed nations are no longer insulated from competition. Once-safe factory jobs have left developed nations. Service occupations are also highly competitive. A worker answering the telephone in Bangladesh can do an airline booking or credit card transaction as well as a worker in Tokyo, Paris, or New York and for a fraction of the cost.

Downsizing has flattened organizational structures, extending work hours for remaining employees, and removed many higher positions in the pyramid to which they could have aspired. Government regulations protect workers from cruel bosses and arrant misfortune, but because they raise costs to employers they have slowed the creation of traditional career jobs. Global corporations are outsourcing work and hiring many temporary workers so as to reduce labor costs and build more flexible workforces.[50]

Despite recent turbulence in employer–employee relations, the outlines of a new employment contract are emerging. In the new contract, employees will trade their time, energy, and skills for compensation and the opportunity to work in a company that provides learning, training, and, perhaps, feelings of self-worth. Unlike the old contract, the employee need not have a high level of loyalty. And the firm, conscious of its need for a lean and flexible workforce, will not promise long-term employment. To attract ambitious people, firms will have to provide training and education for workers who expect to move sequentially from

---

[50] Peter Drucker, "They're Not Employees, They're People," *Harvard Business Review,* February 2002, pp. 70–77.

one employer to another over their working lifetimes. The security of these employees will lie in their marketability, not in promises of a long-term position at one company.

CONCLUDING OBSERVATIONS

In this chapter we discussed five forces acting to change the workplace—demography, technology, competition, structural shift, and government. Demographic and structural changes are uncontrollable but also slow and predictable. Technological change, which is often rapid and unpredictable, is a radical and disruptive force but a source of new jobs. The importance of competition is elevated now in developed nations, where great corporations, expanding into global markets, rush to automate and send their work to low-wage countries. Finally, the importance of government regulation cannot be underestimated. The accumulated workers' protections of the twentieth century are an enormous cost burden on companies, governments, and consumers. Around the industrialized world there is strong pressure to revise labor laws, weakening protections and social welfare for workers.

How will workers fare in these currents of change? Experience suggests that fortunes will be mixed. Yet it is likely that if the global economy prospers, the benefits of rising prosperity will outweigh the costs of occupational dislocations.

Workplace Drug Testing

There is a long record in the United States of drug use in the workplace. However, it was not until the 1980s that drug testing by employers began. The initiative came from the federal government.

The U.S. Navy began the first random drug testing as a result of its discovery of widespread drug use following an accident on the *USS Nimitz* in 1982. Other branches of the federal government quickly followed. In 1986 President Reagan issued Executive Order 12564 requiring all federal agencies to develop a "drug-free workplace" by establishing a program to test for the use of illegal drugs by employees in sensitive positions.

A Conrail engineer who had been smoking marijuana rolled his string of locomotives past a warning light and onto the same track as a high-speed train carrying 600 people. The collision, in

1987, killed 16 people and injured 176. In 1989 the *Exxon Valdez*, a large oil tanker, struck a rock formation and spilled millions of gallons of crude oil in the pristine waters of Prince William Sound in Alaska. There was enormous loss of animal life and destruction to the economic and social fabric of the area. Alcohol was partly responsible for this disaster. Such accidents resulted in the passage of the Omnibus Transportation Employee Testing Act of 1991, requiring the Department of Transportation to test employees in safety-sensitive transportation jobs for drug and alcohol use.

The Department of Energy, the Department of Defense, and the Nuclear Regulatory Commission all have private sector drug-testing requirements for security-sensitive workplaces. Other laws and regulations prompt drug testing. The Occupational

Safety and Health Act, for instance, requires employers to provide safe working environments. The Drug-Free Workplace Act of 1988 requires companies to maintain drug-free workplaces if they want to get contracts from federal agencies. This law covers more than 200,000 companies employing 22 percent of the labor force.

Following this combination of conspicuous accidents and the passage of laws there has been a rapid expansion of drug testing in public and private workplaces. In 1983 only six firms in the *Fortune* 500 were testing their workers for drugs. By 1987, 20 percent of major firms were testing, and in 2001, 67 percent were testing. This last figure represents a drop from a peak of 80 percent in 1996.[1]

Controversy surrounds drug testing. Questions arise over why drug tests are needed, who should be tested, what tests should be given, and how tests should be conducted. The fundamental issue is the conflict between the right of employers to protect their property and the right of employees to be free of unwarranted intrusions on their privacy.

THE COSTS OF DRUG ABUSE

The behavior of drug-using employees imposes costs, including lost productivity, higher insurance premiums, excessive absentee and sick leave rates, the loss of trained workers who are fired or die, the administrative costs of antidrug programs, extra plant security, property damage, declines in employee morale, tarnishing of company images, lawsuits, and thefts of property. The overall cost of drug use at work is unknown but great. The Department of Labor estimates that substance abuse in the workplace costs $100 billion annually.[2] Approximately 40 percent of serious workplace accidents and 40 percent of fatal workplace accidents have drug or alcohol involvement. The Ohio Bureau of Workers' Compensation estimates that substance abusers are 33 to 50 percent less produc-

tive. It reports that they are five times more likely than nonabusers to file worker compensation claims.[3]

BEHAVIOR OF DRUG-ABUSING EMPLOYEES

Drug-addicted employees tend to exhibit one or both of two pernicious effects. The first is distortion of time, which is seen in the inability of the employee to follow normal time patterns for job activities. The second is lack of motivation, which is seen as disinterest in normal performance standards. Both effects stem from imbalances of brain chemistry caused by the chronic presence of marijuana, cocaine, or other drugs in the bloodstream.[4] Supervisors are trained to suspect drug abuse when employees show patterns of behavior such as these:

- Frequent tardiness and absences from work, especially on Mondays and Fridays and near holidays.

- Poor concentration, forgetfulness, missed deadlines, and frequent mistakes.

- Mood changes, including a wide range of states that interfere with personal relationships such as depression, withdrawal, hostility, and overexcitability.

- Risk taking and frequent accidents.

DRUG-TESTING PROGRAMS

Companies must choose what kind of testing to use. There are a variety of drug-testing methods, including the following.

Employee searches may include searches of lockers, workstations, desks, and purses. They seldom include bodily searches, which anger workers and create litigation. Drug-sniffing dogs are extremely effective in locating contraband. But searches are often ineffective. For example, drugs can be se-

---

[1] Data are from American Management Association surveys, reported by Marianne Costantinou, "The American Way," *San Francisco Chronicle*, August 12, 2001.
[2] Kirstin Downey Grimsley, "Great Résumé, Interview, References—Now Here's the Cup," *Washington Post National Weekly Edition*, May 18, 1998.
[3] Reported by D.D.T.A/Services Inc., "Drug Free Workplace Program," http://ddtaservicesinc.com/html/drugfree/html.
[4] William F. Banta and Forest Tennant, Jr., *Complete Handbook for Combating Substance Abuse in the Workplace* (Lexington, MA: Lexington Books, 1989), p. 45.

creted in common areas so that employee ownership is concealed.

Surveillance can detect drug use, but has many pitfalls. It is difficult to keep undercover agents a secret. Spying can shatter employee morale. Surveillance agents can make mistakes, such as striking an employee, that can result in expensive lawsuits.

Written drug tests are available from a dozen or more vendors of employment tests. They ask job applicants and employees whether they have used drugs, what kind, and how often. The validity of these tests is unproven, but they are the least expensive type of drug test.

Polygraphs, or lie detectors, were used frequently in the past, but no more. The accuracy of the results is open to question. Furthermore, the Employee Polygraph Protection Act of 1988 so severely limits their use that most employers no longer use them for drug testing.

Fitness-for-duty exams, sometimes called performance tests, detect impaired acuity. In one test, for example, workers sit in front of a computer screen and turn a knob to keep a moving point centered between two lines. Such tests measure impairment but they do not show the cause, which may be drugs, alcohol, fatigue from staying up with a sick baby all night, or emotional upset. Advocates of performance tests believe they are less physically intrusive than other forms of testing. Critics argue that poor performance invites an employer to ask intrusive questions about private off-work behavior.

Blood tests are useful primarily for alcohol abuse testing. They are expensive and exceptionally intrusive and, because of legal challenges, are rarely used by employers. Their main advantage is that they can determine the approximate time a drug was used.

Saliva tests exist to test for marijuana use but are unreliable. They are useful only up to three hours after marijuana is smoked, and rinsing the mouth can remove detectable residues.

Hair analysis tests can detect use of cocaine, marijuana, or other illegal drugs for as long as three months prior to removing a 1½-inch growth of hair for testing. However, it takes about seven days for substances indicative of drug use to appear in the hair. Few companies use it.

Urinalysis is the most commonly employed testing method. Before discussing urinalysis in some detail, the options about whom to test and the drugs to be tested should be noted.

EMPLOYEES WHO MIGHT BE TESTED

Employers have many testing options. Here are some of the major ones.

- *Those in safety-sensitive positions.* This might refer to national security but also those who could jeopardize the safety of themselves or other employees or the public at large. Included also would be people handling substantial amounts of money or carrying firearms.

- *Those who provide cause.* When employees are frequently absent on Mondays or take periodic unexpected absences, have frequent accidents, display erratic behavior, or show inconsistent job performance, they may be singled out for drug testing.

- *Those who have gone through rehabilitation.* When employees have gone through a drug rehabilitation program, they may be subject to periodic drug testing.

- *Those who apply for employment.* Job applicants, especially for sensitive positions, may be tested.

- *Random testing of all employees.* Random testing makes it harder for employees who use drugs to escape detection, since they cannot arrange to be free of drugs for irregular tests that come by surprise.

DRUGS OF ABUSE TESTED BY EMPLOYERS

In 1988 the National Institute for Drug Abuse (NIDA) issued guidelines on drug-abuse programs for public sector employees. Five drugs were identified for testing: tetrahydrocannabinol, the psychoactive ingredient in marijuana; cocaine; opiates; amphetamines; and phencyclidine. Many employers added other drugs to this list, including barbiturates, benzodiazepines, methadone, methaqualone, and propoxyphene. Some routinely test for alcohol, a legal drug and the most commonly abused.[5]

---

[5] Ibid. pp. 37–38.

Many now test for ecstasy, a drug in the amphetamine and methamphetamine family that has become more widely abused. Ira A. Lipman, chairman and president of Guardsmark, a security and drug testing firm, notes that ecstasy "is dangerous both to the user and to workers. . . [and] can create an unsafe work environment"[6]

URINALYSIS

There are several basic types of urine tests. The first is the *immunoassay test.* This is an inexpensive test costing about $20 to $25 that can be done quickly with modest laboratory equipment and technician training. However, this test is not always 100 percent accurate. For example, it may register positive if a person has recently used any of 10 common over-the-counter drugs.

If the test is positive, a second and much more accurate test may be used to confirm. It involves a different chemical process called *chromatography.* It is more time-consuming and more expensive (about $50 per test) and requires a highly trained technician to interpret results. It is not, therefore, used for mass screening but is held in reserve to double-check a positive result on an immunoassay test.

A third test may be done with a *mass spectrometer.* It is the most accurate test, and the most expensive. Gas chromatography/mass spectrometer tests are so sensitive they have detected cocaine and a by-product, cinnamolycocaine, in the urine of people who have drunk one or two cups of coca leaf teas imported from Peru.

One shortcoming of urine tests is that they can be thwarted by employees who tamper with a sample. A small amount of table salt, bleach, laundry soap, ammonia, or vinegar causes screening tests to miss drug residues in the urine. Consequently, employees giving urine samples must be closely supervised.

There is a cottage industry of companies selling methods to pass drug tests. They have colorfully named websites, such as ezklean.com, urineluck.com, and passyourdrugtest.com. They sell masking products including synthetic urine, herbal concoctions, chemically treated shampoos

(for passing hair tests), and specialty gadgets.[7] Drug-testing companies buy and study these products trying to stay one step ahead of the cheating. Many, of course, do not work as advertised.

A significant problem with urine testing is that it cannot show whether an employee is "high" or impaired. Cocaine and heroin can be detected up to three days after last use and marijuana up to two months after last use. This means that a person who used cocaine at a party Saturday night could be nailed by a drug test Tuesday morning when feeling hale and working productively. But if a colleague had taken LSD that morning and was hallucinating and dangerous, the LSD could not be detected with a simple screening test. An immunoassay test cannot detect hallucinogens such as LSD.

STARTING A DRUG-FREE WORKPLACE PROGRAM

Once a company has chosen from among the options, the Institute for a Drug-Free Workplace recommends the following steps:

1. Identify any federal or state laws with which you must comply.

2. Write a clear, consistent, and fair policy that includes the conditions under which drug testing is to be conducted and the consequences of a "positive" drug test result.

3. If applicable, consult with union representatives and bargain in good faith on the terms and conditions of the drug-testing program.

4. Identify and contact a certified laboratory to set up a drug-testing contract. If possible, go for a visit.

5. Contract with a collection site to receive testing samples.

6. Develop and implement a system to protect the confidentiality of employee drug test records.

[6] PR Newswire, "Guardsmark, Inc., Expands 100% Drug Testing Program to Include 'Ecstasy,' " July 18, 2001.

[7] Costantinou, "The American Way," p. 3.

7. Designate the person who will receive the test results from the laboratory, and make sure that person is aware of confidentiality issues.

8. Have your policy reviewed by legal counsel.

9. Notify employees 30 to 180 days before the testing program goes into effect.

10. Establish procedures for review of all positive drug test results by a medical review officer.

11. Communicate to employees that management also is fully subject to the policy, the specifics of the testing program, what is expected of them as employees, the company's reasons for promoting a drug-free workforce, and the adverse employment consequences of a policy violation.[8]

WHY CORPORATIONS FAVOR DRUG TESTING

First, federal and state laws require drug tests for certain workers and companies. The Drug-Free Workplace Act of 1988, as noted, requires private employers with federal contracts over $25,000 to have comprehensive policies designed to prevent drug abuse. Most states and some cities have laws concerning drug testing. Thus, complying with the law is a major reason for drug testing.

Second, drug testing has beneficial results. For example, SmithKline Beecham reported that the percentage of employees who tested positive for illegal drug use declined from 18 percent in 1987 to 5 percent in 1997.[9] The Department of Labor reported major improvements in job-related performance because of drug-free workplace programs. For example, the Southern Pacific Transportation Company reported that injuries dropped 71 per-

cent.[10] Reductions in workplace drug use also reduce health and insurance costs. The owner of a lumberyard in Georgia with 90 employees reported spending about $1,500 each year for testing. The program paid off if only because it qualified the business for a worker's compensation discount of $4,000.[11]

Third, corporate drug testers argue that urinalysis is a practical method of testing for drug use. Although urine tests are intrusive, they are less so than some alternatives such as drug-sniffing dogs, polygraphs, searches through handbags and desks, undercover investigations, entry and exit searches, and closed-circuit TV monitors in restrooms. When done correctly, urine tests are reliable. Good programs follow the Rule of Two, in which two positive tests are required before action is taken. The first test, an inexpensive screening test, is followed by a second, more sophisticated confirming test on the same vial of urine. Cutoff levels for positive results can be set reasonably high to avoid unnecessarily stigmatizing innocent employees. Errors can also be minimized by using proper procedures for specimen collection and laboratory analysis.

Fourth, there is a social responsibility argument for drug testing. As employers screen applicants and employees, it will become harder for drug abusers to make a living. Employees have no right to use marijuana, cocaine, hallucinogens, PCP, heroin, and designer drugs. Their use is illegal and creates crime, illness, broken families, and broken lives. Thus, business is helping society by combating drug use. From an individual standpoint, if companies can catch a drug-using employee early, it might save his or her career. Many companies refer employees who test positive to assistance programs for treatment rather than terminate them.

Fifth, competitors have drug-testing programs. Hewlett-Packard, for instance, started drug testing because its competitors did so. If Hewlett-Packard

[8] *Annual Corporate Membership Survey,* cited in Marc A. de Bernardo, *Workplace Drug Testing: An Employer's Development & Implementation Guide* (Washington, DC: Institute for a Drug-Free Workplace, 1994), pp. 51–52.
[9] Grimsley, "Great Résumé, Interview, References."
[10] U.S. Department of Labor, "Working Partners for an Alcohol- and Drug-Free Workplace," http://dol.gov/dol/asp/public/programs/drugs/backgrnd.htm, November 6, 1998.
[11] Shannon Lynch, "Popularity of Drug Testing Employees Creates Ethical Dilemma," *Savannah Morning News,* January 30, 2001.

had not done the same, its applicant pool would have filled with drug users unable to get jobs elsewhere.[12]

WHY SOME EMPLOYEES OPPOSE DRUG TESTING

As compelling as these arguments are, drug testing in general and urine testing in particular raise difficult questions. Critics point out that the right of an employer to protect assets and property must be balanced against the rights of individual employees to a reasonable amount of privacy. Opponents make telling points.

First, urine testing is intrusive and an invasion of privacy. To avoid false positive results based on the presence of other drugs in the urine, employees are asked to list all prescription and over-the-counter drugs taken in the last 30 days. This reveals their private, off-duty lives and medical histories. Also, chemical analysis of urine (or blood) can reveal more than drug use. Employers could test it and discover medical conditions such as pregnancy, clinical depression, diabetes, and epilepsy. For all these reasons, civil libertarians believe urine testing smacks of Big Brother.

Second, urine testing is inherently demeaning whether a sample is taken with visual or passive supervision. An author of a law journal article put it this way: "[I]n our culture the excretory functions are shielded by more or less absolute privacy, so much so that situations in which this privacy is violated are experienced as extremely distressing, as detracting from one's dignity and self-esteem."[13]

Third, the tests are unjust because they violate ethical standards of fair treatment. Testing is a dragnet; many innocent people are tested for each drug user detected. A presumption of guilt is placed on everyone, and workers must prove their innocence. If there is an overriding safety justification to prohibit drug abuse—for example, among bus drivers or railroad engineers—then it may be

prudent. But indiscriminate testing of applicants and employees who are not in critical safety-related positions is an evil greater than the drug abuse it seeks to remedy.

Fourth, urine tests are imperfect. Inaccuracies arise from lab errors, mixed-up specimens, and false positives that are due to legal drugs in the body. Errors are too frequent and cast suspicion on employees or cost them their jobs. If scrupulous collection and laboratory procedures are followed, testing is very accurate. But not all companies and labs are that scrupulous. For example, follow-up confirmatory tests after a positive on a simple screening test are expensive, and not every firm is willing to undertake the extra expense for job applicants.

Fifth, drug tests can be misleading and cannot meet reasonable evidentiary standards. The ACLU says "they cannot detect impairment and, thus, in no way enhance an employer's ability to evaluate or predict job performance."[14] The ACLU adds, "Even a confirmed 'positive' provides no evidence of present intoxication or impairment; it merely indicates that a person may have taken a drug at some time in the past.[15] Emphasis should be placed on employee assistance programs not drug testing, says the ACLU.

Finally, drug testing is not cost-effective. For drug testing to be cost-effective it would be necessary, says the ACLU, for it to identify a significant number of drug abusers. In 1990 the federal government spent $11.7 million to test workers in 38 agencies. Of approximately 29,000 tests made, only 153 (.5 percent) were positive. The cost of finding one positive was estimated to be $77,000 per user.[16]

DRUG TESTING AND THE LAW

Legal precedent on drug testing is relatively new and still developing, but the clear trend is to uphold it where it is part of a previously announced

---

[12] Costantinou, "The American Way," p. 4.
[13] Charles Fried, "Privacy," *Yale Law Journal*, January 1968, p. 487.

[14] American Civil Liberties Union, *Drug Testing in the Workplace*, Briefing Paper No. 5, undated.
[15] Ibid.
[16] "Focus on Federal Drug Testing," *Individual Employment Rights*, BNA, April 9, 1991, reported in *Drug Testing: A Bad Investment*, ACLU, undated.

and carefully formulated policy. Here is a short briefing on legal issues.

Since the Bill of Rights in the U.S. Constitution restrains only government actions, public employees are protected by these provisions, but employees in private businesses are not. This is a major legal difference; public employers must meet stricter guidelines for testing. The Fourth Amendment guarantees protection to public employees against "unreasonable searches and seizures," and courts have generally held that urine tests and other forms of testing, such as blood tests for HIV antibodies, are a form of search and seizure. The Fifth Amendment guarantees due process of law and protects against self-incrimination. Public employers must guard against firings that violate these rights.[17] Since 1988 federal agencies have adhered to testing guidelines issued by the Department of Health and Human Services. These guidelines attempt to elevate due process for government employees to an impeccable level and stipulate testing procedures in detail.[18]

There have been many court challenges to federal urine-testing programs, and those that have reached the Supreme Court have been upheld. But the decisions also show that some of the justices have grave misgivings about drug testing and do not believe it is permitted by the Fourth Amendment.

In *Skinner* v. *Railway Labor Executives' Association,* the Court was asked to decide whether railroad workers could be forced to submit to mandatory urine and blood tests for drugs.[19] In a 7–2 decision, the Court held that the clear public interest in railroad safety outweighed the privacy rights of employees. But in a strong dissent, Justice Thurgood Marshall compared the decision with the Court's 1940s decisions upholding the assignment of Japanese to relocation camps during

World War II and noted that "when we allow fundamental freedoms to be sacrificed in the name of real or perceived exigency, we invariably come to regret it."[20]

A second case decided by the Supreme Court, *National Treasury Employees Union* v. *Von Raab,* involved a urine-testing program of the U.S. Customs Service.[21] It required applicants for positions in which they would interdict drugs, carry guns, or work with classified material of interest to criminals to submit to urine tests. In a 5–4 decision, the majority argued that the national drug crisis, together with the special gravity of drug enforcement work, justified weighing the public interest in drug-free customs agents more heavily than the interference with the agents' civil liberties. Thus, testing was "reasonable" under the Fourth Amendment. Justice Antonin Scalia, writing in dissent, warned that the Court was too cavalier in sacrificing basic constitutional privacy rights. He quoted these famous lines written by Justice Louis Brandeis in 1928: "The greatest dangers to liberty lurk in insidious encroachment by men of zeal, well-meaning but without understanding."[22]

In 1995 the Court decided a third case and remained divided about the issue. In a 6–3 decision in *Vernonia School District* v. *Acton,* it upheld the requirement that all student athletes in an Oregon high school submit to urine testing. The majority in *Vernonia* was willing to balance the privacy right of individuals against the legitimate needs of government agencies, in this case, the "substantial need of teachers and administrators for freedom to maintain order in the schools."[23] Writing in dissent, however, Justice Sandra Day O'Connor argued that random drug testing such as that on the high school athletes intruded on privacy where individual grounds for suspicion of wrongdoing did not exist. The Founding Fathers, she stated, clearly intended the Fourth Amendment to prohibit general

---

[17] These rights are extended to state, county, and local employees through the Fourteenth Amendment.
[18] National Institute on Drug Abuse, *Comprehensive Procedure for Drug Testing in the Workplace.*
[19] 57 LW 4324 (1989).

[20] At 57 LW 4324 (1989); the relocation camp cases are *Hirabayashi* v. *United States,* 320 U.S. 81 (1943); and *Korematsu* v. *United States,* 323 U.S. 214 (1944).
[21] 489 U.S. 656 (1989).
[22] In *Olmstead* v. *United States,* 227 U.S. 479 (1928).
[23] *Vernonia School District* v. *Acton,* 115 S.Ct. 2391 (1995).

searches of the population such as this and, therefore, such random drug tests were unconstitutional.

These three cases reveal an undercurrent of discomfort and opposition even though the Court approved testing all three situations that came before it.[24]

Although the Fourth Amendment only applies to government as an employer, the discretion of private sector employers is limited by other legal guidelines. First, many state and local governments have adopted laws that regulate drug testing. These laws vary considerably. For instance, San Francisco prohibits drug testing under most circumstances but permits tests for pre-employment, for suspicion of use, and after accidents. Florida permits testing of job applicants and employees, but if they are tested, the employer must follow specific procedures set forth in the Florida Drug-Free Workplace Act. Many states prescribe mandatory precise testing procedures. Second, private employers are open to common-law actions by employees based on doctrines such as negligence, defamation, assault and battery, emotional distress, invasion of privacy, or wrongful discharge. Employees have sued over drug testing using all these legal theories. Some have won in court, but there is no overall trend to prohibit drug testing programs. Union contracts also may circumscribe drug testing.

In the end, however, private employers are generally free to test, provided they have a well-written company policy that conforms to federal regulations and the laws of states and cities in which they operate.[25] However, there is such a bramble bush of rules on testing and privacy that compliance is a complex problem for corporations that operate in many locations. According to Gerald L. Maltman Jr., chairman of Baker & McKenzie, a global employment law firm:

> It's a real tough nut to crack for employers with sites in multiple states, because you end up having to tailor the intrusiveness of your policy depending on the state in which you're doing your testing. Illinois, for example, is a state that is very pro-employer, whereas California is a state that is very pro-employee on the issue of privacy. Because there is no federal law that governs the privacy issue, you, in essence, have employers subject to very much a patchwork quilt of common law claims.[26]

QUESTIONS

1. Should urine testing, or other types of testing, be permitted among public and private employees to prevent drug abuse? Why or why not?

2. If you believe that urine testing in some form might be acceptable, write down the outlines of a sound testing program. Who should be tested? Employees? Job applicants? Should there be random testing? Should people in all job categories be tested?

3. As a manager with responsibility for conducting a testing program, what would be your response to the following situations?

   a. An employee who tests positively for marijuana on a Monday morning but has a spotless 10-year work record.

   b. An airline pilot who refuses a random test.

[24] In 2000 the Court decided a case in which a truck driver for Eastern Associated Coal Corp. had been discharged after his urine came out positive for marijuana use in random testing. The employee filed a grievance and was reinstated, but he then tested positive for marijuana use a second time and was fired again. However, once again, a union arbitrator reinstated the driver. The company argued that rehiring such an employee violated public policy, specifically, Department of Transportation regulations that required companies to maintain programs guarding against drug use by drivers. In its decision, the Supreme Court upheld the arbitration agreement on the narrow grounds that Department of Transportation regulations did not forbid employing drivers who had tested positive. The justices did not reach the conduct of the drug-testing program in their decision. The case is *Eastern Associated Coal Corp.* v. *United Mine Workers of America*, 531 U.S. 57.

[25] Lee Fletcher, "Employer Drug Testing Has Pitfalls," *Business Insurance*, October 23, 2000.
[26] Quoted in Fletcher, "Employer Drug Testing Has Pitfalls," p. 1.

c. A job applicant who tests positively for cocaine use.

d. An employee who tests positively for cocaine use.

e. An employee who comes to your office the night before an announced urinalysis and admits that he regularly uses a hallucinogenic drug off the job.

f. A productive worker who gives no outward sign of drug use but who is named as a drug abuser at work in an anonymous tip.

g. An employee involved in a serious work accident who refuses to take an immunoassay test based on her belief in the right to privacy.

h. The recommendation of the union that management be given the same tests as workers.

Chapter **Eighteen**

Civil Rights at Work

Johnson Controls, Inc.

Johnson Controls, Inc., of Milwaukee was founded in 1885 by Professor Warren Johnson to manufacture his new invention—the electric room thermostat. The company grew into a large multinational with factories on every continent. In 2001 it had $17.1 billion in revenues and ranked 115 on the *Fortune* 500.

Over the years, the company diversified by moving into auto components. It makes seats, instrument panels, consoles, and other parts and delivers them just-in-time to the assembly lines of the big auto firms. In addition, it is the largest manufacturer of lead-acid batteries in the United States. It was battery making that got the company into a landmark legal fight.

Medical research in the 1980s found that small amounts of lead that were harmless to adults could damage a fetus and cause stillbirth, low birth weight, and retardation. In response, Johnson Controls banned fertile women from certain battery-making jobs where workers breathed particles of lead. Ending a woman's lead exposure when pregnancy was discovered was not prudent because inhaled lead stays in the body a long time—it takes five to seven years for just half of it to be excreted.

Unless women proved that they were infertile, Johnson Controls moved them to other jobs. But sometimes the new jobs paid less and women voluntarily sterilized themselves to avoid losing income. For example, Gloyce Qualls, age 34, was removed from a job welding auto battery posts and given a safer job putting vents in motorcycle batteries. She elected to have a tubal ligation to regain her old job. Elsie Nason, age 50, also chose sterilization after being transferred to a lower-paid job.

What happened at Johnson Controls was typical in firms with so-called fetal protection policies. Many companies, including General Motors, Ford, Dow Chemical, DuPont, and Monsanto, had them. It was believed that if impaired children were born, they could sue corporations for exposing them to lead in the womb. So the policies protected stockholders along with fetal health.

However, some women thought that rules barring them from battery-line jobs were sexist. Eight women at Johnson Controls, joined by their union, filed a legal challenge. They argued that Johnson Controls' policy violated Title VII of the Civil Rights Act of 1964, which bans employment discrimination based on sex.

The company responded that it was a "business necessity" to keep fertile women away from lead to prevent future lawsuits. In addition, the company argued, Title VII allowed exceptions to its general rule against sex discrimination. These exceptions, called *bona fide occupational qualifications* (BFOQs), exist when workers of one or the other sex cannot do a job the right way precisely because of their sex. An advertising agency, for example, can screen out men applying for a job modeling woman's bathing suits. Johnson Controls felt that infertility should qualify as a BFOQ in battery making.

Two lower courts agreed with the company.[1] But in 1991, a unanimous Supreme Court held that the fetal protection policy caused illegal sex discrimination.[2] Women could not be excluded from any battery-making job. Its opinion said that the exclusion of women from work based on their ability to get pregnant violated Title VII, which had been amended some years before to make job actions based on pregnancy illegal. No BFOQ exception existed either, because pregnancy did not hinder the woman's ability to make batteries as efficiently as men. The Court concluded that Johnson Controls should inform women of risks and then let them decide.

The Court also stated that for Johnson Controls, obeying federal civil rights law was a defense against future lawsuits by children impaired in the womb. But *The Wall Street Journal* challenged this assertion, asking: "Is there a jury in the land that would tell an injured child who sues a corporation that, sorry, your mother decided to risk it and you must pay the price?"[3]

Before the decision, Johnson Controls had acted to lower lead exposure in its factories but no available technology eliminated it. It also returned to a voluntary fetal protection policy. Feminist groups were elated; women could chart their own destinies. Gloyce Qualls, however, had married and regretted that she could not have children.

This story illustrates the strong protections available in federal civil rights law for women—and for other protected groups—who claim discrimination. In this chapter we discuss employment discrimination and explain the evolution of laws and methods used to fight it over the years.

---

[1] See 680 F.Supp. 309 (DC–EDW 1988) and 886 F.2d 871 (7th Cir. 1989).
[2] *Automobile Workers* v. *Johnson Controls, Inc.,* 111 S.Ct. 1196. There were three concurring opinions.
[3] "Justices Adopt Fetal Position," *The Wall Street Journal,* March 22, 1991, p. A8.

A SHORT HISTORY OF WORKPLACE CIVIL RIGHTS

The American nation was founded upon noble ideals of justice, liberty, and human rights. Yet for most of the country's history, business practice openly diverged from these ideals and widespread discrimination based on race, color, sex, national origin, religion, and other grounds occurred. In fact, significant protection from employment discrimination has existed for less than 40 years of the 225 years since independence.

The Colonial Era

Employment discrimination can be dated from 1619 when European slave traders first brought African natives to the nation's shores. When the colonies declared their independence from England in 1776, there were already 500,000 slaves, mostly in the southern colonies. In the northern colonies, there was considerable anguish about slavery because it clashed with the ideals of those who had founded them to escape from religious persecution and government tyranny in Europe. These ideals were expressed in the Declaration of Independence in the following words.

> We hold these truths to be self-evident, that all men are created equal, that they are endowed by their Creator with certain unalienable Rights, that among these are Life, Liberty, and the pursuit of Happiness.

These "unalienable" rights are *natural rights,* that is, rights to which a person is entitled simply because he or she is human and that cannot be taken away by government. Natural rights exist on a higher plane than *civil rights,* which are rights bestowed by governments on their citizens. Natural rights are a standard against which the actions of governments and employers must be measured and can be found wanting.

This statement in the Declaration distills a body of doctrine known as the American Creed, which historian Arthur M. Schlesinger Jr. defines as incorporating "the ideals of the essential dignity and equality of all human beings, of inalienable rights to freedom, justice, and opportunity."[4] In the language of the time, the phrase "all men" was a reference to free, white males. Thomas Jefferson included in the original draft a strong statement condemning slavery as a "cruel war against human nature itself, violating its most sacred rights of life & liberty."[5] But this offended slave owners and had to be deleted to preserve unity in the coming revolution against England. Despite the limited inclusiveness of the Declaration's language, its statement of natural rights, notes Schlesinger, challenged whites to live up to its ideals and, if anything, "meant even

---

[4] Arthur M. Schlesinger Jr., *The Disuniting of America* (New York: Norton, 1992), p. 27.
[5] Edward S. Corwin and J. W. Peltason, *Understanding the Constitution,* 4th ed. (New York: Holt, Rinehart and Winston, 1967), p. 4.

more to blacks than to whites, since it was the great means of pleading their unfulfilled rights."[6]

The Constitution also reflected this bifurcated view of civil rights. When it was ratified in 1789, it sanctioned the practice of slavery in five clauses. Article 1, section 2, for example, counted slaves as three-fifths of a person for purposes of apportioning seats in the House of Representatives.[7] Yet the Bill of Rights contained ringing phrases protecting a wide range of fundamental rights.

Civil War and Reconstruction

Beginning at about the time the Constitution was ratified, an antislavery movement originated in a small sect within the Church of England. This movement grew rapidly, and in a century's time, its moral arguments largely swept slavery from the world stage.[8] In the United States, the issue of slavery rose to a crisis in the Civil War fought between 1860 and 1865. In 1865 President Abraham Lincoln issued the Emancipation Proclamation that freed an estimated four million slaves. Following the war, Congress passed three constitutional amendments designed to ensure that the rights of former slaves would be protected in the race-conscious southern culture.

- The *Thirteenth Amendment* in 1865 abolished slavery.

- The *Fourteenth Amendment* in 1868 was intended to prevent southern states from passing discriminatory laws. It reads, in part: "No State shall make or enforce any law which shall abridge the privileges or immunities of citizens of the United States; nor shall any State deprive any person of life, liberty, or property, without due process of law; nor deny to any person within its jurisdiction the equal protection of the laws."

- The *Fifteenth Amendment* in 1870 prohibited race discrimination in voting.

These amendments were supplemented by a series of civil rights acts passed by Congress, most notably one in 1866 to protect blacks against employment discrimination and another in 1875 to protect them from discrimination in transportation and accommodations. Altogether, these amendments and statutes created a formidable legal machinery to implement the rights to which blacks were entitled under the American Creed. If this machinery had been allowed to function, a century of painful

---

[6] Schlesinger, *The Disuniting of America,* p. 39.
[7] See also Article I, section 9, limiting taxation of slaves; Article I, section 9, prohibiting Congress from ending the slave trade before 1808; Article IV, section 2, requiring return of fugitive slaves to owners; and Article V, prohibiting amendment of Article 1, section 9, before 1808.
[8] Thomas Sowell, *Race and Culture: A World View* (New York: Basic Books, 1994), pp. 210–14.

employment discrimination against blacks and other groups might have been prevented. But it was not to be.

There was tremendous resistance to the new laws in the South, but at first much enforcement was possible because of the continuing presence of the Union Army, an occupying force that kept a temporary lid on southern resistance to black rights, which was formidable and violent. Because the troops protected voting rights, for example, 16 blacks were elected to Congress and about 600 to state legislatures. But the presidential election of 1876 ended the era of southern rehabilitation. In the race, the Republican candidate Rutherford B. Hayes lost the popular vote to his Democratic opponent Samuel J. Tilden, but the vote was close in the electoral college and returns from three southern states were contested. Hayes agreed to an "understanding" that if the electoral votes from these southern states were cast for him, he would withdraw the remaining federal troops. History records that Hayes won the election and the soldiers left. An important check on racism went with them.

White racism reaaserted itself in the South in many ways. *Racism,* defined broadly, is the belief that each race has distinctive cultural characteristics and that one's own race is superior to other races. It persists when myths and stereotypes about inferiorities are expressed in institutions of education, government, religion, and business. Racism leads to social discrimination, or the apportioning of resources based on group membership rather than individual merit. It insulates the power of a privileged group—for example, white Americans—from challenge.

Southern states adopted segregationist statutes called Jim Crow laws. These laws institutionalized the idea that whites were superior to blacks by creating segregated schools, restrooms, and water fountains; in literacy tests that disenfranchised blacks; in restrictive covenants, or deeds, that prevented whites from selling property to blacks in certain neighborhoods; and in discriminatory hiring that kept blacks in menial occupations.

Other Groups Face Employment Discrimination

In the meantime, other groups aside from blacks faced extensive and institutionalized employment discrimination as well. Native Americans were widely treated as an inferior race. In the nineteenth century, the federal government spent uncounted millions of dollars to destroy their societies and segregate them on reservations. A large population of roughly 90,000 Hispanics suddenly became residents of United States territory when Mexico ceded Texas in 1845 and huge tracts of southwestern land in 1848. Soon these Mexican Americans were victims of a range of discriminatory actions. They were legally stripped of extensive land holdings and exploited in a labor market where discrimination confined them to lesser occupations. They suffered great violence; more Hispanics were killed in the Southwest between 1850 and 1930 than blacks were lynched in the South.[9]

Beginning in 1851, Chinese laborers began to enter the country. They settled in western states and many owned placer mines. In 1863 several thousand began working on the construction of the Central Pacific Railroads as "coolies" (a word of that era used as a synonym for Chinese labor). Some started businesses such as laundries and restaurants. By the 1870s there were 100,000 Chinese in western states; in California there were 75,000, about 10 percent of the population. Although prejudice existed against them, their presence was tolerated until economic depression set in and the white majority felt them competing for jobs and customers. Then economic and racial discrimination began in earnest. Special taxes passed by state legislatures were used to confiscate their mines and ruin their commercial businesses. Some towns ordered all Chinese to leave. San Francisco passed an ordinance requiring city licenses for all laundries, then denied licenses to Chinese laundries.[10] The California state constitution, adopted in 1874, prohibited Chinese from voting and made it illegal for corporations to hire them. Finally, Congress banned the immigration of Chinese laborers in 1882.

The earliest Japanese immigrants found similar inhospitality. By 1880 there were only 124 Japanese in the United States, but their numbers increased rapidly as employers sought replacements for the cheap Chinese labor supply that had been cut off. By 1990 about 100,000 Japanese immigrants had arrived, most in California. Japanese laborers were typically paid 7 to 10 cents an hour less than whites. Like the Chinese, they ultimately threatened white labor and soon faced violent prejudice in cities. They turned to agricultural work in California's fertile inland valleys, but powerful white farmers resented their presence. California passed laws prohibiting Japanese land ownership, and in 1924 Congress banned further Japanese immigration. Although employers wanted to utilize Japanese labor, social attitudes frequently made this impossible. For example, in 1925 Pacific Spruce Corporation brought 35 Japanese to the small lumber town of Toledo, Oregon, to work in its sawmill. A mob of 500 men, women, and children swarmed the mill and the company had to load the Japanese on trucks that took them to Portland.[11]

As this brief sketch on nineteenth- and early twentieth-century employment discrimination shows, neither the American Creed nor the fine legal mechanism put in place after the Civil War worked to stop racism.

---

[9] John P. Fernandez, *Managing a Diverse Work Force* (Lexington, MA: Lexington Books, 1991), p. 165.

[10] In *Yick Wo* v. *Hopkins*, 118 U.S. 356 (1886), the Supreme Court struck down the ordinance as a violation of the equal protection clause of the Fourteenth Amendment. Had the Court followed up on this precedent, it could have struck down Jim Crow laws in the South.

[11] Herman Feldman, *Racial Factors in American Industry* (New York: Harper, 1931), pp. 89–90.

Why not? The former was eclipsed by broad public prejudice. The latter had to be enforced against the grain of southern racism and was, in any case, soon dismantled by the Supreme Court in two landmark cases—the *Civil Rights Cases* and *Plessy* v. *Ferguson.*

The *Civil Rights Cases*

The Civil Rights Act of 1875 was passed to prevent racial discrimination in "inns, public conveyances on land or water, theaters and other places of public amusement."[12] The law set a fine of up to $1,000 or imprisonment up to one year for violation. Still, there was widespread discrimination against freed slaves by business and soon a series of cases reached the Supreme Court. Two cases involved inns in Kansas and Missouri that had refused rooms to blacks. And in one case, the Memphis and Charleston Railroad Company in Tennessee had refused to allow a woman "of African descent" to ride in the ladies' car of a train. These cases were consolidated into one opinion by the Supreme Court in 1883 and called the *Civil Rights Cases.*[13]

The Civil Rights Act of 1875 was based on the Fourteenth Amendment, and in the Court's opinion, Justice Joseph P. Bradley focused on its wording. Because the amendment reads that "no state" shall discriminate, Bradley held that it did not prohibit what he referred to as a "private wrong." If race discrimination was not supported by state laws, it was a private matter between companies and their customers or employees and the Fourteenth Amendment did not prohibit it. For this reason, Congress lacked the authority to regulate race bias among private parties; therefore, the Civil Rights Act of 1875 was unconstitutional.

The *Civil Rights Cases* so narrowed the meaning of the Fourteenth Amendment that it became irrelevant to a broad range of economic and social bias. Congress and the courts could no longer use it to strike down much of the most brazen race discrimination. It was not necessarily a wrong decision; in fact, many constitutional scholars believe that the Court made a reasonable decision for that day given the clear reference to state action in the Fourteenth Amendment. But in dissent, Justice John Marshall Harlan argued that "the substance and spirit of the recent Amendments of the Constitution have been sacrificed by a subtle and ingenious verbal criticism."[14]

Plessy v. *Ferguson*

Southern states had passed so-called Jim Crow laws that sanctioned race segregation. If the Fourteenth Amendment could not prohibit private individuals from depriving each other of basic rights, did it not still clearly

---

[12] An Act to Protect all Citizens in their Civil and Legal Rights, 18 Stat. At L., 335, section 1.
[13] 109 U.S. 835 (1883).
[14] 109 U.S. 844.

prohibit states from enacting laws that abused the former slaves? The answer was no.

One such law was the Separate Car Act passed by Louisiana in 1890. This statute required all Louisiana railroads to "provide equal but separate accommodations for the white, and colored races, by providing two or more passenger coaches for each passenger train, or by dividing the passenger coaches by a partition so as to secure separate accommodations."[15] This law, like other Jim Crow laws, was based on the *police power* of the state, a presumed power inherent in the sovereignty of every government, to protect citizens from nuisances and dangers that might harm public safety, health, and morals.

On June 7, 1892, Homer Plessy, who was seven-eighths Caucasian and one-eight African, bought a first-class ticket on the East Louisiana railroad to travel from New Orleans to Covington. Boarding the train, he took a vacant seat in the white coach. He was asked by the conductor to move to the "nonwhite" coach. Plessy refused and was taken to a New Orleans jail.

Plessy brought suit, claiming he was entitled to "equal protection of the laws" as stated in the Fourteenth Amendment. In 1896, in *Plessy* v. *Ferguson,* the Supreme Court disagreed, holding that as long as separate accommodations for blacks were equal to those of whites, blacks were not deprived of any rights. Justice Henry B. Brown, writing for the majority, argued that laws requiring race separation "do not necessarily imply the inferiority of either race to the other" and were a valid exercise of police power by state legislatures because they enhanced "comfort, and the preservation of the public peace and good order."[16] This ruling completed the destruction of the Fourteenth Amendment as a mechanism that could guarantee civil rights by imposing upon it the perverse interpretation that legitimized "separate but equal." This doctrine, which became the foundation for legal apartheid in the South, stood for 58 years until reversed in 1954 by the Court in its famous school desegregation case, *Brown* v. *Board of Education.*[17]

Plessy is in retrospect notorious and some say one of the worst decisions ever made by the Court because of its consequences. The justices missed an opportunity to read the Fourteenth Amendment in a way that would protect blacks from the schemes of white racists. They must have thought that a decision striking down Jim Crow would be unpopular and widely disobeyed and may have sought to prevent the Court from being weakened by disregard for its opinions. As in the *Civil Rights Cases,* Justice Harlan was a lone dissenter who kept the light of the American Creed flickering by lecturing the majority. He wrote:

[15] Act 111 of 1890, quoted in Richard Epstein, *Forbidden Grounds: The Case Against Employment Discrimination Laws* (Cambridge, MA: Harvard University Press, 1992), pp. 99–100.
[16] *Plessy* v. *Ferguson,* 163 U.S. 540 (1896), at 544 and 550. John H. Ferguson was the judge who denied Plessy's constitutional claim in the New Orleans Criminal Court.
[17] 347 U.S. 483.

The *Plessy* decision made possible this photograph taken in North Carolina in 1950. These water fountains symbolize a much larger universe of discrimination, including employment discrimination.
© Elliott Erwitt/Magnum Photos.

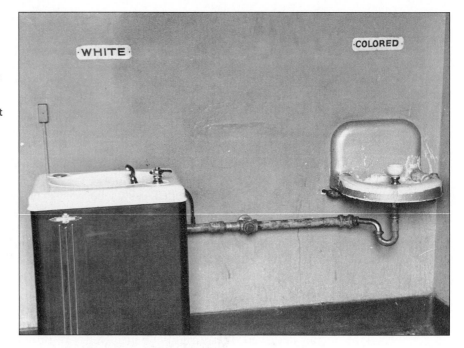

> Our Constitution is color-blind and neither knows nor tolerates classes among citizens. In respect of civil rights, all citizens are equal before the law. The humblest is the peer of the most powerful. The law regards man as man, and takes no account of his . . . color when his civil rights as guaranteed by the supreme law of the land are involved.[18]

Long Years of Discrimination

The nation's civil rights laws were now hopelessly crippled. Southern legislatures were emboldened by *Plessy.* Now needing no special moral justification, Jim Crow laws spread. Black workers faced the most blatant discrimination. They were not allowed to hold jobs such as streetcar conductor or cashier where they would have any authority over whites. Labor unions refused to admit blacks, and a few that did limited them to low-pay occupations. The Brotherhood of Locomotive Engineers, for example, barred blacks from being locomotive engineers. In South Carolina, a law prohibited blacks and whites from working in the same room or using the same plant entrances in the cotton textile industry. Such custom spread to the North. A study of economic opportunity for blacks in Buffalo, New York, told the following tale.

[18] 163 U.S. 537.

A [black] man tells of being made a moulder in a foundry, later to be replaced by a white worker and reduced to the grade of moulder's helper, and finally dismissed when he made a complaint. Another man was given a chance to try out for a skilled-labor job in a stone-cutting concern and, having made good, was given the position temporarily, losing it, however, a few days later when the superintendent "came down through the shop" and, seeing him so employed, told the foreman to put another man on the work.[19]

THE CIVIL RIGHTS ACT OF 1964

This kind of open discrimination continued in the South. A study of 175 firms in New Orleans in 1943 found that almost all of them hired blacks, but then 93 percent segregated their workforces and 79 percent segregated job categories.[20] In the North, many companies refused to hire blacks at all. A study of 14 plants in Chicago in 1952, for example, found that 10 of them, or 71 percent, excluded blacks.[21]

In the late 1950s and early 1960s, a new civil rights movement arose. Under the leadership of blacks such as Martin Luther King, this movement was nonviolent and again focused on making America live up to the ideals in the American Creed. "The American people are infected with racism—that is the peril," said King. "Paradoxically, they are also infected with democratic ideals—that is the hope."[22] The pressures of this movement led to many social reforms, among them passage of the Civil Rights Act of 1964, which is today the cornerstone of the structure of laws and regulations enforcing equal opportunity. Its Title VII prohibits discrimination in any aspect of employment. It reads, in part:

It shall be an unlawful employment practice for an employer:

1. To fail or refuse to hire or to discharge any individual, or otherwise to discriminate against any individual with respect to his compensation, terms, conditions, or privileges of employment, because of such individual's race, color, religion, sex, or national origin.
2. To limit or classify his employees or applicants for employment in any way which would deprive any individual of employment opportunities or otherwise adversely affect his status as an employee, because of such individual's race, color, religion, sex, or national origin. [Section 703(a)]

[19] Quoted in Feldman, *Racial Factors in American Industry,* p. 36.
[20] Logan Wilson and Harlan Gilmore, "White Employers and Negro Workers," *American Sociological Review,* December 1943, pp. 698–700.
[21] Lewis M. Killian, "The Effects of Southern White Workers on Race Relations in Northern Plants," *American Sociological Review,* June 1952, p. 329.
[22] Quoted in Lani Guinier, "[E]racing Democracy: The Voting Rights Cases," *Harvard Law Review,* November 1994, p. 109.

Title VII also created the Equal Employment Opportunity Commission (EEOC), an independent regulatory commission, to enforce its provisions. All companies with fifteen or more employees fall under the jurisdiction of Title VII and must report annually to the EEOC the number of minorities and women in various job categories.[23] If bias exists, employees can file charges with the EEOC. The agency then attempts to resolve charges through conciliation or voluntary settlement, but if that fails, it can sue in a federal court. In 2000 there were 59,588 charges filed under Title VII leading to the recovery of $149 million in monetary benefits to workers suffering discrimination.[24]

The overall purpose of Title VII, which is clear from the congressional debates that preceded its passage, was to remove discriminatory barriers to hiring and advancement and create a level playing field for all workers. As originally enacted, it did not require that minority workers be hired simply because they belonged to protected groups. It did not require employers to redress racially imbalanced workforces or change established seniority systems. No whites would be fired, lose their seniority, or be adversely affected. Simply put, from the day the law went into effect, all bias was to end. Job decisions could be made only on merit.

Disparate Treatment and Disparate Impact

Title VII made overt, blatant employment discrimination illegal. It enforced a legal theory of *disparate treatment.* Disparate treatment exists if an employer gives less favorable treatment to employees because of their race, color, religion, sex, or national origin. For example, a retail store that refused to promote black warehouse workers to sales positions, preferring white salespeople to serve predominantly white customers, would be guilty of this kind of discrimination. Disparate treatment violates the plain meaning of Title VII.

Although the intention of Title VII was to create a level playing field by prohibiting all discrimination, given the entrenched prejudices of employers in the 1960s, expecting that bigotry would instantly vanish was futile. The statute would need to evolve, and it did.

When Title VII went into effect, employers could no longer engage in outwardly visible displays of discrimination. "Whites only" signs came down from windows and discrimination went underground where it was disguised but just as invidious. Instead of openly revealing prejudicial motives, employers hid them. Minority job applicants were simply

---

[23] A 1972 law extended coverage of Title VII to federal, state, and local government employees, so today Title VII covers most workers. Workers at firms with fewer than 15 employees can sue under state and local civil rights laws or, for race discrimination, may seek remedy under the Civil Rights Act of 1866.

[24] U.S. Equal Employment Opportunity Commission, "Title VII of the Civil Rights Act of 1964 Charges: FY 1992–FY 1998," www.eeoc.gov/stats/vii.html.

rejected without comment or were found less qualified in some way. Or employers introduced job requirements that appeared merit-based but were in fact pretexts for discrimination. Female applicants had to meet height, weight, and strength requirements that favored men. Southern blacks were given tests that favored better-educated whites.

This kind of discrimination was hard to eradicate under the existing provisions of Title VII because employers would not admit a discriminatory motive and claimed that their job criteria were neutral and merit-based. The flaw in Title VII was that it contained no weapon to fight *disparate impact*. Disparate impact exists where an employment policy is apparently neutral in its impact on all employees but, in fact, is not job-related and prevents individuals in protected categories from being hired or from advancing. To combat disparate impact, the court initially used a case-by-case judicial test for discrimination. First, the applicant or employee made a charge alleging bias. Then the employer had to set forth a reason why it was a "business necessity" to engage in the practice. Then the burden of proof shifted back to the employee to prove that the employer's reason was phony, which was frequently hard.[25] This back-and-forth dance in which each individual case was separately considered was awkward and time-consuming for the courts and placed the difficult burden of proving the employer's secret motive on individual plaintiffs who lacked the legal resources of corporations. Some other way to fight hidden employer racism was needed. The Supreme Court would create it.

The *Griggs* Case

The Duke Power Company had a steam-generating plant in Draper, North Carolina, where workers had been segregated by race for many years. The plant was organized into five divisions and blacks had been allowed to work only in the lowest-paying labor department. The company had openly discriminated against blacks, but when Title VII took effect, it rescinded its race-based policies and opened all jobs to blacks.

But it also instituted a new policy that required a high school diploma to move up from the labor department to the coal handling, operations, maintenance, or laboratory and test departments. Now black workers could apply for formerly white-only jobs that paid more only if they had finished high school. Alternatively, they could take an intelligence test and a mechanical aptitude test, and if they scored at the same level as the average high school graduate, they could meet the high school diploma requirement. But since blacks in the area were less educated, this requirement frustrated their ambitions. Instead of rejecting blacks for being black, Duke Power now rejected them for lacking education. Black workers filed suit, alleging that the education and testing requirements had

---

[25] This sequence was set up in *McDonnell Douglas* v. *Green,* 411 U.S. 792 (1973).

the effect of screening them out and were, in any case, unrelated to the ability, for example, to shovel coal in the coal handling department.

In *Griggs* v. *Duke Power,* decided in 1971, the Supreme Court held that diploma requirements and tests that screened out blacks or other protected classes were illegal unless employers could show that they were related to job performance or justified by "business necessity." They were unlawful even if no discrimination was intended. The *Griggs* decision, and the legal theory of disparate impact it created, was necessary for Title VII to work. If employers had been permitted to use sinuous evasions and substitute proxies for direct racial bias, Title VII would have been ineffective.

In 1978 the EEOC defined illegal disparate impact for employers with a guideline known as the *80 percent rule.*

> A selection rate for any race, sex, or ethnic group which is less than four-fifths (4/5) or (eighty percent) of the rate for the group with the highest rate will generally be regarded . . . as evidence of adverse impact.[26]

This rule is met if a company has hired minorities at the rate of at least 80 percent of the rate at which it hires from the demographic group (usually white males) that provides most of its employees. If, for example, it hires 20 percent of all white applicants, it must then hire at least 16 percent (80 percent of 20 percent) of black applicants. If it hires less than 16 percent of blacks, this statistical evidence defines unlawful disparate impact. The company is now on the defensive. It must show that the employment practices it uses, such as tests or applicant screening criteria, are a *business necessity.* Using the business necessity defense, it must prove that the test or practice is "essential," and the need for it is "compelling."[27]

With the addition of the theory of disparate impact by the judiciary, Title VII had evolved beyond its original meaning and could be used to strike down a broader range of discrimination. Title VII finally gave blacks and others a potent legal mechanism to get the civil rights on the job that Congress had tried to give them during the Reconstruction era. In a sense, broken promises were repaired. There is little in Title VII that would have been needed if, a century before, the Supreme Court had given good-faith construction to Reconstruction-era laws.

AFFIRMATIVE ACTION

Affirmative action is a phrase describing a range of policies to seek out, encourage, and sometimes give preferential treatment to employees in the groups protected by Title VII. The broad use of affirmative action was

---

[26] 29 CFR 1607.4 D (1989).
[27] Epstein, *Forbidden Grounds,* p. 212, citing *Williams* v. *Colorado Springs School District,* 641 F.2d 835 at 842.

rejected when Title VII was drafted and its congressional backers assured the business community that blacks and others would not have to be given preference over whites. Title VII was designed as a stop sign to end discrimination, not as a green light to engineer racially balanced workforces. Yet no sooner had President Lyndon Johnson signed it than civil rights groups argued that its philosophy of equal opportunity was too weak; blacks and others were so disadvantaged by past rejection that they lacked the seniority and credentials of whites. They could not compete equally in a merit system, and preferential treatment was needed to get justice.

Executive Order 11246

The origin of most affirmative action in corporations is Executive Order 11246, issued by President Johnson in 1965.[28] As originally written, the order simply required federal contractors to refrain from discrimination. It imposed penalties for noncompliance and established an agency in the Department of Labor, the Office of Federal Contract Compliance Programs (OFCCP), to enforce its provisions.

However, in 1971, the Labor Department issued Order No. 4, which requires federal contractors to analyze major job categories—especially officials and managers, professionals, technicians, sales workers, office and clerical workers, and skilled crafts workers—to find out if they are using women and minorities in the same proportion as they are present in the area labor force. If protected groups are underrepresented, companies must set up goals and timetables for hiring, retention, and promotion. About 200,000 corporations, employing 22 percent of the labor force and including nearly all of America's largest firms, have contracts to supply goods and services to government. So in effect, Executive Order 11246, as revised by Order No. 4, imposes widespread affirmative action.

The OFCCP, with one exception, does not establish rigid hiring goals for companies. The exception is in the construction industry, where, since 1980 it has mandated a goal of 6.9 percent females. In other industries, however, it requires contractors to set hiring goals and make a "good faith" effort to achieve them. Adequate progress is usually defined as a final hiring total that meets the 80 percent rule.

The OFCCP conducts zealous compliance reviews. Teams descend on a contractor, looking around, interviewing employees and managers, and auditing all kinds of records from interview notes to payroll slips. Each year the agency does more than 4,000 such audits. At the San Diego Marriott Hotel & Marina, OFCCP team members walked around restaurants, banquet halls, and the front desk and failed to see a single black woman working in a visible position. A look at job applications soon revealed that most black women had been rejected for positions where they would

---

[28] Now codified as 41 CFR 60–30.1 (2001).

interact with hotel guests. Some were better qualified than whites who were hired. Once this information surfaced, the hotel gave job offers, back pay, and benefits—a package worth $670,000—to 34 black women.[29] In extreme cases, the OFCCP can disqualify corporations from receiving federal contracts. This is rare. There have been only 13 debarments since 1990. However, it is common for inspections to uncover violations of antidiscrimination guidelines. In 2001 the agency discovered problems in 53 percent of the 4,716 facilities in which it did a compliance review.[30]

THE SUPREME COURT CHANGES TITLE VII

From the beginning, affirmative action was controversial. Philosophically, it challenges the American Creed in several ways. It affronts the ideal of equality of opportunity by substituting equality of result. It affronts the ideal of achievement based on merit. And it affronts the ideal of individual rights before the law by substituting group preferences. When affirmative action first started, it posed more than a philosophical problem. Corporations were alarmed by its potential for generating lawsuits. If they failed to remedy race and sex imbalances in their workforces, they faced penalties for violating federal laws. If they used affirmative action to increase numbers of minorities and women, they feared reverse discrimination suits by white males.

Affirmative action was bound to provoke fierce legal challenges, and the Supreme Court used these attacks to read revolutionary changes into Title VII. The first high-profile challenge came from Allan Bakke, a white male denied admission to the medical school at the University of California at Davis. In the entering class, 16 places out of 100 had been reserved for minority students. Bakke argued that he was better qualified than some minorities admitted and had suffered illegal race discrimination under Title VII because he was white. In *Regents of the University of California* v. *Bakke,* the Supreme Court ruled in his favor.[31] In a muddled, divided, and verbose opinion, the justices forbade strict quotas. Yet they also held that race and ethnicity could be one factor considered in admissions. This kept affirmative action alive but failed to resolve the dilemma of employers, who still feared reverse discrimination lawsuits.

Then a second case arose from a Kaiser Aluminum and Chemical Corporation plant in Louisiana. The Kaiser plant was near New Orleans where 39 percent of the workforce was black. Few blacks worked at the plant before passage of Title VII, and even with it, by 1974, only 18 percent

[29] Office of Federal Contract Compliance Programs, "OFCCP Egregious Discrimination Cases," www.dol.gov/dol/esa/public/media/reports/ofccp/egregis.htm.
[30] "Accomplishment Data: FY 1990–2001," www.dot.gov/dol/esa/public/media/reports/ofccp/acdata01.pdf.
[31] 438 U.S. 265 (1978).

of the plant's workers were black. Moreover, less than 2 percent of skilled crafts workers were black because Kaiser required previous craft experience and seniority. Blacks had little of either since crafts unions excluded them. Kaiser had federal contracts and, to comply with Executive Order 11246, it adopted an affirmative action plan in 1974 to raise percentages of black workers. One goal was to bring blacks into skilled craft positions, so the plan reserved 50 percent of crafts-training openings for them. This was clearly a race-based quota.

In 1974 a white laboratory analyst, Brian Weber, who had worked for Kaiser for 10 years, applied for a crafts-training program that would place him in a more skilled job and raise his yearly pay from $17,000 to $25,000. To pick the trainees, Kaiser set up dual seniority ladders—one for blacks and another for whites. Names were picked alternately in descending order from the top of each ladder, starting with the black ladder, until positions were filled, with the result that seven blacks and six whites were chosen. Weber was too low on the white ladder and was not selected, whereas two blacks with less seniority than Weber were chosen (see Figure 18.1). This was a classic case of reverse discrimination.

Weber brought suit, claiming that the selection procedure violated the clear language in Title VII that prohibited making employment decisions based on race. He claimed that his Fourteenth Amendment rights to equal treatment under the law had been abridged. Justice William J. Brennan delivered the opinion of the Court in 1979 in *United Steelworkers*

FIGURE 18.1
Selection of Crafts Trainees at Kaiser
Kaiser and the union selected 13 crafts trainees. All candidates met minimum qualifications, but black applicants numbered 6 and 7 had less seniority than whites numbered 7, 8, and 9.

of America v. *Weber*, ruling that Kaiser's affirmative action plan embodied the "spirit of the law," which was to overcome the effects of past discrimination against blacks.[32]

The Court also established important criteria for judging the legality of affirmative action programs that it would frequently use in later years. First, a plan must be designed to break down historic patterns of race or sex discrimination. Second, the plan must not create an absolute bar to the advance of white employees. In the *Weber* case, for example, some whites were still admitted to training. Third, the plan must not require the discharge of white workers. And finally, the plan should be flexible and temporary, so that it ends when goals are met.

The *Weber* decision added an entirely new meaning to Title VII. Henceforth, Title VII no longer stood guard over a neutral playing field. Now, it permitted the very thing that its drafters assured the nation it would not do—it permitted race-conscious preferential treatment for members of protected groups. A strong dissent in *Weber* by future Chief Justice William Rehnquist attacked the majority for adding this meaning to Title VII in contravention of its language, which clearly forbade *all* race discrimination, including that against whites. He referred to Brennan's opinion as "a tour de force reminiscent not of jurists such as Hale, Holmes, or Hughes, but of escape artists such as Houdini."[33]

The *Weber* case squarely raised the issue of reverse discrimination and confirmed that affirmative action plans were legal even if they adversely affected whites. After *Weber,* companies no longer worried about lawsuits by angry white workers. Affirmative action spread.

One year after *Weber*, the Supreme Court upheld race-conscious "set-aside" programs in *Fullilove* v. *Klutznick*.[34] To spur the economy, Congress in 1977 established a $4 billion fund for public works construction. Ten percent of the fund was reserved, or set aside, for minority contractors, who had to get some contracts even when they were not low bidders. When white contractors challenged the set-asides, the Court ruled that they were an appropriate remedy for past discrimination against minority contractors.

The *Bakke, Weber,* and *Fullilove* cases showed that a majority on the Supreme Court supported affirmative action. Yet in each case, there were strong dissents. And even among the justices who supported affirmative action, there was disagreement about its legitimate scope. Thus began many years of contentious jurisprudence in which the Court defined the limits of affirmative action, then began to restrict it.

In the 1980s a liberal majority on the Court established generous boundaries for affirmative action. It held, for example, that seniority sys-

---

[32] 443 U.S. 193.
[33] 47 LW 4859.
[34] 448 U.S. 448 (1980).

tems could not be overridden during layoffs to retain recently hired blacks.[35] In several other cases, it confirmed its decision in *Weber* by upholding affirmative action plans with hiring quotas for blacks.[36] It also upheld affirmative action to increase percentages of women in skilled crafts work.[37] Throughout, a minority of conservative justices vigorously dissented from the opinions of the liberal majority.

By 1988, however, President Ronald Reagan, an opponent of affirmative action, had appointed three new associate justices and a conservative bloc of five justices emerged to dominate the liberals on affirmative action cases.[38] In three cases decided in 1989, this group whittled away at race-conscious preferences.

The five first struck down a program awarding 30 percent of city construction work in Richmond, Virginia, to minority contractors, holding that the city had not adequately documented the past discrimination this program was said to remedy.[39] Next they changed the rules in disparate impact cases. Previously, neutral-seeming practices that led to disproportionate exclusion of minorities were assumed to be illegal unless the company could prove that they were a "business necessity"—an extremely difficult task. Now, said the Court, in a decision favoring an Alaskan salmon cannery where whites dominated the better-paying jobs, the burden was on nonwhites to prove that neutral-seeming rules caused discrimination.[40] Finally, in a case involving the Birmingham Fire Department, which had adopted an affirmative action plan because only 42 of its 5,453 firefighters and none of its 140 officers were black in a city that was more than 50 percent black, the Court held that white firefighters passed over for promotions were entitled to bring reverse discrimination suits.[41]

Advocates of affirmative action were infuriated, and soon Congress sent a clear message of its intent to the Supreme Court by passing the Civil Rights Act of 1991. This statute reversed the Court's narrowing of the grounds for affirmative action. Among other things, it shifted the burden of proof in statistical disparity cases back to employers, and it restricted the ability of whites to challenge preferential hiring and promotion plans.

---

[35] *Firefighters Local Union No. 178* v. *Stotts,* 467 U.S. 561 (1984); and *Wygant* v. *Jackson Board of Education,* 476 U.S. 267 (1986).

[36] *Local 28* v. *EEOC,* 478 U.S. 421 (1986); *Local No. 93* v. *City of Cleveland,* 478 U.S. 450 (1986); and *United States* v. *Paradise,* 480 U.S. 149 (1987).

[37] *Johnson* v. *Transportation Agency, Santa Clara County, California,* 480 U.S. 616 (1987).

[38] This bloc included Chief Justice William Rehnquist and Justices Anthony Kennedy, Sandra Day O'Connor, Antonin Scalia, and Byron White. These five joined to dominate the liberals William Brennan, Thurgood Marshall, Harry Blackmun, and John Paul Stevens. Kennedy, O'Connor, and Scalia were Reagan appointees.

[39] *City of Richmond* v. *J. A. Croson Co.,* 488 U.S. 469 (1989).

[40] *Wards Cove Packing Company* v. *Atonio,* 490 U.S. 642 (1989).

[41] *Martin* v. *Wilks,* 490 U.S. 755 (1989).

Since 1991 there has been a clear majority on the Court for ending affirmative action. President George Bush appointed two more justices who stand with conservatives on civil rights cases, David Souter (1990) and Clarence Thomas (1990); then, President Bill Clinton appointed two liberal-leaning justices, Ruth Bader Ginsburg (1993) and Steven Breyer (1994). Although a five-to-four majority to end affirmative action has existed for many years, the Court has not yet done so, although, in 1995 the five conservatives set up a "strict scrutiny" standard that was more difficult for existing affirmative action programs to meet. The case, *Adarand* v. *Peña,* is the case study following this chapter.[42]

It is no accident that the conservative justices have not overturned affirmative action. Advocates of preferences have been reluctant to risk the policy by appealing a case to the Supreme Court. In fact, civil rights groups raised money to settle one case so that it could be withdrawn before it was decided.[43] The future is uncertain, but if the five-member conservative bloc remains intact, new tests of affirmative action are likely to result in a decision that government-sponsored racial preferences in employment violate the equal protection clause in the Fourteenth Amendment.

The Affirmative Action Debate

The legal debate about affirmative action parallels a broader debate in society. This debate revolves around three basic ethical considerations.

First, there are *utilitarian* considerations. Utilitarian ethics require calculations about the overall benefit to society, as opposed to the costs, of affirmative action. Advocates argue that preferential treatment policies benefit everyone by making fuller use of talent. Critics say that affirmative action has been ineffective or that its meager benefits are outweighed by the fairness problems it raises.

Pinning down the overall effect of affirmative action is difficult. For example, three studies of the impact on blacks when federal contractors changed their hiring practices to comply with Executive Order 11246 showed only small employment increases of 0.8 percent to 1.2 percent.[44] But studies of its effect in some industries show remarkable gains. Statistics cannot resolve the utilitarian argument about whether affirmative action, on the whole, is a net benefit or cost to society.

Second, ethical theories of *justice* raise questions about the ultimate fairness of affirmative action. Norms of distributive justice require that fair criteria be used to assign benefits and burdens. It is widely believed that economic rewards should be distributed based on merit, not on race,

[42] 132 L.Ed.2d 158 (1995).
[43] *Piscataway Township Board of Education* v. *Taxman,* No. 96–679, 118 S.Ct. 595.
[44] Robert Rank and Eleena de Lisser, "Research on Affirmative Action Finds Modest Gains for Blacks over 30 Years," *The Wall Street Journal,* February 21, 1995, p. A2.

ethnicity, or sex. On the other hand, norms of compensatory justice require that payment be made to compensate for past wrongs. Past and current discrimination has handicapped women and minorities and placed them at a disadvantage. It has been estimated from the study of wage gaps, for example, that discrimination in employment has cost blacks $500 billion since 1929 and unjustly enriched whites by the same amount.[45] Thus, discrimination in favor of blacks may be justified to compensate for past deprivation. In 1963 President Lyndon Johnson used a colorful analogy to make this point.

> Imagine a 100-yard dash in which one of the two runners has his legs shackled together. He has progressed 10 yards, while the unshackled runner has gone 50 yards. How do they rectify the situation? Do they merely remove the shackles and allow the race to proceed? Then they could say that "equal opportunity" now prevailed. But one of the runners would still be 40 yards ahead of the other. Would it not be the better part of justice to allow the previously shackled runner to make up the 40-yard gap or to start the race all over again?[46]

However, with affirmative action, the penalty for past injustices falls on the current generation of white males—the least racist of any generation. Retributive justice requires that punishment be proportional to the crime committed. By what proof can it be shown that this generation should inherit the guilt of past generations?

And third, affirmative action may be debated in light of ethical theories of *rights*. Advocates of affirmative action argue that it is appropriate to mint a new civil right for women and minorities, the right to preferential treatment, and to exercise it until equality prevails. Discrimination in favor of protected groups is benevolent of intention, unlike the evil race discrimination of bigoted whites in the past. Opponents of the right to preferences argue that they destroy a more fundamental right—the right of all individuals to equal treatment before the law. Affirmative action can result in rewards being taken from persons who did not discriminate and given to persons who suffered no discrimination.

There is no easy solution to the contradictory appeals of these ethical arguments. Affirmative action is a complex policy with important benefits but also highly visible drawbacks. As a broad public policy, it is aging and past its prime. Four forces work to weaken it. First, the Supreme Court has narrowed its use. Second, the value of nondiscrimination, though hardly universal, is much stronger in the United States today than it was in the 1960s, when racism was more widespread. The nation now is

[45] Richard F. America, "Has Affirmative Action Repaid Society's Debt to African Americans?" *Business and Society Review,* Summer 1995, p. 58.
[46] Quoted in Robert A. Fullinwider, *The Reverse Discrimination Controversy: A Moral and Legal Analysis* (Totowa, NJ: Rowman and Littlefield, 1980), p. 95.

Other Important Antidiscrimination Laws

The problem of employment discrimination is so longstanding that, in addition to Title VII and Executive Order 11246, other laws have been passed to protect women, ethnic or racial minorities, and other disadvantaged groups. They include these:

The Civil Rights Act of 1866 was passed after the Civil War to protect the employment rights of freed slaves. It provides that "All persons . . . shall have the same right . . . to make and enforce contracts . . . as is enjoyed by white citizens."[47] Soon after its passage, the Supreme Court narrowly interpreted it to protect only state employees. For nearly a century, it remained on the books as an emasculated law, but it was revived by the Supreme Court in 1968.[48] Since then, it has been widely used by civil rights attorneys. It protects millions of workers in firms with fewer than fifteen employees against all forms of racial discrimination in employment. Employees of such small firms are not covered by Title VII.

The Equal Pay Act of 1963 prohibits pay differentials between male and female employees with

[47] 42 U.S.C. Sec. 1981, rev. stat. 1977.
[48] *Jones* v. *Alfred H. Mayer Co.*, 392 U.S. 409 (1968). This case overturned the *Civil Rights Cases.*

equal or substantially equal duties in similar working conditions. It does not override pay differences that are due to legitimate seniority or merit systems. It also covers nonwage benefits.

The Age Discrimination in Employment Act of 1967 protects people over age 40. After that age, it is illegal to discriminate against a person in hiring and job decisions because of their age. As the workforce ages, age bias complaints are the fastest-growing kind of discrimination charge. The average charge is brought by a white male in his fifties, dismissed in corporate downsizing, believing that his age was the reason.

The Vietnam-Era Veterans' Readjustment Assistance Act of 1974 requires federal contractors to develop affirmative action programs for hiring, training, and promoting Vietnam veterans.

The Pregnancy Discrimination Act of 1978 prohibits employment discrimination based on pregnancy, childbirth, or related medical conditions. If a woman can still work, she cannot be made to resign or go on leave for any pregnancy-related condition, including having an abortion. If she is temporarily unable to perform her regular duties, the employer must try modifying her work assignments or grant leave with or without pay.

closer to the ideal of equal treatment. Third, expansion of affirmative action weakened its justification. Originally, it was introduced to overcome lingering effects of black slavery and Jim Crow laws in the South. Strong medicine was warranted to reverse this tide of bigotry. Then over the years the same preferences were extended to other groups, including Hispanics, Asians, Pacific Islanders, and women, but there has been less consensus about their need for this advantage. Fourth, the 2000 census revealed the blurring of racial categories. Seven million Americans declined to check boxes for traditional racial categories, showing they preferred to be classified as multiracial.[49] Cumulatively, these changes weaken the case for affirmative action, and long ago public opinion began to move against it. Still, much life remains in this old warhorse of a policy, and it may continue to exist in some form for many years.

[49] Peter H. Schuck, "Affirmative Action: Don't Mend It or End It—Bend It," *Brookings Review,* Winter 2002, pp. 25–26.

The Americans with Disabilities Act of 1990 protects workers with mental and physical impairments, including those with AIDS, from job discrimination and extends to them the protections granted to women, ethnic, racial, and religious minorities in Title VII. In interviews, employers can ask only about the ability to do specific work. Companies must make "reasonable accommodations" for disabled workers, including, for instance, provision of devices that allow deaf workers to communicate visually and readers for blind workers. Companies must also try to accommodate persons with mental illnesses such as major depression, manic depression, schizophrenia, and obsessive compulsive disorder. For example, employers have been required to install soundproofing and set up room dividers for schizophrenic workers who have heightened sensitivity to noise and visual distractions.[50] However, companies are not required to make accommodations imposing an "undue burden" on the business.

The Civil Rights Act of 1991 amended five existing civil rights laws, including Title VII, to extend their coverage in employment situations. It encouraged civil rights lawsuits. Employment discrimination cases are difficult to prove, the evidence is often subtle or hidden in voluminous employment records, and they can take years to complete. Before this law, awards were limited to reinstatement and back pay, so the attorneys trying them were, in effect, low-paid crusaders. Then the 1991 act allowed plaintiffs in class actions to recover up to $300,000 in pain and suffering in addition to back pay and permitted their lawyers to bill losing corporations double their fees. The result was that more lawyers were attracted to bias litigation.

Altogether, this is a thorough body of legislation that, with Title VII and Executive Order 11246, protects *everyone* in the workforce from discrimination.

Sexual orientation is one area in which federal law does not yet provide specific protection against discrimination. Civil rights laws protecting homosexuals and lesbians from bias at work have been enacted by at least eight states and more than 90 cities. In 1996 the Supreme Court struck down a Colorado initiative that prohibited Colorado cities from passing ordinances to protect gay rights.[51] The Court held that the initiative violated the equal protection clause in the Fourteenth Amendment. This made it clear that the Court put discrimination due to sexual orientation on the same plane as discrimination based on other motives such as racism. However, no federal law specifically prohibits job bias against gays and lesbians.

[50] Robert Fear, "Employers Told to Accommodate the Mentally Ill," *The New York Times,* April 30, 1997, p. A15.

[51] *Romer* v. *Evans,* 517 U.S. 620 (1996).

WOMEN IN THE WORKPLACE

The number of working women began to rise early in the century. In 1910 women were only 21 percent of the labor force, and this number crept up very gradually until World War II, when it jumped to 35 percent as women replaced men in defense factories. After the war, the percentage of working women, what statisticians call the "participation rate," resumed its slow growth—never more than 1 percent a year and now less than that.

Today 60 percent of all women work, and they comprise 47 percent of the labor force. These figures are records, and some believe they reflect a recent and striking social change, but the trend they represent is a century old. What is new is the tendency for married women with children to hold jobs. Single women and married women without children have always worked in large numbers but left their jobs for childbearing. In the 1960s, however, the number of women continuing to work while raising children began to grow. In 1960 only 25 percent of mothers worked; by the late 1990s more than 70 percent did.[52] If there is any dramatic element of social change in the gradual trend of women to participate more in the labor force, it is found in this subtrend. The presence of so many mothers at work creates pressure to modify workplaces and forces millions of women to balance motherhood with job demands.

The trend for more women to work is worldwide. Between 1980 and 1999, the percentage of females in the world labor force grew by 1.5 percent to an average of 40.6 percent. Although the entry of more women is almost universal among nations, this slight overall increase masks underlying patterns. In socialist countries such as Vietnam, and in the nations formerly comprising the Soviet Union, for decades women have comprised half the labor force and their participation rates have not risen. The experience in European Union countries closely parallels that of the United States; the percentages of women in their labor forces and the rise in participation rates are comparable.

Some non-Western nations have far fewer working women. Where strong religious and cultural values discourage independent work outside the home, their labor force participation is lower. Islamic nations are an example. Only 15 percent of workers in the United Arab Emirates are women, 16 percent in Saudi Arabia and Oman, 24 percent in Jordan, and 27 percent in Iran. But Islamic women are entering the workforce more rapidly than women in the United States and Europe. Since 1980 women have increased by 5 percent in the U.S. labor force and 4.5 percent in Europe but by 10 percent in the United Arab Emirates, 9 percent in Jordan and Oman, 8 percent in Saudi Arabia, and 7 percent in Iran.[53]

The only part of the world where female participation rates are declining in the workforce is in sub-Saharan Africa. There, strong cultural and religious traditions subordinate females. Women have little access to education. They move into heavy manual labor and into traditionally female work, often experiencing discrimination and sexual harassment. The largest concentration of the world's very poor countries is in this region; these nations have not participated in the growth of world trade and most are in long-term economic decay. To remedy this, some governments have cut spending and subsidized industries that attract international trade. Men move into better-paying jobs in these modernizing sectors, leaving women vulnerable to unemployment as old areas of the economy founder. Thus, as economies decline and change, the percentage of women in the labor forces of about a dozen poor African nations has declined.

[52] U.S. Department of Labor, *Equal Pay: A Thirty-Five Year Perspective* (Washington, DC: Department of Labor, June 10, 1998), pp. 16, 53.
[53] Figures in this paragraph are from World Bank, *World Development Indicators 2000* (Washington, DC: World Bank, 2000), table 2.2.

Gender Attitudes at Work

Throughout recorded history, men and women have been socialized into distinct sex roles. Men were traditionally aggressive, logical, and dominant; they were the breadwinners. Women were objects of sexual desire and homemakers; they were expected to be emotional and submissive. For centuries, these stereotypes dominated perceptions of the sexes, and they were carried from family and social life into the workplace, where they defined male-female relationships.

In the 1960s, however, a worldwide women's movement gained force and challenged male domination in Eastern and Western cultures. Arguing that women could do men's jobs, its advocates attacked cultural impediments to equality. Because of this movement, two competing values clashed in the workplace. The new feminist perspective asserted that working women were entitled to the same jobs, rights, and ambitions as men. Yet men who believed in traditional sex-role stereotypes thought that women were too emotional to manage well; lacked ambition, logic, and toughness; and could not sustain career drive because of family obligations.

There is no evidence that such stereotypes of male and female behavior have a biological basis. Sex-difference studies done over many years show genetic and hormonal differences between men and women but do not confirm behavioral differences. Some studies document, for example, greater aggressiveness in men and greater willingness of women to express a range of emotions. Yet other studies contradict such findings and suggest that, from a statistical standpoint, behavioral overlap is usually more significant than behavioral similarities.[54]

Studies of men and women managers confirm these observations. Some bear out stereotypes, but others fail to support them. One survey of high-level managers found that men tend to use a command-and-control leadership style, whereas women use an "interactive" style with more emphasis on participation, information sharing, and enhancing the self-worth of subordinates.[55] This result confirms a stereotyped view of sex differences. Another study, however, found that female managers were more committed to their careers than males; they were, for example, more willing to rank work over family and more willing to move for promotion.[56] This contradicts the stereotyped view that women are less steady workers because of family obligations. Still other studies show that women are not different in the way they work. An analysis of the decision styles of 300 managers, for example, found that female managers,

[54] Cathy Young, "Sex & Sensibility," *Reason,* March 1999.
[55] Judy B. Rosener, "Ways Women Lead," *Harvard Business Review,* November–December 1990.
[56] Warren H. Schmidt and Barry Z. Posner, "The Values of American Managers Then and Now," *Management Review,* February 1992.

like male managers, were predominantly "left-brain" and tended to use the same decision methods as men.[57] Another survey of men and women found that over a wide range of values and attitudes toward work, there were few sex differences and those that did exist were "of rather small magnitude."[58] In sum, although much is written about how men perceive women differently in the workplace and discriminate against them based on these perceptions, there is no persuasive body of evidence that men and women behave differently as managers. However, several large-scale studies of the performance evaluations of men and women managers in a number of industries found that the women outscored their male colleagues on a majority of rating criteria.[59]

The Persistence of Traditional Stereotypes

Despite lack of evidence for behavior differences at work, stereotypes persist. Surveys documented a marked decline in negative stereotyping following the rapid gains of the women's movement after the 1960s. A survey, taken in 1965 and then repeated in 1985, showed sexist attitudes receding. The number of men expressing an "unfavorable basic attitude" toward female executives fell from 41 percent in 1965 to 5 percent in 1985. The number agreeing that "women rarely expect or want authority" fell from 54 percent to 9 percent. And the number who believed that "the business community will never wholly accept women executives" fell from 61 percent to 20 percent.[60] Other surveys have shown similar changes in male thinking.[61]

However, a gap still exists between how men and women perceive the career chances of women. A survey of female executives and male CEOs at 1,000 large American corporations found a remarkable divergence of opinion about why women advanced so slowly into top jobs. For example, 52 percent of the women felt that male stereotyping stopped their advance, while only 25 percent of CEOs saw this as a problem; 49 percent of women felt that their exclusion from informal male networks was a problem, but only 15 percent of the CEOs agreed.[62]

[57] Alan J. Rowe and James D. Boulgarides, *Managerial Decision Making* (New York: Macmillan, 1992), p. 49. "Left-brain" thinking refers to logical thinking, as opposed to "right-brain" thinking, which is defined as nonlogical, or emotional, thinking.

[58] Joel Lefkowitz, "Sex-Related differences in Job Attitudes and Dispositional Variables: Now You See Them, . . . " *Academy of Management Journal,* April 1994, p. 343.

[59] Rochelle Sharpe, "As Leaders, Women Rule," *Business Week,* November 20, 2000, p. 75.

[60] Charlotte Decker Sutton and Kris K. Moore, "Executive Women—20 Years Later," *Harvard Business Review,* September–October 1985.

[61] See, for example, Alma S. Baron, "What Men Are Saying about Women in Business: A Decade Later," *Business Horizons,* July–August 1989, p. 52.

[62] Belle Rose Ragins, Bickley Townsend, and Mary Mattis, "Gender Gap in the Executive Suite: CEOs and Female Executives Report on Breaking the Glass Ceiling," *Academy of Management Executive,* February 1998, p. 34.

DISCRIMINATORY TREATMENT OF WOMEN

In this section we discuss four areas of work life in which women are treated differently than men.

Occupational Segregation

Women are more likely to work in some jobs than others. Within corporations and in the economy as a whole, traditionally female jobs generally are lower in status and pay than typically male jobs. Women also have less occupational diversity than do men.

In the 1960s, when married women first began to work in large numbers, two-thirds of all women worked in clerical, sales, or low-level service occupations such as domestic worker. Another 15 percent worked in the professions, mainly as teachers and nurses. Since then, women have entered nontraditional occupations. They flow most freely into growing occupations where demand for labor reduces barriers to entry such as sex discrimination. For example, they have moved in large numbers into management positions in service industries, now holding 47 percent of such positions. Because jobs in the manufacturing sector have not been increasing since the 1960s, women have had far less success moving into skilled blue-collar occupations. For example, women hold only 9 percent of precision production, craft, and repair jobs.

Table 18.1 shows the detailed occupations at which the largest numbers of women work. The nine jobs shown account for more than 20 percent of all women working full-time. The percentage figures in the right-hand column show the predominance of women in each occupation. Numerically, more women work in the broad occupational category of executives, administrators, and managers, but only one specific occupation, accountants and auditors, employs enough women to make the list. However, 49 percent of women who work are executives, managers, and administrators. Other occupational categories, including traditionally male jobs, have far fewer women. Although women are moving into nontraditional occupations, they do so in small numbers. They are, for example, only 10 percent of engineers, 4 percent of airline pilots, 4 percent of firefighters, and 4 percent of precision machinists.

Labor statisticians have developed a *difference index* to measure occupational differences between men and women over time and throughout the labor force. Between 1985 and 1995, the difference index fell from 58 to 54.[63] This means that because women are so highly concentrated in a few traditionally female occupations, for men and women to have an equal share of every occupation, 54 percent of women would have to

---

[63] Barbara H. Wootton, "Gender Differences in Occupational Employment," *Monthly Labor Review,* April 1997, p. 17. See this article for a description of the difference index.

TABLE 18.1
The Top Nine Jobs Held by Women: 2000*

Source: Bureau of Labor Statistics, Current Population Survey.

Occupation	Number of Women (in thousands)	Women as a Percentage of Total Number of Workers in Occupation
1. Secretary	2,002	99%
2. Elementary school teacher	1,563	83
3. Registered nurse	1,385	91
4. Nursing aid, orderly, or attendant	1,267	88
5. Cashier	1,046	77
6. Health technologist or technician	1,023	78
7. Bookkeeper, accounting, or auditing clerk	1,014	91
8. Accountants and auditors	785	60
9. Receptionist	688	97

*Based on number of women working full-time as wage and salary workers in detailed occupational categories.

switch to another occupation. The rate of decline in the index is so slow that decades will pass before any approximation of parity in occupations across the board is achieved. Sex discrimination may explain an indefinable part of this slowness in achieving parity.

Subtle Discrimination

Women face discriminatory male attitudes. Many workplace cultures are based on masculine values. In them, the expectation is that women will behave according to traditional male–female stereotypes. Men holding these stereotypes are conditioned to see women in the role of lovers, wives, or daughters; they subconsciously expect female co-workers to act similarly and be supportive and submissive.

In blue-collar settings, sexism may be blatant; some men will openly express biases. In managerial settings, sex discrimination is usually subtle, even unintentional. Men may assume that women are secretaries. In groups, men address other men first. They discount or ignore women's ideas. They make women uncomfortable with locker-room humor. They fail to include women in after-hour socializing. A female bond trader at Morgan Stanley Dean Witter in New York tells of hosting a dinner for her clients, all male, and some male co-workers. Afterward, the men politely called a taxi for her safe return home, then went to a club with topless dancing, where they spent the rest of the evening. The following day, the men recounted stories of revelry with her clients.[64]

[64] Patrick McGeehan, "Wall Street Highflier to Outcast: A Woman's Story," *The New York Times,* February 10, 2002, p. 1.

Masculine cultures underlie many kinds of differential treatment. The norms in these cultures are usually not blatantly sexist. They can be nearly invisible, manifest only as practices that seem innocent and neutral. The problems they cause for women are often unintended. At one global retailing corporation dominated by men in the top ranks, a culture of flexible operations had grown up in which meetings were held spontaneously, often at the last minute or late in the day. Important decisions were made quickly. This culture was highly successful because it facilitated fast reaction to markets and minimized bureaucratic inefficiencies. However, it was hard on women who bore heavier responsibilities for households and children than the men. When a meeting suddenly materialized for the early evening, some women could not stay, and if they did not they were left out of critical decisions and unable to defend their turf.[65]

Deborah Tannen studied the linguistic styles of men and women at work.[66] According to Tannen, men and women learn different ways of speaking in childhood. Boys are taught by peers and cultural cues to use words in ways that build status and emphasize power over other boys. Girls, on the other hand, use language to build rapport and empathy with their playmates. Unlike boys, girls will ostracize a playmate who brags and asserts superiority in a group. Later in life, these conversation styles carry over into the workplace, where they can place women at a disadvantage. In meetings, women may be reluctant to interrupt or criticize the ideas of another, whereas men push themselves into the conversation and engage in ritual challenges over the validity of ideas. Men hear women make self-effacing or apologetic remarks and conclude that they lack self-confidence. Tannen thinks that the female linguistic style makes it harder to make a firm impression in male-dominated groups, so they are more often interrupted in meetings and their ideas may be pushed aside. "I have yet to talk to any woman who doesn't report an anecdote about this issue," she says.[67] Tannen recommends demonstrative speech, but many women report that men react negatively to aggressive behavior.

Compensation

Women are paid less than men. Before the Equal Pay Act was signed in 1963, newspapers openly ran help-wanted ads with separate male and female pay scales for identical jobs, and in that year, across all occupations, the average woman earned only 59 cents for every dollar earned

---

[65] Debra E. Meyerson and Joyce K. Fletcher, "A Modest Manifesto for Shattering the Glass Ceiling," *Harvard Business Review,* January–February 2000, pp. 128–29.

[66] Deborah Tannen, "The Power of Talk: Who Gets Heard and Why," *Harvard Business Review,* September–October 1995.

[67] Quoted in Ralph D. Ward, *Improving Corporate Boards* (New York: John Wiley & Sons, 2000), p. 215.

by a man. The Equal Pay Act, which forbids pay differences based on sex, has been effective in narrowing the earnings gap between the sexes. By 2000 women earned 76 cents for every dollar earned by a man.[68]

Why though, after almost 40 years of enforcing the law, does any discrepancy remain? Overall, women have entered the labor force more recently than men, so they are younger and have less seniority. In addition, they have less education and take more degrees in lower-paying fields such as education and nursing. However, for many years women have been moving into higher-paid occupations. In 2000 they were 49 percent of executives, administrators, and managers, up from 34 percent in 1983, and they held 52 percent of jobs in professional specialty occupations, up from 47 percent in 1983. Yet within these broad occupational categories, men still far outnumber women in the most lucrative specialties. While women dominate as registered nurses and elementary school teachers, this work pays far less than that of architects, who are 79 percent men, and aerospace engineers, who are 94 percent men. Until larger numbers of women move into such better-compensated occupations, aggregate pay statistics will continue to show a male–female gap.

The earnings gap narrows when women and men of similar age, occupational experience, and educational background are compared. Still, it does not disappear. In one study of men and women holding degrees in 130 professional fields, women were paid equally with or made more than men in only 11 fields employing just 2 percent of the women. In all the remaining fields, women averaged only 73 percent of men's pay.[69] Nothing in the statistical analysis of men's and women's characteristics, besides sex, accounts for this shortfall. Its cause defies statistical explanation and is either discrimination or another, undiscovered, factor.

The pay gap between men and women is worldwide. A study by the International Labor Organization showed that women were paid less than men for comparable work in every nation. Depending on the country, they earned between 50 percent and 96 percent of men's wages in 1995.[70] The United Nations reports that for the period 1994 to 1999, women's wages in manufacturing work were lower than men's in 38 of 39 countries studied. In 27 of these countries, they were only 20 to 50 percent those of men.[71]

---

[68] This figure is calculated by the Bureau of Labor Statistics based on median weekly earnings of full-time wage and salary earners. Unless otherwise attributed, figures in this section are from Bureau of Labor Statistics, *Highlights of Women's Earnings in 2000,* Report 952, August 2001.
[69] Daniel E. Hecker, "Earnings of College Graduates: Women Compared with Men," *Monthly Labor Review,* March 1998, p. 63.
[70] International Labor Organization, "Women Work More, but Are Still Paid Less," press release, August 25, 1995, p. 1.
[71] United Nations, *The World's Women 2000: Trends and Statistics* (New York: United Nations, August 2000), table 5.G. The lone exception was Myanmar, where women's wages were 112 percent those of men.

Top-Level Promotions

In 2000 there were 7.2 million women working with 8.1 million men in occupations classified as executive, administrative, and managerial. Yet few women reached top positions. They were only 12.5 percent of officers in *Fortune* 500 companies, up from 10.6 percent in 1998. At 50 of these companies, women were 40 percent or more of the officers, but in 90 companies there were no women in such positions.[72] Only 7.3 percent of women officers were in line positions with profit-and-loss responsibility. In 2001 women held only 12.4 percent of the seats on boards of *Fortune* 500 companies, up from 10.2 percent in 1996.[73] The small number of women in top positions leads some to say that women have hit a *glass ceiling,* or an invisible barrier of sex discrimination thwarting career advancement to the highest levels.

One survey of male CEOs and female top managers found that the women saw "male stereotyping and preconceptions" as the most important barrier they faced, while the CEOs thought that lack of experience was the biggest barrier. The CEOs believed promotion processes were neutral and that as women gained more seniority, they would prevail. Yet women saw the process as tilted against them. The authors concluded that "the majority of CEOs surveyed apparently are unaware of the corporate environment faced by their women."[74]

Like the pay gap, the glass ceiling is worldwide. The International Labor Organization estimated in 1995 that at the existing rate of progress, it would be 475 years before parity between men and women was achieved in executive positions.[75]

SEXUAL HARASSMENT

Many women experience sexual harassment at some time in their careers. In a recent survey, 34 percent of employees in six industries stated that they had observed some form of it in the past year.[76] Various forms of harassment exist, and same-sex harassment is prohibited by the same laws that bar male–female harassment. However, the major workplace problem is harassment of women by men. In a landmark book, *Sexual Shakedown,* Lin Farley defined this form of harassment as "unsolicited

---

[72] Catalyst, "Catalyst Census Finds 50 Companies with Significant Numbers of Women Corporate Officers, a 100 Percent Increase Since 1995," press release, November 13, 2000.
[73] Catalyst, "Catalyst Charts Growth of Women on America's Corporate Boards," press release, 2001, p. 1.
[74] Ragins, Townsend, and Mattis, "Gender Gap in the Executive Suite," p. 37.
[75] International Labor Organization, "Women Work More," p. 2.
[76] KPMG Integrity Management Services, *2000 Organizational Integrity Survey: A Summary* (New York: KPMG, 2000), p. 2.

FIGURE 18.2
The EEOC Guidelines on Sexual Harassment

Source: 29 CFR 1604.11(a).

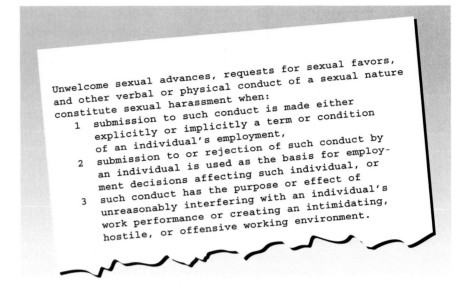

Unwelcome sexual advances, requests for sexual favors, and other verbal or physical conduct of a sexual nature constitute sexual harassment when:
1 submission to such conduct is made either explicitly or implicitly a term or condition of an individual's employment,
2 submission to or rejection of such conduct by an individual is used as the basis for employment decisions affecting such individual, or
3 such conduct has the purpose or effect of unreasonably interfering with an individual's work performance or creating an intimidating, hostile, or offensive working environment.

nonreciprocal male behavior that asserts a woman's sex role over her function as a worker."[77]

Sexual harassment of women encompasses a wide range of behavior. It can be very subtle, as when older men treat younger women like daughters, an approach that diminishes the authority of a female manager. More direct forms of harassment are staring, touching, joking, and gratuitous discussions of sex. The most serious forms include demands for sexual favors or physical assaults. These behaviors reinforce male power in work settings. By treating a woman as a sex object, a man places her in the stereotyped role of submissive female, thereby subordinating and marginalizing her. The message is, "You're only a woman, that's the way I see you. And at that level you're vulnerable to me and any man."[78]

In 1980 the EEOC issued guidelines (see Figure 18.2) making sexual harassment a form of sex discrimination under Title VII. The guidelines define two situations where harassment is illegal. One is the *quid pro quo*, when submission to sexual activity is required to get or keep a job. The other is a *hostile environment*, where sexually offensive conduct is so pervasive that it becomes unreasonably difficult to work. The range of conduct that can create a hostile environment has expanded to become very broad, but is not subject to precise definition. At first, courts often held that coarse language, innuendo, and pinups were part of some

[77] Lin Farley, *Sexual Shakedown* (New York: McGraw-Hill, 1978), pp. 14–15.
[78] Cynthia Cockburn, *In the Way of Women: Men's Resistance to Sex Equality in Organizations* (Ithaca, NY: ILR Press, 1991), p. 142.

work environments and that Title VII could not magically dignify the manners of male workers throughout America.[79] Then, in a landmark case, a female welder named Lois Robinson, one of only seven women among 1,010 skilled craftsworkers in a Florida shipyard, complained that suggestive and lewd pinups, drawings, and cartoons created a hostile working environment. A Florida court agreed with her, holding that even if men enjoyed this decor, it nevertheless created an abusive climate for Robinson.[80]

In 1993 the Supreme Court set up a test for hostile environments. Teresa Harris, a manager in a Nashville company that rented forklifts, filed an EEOC complaint due to the behavior of the company president, Charles Hardy. Over several years, Hardy engaged in a pattern of vulgar and demeaning behavior that targeted Harris as a woman. He made derogatory remarks such as "You're a woman, what do you know?" and "We need a man as the rental manager." He made her serve coffee in meetings. He asked Harris and other female employees to fish coins out of his front pants pockets and sometimes threw objects on the floor, asking the women to pick them up while he commented on their breasts and clothing. He proposed negotiating Harris's raise at a Holiday Inn and suggested that she try giving sexual favors to get forklift rentals. When Harris complained and threatened to quit, Hardy apologized and she stayed, but his boorishness resumed.

Other women at the company testified that Hardy's behavior was all part of a ribald, joking atmosphere that everyone understood and enjoyed. Did Forklift Systems contain a hostile working environment? A lower court did not think so, ruling that although it was a close call and Hardy was a vulgar man, there was no proof that his conduct created a situation so intimidating that it interfered with Harris's ability to do her job.[81] However, when the case reached the Supreme Court, the justices created new criteria for defining a hostile environment.

In *Harris* v. *Forklift Systems,* they held that the guideline was whether sexual harassment created "an environment that a reasonable person would find hostile or abusive." There was no "mathematically precise test" for what constituted a hostile environment, but harassing conduct should be examined with respect to its "frequency" and "severity," whether it is "physically threatening or humiliating," and whether it "unreasonably interferes" with work.[82] The Supreme Court sent the *Harris* case back to a lower court for rehearing based on these criteria, and, a year later, that court ordered the company to set up a sexual harassment policy and to pay Harris's attorney fees. Forklift Systems appealed, but

[79] See, for example, *Rabidue* v. *Osceola Refinery Co.,* 805 F.2d 611 (CA–6 1986).
[80] *Robinson* v. *Jacksonville Shipyards,* 760 F.Supp. 1486 (M.D. Fla. 1991), at 1524.
[81] *Harris* v. *Forklift Systems, Inc.,* No. 3–89–0557 (M.D. Tenn. 1990).
[82] 510 U.S. 23 (1993).

the litigants ultimately made a nonpublic, out-of-court settlement to end the case.

In the year following the *Harris* decision, the number of harassment charges filed with the EEOC jumped by 21 percent, but since then they have leveled off. In 2001 the agency received more than 15,000 complaints. Women filed most charges, but 14 percent came from men.[83] Enforcement of sexual harassment law has led to some big damage awards. In 1998 Mitsubishi Motor Manufacturing of America settled the most expensive case to date, paying $34 million to 400 women at an Illinois assembly plant. In 1999 Astra USA, a pharmaceutical company, paid $10 million to 120 women who had been verbally teased, touched, fondled, and solicited for sex by a group of executives.

In 1998 the Supreme Court further elaborated the law of sexual harassment. It made corporations liable for damages when employees create a hostile environment. They can escape liability only if management proves that it tried hard to prevent and remedy harassment and, in addition, that the aggrieved employee neglected to make a complaint.[84] Now, most companies have formal policies that prohibit sexual harassment and set up complaint channels.

CORPORATE EFFORTS TO PROMOTE DIVERSITY

Employment decisions are now heavily regulated to protect workers from discrimination. While most companies, particularly smaller ones, simply try to comply with all the laws and regulations, many large firms broaden their efforts beyond compliance to promotion of diversity. *Diversity management* refers to programs that increase worker heterogeneity and change corporate cultures, making them hospitable to employees regardless of race, ethnicity, gender, age, religion, sexual orientation, or disability. In 2001 three out of four *Fortune* 1000 corporations had such programs.[85]

Diversity management is a much broader effort than affirmative action. Affirmative action is compliance-oriented hiring of individuals from a narrow range of racial and ethnic categories. Once hired, the law requires nondiscrimination and, sometimes, promotion to fill quotas, but

---

[83] Equal Employment Opportunity Commission, "Sexual Harassment Charges, EEOC & FEPAs Combined: FY 1992–FY 2001," www.eeoc.gov/stats/harass.html.

[84] See *Burlington Industries, Inc.* v. *Ellerth,* 524 U.S. 742 (1998); and *Faragher* v. *City of Boca Raton,* 524 U.S. 775 (1998). As a result of these cases, the EEOC issued new guidelines for employers. See EEOC, "Enforcement Guidance: Vicarious Employer Liability for Unlawful Harassment by Supervisors," Notice 915.002, June 18, 1999. These guidelines cover all forms of harassment prohibited under Title VII, including that based on race, ethnicity, national origin, and religion as well as sexual harassment.

[85] Cora Daniels, "Too Diverse for Our Own Good?" *Fortune,* July 9, 2001, p. 116.

there is no requirement that people's differences be indulged. Women and minorities are often required to assimilate into a white-male corporate culture that has little tolerance for differences. They get in, but to prosper and advance they must mirror the values and behavior of the dominant group. Diversity management, on the other hand, is based on the belief that people in a wide range of identity groupings have dissimilar backgrounds and social experiences. Their behavior does not always conform to the norms of a single corporate culture. Therefore, the corporation should recognize the differences and change to accommodate them. There are countless identity groupings. Federated Department Stores, for instance, recognizes 26 groups in its diversity program, including racial and ethnic categories and, among others, disabled, atheist, devout, homosexual, married, single, and older employees.[86]

Advocates of diversity management promote it using two arguments. They say that it is an ethically right action needing no justification beyond its inherent goodness. And they say that it pays off in several ways. First, it lowers costs of recruiting, turnover, absenteeism, and lawsuits. Minorities and women have higher turnover than white men and often have higher absenteeism due to the presence of hurdles the corporation fails to see and remove. Less frustration raises both tenure and productivity and can prevent discrimination charges. Second, diversity improves understanding of markets and customers. At Merck, an anticoagulant drug sold poorly in Hispanic markets until a Hispanic manager noticed that the package insert was written only in English. After translation into Spanish, sales rose. The idea was simple, but nobody else thought of it.[87] Third, diversity efforts reduce friction between workers with different backgrounds. There is evidence that diverse teams also make better decisions because they consider more perspectives.[88] Recent studies show that diversity is positively associated with some measures of corporate performance.[89]

To succeed, a diversity management program must be part of the corporate management system.

- *Leadership* is critical. Without it, diversity efforts will not be seen as central to business strategy. Taylor Cox Jr., a diversity management consultant, tells how leaders go wrong. Managers commit to attending meetings about diversity tasks but change their plans when operations

---

[86] Ibid.

[87] Margaret A. Hart, *Managing Diversity for Sustained Competitiveness* (New York: The Conference Board, 1997), p. 5.

[88] Faye Rice, "How to Make Diversity Pay," *Fortune,* August 8, 1994, p. 79.

[89] See, for example, Orlando C. Richard, "Racial Diversity, Business Strategy, and Firm Performance: A Resource-Based View," *Academy of Management Journal,* April 2000, pp. 164–175; and Larry Bellinger and Amy J. Hillman, "Does Tolerance Lead to Better Partnering?" *Business & Society,* September 2000, pp. 323–37.

make competing demands on their time. A manager picked to open a diversity training session, welcomed attendees and then said, "I'm sorry you have to be here today and sit through all of this."[90] When asked at a diversity meeting whether anyone in the company had been promoted or passed over because of performance on diversity, a senior vice president of human resources could not think of anyone. Glen Hiner of Owens Corning, Inc., set a different example. When he came into the company, he stated in the first meeting with senior executives, "We are too white and too male, and that will change." He followed this by taking large and small actions, from appointing women and minorities to high positions to requiring a statement about the dignity of individuals printed on all business cards.[91]

- *Change in the organization structure* creates focal points for diversity efforts. Many companies have corporate diversity officers. In large companies, coordinators in business units often support these staff executives. Sometimes a steering committee of top managers runs the program. Coordinating committees are common in divisions of large firms. An example is the Diversity Leadership Council at Lockheed Martin's Missiles & Space Division, which consists of diversity coordinators, managers from the division's business units, and representatives of six formally recognized employee groups. Among these groups a gay, lesbian, or bisexual group with 30 members helps employees to "feel more free to be 'out.' "[92] An Asian American and Pacific Islander group promotes training to combat the stereotype that Asians are not assertive.

- *Training programs* sensitize employees to prejudices and cultural differences. A recent study found that 73 percent of 108 companies surveyed conducted diversity training. The typical training course averaged 25 people and lasted 10 hours. Topics covered, in order of frequency, were workplace discrimination, stereotypes, ways of making people from diverse groups welcome, the contribution of diversity to productivity, nondiscriminatory promotions and evaluations, white-male resistence, and the cultures of a range of groups.[93]

- *Mentors* can be assigned to women and minorities to overcome isolation in firms where the hierarchy is predominantly white and male. A recent study of successful managers in large companies found that

---

[90] Taylor Cox Jr., *Creating the Multicultural Organization* (San Francisco: Jossey-Bass, 2001), p. 41.
[91] Marc Bendick Jr., Mary Lou Egan, and Suzanne M. Lofhjelm, "Workforce Diversity Training: From Anti-discrimination Compliance to Organizational Development," *Human Resource Planning*, January 2001, p. 10.
[92] *Lockheed Martin Today*, "Common Ground: Workplace Evolving to Support Increased Employee Diversity," 2000, www.lockheedmartin.com/diversity/common.html.
[93] Bendick, Egan, and Lofhjelm, "Workforce Diversity Training," p. 10.

high-potential minorities were often discouraged by mid-career. They tended to move up more slowly than high-potential whites, who were put on fast tracks earlier. As whites got key assignments and promotions, the minority managers often felt discouraged. A key to their ultimate success was the support of mentors who opened doors for them.[94]

- *Data collection* is needed to define issues and measure progress. Many companies conduct surveys. Twice a year, for example, Allstate Insurance Co. surveys its employees to learn how they feel they are being treated.[95] Related to data collection is measurement. Because of the pervasive philosophy in business that what gets measured gets done, many companies quantify diversity goals. The Quaker Oats Company created a statistic called the "best-practices index" that registers points for every program and action taken in each of its plants. Its diversity administrator argues that "Most CEOs may not know a lot about diversity, but they understand numbers. They can tell the difference between a facility with 1000 points on the best-practices index, and a facility with 500 points."[96]

- *Policy changes* establish new rules. Following a public relations disaster when tapes of executives making racially biased remarks were leaked to the press and a $115 million settlement of a race discrimination lawsuit, Texaco set up a program to reform its corporate culture. Many policies changed as a result. One example is a new rule that no human resource committee meeting can take place unless attended by a minority or a woman. If such a person is sick or delayed, the meeting is postponed.[97]

- *Reward systems* encourage managers to achieve diversity goals. Diversity can be one element of performance reviews. Division managers at ExxonMobil are required at annual reviews to present career development plans for 10 females and 10 minority males. At Coca-Cola, CEO Douglas Daft bases 25 percent of each manager's compensation, including his own, on achieving diversity goals.[98]

Resistance to diversity projects comes from white males who feel blamed for problems and perceive a zero-sum game in which the advance of others precludes their success and from some women and minorities

---

[94] David A. Thomas, "The Truth about Mentoring Minorities: Race Matters," *Harvard Business Review,* April 2001, pp. 99–107.

[95] Louisa Wah, "Diversity at Allstate: A Competitive Weapon," *Management Review,* July–August 1999, p. 28.

[96] Hart, *Managing Diversity for Sustained Competitiveness,* p. 8, citing I. Charles Mathews, vice president of diversity management.

[97] Kenneth Labich, "No More Crude at Texaco," *Fortune,* September 6, 1999, p. 208.

[98] Betsy McKay, "Coke CEO to Tie Pay to Diversity Goals, Create Post on Promotion of Minorities," *The Wall Street Journal,* March 10, 2000, p. B7.

hoping to deemphasize their differences and assimilate into the dominant company culture. Yet, growing diversity in workforces and markets ensures that these programs will remain strong because there is a business rationale for them. Nondiscrimination has moved from a social responsibility, to a legal duty, to a business imperative. In the end, it may be the latter consideration that closes any remaining gap between the promises of natural rights in the Declaration of Independence and the abridgement of them in practice.

CONCLUDING OBSERVATIONS

Workplace discrimination has existed throughout American history. The first national effort to end it began during the Civil War, with the Emancipation Proclamation freeing slaves, and included constitutional amendments and civil rights laws passed after the war. This effort floundered because societal values hindered enforcement of the laws.

In the 1960s, a second effort to eradicate discrimination began with passage of the Civil Rights Act of 1964. Since then, more laws and thousands of agency and court decisions have greatly reduced, but not eliminated, job bias against minorities and women. Today, the accumulated corpus of antidiscrimination law is massive, complex, and controversial where it embodies preferential treatment. But overall, and unlike the reconstruction-era effort, it works. Along with government, corporations are taking many actions—both voluntary and legally mandated—to make progress.

Yet more needs to be done. There is widespread evidence of continuing discrimination. Research on wage gaps, studies of job applications, and the continued existence of many discrimination suits attest to it.

Adarand v. *Peña*

This is the story of an affirmative action case that made its way to the U.S. Supreme Court. When the Court announced that it would hear *Adarand* v. *Peña*, there was considerable speculation about the outcome. The plaintiff, a white male, argued that preferential treatment for minority and female contractors was unconstitutional. Would the justices agree?

In due course, the nine-member Court issued a lengthy (21,800 words) split decision, showing itself to be as fractured as the public in its thinking. It divided 5 to 4, with six separate opinions—a majority opinion, two concurring opinions, and three dissents. The result? Affirmative action lived on but became harder to justify. With the support of affirmative action foes in the legal community, Adarand Constructors tried to carry the case farther, refusing to give up until the Court killed affirmative action in all its forms. The case bounced around the federal court system for another six years until fizzling out in 2001 when the Supreme Court dismissed it.

THE GUARDRAIL SUBCONTRACT

In 1987 Congress appropriated a huge sum, more than $16 billion, to the Department of Transportation (DOT) for highway construction across the nation.[1] Ten percent, or $1.6 billion, was earmarked for small businesses run by "socially and economically disadvantaged individuals."[2] *Socially disadvantaged persons* were defined as "those who have been subjected to racial or ethnic prejudice or cultural bias" and *economically disadvantaged persons* were defined as those "whose ability to compete in the free enterprise system has been impaired due to diminished capital and credit opportunites as compared to others in the same business area who are not socially disadvantaged."[3] It was to be presumed that black, Hispanic, Asian Pacific, subcontinent Asian, and Native American persons and women were both socially and economically handicapped. Any small business with 51 percent or greater ownership by persons in these categories could be certified as a *disadvantaged business enterprise,* or DBE. Then, Congress put monetary incentives to hire DBEs into the highway construction law. The story here illustrates how these incentives worked.

[1] The Surface Transportation and Uniform Relocation Assistance Act of 1987, P.L. 100–17.
[2] Section 106(c)(1).
[3] Section 106(c)(2)(B).

In 1989 Mountain Gravel & Construction Company received a $1 million prime contract to build highways in the San Juan National Forest of southwest Colorado. It requested bids from subcontractors to install 4.7 miles of guardrails. Two small companies that specialize in guardrail installation responded. Adarand Constructors, Inc., a white-owned company, submitted the low bid, and Gonzales Construction Company, a firm certified as a DBE, submitted a bid that was $1,700 higher. Ordinarily, Mountain Gravel would have chosen the low bidder, but the prime contract provided that it would be paid a bonus, up to 10 percent of the guardrail subcontract, if it picked a DBE. On this subcontract, the bonus payment was approximately $10,000, so even by accepting a bid $1,700 above the low bid, Mountain Gravel came out $8,300 ahead. Gonzales Construction, the high bidder, got the nod.

The part of the prime contract that caused Mountain Gravel to reject Adarand Constructors' low bid was called a *subcontractor compensation clause.* It provided that a sum equal to 10 percent of the subcontract would be paid to Mountain Gravel, up to a maximum of 1.5 percent of the dollar amount of the prime contract, if one DBE subcontractor was used. If two DBE subcontractors had been used, the extra payment could have been as much as 2 percent of the prime contract.

Losing the guardrail job angered Randy Pech, the white male co-owner and general manager of

Randy Pech of Adarand Constructors.
© Gaylor Wampler/Corbis Sygma.

Adarand Constructors. "It was very discouraging to run a legitimate, honest business," said Pech, "to go to a lot of trouble of bidding on a project—to know you did a great job and come in the low bid—and then find out they can't use you because they have to meet their 'goals.' "[4] Pech's lawyer, William Pendley, spoke more bluntly about the subcontractor compensation clause. "It works like a bribe," he said.[5] This was not the first time Adarand Constructors had faced this situation. It was one of only five Colorado contractors specializing in guardrails. The other four, Cruz Construction, Ideal Fencing, C&K, and Gonzales Construction, were minority-owned and, by virtue of that, designated as DBEs. These four competitors were all stable businesses at least 10 years old, and on nonfederal highway projects, they sometimes beat Adarand Constructors with lower bids. Yet when federal highway dollars were being spent, Adarand Constructors frequently lost—even with the lowest bid. Later it would be documented that because of the subcontractor compensation clause, prime contractors had rejected the company's low bids five times to favor its DBE competitors. Mountain Gravel's bid estimator verified that Adarand Constructors' low bid on the 4.7 mile guardrail job would have been accepted if the extra payment had not existed. Fed up, Randy Pech sued the federal government.

In his suit, Pech claimed that the subcontractor compensation clause violated his constitutional right to equal treatment under the law. This right is found in the Fifth Amendment of the Constitution, which reads: "No person shall . . . be deprived of life, liberty, or property, without due process of law." Although this wording does not literally state that citizens are entitled to equal treatment, the Supreme Court has held that its meaning protects citizens from arbitrary or unequal treatment by the federal government in the same way that the Fourteenth Amendment prohibits states fom denying "equal protection of the laws" to their citizens. Pech did not seek monetary damages, but requested an injunction, or a court-ordered halt, to any future use of contract clauses providing extra payments on subcontracts given to DBEs.

Things got off to a bad start for Pech when the U.S. District Court for the District of Colorado ruled against him.[6] The court held that it was within the power of Congress, when it enacted the highway bill, to use race- and gender-based preferences to compensate for the harmful effects of past discrimination. Pech appealed to the Tenth Circuit Court of Appeals, but, two years later, it affirmed the district court's decision.[7] Pech then took the next step and appealed to the Supreme Court, which agreed to decide the case. Because the lawsuit named Transportation Secretary Federico Peña as a defendant, it was entitled *Adarand* v. *Peña.*

THE CONSTITUTION AND RACE

The Court was being asked to decide whether classifying citizens by race in order to treat them differently was constitutionally respectable for the federal government. This was not a new question; neither was it one that has ever been resolved with clarity. Affirmative action has deeply divided the Court, but it is not the first race-based classification scheme to raise constitutional problems.

Between 1884 and 1893, the Court decided a series of challenges to exclusionary laws passed by Congress stopping the immigration of Chinese laborers and restricting the civil rights of resident Chinese. At first, the justices struck down laws that treated Chinese differently from American citizens.[8] Eventually, however, the Court went along with a wave of public hysteria over the Chinese and in key decisions upheld laws that denied them equal treatment.[9]

---

[4] Marlene Cimons, "Businessman Who Brought Lawsuit Praises Ruling by Justices," *Los Angeles Times,* June 13, 1995, p. A15.

[5] David G. Savage, " 'Colorblind' Constitution Faces a New Test," *Los Angeles Times,* January 16, 1995, p. A17.

[6] *Adarand Constructors, Inc.* v. *Samuel K. Skinner,* 790 F.Supp. 240 (D.Colo. 1992). Then-Secretary of Transportation Skinner was named as the defendant.

[7] *Adarand Constructors, Inc.* v. *Federico Peña,* 16 F.3d 1537 (10th Cir. 1994). By this time, Peña was Secretary of Transportation.

[8] *Chew Heong* v. *United States,* 112 U.S. 536 (1884); and *United States* v. *Jung Ah Lung,* 124 U.S. 621 (1888).

[9] *Lee Joe* v. *United States,* 149 U.S. 698 (1893).

A few years later, in 1896, the Court had an opportunity to strike down the Jim Crow laws of the old South in *Plessy* v. *Ferguson* but failed to do so. Instead, it upheld the Louisiana statue requiring segregation of whites and nonwhites in separate railroad cars and fixed in place the infamous "separate but equal" doctrine. In a lone dissent that rang across decades, Justice John Marshall Harlan called the Constitution "color blind" and said that race was not a valid criteria for making law.

> In respect of civil rights, common to all citizens, the Constitution of the United States does not, I think, permit any public authority to know the race of those entitled to be protected in the enjoyment of such rights. . . . [T]he common government of all shall not permit the seeds of race hate to be planted under the sanction of law.[10]

During World War II, the Court was once again called upon to decide the question of a race-based government action. In early 1942, President Franklin Roosevelt issued an executive order, which Congress ratified, requiring the relocation of 70,000 persons of Japanese descent, both American citizens and resident aliens, from homes on the West Coast to inland evacuation camps. This policy was challenged as depriving the Japanese Americans of their Fifth Amendment guarantee of equal protection of the laws. However, the Court was once again willing to uphold a racial classification scheme used by government. In the majority opinion, Justice Black conceded that "all legal restrictions which curtail the civil rights of a single racial group are immediately suspect" and must be subjected "to the most rigid scrutiny."[11] Nevertheless, the evacuation order passed this "rigid scrutiny," because the president and Congress were taking emergency actions in time of war to prevent sabotage and avert grave danger. In dissent, Justice Frank Murphy argued that the evacuation "goes over 'the very brink of constitutional power' and falls into the ugly abyss of racism."[12]

In 1954 the Court finally reversed its decision in *Plessy*. In the landmark school desegregation case, *Brown* v. *Board of Education*, it agreed that under the "separate but equal" doctrine, the states had provided grossly unequal schools for blacks.[13] During oral arguments in the case, Thurgood Marshall, destined to be the first black Supreme Court justice, invoked the principle of a color-blind Constitution. A unanimous Court struck down "separate but equal" as a violation of the equal protection clause in the Fourteenth Amendment.

The *Brown* decision, however, did not mean that the Court saw a completely color-blind Constitution. In the 1970s, suits by whites who had suffered reverse discrimination as a result of affirmative action began to reach its docket. In the first such cases, a divided Court upheld affirmative action, but was obviously troubled by it and tried to define its limits. There was also an ideological split among the justices, with a liberal bloc condoning race-based affirmative action and a conservative bloc inclined to severely limit or prohibit it.

THE FULLILOVE CASE

In 1980 the Court heard for the first time a challenge to a set-aside program for minority businesses. In the Public Works Employment Act of 1977, Congress authorized $4 billion for public works projects such as dams, bridges, and highways. At least 10 percent of this sum was set aside for businesses owned by "minority group members," who were defined as "Negroes, Spanish-speaking, Orientals, Indians, Eskimos, and Aleuts."[14] The law was challenged by several associations of white contractors, who claimed to have lost business and argued that the set-aside violated their constitutional rights to equal protection. But in *Fullilove* v. *Klutznick*, the Court held that Congress could use racial classification schemes to strike at racist, exclusionary practices used by prime contractors on federally funded projects.[15]

Over the years, courts have developed standards for testing the constitutional validity of laws that classify citizens. All such laws must withstand one of three levels of scrutiny by a skeptical

[10] 163 U.S. 554, 560.
[11] *Korematsu* v. *United States*, 323 U.S. 214.
[12] 323 U.S. 242.
[13] 347 U.S. 483.
[14] Section 103(f)(2).
[15] 448 U.S. 448.

judiciary. The lowest level is *ordinary scrutiny*, which requires that government prove its classification scheme is "reasonably" related to a "legitimate interest." For example, classifying citizens by income for purposes of tax collection would pass this minimum test. The second level is *intermediate scrutiny*, a heightened standard requiring that the law be "substantially related" to an "important government objective." In the past, intermediate scrutiny was typically used for laws related to gender, for example, the law drafting men for military service but not women.

The final, and most exacting, level of scrutiny, called *strict scrutiny*, is reserved for racial classifications regarded as pernicious and undesirable. When strict scrutiny is used, it is presumed that the law in question is unconstitutional unless the government can prove that it serves a "compelling" government interest and is "narrowly tailored," that is, not more extensive than it needs to be to serve its purpose. There are no fixed definitions of the words "reasonably," "substantially related," and "compelling," but they represent an escalating standard of proof.

The majority opinion in *Fullilove* showed that neither Chief Justice Warren Burger nor the five other justices who joined and concurred with him were particularly alarmed about race-based set-asides for minority contractors. The chief justice subjected the minority business program in the Public Works Employment Act to only an intermediate level of scrutiny. This was unusual for a race-based classification, but reflected the view that discrimination against whites to make up for past racism was not as harmful as old-style, direct discrimination against minorities.

THE CROSON AND METRO CASES

After *Fullilove*, nine years passed before the Court looked at set-asides again. During the interim, President Ronald Reagan appointed three new conservative justices and the liberal bloc lost its ability to form a five-member majority on affirmative action cases. Hence, in 1989 the Court struck down an affirmative action contracting plan used by the city of Richmond, Virginia. This plan required that 30 percent of city construction work be awarded to minority contractors. In *Richmond* v.

Croson, the Court held that because the city's plan was a suspect racial classification, it should be subject to strict scrutiny.[16] And when the two tests required by strict scrutiny were applied, the plan could not pass constitutional muster. First, although the population of Richmond was 50 percent black and less than 1 percent of city contracts were awarded to black firms, the city had not proved a "compelling" interest because it had never conducted studies to show that this statistical discrepancy was caused by race discrimination. Without proof of past discrimination, no "compelling" justification for raced-based remedial action existed. And second, the plan was not "narrowly tailored"; in addition to giving preference to black contractors, it entitled Hispanic, Asian, Native American, Eskimo, and Aleut contractors located anywhere in the United States to take advantage of preferential bidding rules. This scheme of inclusion was too broad. The Court ruled that for white contractors, the Richmond plan violated the Fourteenth Amendment guarantee of equal protection under the law.[17]

In the wake of the *Croson* decision, more than 200 set-aside plans around the country were dropped or changed for fear that they would be challenged and struck down. In Richmond, the percentage of contract dollars awarded to minority businesses plummeted from 30 percent to "the low single digits."[18]

A year later, in 1990, the Court confronted a case in which white-owned broadcasters challenged a congressional statute requiring that the Federal Communications Commission give certain preferences to minority radio and television companies

[16] *City of Richmond* v. *J. A. Croson Co.*, 488 U.S. 469 (1989).
[17] The Fourteenth Amendment protects American citizens from unjust actions by state governments. It reads: "No State shall . . . deny to any person within its jurisdiction the equal protection of the laws." The City of Richmond, being chartered by the state of Virginia, was therefore a governmental actor falling under the reach of the Fourteenth Amendment.
[18] Paul M. Barrett and Michael K. Frisby, "Affirmative-Action Advocates Seeking Lessons from States to Help Preserve Federal Programs," *The Wall Street Journal*, December 7, 1994, p. A18.

when it issued broadcast licenses. Congress declared that its purpose was to promote diversity in programming. In *Metro Broadcasting* v. *FCC,* a five-member majority of the Court composed of four remaining liberals and the usually conservative Justice Byron White held that "benign race-conscious measures" undertaken by Congress to compensate victims of discrimination need be subject only to the standard of "intermediate scrutiny."[19] Creating diversity in broadcasting was an "important governmental objective," and preferences for nonwhite and female broadcasters were "substantially related" to achieving this objective. In dissent, Justice Anthony M. Kennedy sought to refocus the Court on the mistake made in the *Plessy* case. "I regret," he wrote, "that after a century of judicial opinions we interpret the Constitution to do no more than move us from 'separate but equal' to 'unequal but benign.' "[20]

TWO LINES OF PRECEDENT

This was where matters stood until 1994, when *Adarand* came before the Court. The Supreme Court likes to follow precedent and generally adheres to the rule of *stare decisis* (STARE-ray da-SEE-sis), a Latin term meaning to stand as decided. The judicial system is based on the principle that once a matter of law is settled, courts should follow the established path. Judges believe that this should be the case even though a court would decide the question differently if it were new. *Stare decisis* preserves one of the law's primary virtues, its predictability.

However, two different precedents had been established for minority preferences in contracting. In *Croson,* the Court had applied strict scrutiny to a city plan and declared it unconstitutional. But *Adarand* was not about a city plan; it involved a plan enacted by Congress. Traditionally, the Supreme Court recognizes that Congress represents the will of the American people and thus its actions deserve great deference. Supreme Court justices, who are appointed rather than elected, are reluctant to substitute their views in place of congressional intent. The line of precedent closest to

the issue in *Adarand* was that emerging from *Fullilove* and *Metro.* In both cases, the Court had applied only intermediate scrutiny to congressional affirmative action plans and in both cases the plans were upheld. This result was consistent with the Court's studied deference toward Congress.

THE DECISION

Attorneys for each side in *Adarand* v. *Peña* presented 30 minutes of oral argument before the nine justices on January 17, 1995.[21] On June 12, 1995, the Supreme Court released a 5–4 decision in favor of Adarand Constructors.[22] The majority opinion, written by Justice Sandra Day O'Connor, departed from the line of precedent running from *Fullilove* and *Metro* and instead returned to *Croson* and ruled that the Department of Transportation plan giving preferences in bidding to minority subcontractors would have to withstand the test of strict scrutiny. The majority held that the plan was a race classification and presumed to be unconstitutional unless it was "narrowly tailored" to meet a "compelling government interest." Justice O'Connor wrote as follows.

> [W]e hold today that all racial classifications, imposed by whatever federal, state, or local governmental actor, must be analyzed by a reviewing court under strict scrutiny. In other words, such classifications are constitutional only if they are narrowly tailored measures that further compelling governmental interests. To the extend that *Metro Broadcasting* is inconsistent with that holding it is overruled.[23]

Justice O'Connor justified departing from the *Fullilove* and *Metro* precedents by citing Justice Felix Frankfurter, who 55 years earlier had written that "*stare decisis* is . . . not a mechanical formula of adherence to the latest decision, however recent and questionable, when such adherence involves

---

[19] 497 U.S. 547.
[20] 497 U.S. 637–38.

[21] This oral argument can be heard in CSPAN's recorded archives at www.cspan.org/guide/courts/historic/oa072598.htm.
[22] 132 L. Ed. 2d 158, 515 U.S. 200 (1995).
[23] 132 L. Ed. 2d 182.

collision with a prior doctrine more embracing in its scope, intrinsically sounder, and verified by experience."[24] The Court's longstanding, deep suspicion of any race classification, wrote O'Connor, should override the recent efforts of some liberal justices to apply more lax scrutiny to forms of discrimination they called "benign." She expressed deep skepticism about the ability of Congress to distinguish between race classifications generated by "benign" or remedial motives and race classifications resulting from illegitimate motives or racially charged politics.

However, the majority was unwilling to say that no scheme of race-conscious preferences could withstand strict scrutiny. Using affirmative action might still be possible for the government. O'Connor wrote:

> Finally, we wish to dispel the notion that strict scrutiny is "strict in theory, but fatal in fact. . . ." The unhappy persistence of both the practice and the lingering effects of racial discrimination against minority groups in this country is an unfortunate reality, and government is not disqualified from acting in response to it.[25]

This completed the majority opinion. The Court did not uphold or strike down the Transportation Department's subcontractor bidding clauses. Instead, it remanded, or returned, the case to the Tenth Circuit Court of Appeals to be redecided using the strict scrutiny test instead of the lesser test of intermediate scrutiny.[26] The result of this tougher review would determine whether the equal protection rights of Randy Pech at Adarand Constructors had been violated. Thus, as in many cases that come before the high court, the justices avoided deciding the specific question and decided only matters of law.

JUSTICE SCALIA CONCURS

Justice Antonin Scalia, a conservative and longtime foe of affirmative action, wrote a concurring opinion in which he agreed with the application of strict scrutiny but took the extreme position that "government can never have a 'compelling interest' in discriminating on the basis of race in order to 'make up' for past racial discrimination in the opposite direction."[27] He elaborated:

> Individuals who have been wronged by unlawful racial discrimination should be made whole; but under our Constitution there can be no such thing as either a creditor or a debtor race. The concept of racial entitlement—even for the most admirable and benign of purposes—is to reinforce and reserve for future mischief the way of thinking that produced race slavery, race privilege and race hatred. In the eyes of government, we are just one race here. It is American.[28]

Justice Scalia concluded that it was very unlikely and probably impossible that the Department of Transportation program could pass the strict scrutiny test.

JUSTICE THOMAS CONCURS

Justice Clarence Thomas, the Court's only black member, agreed with the majority opinion, but wrote separately to underscore the principle that the Constitution requires all races to be treated equally. In his eyes, there was no moral difference between a law designed to subjugate a race and a law passed to give it benefits.

> That these programs may have been motivated, in part, by good intentions cannot provide refuge from the principle that under our Constitution, the government may not make distinctions on the basis of race. As far as the Constitution is concerned, it is irrelevant whether a government's racial classifications are drawn by those who wish to oppress a race or by those who have a sincere desire to help those thought to be disadvantaged.[29]

Many observers of Justice Thomas's appointment believed that he was not the most qualified jurist available for the Supreme Court at the time and that his race played a part in President Bush's

---

[24] 132 L. Ed. 2d 184, citing *Helvering* v. *Hallock*, 390 U.S. 106, at 119.
[25] 132 L. Ed. 2d 188.
[26] 16 F.3d 1537, vacated and remanded.

[27] 132 L. Ed. 2d 190.
[28] 132 L. Ed. 2d 190.
[29] 132 L. Ed. 2d 190.

decision to nominate him. Whether that is correct or not, Thomas used his concurrence in *Adarand* to argue that affirmative action degrades the very individuals it tries to help.

> So-called "benign" discrimination teaches many that because of chronic and apparently immutable handicaps, minorities cannot compete with them without their patronizing indulgence. Inevitably such programs engender attitudes of superiority or, alternatively, provoke resentment among those who believe that they have been wronged by the government's use of race. These programs stamp minorities with a badge of inferiority and may cause them to develop dependencies or to adopt an attitude that they are "entitled" to preferences.[30]

THE DISSENTERS

Three separate dissenting opinions were written, joined in by four justices. In the first, Justice Stevens, joined by Justice Ginsburg, objected to the departure of the majority from established precedent and argued that the Court had a duty to uphold the intermediate scrutiny standard. Stevens also disagreed with the majority that all discrimination was the same in principle.

> There is no moral or constitutional equivalence between a policy that is designed to perpetuate a caste system and one that seeks to eradicate racial subordination. Invidious discrimination is an engine of oppression, subjugating a disfavored group to enhance or maintain the power of the majority. Remedial race-based preferences reflect the opposite impulse: a desire to foster equality in society. No sensible conception of the Government's constitutional obligation to "govern impartially" . . . should ignore this distinction. . . . The consistency that the Court espouses would disregard the difference between a "No Trespassing" sign and a welcome mat.[31]

A second dissent was written by Justice Souter, in which Justices Ginsburg and Breyer joined. Souter objected to the Court's departure from the *Fullilove* and *Metro* precedents. He argued that

more deference was owed to Congress and affirmed his approval for laws that try to redress persistent racism.

The third dissenting opinion came from Justice Ginsburg, joined by Justice Breyer. She wrote to underscore the lingering effects of "a system of racial cast" in American life. According to Ginsburg:

> White and African-American consumers still encounter different deals. People of color looking for housing still face discriminatory treatment by landlords, real estate agents, and mortgage lenders. Minority entrepreneurs sometimes fail to gain contracts though they are the low bidders, and they are sometimes refused work even after winning contracts. Bias both conscious and unconscious, reflecting traditional and unexamined habits of thought, keeps up barriers that must come down if equal opportunity and nondiscrimination are ever genuinely to become this country's law and practice.
>
> Given this history and its practical consequences, Congress surely can conclude that a carefully designed affirmative action program may help to realize, finally, the "equal protection of the laws" the Fourteenth Amendment has promised since 1868.[32]

THE CASE MOVES ON

The Supreme Court elected to decide principles of law. It declined to settle the specific question of whether the subcontractor compensation clause was constitutional. Therefore, it sent the case back to the Tenth Circuit, with instructions to decide the constitutionality question. The Tenth Circuit, in turn, sent the case down to the U.S. District Court in Colorado where it had originated in 1992.

In 1997, almost two years after the Supreme Court's decision, the district court issued an opinion. Judge John L. Kane Jr. applied the strict scrutiny test to the subcontractor compensation clause, and the result invalidated the clause. The clause passed the part of the test requiring the government to show a compelling interest. Judge Kane stated that there was sufficient evidence of bias in contracting before Congress when it passed the

[30] 132 L. Ed. 2d 191.
[31] 132 L. Ed. 2d 192, 193.

[32] 132 L. Ed. 2d 212.

law. However, the clause failed the test of narrow tailoring. Judge Kane held that basing social and economic disadvantage solely on race was unfair. Under the existing criteria for selecting DBEs, a multimillionaire who immigrated from Hong Kong and became a U.S. citizen one day before applying would automatically qualify, but a poor white man who had lived in the United States his entire life could not. So the set-aside program was overinclusive and unconstitutional. Since Colorado was administering the program for the federal government, Judge Kane issued an injunction ordering the state to stop using the objectionable regulation.[33]

Pech and his company had won, but defenders of affirmative action wanted to put up a fight. The Department of Transportation appealed the decision back to the Tenth Circuit. Then Colorado refused to comply with Judge Kane's ruling. Governor Roy Romer argued, disingenuously, that a federal court order did not apply to a state government. Adarand Constructors immediately sued the state to force its obedience. When the case came before Judge Kane, Colorado argued that it had changed its contracting program. It no longer used the subcontractor compensation clause, and it allowed all contractors, including white males, to get DBE status if they could show disadvantage.

Judge Kane was furious at the recalcitrance of Colorado officials. Instead of retrying the entire issue, he declared that Adarand Constructors had suffered years of discrimination and financial hardship at the hands of a government enforcing an unfair, unconstitutional law. He decreed that the company was eligible for DBE status.[34] Pech applied for it, and it was granted by Colorado in 1998.

Meanwhile, the *Adarand* decision had sparked a national debate. The federal government had approximately 160 preference programs for businesses certified as disadvantaged. In the year that *Adarand* was decided, $10 billion in contracts earmarked for minority and female vendors was distributed through various preference schemes. Opponents of affirmative action felt that, because of the decision, such practices should cease.

There was no doubt that *Adarand* cast a shadow over these arrangements, but their supporters had no intention of conceding defeat. Instead, President Clinton promised to "mend, not end" affirmative action. What he had in mind was revising preferential treatment rules so that the programs would withstand legal challenge.

Meanwhile, congressional opponents of affirmative action started a floor fight trying to kill a 10 percent set-aside provision in a new highway funding bill. In March 1998 strident debate erupted in the Senate over an amendment to delete the set-aside, but the amendment was defeated, leaving more than $17 billion of new highway funds earmarked for DBEs.[35]

In 1999 the Department of Transportation issued revised rules for awarding federal highway contracts to DBEs.[36] These regulations ran 64,500 words in the *Federal Register,* the equivalent of about 114 pages of the case you are now reading. They stated that the 10 percent of highway funding reserved for DBEs was not a "quota" or a "set-aside" but an "aspirational goal at the national level." The DBE participation level in each state receiving highway funds could be higher or lower. To meet DBE goals, the states were required to first use "race-neutral" measures, that is, to do things to help all small businesses, including both DBEs and white-male-owned companies. These measures did not require race–gender classifications and included, for example, training and advice in bidding and contract work, bonding assistance, and breaking large contracts into pieces that small businesses could more easily handle. However, if such methods did not fully achieve DBE goals and "egregious" discrimination existed, then "race-conscious" methods that gave preferences to DBEs, including set-asides on which only DBEs could bid, could be used.

[33] *Adarand Constructors, Inc.,* v. *Peña,* 965 F. Supp. 1556 (D. Colo. 1997).
[34] *Adarand Constructors, Inc.* v. *Romer,* Civ. No. 97–K–1351 (June 26, 1997).
[35] Amendment No. 1708, 144 Cong. Rec. S1395.
[36] Department of Transportation, "Participation by Disadvantaged Business Enterprises in Department of Transportation Program," 64 FR 5096–5148.

The states were required to do studies pinpointing discrimination, so that there would be a compelling rationale for race-conscious actions if they were needed. The rules also tightened qualifications for persons designated as "economically disadvantaged." This status was from now on denied to persons with a net worth of $750,000 or more (calculated as personal net worth minus the value of a primary residence and the ownership interest in the contracting business). The rules allowed white males to apply for socially or economically disadvantaged status. However, unlike minorities and women who are still automatically included (unless worth more than $750,000), the burden is on white males to prove that they have suffered financial hardship from discrimination.

These changes significantly scaled back affirmative action in highway programs. Later, President Clinton issued an executive order that introduced similarly constricted affirmative action methods in all federal contracting.[37]

[37] Executive Order 13170, "Increasing Opportunities and Access for Disadvantaged Businesses," October 6, 2000.

ADARAND KEEPS GOING

Although the use of preferences was being scaled back, through it all Pech persisted in the belief that any race- and sex-based preferences at all were unconstitutional. The case continued its odyssey through the federal courts. The Department of Transportation had appealed Judge Kane's 1997 ruling that the subcontractor compensation clause was unconstitutional. In 1999 the Tenth Circuit ruled that the case was now moot because Colorado had changed its contracting guidelines and no longer used the bonus clause. In addition, the court noted that Colorado had classified Adarand Constructors as a DBE.[38] Adarand, which argued that the Colorado guidelines were still unconstitutional, appealed to the Supreme Court. In 2000 the Supreme Court reversed the Tenth Circuit's decision and sent the case back with instructions to decide the constitutionality of the Colorado contracting guidelines.[39]

[38] *Adarand Constructors, Inc.,* v. *Slater,* 169 Fed 1292 (10th Cir. 1999).
[39] *Adarand Constructors, Inc.,* v. *Slater,* 528 U.S. 216 (2000).

Who Is Disadvantaged?

Any person who is a citizen and falls into one of the following categories is presumed to be socially and economically disadvantaged (beginning in 1999, persons with a net worth of $750,000 or more were disqualified). If the person has 51 percent ownership or greater in a company applying for a federal highway construction contract, that company qualifies as a "disadvantaged business enterprise" and can receive preferential treatment on federal highway contracts.

Black. Includes persons having origins in any black racial groups in Africa.
Hispanic. Includes persons of Mexican, Puerto Rican, Cuban, Dominican, Central or South American, or other Spanish or Portuguese culture or origin, regardless of race.

Native American. Includes American Indians, Eskimos, Aleuts, or Native Hawaiians.
Asian-Pacific Americans. Includes persons whose origins are from Japan, China, Taiwan, Korea, Burma (Myanmar), Vietnam, Laos, Cambodia (Kampuchea), Thailand, Malaysia, Indonesia, the Philippines, Brunei, Samoa, Guam, the U.S. Trust Territories of the Pacific Islands (Republic of Palau), the Commonwealth of the Northern Marianas Islands, Macao, Fiji, Tonga, Kirbati, Juvalu, Nauru, Federated States of Micronesia, or Hong Kong.
Women. All women are included.

Source: 49 CFR §26.1 (2000); 64 FR 5128 (1999).

FIGURE 1

The *Adarand* Odyssey.

This diagram shows the path of the case as it moved through levels of the federal court system over nine years. Twice the Supreme Court remanded the case, that is, sent it back to a lower court for deliberation consistent with legal principles it set forth. Name changes occurred as each new Secretary of Transportation was named as the defendant.

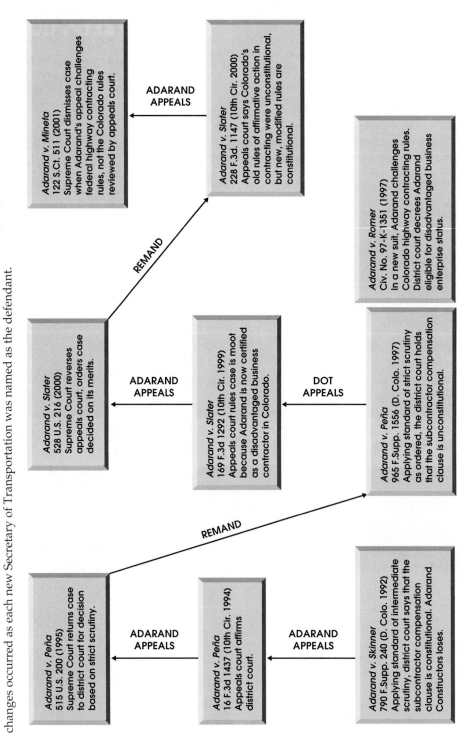

Later that year, the Tenth Circuit responded, deciding that although the original Colorado highway contracting rules had been unconstitutional, the states' new rules were narrowly tailored to meet a compelling government interest, therefore, constitutional. Again, Adarand Constructors appealed the decision to the Supreme Court, which took the case under review. It argued that the Tenth Circuit had erred in its constitutional analysis because no rules that used race or sex as a criterion for awarding government funds could pass the strict scrutiny standard. In its brief, it argued the arbitrariness of the rules:

> [E]very single legally admitted permanent resident or citizen of the United States who happens to be female or who can trace his origins to any of 42 specifically designated countries is automatically presumed to have attempted to enter the American highway construction business and to have experienced racial prejudice that somehow hindered that attempt.[40]

Adarand Constructors urged the Court to adopt the position of Justice John Marshall Harlan that the Constitution is color-blind. It believed that both Congress and the states continued to "trample the constitutional rights of countless innocent individuals."[41] Conservative foes of affirmative action cheered the case on. John O'Sullivan, writing in the *National Review,* articulated their view.

> Today, . . . preferences bestow benefits on something like 65 percent of Americans by extracting a sacrifice from the remaining 35 percent who happen to be white males. Their injustice is now real and concentrated. In other words, they are now plainly and undeniably [victims of] an official program of negative discrimination against a minority: the sole remaining example of institutionalized racism in the United States.[42]

Adarand was a major challenge to affirmative action, but there would be no decision on it. In late 2001 the Supreme Court, after hearing oral arguments, dismissed the case without a decision, saying that it should never have accepted it in the first place. The reason was something of a technicality. In an unsigned opinion, a unanimous Court explained that in the case Adarand Constructors was not challenging the Tenth Circuit's decision about Colorado's contracting rules. Instead, it was arguing that federal guidelines were unconstitutional. The Tenth Circuit decision had not addressed federal guidelines. Therefore, since the Supreme Court was "a court of final review and not first review," it declined to take up the merits of Adarand's arguments and the case was "dismissed as improvidently granted."[43]

With this dismissal the litigation epic of the *Adarand* case, shown in Figure 1, came to sudden end. The merits of its final appeal are still up for debate, if not for a formal decision.

QUESTIONS

1. What constitutional issue is raised in the *Adarand* litigation?

2. After the Supreme Court's 1995 decision in *Adarand* v. *Peña* what requirements did an affirmative action program have to meet to be constitutional?

3. Was the decision of the Court majority correct? Why or why not?

4. In a concurring opinion, Justice Scalia said that race classifications by government were never legitimate. In dissenting opinions, Justices Stevens, Souter, and Ginsburg argued that race-conscious remedies were justified. What were their arguments? With whom do you agree? Why?

5. Following *Adarand* v. *Peña,* the district court held that the affirmative action program in federal highway contracts was unconstitutional. Do you agree with this decision? Why or why not?

6. Do you believe that the Department of Transportation's current rules for helping DBEs get highway construction contracts pass the strict scrutiny requirement?

---

[40] Petitioner's Brief on the Merits, June 11, 2001, p. 11.
[41] Ibid., pp. 19–20.
[42] John O'Sullivan, "Preferred Members," *National Review,* September 3, 2001, p. 20.

[43] *Adarand Constructors, Inc.,* v. *Mineta,* 122 S. Ct. 511, at 514 and 515. Norman Mineta, a new secretary of transportation, was now the respondent.

Part Nine

Corporate Governance

Chapter **Nineteen**

Corporate Governance

Enron's Governance Debacle

Enron Corp. for years was a favorite of stockholders who enjoyed the rise of its stock price from a low of $19.10 at the beginning of 1999 to a high of $90.80 in 2000. Until the 1990s the company was one of the world's largest natural gas, oil, and electricity producers. Then, in that decade, the company's business model changed radically as it evolved into the world's largest energy-trading company. It also created an unknown but large number of limited partnerships and other financial entities, numbering in the hundreds, perhaps in the thousands, dealing with commodities and services.

It its 2000 *Annual Report,* the company said its revenues had increased from $13.2 billion in 1996 to $100.8 billion in 2000, with a growth of profits from $1 million in 1996 to $1.1 billion in 2000. This bright picture clouded in October 2001, when Enron announced a $544 million after-tax charge against earnings related to the transactions of some partnerships. A month later the company said it was revising its financial statements from 1997 to 2001 to reduce net income by more than $1 billion. The reason was that the company had been reporting income from some of its trading arrangements that was not real. And billions of dollars in debt had been hidden in so-called off-the-books accounts. Investors lost confidence in Enron, and cash flow declined to the point where the company could not meet its debt obligations. Finally, on December 2, 2001, the company filed for bankruptcy. It was the largest bankruptcy in U.S. history.

What happened? A swarm of congressional committees announced hearings to discover the answer, but they were frustrated by top Enron executives who chose to exercise their Fifth Amendment right to remain silent rather than incriminate themselves. Faced with a complex investigative task, those needing reasons could at least agree with Arthur Levitt Jr., a former SEC chairman, who offered the sweeping explanation that "all systems failed in the Enron debacle."[1] In all likelihood he had in mind the board of directors, top management, internal auditors, outside auditors and lawyers, investment analysts, the SEC, and business journalists. As Nora Brownell, commissioner of the Federal Energy Regulatory Commission put it, "Everyone who has touched Enron should be looking in the mirror."[2] In this brief introductory story we cannot unravel the failures of all these parties. Instead, we focus on the massive failure of corporate governance, primarily by the board of directors and to a lesser degree on top managers.

The Board of Directors and Top Management

Enron's board was composed of individuals with distinguished backgrounds (see the box). This board obviously had enough collective acumen that its oversight should have prevented the ignominious collapse of its charge. In October 2001, a Special Committee was created by the board to look at transactions between Enron and investment partnerships created and managed by Andrew S. Fastow, the company's chief financial officer. This action was triggered by huge losses in these partnerships contributing to the escalating financial problems of the company.

The Special Committee submitted its 218-page report to the board of directors on February 1, 2002.[3] In reviewing the extremely complex world of Enron's partnerships, it cast a critical eye on the governance structure of the company beginning with the board of directors.

The board had approved Fastow's creation of partnerships even though, in some cases, they created a conflict of interest. The problem was that in some of the partnerships he was both a manager for Enron and an investor in an outside entity that engaged in financial transactions, such as the buying and selling of assets, with Enron. Which interest would be his priority, Enron's or his own? The rules of the Financial Accounting Standards Board (FASB), an organization that sets guidelines for accounting practices, are that if an outside investor puts in 3 percent or more of the capital in a partnership, the corporation, even if it provides the other 97 percent, does not have to declare the partnership as a subsidiary. Therefore, assets and debt in the partnership can be withheld from the corporation's balance sheet.

[1] Arthur Levitt Jr., "All Systems Failed in the Enron Debacle," *Los Angeles Times,* January 24, 2002.
[2] John R. Emshwiller and Rebecca Smith, "Murky Waters: A Primer on Enron Partnerships," *The Wall Street Journal,* January 21, 2002, p. C14.
[3] William C. Powers Jr., chair; Raymond S. Trobh, and Herbert S. Winokur Jr., *Report of Investigation by the Special Investigative Committee of the Board of Directors of Enron Corp.,* February 1, 2002. Powers was chairman of the committee and dean of the University of Texas School of Law. Powers and Trobh were admitted to the board after the committee was formed. Winokur had been a member of the board for some time.

Enron's Board of Directors

ROBERT A. BELFER
New York, New York
Chairman, Belco Oil & Gas Corp.

NORMAN P. BLAKE, JR.
Colorado Springs, Colorado
Chairman, President and CEO, Comdisco, Inc.,
and Former CEO and Secretary General, United
States Olympic Committee

RONNIE C. CHAN
Hong Kong
Chairman, Hang Lung Group

JOHN H. DUNCAN
Houston, Texas
Former Chairman of the Executive Committee
of Gulf & Western Industries, Inc.

WENDY L. GRAMM
Washington, D.C.
Director of the Regulatory Studies Program of
the Mercatus Center at George Mason University
Former Chairman, U.S. Commodity Futures
Trading Commission

KEN L. HARRISON
Portland, Oregon
Former Chairman and CEO, Portland General
Electric Company

ROBERT K. JAEDICKE
Stanford, California
Professor of Accounting (Emeritus) and Former Dean,
Graduate School of Business, Stanford University

KENNETH L. LAY
Houston, Texas
Chairman, Enron Corp.

CHARLES A. LEMAISTRE
San Antonio, Texas
President Emeritus, University of Texas M.D.
Anderson Cancer Center

JOHN MENDELSOHN
Houston, Texas
President, University of Texas M.D. Anderson
Cancer Center

JEROME J. MEYER
Wilsonville, Oregon
Chairman, Tektronix, Inc.

PAULO V. FERRAZ PEREIRA
Rio de Janeiro, Brazil
Executive Vice President of Group Bozano
Former President and COO, Meridional Financial
Group, and Former President and CEO, State Bank
of Rio de Janeiro, Brazil

FRANK SAVAGE
Stamford, Connecticut
Chairman, Alliance Capital Management International
(a division of Alliance Capital) Management L.P.)

JEFFREY K. SKILLING
Houston, Texas
President and CEO, Enron Corp.

JOHN A URQUHART
Fairfield, Connecticut
Senior Advisor to the Chairman, Enron Corp.,
President, John A. Urquhart Associates, and Former
Senior Vice President of Industrial and Power Systems,
General Electric Company

JOHN WAKEHAM
London, England
Former U.K. Secretary of State for Energy and Leader
of the Houses of Lords and Commons

HERBERT S. WINOKUR, JR.
Greenwich, Connecticut
President, Winokur Holdings, Inc., and Former Senior
Executive Vice President, Penn Central Corporation

Source: Enron *Annual Report* 2000, pp. 54–55.

Using this device, Enron was able to hide losses and debt totaling hundreds of millions of dollars.[4]

The directors recognized that it was a conflict of interest for Fastow to be an outside investor but defined it as a modest problem in light of the great potential gain for Enron, and they thought that it could be handled by certain controls specified by the board. These controls required the approval of top executives and the board on partnership deals. This policy was a mistake. The approval requirement gave a green light to expansion of the partnerships beyond anything envisioned by the board. The controls on Fastow were never properly implemented. The Special Committee found that board committees, such as the audit committee, "were severely hampered by the fact that significant information was withheld from them."[5] Observers outside the company have not been as charitable, placing much of the blame for Enron's failure on the audit committee.[6] The Special Committee reached the obvious conclusion that proliferation of the partnerships had exposed the company to enormous risks. At the same time, Fastow had been able to orchestrate side deals netting him more than $30 million as an individual.

The Special Committee did not place sole blame for Enron's failure on its directors, but it accused the board of failing to exercise its oversight responsibility. The committee said: "The Board of Directors was denied important information that might have led it to take action, but the Board also did not fully appreciate the significance of some of the specific information that came before it."[7] Some partnership arrangements were presented to the board that involved substantial sums of money and risk and the board failed to give them the scrutiny they deserved. Some of these intricate deals had received only 10 or 15 minutes of attention at board meetings. The board cannot be faulted, said the Special Committee, for not acting if it had no or insufficient information. It could be faulted, however, for limited scrutiny and probing.

The board had also approved procedures for management appraisal of partnerships and other, similarly arcane, arrangements such as limited-liability companies set up by Enron. For example, it directed its audit committee to conduct annual reviews of all partnership transactions. The committee, however, failed to probe deeply into the intricate transactions being generated. The board charged the chief accounting officer with the responsibility of reviewing and approving all transactions between Enron and its partnerships. Here again, the review was inadequate. What it all amounted to, said the Special Committee, was that top management was not "watching the store."

---

[4] Emshwiller and Smith, "Murky Waters," p. C1.
[5] Powers, Trobh, and Winokur, *Report of Investigation,* p. 159.
[6] Louis Lavelle, "Enron: How Governance Rules Failed," *Business Week,* January 21, 2002, p. 28.
[7] Ibid., p. 148.

Financial Impacts

Enron's collapse resulted in mass layoffs. That, of course, was devastating to those who lost a job and found it difficult to get another. To compound that disaster, many employees whose 401(k) retirement accounts were heavily invested in Enron stock saw their savings disappear. Janice Farmer of Orlando, Florida, for example, an Enron retiree, told the Senate Commerce Committee she at one time had $700,000 in her employee stock plan but now had only $4,000.[8]

In contrast, top managers were enriched by tens of millions of dollars as the financial fortunes of Enron declined. Days before it filed for bankruptcy, the company disbursed $55 million in bonuses to about 500 employees.[9] Fastow's gains were noted above. Michael Kopper, who worked for Fastow, invested $125,000 in one partnership and received more than $10 million in return. Throughout 2001, managers sold millions of shares of Enron stock at relatively high prices. Kenneth Lay, Enron's chairman, sold over $123 million of Enron stock in 2000 and $23 million in 2001.[10] Other top managers also made tens of millions of dollars in capital gains by selling before the fall.

This story illustrates what can happen when a company's board and top managers fail in their governance responsibilities. It is a lesson for all companies to stress effective and efficient governance.

We begin the chapter with a definition of governance and contrast it with management. Then the corporate charter as the legal basis for governance authority is described. This is followed with a review of current structures of boards and the duties of directors. We note some important criticisms leveled at boards and discuss recommendations for reforming them. Special attention is then given to compensation of CEOs. Finally, we examine the question: To whom are directors accountable?

CORPORATE GOVERNANCE DEFINED

Corporate governance is the overall control of activities in a corporation. It is concerned with the formulation of long-term objectives and plans and the proper management structure (organization, systems, and people) to achieve them. At the same time, it entails making sure that the structure functions to maintain the corporation's integrity, reputation, and responsibility to its various constituencies.

[8] Robert L. Jackson, "Tearful Tales of Investors' Losses Fill Senate Panel Hearing on Enron," *The New York Times,* December 19, 2001, p. C3.
[9] Richard A. Opell Jr., and Kurt Eichenwald, "Enron Paid $55 Million for Bonuses," *The New York Times,* December 6, 2001, p. 81.
[10] Marianne Lavelle and Matthew Benjamin, "The Biggest Bust," *U.S. News & World Report,* December 10, 2001, p. 34.

In this definition, governance is the concern of the board of directors. However, top management is also clearly involved. But management has other dimensions that are quite distinct from the operations of the typical board of directors. Management is a hands-on operational activity. It is concerned with supervising day-to-day action and the prudent use of scarce resources to achieve desirable aims. The typical board of directors does not become involved in such activities. While governance is shared by boards and top management, our focus in this chapter is essentially but not exclusively on boards of directors.

THE CORPORATE CHARTER

The *corporate charter* is the legal authority for corporate managers and directors to function in conformance with the above definition. All American corporations except a few quasi-public enterprises chartered by the federal government (for example, the Tennessee Valley Authority) are chartered by the state in which they incorporate. At the Constitutional Convention of 1787, the Founders debated a federal chartering power but decided that existing state controls were adequate to regulate corporate activity.

All states have general incorporation laws and compete with one another to attract the tax revenues of large corporations. Delaware is the longtime victor in this competition and charters almost half the largest industrial corporations in the United States. The attraction of Delaware, despite the fact that costs of incorporation there are higher than in most states, is the business-friendly corporate laws in the state. It has been said that Delaware will not be underregulated, meaning that its laws are less restricting of corporate activities. Also, its Chancery Court, which handles only business cases, is very accommodating to corporate interests.

Corporate charters specify the rights and responsibilities of stockholders, directors, and officers. Fundamentally, corporate charters lodge control over the property of the enterprise in stockholders who own shares in the assets of the company and vote those shares in naming a board of directors to run the firm. The directors have a fiduciary responsibility to protect the interests of the shareholders. They are responsible for appointing officers to run the day-to-day affairs of the company. The legal line of power runs from the state, to shareholders, to directors, to managers.

The charters also include detailed provisions about such matters as annual meetings, methods of choosing directors, and authority of directors to issue stock. For instance, charters are specific about calling meetings of shareholders, declaring dividends, electing and removing officers, proposing amendments of the articles of incorporation, and so on. Such charter provisions are meant to protect the interests of shareholders. A vast body of law that seeks to do the same thing has also been created over time.

THE STRUCTURE OF BOARDS OF DIRECTORS

In 2000 the average corporate board had 11 members, according to a comprehensive study by Korn/Ferry Internatonal.[11] The number varies in different industries. Banks, for example, average 17 members. Aerospace companies average 13 members. These numbers would be excessive for Giovanni Agnelli, the founder of Italy's huge Turin-based Fiat conglomerate. He once observed: "Only an odd number of directors can run a company, and three are too many."[12] This is an extreme position, of course, but most small firms and many large ones do have small boards of directors. Banks and other financial institutions tend to have large boards, but the general trend is for smaller boards.

Board membership may include both inside (management) directors and outside (nonmanagement) directors. In recent years, the number of outside directors on boards has grown until today the average corporate board has nine outside and two inside directors. Seventy-four percent of the companies studied by Korn/Ferry International had at least one woman board member. This compared with 69 percent in 1995. Sixty-five percent had one or more ethnic minority directors, compared with 47 percent in 1995. Fifteen percent of the boards had non-U.S. citizens as directors, compared with 17 percent in 1995. Korn/Ferry's report commented on this decline as follows: "Once touted as necessary for successful globalization, challenges such as logistics, availability of qualified individuals and board cultural assimilation may have lessened the demand. Only 4 percent of survey respondents say their boards plan to add a foreign national to the directorship."[13]

In the past, board members were usually suggested by the CEO to the board for approval. Today, nominating committees on most boards have this responsibility, but CEOs still play a prominent part in the process. Once selected, the names of the nominees are presented to the shareholders for their approval or disapproval at the annual stockholder meeting.

Boards are divided into committees. Here are committees most frequently found on boards as reported by the Korn/Ferry report.[14] Audit (100%), compensation (99%), stock options (87%), nominating (73%), executive (57%), board organization (46%), finance (40%), succession planning (32%), corporate responsibility (22%), investment (21%), and director's compensation (21%). Other committees sometimes found on boards are public affairs, corporate ethics, employee pensions and benefits,

---

[11] Korn/Ferry International, *28th Annual Board of Directors Study,* 2001, p. 10.
[12] Quoted in Paul Betts, "Heads Begin to Roll at Fiat," *Paris Financial Times,* June 18, 1990.
[13] Korn/Ferry International, p. 11.
[14] Ibid., p. 12

human resources, environment, science and technology, corporate contributions, legal affairs, and social responsibility.

Board Structures in Foreign Countries

Board structures in European countries are considerably different from those in the United States. German companies have "two-tier" boards that consist of an upper supervisory board and a lower management board. The supervisory board exercises broad control over the company. Its members, which include representatives of banks, major shareholders, trade unions, and suppliers, are appointed at an annual meeting of stockholders. This board supervises the management board. It elects members of the management board whom it can remove anytime. The lower board manages the detailed operations of the company. The EU has debated whether this model should be mandated in a European Community statute, but no decision has been made.

In recent years, Japanese companies have drastically reduced the number of their directors to improve decision making. For example, Sony had 38 directors in 1997 and now has only 10. Sony changed the title of 31 directors to "corporate executive officer," which corresponds with vice president in the United Sates. In 1999 Hitachi reduced the number of its directors from 30 to 14 and created 21 corporate executive officers. The same pattern has been adopted in other large Japanese companies. In all these changes, no outside directors were appointed. In Japan, the real power to decide rests with the CEO and staff and not with the board of directors.[15]

The Duties of Directors

Inside U.S. companies, boards of directors have ultimate authority except for matters that must have the approval of shareholders, such as the election of the board itself or an increase in capitalization. In recent years, many boards have been strongly criticized for not paying proper attention to their responsibilities, and codes of conduct have appeared like dandelions in the spring. Because of the Enron debacle, this trend undoubtedly will continue and be reinforced with new laws. The fundamental responsibilities and duties, however, remain essentially the same as in the past.

We begin with a 1990 policy statement on corporate boards of directors issued by the Business Roundtable, an organization of CEOs of the largest companies in the United States.[16] Overall, said the policy statement, "the

---

[15] Toyohiro Kono and Stewart Clegg, *Trends in Japanese Management* (London: Palgrave, 2001), p. 59.

[16] The Business Roundtable, *Corporate Governance and American Competitiveness* (New York: Business Roundtable, March 1990), p. 7.

principal responsibility is to exercise governance so as to ensure the long-term successful performance of their corporation." Specific responsibilities are as follows:

1. Select, regularly evaluate, and, if necessary, replace the chief executive officer. Determine management compensation. Review succession planning.

2. Review and, where appropriate, approve the financial objectives, major strategies, and plans of the corporation.

3. Provide advice and counsel to top management.

4. Select and recommend to shareholders for election an appropriate slate of candidates for the board of directors; evaluate board processes and performance.

5. Review the adequacy of systems to comply with all applicable laws/regulations.

In a similar statement in 1978, the Business Roundtable advocated these specific duties for boards: "It is the board's duty to consider the overall impact of the activities of the corporation on (1) the society of which it is a part, and (2) the interests and views of groups other than those immediately identified with the corporation. This obligation arises out of the responsibility to act primarily in the interests of the share owners—particularly their long-range interests."[17]

Cutting across these functions, it seems to us, are requirements to make sure that there is an appropriate flow of information to the board and that internal policies and procedures of the company are fully capable of responding to board decisions. Peter Drucker has added the following other dimensions to these functions if a board is to be effective: asking critical questions; acting as a conscience, a keeper of human and moral values; serving as a window on the outside world; and helping the corporation to be understood by its constituencies by the outside community.[18]

How individual boards and members perform these duties will vary much. Jay Lorsch, a professor at Harvard Business School, observes, "Traditionally, corporate leaders have considered a powerful, active board to be a nuisance at best and a force that could improperly interfere in the management of the company at worst. They have preferred directors who are content to offer counsel when asked and to support management in times of crisis."[19] That is becoming less true as pressures

[17] The Business Roundtable, *The Role and Composition of the Board of Directors of the Large Publicly Owned Corporation* (New York: Business Roundtable, 1978), pp. 11–12.
[18] Peter F. Drucker, "The Bored Board," *Wharton Magazine,* Fall 1976.
[19] Jay W. Lorsch, "Empowering the Board," *Harvard Business Review,* January–February 1995, p. 107.

have led to more active boards. Still, many companies' boards today perform in the traditional way.

Criticisms of Boards of Directors

Historians may look back on the 1980s and 1990s as a period when corporate boards were under siege. Several significant forces energized the critics. One was widespread publicity about excesses in the merger movement, such as greed-driven leveraged buyouts and "greenmail."[20] The savings and loan crisis in the mid-1980s, with its widespread bankruptcies, also raised public questions about corporate governance. At the same time, there was a major change in the composition of corporate shareholders because of the extraordinary growth of pension funds.

Complaints of individual stockholders and institutional investors arising in the 1980s and 1990s still resonate. Today there are complaints that in too many companies, board performance in enhancing equity investment is inadequate. Some critics assert that other stakeholders, such as employees, communities, and society as a whole, are not given the power in decision making they deserve. Indeed, it is said, decisions are often diametrically opposed to the best interests of these groups. It is asserted that boards do not properly evaluate the performance of managers and permit all sorts of unethical practices to exist in their companies. Board members do not spend enough time on company business and are, in effect, used as rubber stamps by the company's chief executive officer. To make matters worse, directors are egregiously overpaid. Critics also complain that boards lack sufficient diversity.

Individual shareholders have tried without much success to influence board performance through stockholder proposals. Significant board reform, however, has been initiated primarily by government agencies such as the SEC; by pension funds; and by some business groups such as the Business Roundtable and the National Association of Corporate Directors. Academics have not been silent in making recommendations for reform.[21]

The SEC has issued many new rules to make it easier for individual shareholders to be heard in corporate offices. For instance, the SEC has mandated disclosure of information about corporate officer compensation, finances, stock issuances, and accounting procedures. These changes have been important in giving individual shareholders more information and power. In addition, pension funds have become a significant new source of pressure on corporations to improve performance.

---

[20] Greenmail is a name given to a transaction in which a company agrees to buy back a corporate raider's stock at a premium price over the market. Some critics use harsher words, such as "legalized corporate blackmail." The idea, of course, is to get the raider to go away.

[21] See for example Jay A. Conger, Edward E. Lawler III, and David L. Finegold, *Corporate Boards: New Strategies for Adding Value at the Top* (San Francisco: Jossey-Bass, 2001).

INSTITUTIONAL INVESTOR PARTICIPATION IN GOVERNANCE

The growth of pension and mutual fund assets has given these entities new power in corporate governance. Their total assets rose from $70 billion in 1980 to $9.8 trillion in the third quarter of 2001. The investments of these funds in corporate equities rose from $267.5 billion in 1980 to $5.1 trillion in 2001. At that time, the total value of corporate equities on the market was, according to the Federal Reserve System, $13.6 trillion.[22] The stock holdings of these institutions give them a majority of the common shares in many companies, which, of course, gives them power to influence corporate governance, and they have used it.

Before the mid-1980s, pension fund managers were passive investors and usually went along with the decisions of corporate managers. Their activism in corporate governance began in 1985 when Jesse Unruh, treasurer of the State of California and manager of the state's two large pension funds, decided to wield the ownership power of the funds to influence governance. His motivation stemmed from losses incurred when managers at Disney and Texaco paid "greenmail" to get rid of corporate raiders. Unruh proclaimed, "We can't just sit there and watch the action pass by, and yet that's exactly what we're all doing." He added, "Up to this point, we have all been used and generally abused by everybody—corporate raiders, arbitragers (takeover speculators) and management—because we are all so ignorant and ineffective in these situations."[23] Unruh's ire led to formation of the Council of Institutional Investors (CII) by 31 pension fund managers who controlled at that time approximately $200 billion of assets. The CII endorsed a "Shareholder's Bill of Rights" that demanded a voice in all "fundamental decisions which could affect corporate performance and growth.[24]

Should pension fund managers seek to influence corporations? If not, why not? If so, in what way? The interest of many pension fund managers is essentially short-term improvement in the value of the stock they hold or manage. If they are not satisfied with the management of the companies whose stock they hold, the shares can be sold. This is possible when the shares owned in any one corporation are small. But when a pension fund such as the California Public Employee's Retirement System (CalPERS) owns a large percentage of stock in any one company, it is essentially locked in as an owner-investor of that company. Fundamentally, said former manager of CalPERS Dale Hanson, the security owner should take the long view of investment, not the short view. In

---

[22] Board of Governors of the Federal Reserve System, *Flow of Funds Accounts of the United States: Flows and Outstandings, Third Quarter 2001* (Washington, DC: Board of Governors of the Federal Reserve System, 2001).

[23] In Debra Whitefield, "Unruh Calls for Pension Funds to Flex Muscles," *Los Angeles Times,* February 3, 1985, p. E3.

[24] Council of Institutional Investors (New York: Council of Institutional Investors, undated).

this light, it makes sense to seek to influence companies whose performance is deficient but whose long-term promise is bright. CalPERS and other major pension fund managers agree.

The largest pension funds do not attempt day-to-day management of companies but seek to encourage them to improve their procedures and, on occasion, basic strategies. For example, CalPERS had some influence, along with other pension funds, over top management changes at General Motors, IBM, and Eastman Kodak. How much is not publicly known. Other large pension funds also have initiated change in top management. For example, Teachers Insurance and Annuity Association–College Retirement Education Fund succeeded in ousting the entire board of Furr's/Bishop's Inc., a cafeteria company.

CalPERS

CalPERS is the nation's largest public pension fund, with assets of $146.6 billion in 2001, and since Unruh's day it has been a leader in pension fund governance activism. CalPERS's initiatives have developed through several stages and are still evolving. The earliest focus was the elimination of greenmail and other techniques used by companies to combat hostile takeovers. Then, beginning in 1993, the fund identified each year a list of 10 companies in its portfolio whose stocks underperformed general stock market indexes. CalPERS urged the boards of targeted companies, sometimes privately and sometimes publicly, to improve governance and enhance long-term stock performance. Surveys show that targeted companies outperformed the Standard & Poor's 500 Index by substantial percentages. One study cited by CalPERS showed that five years after being targeted, the companies outperformed the S&P index by 52.5 percent.[25]

New Governance Guidelines

In 1997 CalPERS embarked on a new program called "Corporate Governance Core Principles and Guidelines." This is a set of standards for a model corporate board. The fund said, in initiating these standards, "CalPERS does not expect nor seek that each company will adopt or embrace every aspect of either the Principles or Guidelines . . . (the purpose is) to advance the corporate governance dialogue by presenting the views of one shareowner, but not to attempt to permanently enshrine those views."[26] Here are brief descriptions of some principles and guidelines:

- Majority of board should be independent directors.

- Independent directors meet periodically without the CEO.

[25] CalPERS, "Corporate Governance Core Principles & Guidelines," Sacramento, CA, April 13, 1998, www.corpgov.net/forums/commentary/ending.html.
[26] Ibid., p. 3.

- When the CEO is also the chair of the board, the board should elect an independent "lead" director.

- Some board committees, such as director nomination, board evaluation, and CEO evaluation, should be entirely composed of independent directors.

- No director can serve as a consultant to the company.

- Director compensation is cash and stock of the company.

- The board regularly evaluates itself.

- The board regularly reviews the CEO's performance.

- The board establishes guidelines limiting the number of other board seats each director may hold.

- The board should consider setting tenure rules.

- When selecting a new CEO, the board should consider separating the CEO and board chair positions.

- Generally, the retiring CEO should not continue on the board.

In subsequent years CalPERS expanded its statement of governance principles. In 1998 a new set of principles moved beyond the structure of the board of directors to include individual director characteristics and shareowner rights. (CalPERS prefers the word *shareowner* to *shareholder*.) In 1999 CalPERS accepted a "Statement of Global Corporate Governance Principles," adopted by the International Corporate Governance Network (ICGN). This organization was founded in 1995 at the initiation of major institutional investors, academics, and other parties interested in the betterment of global corporate governance practices. CalPERS's board of directors said it "believes that the global governance dialogue will now be most advanced through coalescence of thought around a single set of standards." To this end, CalPERS said it embraces the "Statement of Global Corporate Governance Principles, adopted in 1999 by the International Corporate Governance Network."[27] These principles are set forth in a 25-page document of fine print in the OECD Principles of Corporate Governance.[28]

COMMENTS ON SOME PROPOSED BOARD REFORMS

Many thoughtful proposals for reform have been made in recent years from such organizations as the National Association of Corporate Directors. Institutional investor groups in foreign countries, individual corpo-

[27] CalPERS, "Global Corporate Governance Principles," www.calpers-governance.org/principles/international/global/page 04.asp, undated, p. 1.
[28] Organisation for Economic Co-operation and Development, Directorate for Financial, Fiscal, and Enterprise Affairs, Paris, France, April 16, 1999.

rations, academics, and activist groups in the United States have prepared codes, guidelines, and principles to improve corporate performance as they define the term. Many are similar to those principles noted above. Each proposal deserves evaluation, but space limits discussion to only a few that focus on directors.

Selecting Directors

If the board has an outside director as chairperson, it would be his or her responsibility to ensure that the nominating committee was finding appropriate people for membership. The advice and counsel of the CEO would still be sought, of course. However, this process would end the misperception, if there was one, that board members were appointed by the CEO and, therefore, were in some sense beholden to that person.

Some suggest that boards be composed almost completely of independent outside directors. In our experience serving on boards, this would be a mistake. It is important that the board be well informed about the details of the operation of the business. Insiders should be present to provide company information to the board.

Ram Charan, a consultant to CEOs and boards, emphasizes the point that for an effective board there must be carefully defined criteria for selection of new board members. He suggests that each director be asked to complete a form of 22 special criteria by checking each with a simple "yes" or "no." The criteria are organized under three major questions, as follows: "How will this individual add to the composite perspective of the group of outside directors?" "Will this individual enhance the dynamics of interaction among directors . . . in challenging management and directors, stimulating creative thought, contributing incisiveness to discussions, and helping bring closure to debate?" "Does this person have a record of leadership in his/her area of activity and have the gut instincts of a CEO?"[29]

Selecting the CEO

As noted previously the Business Roundtable in listing the responsibilities of directors specified the selection of the CEO first. This is, indeed, a major responsibility of directors. As Warren Bennis and James O'Toole, two experts on the subject, point out: "The right CEO can make or break a company, yet boards often go about CEO selection all wrong. The problem is simple: they don't understand what defines real leadership today–or if they do, it scares them." In an article in the *Harvard Business Review,* they set forth major guidelines for directors in their selection of the company's CEO.[30]

[29] Ram Charan, *Boards at Work* (San Francisco: Jossey-Bass Publishers, 1998), pp. 98–99.
[30] Warren Bennis and James O'Toole, "Don't Hire the Wrong CEO," *Harvard Business Review,* May–June 2000, p. 17.

Evaluating the CEO's Performance

Most boards say this is one of their major functions. There is a question, however, about how well defined are the board's objectives for evaluation, how comprehensive, and how thorough are evaluations in practice. Too frequently, evaluation is casual, if performed at all, and any negative feedback is minimal.

There are, however, many companies whose boards have detailed evaluation criteria. Criteria for an effective evaluation of CEOs would include the following:

• The board should develop a clear job description for the CEO position.

• The board and the CEO should meet and agree upon the CEO's performance objectives.

• The performance evaluation should be conducted annually.

• Specific board meetings should be established for the CEO evaluation.

• The long-term performance of the company should be compared with similar organizations.

• The CEO's performance should be evaluated against the goals set for the company.

• The CEO should appraise his or her performance and present it to the board.

• The CEO should have an opportunity to discuss the evaluation with the entire board.[31]

Board Self-Evaluation

This is an extremely important function. About half the respondents to the Korn/Ferry survey said the entire board's performance was formally evaluated on a regular basis.[32]

There are, of course, many ways to perform a self-evaluation. For example, a questionnaire may be completed by outside directors, the full board may discuss specific questions, and an outside consultant may be asked to conduct a survey. The preferred methodology should invite responses to specific questions. Companies that make such evaluations usually have such a list. Here are areas of assessment that should be included:[33]

• Board procedures.

• Quality of board discussions.

[31] Report of the NACD Blue Ribbon Commission on *Performance Evaluation of Chief Executive Officers, Boards, and Directors* (Washington, DC: National Association of Corporate Directors, 1994).
[32] Korn/Ferry International, p. 22
[33] NACD Blue Ribbon Commission.

- Board relationship to senior management.
- Evaluations of the CEO.
- Board role in company strategy.
- Director selection and retirement.
- Preparation to deal with an unforeseen crisis.
- Board leadership.
- Director compensation.
- Definition of independence of outside directors.
- Adequacy of information given to board.

Understanding and Approving Major Company Strategies

It is difficult to understand how a board can feel comfortable in its performance unless it is certain that it understands, reviews, and approves the major strategies designed for the company. In a number of companies, this process is conducted at a two- or three-day offsite meeting of the board to discuss only strategy.

The question arises, of course, at what point does such a legitimate process encroach upon the detailed management of the company? This is a difficult line to draw, but one that must be understood and drawn in such a way that the CEO feels comfortable.

Separate the CEO and Board Chairman

In most large American corporations, the CEO is also the chairperson of the board. Some observers believe the two jobs should be separated, but there is much opposition to the idea, especially among CEOs.

Many directors believe that when CEOs also chair the board, they have too much power. The power to control the agenda and the information that directors get is overwhelming, they say.

After a three-year study in which hundreds of directors participated, Professor Jay W. Lorsch of the Harvard Business School concluded that separating the two jobs would go a long way to help directors perform better. It would help prevent crises because, with an outside director as chairperson, the board would likely get more and better information about company affairs. Also, in the event of a crisis involving the CEO, the board would be more organized to deal with it. But beyond that, splitting the jobs would underscore the notion that managers serve at the discretion of directors, not the other way around. At board meetings, directors would feel freer to raise questions and be critical of management.[34] Many top executives support this view.

[34] Jay W. Lorsch, *Pawns or Potentates* (Boston, MA: Harvard Business School Press, 1989).

Critics of this proposal point out that although the two top people usually get along well, there are many unpublicized cases of failure. If the CEO and chairperson positions are split, and if rivalry or dislike develops between the two, then the split works to the detriment of the business and the board functions less well. CEOs say that to split the roles would complicate their jobs. They are concerned that their immediate predecessors might be appointed chairperson. That situation would indeed be fraught with danger and should not be permitted by a board where the split has taken place.

Ram Charan, a consultant to corporate CEOs and boards of directors, is critical of the separation of the two jobs. He says: "Separating the role of CEO and chairman can create confusion and blur accountability. Outsiders might begin to wonder who is really in charge or whether the CEO is on the way out. Any misperceptions outside can erode the CEO's decision-making power internally as well."[35]

Enron Inspired Reform

The focus of the above discussion was on boards of directors. It should be noted, in addition, that the Enron debacle energized Congress, the SEC, the FASB, lawyers, corporations, and other groups to establish laws and write new rules within their authority to improve the governance of corporations and prevent another Enron disaster. How much of this activity will actually result in new mandates will depend on a number of factors such as the degree to which the public is concerned and the power of lobbies. At any rate, here are a few measures, beyond those noted above, that are being considered.

- Bar outside auditors from accepting consulting fees from the company.

- Bar members of the audit committees from accepting consulting fees from the company.

- Limit the amount of company stock that employees can hold in their 401(k) plans.

- Bar directors who violate ethics from serving on boards.

- Improve the readability of corporate financial statements.

- Mandate prompt disclosure of more financial information to the public.

- Relax the cloak of confidentiality between lawyers and their clients to permit them to report crimes that could cause severe financial damage to shareholders, the corporation, and creditors.

- Mandate that directors and top managers report stock trades the next business day to the SEC and the day after that to the public.

[35] Ram Charan, *Boards at Work,* p. 51.

COMPENSATION ISSUES

We now turn to a very controversial subject: director and executive compensation.

Compensation of Directors

Korn/Ferry reported the average compensation (annual retainer fee plus fees for attending separate board committee meetings) of outside directors was $40,667 in 2000. For the largest companies, those with annual revenues more than $20 billion, the average was $51,774.[36] Director compensation can take forms other than cash. In recent years, more companies have added stock options to cash stipends. The assumption is that directors will be more diligent in their responsibilities when their interests are aligned with shareholders. When the value of stock options is added to cash compensation, the total can be rather large. For instance, analysts at Pearl Meyer & Partners, an executive compensation consultant in New York, reviewed 72 proxy statements. Topping the list was an estimated $637,536 for each director at Cisco Systems when the value of stock options was calculated at the time of the company's 2000 annual meeting.[37] The average for directors of the 200 largest industrial and service companies was much less, $137,400 in cash and equity awards. Other benefits sometimes offered outside directors include pensions, life insurance, medical benefits, donations to a director's charities, paying a spouse's travel fare to board meetings, and use of the corporate airplane.

The basic recommendation of critics is that compensation should be adequate and that it should be tied in some way to the long-range not the short-range performance of the company. What is adequate will vary among companies and will always remain controversial. How to link pay to performance is challenging. This probably is done best through stock options that can be redeemed at a specified time.

How Much Are CEOs Paid?

First of all, it must be recognized that it is difficult to accurately calculate the exact amount of all pay and benefits paid to a chief executive. The salary paid to a CEO as well as any annual bonus is clear enough and publicly reported. Problems arise in calculating the value of stock options, which are a large part of most CEO compensation, and other benefits such as deferred pay and perquisites. A stock option, as noted previously, is a right to buy the company's stock at a fixed price and under conditions determined by the board of directors. Usually the price is set at or close to the current price and there is a limit on the time granted to

---

[36] Korn/Ferry International, p. 14.
[37] Reported by Reed Abelson, "As the Market Goes, So Go the Rewards of Many Company Directors," *The New York Times,* April 1, 2001, p. 6.

the receiver to buy the stock, usually 10 years. Thus, if the stock of XYZ corporation today is $10 and rises to $50 dollars within the time limit, say 10 years, the CEO can buy that stock at $10 and reap the gain between this price and the future market price. If the stock does not rise above $10, the option is worthless. See page 691 for more on options.

Nearly all corporations have compensation committees that set the pay and benefits of top executives. Perceptions of excessively generous pay and benefits for CEOs inspire widespread popular outrage. This is an old story. In 1939 President Franklin D. Roosevelt railed against the "entrenched greed" of corporation executives, and the criticism has periodically arisen since. By today's standards, CEO pay in President Roosevelt's era was modest. Eugene G. Grace, president of Bethlehem Steel, was the highest paid executive in 1929. He received a salary of $12,000 and a bonus of $1.6 million. In 1949 the highest paid executive was Louis B. Mayer, first vice president of Lowe's Inc., who got $509,622. This contrasted with the average pay of $2,612 for workers. In 1968 the highest paid executive was James M. Roche, chairman of General Motors, who got $795,000 while the average worker was paid $5,602.[38]

In 2000 the total stock market declined 12 percent. Corporate executives, on average, increased their compensation of salary and bonuses by 22 percent and stock options by 14 percent over 1999.[39] The average realized compensation differed substantially among industries. For example, total median compensation (cash, bonus, and stock) for executives in basic materials was $1.5 million. To this sum could be added the unrealized potential value of stock options, which was $2.9 million. Technology executives received average compensation of $3.4 million and had potential option compensation of $59.7 million.[40]

The highest paid CEO in 2000 was Sanford I. Weill, of Citigroup, Inc., with total compensation of $224.4 million. That included $196.2 from the exercise of stock options. John T. Chambers, of Cisco Systems Inc., was the second highest with compensation of $157.3 million. The third highest was Kenneth L. Lay of Enron Corp., whose compensation was $140.4 million. The fourth was L. Dennis Koztowski of Tyco International Ltd., who received $125.3 million. And the fifth was John F. Welch Jr., CEO of General Electric Co., with $122.5 million.[41]

---

[38] "Executive Pay, Up, Up, and Away," special supplement, *Business Week,* undated, circa 2001.
[39] These numbers were calculated by Executive Compensation Advisory Services, which conducted a survey of pay at 200 companies. The figures were reported by David Leonhardt, "For the Boss, Happy Days Are Still Here," *The New York Times,* April 1, 2001, p. 1.
[40] William M. Mercer Inc., survey of 350 proxy statements of large U.S. companies made for *The Wall Street Journal,* reported in "Executive Pay," *The Wall Street Journal,* April 12, 2001, p. R11.
[41] These numbers were calculated by William M. Mercer Inc. reported by Joann S. Lublin, in "Hedging Their Bets," *The Wall Street Journal,* April 12, 2001, p. R1.

Compensation of European CEOs

When shareholders ask about the compensation of Jurgen Schrempp, chief executive of DaimlerChrysler, they are told it is a secret and will likely remain so. This lack of transparency in Germany is traditional in many other European countries, including France, Spain, and Italy. Great Britain is an exception. CEO compensation in Europe tends to be low when compared with the pay of top executives in the United States. Compensation for CEOs in large automobile companies, for example, ranged from $500,000 to $2 million, small compared with U.S. standards. In Great Britain the salaries of senior executives rose almost 20 percent in 2000 to average about $1 million. There is public resentment of high corporate salaries, but, as in the United States, executive compensation is rising nonetheless.[42]

Criticisms of CEO Compensation

A widespread criticism of CEO compensation is that it is far too high. In addition, for most CEOs, the compensation has almost no relation to performance. This criticism is sharpened by stories of executives who have been handsomely rewarded when fired by their boards. For example, Jill Barad, Mattel's CEO, was asked to leave after three years on the job for poor performance. She left with a reported $50 million severance package. It included $12.8 million in cash, retirement benefits, forgiveness of a home loan, and 52 Barbie dolls, among other things. Graef Crystal, a compensation consultant, observed: "There are two ways in America that you can make a ton of money as a CEO. One is to perform magnificently. The other is to screw up big time and get fired."[43] Many other executives have been fired and received handsome settlements. For example, when Douglas Ivester was asked to leave his job as CEO of Coca-Cola he wound up with an astronomical package estimated at $166 million. Companies have declared bankruptcy but managed to compensate executives generously. The story of Enron illustrates but one instance. A corporate collapse similar to Enron's is that of Global Crossing Ltd. Gary Winnick founded the company in 1997, took it public in 1998, and sold shares worth $734 million before the company declared bankruptcy.[44]

Critics charge that in too many compensation committees, the members are CEOs of other corporations, cronies of the CEO, or consultants who have profited from business with the company. In such cases, it is alleged, the bias is clearly in favor of boosting CEO compensation.

[42] Alan Cowell, "Overseas, Salaries Are Kept Hush-Hush," *The Wall Street Journal,* April 1, 2001, Section 3, p. 7.
[43] Margarete Loftus, "Golden Parachute Barbie," *U.S. News & World Report,* May 15, 2000, p. 12.
[44] Geraldine Fabrikant and Simon Romero, "How Executives Prospered at Global Crossing," *The New York Times,* February 11, 2002, p. 1.

Critics are concerned that stock options, if large compared with total shares outstanding, depress the price of stocks on the market. When exercised, such options add to the number of shares outstanding and dilute both the market price and the voting power of other shareholders.

Labor unions are disturbed by the large and growing gap between salaries of workers and executives. According to the AFL-CIO, the average U.S. chief executive made 475 times as much as the average blue-collar worker. This contrasts with 24 times the average in Great Britain and 15 times in Germany.[45]

In Defense of CEOs

Executives defend high pay on several grounds. First, stock options have become a larger part of their compensation in recent years. As a result, the bull market in stock prices in the 1990s provided opportunities for executives to exercise options granted at much lower prices years earlier. If these past option grants are exercised and compensation is calculated for the year in which they are exercised, say the CEOs, of course the amounts look large.

Second, CEOs and their defenders say many large compensation packages were justified by the gains of stockholders during their tenure. Sometimes, this is correct. It clearly applies in the case of John Welch—the price of GE stock rose significantly while he was CEO. Another case is that of Michael Eisner, CEO of Walt Disney, who became head of that company in 1984 when net income was barely at the break-even point and its stock price was low. By 1992 revenues of the company were $7.5 billion and profits were $816 million. Eisner cashed options in 1992 with a value of $175 million. He had received the options at $3.59 and sold them at $40. By 1997 the company's revenues reached $22.5 billion, the price of the stock soared, and shareholders profited. So did the value of Eisner's stock options. During the 1990s, U.S. corporations expanded globally, and that significantly increased total revenues and profitability. Many CEOs were responsible for devising and implementing strategies that produced these results. They are now being compensated accordingly.

Third, boards of directors point out that if they do not pay their CEOs what executives in comparable companies get, they stand to lose them, and that would be costly. Anyway, they say, the compensation is not out of line with comparable professionals, such as top lawyers and Wall Street investment bankers.

What Should Directors Do about Compensation?

There are several reforms that can be introduced to improve the system for setting executive compensation. First, the compensation committee membership must be made independent from the influence of the CEO

45 Cowell, "Overseas, Salaries Are Kept Hush-Hush."

and other biased interests. The committee should be composed solely of outside directors and in large companies have an outside compensation consultant.

The criteria for determining compensation should be designed to provide greater incentives for the CEO to meet company objectives, which, among other things, should be formulated with the long term in view. This can be done in a number of ways. For example, if stock options are given, the time after which they may be exercised can be extended. Cash compensation may be related to achieving specific goals, such as corporate profits.

Other Reforms and Proposals for Reform

In response to widespread criticism, the SEC issued new regulations concerning executive pay in 1992 that require companies to show in charts and graphs precisely all details of senior executive compensation. The board of directors compensation committee is required to explain the performance factors used in determining pay. As we have said, there is no generally accepted formula for calculating the value of unexercised options. However, the SEC now requires that companies calculate and report to stockholders a range of values.

Criticism of compensation also initiated action by Congress. A 1994 tax law bars publicly held corporations from deducting as a cost of doing business a top officer's compensation in excess of $1 million a year. Nevertheless, many corporations pay executives more despite the fact that it is not tax deductible as an expense. The Financial Accounting Standards Board has been considering what to do about stock options. The recommendation to them is to account for stock options as an expense, the same as other compensation. The big problem, of course, is how the cost of the options should be calculated.

TO WHOM ARE DIRECTORS ACCOUNTABLE?

Jay Lorsh in his study found that" the majority of directors felt trapped in a dilemma between their traditional legal responsibility to shareholders, whom they consider too interested in short-term payout, and belief about what is best, in the long run, for the health of the company."[46]

The laws are clear that directors are accountable to stockholders. It is their duty to protect stockholder interests and provide an adequate return on their investment. But to which shareholders do directors owe this responsibility? Short-term stock traders? Corporate raiders interested in a "fast buck"? Employees in stock option plans? Individual long-term stock investors?

[46] Jay W. Lorsch, *Pawns and Potentates,* p. 49.

In response to unfriendly takeovers in the 1980s, 25 states, not including Delaware, enacted laws that broaden the legal authority of boards to consider in their deliberations stakeholders other than shareholders. These other stakeholders may be communities, governments, suppliers, lenders, employees, and others. What these states are saying, and others will likely follow, is that corporations exist to provide more than a return to owners. This legal position, in contrast to the stark doctrine of stockholder supremacy, focuses the accountability of directors on the overriding role of the corporation in society. Directors obviously face difficult problems in balancing claims of different stakeholders and in defining their responsibility to them.

These considerations inject considerable ambiguity into the question: To whom are directors accountable? Lorsch suggests that directors should develop decision criteria for dealing with the dilemmas they face.

CONCLUDING OBSERVATIONS

The roles of boards of directors have changed dramatically in the past few years, a trend destined to continue in the future. Years ago, membership on a typical large corporation board was viewed as an honorary position with few responsibilities and a chance to get away from the office to socialize with peers. Today, more and more boards are asserting firm authority over corporate governance.

In this chapter we discuss reforms that have been suggested for more effective board governance. The successful implementation of these reforms will improve corporate governance and raise public confidence in the leadership of corporations.

Disney Shareholders Attack Executive Pay

The Walt Disney Company is headquartered in Burbank, California. Its home is a cluster of unusual architectural forms rising just north of the 134 Freeway, including one building crowned by Mickey Mouse's ears and another resembling a strip of celluloid film. However, the company decided to hold its 2002 annual meeting of shareholders in Hartford, Connecticut, 2,900 miles away. When asked why, Michael Eisner, Disney's chairman and chief executive officer, said the meeting was in Hartford "because of its proximity to Bristol, home of the greatest four letters in sports entertainment—

ESPN," a reference to the profitable sports network owned by the company's ABC subsidiary.[1] A Disney public relations executive told the press that the location was logical because many of Disney's 909,000 stockholders lived nearby in Boston and New York City.[2] Scott Klinger, co-director of a

---

[1] Richard Verrier, "Walt Disney Investors Get Upbeat Report, Entertainment," *Los Angeles Times*, February 20, 2002, p. C2.
[2] Virginia Groark, "For One Day, Disney Is Coming to Hartford," *The New York Times*, February 17, 2002, p. 3.

group called Responsible Wealth, had a different theory. He believed Disney had moved its meeting to Hartford because there were few activists in the area. "L.A. would be a place that would attract a lot of sweatshop interests pretty easily," he told a reporter.[3]

RESPONSIBLE WEALTH

Responsible Wealth is a progressive group with links to labor and religious activists. In its own words, it is "devoted to putting a spotlight on the dangers of excessive inequality of income and wealth in the United States."[4] The group describes its members as leaders from "among the wealthiest 5% of Americans, the primary beneficiaries of the robust growth of the American economy" who are "united by our common concern that despite a booming economy, many are not sharing in the prosperity."[5]

In the past four years, Responsible Wealth had put 40 proposals before shareholders of large corporations asking for moderation and accountability in executive pay. At AOL Time Warner it sought to freeze the CEO's pay when the company was downsizing. At Citigroup it asked stockholders to vote for linking CEO pay to a reduction in predatory lending. All of its proposals had been voted down by large majorities. About 20 members planned to attend the Hartford gathering in support of a proposal to limit the stock options given to Disney's top executives.

THE PROPOSAL

On Tuesday, February 19, 2002, approximately 2,200 shareholders converged on the Hartford Civic Center.[6] CEO Eisner showed nearly an hour of film clips about Disney's studio productions and famous brands. He gave an optimistic talk about the

corporation's future, then fielded questions of varying incisiveness from the audience, including one from a shareholder who complained that Disney World rides made too much noise. When the time came, Marnie Thompson of Responsible Wealth presented the group's resolution.[7]

WHEREAS, Disney's compensation policies concentrate large amounts of stock options in the hands of small numbers of executives. According to Disney's SEC filings, the company's top five officers (0.004% of Disney's workforce), control 18.6% of outstanding options;

WHEREAS, in 1996, Disney granted CEO Michael Eisner 24 million stock options (split adjusted) in order to align the interests of Mr. Eisner and shareholders. This option grant represented 26.2% of the total options granted by Disney that year;

WHEREAS, while Mr. Eisner personally has seen the value of his stock options rise by hundreds of millions of dollars since 1996, Disney shareholders have seen the value of their investment perform poorly compared to the overall stock market. From September 30, 1996 (the date of Eisner's 24 million share grant) through August 31, 2001, the total return of Disney's stock was 24.1%, compared with a 77.0% rise in the Standard & Poors 500 index and a 97.5% rise in the S&P Entertainment Index;

WHEREAS, over the 1998–2000 period, *Business Week* ranked Mr. Eisner the second worst CEO in terms of delivering shareholder value relative to the size of his $699 million pay package. (*Business Week,* April 16, 2001);

WHEREAS, there is a growing body of research confirming that firms with broad-based employee ownership grow faster, create more jobs, and retain higher quality employees than firms with narrowly concentrated ownership. According to "Unleashing the Power of Employee Ownership," a 1999 report by Northwestern's Kellogg School of Management and the management consulting firm Hewitt Associates, firms with broad-based stock ownership delivered

[3] Ibid., p. 3.
[4] Responsible Wealth, "Who We Are," www.responsiblewealth.org/aboutrw/index.html.
[5] Ibid.
[6] Dan Haar, "Disney in Realityland," *The Hartford Courant,* February 20, 2002, p. E1.
[7] Thompson represented Garold Faber and Michele McGeoy, two Disney stockholders who sponsored the proposal.

superior stock market performance and profitability relative to peer firms without employee ownership. Kellogg/Hewitt studied all 380 public firms that established employee stock ownership plans (ESOPs) between 1971 and 1991 and found that in the four years following the adoption of an ESOP firms saw their stock price cumulatively outperform peer firms without widespread employee ownership by 7%. In addition, the return on average assets of firms with broad-based ownership exceeded concentrated ownership firms by 3% per year;

WHEREAS, research confirms that sustained superior performance is due to contributions across a broad range of employee skills, along with shared values within a firm, and not to the efforts of a single employee;

RESOLVED, that the Board limit the stock options received: (1) by any single executive officer to no more than 5% of the total options granted in a single year, and (2) by the group of executive officers to no more than 10% of the total options granted in a single year.

SUPPORTING STATEMENT

Disney's executive compensation policies have failed to deliver their promise of enhanced shareholder returns. While executives have become rich, shareholders have suffered mediocre returns over the last six years. It is time for the company to try a different approach. The financial benefits of broad-based employee ownership are well documented and offer an attractive alternative to the current failed policies of concentrating stock ownership in the hands of a few corporate leaders.

Last year, 9.8% of shareholders supported this resolution.[8]

In presenting the proposal, Thomson remarked that "while shareholders' return has been poor, Disney's executives have gotten rich," drawing booming applause.[9]

[8] The Walt Disney Company, *Proxy Statement,* January 4, 2002, p. 29.
[9] Verrier, "Walt Disney Investors Get Upbeat Report," p. C2.

SHAREHOLDER PROPOSALS

Common shareholders are entitled to one vote for each share they own. Under the laws of most states, including Delaware, where Disney is incorporated, shareholders have the right to vote on certain matters. They can come to the annual meeting to vote their shares in person. But most mark their votes on a proxy form sent out by management to be returned before the meeting. At the Disney annual meeting, shareholders were asked by the company's management to elect the company's 16 directors, to ratify the choice of PricewaterhouseCoopers LLP as its accountant, and to approve the executive pay plan prepared by the board of directors. In addition, shareholders, including members of Responsible Wealth, had written four proposals and the company was required to put them to a vote.[10]

Shareholder proposals are allowed by the Securities and Exchange Commission (SEC) if certain conditions are met.[11] The shareholder must own $2,000 or more of the company's securities for at least one year. The proposal cannot exceed

[10] The three other proposals were (1) that the independent accounting firm hired by Disney to audit its books not be allowed to provide other services to the company, (2) that Disney adhere to a set of 11 human rights standards for doing business in China, and (3) that Disney's board of directors prepare a report on amusement park safety. All three failed to pass, although 42 percent of shareholders were in favor of the first proposal, to prevent independent auditors from having other business with the company. Prior to the annual meeting, Disney management announced that it accepted this recommendation, making the vote moot. In the previous year, Disney had paid PricewaterhouseCoopers LLP $8.7 million in audit fees and $32 million in additional fees for consulting on taxes and Internet purchasing. The recent Enron Corp. scandal created pressure to avoid such apparent conflicts of interest.
[11] 17 C.F.R. 240.14a–8 (2000). The regulations were created by the SEC under authority found in the Securities and Exchange Act of 1934. They have been revised many times by the Commission, most recently in 1998. See Release No. 34040018 dated May 21, 1998 at www.sec.gov/rules/final/34–40018.htm.

500 words. Its submission must comply with certain formal procedures and deadlines. And the shareholder must be at the annual meeting to present it.

Hundreds of such proposals are advanced annually. Many come from public and union pension funds owning large blocs of a company's securities. Their proposals tend to focus on matters of corporate governance such as takeover defenses, executive compensation, and option repricing. Each year some governance proposals get a majority vote. Many other proposals come from progressive activists, religious groups, labor unions, and miscellaneous critics of business who often own only a small number of shares. These proposals raise corporate social responsibility issues.[12] They lack any chance of approval; not one has ever passed when opposed by the company. But they are useful for broadcasting the political and ideological views of their sponsors.

Management can petition the SEC to exclude proposals on a variety of grounds. If, for example, they relate to a trivial aspect of the company's operations, bring a personal claim or grievance against the company, contain false statements, or would require breaking a law, they can be left out. Otherwise, they must be put before all the shareholders for a vote. This can be expensive for a large corporation. Each shareholder resolution costs an average of $87,000 for legal consultation, administrative work, printing, distribution, and vote counting.[13] After spending this much, the firm ends up including views that it strongly disagrees with in its communications to stockholders. As a rule, there is considerable tension between shareholder activists and corporate managements.

---

[12] For background on the rise of social responsibility shareholder proposals, see David Vogel, *Lobbying the Corporation: Citizen Challenges to Business Authority*, (New York: Basic Books, 1976).
[13] Roberta Romano, "Less Is More: Making Institutional Investor Activism a Valuable Mechanism of Corporate Governance," *Yale Journal on Regulation*, Summer 2001, p. 174. This estimate is based on a 1997 survey of corporations by the SEC.

DISNEY MANAGEMENT OPPOSES RESPONSIBLE WEALTH

The SEC permits companies to make written statements of opposition. Disney responded to the Responsible Wealth proposal by printing this rejoinder in the proxy statement sent to all shareholders.

The Board of Directors of the Company recommends a vote "AGAINST" this proposal for the following reasons:

The Board of Directors has long considered the encouragement of broad employee ownership of Company common stock to be in the interest of all shareholders, as a means of promoting focus on the long-term increase in shareholder value. The Company's Employee Stock Purchase Plan, open to all Disney cast members, offers one cost-efficient means of acquiring and maintaining Disney shares, and the Company's various 401(k) plans provide an additional opportunity for many cast members to acquire and hold shares.

As noted in the Report of the Compensation Committee and the Executive Performance Subcommittee, the Company also uses grants of stock options as a means of aligning the interests of key employees with shareholders. Option grants are also a key element of the Company's constant drive to obtain and keep the creative, operational and managerial talent that is critical to our success across all business operations.

We believe it is essential that the Compensation Committee and the Executive Performance Subcommittee retain their current ability to develop and implement a balanced approach to compensation and the promotion of shareholder interests through a carefully designed program of stock option grants. In this respect, it is also important that the Committees retain sufficient flexibility to make option grants in a manner that they determine necessary to meet competitive challenges and to promote the best interest of all shareholders. The Board of Directors therefore believes that artificial constraints advocated in this proposal are thus not in the Company's best interest.

Accordingly, the Board of Directors recommends that you vote "AGAINST" this proposal, and your proxy will be so voted if the proposal is presented unless you specify otherwise.[14]

This was the second time that Responsible Wealth had presented the proposal to Disney shareholders. At the annual meeting in 2001, the same proposal had been brought forth. During its discussion, Eisner remarked that he would not give stock options to parking lot attendants and people in similar positions.[15] As noted, the proposal had received only 9.8 percent of the votes cast.[16] However, under guidelines set up by the SEC, if a proposal gets 3 percent or more of the votes it is eligible to be put forward again in another year. So Responsible Wealth went through the steps necessary to qualify it for the 2002 annual meeting. This time it would need 6 percent of the votes to be eligible for inclusion in the company's proxy materials a third time. After that, it would need to get 10 percent or more to be included in additional years.

EXECUTIVE COMPENSATION AT DISNEY

Although the resolution seemed to stand little chance of passing, the group was not discouraged. It viewed shareholder resolutions as educational tools, tools that could be used to teach the shareholders of large corporations about wealth disparities in American society. Responsible Wealth picked Disney as the target for a resolution because its CEO, Michael Eisner, seemed to typify excess in executive compensation.

Eisner took the top position at Disney in 1984 and over the years his paychecks had attracted attention. The board of directors at Disney sets Eisner's compensation. Its compensation committee, composed of seven outside directors, creates the ground rules about how and when he and other executives are paid. The Disney board has been criticized as one of the most feckless by critics who believe that current corporate governance arrangements are inadequate to check runaway CEO paychecks. Writes one:

> With notable exceptions, the "independent" directors on most corporate boards are a well-known sham—typically handpicked by the CEO and loyal to him, even when serving on the executive compensation committees that ratify bloated CEO pay packages. The poster boy for this charade is Michael Eisner of Disney. As CEO, he must answer to a board of directors that includes the principal of his kids' elementary school, actor Sidney Poitier, the architect who designed Eisner's Aspen home and a university president whose school got a $1 million donation from Eisner.[17]

However, throughout Eisner's tenure the compensation committee has maintained a strong connection between pay and performance. Eisner and four other top executives are paid modest base salaries, but when the company meets profit goals they get large annual bonuses and are awarded generous stock options. If the price of Disney shares rises, they can make extraordinary income. If it does not, they earn only a modest salary.

Eisner has prospered under this compensation philosophy. Between 1987 and 1992 he exercised stock options netting him $229 million. In 1997 he exercised options worth $552 million. During these years, his income was extraordinary, even when compared with other top-earning executives, but his actions rewarded shareholders as well. As he built a larger and more profitable corporation, Disney shares outperformed the Standard & Poor's 500 index.

EISNER'S OPTIONS

In 1997 Eisner entered an employment agreement with the company that runs through September 2006. Under the agreement, he is paid a base salary of $1,000,000 a year and is eligible for bonuses of up to $18,750,000 a year. He also received options on 24,000,000 common shares.

---

[14] The Walt Disney Company, *Proxy Statement,* p. 30.

[15] Responsible Wealth, "Shareholders Ask Disney to Spread the Wealth," press release, March 1, 2000.

[16] "2001 Proxy Season Report," *The Corporate Examiner,* August 20, 2001, p. 4.

[17] William Greider, "Crime in the Suites," *The Nation,* February 4, 2002, p. 11.

Michael Eisner, chairman of the board and chief executive officer of Disney since 1984.
© Susan Goldman/The Image Works.

Here is how options work. Stock options give Eisner the right to buy from the company a specified number of Disney's common shares for a specified price at a future date. On this date the options *vest*, that is, the person who holds them may buy the stock at the *exercise price*, or the market price of the shares on the day the options were granted. Options have an *expiration date*. They can no longer be exercised at some point, typically one to ten years, after they vest. The options must be taken advantage of during an *exercise period*, or a period of years between vesting and expiration. If the market price of the shares is higher than the exercise price anytime during the exercise period, Eisner can *exercise* the options, that is, he can buy shares at the exercise price. If the market price is lower than the exercise price when the options vest, they are worthless. Here is how the 24,000,000 option shares granted to Eisner in 1997 were structured. He received

- 3,000,000 shares with an exercise price of $21.10 to vest on June 30, 2000, which expire on September 30, 2008, and which, if exercised, must be held until at least September 30, 2003.
- 6,000,000 shares with an exercise price of $21.10 to vest on September 30, 2001, which expire on September 30, 2008, and which, if exercised, must be held until at least September 30, 2003.

- 6,000,000 shares with an exercise price of $21.10 to vest on September 30, 2002, which expire on September 30, 2008, and which, if exercised, must be held until at least September 30, 2003.
- 3,000,000 shares with an exercise price of $26.38 (125 percent of the market price at the time of the grant) to vest on September 30, 2003, which expire on September 30, 2011, and which, if exercised, must be held until at least September 30, 2004.
- 3,000,000 shares with an exercise price of $31.66 (150 percent of the market price at the time of the grant) to vest on September 30, 2004, which expire on September 30, 2011, and which, if exercised, must be held until at least September 30, 2005.
- 3,000,000 shares with an exercise price of $42.41 (200 percent of the market price at the time of the grant) to vest on September 30, 2004, which expire on September 30, 2011, and which, if exercised, must be held until September 30, 2006.[18]

This options structure closely aligns Eisner's interests with those of Disney shareholders. The large number of options gives him an enormous incentive to increase share price. Every $1 rise in Disney shares above the exercise prices of his options is ultimately worth millions of dollars to him. And he is only rewarded by long-term price increases. He cannot capitalize on short-term price moves because after exercising options he is required to hold shares for one to three years. And some shares can be exercised only at prices that are 125 to 200 percent above the exercise price set in 1997, meaning that Eisner must accomplish a significant price rise in Disney's shares before these options are worth anything.

There are other generous provisions in Eisner's employment agreement. If fired, he is entitled to receive a $6,000,000 bonus each year (unless he takes a position with another major entertainment company) until the agreement ends in 2006. If Eisner decides to leave Disney "for good reason" he will still receive the $6,000,000 annual bonuses. The agreement allows him to resign for good reason if his duties are substantially reduced, if he is required to work outside the Los Angeles area, or if he is no longer the CEO in a combined company after the sale or merger of Disney assets. If he decides to retire, he is eligible for a substantial annual income. Had he retired in 2002 it would have been $803,269 a year.

THE PAY–PERFORMANCE CONNECTION GROWS TENUOUS

Although Disney shareholders were pleased with Eisner's performance through 1997, for the five-year period leading into the 2002 annual meeting the company's shares did poorly compared with alternative benchmarks. Table 1 shows how someone investing $100 in September 1996 would have fared in Disney stock versus three index investments. The steep decline between September 2000 and September 2001 was caused by declining revenue in the wake of the September 11, 2001, terrorist attacks, closure of Disney's Internet portal go.com, and costs incurred laying off 4,000 employees. The company ended 2001 with a net loss of $158 million on revenues of $25.3 billion.[19]

Disney's top executives lost financially as the company's fortunes declined. Eisner in 1999, and again in 2001, received only his base salary, failing to qualify for a bonus or additional stock options. In 2000 his total compensation was $60,531,000, including $12,317,482 in base salary and bonus, and option grants of 387,060 shares valued at $48,688,162. He suffered a paper loss of $266 million as share prices fell in 2001. However, his net worth was estimated at $720 million in January 2002, and he continued to hold more than 13 million Disney shares.[20]

REJECTION, BUT THE CAUSE LIVES ON

When all the votes were counted, the Responsible Wealth proposal was defeated. It received only 6.9 percent of the vote, less than the year before. Of the approximately 2.1 billion shares of Disney common stock outstanding, about 1.1 billion votes were cast, most with proxies sent in by shareholders before the meeting. The Responsible Wealth proposal got about 16.3 million votes. Compensation policy at Disney remained unchanged. However, the formal accusation of excessive and unfair distribution of options lived on because the proposal, having received more than 6 percent of the vote, was eligible for inclusion again at the 2003 annual meeting.

[19] The Walt Disney Company, *Form 10-K*, fiscal year ending September 30, 2001, p. 20.

[20] Richard Verrier, "Eisner's Paycheck Humbled in 2001," *Los Angeles Times*, January 5, 2002, p. C1.

TABLE 1 Comparison of Five-Year Cumulative Total Return (based on reinvestment of $100 beginning September 30, 1996)

Source: The Walt Disney Company.

	9/96	9/97	9/98	9/99	9/00	9/01
The Walt Disney Co.	$100	$128	$122	$125	$186	$91
S&P 500	$100	$140	$151	$202	$231	$186
S&P Entertainment & Leisure Composite*	$100	$121	$138	$179	$204	$136
Custom Composite Index (four stocks)†	$100	$117	$187	$254	$357	$183

*A published index of companies in the entertainment, resort and leisure, and restaurant industries that includes Disney.
†An index created by Disney composed of AOL Time Warner Inc., King World Productions, the News Corporation Ltd., and Viacom Inc.

QUESTIONS

1. Do you believe that compensation policy at Disney is flawed? If so, what changes would you suggest?

2. Do you believe that Michael Eisner is paid too much?

3. If you had been a Disney shareholder, would you have voted in favor of or against the Responsible Wealth proposal?

4. What are the pros and cons of allowing shareholder proposals such as the one advanced by Responsible Wealth?

Index